The Complete
Walt Disney
World® 2008

Julie and Mike Neal

coconut
press

COCONUT PRESS
Sanibel Florida

The Complete Guide to Walt Disney World® 2008

ISBN 978-0-9709-5969-0

ISSN 1547-8491

Library of Congress Control No: 2007908586

PUBLISHED BY COCONUT PRESS

Media Enterprises Inc., Sanibel Island, Florida

Contact us online at info@coconutpress.com

WRITING AND RESEARCH: Julie Neal

PHOTOGRAPHY AND DESIGN: Mike Neal

ADDITIONAL RESEARCH: Micaela Neal

This book is not endorsed or sponsored by the Walt Disney Co. or Disney Destinations LLC, or connected in any way to those companies.

IMAGES

Unless indicated all images © 2007 Media Enterprises Inc. La Nouba performance photos used under rights granted by Cirque du Soleil. All maps © 2007 Media Enterprises Inc., illustrations by Vince Burkhead.

ACKNOWLEDGMENTS

WALT DISNEY WORLD PUBLIC RELATIONS: Our thanks to Jonathan Frontado, Jason Lasecki, Dave Herbst, Juliana Cadiz, Liz Benz, Darrell Fry and David Hillstrom, who helped arrange interviews, backstage access, photo rights, photo shoots and much more.

OTHER ACKNOWLEDGMENTS: We also thank everyone else who supplied information, materials and resources, including: Rosa Acosta, Ross Adams, Craig Albert, Ngonba Anadou, Odalys Aponte, Karen Aulino, Jasmine Barczyk, Jane Berry, David Brady, William Burke, Shawn Cannon, Shelly Carter, John Chenciner, Steve Christ, the Cleary family and their beautiful princesses, Lee Cockerell, the Connells (Matthew, Sherri, Anna), Brian Cotten, Elise Cottle, Amy and Mitch Crews, Karen Derose, the Dix family, Jamie Entwistle, Catherine Ewer, Aiden Feeback, Andrea Finger, Jay Garcia, Susan Germer, Keith Gimbel, Michelle Ginesin, Aurélie Grand, Jeff Green, Barbara Gross, Dana Hall, Liz Hall, Robert Hargrove, Trina Hofreiter, Mark Hoevenaars, Roger Isako, Rob Iske, Jennifer Jacobsen, Eric Jacobson, Kristie A. Jones, Kristine Jones, Traci Kennedy, Mary Kenny, Tommy King, Kelly Knowlen, Daniel Lahr, Jeff Lindberg, Josh Little, Kathy Mangum, Tony Marotta, Roberto Martinez, Carrie Matlack, Amanda Maure, Jennifer McKay, Suzan Meaux, Sherri Mercer, Bob Miller, Bo Morris, Nenette Mputu, Kim and Diane Nelson, David Njoroge, Sanja Novakovich, Tina Pankow, Sunni Petty, Thabo Pheto, Brian Piasecki, Ernie Porterfield, Honor Rasch-Gush, Jodi Rauer, Michelle Reeves, Mark Renfro, Kevin Renzi, Alfonso Ribeiro, Laura Richeson, Charles Ridgway, Joe Rindler, Wally Robinson, Todd Roby, Kathy Rogers, Catherine Roth, Hanns-Claudius and Monika Scharff, Shannon Shelton, Brandon Sims, Theron Skees, Jennifer Smith, Lynne Smith, Courtney and Jerry Soares, Brian Spitler, Jason Surrell, Rheo Tan, Gary Terry, Dikeledi Tlhako, the Turners (Jeff, Anna, Laura, Michael, Andrew), Michelle Valle, Kim Veon, Jon Wagner-Holtz, Jenn Wakelin, Robin Walker, Andy Warren, Christopher White, Dave Williams, George Willis and all the various resort managers and park duty managers.

Opening page: Nicola Lambo prepares for her role as Princess Kibibi in the Festival of the Lion King.
Previous page: Orlando's Sunny Christiansen, 6, learns an African dance at Disney's Animal Kingdom

ABOUT THE AUTHORS

After writing a guidebook about their hometown islands of Sanibel and Captiva, Florida, Julie and Mike Neal decided to spend a year and write one about Walt Disney World. Five years later they finished, only to learn they need to return weekly to keep things up to date. As a result, they've visited Disney World over 1,000 times. Back on the islands, Julie coaches both a rec and middle-school soccer team, and is famous for her cooler full of ice pops. Mike is known for never getting around to putting his boat in the water. When not at Disney riding Big Thunder Mountain, their teenage daughter, Micaela, loves to boogie-board and fish at the beach. The family lives with their chocolate lab, Bear.

MICAELA NEAL

Authors Julie and Mike Neal

Walt Disney World® is officially known as the Walt Disney World Resort.® Walt Disney World® is a trademark of the Walt Disney Co.

To Karen, who helped us so much.

About this book

One thing you'll notice right away: there's so much stuff. And no wonder — this book has the most detailed information ever published about Walt Disney World. Completely updated for 2008, it combines a thorough description of everything the resort has to offer with a cornucopia of advice to help you enjoy it. In other words, **this guide is a handbook on how to have fun.**

In addition, more than 400 color photos show you every aspect of Walt Disney World, from backstage dressing rooms to fireworks.

A comprehensive overview kicks off the book. It includes background articles about the life of Walt Disney, his classic cartoon characters, the company's Imagineers, even the history of monorails.

A step-by-step planning chapter makes organizing your Disney trip easy. It features practical information on subjects such as what to pack and how to meet characters, and straightforward explanations of such key Disney concepts as Fastpass and Extra Magic Hours.

Most of the book is devoted to Disney's theme parks, water parks and recreational activities. Comprehensive chapters are devoted to the Magic Kingdom, Epcot, Disney's Hollywood Studios and Disney's Animal Kingdom. There are also separate chapters for Walt Disney World's water parks as well as Downtown Disney.

The attraction coverage is unprecedented, with exclusive tips, story lines, back stories, fun finds and fun facts unlike those in any other Disney guide book. You'll get a clear understanding of every attraction, so you can enjoy each one to the fullest.

Every park chapter also has at least one Magical Day plan: an hour-by-hour itinerary designed to give you a relaxed, enjoyable experience. Each schedule requires you to start your day bright and early, but follow it and you'll have a terrific time.

Like variety in your vacation? Check out our Diversions chapter for options such as golf, water sports and backstage tours.

The back of the book includes a greatly expanded accommodations chapter, a brand-new restaurant chapter with reviews of every Walt Disney World eatery, descriptions of special events and festivals and a list of Walt Disney World's Hidden Mickeys, those secretly placed three-circle shapes that hide in the architecture, art and landscape.

Extras include a 10-page animal guide for Animal Kingdom and bonus articles that tell the surprising histories of the Cinderella and Beauty and the Beast fairy tales.

Want to have a *great* time on your Disney trip?

This is the book for you.

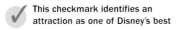

✓ This checkmark identifies an attraction as one of Disney's best

✔ This checkmark identifies a top restaurant or live-entertainment option

Expedition Everest
Disney's Animal Kingdom **194**

Soarin'
Epcot **112**

La Nouba
Downtown Disney **240**

SOARIN' PHOTO © DISNEY

Contents

Magic Kingdom

Epcot

Disney's Hollywood Studios

Disney's Animal Kingdom

Water Parks

Downtown Disney

Diversions

Accommodations

Restaurants

Special Events

Hidden Mickeys

142 High School Musical 2: School's Out
Disney's Hollywood Studios

312 Character dining
Norway pavilion, Epcot

55 It's a Small World
Magic Kingdom

CHARACTER DINING, IT'S A SMALL WORLD PHOTOS © DISNEY

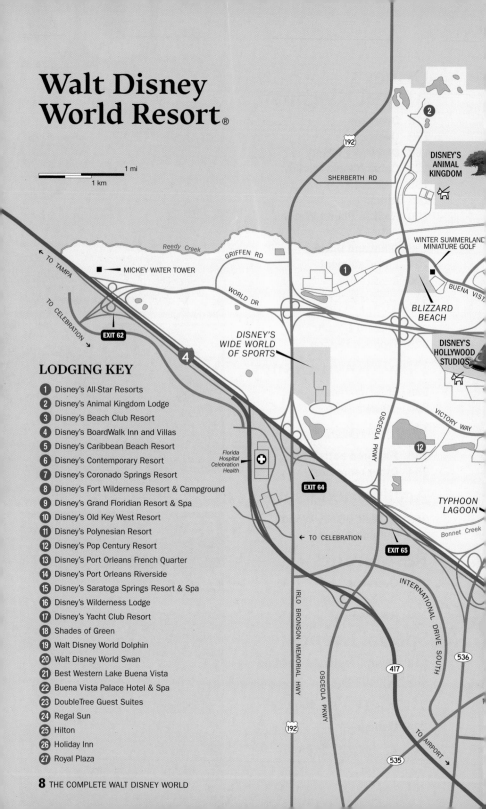

Walt Disney World Resort®

1 mi

1 km

TO TAMPA →

TO CELEBRATION ↗

EXIT 62

■ → MICKEY WATER TOWER

Reedy Creek

GRIFFEN RD

WORLD DR

4

SHERBERTH RD

192

DISNEY'S ANIMAL KINGDOM

①

WINTER SUMMERLAND MINIATURE GOLF

■

BUENA VIST

②

BLIZZARD BEACH

DISNEY'S HOLLYWOOD STUDIOS

DISNEY'S WIDE WORLD OF SPORTS

VICTORY WAY

12

OSCEOLA PKWY

Florida Hospital Celebration Health ✚

EXIT 64

← TO CELEBRATION

TYPHOON LAGOON

Bonnet Creek

EXIT 65

IRLO BRONSON MEMORIAL HWY

INTERNATIONAL DRIVE SOUTH

536

417

OSCEOLA PKWY

192

TO AIRPORT ↘

535

LODGING KEY

1 Disney's All-Star Resorts
2 Disney's Animal Kingdom Lodge
3 Disney's Beach Club Resort
4 Disney's BoardWalk Inn and Villas
5 Disney's Caribbean Beach Resort
6 Disney's Contemporary Resort
7 Disney's Coronado Springs Resort
8 Disney's Fort Wilderness Resort & Campground
9 Disney's Grand Floridian Resort & Spa
10 Disney's Old Key West Resort
11 Disney's Polynesian Resort
12 Disney's Pop Century Resort
13 Disney's Port Orleans French Quarter
14 Disney's Port Orleans Riverside
15 Disney's Saratoga Springs Resort & Spa
16 Disney's Wilderness Lodge
17 Disney's Yacht Club Resort
18 Shades of Green
19 Walt Disney World Dolphin
20 Walt Disney World Swan
21 Best Western Lake Buena Vista
22 Buena Vista Palace Hotel & Spa
23 DoubleTree Guest Suites
24 Regal Sun
25 Hilton
26 Holiday Inn
27 Royal Plaza

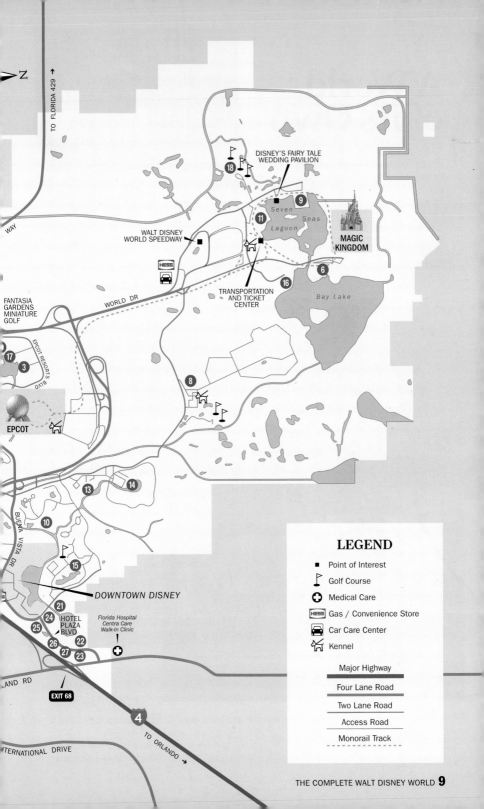

N

TO FLORIDA 429

18

DISNEY'S FAIRY TALE
WEDDING PAVILION

9

Seven
Seas
Lagoon

11

MAGIC
KINGDOM

WALT DISNEY
WORLD SPEEDWAY

HESS

6

16

Bay Lake

WAY

FANTASIA
GARDENS
MINIATURE
GOLF

WORLD DR

TRANSPORTATION
AND TICKET
CENTER

EPCOT RESORTS BLVD

17
3

8

EPCOT

13   **14**

BUENA VISTA DR

10

15

DOWNTOWN DISNEY

21
24   HOTEL
25   PLAZA
BLVD
26
27   **22**
23

Florida Hospital
Centra Care
Walk-In Clinic

LAND RD

EXIT 68

4   TO ORLANDO

INTERNATIONAL DRIVE

LEGEND

■ Point of Interest

⚑ Golf Course

✚ Medical Care

HESS Gas / Convenience Store

🚗 Car Care Center

🐕 Kennel

Major Highway

Four Lane Road

Two Lane Road

Access Road

Monorail Track

A World of its Own

There's no place else like it. Twice the size of Manhattan — 47 square miles — Walt Disney World is unlike any other spot on earth. The world's largest collection of theme parks, water parks and resorts, this family-friendly vacation kingdom is also so, well, *inspiring*. A trip here is not just a way to spend time with your kids, not just an escape from day-to-day doldrums. It's a reawakening of that free-spirited, good-natured soul who lives deep inside you — the

one your spouse married, the one you want your kids to emulate. Yes it can be crowded, yes it can be expensive, yes it takes a good plan to see it all, but what other man-made vacationland so deliberately embraces creativity, optimism and a sense of wonder about the world?

Populated daily by more than 100,000 visitors as well as 54,000 "cast members," it

Clockwise from top right: The namesake of the movie that funded much of Walt Disney World, Mary Poppins poses at Epcot; lifeguards take a break at Disney's All-Star Music Resort; the Dapper Dans perform on Magic Kingdom's Main Street U.S.A.; the restored Spaceship Earth, the icon of Epcot

truly is a world of its own, and the No. 1 vacation destination on the planet.

It's only 122 acres, 0.5 percent of the property, but to many folks the **Magic Kingdom**

Clockwise from right: Swaying dancers at Beauty and the Beast Live on Stage; nighttime fun at Pleasure Island; a pirate girl at a Magic Kingdom party; a young Chinese acrobat poses for the camera crowd at Epcot

is Walt Disney World. A spacious version of California's Disneyland, Magic Kingdom re-imagines that park's Main Street U.S.A., Adventureland, Fantasyland, Frontierland and Tomorrowland. Altogether, this family favorite has more than 40 attractions, including classics such as It's a Small World and Space Mountain. It's the most popular theme park in the world.

A permanent World's Fair, the 300-acre **Epcot** park is divided into the science-themed Future World and the international pavilions of the World Showcase. Top Future World attractions include realistic simulators that give you the sensations of hang gliding (Soarin') and astronaut training (Mission Space). A globe-hopping tour of 11 countries, the World Showcase is highlighted by its architecture, entertainment, dining and shopping. Changes for 2008 include a revamped Spaceship Earth attraction, new Japanese and Italian restaurants, and a new film in the Canada pavilion.

Also divided in half is the show-business-themed **Disney's Hollywood Studios,** formerly known as Disney-MGM Studios. The front is a tribute to Old Hollywood, with re-created 1940s-era icons such as Hollywood Boulevard and Grauman's Chinese Theatre. The rear was originally a working studio, and still carries that theme. This 135-acre park includes two of Disney's best thrill rides — the Twilight Zone Tower of Terror and the Rock 'n' Roller Coaster Starring Aerosmith. The park will be introducing a number of new attractions in 2008, including a new parade, an indoor ride based on the "Toy Story" films, and a revamped Playhouse Disney stage show.

The 500-acre **Disney's Animal Kingdom** combines exotic animals with quality at-

tractions such as Expedition Everest, a roller coaster that travels backward into a mountain; Kilimanjaro Safaris, an exploration into a replicated African preserve aboard an open-sided truck; and Festival of the Lion King, a show with energetic acrobats, dancers, singers and stilt walkers. The centerpiece of the park is the Tree of Life, a 145-foot man-made sculpture.

Beyond the theme parks, Disney World offers many entertainment, recreation and shopping options. It's hard to beat the family fun at the two themed water parks, **Blizzard Beach** and **Typhoon Lagoon.** Disney has four championship golf courses as well as a 9-hole, two miniature golf courses and many tennis courts, and offers organized fishing, horseback riding, stock-car driving, surfing and water sports.

Downtown Disney is a commercial center at the eastern edge of the property. The 120-acre site is made up of the Marketplace outdoor mall, Pleasure Island nightclub complex and West Side dining, entertainment and shopping district.

Disney's Wide World of Sports complex is 220 acres of sports facilities that host amateur — and some professional — competitions. It includes a baseball stadium, fieldhouse and many outdoor fields.

Distant lands and forgotten eras are the themes at most of Disney's 19 **themed resorts.** Accommodations range from campsites to luxurious multilevel suites.

PROJECT X

Rumors of a mystery major land buyer began swirling around Orlando in 1964. And it was true. A company *was* buying up parcels 20 miles southwest of the town, but it was being done in secret, with false names and dummy corporations. Who could it be? Many folks had it figured out from the start: it had to be Boeing. Or maybe Lockheed. Absolutely something related to NASA.

But it wasn't. In October, 1965, the Orlando Sentinel-Star reported the buyer was Walt Disney, who was planning a huge secret development, internally designated as Project X. A month later, Walt and his brother, Roy, confirmed the project at an Orlando press conference. Walt's vision was an Experimental Prototype Community of Tomorrow, a futuristic city where solutions to urban problems could be explored. There would be a theme park, too, an East Coast version of Disneyland. After Walt's sudden death in 1966, his successors got to work.

Construction started in 1969. The largest private construction project in the history of the United States, it was led by two military men — former Army General Joe Potter, who had overseen operations at the Panama Canal and the 1964 World's Fair,

GINGERBREAD MEN PHOTO © DISNEY

Clockwise from top left: A window of Minnie's house, Animal Kingdom's DiVine, Richard Petty stock cars, Magic Kingdom gingerbread men in a Christmas parade

and former Navy Admiral Joe Vallor, who had supervised the building of Disneyland.

Charged with taming what was at the time considered worthless "swampland," Potter, Vallor and 9,000 workers moved 8 million cubic yards of dirt and built 47 miles of canals and 22 miles of levees.

They cleaned the 406-acre Bay Lake, and created the 172-acre Seven Seas Lagoon.

Clockwise from left: A caricaturist sketches the authors' daughter at Animal Kingdom; a cast member sells Haunted Mansion merchandise; a Citizen of Hollywood at Disney's Hollywood Studios; Magic Kingdom's Notorious Banjo Brothers and Bob

Kingdom, the Contemporary and Polynesian Resorts and the Fort Wilderness Resort & Campground. Disney's Golf Resort (today's Shades of Green military center) was built in 1973. Lake Buena Vista Village (today's Downtown Disney Marketplace) opened in 1975.

What about EPCOT?

The Disney company wrestled with the idea through the early '70s, but the vision just wasn't clear without its visionary. Finally, in 1976 Disney announced plans for Epcot Center, a dramatically scaled-down theme-park version of Walt Disney's grand idea. Announced as a park that featured "demonstration concepts" as well as an "international people-to-people exchange," it opened in 1982.

They built roads, maintenance shops, a food distribution center, phone company, power plant, sewage plant and a tree farm.

Walt Disney World opened to the public on Oct. 1, 1971. It consisted of the Magic

BUILDING BOOM

For everything Disney built on its property during the space-race and disco eras, it has created far more since. It opened Disney-MGM Studios, Pleasure Island and Typhoon Lagoon in 1989. The Osprey Ridge and Eagle Pines golf complex debuted in 1992. Blizzard Beach arrived in 1995. Downtown Disney's West Side and Disney's Wide World of Sports opened in 1999.

That same period saw a huge expansion in Disney World hotels, when the number of rooms on the property grew from 2,000 to 31,000.

Disney's Caribbean Beach and Grand Floridian resorts opened in 1988, then 13 new lodging facilities were built during the 1990s. They included the Yacht and Beach Club and independent Walt Disney World Swan and Dolphin complexes (1990), the Port Orleans French Quarter and Old Key West resorts (1991), Dixie Landings (now Port Orleans Riverside, 1992), All-Star Sports Resort and Wilderness Lodge (1994), All-Star Music and BoardWalk (1995), Coronado Springs (1997) and All-Star Movies (1999). Disney's newest hotels are Animal Kingdom Lodge (2001), Pop Century (2003) and Saratoga Springs (2004). The southwest corner of the property was developed as a residential community, Celebration. It broke ground in 1996.

Clockwise from top left: Italian columns in Epcot; a trick-or-treating Tweedledum; Cinderella Castle at Christmas; a Lights Motors Action stunt

FUN FACTS ⟩⟩ Walt Disney World buses log more than 15 million miles a year. ⟩⟩ Disney World is the world's largest consumer of fireworks, burning through a million shells a year. ⟩⟩ Disney World's employee wardrobe consists of 1.8 million pieces. Cast members wear 2,500 different "costumes" (there are no "uniforms.") ⟩⟩ Walt Disney World sells enough Mouse Ear caps each year to cover the head of every man, woman and child in Portland, Oregon. The number of character T-shirts sold each year would clothe everyone in Chicago.

Making the Magic

How Disney 'Imagineers' combine space-race ingenuity and cutting-edge technology to create A WHOLE NEW WORLD.

When you think of Walt Disney World, do you think of attractions that tell stories, high-tech experiences, or themed architecture? If so, you're thinking about the work of the company's "Imagineers," a word coined by Walt Disney to describe his team of imaginative engineers, architects, artists, programmers, sculptors, special-effects designers and script writers that created California's Disneyland.

Originally known as WED Enterprises (for Walter Elias Disney), the company is known today as Walt Disney Imagineering (WDI). It employs 1,400 people. Based in California, it has a field office at Walt Disney World.

Imagineering's best attractions often feature innovative high-tech concepts. At Magic Kingdom, Space Mountain was not only the world's first roller coaster in the dark, but also the first computer-controlled thrill ride. In that park's Fantasyland,

John, the father at the Carousel of Progress, is among the Audio Animatronic characters that move through the manipulation of pressurized air, gas or fluid, which triggers actuators that move eyes, pinch lips or twist torsos. Electrical cables run from each figure to a backstage operations center, where a computer system uses flash memory cards to store the character's program. Each movement is timed to coincide with prerecorded dialogue, music or sound effects. In more recent characters, compliance circuits control the force that pushes or pulls each movement, and add a natural-style inertia that makes the motions more realistic.

Mickey's PhilharMagic features the world's largest wraparound projection screen.

The group's best known creation is its collection of what it calls "Audio Animatronic" characters, the robotic people and animals that populate such attractions as the Carousel of Progress, Pirates of the Caribbean and The Great Movie Ride. Basically, Disney's version of a robot is simply an electrical machine that has the appearance of a living creature. It doesn't really do much, but moves so realistically it often seems to have an actual personality.

The concept began in the 1950s, when scientist Wernher von Braun gave Walt Disney some magnetic computer tape he was using to synchronize the steps of rocket launches at Florida's Cape Canaveral. In 1961, Disney's engineers used similar tape to synchronize the sounds and movements of mechanical birds, flowers and Tiki carvings in the Disneyland attraction The Enchanted Tiki Room. And just like von Braun secured his computer in a nearby bunkhouse, Disney hid his backstage.

Humanistic characters debuted a few years later. The most famous Audio Animatronic figure, Abraham Lincoln at the Hall of Presidents, is a copy of a figure that stunned audiences at the Illinois pavilion at the 1964 New York World's Fair.

Walt Disney World has more than 1,600 Audio Animatronic characters. The most complex figures include a spitting Stitch at Stitch's Great Escape, a walking Ben Franklin at The American Adventure and a Wicked Witch at The Great Movie Ride who looks amazingly real. Fanciest of all is Hopper, an 8-foot grasshopper with 68 functions at It's Tough to be a Bug, and the gigantic Yeti at Expedition Everest. It has 19 axes of motion.

Back to the Future

It's the future of transportation, as imagined in rural Pennsylvania in the 1870s. It's the ELEVATED MONORAIL.

The concept of a small train straddling an elevated beam debuted in 1876, at Pennsylvania's American Centennial Exposition. Inventor LeRoy Stone argued that a single beam was cheaper than a two-rail system, and that elevating it made it fit into America's growing cities.

Two years later his idea became the world's first commercial monorail, a 4-mile system that ran between Bradford and Gilmore, Penn. The train was a hit — until it blew off of its tracks.

The idea reemerged after World War II. As traffic jams began to clog rebuilt German cities, Swedish industrialist Dr. Axel Wenner-Gren introduced a monorail train with additional horizontal wheels. They hugged its beam, making monorail trains stable even in strong winds. Working at a test track near Cologne, Germany, he built a full-scale test train in 1957.

A few months later, who should come driving through the Cologne countryside but the vacationing Walt and Lillian Disney. Glancing out his side window, Walt noticed "a huge loaf of bread" (as he called it) gliding above the treetops. He followed it to a service yard, where he found the office of Dr. Wenner-Gren and his company, Alweg Research.

Wenner-Gren had his first sale. Making just one change — the bodies would be redesigned to resemble Buck Rogers spaceships — Disney ordered an Alweg system for his new California theme park, Disneyland. In 1959, it became a ride in that park's Tomorrowland. Meant as a serious model of a future transportation system, the system's 4,200-foot track featured overpasses, steep grades and tight turns.

Alweg built two other demonstrators. The 1961 Expo Italia fair in Turin, Italy, used one to connect its pavilions, and Seattle featured one at its 1962 Century 21 Expo. The company made proposals to Cologne, Hamburg, Los Angeles and Mexico City, but never signed a real deal. Wenner-Gren died in 1961. In 1967, his track was demolished to make room for a subdivision.

One Alweg-inspired system, however, came close to the doctor's dreams. The Walt Disney World monorail is a real transportation system. Used by 200,000 passengers a day, the two-track, 14-mile "highway in the sky" has six public stations and a backstage service hangar.

Today's Disney World trains are built by Bombardier, a company whose Learjets share a similar style. Each train has six cars, is 203 feet long, can carry 360 passengers, is powered by eight 113-hp motors and, thanks to its fiberglass body, weighs a total of only 800 pounds without equipment. Top speed is 45 mph.

The trains travel on 26-inch concrete beams supported by tapered columns. As trains move, they pick up electrical power from metallic buss bars. Each train can be controlled from either end. Sometimes, after the parks close, drivers run them "blindly" backward.

Disney's monorails are powered by a 600-volt electrical system. Motors turn unseen tires that roll along the top of the beam, while horizontal stabilizing wheels hug its sides.

Walt Disney

Raised on a Missouri farm, this self-made man kept on believing in his ideas, and saw most of his dreams come true

A tycoon with the mind of a farm boy. A storyteller who didn't finish high school. An artist who thought like an engineer. A visionary who loved the past. A mix of contradictory characters, Walt Disney was an American icon and the personification of the American dream. He introduced sound and color cartoons, perfected animated movies and invented theme parks.

Disney received hundreds of accolades, including 32 personal Academy Awards and honorary degrees from Harvard and Yale. But just as he started his grandest dream... he died.

COWS AND CIGARS

The namesake of Walt Disney World was born in Chicago on Dec. 5, 1901. He had three older brothers and a younger sister.

Disney lived on a farm during his most impressionable years. Between the ages of 4 and 10, from 1905 to 1911, he was raised on 45 acres near Marceline, Mo., an isolated town in the middle of the state.

Clad in overalls, the young boy spent much of his time playing with the farm animals, swimming in a pond, picking apples, or daydreaming under a cottonwood tree. He often ignored his homework to doodle animal pictures, and once talked his sister into helping him tar (he called it "paint") the side of the family barn.

When still in grade school, Disney sold cigars, gum and soda pop to passengers at the town's railroad depot. His uncle was a train engineer. Free to roam, the boy came to know an elderly Civil War veteran who told him dramatic old stories.

CHAPLIN AND CHICAGO

When his family moved to Kansas City, Disney impersonated Charlie Chaplin in skits he put on with other neighborhood kids. When they moved back to Chicago, Disney started high school (he would attend for just one year), contributing cartoons and photos to the school paper. He took night courses at Chicago's Academy of Fine Arts.

OUT ON HIS OWN

At 16, Disney dropped out of high school and left home. Germany had just signed an armistice ending World War I, but he still tried to enlist in the Army. Rejected because of his age, Disney instead snuck into the Red Cross, which sent him to France to drive an ambulance.

He took up smoking.

Returning to Kansas City, Disney formed his first business at age 20. Using a borrowed camera and working in a shed, he made "Laugh-O-Gram" cartoons of a live girl in an animated world. When his distributor went bankrupt, Disney brought in cash with a dental-health film ("Tommy Tucker's Tooth"), but soon he went under, too.

ALICE AND THE RABBIT

After raising train fare by going door-to-door photographing babies, Disney left Missouri and headed for Hollywood. "There was just one thing I wanted to do," he later recalled. "I wanted to be a director." His brother Roy was already there.

Carrying a print of his last Kansas City cartoon, an unfinished extravaganza called "Alice's Wonderland," Disney applied at every major studio. Finally, a New York distributor agreed to market his work. He was in business again.

Forming the Disney Bros. Studio, Walt and Roy set up shop in the rear of a real estate office. Running the business side of the operation, Roy soon insisted its name should be changed to the Walt Disney Studio, today's Walt Disney Company.

The new business prospered. Disney celebrated by buying a Moon roadster, growing a mustache and, in 1925, getting married to a young woman he had hired to ink and paint celluloids, Lillian Bounds. The couple later raised two daughters, Diane and the adopted Sharon.

In 1927, Disney created a new character: Oswald the Lucky Rabbit. He produced 26 Oswald cartoons, which were distributed by Universal and popular enough to spawn an Oswald candy bar and some merchandise. But a year later, on a trip to New York to renew his contract, Disney learned of a clause in his deal that gave Universal ownership of his character. Devastated, on the train ride back to California he realized he needed a star he owned outright.

Remembering a friendly mouse that used to climb up on his desk in Kansas City, Disney turned to his wife and said "I think it will be a mouse, and I think I'll call him Mortimer."

"Mortimer?" Lillian asked. "I don't like it. What about Mickey?"

OF MOUSE AND MAN
Using many of the visual cues of Oswald, Disney and partner Ub Iwerks designed their new mouse and cranked out two cartoons. Inspired by the fame of Charles Lindbergh, the first was a gag-filled short called "Plane Crazy." The second, titled "The Gallopin' Gaucho,"

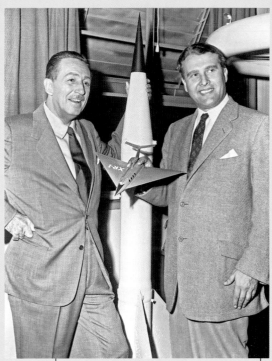

NASA

Walt Disney (left) with Dr. Wernher von Braun, 1954

cast Mickey as an Argentine outlaw. Neither sold.

Disney's solution? Make one with sound. To raise cash, Disney sold his roadster. He figured that, with the recent success of "The Jazz Singer," distributors would want a cartoon with sound, too.

He was wrong. Again and again, distributors still said no. When a promoter offered to run the cartoon for free just for the publicity value, Disney, with no other options, reluctantly agreed.

The first synchronized sound cartoon, "Steamboat Willie" premiered at New York's Colony Theatre on Nov. 18, 1928. The public loved it, but only one distributor showed interest: Universal.

Walt said no.

Finally, Disney did strike a distribution deal — with a sound-machine salesman.

COLOR, DEPTH AND 'WALT'S FOLLY'
As his Mickey cartoons took the country by storm, Disney put his profits back into his company. To ensure his artists were highly skilled, he paid for them to attend

art school and later set up an in-house training center. Disney introduced Technicolor to animation with the 1932 Silly Symphonies cartoon "Flowers and Trees." In 1937 he released "The Old Mill," which used a "multiplane" camera to add realistic depth to animation.

All of that, however, was simply a warm-up for Disney's next idea: an animated feature film. The idea had been tried in Europe (the box-office bomb "Lotte Reiniger's Adventures of Prince Achmed") but never in the States. Disney knew he had the story, a dramatic, romantic, sympathetic fairy tale he had seen as a kid as a silent film: "Snow White." Though Hollywood scoffed at the idea, dubbing it "Walt's Folly," Disney mortgaged his home to help cover expenses.

The gamble paid off. Premiering December 21, 1937, "Snow White and the Seven Dwarfs" was such a smash that within six months the Disney company had millions in the bank. The film went on to gross $8 million, at a time when a child's movie ticket was just 10 cents.

HARD TIMES

Refusing to make a sequel, Disney instead created 1940's "Fantasia" and "Pinocchio," 1941's "Dumbo" and 1942's "Bambi." All lost money. They couldn't break even without a European market, which had disappeared with the outbreak of World War II.

And there was more trouble. Rumors spread throughout the studio that major salary cuts and layoffs were coming. Soon, union organizers appeared at the studio, and on May 29, 1941, many of the company's animators went on strike.

The walkout ended in just a few weeks, but Disney firmly believed the strike was inspired by communists. In 1947 he testified before the House Un-American Activities Committee that there was a threat of Communism in the motion-picture industry, though he added "I don't think they have gotten very far, and I think the industry is made up of good Americans, just like in my plant — good, solid Americans."

For awhile it seemed Disney couldn't catch a break. "Dumbo" was scheduled to appear on the cover of Time magazine the first week of December, 1941, until Japan bombed Pearl Harbor. During the war the U.S. military took over the studio in an effort to protect a nearby Lockheed aircraft plant, an act which essentially shut down Disney's commercial business for years.

By now Disney was a chain smoker. Studio workers could tell if he was coming down the hall by listening for his cough.

A DECADE ON TOP

Walt Disney's golden touch returned during the 1950s. Animated films included 1950's "Cinderella," 1951's "Alice in Wonderland" and 1953's "Peter Pan." The 1954 movie "20,000 Leagues Under the Sea" was the company's first live-action film and the first to feature major stars, in this case Kirk Douglas, James Mason and Peter Lorre. Unlike many studio chiefs, Disney embraced television and found success with shows such as "The Mickey Mouse Club" and "Zorro."

During the decade Disney also created a series of shorts on science and technology. Broadcasts of the "Disneyland" television show included three films produced with rocket designer Dr. Wernher von Braun. A 1957 episode of the show featured "Our Friend the Atom," a collaboration with the U.S. government designed to enhance the image of nuclear energy.

Back during the war, Disney would take his daughters to Hollywood's Griffith Park, 10 miles from his home. As the girls rode the carousel he would sit on a dirty bench, eating peanuts. "As I'd sit there," he later recalled, "I felt there should be something built, some kind of an amusement enterprise, where the parents and the children could have fun together."

In 1951 he visited Copenhagen's Tivoli Gardens, a lushly landscaped park with fireworks, parades, a railroad and exotic buildings, many with little white lights. "Now this is what an amusement place should be!" Disney told his wife.

Two years later Disney bought 160 acres near Anaheim. Gathering some of his best motion-picture talent, he set about building Disneyland, the world's first theme park. Disney decided its central attraction would be a castle, and that its entrance would be a re-creation of a turn-of-the-century small town. As budgets increased Disney hocked his life insurance to get more cash. Construction began in July of 1954, and the park opened just one year later. It was a huge hit.

IT ALL COMES TOGETHER

Success continued in the 1960s. In 1961 "One Hundred and One Dalmatians" was the year's No. 1 movie, and Disney's "Wonderful World of Color" was among the first color television programs. Walt and Roy even entered the field of education. They provided the funds to merge the Los Angeles Conservatory of Music with the Chouinard Art Institute (where Disney had earlier sent his animators) to create the California Institute of the Arts. It would be the nation's first art institute to grant undergraduate and graduate degrees.

Everything came together in 1964. The New York World's Fair opened in April, and Disney's contributions, including the Audio Animatronic showcases Carousel of Progress, Great Moments with Mr. Lincoln and It's a Small World, became its most popular attractions. In August "Mary Poppins" premiered at Grauman's Chinese Theatre and soon became the studio's biggest hit ever.

In September President Johnson invited Disney to the White House to receive the Presidential Medal of Freedom, the nation's highest civilian honor. The man who 40 years earlier was bankrupt was now not only rich, but a national hero.

By then 62 years old, Disney had one dream left: to fix America's cities.

'I LIKE TO CREATE NEW THINGS'

In 1965, Disney turned his attention toward the problem of improving urban life in America. His idea: Combine the money he made from "Mary Poppins" with corporate sponsorships, and then — using 43 square miles of land he had secretly purchased in Florida — build an experimental city. Filled with technological advancements, it would demonstrate how communities could solve their problems of housing, pollution and transportation.

Disney called it the Experimental Prototype Community of Tomorrow.

EPCOT for short.

"I don't believe there is a challenge anywhere in the world that is more important than finding the solution to the problems of our cities," he said. "We think the need is for starting from scratch on virgin land and building a community that will become a prototype for the future. Epcot will be a community of tomorrow that will never be completed, but will always be introducing and testing and demonstrating new materials and new systems."

The design called for a 50-acre town center enclosed in a dome, an internationally themed shopping area, a 30-story hotel and convention complex, office space, apartments, single-family homes, monorail and PeopleMover systems, an airport and underground roads for cars and trucks. Disney even planned for a nuclear power plant. To make money he'd have a theme park, too, a larger version of Disneyland. Disney planned to finish the project by 1985.

On Nov. 15, 1965, Walt and Roy held a press conference in Orlando to announce the project. "I'm very excited about it," Walt said to the media, "because I've been storing these things up over the years. I like to create new things."

Less than a year later, he got sick. The smoking had caught up with him.

In November, 1966, doctors found a tu-mor the size of a walnut in Disney's left lung. But when they operated, they discovered the cancer had spread through the lung, and the entire organ had to be removed. Afterward Disney checked out of the hospital and went back to work, but he had to check back in just two weeks later. His body wasn't recovering.

On the night of December 14th, Disney lay in his hospital bed and discussed his Florida project with Roy, who sat at his side. Using the acoustical tiles on the ceiling above, Walt showed Roy his detailed, if imaginary, vision of the undertaking — the roads, airport, everything.

The next morning, Walt Disney died.

Some called Walt Disney too naive, a boy who never really became an adult.

But to him that was just the point.

"The American child is sensitive, humorous, open-minded, eager to learn, and has a strong sense of excitement, energy, and healthy curiosity about the world in which he lives," he wrote in 1963. "Lucky indeed is the grown-up who manages to carry these same characteristics into adult life. That's the real trouble with the world. Too many people grow up."

FUN FACTS ❯❯ Married in 1888 in Acron, Florida, 40 miles north of today's Walt Disney World, Walt Disney's parents later grew oranges and ran a hotel in nearby Kissimmee. ❯❯ In school, when one art assignment called for drawing a still life of flowers, Disney drew his with faces and arms. His teacher didn't approve. ❯❯ The Disney company regained the rights to Oswald in 2006. Universal gave the bunny back in exchange for sportscaster Al Michaels. Really. ❯❯ In 1949 Disney built a scale-model live-steam railway in his backyard. The half-mile layout included a 46-foot-long trestle, overpasses and a 90-foot tunnel underneath his wife's flower beds. ❯❯ His favorite meal was chili and beans with tomato juice. ❯❯ He was unable to pronounce the word "aluminum." When Disney hosted his television show, writers made a point not to include it. ❯❯ According to legend, Disney's last words came as he looked out of his hospital window and remarked how shabby the company water tower looked. Since then, company execs have made sure the tower is regularly repainted, as is its replica at Disney's Hollywood Studios. ❯❯ Had he not smoked, Disney may have lived into the 21st century, easily long enough to finish his EPCOT city. One of his brothers lived until 98; his sister died at 92. He was born exactly one year earlier than U.S. Sen. Strom Thurmond, who died in 2003.

SOURCES FOR THIS ARTICLE INCLUDE "WALT DISNEY: AN AMERICAN ORIGINAL" BY BOB THOMAS AND "WALT DISNEY AND THE QUEST FOR COMMUNITY" BY STEVE MANNHEIM

The Disney Fab Five

An introduction to Donald Duck, Goofy, Pluto and that scandalous couple, Mickey and Minnie Mouse

MICKEY MOUSE

Since his debut in 1928's "Steamboat Willie," Disney's cartoon titan has been a pop-culture icon. Modeled in part on silent-film star Charlie Chaplin, Mickey Mouse was an underdog who dreamed big — a character everyone could root for. In the 1930s, his optimistic attitude was an antidote to the Great Depression. During World War II he become symbolic of the can-do attitude of the United States. During the 1960s Mickey Mouse was embraced by the counterculture.

Today he's still enormously popular — the most recognized and celebrated cartoon character in history. Sure he's a corporate symbol, but Mickey's also an honest, pure piece of Americana.

When his cartoons debuted in the late 1920s, an opening short had been a common feature at movie theaters for more than a decade. Mickey's, though, were different. They had sound (a novelty at the time) and Mickey had a strong personality, a happy-go-lucky approach to life that was said to be Walt Disney's alter ego. At many theaters, a 7-minute Mickey short would draw more of a crowd than the main feature, and the name "Mickey Mouse" would be the largest on the marquee. "Mickey Mouse is an international hero," Fortune magazine wrote in 1934, "better known than Roosevelt."

After World War II Mickey became so popular with children artists found it difficult to give him interesting behaviors. If he misbehaved, parents would complain. In 1955 Mickey became the walk-around host of California's Disneyland. In the 1960s his kindhearted innocence made him a symbol of the counterculture.

MINNIE MOUSE

Minnie is Mickey's girlfriend. She's always around to flatter, giggle at and swoon over her main squeeze. Still, she does have her own life. Quick-witted and energetic, she loves animals, cooking and gardening, and can play the harmonica, guitar and piano.

She also gets mad. After Mickey forces her to kiss him in 1928's "Plane Crazy," Minnie slaps him, then jumps out of their open-cockpit airplane, forcing it to crash. She smashes a lamp on Mickey's head when he pulls her nose in 1930's "The Cactus Kid." And when she mistakenly thinks Mickey has given her a bone for a present in 1933's "Puppy Love," she kicks Mickey out of her house and sobs "I hate him! I hate all men!"

They always make up. Mickey, in fact, rules Minnie's world. In 1995's "Runaway Brain," she goes shopping for a swimsuit. "Oh my!" she says, looking in a mirror as she eyes a skimpy two-piece number. "What would Mickey think?"

As portrayed in the 1928 cartoon "The Gallopin' Gaucho," the couple first lays eyes on each other in a bar in Argentina. When Minnie, a flirty dancer, bats her eyes at Mickey, a cigarette-smoking outlaw, he watches her perform, chugs a beer, then grabs her for a tango. Minnie has an old flame (suave, tap-dancing Mortimer) in the 1936 cartoon "Mickey's Rival." In 1933's "Mickey's Steam Roller," she has kids.

DONALD DUCK

He's rude, he's crude, he doesn't wear pants. He shouts, he pouts and loses his temper at the drop of a pin. He has a serious eye for the ladies, and often just likes to be mean.

Yet who doesn't love Donald Duck? He responds to life the way we are tempted to, but never dare. Created in 1934 as a foil for the then-gentlemanly Mickey, Donald soon emerged as Disney's most popular star. Besides his bombastic personality, Donald is known for his nearly unintelligible voice, originally done by bird impressionist Clarence "Ducky" Nash. The "duck with all the bad luck" is also famous for his "hopping mad" boxing stance, a leaning, jumping posture with one arm straight and the other twirling like a windmill. (Watch closely during "The Lion King" segment of Mickey's PhilharMagic and you'll see it.)

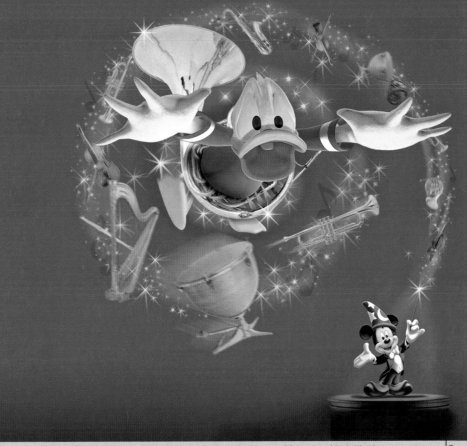

Mickey Mouse and Donald Duck star in Mickey's PhilharMagic, a 3-D movie at Magic Kingdom

GOOFY

A good-hearted simpleton, Goofy appeals to your inner idiot. He's clumsy and gullible, has a hard time concentrating and seldom finishes what he starts (just like many husbands). He has lousy posture, his clothes don't fit, his stomach is too big — yet he always mugs for a camera.

Originally known as Dippy Dog, Goofy made his debut in 1930. He later became the host of a series of "How To" sports parodies. As for the eternal Goofy question — man or dog? — the answer is... both! Unlike Pluto, Goofy is an upright talking character. But he has the physical characteristics of a dog, including floppy ears and a long snout.

PLUTO

One of the greatest dogs in Hollywood history, Pluto brings the unique personality of Man's Best Friend to life. The only Five Fab character with no human traits, Mickey's pet doesn't speak or, except at the theme parks, walk upright. Instead, the gangly yellow hound licks, sniffs, romps and runs in a fashion instantly recognizable to dog lovers everywhere. In cartoons Pluto is known for his vivid facial expressions, as he is always thinking.

FUN FACTS ›› Walt Disney originally did the voices for Mickey and Minnie. ›› President Roosevelt showed Mickey cartoons at the White House in the 1930s. ›› In 1933 Mickey received 800,000 fan letters, the most of any Hollywood star. ›› During World War II, the password of the Allied forces on D-Day was "Mickey Mouse." ›› Mickey was banned in Nazi Germany in 1933, the Soviet Union in 1936, Yugoslavia in 1937, Italy in 1938 and East Germany in 1954. ›› In the 1950s Disney transformed Goofy into George Geef, a suburban everyman often drawn without ears. ›› Pluto once spoke. In the 1931 short "The Moose Hunt," the dog got down on his knees and, impersonating Al Jolson, proclaimed "Mammy!" Moments later, Pluto looked into Mickey's eyes and whispered "Kiss me!"

Planning Your Trip

Planning your Walt Disney World vacation takes some thought, but it isn't brain surgery. All it takes is this book, access to the Internet, a cell phone and a couple of hours of your time. You can do it at Starbucks. Ideally you should put your plan together seven months early. Here's how to do it:

1 DECIDE WHEN TO GO

You can have a good time at Disney World any day of the year, but if you've got the flexibility, the first two weeks of December is the **best time to go.** It's not crowded, and there's more to see and do than any other time of the year, thanks to the holiday decor and entertainment. Crowds are also light, and hotel rooms often less expensive, from the middle of January to Valentine's Day, late April to late May and the weeks between Labor Day and mid-November (but it's not all good: some attractions shut down during these periods and the Magic Kingdom often closes at 6 p.m.). The least crowded week is the one after Labor Day.

The **worst times to visit?** July and early August, when crowds are thick and the air even thicker, and between Christmas and New Year's, when the crowds are incredible. In general, the parks can be packed any time schools are not in session. In fact, many families take their kids out of school to visit Disney in a less-crowded period. If you must come during a peak time, you do get the benefit of the parks being open late. For detailed **yearly weather data** log on to weather.com, type in the ZIP code 32830 and then scroll down to the tab "Averages."

2 DECIDE HOW LONG TO STAY

Want to see the best of everything Disney has to offer? You'll need **at least a week.** Each theme park takes at least a day to fully enjoy, and you can easily spend a day at each water park. Diversions such as golf, fishing and horseback riding add variety to your trip, and then there's the nightlife of Downtown Disney. And remember, it's a vacation. You're supposed to *relax.*

Longer stays also cost less per day, as there's not much difference between a basic 3-day park ticket ($203 for adults) and one that's good for a week ($225). Because of this, a family of four typically spends about $525 a day on its hotel room, food and tickets during a three-day Disney vacation, but only $425 a day if it stays a week. If you can't stay that long, **three days is enough** to get a good dose of Disney World, especially if you know just what to do. The column on the next page lists all of Disney's theme and water parks and other entertainment centers and recreation options.

3 DECIDE WHERE TO STAY
As for accommodations, you have plenty of choices. Disney itself owns 19 resorts. There are ten others on Disney World property, and many major-chain properties within 10 miles. What's the difference? **Disney resorts** have elaborate theming and offer benefits such as more time in the parks, free transportation options and packaged dining and recreation plans. Disney resort guests also get first crack at Disney restaurant reservations. They can make them 190 days early, compared to 180 days for the general public. Rates range from $80 to $2,000 a night, though most rooms go for $100 to $300. Also on Disney World property: the **Walt Disney World Swan and Dolphin** (run by Starwood), two convention hotels within walking distance of Epcot and Disney's Hollywood Studios; **Shades of Green,** an Armed Forces Recreation Center near Magic Kingdom; and the **Downtown Disney resorts,** a group of older, brand-name hotels at the eastern edge of the property which offer larger rooms and usually have availability when Disney itself doesn't. Dozens of hotels and resorts **outside of Disney** offer good rates and availability, sometimes with free breakfast. A few are spectacular. *For complete details see the Accommodations chapter.*

4 CHOOSE YOUR TICKETS
With park tickets, besides the number of days you want, you also need to consider three options. The **Park Hopper** ($45) lets you visit more than one park a day. **Water Park Fun & More** ($50) adds visits to Blizzard Beach, Typhoon Lagoon, DisneyQuest, Pleasure Island and/or Disney's Wide World of Sports. **No Expiration** ($15–$180, depending on how many days your ticket includes) means unused days never expire. You can add the No Expiration choice anytime within 14 days of your first use. The easiest way to go: buy the Park Hopper, and, if you're going to be here awhile, the Water Park Fun & More. *Once you purchase your tickets, you can always upgrade them (but can't downgrade them) by visiting a ticket location at a theme park, Downtown Disney or Disney resort. Details at 407-W-DISNEY (934-7639) or at disneyworld.com.*

Plan on visiting more than once this year? Consider an **annual pass.** The basic model includes 365 consecutive days of unlimited admission to the four theme parks, plus perks such as free theme-park parking and a smattering of dining, entertainment and merchandise discounts. A Premium Annual Pass adds admission to the water parks, Pleasure Island, DisneyQuest and Wide World of Sports.

Disney offers many ticket **discount plans.** Florida residents have a variety of options. They can get discounted 3- and 4-day tickets (with 6-month expiration periods) and annual passes, can buy a special Seasonal Pass, and save 50 percent on the Park Hopper and Water Park Fun & More options.

DISNEY WORLD WEATHER
Temperatures

■ Average daily range
■ Record monthly range

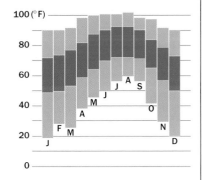

SOURCE: The Weather Channel

What there is to do

THEME PARKS

Magic Kingdom. The signature Walt Disney World park has Cinderella Castle, Main Street U.S.A. and the most attractions. *Page 34.*

Epcot. A permanent World's Fair, Epcot showcases nature, science and technology in its Future World and highlights 11 countries in its World Showcase pavilions. *Page 96.*

Disney's Hollywood Studios. Formerly known as Disney-MGM Studios, this intimate park celebrates show biz with stage musicals, stunt performances and thrill rides. *Page 132.*

Disney's Animal Kingdom. This lush park includes live animals, elaborate attractions and African and Asian villages. *Page 172.*

WATER PARKS

Blizzard Beach. Big, thrilling slides highlight this "melting ski resort." *Page 221.*

Typhoon Lagoon. Includes a surf pool, a water coaster and snorkeling with fish. *Page 228.*

DOWNTOWN DISNEY

AMC Theater. *Page 239.*

DisneyQuest. A high-tech arcade. *Page 239.*

House of Blues. Live concerts. *Page 239.*

La Nouba. A European circus. *Page 240.*

Pleasure Island. Nightclubs. *Page 243.*

DIVERSIONS

Bicycle and surrey rentals. *Page 254.*

Boat charters. *Page 254.*

Boat rentals. *Page 254.*

Campfire. *Page 254.*

Carriage and wagon rides. *Page 254.*

Disney's Wide World of Sports. *Page 257.*

Diving and snorkeling. *Page 254.*

Dolphin encounter. *Page 255.*

Fishing. *Page 255.*

Golf. *Page 248.*

Horseback riding. *Page 256.*

Jogging. *Page 256.*

Miniature golf. *Page 250.*

Spas. *Page 256.*

Stock car driving. *Page 252.*

Surfing lessons. *Page 251.*

Tennis. *Page 257.*

Tours. *Page 256.*

Water sports. *Page 253.*

DINING

Theme-park restaurants. *Page 300.*

Resort restaurants. *Page 305.*

Character meals. Disney characters visit your table as you eat. *Page 312.*

Dinner shows. A Polynesian luau, Western stage show and outdoor barbecue. *Page 315.*

Downtown Disney restaurants. *Page 316.*

SHOPPING

Theme parks. *Pages 73, 116–129, 157, 185.*

Downtown Disney. *Page 244.*

Floridians also save 10 percent on one-day base tickets if they buy them over the phone or online *(407-W-DISNEY, disneyworld.com)* or at a Florida Disney Store or military base. Convention attendees can often get special theme-park tickets (good only after 2 p.m. or 4 p.m.) through their hotel. Military personnel can buy discounted tickets at the Shades of Green resort. AAA members can get discounts through that organization.

5 WANT A PACKAGE DEAL?

If you're going to stay at a Disney resort, you may want to consider one of Disney's pre-paid dining and recreation packages. If you use them wisely, these plans can help control costs and save money. The **Disney Dining Plan** (also known as "Magic Your Way Plus Dining," about $40 per day per adult, $11 per child) gives you one table-service meal, one counter-service meal and one snack per day. You can choose from over 100 restaurants, including some with character meals. Is it a good deal? Yes, if you order the fancy stuff at the table-service restaurants. Want to really chow down? Choose the **Disney Deluxe Dining Plan** (about $70 per day per adult, $20 per child), which lets you eat all three of your daily meals at table-service restaurants and comes with two snacks (that's a lot of food!). If you want an active vacation but don't need to spend much time in the parks, the **Disney Premium Plan** (about $150 per day per adult, $100 per child) can be a great deal. It gives you unlimited use of many recreation options, including golf and water sports. Like the Deluxe plan, you get three meals a day and all can be in table-service restaurants. The package even includes vouchers to La Nouba, unlimited use of child-care facilities and unlimited theme-park tours. You do need to buy at least a one-day park ticket. Book this plan six months early to cherry-pick your dining times, tee times, etc. The **Disney Platinum Plan** (about $200 per day per adult, $130 per child, available only to guests of Disney Deluxe and Vacation Club resorts) includes everything in the Premium Package and adds such extras as an itinerary planning service, a spa treatment, fireworks cruise and reserved seating for Fantasmic. Each package has some complications and restric-

tions. As of 2008, the plans no longer include gratuities. For more information see our Restaurants chapter.

Another way to save on food is the **Disney Dining Experience** (DDE) card *($65–$85 annually)*, available to annual passholders and Florida residents. It saves its holder and up to nine guests 20 percent off food and beverages during non-holiday periods at most Disney table-service restaurants and a handful of other spots, including the food courts at Value Resorts. As of 2008, an automatic 18 percent gratuity is added to all DDE transactions. *For information call 407-566-5858, weekdays 9 a.m. to 5 p.m.*

6 BOOK IT!

To book tickets, a Disney room or a dining/recreation package go to disneyworld.com or call 407-W-DISNEY (934-7639) from 7 a.m. to 10 p.m. Eastern time. Other resort numbers are in our Accommodations chapter. Note: Annual passes are not sold online.

7 PLAN YOUR DAYS

First, determine what days to go to what theme parks. **Log on to disneyworld.com** and click "Calendar" to find the hours, Extra Magic Hours, special events and parade and fireworks times of the parks during your stay (available six months in advance). Check pages.prodigy.net/stevesoares for Disney's live entertainment schedules.

Not everyone jumps for joy when it rains, but the parks are usually less crowded and most attractions are indoors anyway. Most gift shops sell ponchos. The best thing to bring? A happy-go-lucky attitude.

Then **make your restaurant and recreation reservations** around that schedule. Dinner shows take reservations a year in advance, restaurants 180 days early (190 days if you're staying at a Disney resort). For recreation, you can book fishing and surfing a year out, tours and stock car driving six months in advance, boat cruises and golf tee times 30 days early (90 days for Disney resort guests) and water sports 30 days early. Other reservations to consider: Birthday parties, florist services, special events, and stroller and ECV rentals (offered with reservations from outside vendors). For phone numbers see the directory on the last page.

When planning your days, keep in mind the most common mistakes guests make when they visit Walt Disney World: ❶ They don't make dining reservations before they leave home. ❷ They don't get to a park before it opens. ❸ They don't take advantage of Fastpass. ❹ They underestimate how long it takes to travel on Disney transportation. ❺ They try to go to too many parks in one day. ❻ They wear themselves out.

GRAND GATHERINGS are unique events for groups of eight or more. They include a special breakfast at Magic Kingdom, unusual dinners at Epcot and Disney's Animal Kingdom and a Wishes fireworks cruise, all with character appearances and entertainment. For details call 407-939-7526.

Practical information

What to pack

Let's see. You're going to the hottest state in the country and plan to spend all day outside walking on pavement. Sounds like fun! Actually, it doesn't have to be that bad, and you don't need to look like a frump. Just be prepared, and dress light and comfortably. **Fundamental** are T-shirts, loose-fitting cotton tops, capris and shorts with large pockets, baseball caps and swimsuits, and broken-in walking shoes. Pack two pair of shoes per person, so if it rains everyone can still have a dry pair. During the winter you'll need clothes you can layer, such as jackets, sweaters and sweatshirts, as days start off cool but warm quickly. January mornings can be below freezing at 9 a.m. but 60 degrees by noon. Temperatures at 7 p.m. will be in the 50s through March. As for **other essentials**, pack an umbrella, sunglasses and sunscreen (sweat-proof, SPF rating at least 30). Instead of a purse, try a waist pack to keep your hands free. Don't forget tickets and confirmations. **Dress your kids** like you dress yourself, casually and comfortably, but protect them more from the sun. Wide-brimmed hats help. Bring snacks (granola bars, raisin boxes) and, for autographs, a Sharpie pen.

Getting here

BY AUTOMOBILE Two major highways border Walt Disney World. **Interstate 4** runs along the southern edge of the property, connecting it to Orlando (18 miles northeast) and Tampa (53 miles southwest). An interstate-like toll road opened in 2007, **Florida 429** runs along the western edge of Disney World, creating a short-cut for travelers coming from the north on Florida's Turnpike. It saves about a half-hour in travel time compared to taking the turnpike all the way into Orlando, and instead of congested urbania offers a pleasant, almost traffic-free drive past farms and orange groves. To use it, take the turnpike south to Exit 267A, then head southeast on Florida 429 11 miles to Exit 8, which brings you to Disney's new Western Way entrance road. The toll for 429 is $1. As you travel the new

highway, notice the view to your left. After about 4 miles you can see Cinderella Castle, Space Mountain, the Contemporary Resort, Spaceship Earth and the Walt Disney World Dolphin Resort in the distance.

FROM THE AIRPORT Walt Disney World is 19 miles southwest of the Orlando International Airport. You can get to Disney by taxi *($40–$60, Yellow Cab: 407-699-9999)*, town car *($60–$90, Mears: 407-423-5566)*, bus or van *($18 per person, Mears: 407-423-5566)* or by renting a car *(Hertz: 800-654-3131. Avis: 800-331-1212. National: 800-227-7368.)*. **The simplest route** (25 min.): take the airport's South Exit road 4 miles to Florida 417 ($2 toll), go west on 417 13 miles to Osceola Parkway (Exit 3), then west again 2 miles. Guests staying at a Disney-owned resort can take one of Disney's free Magical Express buses *(see Accommodations chapter)*.

Getting around

You can get around the 47-square-mile Disney property via a network of two- and four-lane roads (see map, page 8) or by using Disney's free transportation system.

A complimentary **bus system** connects all Disney resorts with the theme and water parks as well as Downtown Disney, and travel between some parks. Other buses take guests to character breakfasts. The famous **monorail** track forms a giant Figure 8. The top loop connects the Transportation and Ticket Center (TTC) with the Magic Kingdom and the Polynesian, Grand Floridian and Contemporary resorts. The bottom loop connects the TTC to Epcot. **Ferry boats** connect the Magic Kingdom with the TTC and resorts that front Seven Seas Lagoon and Bay Lake; Epcot and Disney's Hollywood Studios with the resorts between those parks; and Downtown Disney with the Port Orleans, Old Key West and Saratoga Springs properties.

There are three Hess **gasoline stations** on Disney property — just outside the Magic Kingdom parking lot, near an entrance to Disney's Hollywood Studios and across from Downtown Disney. The map on page 8 shows their exact locations.

▶ The most important item to pack? Broken-in shoes. You can't buy them here.

Meeting characters

Meeting a Disney character can make a lifelong memory. Though some fantasy-free parents may not appreciate it, the Disney characters are real. That's not a sweaty young woman in a fur suit, it's Pluto. Just ask your kids. There are three ways to meet characters: at meet-and-greet lines, parades and character meals. Sometimes you just come upon one.

FACE OR FUR? Disney has two types of characters. Face characters, such as Cinderella, show the performer's actual face. Fur characters, such as Winnie the Pooh, are fully costumed. Though face characters rarely intimidate, the odd, huge heads of the fur family sometimes do. To help your child feel comfortable, talk with her beforehand so she knows what to expect. For meet-and-greet lines, buy her an autograph book to give her something to focus on besides the face-to-fur encounter. Don't push her; the characters are super patient. Watch your time: each park has so many autograph lines that stopping at them all could take all day.

FINDING CHARACTERS Though Mickey, Minnie, Donald, Goofy and Pluto seem to pop up everywhere, many characters appear in only one or two places. Still, it's easy to find the one you want. Each park's free Times Guide has an overview of character locations, and most cast members can track down the schedule of any character. If those ideas don't work, try a Guest Relations office. Also check out the Character Meal section of this book's Restaurants chapter.

Wide-eyed wonder. Though they usually love to meet Disney characters (here, Pinocchio), many children still tend to back away.

Childcare

THEME PARKS Each Disney theme park has a **Baby Care Center** with private nursing areas, rocking chairs and a microwave oven. Each sells supplies and over-the-counter medications. Moms can **nurse** their children in public throughout the property.

RESORT CENTERS Five Disney-owned resorts include an evening **childcare center.**

'You can't get there from here'

Despite its benefits, Disney's bus system has a few irritating facets: ❶ Though they run from theme park to theme park, and from any theme park to Blizzard Beach, the buses do not go from theme parks to Downtown Disney or Typhoon Lagoon. ❷ There is no direct service *between* resorts. You can, however, take a bus to a theme park or Downtown Disney, then transfer to another one that goes to another resort. (Downtown Disney buses often aren't as crowded, and run until after 1 a.m.) ❸ Buses do not run from the Epcot resorts to Epcot, or to Disney's Hollywood Studios. Guests staying at the BoardWalk, Yacht and Beach Club or Walt Disney World Swan and Dolphin can get to those parks via a ferry boat or on foot. They enter Epcot through that park's rear "International Gateway" entrance. (During thunderstorms, when the boats can't run, the buses do.) ❹ Disney buses do not serve Disney's Wide World of Sports except from (but of course!) Disney's Hollywood Studios (8 a.m. to 8 p.m.).

▶ The easiest thing to forget to pack? The charger for your cell phone or camera.

Disney's Animal Kingdom Lodge, Beach Club, Grand Floridian, Polynesian and Wilderness Lodge resorts each have a special, secure room staffed with childcare professionals and filled with arts and crafts, books, games, toys and videos. Rates are $10 per hour per child with a two-hour minimum charge, and include dinner from 6 to 8 p.m. Children must be fully toilet trained (no pull-ups) and between 4 and 12 years old. Hours are 4 or 4:30 p.m. to midnight daily. For details or reservations call 407-WDW-DINE.

IN-ROOM CARE Disney works with two in-room childcare services. **Kids Nite Out** (*800-696-8105, 407-828-0920, kidsniteout.com)* provides baby-sitting and childcare for kids ages 6 weeks to 12 years, including those with special needs. Caregivers arrive prepared with age-appropriate toys, activities, books, games, and arts and crafts. Rates start at $14 per hour with a 4-hour minimum charge, plus a $10 transportation fee. **All About Kids** (*800-728-6506, 407-812-9300, all-about-kids.com)* offers child-sitting services; services for adults, those with special needs and pets; and rents car seats, high chairs, playpens, toys and other baby and children's equipment. Childcare rates start at $12 per hour with a 4-hour minimum charge, plus a $10 transportation fee.

Photos and video

Keeping a camera with you is a good idea. Besides letting you photograph the landmarks and characters, it allows you to capture spontaneous and silly moments that create treasured memories. Whatever shots you snap, take turns being the photographer. If dad takes all of the pictures, none of them will include dad. Also, consider disposable cameras for your kids, and waterproof cameras for the water parks. The results are almost sure to add to your memories.

CAMERA SUPPLIES Every theme park has a Camera Center which sells still and video cameras, batteries, memory cards and other supplies. Each is easy to find: it's just inside the park, in the first building on your right. At Magic Kingdom it's in Exposition Hall on Main Street U.S.A.; at Epcot it's Gateway Gifts under Spaceship Earth; at Disney's Hollywood Studios it's the Dark-

room on Hollywood Blvd.; at Animal Kingdom it's inside Garden Gate Gifts. At the water parks, camera supplies, including waterproof disposable cameras, are sold at the main gift shops. *Guest Relations offices will charge your batteries at no charge — if you have the charger.*

DIGITAL IMAGING Three Disney theme parks have **Kodak PictureMaker kiosks**, which let you create CDs of your digital files (200 images for $11.99) or make 4-by-6-inch prints (69 cents). Simplified versions of machines found in drug and grocery stores, these touch-screen kiosks accept nearly every type of storage device. You'll find them at the Camera Centers at Magic Kingdom and Disney's Hollywood Studios and in the Imageworks area inside Epcot's Imagination pavilion.

PHOTOPASS With this service Disney photographers take shots of you and your group, but you pay for only the images you choose. Here's how it works: The photographers are stationed in front of each theme-park icon, most character locations and other key spots, as well as Downtown Disney and some hotels. Whenever you like, you have him or her take your picture, using a credit-card-like PhotoPass that all photographers hand out for free. Disney applies no sales pressure. You view the images at theme-park Camera Centers or at disneyphotopass.com, and decide which, if any, you want to purchase. You can order single photos, photo packages, CDs, custom scrapbooks (that can include photos from your own camera), even DVD slideshows. You can view your images for up to three days at any Camera Center or up to 30 days online.

Though it has its benefits, PhotoPass is not a replacement for your own camera: the photographers shoot only posed photos at particular locations. If you use it, write down your Photopass ID number on a sheet of paper. That way, if you lose your card you won't lose your images.

SOUVENIR RIDE PHOTOS At some attractions an automated camera takes your picture at a climactic moment, then an exitway gift shop offers to sell you the souvenir. This happens at Splash Mountain and Buzz Lightyear's Space Ranger Spin at the Magic Kingdom, Test Track at Epcot, Rock 'n'

▶ The most important item to pack? Broken-in shoes. You can't buy them here.

Roller Coaster Starring Aerosmith and The Twilight Zone Tower of Terror at Disney's Hollywood Studios and Dinosaur and Expedition Everest at Animal Kingdom. The system is now being updated to let you add these images into your PhotoPass account.

Avoiding long lines

FASTPASS You'll skip the line at the most popular attractions with this free service. It's an automated reservation system that saves you a place in line at a time window later in the day.

Here's how it works: When you place your park ticket into a Fastpass machine (located at attraction entrances), you get your ticket back plus a slip of paper that shows your reservation time, which is a one-hour window. When you return at that time, you enter the attraction through a separate, Fastpass-only entrance that has little or no wait. You can't pick your

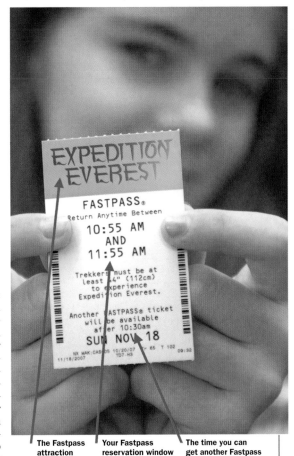

The Fastpass attraction · Your Fastpass reservation window · The time you can get another Fastpass

time, but a display sign shows you what it will be before you get your pass. Each ticket-holder can get only one Fastpass at a time, but can accumulate many throughout a day. The service is free but not well promoted, so only about half of all visitors use it. Those that do see 25 to 75 percent more attractions, depending on crowds.

Here's how to take full advantage of it: ❶ Designate someone in your party as your Fastpass supervisor. This person will hold all your park tickets, go off to get Fastpasses for your entire party throughout the day and watch the time. Hello, Dad? ❷ Always hold at least one Fastpass, so you're always "on the clock" for at least one attraction. Get one when you get in the park, then others as often as possible through the day. ❸ Don't sweat it if you miss the return time. Disney rarely en-

forces it. ❹ Use the service for every Fastpass attraction except those you'll be riding before 10 a.m. or very late at night.

CHILD SWAP Another way to cut time in line is to use Disney's Child Swap system. At attractions with minimum-height requirements, if a child doesn't meet the restriction one parent can wait with him at the loading area, while the rest of the group goes on the ride or sees the show. When it's over the parents switch. The second parent boards immediately, without waiting in a second line. Child Swap is free of charge, but not publicized. To use it, simply ask the cast member at the attraction entrance. *Child Swap is not available at Magic Kingdom's Tomorrowland Indy Speedway. Though that attraction requires guests to be 52 inches tall to take a car out alone, it has no restrictions on simply riding in one.*

▶ Fastpasses can 'sell out' by noon at hot rides such as Expedition Everest and Soarin'.

SINGLE RIDER LINES A third way to bypass a line is to enter an attraction through its Single Rider line, a special line at a handful of attractions that Disney uses to fill the random leftover seats in ride vehicles. Each person in your group will be sitting with strangers, but during peak periods choosing an attraction's Single Rider line can save you up to an hour or more in waiting time compared to its Standby Line. Single Rider lines are at four Disney World attractions — Mission Space and Test Track at Epcot, Rock 'n' Roller Coaster Starring Aerosmith at Disney's Hollywood Studios and Expedition Everest at Animal Kingdom — as well as the chair lift that carries guests up Mt. Gushmore at Blizzard Beach.

EXTRA MAGIC HOURS The easiest way to avoid a long line is to simply go to a park when less people are there, and if you're staying at a Disney-owned-and-operated resort, there's an easy way to do just that. Each day one of the theme parks, water parks or both opens an hour early, or stays open up to three hours later, for guests staying at Disney resorts, the Walt Disney World Swan and Dolphin, Shades of Green and the Hilton on Hotel Plaza Blvd. To get in early you'll need a resort ID (and a park ticket); to stay late you'll need a resort ID and a wristband, which you get at a table at the park. Not every attraction, restaurant and shop is open during the extended hours, but most major ones are. *If you're not going to take advantage of a park's early-open benefit, don't go to it at all that day. It will be extra crowded all day long. If you're going to a park with nighttime Extra Magic Hours, you do NOT have to be in the park before the normal closing time.*

Money matters

There's at least one **ATM** at every theme park and resort. *Most debit and credit cards are accepted. $2–$2.50 fee per transaction.* Across from the Downtown Disney Marketplace, SunTrust Bank handles **cash advances** (Discover, MasterCard or Visa) and wire transfers. *Open 9 a.m.–4 p.m. weekdays, until 5:30 p.m. Thursdays. 407-828-6103.* In the nearby CrossRoads shopping center, Gooding's Supermarket handles **Western Union transfers.** *8 a.m.–*

10 p.m. daily. 407-827-1200. All Disney charge locations accept these **credit cards:** American Express, Diner's Club, Discover, JCB, MasterCard and Visa. Character-faced **Disney Dollars** are accepted as currency at the theme parks and Disney-owned resorts and gift shops. They're sold at Guest Relations centers, Disney concierge desks and the World of Disney store at Downtown Disney. Nearly any purchase can be made with a **traveler's check.** SunTrust Bank handles the AmEx brand. Guest Relations centers will **exchange foreign currency** up to $100.

Guest Assistance Cards

Each Guest Relations office has complimentary Guest Assistance Cards that its cast members hand out to visitors who require special assistance. There are different cards for different disabilities. Each about the size of a Pop Tart, these cards are easy to get, but the particular one you receive depends entirely on how well you communicate your situation, and, in some cases, how well the desk attendant understands the policy.

For example, if your child is autistic, you want the card that lets your party enter attractions through their Alternate Entrances (the way to make sure you get it: when you're speaking with the Guest Relations cast member, make sure you say the word "Autism"). Known internally by many cast members, in fact, as the "Autistic Card," the Alternate Entrance Card doesn't provide front-of-the-line access, but at many attractions it lets you enter through a separate entrance which will have a shorter wait. For example, at Magic Kingdom's It's a Small World you'll board through the wheelchair entrance, and at Animal Kingdom's Kilimanjaro Safaris you'll be put in the Fastpass line. It won't help at smaller attractions such as Dumbo, or at shows, or at character greeting lines, and it won't get you seated any faster at a restaurant. It is good for a party of up to six people.

You can get a card at any Guest Relations office, which are located at the front of each theme park as well as at Downtown Disney. A card is good for the length of your stay, or up to six months for annual passholders. And, believe it or not, you do not need a let-

▶ If you ask, Child Swap may be "unofficially" available at nearly any attraction.

ter from a doctor. Disney simply trusts you. If you have a problem getting your card, stay polite but ask to speak to a manager or supervisor. If you're planning to get your card at a theme park, consider getting to the park one hour before it opens. The Guest Relations walk-up windows just outside the park will be open, so you'll have plenty of time to work things out while still beating the crowds.

Pets

Five small kennels — at **Magic Kingdom** *(407-824-6568)*, **Epcot** *(407-560-6229)*, **Disney's Hollywood Studios** *(407-560-4282)*, **Disney's Animal Kingdom** *(407-938-2100)* and **Fort Wilderness Resort & Campground** *(407-824-2735)* — offer daytime and overnight caged boarding for dogs, cats, rabbits and other small creatures. The animals are not exercised; dog owners must stop by twice a day to walk their pet (three times for puppies). You get 24-hour access. *Day boarding: $10 per day. Overnight: $15 ($13 for Disney resort guests). No reservations. Vaccinations req. Cats and dogs must be 8 weeks. Fort Wilderness campers may keep their pet with them for $5 per day. Except for Fort Wilderness, only service animals are allowed in Disney resorts, theme parks, water parks or Downtown Disney.*

Birthdays

Free "It's My Birthday Today" **buttons** available at Guest Relations offices will cue cast members to recognize your birthday boy or girl — of any age. **Goofy will call** your Disney hotel room with a free birthday greeting; to arrange it call 407-824-2222. Many table-service restaurants will bring out a "surprise" 6-inch **birthday cake** ($12.50) with advance notice. The cakes can be personalized with 48 hours notice at 407-824-7091. You can arrange a **birthday party** at the Winter Summerland miniature golf course or Blizzard Beach water park *($16–$20 per person, includes cake and either hot dogs or pizza)* or a special **fireworks cruise** at Epcot. *Details: 407-WDW-BDAY (939-2329).*

Makeovers

A young girl can be made up as pretty as a princess at Disney's two **Bibbidi Bobbidi Bou-**

tiques, inside Magic Kingdom's Cinderella Castle and at Downtown Disney's World of Disney store. Services include hair styling, makeup and nails. Each package comes with a sash. Boys can become "cool dudes." *$45–$180. Ages 3 and up. Reservations: 407-WDW-STYLE (939-7895).*

Weddings and honeymoons

Up to a dozen couples tie the knot at Walt Disney World every day. And no wonder: from a practical standpoint it has unrivaled facilities for a family gathering, great year-round weather and the one-stop shopping of its **Fairy Tale Weddings** division. To many couples Disney World is also a home of romance, most of it fictional and childish to be sure, but still meaningful nonetheless. The average wedding costs $26,000 and includes 100 people, but prices for small affairs start at $2,450. **Honeymoon packages** include an online registry, which allows couples to create a wish list for its trip and have family and friends contribute toward the particulars. *For details call 877-566-0969 or go online to disneyweddings.com or disneyhoneymoons.com.*

▶ Have more questions? Call the Disney World information line at 407-824-2222.

Maleficent contemplates a dastardly deed during the Dream Along with Mickey castle show

Magic Kingdom

i t's a world that, if real, you'd love to escape to. A land straight out of your imagination, filled with barbershop quartets and hoop skirts, small towns and clean streets, charming pirates and cute little dolls. A kingdom where everyone is always glad to see you. The definitive theme park experience, Magic Kingdom has a universal appeal. For newcomers it's a postcard come to life; for veterans it's like seeing an old friend.

LAY OF THE LAND The park is laid out like a spoked wheel. You enter via Main Street U.S.A., which leads to a hub in front of Cinderella Castle. From there paths lead to Adventureland; Liberty Square and Frontierland; Fantasyland; Mickey's Toontown Fair; and Tomorrowland.

Walt Disney's childhood home of Marceline, Mo., helped inspire **Main Street U.S.A.,** a thoroughfare from a hundred years ago. It's complete with horse-drawn trolleys, period entertainers, even a vintage barbershop. The sound of beating drums introduces you to **Adventureland,** an eclectic mix of African jungles, Arabian nights, Caribbean architecture and South Seas landscaping. Major attractions include Jungle Cruise and Pirates of the Caribbean. **Liberty Square** honors our Colonial heritage. Federal and Georgian architec-

> **"It's easy to be snippy about the Magic Kingdom, but once you're here you have to open your mind to it."**
> — *Alan Cumming, actor*

ture brings back the time of the Revolutionary War. The main attractions: the Haunted Mansion and the Hall of Presidents. **Frontierland** looks to be a 19th-century rural American village. Theatrical touches include raised wooden sidewalks, rocking chairs, checkerboard tables and lots of banjo and fiddle music twangin' from the trees. Attractions here include Big Thunder Mountain Railroad and Splash Mountain.

Crowds typically mob Fantasyland after 11 a.m., but are often light early in the morning

▶ Consider using the resort monorail instead of the express. There's often no line.

A DAILY PLAN

Can you absolutely get to the park by 8:30 a.m.? If so, here's a great plan. The key? Riding the first or second Dumbo of the day.

8:30 ARRIVE AT THE PARK

9:00 FANTASYLAND See, in order: Dumbo, Peter Pan's Flight, It's a Small World, Mickey's PhilharMagic.

9:55 GET FASTPASSES for The Many Adventures of Winnie the Pooh.

10:00 MICKEY'S TOONTOWN FAIR Meet Mickey Mouse, then more characters at the Toontown Tent.

10:30 THE MANY ADVENTURES OF WINNIE THE POOH

11:45 GET FASTPASSES for Space Mountain.

12:00 LUNCH at Tony's Town Square.

1:00 GET FASTPASSES for Buzz Lightyear's Space Ranger Spin.

1:05 SPACE MOUNTAIN

1:45 GET FASTPASSES for Splash Mountain (send dad while you wait).

2:05 BUZZ LIGHTYEAR'S SPIN

3:05 PIRATES OF THE CARIBBEAN

4:05 GET FASTPASSES for Big Thunder Mountain Railroad.

5:05 SPLASH MOUNTAIN

6:00 DINNER with Cinderella at the Grand Floridian Resort. (Make your reservations months in advance.)

8:00 SPECTROMAGIC

9:00 WISHES

9:30 BIG THUNDER MOUNTAIN RAILROAD

Assumes park hours of 9 a.m. to 10 p.m.

"Partners," a statue of Walt Disney and Mickey Mouse, anchors the hub in front of the castle

Set within the stone walls of Cinderella's castle estate, **Fantasyland** resembles a royal courtyard during a Renaissance fair. Some buildings are designed as tournament tents; others blend in styles from Great Britain and Germany. Ideal for preschoolers, it has nine attractions, including Dumbo the Flying Elephant, It's a Small World, the Many Adventures of Winnie the Pooh and Mickey's PhilharMagic.

Themed to be a rural town that's holding a county agricultural exhibition, the two-acre **Mickey's Toontown Fair** also has the country homes of Mickey and Minnie Mouse. Built with cartoonish "Squash and Stretch" architecture, it has the park's only indoor, air-conditioned spots to get character autographs.

The theme of **Tomorrowland?** An intergalactic spaceport, a nostalgic trip back to the future as envisioned by 1930s comic books

GO WEST, YOUNG VISITOR You move both literally and figuratively from east to west as you travel from the start of Liberty Square to the end of Frontierland. You start off in New York, in the Hudson Valley of the Haunted Mansion. The Columbia Harbour House is Boston; the Hall of Presidents Philadelphia. The Diamond Horseshoe represents St. Louis, Grizzly Hall is Colorado, the Pecos Bill Tall Tale Inn is Texas and Big Thunder Mountain is Utah. (Splash Mountain is Georgia, apparently washed away from the South.)

and sci-fi films. The concept applies mostly to the architecture. It's best appreciated at night, when the brushed-metal curves of the buildings are lit by colorful beacons, lasers and neon. Calling cards include the classic Space Mountain, Buzz Lightyear's Space Ranger Spin and the new Monsters Inc. Laugh Floor high-tech theatrical show.

With many modern attractions, Tomorrowland appeals to older children and young adults

TOURING TIPS There are three secrets to having fun at Magic Kingdom. First, get to the gate 30 minutes before the park opens. You'll avoid the crush of people going through the security check, get to see the "Singin' in the Rain"/"Dumbo" inspired opening ceremony and then find no line at any attraction. Magic Kingdom has dozens of attractions, but most take only a few minutes to experience. Get here first thing in the morning and you'll be able to zip through many of them during the first hour.

Second, use the Fastpass system. Take advantage of it and you'll rarely, if ever, wait in a line. See page 31 for details.

Third, consider leaving after lunch. Go back to your hotel for a swim or a nap, and come back after dinner. Magic Kingdom can be hell during a hot, crowded afternoon, but your hotel bed, pool and shower will seem heavenly. Come back at dusk for the nighttime parade and fireworks.

FUN FINDS ❶ A topiary of Elliot, the star of 1977's "Pete's Dragon," swims through the grass of the plaza in front of Tomorrowland. ❷ In front of the Jungle Cruise, six Tiki statues sync water squirts to African rhythms. ❸ Crates stacked alongside the Liberty Square entrance recall the 1773 Boston Tea Party, when colonists boarded the ships of Britain's East India Tea Co. and threw the cargo into the sea. ❹ Streams of brownish pavement on the Liberty Square walkways symbolize sewage that often flowed along 18th-century building fronts and down streets. ❺ Across from the Hall of Presidents is a cast of the actual Liberty Bell. It was created in 1987 in recognition of the U.S. Bicentennial. ❻ Adjacent is Disney's Liberty Tree, a 160-year-old live oak that recalls a historic Boston elm. ❼ Stocks for adults and children stand in front of the Riverboat dock. ❽ The exterior surround-

The underworld

When you stroll through the Magic Kingdom you're actually walking on its second floor. Underneath you — beneath the trees, flowers, grass, dirt and, yes, waterways — are nine acres of warehouse-sized rooms, hallways and office space. Called the park's "utilidor," this network of interconnected service areas forms a unique support basement. Completely hidden from guests, it serves two roles.

First, it helps keep the Kingdom magical, as its one-and-a-half miles of color-coded tunnels give cast members and characters a way to travel from spot to spot without being seen by guests.

Second, the utilidor is the park's nerve center. Rooms off to the sides (all windowless, of course) include an employee lounge (with lockers, ping-pong tables and video games), barber shop, cafeteria, paycheck center and wardrobe headquarters; merchandise storage areas; utility hubs; and a huge computer center that controls virtually everything in the park, from the hundreds of audio recordings and projection systems in each attraction, to the water pressure needed to push various boats through each ride track, to all the fireworks and parade operations.

Whooshing above on the ceiling is the Magic Kingdom's Automated Vacuum Assisted Collection system. Every 15 minutes — after above-ground maintenance workers empty the park's trash cans into several backstage collection sites — the garbage is drawn through the tubes at speeds up to 60 miles per hour, on its way to a giant central trash terminal behind Splash Mountain.

Guests over 12 go into the utilidor on the park's Keys to the Kingdom Tour (see Diversions chapter).

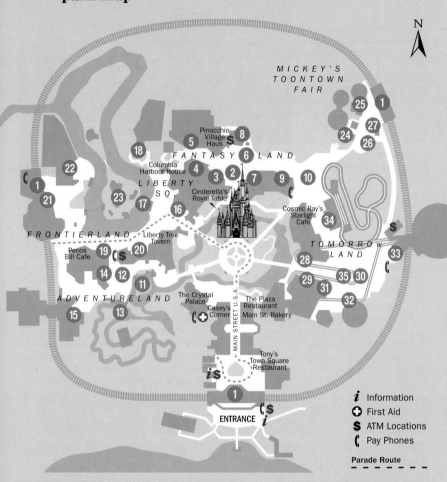

N

i **Information**
✚ First Aid
$ ATM Locations
(Pay Phones

Parade Route — — — —

ATTRACTIONS

1. Walt Disney World Railroad
2. Cinderella's Golden Carrousel
3. Mickey's PhilharMagic
4. Peter Pan's Flight
5. It's a Small World
6. Dumbo the Flying Elephant
7. Snow White's Scary Adventures
8. Ariel's Grotto
9. The Many Adventures of Winnie the Pooh
10. Mad Tea Party
11. Swiss Family Treehouse
12. The Magic Carpets of Aladdin
13. Jungle Cruise
14. The Enchanted Tiki Room — Under New Management
15. Pirates of the Caribbean
16. The Hall of Presidents
17. Liberty Square Riverboat
18. The Haunted Mansion
19. Country Bear Jamboree
20. Frontierland Shootin' Arcade
21. Splash Mountain
22. Big Thunder Mountain Railroad
23. Tom Sawyer Island
24. Minnie's Country House
25. Mickey's Country House
26. The Barnstormer
27. Donald's Boat
28. Stitch's Great Escape
29. Monsters Inc. Laugh Floor
30. Astro Orbiter
31. Buzz Lightyear's Space Ranger Spin
32. Walt Disney's Carousel of Progress
33. Space Mountain
34. Tomorrowland Indy Speedway
35. Tomorrowland Transit Authority

Big Thunder Mountain Railroad is a family-friendly Frontierland roller coaster

ing the Hall of Presidents has three references to Colonial times and the American Revolution: Two lanterns in a second-story window facing the Haunted Mansion represent the famous line from the 1860 Longfellow poem "Paul Revere's Ride" ("One, if by land, and two, if by sea") that described how villagers signaled the patriot

---

"I like the classic attractions best. I was introduced to them as a kid, and they are still in my bones."

— *Daphne Zuniga, actress*

---

about invading British troops. ❾ A rifle sits in a window to the right, sending a message that the owner is home and ready to fight. ❿ Closer to the Hall's front door, a marble step beneath a blue townhouse door (No. 26) symbolizes Jefferson entering the hall to write the Constitution. ⓫ Showing four interlocking hands, a firemen's fund plaque is mounted on a set of green stable doors to the left of the Hall of Presidents. As some Colonial fire departments were, in essence, insurance companies, policyholders were given plaques that would tell arriving firefighters their fees had been paid. ⓬ The

ATTRACTION TIMELINE

1971 Original attractions: *Adventureland:* Jungle Cruise, Swiss Family Treehouse, Tropical Serenade. *Fantasyland:* Cinderella's Golden Carrousel, Dumbo the Flying Elephant, Peter Pan's Flight, Mad Tea Party, The Mickey Mouse Revue, Mr. Toad's Wild Ride, It's a Small World, Snow White's Adventures, Skyway, 20,000 Leagues Under the Sea Submarine Voyage. *Liberty Square:* Mike Fink Keel Boats, The Hall of Presidents, The Haunted Mansion, Liberty Square Riverboats. *Frontierland:* Frontierland Shootin' Gallery, Country Bear Jamboree. *Tomorrowland:* America the Beautiful, Flight to the Moon, Grand Prix Raceway. *Main Street U.S.A.:* Main St. Vehicles, Main St. Cinema, Plaza Swan Boats, Walt Disney World Railroad.

1972 If You Had Wings.

1973 Pirates of the Caribbean, Tom Sawyer Island.

1974 StarJets, Magic Carpet 'Round the World replaces America the Beautiful.

1975 Space Mountain, Carousel of Progress, WEDway PeopleMover, Mission to Mars replaces Flight to the Moon, America the Beautiful replaces Magic Carpet 'Round the World.

1979 Magic Carpet 'Round the World replaces America the Beautiful.

1980 Big Thunder Mountain Railroad.

1984 American Journeys replaces Magic Carpet 'Round the World.

1986 Magic Journeys replaces Mickey Mouse Revue.

1987 If You Had Wings renamed If You Could Fly.

1988 Mickey's Birthdayland.

1989 Delta Dreamflight replaces If You Could Fly.

1990 Mickey's Birthdayland begets Mickey's Starland.

1992 Splash Mountain.

1994 Legend of The Lion King replaces Magic Journeys, The Timekeeper replaces American Journeys.

1995 Mission to Mars becomes ExtraTERRORestrial Alien Encounter, StarJets begets Astro Orbiter. WEDway PeopleMover renamed Tomorrowland Transit Authority.

1996 Ariel's Grotto. Grand Prix Raceway renamed Tomorrowland Speedway. Delta Dreamflight renamed Take Flight. Mickey's Toontown Fair replaces Mickey's Starland (adds Donald's Boat and The Barnstormer).

1998 Buzz Lightyear's Space Ranger Spin replaces Take Flight, Tropical Serenade becomes The Enchanted Tiki Room Under New Management.

1999 The Many Adventures of Winnie the Pooh replaces Mr. Toad's Wild Ride.

2000 Tomorrowland Speedway renamed Tomorrowland Indy Speedway.

2001 The Magic Carpets of Aladdin.

2003 Mickey's PhilharMagic replaces Legend of The Lion King.

2004 Stitch's Great Escape replaces ExtraTERRORestrial Alien Encounter.

2007 Monsters Inc. Laugh Floor Comedy Club replaces The Timekeeper.

Freaky Tiki. A statue squirts water in Adventureland.

hanging sign for the Columbia Harbour House Restaurant features a U.S. shield with its eagle crying and holding arrows in its right claw, signs the country is at war on its own soil. ❸ An invisible Tinker Bell flies around Tinker Bell's Treasures, spreading pixie dust on the gift shop's walls. Peek through the keyhole of a vanity on the left to see a flash of light. ❹ Jousting lances form the canopy supports of the Small World building. ❺ Donald Duck's great-great-grandfather is honored by a statue at Mickey's Toontown Fair. According to tales told in 1989 comic books, Cornelius Coot founded the frontier outpost of Duckburg by popping some sweet corn to frighten away Spanish invaders. His deed was commemorated with this sculpture. ❻ The key to the restroom at Pete's Garage is floating inside the gas pump. ❼ Standing between the entrances of the Tomorrowland Transit Authority and Astro Orbiter, a Galaxy Gazette hawker talks ("Extra Extra! Read all about it!") when you stand directly in front of him. He may insult you, with a line such as "Would you get a load of you! It's times like this I wish I didn't have X-ray vision!"

BY THE NUMBERS ❱❱ **100** Number of sunglasses turned in to Guest Relations daily. ❱❱ **122** Size of the Magic Kingdom, in acres. ❱❱ **11,000** Spaces in the Magic Kingdom parking lot.

Walt Disney World Railroad

With stations at Main Street U.S.A., Frontierland and Mickey's Toontown Fair, this leisurely 1.5-mile trip offers a foot-free way to get around the park. The streetcar-styled passenger cars are pulled by four steam locomotives, which chug along at 10 to 12 miles per hour. As you ride you get a heapin' helpin' of banjo pickin' and a folksy narrator. "Be on the lookout!" he warns along Adventureland. "You never can tell when a man-eatin' tiger, or train-chasin' tiger, might show up!"

The engines are antiques, assembled by Philadelphia's Baldwin Locomotive Works between 1916 and 1928. They were used by the United Railway of the Yucatan to haul passengers, jute, sisal and sugar cane.

20 min. (roundtrip). Capacity: apx. 360. Avg. wait: 5 min. early morning, 10 min. peak afternoon. No service during parades, fireworks or thunderstorms. No Disney rental strollers are allowed onboard; but folding strollers are OK. ECV users must transfer. Handheld video captioning available. Debuted: 1971.

FUN FINDS ❶ Some Disney characters have lost their luggage on the train. Items such as Pluto's bone, Capt. Hook's hook and Chip 'n' Dale's acorns are stored on shelves in the lower lobby of the Main Street depot. ❷ The red bridge (along the track between Main Street and Frontierland) is an old train bridge from the old Florida Flagler line. It was originally two tracks wide. ❸ Some trees past the Indian village have charred trunks. They're from falling fireworks during performances of Wishes.

Above: The Walter E. Disney locomotive blows off steam. **Below:** Indians build a fire along the track.

▶ Sit on the right for the best views, which include a couple of glances backstage.

Main Street U.S.A.

You enter the park with a stroll through a small, 1900s-era county seat. The past made perfect, Main Street U.S.A. is a world of Victorian buildings, barbershop singers, horse-drawn streetcars and horseless carriages. It's an ideal introduction to the Magic Kingdom.

A central Town Square green is surrounded by the town's key civic buildings — its courthouse (or city hall), firehouse, train station and exhibition hall. In the center is a statue of the founding father. In this case that means Roy Disney, who supervised Walt Disney World's creation after his brother's death.

Next is Main Street itself. Fronted with flowers and trees, the building facades use the motion-picture technique of forced perspective to appear larger than they are. Each has its first floor at full scale, its second at 80 percent, its third 80 percent of that. Upper story windows identify the offices of fictional business folk (actually Disney alumni).

Many of the 51 facades use Cape Cod-style clapboard and gingerbread trim; some include prefabricated metalwork, an

Top: Main Street U.S.A. recalls a mythical Eastern seaboard town at the end of the 19th century.
Above: Inspired by late-1800s street cars, a Main Street horse trolley pulls away from Town Square.

Industrial Age invention. Each has its own window framing, frieze work and cornice. The interiors have tin ceilings, brick floors and some huge chandeliers.

It's a town in transition. Horse hitches are giving way to bus stops. Streetlights are changing from gas to electricity.

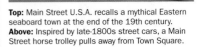
▶ Catch one of the first trolleys of the day and the Dapper Dans may serenade you.

The faces of Main Street. **1.** A Casey's Corner pianist plays a ragtime number. **2.** Casey's pitcher holds a ball, ready to pitch the final strike. **3.** A huge bass saxophone adds depth to Mickey's Toontown Tuners. **4.** One of the street's many friendly cast members sells balloons. **5.** A spirited Trolley Parade performer. **6.** Effervescent Victoria Trumpetto belts out a song to passersby. **7.** A drumstick through the head hints at the wacky mentality of the Main Street Philharmonic. **8.** A cook at the Main Street Confectionery brings out a fresh batch of caramel apples.

OLD-FASHIONED ENTERTAINMENT Realistic down to their bells and horns, the **Main Street Vehicles** include trolleys, horseless carriages, jitneys, a double-decker bus and a small fire truck, all ready to take you down Main Street. Though the loading area looks crowded (with guests waiting to meet characters), there's never a line. *Typically until 12:30 p.m. Duration: apx. 3 min., depending on traffic (and, with trolleys, the particular horse). Avg. wait: 5 min. Must be ambulatory. No horse petting. Debuted: 1971.*

The **Casey's Corner Pianist** bangs out honky tonk, rag and requests on an upright piano. The **Dapper Dans** barbershop quartet mixes its harmonically perfect repertoire with chimes, tap dancing and corny humor. They'll do "Happy Birthday" on request. A troupe of professional, improvisational actors, the **Citizens of Main Street** portray the boulevard's living, breathing townsfolk, including its mayor, fire chief, news reporter, music teacher and assorted socialites. They chat, joke, sing and even dance with guests of all ages between 10 a.m. and 2 p.m. New for 2008 is a fun Mayoral Campaign Rally Tuesday, Wednesday and sometimes Thursday at 9:45 and 10:45 a.m. The **Main Street Philharmonic** often grabs a perky female out of its audience to help out with "Hold That Tiger." So strange but so Disney, the **Main Street Trolley Parade** consists of five to seven Gay '90s couples who soft-shoe and *lip-synch* to "The Trolley Song" and a couple of service numbers a few times each morning. Sax quintet **Mickey's Toontown Tuners** appears a couple of times each day, harmonizing deftly on ragtime, jazz and Disney tunes.

You can **watch cooks make candy** at the Confectionery until about 7 p.m. Working **antique arcade games** inside the train station's second-floor waiting room include a mutoscope showing the San Francisco adventures of "The Goddess of the Silent Screen" (and Drew Barrymore's grandmother) Dolores Costello. In the back of the Exposition Hall, the **Milestones in Animation** exhibit includes a small padded-seat theater that shows a 25-minute loop of classic Disney cartoons. In the hall, a **Kodak camera display** shows two dozen models dating from 1889. Tucked between the Plaza Ice Cream Parlor and Cinderella

Castle, the **Plaza Rose Garden** includes a number of Floribunda and Hybrid Tea prize winners. During the evening **Flag Retreat,** a guest military vet often helps a color guard lower Old Glory down the Town Square flagpole.

FUN FINDS ❶ "Well, howdy!" says a statue of Goofy every 30 seconds, sitting on a bench in front of Tony's Town Square Restaurant. **❷** The stars of 1955's "Lady and the Tramp" have put their paw prints in the sidewalk in front of Tony's patio. **❸** A window next to the front door of the Emporium identifies its proprietor as Osh Popham, the general-store owner played by Burl Ives in the 1963 film "Summer Magic." **❹** The sounds of a practicing singer and dancer come from two open Center Street windows marked "Voice and Singing Private Lessons" and "Music and Dance Lessons, Ballet Tap & Waltz." **❺** Antique baseball paraphernalia lines the walls of the Casey's Corner eating area. **❻** At night many second-story windows are lit. **❼** Swan topiaries mark the rose-garden entrance to the Plaza Swan Boats, a ride that closed in 1983.

Main Street west (above) and east (below)

FUN FACTS » The entrance is designed to give the experience of going to a movie theater. The train station is the curtain. As it opens (i.e., as you walk through its tunnel) you see some Coming Attraction posters and smell popcorn. **»** Belgian, Clydesdale and Percheron horses pull the trolleys. Each works a few mornings a week. The animals live at the Fort Wilderness Campground. **»** The horseless carriages are modeled after 1903–1907 Franklins. **»** The omnibus recalls New York City double-deckers of the 1920s. **»** All vehicles are Disney's original machines from 1971. **»** The Toontown Tuners saxophones include a 1926 curved soprano and a 1929 bass. **»** The Harmony Barber Shop has 1920s barber chairs and a shoeshine chair from the 1870s. **»** The symbol on Walt Disney's tie tack on the Partners statue is that of the Smoke Tree Ranch, a rustic Palm Springs retreat where he owned a cottage. **»** Much of the background music is from the 1988 CD "The Whistler and His Dog" by the Paragon Ragtime Orchestra. The instrumental "Beautiful Beulah" comes from the soundtrack of the 1963 film, "Summer Magic." **»** Exposition Hall replicates the look of the 1877 Adelphi Hotel in Saratoga, New York. **»** The Crystal Palace combines the glass dome of San Francisco's 1879 Conservatory of Flowers with the greenhouse interior of London's Crystal Palace, an 1851 exhibition hall. **»** The 850-foot-long street rises about 6 feet from the train station to the castle.

Cinderella Castle. The two tallest spires, as well as the tops of several turrets and towers, are coated in real gold leaf.

Cinderella Castle

A symbol of imagination, innocence and romance

One of the most photographed buildings in the world, Cinderella Castle has its picture taken 30,000 times a day. And no wonder. It's not only a world-famous landmark, but also quite a piece of fantasy architecture.

Its design combines the looks of a medieval fortress and Renaissance castle. Heavy lower walls have saw-toothed battlements like those that hid artillery atop 11th-century stone forts. The top has the turrets, spires and Gothic trim of French castles of the 14th, 15th and 16th centuries. Accents include 13 winged gargoyles and a portcullis, an iron grate over the entrance that appears ready to drop at a moment's notice.

Though the castle appears to be a 300-foot-tall stone fortress, it is actually a 189-foot steel frame covered in fiberglass. The building was designed to be seen from a mile away, so guests arriving on ferries and monorails can spot it with anticipation.

Top: Toronto's Madison Greco and Shelby Devine, both 5, view the castle mosaic. **Above:** Cinderella.

The interior includes a restaurant and gift shop, security rooms, three elevators and a fourth-floor apartment that, though planned for the use of the Disney family, re-

▶ Three windows of the castle apartment peer out from the right rear, halfway up.

War and Pieces

Inside Cinderella Castle is a terrific mosaic. Created out of 500,000 bits of glass in 500 colors, a five-panel piece tells the Cinderella story. The 15- by 10-foot arches were crafted by a team led by acclaimed artist Hanns-Joachim Scharff, based on a design by Disney's Dorothea Redmond (both signed the mosaic at its bottom right corner).

It took two years to create. Redmond's paintings were redrawn to life-size proportions on heavyweight brown craft paper. These images were cut up into 50 or so jigsaw-puzzle-like pieces. Scharff used smooth and uneven glass, a third of the pieces fused with silver and gold. Many were hand cut and shaped with a power grindstone. Thin glass strips were used to outline hands and faces. Multihued rods were chopped crosswise for other effects.

Scharff was a fascinating man in his own right. Born in Germany in 1907, he became a Luftwaffe interrogator of captured American Air Force fighter pilots during World War II. Still considered one of the best interrogators in the history of armed combat, he treated his prisoners with kindness and respect, which led them to unwittingly reveal pieces of military information which fit into a bigger strategic picture for the Germans.

Scharff saved six U.S. prisoners from execution by proving their innocence to the Gestapo. At one time, Scharff was investigated by the Gestapo for collaboration with the enemy because of his unusual treatment of prisoners.

After the war Scharff met and befriended many of his former prisoners in the United States. He soon moved to New York, where out of a pre-war hobby he started a mosaic studio. A Neiman Marcus order of 5,000 mosaic tables gave the artist the funds to move to California and set up a new mosaic studio, where he was credited with introducing the smooth-surface Venetian glass form of mosaic art to this country in 1952.

Scharff died in 1992, but his studio continues under the stewardship of his daughter-in-law, Monika. She started her mosaic apprenticeship by working on these five Cinderella murals, and later led the team that created the mosaics at The Land pavilion at Epcot.

Hanns-Joachim Scharff is still widely respected today, especially by U.S. military veterans who argue against the torture of terrorist suspects.

In this family snapshot from 1971, artist Hanns Scharff compares a reference painting to his working mosaic for Cinderella Castle at his California studio

mained unfinished until 2006. Today it's the 650-square-foot Cinderella Castle Suite, a foyer, salon, bedroom and bath that's often offered to guests. Above a fireplace, a portrait of Cinderella magically changes into a flat-screen television. The bedchamber includes a 17th-century desk with inlaid computer hookups. Bath sinks resemble wash basins; faucets look like hand pumps. A cut-stone floor recalls the castle mosaic (see left). Guests access the suite through a door in the breezeway. An elevator leads to a foyer decorated with original "Cinderella" movie concept art by artist Mary Blair and a display case holding a glass slipper.

FUN FINDS ❶ In the mosaic, stepsister Drusilla's face is green with envy, while Anastasia's is red with anger. **❷** The columns alongside the mosaic are topped with molded sculptures of Cinderella's animal friends. **❸** Her wishing well is to the right of the castle, on the walkway that leads to Tomorrowland. **❹** Her fountain is behind the castle to the left. Thanks to a wall sketch behind it, toddlers who stand in front of the fountain see the princess wearing her crown.

FUN FACTS ❯❯ Two of the mosaic faces are those of real people. The page holding the slipper has the profile of castle artist Herb Ryman. His assistant is John Hench, who helped create the Walt Disney World master plan. **❯❯** Until 2006 the castle's apartment was used as a radio room, a switchboard center and, finally, a dressing room for performers on the Castle Forecourt Stage.

HANNS-CLAUDIUS AND MONIKA SCHARFF

If The Shoe Fits

The classic rags-to-riches tale, "Cinderella" began as a **Chinese fable.** In the 9th-century "Yeh-Shen," a stepmother and two step-sisters humiliate a hard-working girl. But when a 10-foot fish gives her food, a beautiful dress and tiny slippers*, she gains confidence.

Often sweeping the fireplace, the girl gets so covered in ash her stepsisters call her Cinderella ("cinder girl") in **Charles Perrault's** French version, written to entertain the 17th-century court of Louis XIV. When a king wants his son to wed, he has the prince invite all the land's maidens to a two-night ball. Cinderella's stepmom won't let her go, but then her fairy godmother (the spirit of her real mom) appears. Waving a magic wand, she turns a pumpkin into a coach, mice into horses, rats and lizards to footmen, and the girl's ragged dress into a ball gown, with glass slippers. Cinderella can go to the ball, the godmother says, but the magic wears off at midnight. The first night the girl mesmerizes the prince and leaves on time, but the next night she stays until the moment the clock strikes twelve. Rushing out, she loses a slipper, which the prince recovers. Determined to find her, he orders his Grand Duke (chief of staff) to test the shoe on every girl in the kingdom. On Cinderella's foot it slides on perfectly.

The story got bloody when Germany's **Brothers Grimm** published their version, "Aschenputtel," in 1812. When the slipper won't fit the stepsisters, their mom has them slice off their heels and toes and try again. During Cinderella's wedding, birds peck out the sisters' eyes.

Disney's 1950 film gave Perrault's tale new life. It cleaned up the plot, added a supporting animal cast, scored it with catchy songs and beefed up the finale. Disney's stepmother locks Cinderella in her room when the Grand Duke arrives. The girl's mice pals unlock it, but then the stepmom trips the Duke, causing him to drop the slipper and break it. Cinderella, however, reaches into her pocket and pulls out the mate.

Walt Disney produced **the first animated Cinderella** in 1922, when his Laugh-O-Grams Co. produced an "Alice" silent cartoon based on the tale. **Betty Boop** danced her way through 1934's "Poor Cinderella." **Rodgers and Hammerstein's** 1957 musical "Cinderella" is still the most popular television special ever. Starring Julie Andrews, it drew 71 percent of all Americans with a TV set. The production was remade with Lesley Ann Warren in 1965, and with Brandy in 1997. Jerry Lewis learns geeks, too, have charms in 1960's **"Cinderfella"** when a Disney-like Cinderella pops out of the past to flirt with him: "If I weren't a married woman," she purrs, "Grrrrr!"

Hollywood ignored the fable for decades, but in the '90s Cindy was back and always in charge. In 1998's **"Ever After,"** the princess-to-be (Drew Barrymore) escapes her step family and enlightens the prince about social policy. A feisty "Ella" breaks out into Queen's "Somebody to Love" in the 2004 musical **"Ella Enchanted."** And she's no passive patsy in 2004's **"A Cinderella Story."** After dressing as Cinderella for a high-school ball, Hilary Duff gains the courage to simply walk out on her step family and her princely quarterback, until he decides to join her. Then they're off to their dream college: Princeton.

Top to bottom: The Betty Boop cartoon, Andrews, Warren, Duff with co-star Chad Michael Murray

* In ancient China tiny feet were a status symbol. The practice of foot binding started with palace dancers, but was soon used by wealthy parents to fashion their daughters for marriage. The painful process began when a girl was about 5 years old. Each foot was wrapped in a long bandage (compressing her arches and bending under all of her smaller toes) then jammed into a shoe far too small. As the girl grew, her feet could not. Eventually they would deform into hoof-like clubs just a few inches long.

From left: Sleeping Beauty, Cinderella and Snow White in Dream Along with Mickey

Castle shows

DREAM ALONG WITH MICKEY
Forecourt stage
When Mickey and Minnie Mouse throw a party to celebrate the power of dreams, the guests include Cinderella, Snow White, Sleeping Beauty and nearly the entire cast of "Peter Pan" in this song-and-dance revue. Trouble brews when Donald Duck says he doesn't believe in dreams, then Maleficent (the evil fairy from the 1959 movie "Sleeping Beauty") shows up with a dream of her own: to turn the Magic Kingdom into a place where nightmares come true. With help from the audience, that doesn't happen. Songs include "Some Day My Prince Will Come," "A Dream is a Wish Your Heart Makes" and "A Pirate's Life." Unlike most Disney shows, all vocals in the performance are prerecorded. In a Disney first, the eyes and mouths move on the giant heads of Mickey, Minnie, Donald and Goofy. Donald's eyebrow expressions are hilarious. Another fun find:

Goofy wears a puffy shirt that would make Jerry Seinfeld jealous. *20 min. Guests may stay in wheelchairs, ECVs. Best ages: 3–10. Debuted: 2006.*

STORYTIME WITH BELLE
Fairytale Garden Theater
The heroine from 1991's "Beauty and the Beast" is just a few feet away from you in this cozy show. Tucked into a shady alcove between Main Street and the Mad Tea Party, her stage sits just off the ground, in front of only four rows of benches. Six children and one adult join Belle onstage to act out her story. To give your child the best chance of getting picked, sit to the far left directly in front of the stage steps and have your child shout out the answers to Belle's early questions ("Who did I live with in my quiet little village?"). Sit at the far

right to be among the first in line for an autograph when the show ends. *15 min. Capacity: Apx. 75 seats, plus standing room for another 50. Arrive 30 min. early to pick your seats, 15 min. early to get any seat. Guests may stay in wheelchairs, ECVs. Best ages: 3–10. Debuted: 1999.*

"Marry me, Belle!" orders a young Gaston in Storytime with Belle

▶ See Dream Along with Mickey after dark, when spotlights add a theatrical flair.

Cinderella's Golden Carrousel

A true antique, this 1917 merry-go-round was one of the fanciest of its day. One of only four five-row carrousels built by the Philadelphia Toboggan* Co., this "Liberty" model was adorned with carved flowers, medieval weapons and patriotic images. Its 72 hard-maple horses and six chariots rode under a lavish cresting featuring Miss Liberty, a crowned blonde in a robe and sandals. Craftsmen built five sizes of horses, and placed the largest and most ornate on the outside rim.

Built for the Detroit Palace Garden Park in Michigan, the ride moved in the 1920s to Maplewood, N.J.'s Olympic Park, where it stayed until Disney bought it in 1967. To follow Walt Disney's belief that every rider should feel like a hero, the company painted each horse white, repositioned its legs so it canters instead of prances and took out the chariots to add more horses. It designated the steed with a gold ribbon on its tail (No. 37) as Cinderella's and themed everything to the princess, repaint-

* At the time, the word for a wooden roller coaster

Miss Liberty decorates the chariot. **Top:** Toronto's Elise Meiers, 2, rides with her mom, Terri.

ing the carrousel — including the patriotic pieces — gold, pink, purple and blue.

Today's 87 horses are fiberglass replicas, but one of the original wooden chariots has returned. Reinstalled in 1997, it offers the only truly antique seats on the ride.

By the way, the outside horses move at 7 mph; those on the inside at 3.5 mph.

2 min. Capacity: 91. Avg. wait: 5 min. early morning, 30 min. peak afternoon. Must be ambulatory. Debuted: 1971.

▶ Look up, down and to your left to see the original carvings and structural pieces.

Donald Duck searches for the Sorcerer's Hat in the "Beauty and the Beast" dining hall

© DISNEY

Mickey's PhilharMagic

✓ The most fun 3-D movie made to date, Mickey's PhilharMagic gives you the same delight you get from flipping through a Viewmaster — marvelous 3-D views that fill your field of vision. But here the scenes are videos, filled with beloved songs and characters. There's nothing scary for kids.

Many items seem to fly over your head, others hang in front of you. In-theater effects help immerse you in the action — you smell a fresh-baked pie, feel champagne corks pop, and get spritzed with water. Strobes flash when Donald kisses an eel,

> "I'm still thinking about PhilharMagic. I've never experienced anything like it."
> — John Corbett, actor

and when Simba is "in the spotlight" so are some audience guests.

The plot? When Mickey Mouse plans to conduct a magical orchestra, Donald insists on trying it himself. When his scheme fails, he (and you) are sent on a madcap adventure through the best scenes from Disney's best musicals, reprising songs such as "Be Our Guest," "Part of Your World," "I Just Can't Wait to be King" and "A Whole New World."

The animation is delightful, especially the first three scene transitions. The "Be Our Guest" feast falls into the "Sorcerer's

Apprentice" workshop... where the water from the brooms' buckets washes into the sea of Ariel's grotto... where the sunlight at the surface turns into the sun of Simba's Africa. The following "Lion King" sequence is, as in the 1994 film, a kaleidoscope of flat 2-D cutouts, but here they twist and turn with 3-D realism.

Actor John Corbett compares the show to another Disney classic. "I loved the Tower of Terror," he says. "I did it three times. But after you get that thrill you don't think about it again. I'm still thinking about PhilharMagic. I've never experienced anything like it."

12 min. Capacity: 450. Avg. wait: 10 min. early morning, 30 min. peak afternoon. Fastpass available. Guests may remain in wheelchairs, ECVs. Assistive listening, reflective captioning. Debuted: 2003.

FUN FINDS ❶ There's a murmur in the theater crowd even when there's no one there. Faint audience noise plays from the loudspeakers. ❷ As Goofy walks behind the crowd, he hums the "Mickey Mouse March" and steps on a cat ("Sorry little feller!"). ❸ The instruments gasp when Donald grabs the flute, watch as he throws it into the audience and laugh when it whops him on the head. ❹ When Lumiere rolls out toward you he's on a tomato that wasn't there a moment earlier. It arrived when Donald blocked your view to ask, "Where's my hat?" ❺ Ariel giggles as she

▶ The best seats are in the middle rear, directly in front of the main projector.

swims onscreen. **❻** When a crocodile sends Donald flying (on the line "Everybody look right!") you hear the duck circle behind you before he returns to the spotlight. **❼** A pull chain falls into view as Simba sings "I'm standing in the spotlight!" Zazu pulls it to turn the light off. **❽** Jasmine waves to a guest in the audience as she starts to sing. **❾** When she and Aladdin wave goodbye to Donald, so does their carpet. **❿** Once Mickey regains control of the orchestra, the flute wakes up the tuba then trips Donald into it. **⓫** As you exit past the gift shop, Goofy says goodbye to you in five languages ("Sigh-a-NAIR-ee!").

CLASSIC DISNEY Enchanted as part of a spell on their owner, all of a castle's household objects — including the candelabrum — are alive in 1991's **"Beauty and the Beast."** When they get a visitor, they put on a floor show as they prepare a meal. In 1940's **"Fantasia,"** sorcerer's apprentice Mickey gets out of washing a floor by putting on his mentor's magical hat and casting a spell on a broom. At first it works: the broom marches out to a fountain, fills its bucket with water, marches back in and splashes it on the floor. Unfortunately, it never stops, and the workshop soon begins to fill with water. Desperate, Mickey chops the broom into pieces, but each splinter turns into its own marching, splashing broom. Teenager Ariel collects every human object that floats down to her in 1989's **"The Little Mermaid."** Fish friend Flounder keeps her company, but she wants to be where the people are. A young cub just can't wait to be the king of beasts in 1994's **"The Lion King."** Simba's brushing up on looking down, but that's not enough to convince his father's advisor, the hornbill Zazu. In 1953's **"Peter Pan"** a boy can fly... and his friends can, too, if they get a sprinkling of dust from his pixie Tinker Bell. One night he convinces the children of London's Darling family to go with him to Never Land, a world where kids never grow up. "Here we go!" he yells, and they all soar over the moonlit city. They stop for a moment on the minute hand of Big Ben, the city's clock tower. **"Aladdin,"** a young streetwise commoner in 18th-century Iraq, falls in love with princess Jasmine in Disney's 1992 hit. To win her heart he disguises himself as "Prince Ali" and shows her a new, fantastic point of view as they ride on his magic carpet. Out to destroy his plans is Iago, the cranky red parrot of the king's advisor. **"The Mickey Mouse Club"** weekday TV show was a 1950s staple. Every kid knew the last line of its theme song: "M-I-C... See ya real soon!... K-E-Y... Why? Because we like you!... M-O-U-S-E."

FUN FACT 》 The screen starts out 16 feet high and 40 feet wide. It expands to 28 by 150.

Déjà Donald

With just a few exceptions (for example, his humming of "Be Our Guest"), Donald Duck's lines come from the master audio tracks of animated shorts of the 1930s and 1940s, as recorded more than 60 years ago by the original voice of Donald, Clarence "Ducky" Nash.

DONALD'S LINE...	COMES FROM...
"OH BOY OH BOY!," said when he realizes Mickey has left the Sorcerer's Hat unattended...	1942's "Sky Trooper," said when he realizes he can train to be a pilot if he peels some potatoes.
"ATTEN... TION!," said to the PhilharMagic orchestra as he begins to conduct it...	1940's "Fire Chief," said to nephews Huey, Dewey and Louie as he teaches them to be firemen.
"I'LL SHOW YOU WHO'S BOSS!," shouted at an unruly flute before he tosses it into the audience...	1941's "Early to Bed," shouted at a noisy alarm clock before he tosses it across his bedroom.
"WHO DID THAT?," said after the flute returns from its flight over the audience and hits him on the head...	1941's "Orphan's Benefit," said after a boy blows his nose during Donald's recitation of "Little Boy Blue."
"BLIBA-BLIBA-BLIBA," blubbered after the Sorcerer's brooms throw buckets of water on him...	1937's "Don Donald," blubbered after early girlfriend Donna Duck pushes him into a fountain.
"YOO-HOO!," yelled up to Ariel so the mermaid will slow down and wait up for him...	1940's "Window Washers," yelled down to Pluto so the dog will wake up and help him wash windows.
"NOTHIN' TO IT!," said after Peter Pan sprinkles Tinker Bell's pixie dust on him, allowing him to fly...	1944's "Commando Duck," said after he learns to bend his knees when he lands, allowing him to parachute.
"FASTER! FASTER!," said to his magic carpet while flying it through the narrow streets of Agrabah...	1937's "Don Donald," said by Donna Duck to Donald, while riding in his car through the desert.
"AH, PHOOEY!," said at the end of the show, after he falls through the back wall of the theater...	1942's "Donald Gets Drafted," said at the draft board, after he learns he has to pass a physical.

Peter Pan's Flight guests fly miniature pirate galleons over London and off to Never Land

"My favorite ride is Peter Pan's Flight. Of course, I always liked Peter best." — Maureen "Marsha Brady" McCormick

Peter Pan's Flight

Soar over London in this timeless Disney dark ride

Originally built for Disneyland in 1955, this ride is timeless in its charm. Flying in a single-seat pirate ship, you swoop through scenes from 1953's "Peter Pan."

You start off in the upstairs nursery of the Darling home. As daughter Wendy reads her brothers a bedtime story, Peter beckons them (and you) to fly off with him to Never Land. Once Tinker Bell sprinkles you with pixie dust, you soar... over the Darling's backyard and then the twinkling streets of London. The kids fly ahead of you; you can see their shadows on the moon.

Soon you come to Never Land, an island of flowers, mountains, waterfalls, even a volcano. Captain Hook waits for you on his ship down below. "Fire, Mr. Smee!" he commands. Fortunately, Smee misses.

Rounding a corner, you pass the Lost Boys, dressed as animals sitting around a campfire. Continuing your island tour, you pass three sirens on the rocks of Mermaid Lagoon, princess Tiger Lily with her dad and four braves at the Indian Encampment, and Skull Rock, a skeleton-faced cliff.

Next you set out to sea, to Hook's ship, where the pirate has kidnapped the Darling kids and the Lost Boys. Peter is dueling the Captain on the mainsail; the crew is making Wendy walk the plank.

As the ticking crocodile hints, however, Hook's time is up. As you round a corner, Peter stands triumphantly at the helm, with Wendy and her brothers alongside.

Hook, meanwhile, is in the water. "Help me Mr. Smee! Help me!" he calls, straddling the croc's snapping jaws. As you near the exit, a mural shows the pixie-dusted ship flying the kids back home.

3 min. Avg. wait: 5 min. early morning, 90 min. peak afternoon. Fastpass available. Must be ambulatory. Handheld captioning. Debuted: 1971 (Disneyland, 1955).

FLIGHTS, FIGHTS AND TIGHTS Based on a 1904 play by English author James Matthew Barrie, Disney's 1953 film "Peter Pan" follows the adventures of a boy who refuses to grow up. One night he arrives at the London home of the Darling family and convinces daughter Wendy and her brothers John (who wears a top hat) and Michael to fly off with him to Never Land, a remote island where children don't age. Sprinkled with magic dust from moody pixie Tinker Bell, the kids join Peter's gang of Lost Boys (each lost by his parents when he fell out of his pram) for a series of adventures.

▶ Go first thing in the morning or use a Fastpass. The afternoon wait can be an hour.

It's a Small World

A baby mobile, a political statement, a pop-art parade

✓ Filled with colorful dolls, fantastical animals, imaginative sets and layers of abstract art, this whimsical indoor boat ride promotes international brotherhood as it takes you on a trip around the world. A Disney classic, it has something for everyone, and works on at least three levels.

First, it's terrific for children. To infants it's a world of their dreams, an exciting journey filled with happy, goofy faces and funny animals, accented with gentle music and the largest crib mobiles they've ever seen. To preschoolers it's a place to bond with their parents, as there's no narration and lots of time to chat ("Where are we now, mom?" "Hawaii!"). Artistic older kids will like the ride's conceptual playfulness and explosion of colors.

Second, it has a great message — honoring diversity while celebrating shared humanity. Color schemes underline regional differences, and each doll, with a skin tone that reflects its homeland, wears authentic cultural clothing. Yet the faces are more similar than different, and though the dolls speak different languages, they all sing the same song.

In today's times, the message is also one of reassurance.

"It's a Small World portrays the world as we would like it to be," says Imagineer Jason Surrell. "It's a childlike view, yes, one which is pure and innocent and optimistic."

The attraction also succeeds as a work of art. As created by illustra-

tor Mary Blair — the artist behind the vibrant backgrounds of films such as "Cinderella" and "Alice in Wonderland" — the sets alone form a stylized pop-art collage that communicates a simple yet sophisticated innocence.

There is no color unused, no shading within a color. The shapes are both organic and geometric. The pieces combine cartoonish styles (the giant squiggle that forms the Swiss Alps) with cultural motifs (the patterns on the Mexican pyramids).

The elaborate costumes rival those of a Broadway show. Each is its own mix of embroidery, feathers, lace, satin, sequins and

The finale of It's a Small World unites the world's children in Denmark's Tivoli Gardens

© DISNEY

FUN FACTS ❯❯ The attraction includes 289 human dolls and 210 animals and toys. ❯❯ The dolls sing in English, Italian, Japanese, Spanish and Swedish. ❯❯ They wear 2,296 garments. ❯❯ The ride has four types of American dolls: cowboy, Hawaiian, Inuit and Native American. ❯❯ Being a Small World ride operator was named one of the "Fifty Jobs Worse Than Yours" in a 2004 book by that title.

▶ Sit in the front row of the boat. You'll see more details and have more legroom.

At home in the African jungle of It's a Small World, a bright-eyed hippo lets pick-pick birds rest on its back

ribbons. There's nearly every type of hat and shoe known to man.

A WORLD CRUISE You start off in Europe, a two-minute sensory overload filled with dozens of dancing, singing, swinging, marching, unicycling, even yodeling dolls and creatures. Then you cross Asia, a trip through oranges and yellows that passes belly dancers, Greek and Russian folk dancers and an Indian snake charmer. Above you are Arabian flying carpets and Chinese kites. Cool blues and greens lead you into Africa, a hip jungle of wild animals diggin' a Dixieland band.

Chilean penguins lead you to the Western hemisphere, where Latin America is an orange-hot party spot. Rio's Carnivale is on your left; Mexico's Day of the Dead celebrates on your right.

Next is the blue and green Brazilian rainforest, a world of twirly-headed birds and nary a doll at all. As the rain falls (symbolized by hanging strips of clear plastic), a crocodile and jaguar bring out umbrellas.

Polynesian percussion takes you to the green and purple South Pacific, then finally you arrive back in Europe. This time, all the world's children sing in unison, now dressed all in pale blues and whites. They play and perform at a re-creation of Denmark's Tivoli Gardens, the world's oldest amusement park that's famous for its roller coaster, sparkling white light... and being Walt Disney's inspiration for Disneyland.

Renovated in 2005, the ride now has smooth robotics, crisp music and rich lighting. In the loading area, the smiling face of a whimsical two-story clock rocks to and fro as a gentle "tick-tock" echoes throughout the room. The clock comes to life every 15 minutes.

11 min. Capacity: 600. Avg. wait: 5 min. early morning, 60 min. peak afternoon. ECV users must transfer to a wheelchair. Handheld captioning. No flash photography. Debuted: 1971 (Disneyland 1966), refurbished 2005.

FUN FINDS **Europe: ❶** As you enter the ride, a high-wire unicyclist crosses above you. ❷ A purple-haired clown floats in a wicker balloon basket. ❸ A diamond-eyed pink

'I want to get off!'

Despite its qualities, It's a Small World is so iconic many people love to poke fun at it. In "Selma's Choice," a 1993 episode of **"The Simpsons"** television program, Aunt Selma takes Bart and Lisa to the Disney World-like Duff Gardens, a park where every attraction is themed around Duff Beer. When they board the indoor boat ride Little Land of Duff, they find hundreds of manic dolls singing the one-verse theme song "Duff Beer for me, Duff Beer for you, I'll have a Duff, You have one, too!"

"I want to get off!" Bart yells. "You can't," says Selma. "We have five more continents to visit!" After Bart dares Lisa to take a drink of the water, she begins hallucinating that the dolls are coming after her. "They're all around me! There's no way out! No way out, I tell you! I am the lizard queen!"

Even Disney cracks jokes. Some **Jungle Cruise** skippers tell their guests that any children left on board will be taken to It's a Small World, have their feet glued to the floor and be forced to sing the theme song "over and over for the rest of their lives." Small World dolls help destroy the theater during the **MuppetVision 3-D** finale at Disney's Hollywood Studios. The song is also dissed in the 1994 film **"The Lion King."** After evil lion Scar takes over the kingdom, Zazu the hornbill begins to sing "Nobody Knows the Trouble I've Seen." When the new king demands something more upbeat, the bird chirps "It's a small world after all; It's a small world after all..." "No, no, no!" cries Scar. "Anything but that!"

poodle wags its tongue as it watches the cancan girls. ❹ A Mary Blair doll appears under the Eiffel Tower. ❺ A British Bobby guards the Tower of London with a cork gun. ❻ One of Big Ben's hands spins backward. ❼ A Beefeater blinks as he guards the Tower. ❽ A bagpiper drones out the song. ❾ Three geese wag their tails and quack to the theme song. ❿ Crazy-eyed Don Quixote tilts at a windmill while dismayed pal Sancho Panza looks on. ⓫ An ax-wielding yodeler warbles the song. **Asia:** ⓬ Balkan folk dancers do a jig in a circle. ⓭ Three Russian boushka dancers perform at the Kremlin. ⓮ Israeli newlyweds dance in a tent. ⓯ One flying carpet has a steering wheel. **Africa:** ⓰ Cleopatra winks at you as she lies on a barge. ⓱ The eyes of three tongue-wagging frogs spring out of their sockets. ⓲ A pink elephant hoists a Dixieland trio. **Latin America:** ⓳ A pink pig piñata hangs above you. ⓴ Three butterflies flutter on a flower cart. ㉑ A horse and a cow sing the song. ㉒ So does a ball-necked yellow, orange and turquoise ostrich. ㉓ Three singing basket people ride basket horses. ㉔ A saguaro cactus plays a guitar. **Brazilian rain forest:** ㉕ Three wind-up birds spin their cranks. **South Pacific:** ㉖ Eight lace-winged butterflies fly above you. ㉗ Two purple Moais stand stoically on Easter Island. **Tivoli Gardens:** ㉘ Four sparkly-eyed girls hold flowered umbrellas as they float above your boat. ㉙ Also up high, eleven flowered clouds turn like fans in the sky. ㉚ Two Asian plate spinners sing and dance as they perform. ㉛ A German band oompahs on top of a riverboat. ㉜ A jewel-eyed acrobat is hanging from an overhead unicyclist. ㉝ A bicycle act performs above you on a high wire.

SECOND VERSE, SAME AS THE FIRST Lyrically, there's only one verse* and the chorus is simply three takes of "It's a small world after all" followed by "It's a small, small world." Musically, it's just ten notes that repeat twice, four that repeat four times, then seven that repeat three times. On the ride, though, the song "It's a Small World" isn't that bad. Though it plays constantly, it's usually an instrumental and sometimes just a rhythm track. When the dolls sing, half the time they're not speaking English. You hear the words "small world" only about every 30 seconds. * *The song actually has two verses, but only the first is used on the ride.*

Blame it on Rio

The history of It's A Small World dates back to 1941. Working on location in Brazil, Disney illustrator Mary Blair created dozens of concept paintings for the animated film "The Three Caballeros," which told the story of Donald Duck's visit to Central and South America. Filled with color, the abstract, collage-style pieces had a vibrancy rarely seen in commercial art. "Brazil is really a very colorful country," Blair said. "The jungle... the costumes and native folk art are really bright and happy."

Twenty-two years later, Pepsi-Cola wanted Disney to create its children-themed UNICEF pavilion at the upcoming 1964 World's Fair, which was only nine months away. "One of our executives actually declined," says Disney Imagineer Jason Surrell. "Walt found out about it and said 'I'm the one who makes these decisions. Tell Pepsi we'll do it.'"

Needing ideas quickly, Walt remembered Blair's work from "Caballeros." Though she had left the company in 1953, Blair returned to create dozens of collages of wallpaper cuttings, cellophane and acrylic paint. Disney animator Marc Davis added in his own playful mechanical animals. All of it was personally approved by Walt Disney. "Mr. Disney treats it like his baby," Pepsi President Donald Kendall told the New York Times, "because it is."

As for the dolls, Blair and Davis created three-dimensional versions of the "Mary Blair kid," a child with a large head and simple, smiling face that Blair had earlier used in the "Caballeros" sister film "Saludos Amigos" (1943) as well as 1950s advertisements for such products as Dutch Boy Paint and Meadow Gold Ice Cream.

At first, each of the doll groups was programmed to sing its own national anthem — the U.K. dolls sang "God Save the Queen," the French children "La Marseillaise," the Spanish kids the "Marcha Real." When that sounded awful, Disney songwriters Richard and Robert Sherman created a roundelay — a short, simple song with a catchy refrain that all the dolls could sing in unison.

To move its guests from scene to scene, Disney decided on a waterway, developing a new flume system that used tiny water jets to propel a series of free-floating, open-top boats.

The result was sensational. Though the World's Fair had more than 50 pavilions that charged a fee, It's a Small World accounted for 20 percent of the fair's total paid admissions (a Small World ticket cost 95 cents for adults, 65 cents for children). Guests voted the ride the "Most Charming" attraction at the fair, which drew 51 million people over its two-year run.

The ride even spawned its own non-Disney merchandise, including UNICEF-approved toy dolls that were sold by the Women's International League for Peace and Freedom in a fund-raising effort against the Vietnam War.

All ages enjoy the Dumbo experience. Below, a clown puzzle post along the queue.

Dumbo the Flying Elephant

✓ Cynics who dismiss this as just another carnival ride need to wake up and smell the elephant. As anyone with an inner child knows, this is Dumbo, the sympathetic star of Disney's touching 1941 classic. His story is so sweet, his face so cute, he transforms this basic attraction into something special.

But Dumbo or not, this is no midway ride. It's clean, free from grease or grime. The ride itself is not harsh but cushy, with a view not of weeds and trash but of flowers, trees and the Cinderella carrousel.

In fact, that's the best part. Strapped in with your child, looking down upon Fantasyland, you realize that you're finally here, on vacation, at the iconic epicenter of the Walt Disney World experience.

Designed for Disneyland Paris, the ornate hub is straight off the drawing board of Jules Verne. Details include spinning pinwheels, gilded trim, even hanging frames that show the stork delivering the baby. Atop it all, Timothy holds Dumbo's feather. The trim pieces surrounding the ride feature small elephant pyramids.

Come here during a busy, hot afternoon and the ride is nothing special; the long wait just isn't worth it. But stop by first thing in the morning or very late at night, when the air is cool and the line short, and Dumbo is magical.

90 sec. to 2 min. Capacity: 32. Avg. wait: 20 min. early morning, 90 min. peak afternoon. Shaded queue. Must be ambulatory. Fear factor: None. The vehicles don't even tilt. Debuted: 1971, revised 1993 (Disneyland, 1955).

JUMBO JR. When a stork delivers a baby boy to circus elephant Mrs. Jumbo in 1941's "Dumbo," she names him Jumbo Jr., but his huge ears soon earn him the nickname Dumbo. He fails at being the top of an elephant pyramid, but when his mouse friend Timothy convinces him that holding a feather will let him fly, Dumbo becomes the star of the circus. Later the baby elephant learns to fly whenever he wants, magic feather or not.

▶ Bring a camera. Dumbo has no Disney photographers or souvenir photo stand.

Ariel's Grotto

You may wait an hour to see the star of 1989's "The Little Mermaid" at this outdoor meet-and-greet spot, but your line time can still be fun. The secret: use the queue as your break. Before you go in, stop at the adjacent Scuttle's Landing snack stand, then bring your food in with you as you sit along the line's low, shady side wall. As you eat, your kids can romp in the soft-floored water area. Finally, of course, you meet a girl with a tail (only at Disney!). The experience can be a highlight of your daughter's day. When the grotto opens (usually at 10 a.m.) there's no wait at all.

Snow White's Scary Adventures

Designed in 1954, this indoor ride is a Disney take on a carnival spook house. Guided by a rail, a jerky wheeled vehicle takes you through a series of dark rooms filled with scary scenes. You travel through a predatory dark forest, see Snow White being offered the poisoned apple ("That's right dearie, take a bite…") and hear the old hag fall to her death. The effects are basic (the mouths of the "talking" characters don't move), but one illusion — when the Queen turns and becomes the old hag — is an ingenious Disney classic.

Snow White's animal friends lift her spirits

Originally the ride had guests playing the role of Snow White, experiencing her adventures for themselves. The princess didn't appear until the last scene, lying on the casket. But the attraction didn't *tell* its guests they were Snow White, and many children thought the ride ended with the young girl dead. Disney redid things in 1994, adding in the princess on the mural in the woods and standing next to the witch holding the apple. To clarify that Snow White doesn't die, Disney added a final mural, showing her very much alive.

Still, so much of the first-person terror remains (the crocodiles and trees still chase you through the woods) that some kids are still scared witless. As one dad told us, "My 2-and-a-half-year-old stomped up to a cast member and said, 'I did not like that! Not good! Bad ride!'"

2 min, 30 sec. Capacity: 66. Avg. wait: 5 min. early morning, 60 min. peak afternoon. Must be ambulatory. Handheld captioning available. Fear factor: Scares many young children. Many threatening scenes, some with loud screams. Debuted: 1971, revised 1994 (Disneyland, 1955).

ONE BITE, LONG NIGHT When a fair-featured girl's father dies, she's forced to contend with her evil stepmother, the Queen, and is relegated to doing menial chores such as scrubbing the steps of the castle in Disney's 1937 film, "Snow White and the Seven Dwarfs." Obsessed with her own looks, the Queen gets jealous when a magic mirror tells her Snow White has become "the fairest one of all." The Queen orders a huntsman to take the girl to a forest and kill her, but instead he tells Snow White to "run away, and never come back!" She takes refuge in the cottage of the Seven Dwarfs, a group of men who work in a diamond mine. Learning of Snow White's escape, the Queen transforms herself into an old hag, tracks down the girl and gives her a poisoned apple, which makes her faint and appear to be dead. Once the hag falls to her death while trying to crush the dwarfs with a boulder, they plan to bury the girl. Just in time, a prince arrives and gives Snow White her first kiss, breaking the spell.

▶ **Ask to sit in the front seat. Many scenes take place directly in front of you.**

"They steal honey!" Tigger warns Pooh of hefflalumps and woozles

The Many Adventures of Winnie the Pooh

A modern dark ride takes you through the Blustery Day

✓ This storybook-style adventure combines the cute style of the Pooh films with imaginative visuals and effects. Hidden behind swinging doors, the scenes each come as a surprise. Better still, your vehicle travels through each diorama all by itself.

The story is taken, mostly, from "Winnie the Pooh and the Blustery Day," the 1968

WINNIE, WINDY AND WET Based on an A.A. Milne story about the stuffed animals of his son Christopher Robin, the 1968 Disney featurette "Winnie the Pooh and the Blustery Day" tells of the group's adventure in a thunderstorm. Leader Pooh is a cheerful teddy who loves honey. His pals include excavation expert Gopher (a Disney invention), timid Piglet, fastidious gardener Rabbit, motherly Kanga and adventurous son Roo, gloomy donkey Eeyore, self-important Owl and the ebullient Tigger, who loves to bounce. Pooh's enemies, he thinks, are hefflalumps and woozles, the elephants and weasles Tigger says steal honey. The chubby cubby has never seen one, but in his nightmares the crazy beasts blow smoke rings and morph into hot-air balloons and watering cans.

featurette that was part of the 1977 full-length feature film "The Many Adventures of Winnie the Pooh."

As the ride starts, Gopher pops up to greet you with "Happy Windsday!" Sweeping leaves, Piglet can barely hang on to his broom. Gardening Rabbit has been blown into his wheelbarrow. Roo swings gleefully from his scarf, which mom Kanga holds like a kite.

Meanwhile, Pooh hunts honey. In a scene from the 1966 featurette "Winnie the Pooh and the Honey Tree," Pooh grips the string of a balloon, hoping to rise up to a beehive.

Next you enter Owl's toppling tree house. The walls are falling in, a limb has crashed through the roof, shelves and pictures are on the floor. Perched above, the oblivious Owl drones on about the big wind of '67 — or was it '76?

As night falls you're back outside, when suddenly up pops Tigger. "Come bounce with me!" he says. You rock as he trounces, flounces, pounces... and disappears for a

▶ Watch the 'Blustery Day' segment of the movie first to fully enjoy the attraction.

second before dropping down from a tree. "I almost bounced clear out of the ride!" Tigger explains.

The bouncefest leads to Pooh's house, where Tigger warns him of honey-stealing heffalumps and woozles. Guarding his honey, Pooh paces with his popgun but dozes off. You see him magically rise in the air.

As Pooh floats over your head, you enter his nightmare — a world of evil heffalumps and woozles. One heffalump blows a smoke ring at you, a woozle having lit its firecracker head. Another plays a honey harp. A third, now a hot-air balloon, blasts you with air. Finally, two watering-can heffalumps rise to start a storm.

Next is the Floody Place, a fiber-optic deluge that's all but real. As you sway in a loose glide Pooh wakes up, and uses the rising water to finally get to the top of that honey tree. The others rescue Piglet, who's about to tumble over a waterfall.

"At last the rain went away," the narrator says, "and everyone gathered together to say..." "Hooray!" the gang shouts, as a door opens onto a celebration. Where's Pooh? "Start the party without me," he calls, happily stuck in the honey tree.

3 min. 30 sec. Avg. wait: 5 min. early morning, 60 min. peak afternoon. Fastpass available. ECV users must transfer to a wheelchair. Debuted: 1999.

FUN FINDS ❶ Wind blows the words off the storybook page in the attraction's first scene. ❷ As you enter the Floody Place, the air chills as words appear to wash off another page. ❸ Items floating alongside you in the water include a once-bitten sandwich on your right, a rubber ducky on your left.

MR. TOAD'S WILD FANS You get drunk, steal a car, mouth off to a cop... then go to hell! That was the storyline of this building's former attraction, Mr. Toad's Wild Ride. The attraction had ardent fans. In fact, when Disney announced its closing in 1997 some picketed inside the park. The last day of the ride, the Orlando Sentinel interviewed guests to get their feelings. One mom asked, "Who the heck is Mr. Toad?" Photos of Toad are still in the attraction. As you travel through Owl's house, look on the left wall for a picture of him handing over the deed to the space to Owl. Another picture, of Toad bowing to Pooh, rests on the right floor.

Raise your arms in the air on the Mad Tea Party and you'll slide right into each other, as New York's Jeffrey, Robin and Mikayla Reis demonstrate

Mad Tea Party

This carnival ride whirls you around in a teacup that circles on a disk, which itself spins on the floor. Kids, of any age, love it. It's based on 1951's "Alice in Wonderland," in which a prim and proper Alice eats a magic mushroom, shrinks, then attends

> **"My favorite Disney ride has always been and always will be the teacups. From the time I was little I've loved to jump in and make people sick."**
> — *Kyle Petty, NASCAR driver*

the Mad Hatter and March Hare's Unbirthday Party, a nonsensical tea time in the woods that leaves her dazed and confused. Details include the film's soused mouse as well as its Japanese tea lanterns. The landscape features gigantic leaves, tulips and an Unbirthday Party topiary.

2 min. Capacity: 72. Avg. wait: 5 min. early morning, 30 min. peak afternoon. Must be ambulatory. Debuted: 1971 (Disneyland 1955).

▶ **Pooh's Thotful Spot gift shop carries hard-to-find heffalump and woozle plushies.**

A suspension bridge leads to the tree

Even teens enjoy the carpets' gentle thrills

Swiss Family Treehouse

The ultimate treehouse — circa 1962 — this 62-step climb-through attraction is filled with ingenious ideas on how to live in the wild. Some are obvious (the suspension bridge, the bamboo-and-barrel water system), some less so (the shell sinks, the vine handrails). The dining room's pull-stop organ is a real antique. The attraction shows its age. It has no interactive elements, and its steps can exhaust those who aren't fit.

Based on a banyan tree, a tropical variety that puts down vertical roots to support its outlying branches, the 60-foot "hardwood" is made from cement and steel. It's most realistic at night.

Allow 15 min. Capacity: 300. Avg. wait: None. Must be ambulatory. Debuted: 1971 (Disneyland, 1962).

A HOMEMADE HIGHRISE In Disney's 1960 movie "Swiss Family Robinson," a dad, mom and their three sons (Fritz, Ernst and little Francis) are the sole survivors of an 1805 shipwreck on an uncharted tropical island. The males use salvage from the boat to build an imaginative home in a huge tree. The story is based on an 1812 compilation of morality lessons Swiss pastor Johann Wyss wrote for his sons, who were fans of Daniel Defoe's 1719 novel "Robinson Crusoe."

The Magic Carpets of Aladdin

Inspired by Disney's 1992 animated feature, this carnival-style hub-and-spoke ride is geared to young children. Circling around a giant genie bottle, you fly a carpet which climbs, dips and dives at your command.

Just another Dumbo? Not exactly. Here the vehicles seat four, so the line moves twice as fast and small families can ride together. As you fly, a magic scarab controls both your height and pitch, which adds to the fun. The base of the ride is a pool of water, so as you fly you look down at your reflection, just as Aladdin and Jasmine do in the film. Music — instrumental versions of the movie's best songs — fills the air.

Two golden camels spit water at riders and spectators alike. Want to get hit? Stand on the wet spots in the pavement in front of the attraction's sign. On the ride, fly about halfway high. You'll be in line for the camel who faces the genie bottle.

90 sec. Capacity: 64. Avg wait: 5 min. early morning, 30 min. peak afternoon. ECV users must transfer to a wheelchair, then a carpet. Debuted: 2001.

A NEW FANTASTIC POINT OF VIEW In 1992's "Aladdin," a beetle-shaped amulet leads its holder to the Cave of Wonders, where street orphan Aladdin finds a magic carpet. Later, as it takes him and princess Jasmine on a flight above the city of Agrabah, they see their reflection in the water below.

Calm or crazy, Jungle Cruise skippers tell an endless stream of shameless jokes

Jungle Cruise

Sophomoric humor and, if you're lucky, a wild-eyed young skipper turn this dated river safari into a trippy tongue-in-cheek adventure. Spewing out a constant stream of puns, your guide leads you down the rivers of four continents. Exploring the South American Amazon, the African Congo, the Egyptian Nile and Southeast Asia's Mekong (all surprisingly narrow!) you learn such facts as "the Nile River goes for Niles and Niles and Niles. If you don't believe me, then you're in de-Nile."

To a child the ride offers a lot, as it's fun but not scary. Scenes along the riverbank are often silly; one of gorillas sacking a camp was re-created in Disney's 1999 film "Tarzan." Rising hippo heads and squirting elephant trunks add some excitement.

When you encounter headhunters, you learn that their cache of skulls are "my last crew. They didn't laugh at my jokes, either!" You'll also enter a Cambodian temple. Its fallen beams are "man's first attempt at building a monorail."

Designed in the 1950s, the ride isn't exactly modern. Many of its animals don't move, the ones that do never change expression. And not only is the cultural stuff often mixed up (the designs on the Congo canoes are Polynesian), the theme of the attraction is, at its heart, colonialism.

Nevertheless, taken with a grain of salt the cruise can be a jolly good time. The best quips come at the end. "After five years of college you too can become a Jungle Cruise skipper!" guides often tell their guests. "My parents are so proud."

10 min. Capacity: 310. Avg. wait: 10 min. early morning, 60 min. peak afternoon. Fastpass available. Guests may remain in wheelchairs, ECVs. Assistive listening;

▶ If you ask just as you board, your child may be able to help "steer" the boat.

Sights along the Jungle Cruise include signs of headhunters and playful, water-squirting elephants

handheld captioning available. Fear factor: Low. The only slightly scary moment comes when the right side of the boat comes close to some artificial snakes in the dark temple. Debuted: 1971 (Disneyland 1955).

FUN FINDS ❶ A sign along the queue honors the cruise company's latest Employee of the Month: E.L. O'Fevre. ❷ Toward the end of the queue area, a cage holds a giant (fake) tarantula. It occasionally jerks and rears up. Next to it are crates labeled "arachnid sedative." ❸ On the boarding dock, a chalkboard lists the crew's weekly lunch menu as fricassee of giant stag beetle, BBQ'd 3-toed skink, consomme of river basin slug and fillet of rock python. All, reportedly, taste like chicken. ❹ The invading headhunters end their chant with a shout of "I love disco!" It's usually drowned out by the skipper's spiel. ❺ After you leave the dock, a chalkboard list of missing persons includes "Ilene Dover" followed by "Ann Fellen." ❻ Two crates just

outside the exit were once part of the Swiss Family Treehouse landscape. One is addressed to "Thomas Kirk Esq." and "M. Jones" on the island of "Bora Danno," references to Tommy Kirk (a star of the 1960 film "Swiss Family Robinson" and the title character of the 1964's "The Misadventures of Merlin Jones") and James MacArthur (a "Swiss" star who went on to play "Danno" Williams in the 1968-1980 TV series "Hawaii Five-O"). The other is addressed to "Swiss" director Kenneth Annakin.

BUT SERIOUSLY, FOLKS... Premiering at Disneyland shortly after that park's opening in 1955, the Jungle Cruise was originally a serious attraction — an educational tour of regions most Americans had never seen, even in pictures. The humor began in the 1960s, with the addition of the playful bathing elephants (1962) and the safari party being chased up the tree (1964). By the time the Florida version opened in 1971, the whole thing was being played for laughs. In 1994 the queue got its radio broadcast and some new props. In 1998 the boats received their current vintage design, a look that includes cooking gear hanging from a roof net.

SHRUNKEN NED'S JUNIOR JUNGLE BOATS You steer a miniature Jungle Cruise boat through obstacles at this diversion at the ride entrance. The boats are hard to control. If you play, pick one that's already in a fun spot and not stuck behind something. Rely on your forward gear. *$1 for 2 minutes.*

FUN FACTS ❯❯ The plane is half of an old MGM stage prop. The other side is at Disney's Hollywood Studios in The Great Movie Ride's "Casablanca" scene. ❯❯ The river is 3 feet deep. ❯❯ The water is dyed its dark, murky color. ❯❯ Walt Disney originally wanted the trip to have live animals. The robotic versions were Plan B. ❯❯ The boat is on a track. Your skipper controls its speed, but not its course.

▶ **Try a night cruise. The line will be short and the boat's spotlight adds to the fun.**

The Enchanted Tiki Room — Under New Management

When new owners Iago (from 1992's "Aladdin") and Zazu (1994's "The Lion King") take over this classic show of singing birds and flowers, Iago wants to toss it for something more current. But when he insults the Tiki gods Iago learns that, as Zazu proclaims, "you cannot toy with the Enchanted Tiki Room."

Songs include "Hot Hot Hot," "Conga," and, from the mouths of the wooden Tiki poles, "In the Still of the Night."

An outdoor preshow stars two talent-agent parrots who trade bird-themed barbs (Are you cuckoo?" "You birdbrain!" "Stop grousing!") over which one's client is the attraction's new owner. William (voiced by Don Rickles) represents Iago, while Morris (Phil Hartman) argues for Zazu.

9 min. Capacity: 250. Avg. wait: 5 min. early morning, 15 min. peak afternoon. Guests may remain in wheelchairs, ECVs. Assistive listening; handheld captioning. Fear factor: Lightning, thunder scare some preschoolers. Debuted: 1998; original version 1971 (Disneyland 1963).

Zazu looks on in disgust as Iago changes the show

FOWL PHRASES ❶ Iago: Don't you guys ever fly to the movies? **José:** We don't get out much. **Pierre:** Oui, oui. We are... how do you say?... attached to the place. **❷ Iago:** No more worries! **Zazu:** Well, where I come from, that's called Hakuna Matata. **Iago:** Hunky tuna tostada? What a stupid phrase! **❸ Iago (after the show ends):** Come on, everybody out! Migrate people, migrate! **Birds (singing):** Heigh ho, heigh ho! It's out the door you go! **❹ Iago (just before the exit doors close):** Boy, I'm tired. I think I'll head over to the Hall of Presidents and take a nap.

FUN FACTS ❯❯ Does Pierre sound like Lumiere, the candelabrum from "Beauty and the Beast"? Both were voiced by Jerry Orbach, Det. Lennie Briscoe on TV's "Law & Order." **❯❯** The bird sounds were all voiced by one man. A. Purvis Pullen was known for his ability to imitate 1,000 creatures. He was the voice of Cheetah in the 1930s Johnny Weissmuller Tarzan films, the birds in Disney's 1937 "Snow White and the Seven Dwarfs" and 1959's "Sleeping Beauty," even Bonzo the chimp in the 1951 Ronald Reagan flick "Bedtime for Bonzo." Pullen was proud of his Tiki Room legacy. "It's my favorite accomplishment," he once said, "the one that's gonna last." **❯❯** Originally conceived as a restaurant, the Disneyland Tiki Room debuted in 1963 as Disney's first Audio Animatronic attraction. After a bird barker out front enticed guests to "Come to the Tiki Room," everyone sang along to 18 minutes of "Let's All Sing Like the Birdies Sing" and other old-time tunes. Disney World's duplicate version opened in 1971, but by the 1990s few guests bothered to see it. Disney redid things in 1998, creating today's shorter, sarcastic storyline with more familiar songs and characters. **❯❯** Once the cockatoos arrive and start singing "Conga" the parrot José says "I wonder what happened to Rosita," a reference to a bird from the original attraction who is no longer in the show. **❯❯** The upside-down masks on the walls depict Negendei, the Earth Balancer, who is always portrayed standing on his head. **❯❯** In Polynesian mythology, "Tiki" is the god who created man. The Maori people of New Zealand use the word to refer to a carved or sculpted human image.

▶ **Sit on the left, three rows back. You'll face the goddess and see all the action.**

Pirates of the Caribbean

✔ A rowdy, rum-soaked version of It's a Small World, Pirates of the Caribbean sends you on a slow-moving cruise through stage sets filled with robotic characters. But instead of cute little dolls, here you get big-boy pirates who, as the jaunty theme song reports, *"pillage and plunder... rifle and loot... kidnap and ravage and don't give a hoot."*

AYE, A STORY THERE BE! After a 2006 update, the ride does have a storyline: When Capt. Hector Barbossa invades a Spanish fortress looking for gold, he finds his crafty nemesis Capt. Jack Sparrow one step ahead. Barbossa's men sack the town, but Sparrow sneaks a glance at their treasure map and discovers a room filled with gold. You witness the fable firsthand. Despite the warnings of a ghostly Davy Jones (the octopus-faced ruler of the ocean, who materializes here in a waterfall), you set sail back in time to explore the age of piracy.

Literally falling into an old Caribbean harbor, you sail into the middle of the first scene, smack between the battling cannons of an Audio Animatronic Barbossa and the stone fort. "It's Capt. Jack we're after," Barbossa yells, "and a fortune in gold!" Cannonballs splash close to your boat.

Rounding a bend, you see Barbossa's men in a courtyard, interrogating the mayor by dunking him in a well. "Where be Capt. Jack Sparrow and the treasure, ya bilge rat?" one demands. The robotic Sparrow (looking just like Johnny Depp) peers out nearby, from behind some dressmaker forms.

Meanwhile, other pirates are auctioning off some town maidens to some raucous hecklers. Again you sail through the scene, women on your left, drunks on your right. Another turn sends you into the village itself, where women are chasing pirates who have stolen some chickens and plates.

A GREAT BIG BEAUTIFUL SMALL SCURVY WORLD. Conceived as a wax museum, Pirates became an Audio Animatronic flume ride after the success of the Carousel of Progress robotics and It's a Small World boat system at the 1964 World's Fair.

In front sits an old salt holding a treasure map. As he rambles ("What I wouldn't give to see the look on Capt. Jack Sparrow's face when he hears tell tis only me that gots the goods..."), Sparrow himself pops up behind him. Hiding in a barrel, Jack sneaks a peek at the map before ducking back out of sight.

Other scenes show pirates setting fire to the town and trying to escape from a burning jail by luring a dog that holds its keys. In the finale a giddy Sparrow has found the village gold stash and basks in its glory. Lolling on an ornate rocking chair, leg draped over one of its arms, he sings, slurs, and chats with a parrot.

A new sound system adds a distinctive "whumph" to each cannon shot, while remastered vintage tracks make the pirates' dialogue easier to understand. There's a new soundtrack, and new lighting.

As for flaws, there is a big one. "There is nothing politically correct about Pirates of the Caribbean," says Disney Imagineer Eric Jacobson. "Much of it is patently offensive." It's also all in good fun, but even the most carefree parent may wonder if scenes showing torture, heavy drinking and the selling of women are sending the best messages to boys and girls. In fairness, the attraction does show, vaguely, the results of such behavior. As the first scene illustrates, the pirates end up dead.

To most, though, the ride is a hoot. As we heard some college girls sing as they waited in line (to the tune of "It's a Small World"):

"It's a world of fog and a world of caves.
It's a world of torture and of sex slaves.
But there's gold, and there's rum!
Johnny Depp? He's no bum!
It's the Disney pirates ride!"

Developed by Walt Disney, the essence of the ride combines a Missouri farm boy's view of high-seas adventure with a Hollywood showman's use of theatrics. "Walt came from a world of movies," explains Imagineer Jason Surrell. "He wanted rides that use lighting and backdrops, establishing shots and lots of characters — up-close ones who are most important, and faraway characters who are less so."

> ▶ If you must wait in a line, this is a good one. It's covered, cool and moves quickly.

❭ What is a pirate's favorite cookie? Ships Ahoy. ❭ What type of socks does a pirate wear? Aaaaarrrgyle. ❭ How much does a pirate pay for corn on the cob? A buck-an-ear.

"YO HO (A PIRATE'S LIFE FOR ME)" LYRICS © WONDERLAND MUSIC COMPANY INC.

9 min. Capacity: 330. Avg. wait: 10 min. early morning, 60 min. peak afternoon. ECV and wheelchair users must transfer. Handheld captioning available. Fear factor: Darkness, cannon fire may scare toddlers. No flash photography. Debuted: 1973, revised 2006 (Disneyland 1967).

Capt. Jack's Pirate Tutorial. The famous Disney pirate instructs a future swashbuckler in a show held along the walkway to the left of the attraction.

FUN FINDS Entrance: ❶ Visible through some windows on the right of the right queue, two chess-playing pirates in a dungeon apparently reached a stalemate some time ago. Their skeletons stare at the board. **Caverns:** ❷ A crab on your left rears as it moves its eyes, claws and pinchers. **Harbor attack:** ❸ A sign on the ship's stern reveals its name: the Wicked Wench. ❹ Barbossa yells "Strike yer colors, ye bloomin' cockroaches!" ❺ The Spanish speak en español: "¡Apenten! ¡Disparen! ¡Fuego!" ("Ready! Aim! Fire!"). **Interrogation:** ❻ The captain has a hook for a hand. ❼ When the pirates ask the mayor where Jack is, his wife calls from the window "Don't tell him Carlos! Don't be chicken!" ❽ He responds "I am no chicken! I will not talk!" ❾ Jack's hands rest on the derrieres of the female forms around him. **Bridal auction:** ❿ A crate on your left is filled with bobbing, clucking chickens. ⓫ The first woman in line is beaming, happy to be sold. ⓬ The auctioneer refers to her overweight figure as "stout-hearted and cornfed" and asks her to "shift yer cargo, dearie. Show 'em yer larboard side." ⓭ Impatient to be next, a buxom redhead pulls up her skirt to show her leg. ⓮ The auctioneer tells her to "Strike yer colors you brazen wench! No need to expose yer superstructure!" ⓯ The second to last woman is crying. **Chasing scene:** ⓰ At the end of the scene, a drunken pirate to your right invites two gray cats to join him in "a little ol' tot of rum." **Burning town:** ⓱ On your left, a dog barks along to the cantina band. ⓲ On the right a drunk, snoring pirate lolls in the mud with three intoxicated pigs. His chest heaves. ⓳ As you leave the scene, the hairy leg of a pirate above dangles toward your face. ⓴ His parrot squawks "A parrot's life for me!" **Dungeon:** ㉑ Frustrated that the dog won't respond, a prisoner demands "Hit him with the soup bone!" ㉒ As the dog looks at you, another captive says "Rover, it's us what needs yer ruddy help, not them blasted lubbers." **Treasure room:** ㉓ Jack says the loot is "my reward for a life of villainy, larceny, skullduggery and persnickety." ㉔ After he sings the "Yo, Ho" phrase *"maraud and embezzle and even hijack"* his parrot interrupts with "Hi Jack! Hi Jack!" ㉕ Jack refers to the bird as "my chromatic winged beast." **Exit area:** ㉖ On the exit ramp, a peg-leg print takes the place of a left shoe print.

FUN FACTS ❯❯ The fog screen of Davy Jones consists of droplets of water so small you stay dry as you pass through. It's held in place by columns of air. ❯❯ The fall drops 14 feet. ❯❯ The voices of Davy Jones and Capts. Barbossa and Sparrow are those of Bill Nighey, Geoffrey Rush and Johnny Depp. ❯❯ The auctioneer is voiced by Paul Frees, the Haunted Mansion's ghost host. ❯❯ In reality, the redhead is, from the waist down, little more than a pole. ❯❯ The ride has 65 Audio Animatronic people and 60 animals. ❯❯ The exterior is based on the 16th-century San Juan fortress of El Morro.

MISS SWANN WOULD HAVE DECKED HIM. Where today's women are chasing pirates, pirates once chased them, in what California-based Disney Imagineer Eric Jacobson calls the original ride's "Schwarzenegger moment." And that barrel that now holds Capt. Jack? Originally a woman hid there, while the pirate in front spoke not of a treasure map, but (as he held her slip in his hand) his desire to "hoist me colors on the likes of that shy little wench. I be willin' to share, I be!"

▶ The right queue has the most fun detail, including some chess-playing skeletons.

The Hall of Presidents

✓ A bunch of old men stand stoically. Two talk. That's the highlight, and it's a good one, of this inspirational movie and patriotic stage show. It combines a decent film with Audio Animatronic versions of every United States president from George Washington to George W. Bush.

First is the film. Projected on a 180-degree screen that fills your field of vision, the 10-minute movie recounts how our country's early leaders argued about slavery, from the Constitutional Convention to the Lincoln-Douglas debates.

Then the screen slides apart to reveal our 42 commanders-in-chief. As a roll call introduces each president, he responds with a dignified nod or wave.

Left to right: John Quincy Adams (in brown), Thomas Jefferson (green) and John Adams (gold) listen to George W. Bush

Next, Bush and Lincoln speak. "Let us do nothing that will impose upon another creature," Lincoln says. "True democracy makes no inquiry about the color of the skin, or place of birth, or any other circumstance or condition."

The presidents stand like real people, shifting their weight from hip to hip, fidgeting, looking around, sometimes whispering to each other. Many look amazingly like their human subjects. In fact, one Disney publicist used to tell visiting members of the press that some of the presidents were real — that since there were always a few robots out for repairs, each show had at least one human stand-in. When he asked Walter Cronkite to spot the live actor, the veteran newsman just laughed. A minute later he turned back and said, "Jefferson?"

20 min. Capacity: 740. Avg. wait: 10 min.

Guests may stay in wheelchairs, ECVs. Assistive listening; reflective captioning. No flash photography. Debuted: 1971; updated after the election of each new American president.

© DISNEY

FUN FACTS ❯❯ Each costume was hand-tailored with period techniques. ❯❯ The Lincoln figure is a simplified remake of an ambitious, though problematic, creation that debuted at the 1964 World's Fair. Whenever there was a spike in current, Disney's first Abe would flail its arms, hit itself repeatedly in the head and then slam down in its chair. ❯❯ The attraction was parodied on a 1993 episode of the television series "The Simpsons." In "Selma's Choice," Aunt Selma takes Bart and Lisa to the Disney World-like Duff Gardens, a theme park where every attraction is themed around Duff Beer. At the Duff Hall of Presidents, Lincoln says "Four score and seven years ago, our forefathers brewed a refreshing drink from hops and barley" as he holds up a can of the beer. Then he takes a swig and starts to rap — "We-e-ll, I'm Rappin' A.B. and I'm here to say, if you want to drink beer, well Duff's the only way! I said the only way!" — before mindlessly smashing the can on his head. Lisa calls the show a disgrace, but Selma has another view. "If it's this bad, it has to be educational."

▶ The Hall of Presidents opens at 10 a.m., with shows on the hour and half hour.

Liberty Square Riverboat

This steam-powered stern wheeler takes you on a slow cruise around Tom Sawyer Island and Fort Langhorn. The sights aren't that special — there's a burning cabin, an old fisherman, an Indian village and a few remarkably stoic moose and deer — but the boat, a working paddlewheeler named the Liberty Belle, is pretty cool. A three-tiered vessel with a functioning boiler room, steam engine and paddle wheel on its first deck, it is for the most part the real deal. Up on top there's a working smokestack and a real steam whistle. Wander around and you'll find the captain's quarters and a small stateroom.

The half-mile trip is themed as a journey down the "Rivers of America" during the late 1800s. As you ride, you hear captain Horace Bixby (in real life, the name of the riverboat pilot who taught the skill to Samuel Clemens) direct his crew. "Steady as she goes!" he commands, navigating the vessel through the shallows. He explains to you what you're passing.

By the way, the helmsman is exaggerating when he calls out "Mark Twain!" indicating the water is two fathoms — 12 feet — deep. These rivers run only 9 feet.

Lower-level benches down front offer a way to get off your feet, but the best views are from the top deck. From there you can often see egrets and herons flying beneath you, especially just as the boat leaves the dock.

Built by Disney at a backstage shop, the boat isn't free-floating. It rides on a steel rail that runs along on the bottom of the riverbed. The boat was named the Richard F. Irvine until 1996. It originally had a twin, the Admiral Joe Fowler, until that vessel was dropped by a crane during a 1980 refurbishment. Irvine and Fowler were Disney designers. Today, the names are used by ferry boats in the Seven Seas Lagoon.

13 min. Capacity: 400. Avg. wait: 9 min. Guests may remain in wheelchairs, ECVs. Debuted: 1971.

A symbol of Americana, the Liberty Belle passes old-time settings (below) on the Rivers of America

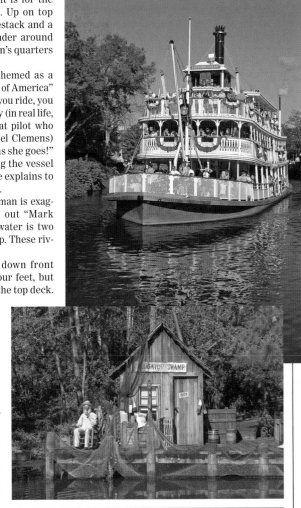

▶ Don't miss the engine. It's on the lower deck, just in front of the paddle wheel.

The Haunted Mansion

✓ Packed with special effects and loaded with detail, this tour of a ghostly retirement home is fun for the whole family. A dark indoor ride, it's plenty awesome for guests of any age but never really scary. Welcome, foolish mortals, to a campy Disney classic.

The show starts at the gate. As you walk toward a hilltop mansion, you're received by a lifeless servant, a cast member trained not to smile. The grounds are unkempt. A hearse is there. A wolf howls in the distance.

You enter the home through a side foyer. A spooky voice — your "ghost host" — intones that spirits are present, "practicing their terror with ghoulish delight." Their first trick: transforming the mantlepiece portrait from a young man to a corpse.

Next up is a portrait chamber, where again the ghosts are pulling pranks. When the door shuts, it disappears, leaving you with no way to escape. Then the walls start to stretch, the lights go out, and the ceiling disappears, revealing a hanging body above you. Fortunately a wall opens, and you board a "doom buggy" (big enough for two adults and a child) for the rest of your tour.

Soon you learn the ghosts want you to join them. "We have 999 happy haunts here," your host says, "but there's room for a thousand. Any volunteers?" In the library, the busts look you over you as you pass.

The Haunted Mansion's exterior recalls 19th-century homes in New York's Hudson River Valley

After that, you see some of the ghosts' earlier attempts to land a new resident. In the conservatory, a live man is trapped in a casket. In a hall, you pass locked door handles that twist and turn, and hear increasingly desperate knocks. One door flexes so much it appears to breathe.

Moments later you're at a seance, where a spiritualist — a disembodied head in a floating crystal ball — beckons serpents, spiders "and the tail of a rat" to "call in the spirits, wherever they're at." She wants the ghosts to materialize.

And then they do. You first see the ghosts in the ballroom, where they've gathered for a rollicking "death-day" party. You pass more morbid merrymakers out in the graveyard, where the midnight madness includes a medieval minstrel band, a disembodied barbershop quintet, a British tea party, even some opera singers dressed as Vikings.

As you enter a crypt a trio of spirits shows up to thumb for a ride. One appears to get in your vehicle.

As you near the exit, a tiny bride appears and urges you to come again. "Hurry back... hurry back..." she coos, standing on a ledge above you, a dead bouquet in her arms, her veil blowing in the breeze. Once you get out of your doom buggy, listen closely and you'll hear the ghosts faintly singing to you one final time. *"Mortals pay a token fee,"* they slowly plead, making their sales pitch one final time. *"Rest in peace, the haunting's free. So hurry back, we would like your company."*

Your tour also includes a music room where a spirit plays a piano; an endless hallway with a floating chandelier; and a trip through the attic, a room with its own, separate storyline (see box).

Completely refurbished in 2007, the attraction now features many new enhancements. The subjects of new paintings in the portrait corridor transform into eerie alternate images (the old por-

▶ Is it scary? Only for preschoolers. There are no drops, chain saws or hockey masks.

traits are now hung in the boarding area). There's a new room full of converging staircases, a nod to the art of M.C. Escher. The ride's bat-eyed wallpaper now morphs from dozens of moving, blinking eyes of hissing bats, while the crystal ball not only appears to float, its talking head now sports fiberoptic green and purple hair.

The attic is all-new (see box, next page).

Other changes include more movements in the suit of armor, better lighting, more colorful ghosts and fantastic new sound, especially in the stretching portrait chamber. *11 min. Capacity: 320. Avg. wait: 10 min. early morning, 45 min. peak afternoon. Must be ambulatory. Handheld captioning. Debuted: 1971, revised 2007.*

FUN FINDS Outside: ❶ Horseshoe prints and wagon wheel tracks lead from the barn to the hearse, which is hitched to an invisible horse. ❷ Dead roses lie inside the hearse. ❸ Madame Leota's eyes open and close on her sculpted tombstone face, which

Transforming before your eyes, a portrait in the foyer portrays a young man aging into a corpse

tilts toward you. **Foyer:** ❹ The fireplace grate forms a cross-eyed, arrow-tongued face. **Stretching room:** ❺ Grates along the bottom of the walls form monstrous faces. **Loading area:** ❻ Toothy brass bats top the waiting line's chain stanchions. **Portrait corridor:** ❼ The transforming paintings include a woman who becomes the Greek goddess Medusa. **Library:** ❽ A bat face is carved into the paneling between each set of busts. **Music room:** ❾ The window frame is decorated with coffins. **Endless hallway:** ❿ Fangbaring serpents extend from the frame molding. **Conservatory:** ⓫ The coffin handles are bats. **Corridor of doors:** ⓬ The grandfather clock is a demon. The casing forms its hair and eyes; the clockface is its mouth. The pendulum is a tail. **Grand dining hall:** ⓭ On the mantle, a ghost in a top hat has his arm around a bust. ⓮ The fireplace grate includes the silhouettes of two black cats. ⓯ In front of the fireplace, an old woman knits in a rocking chair. ⓰ Five ghosts float in from a coffin, which has fallen out of a hearse that has pulled up to an outside door. ⓱ Mr. Pickwick (from the 1836 Charles Dickens novel "The Pickwick

▶ For the shortest wait, go before 10:30 a.m. or late at night.

liberty square

Papers") swings out from the chandelier. **18** Marc Antony and Cleopatra sit next to him. **19** Julius Caesar sits at the far left end of the table. **20** The sheet-music stand is a leering bat. **Graveyard: 21** A band of medieval minstrels includes a flutist emerging from his tomb... **22** a drummer using bones to tap out a beat on the flute player's crypt cover... **23** a bagpiper in a kilt... **24** a soldier playing a small harp... **25** and a trumpeter wearing pajamas and a stocking cap. **26** When the trumpeter rears back, two owls perched above him do, too. **27** Sitting on a tomb, five cats yowl and hiss to the beat. **28** A skeletal dog howls on a hill. **29** A ghostly king and queen ride a makeshift seesaw: a board balanced on a tombstone. **30** Swinging from a tree branch, a princess sips tea behind them. **31** A British duke and duchess toast each other at a candle-lit table. **32** Behind them, four ghosts ride their bicycles in a circle. **33** Wearing hoop earrings, a pirate near you raises his teacup, sometimes his head, from behind a grave. **34** Floating above the ground, a teapot pours tea into a cup. **35** Tracks from a hearse veer off your path. **36** The driver chats with a duchess, who sits atop the hearse sipping tea. **37** A ghost sits up from the hearse's coffin, which has fallen out the back. **38** He's chatting with a sea captain. **39** A dog sniffs an Egyptian sarcophagus. **40** Its mummy is sitting up stirring his tea, mumbling through his bandages. **41** "What's that? Louder! I can't hear you! Eh?" says an old bearded man to him, holding a horn to his ear. **42** The Grim Reaper floats inside a crypt to your far right. The Reaper's beady eyes stare at you from inside his hood. **43** Dressed as Vikings, a male and female opera singer each belt out a loud, exaggerated solo. **44** Holding his severed head in his hand, a knight cheerfully sings a duet alongside his gravelly voiced executioner. **45** Shackled at his feet with a ball and chain, a pint-sized prisoner harmonizes with them. **46** The party over, an arm of a ghost uses a trowel to brick itself back into its crypt. **Crypt: 47** Human arms hold up the wall sconces here and in the unload area. **Outside the exit: 48** Each of the 20 mausoleum occupants has a pun for a name. They include Hal Lucinashun, I. Emma Spook, Wee G. Bord. **49** Dogs and snakes appear in the side frames of the benches in front of the hillside pet cemetery. **50** Mr. Toad is buried in the pet cemetery.*

* J. Thaddeus Toad is "dead" because his attraction, Mr. Toad's Wild Ride, is no longer at the Magic Kingdom. An original park attraction, it was replaced by The Many Adventures of Winnie the Pooh in 1998.

MANY OF THE VOICES are supplied by Hollywood talents. The ghost host is **Paul Frees,** who voiced Boris Badenov in the 1959–1964 television series "The Adventures of Rocky and Bullwinkle" and, incredibly, Pillsbury Doughboy Poppin' Fresh. He's also the Pirates of the Caribbean auctioneer, Carlos, concertina player, nearby dog and bridge parrot. The voice of the spiritualist is **Eleanor Audley,** Lady Tremaine in 1950's "Cinderella" and Maleficent in 1959's "Sleeping Beauty." The group singing "Grim Grinning Ghosts" is the **Mellomen,** a quartet who sang on many 1940s and 1950s pop hits (such as Rosemary Clooney's 1954 "Mambo Italiano") and were Elvis Presley's backup singers in the 1963 movie "It Happened at the World's Fair," 1964's "Roustabout" and the 1966 film "Paradise Hawaiian Style." The graveyard's singing busts feature Mellomen lead **Thurl Ravenscroft** (second from left). Also the voice of Country Bear Jamboree buffalo head Buff and the Enchanted Tiki Room's Fritz the parrot, he sang "You're A Mean One, Mr. Grinch" in the 1966 TV special "How the Grinch Stole Christmas!" and was the voice of Tony the Tiger for Kellogg's Frosted Flakes cereal. The graveyard's singing executioner is voiced by **Candy Candido,** the man who played the angry apple tree in 1939's "The Wizard of Oz" ("Are you hinting my apples aren't what they ought to be?") as well as the Indian chief in Disney's 1953 "Peter Pan" and a goon in 1959's "Sleeping Beauty."

The 'princess with the ax'

The attic has its own storyline, of a woman who spent her life marrying wealthy men then chopping off their heads to collect their fortunes. You pass each of her wedding portraits, which transform to show each groom losing his head. The bride herself stands at the end of the room. Sarcastically reciting wedding vows — "in sickness and in health" becomes "in sickness and in wealth" — she's holding an ax. Another state-of-the-art Disney illusion, the woman looks real, though she's actually a video projection on a three-dimensional figure. Some children, however, don't realize she's a bride. As one 8-year-old said to her dad afterward, "Did you see that princess with the ax? She was awesome!"

Magic Kingdom shopping guide

APPAREL

CHARACTER COSTUMES The Emporium (*Main Street U.S.A.*), Tinker Bell's Treasures (*adjacent to Cinderella Castle, Fantasyland*) and County Bounty (*Mickey's Toontown Fair*) have princess and other costumes. Pirate's Bazaar (*at Pirates of the Caribbean, Adventureland*) has the most pirate items.

CHILDREN'S WEAR The best children's and babywear are at Disney Clothiers (*Main Street U.S.A.*), Pooh's Thotful Shop (*at The Many Adventures of Winnie the Pooh, Fantasyland*) and County Bounty (*Mickey's Toontown Fair*).

FASHION Disney Clothiers (*Main Street U.S.A.*) is the park's main fashion store. Island Supply (*across from Swiss Family Treehouse, Adventureland*) has beach-themed apparel.

SANDALS You'll find sandals at Disney Clothiers (*Main Street U.S.A.*), Island Supply (*across from Swiss Family Treehouse, Adventureland*) and Sir Mickey's (*adjacent to Cinderella Castle, Fantasyland*).

SPORTS APPAREL Disney Clothiers (*Main Street U.S.A.*) is the park's sportswear shop.

T-SHIRTS AND HEADWEAR The Emporium (*Main Street U.S.A.*) has the most T-shirts. Attraction T-shirts are at the Briar Patch (*at Splash Mountain, Frontierland*), Buzz Star Command (*indoors, at the exit to Buzz Lightyear's Space Ranger Spin, Tomorrowland*), Fantasy Faire (*Mickey's PhilharMagic, Fantasyland*) and the Space Mountain shop (*Tomorrowland*). Hats and caps are sold nearly everywhere including from many carts; monogrammed Mickey ears are sold only at The Chapeau (*Main Street U.S.A.*) and Sir Mickey's (*adjacent to Cinderella Castle, Fantasyland*).

OTHER MERCHANDISE

ART The Art of Disney (*new for 2008, located inside the Main Street Cinema, Main Street U.S.A.*) has quality lithographs, posters, prints and two-foot-tall figurines of Mickey Mouse, Donald Duck and other characters. China figurines are at Uptown Jewelers (*Main Street U.S.A.*) and The Yankee Trader (*Liberty Square*). The expanded Crystal Arts (*Main Street U.S.A., in the former Market House*) and La Princesa de Cristal (*Caribbean Plaza, Adventureland*) offer crystal and glass figurines.

BOOKS Disney titles are available at The Emporium (*Main Street U.S.A.*) and at County Bounty (*Mickey's Toontown Fair*). Classic Pooh children's books are at Pooh's Thotful Shop (*at The Many Adventures of Winnie the Pooh, Fantasyland*). Heritage House (*Liberty Square*) has United States history titles, while the Briar Patch (at Splash Mountain, Frontierland) has a small but satisfactual selection of Brer Rabbit and Uncle Remus books.

CANDY The Main Street Confectionery (*Main Street U.S.A.*) makes its own fudge, Rice Krispy treats, candy and caramel apples, cotton candy and peanut brittle, all within view of guests. The treats are also sold at County Bounty (*Mickey's Toontown Fair*) and Prairie Outpost & Supply (*Frontierland*).

CHRISTMAS ITEMS Ye Olde Christmas Shoppe (*Liberty Square*) is the park's holiday store. "Nightmare Before Christmas" items are at Madame Leota's Cart (*at the Haunted Mansion, Liberty Square*).

HOUSEWARES Disney has dramatically reduced its kitchen and cooking merchandise in the past year, but some are still sold at The Yankee Trader (*Liberty Square*). Pooh's Thotful Shop (*at The Many Adventures of Winnie the Pooh, Fantasyland*) has Pooh items.

JEWELRY AND WATCHES Artists at Uptown Jewelers (*Main Street U.S.A.*) draw personalized sketches of Disney characters and reduce them onto watch dials. The store also has conventional watches, fine jewelry, best-friend charms, earrings and name and birthstone necklaces. You'll also find watches at Disney Clothiers (*Main Street U.S.A.*). The Emporium (*Main Street U.S.A.*) and Tinker Bell's Treasures (*adjacent to Cinderella Castle, Fantasyland*) have costume jewelry. Island Supply (*across from Swiss Family Treehouse, Adventureland*) has beach jewelry. Bwana Bob's cart (*at Adventureland's main entrance*) and Pirate's Bazaar (*Pirates of the Caribbean, Adventureland*) have shell, skull and pirate jewelry.

PET PRODUCTS The park's largest selection of pet products is inside the Engine Co. 71 building at the Firehouse Gift Station (*Main Street U.S.A.*). It carries bandanas, bowls, clothes, collars, dishes, leashes, toys and treats.

PINS The Magic Kingdom's pin central is Frontier Trading Post (*Frontierland*). Exposition Hall and Uptown Jewelers (*both Main Street U.S.A.*) have decent selections.

TOYS The big Magic Kingdom toy store is The Emporium (*Main Street U.S.A.*). Among the lures: princess dolls, action figures and a wide range of plushies. County Bounty (*Mickey's Toontown Fair*) has just about every other Walt Disney World plaything. Pooh's Thotful Shop (*at The Many Adventures of Winnie the Pooh, Fantasyland*) carries Pooh toys and plushies. Pirate's Bazaar (*at Pirates of the Caribbean, Adventureland*) has a treasure trove of Pirates of the Caribbean toys. Pal Mickey is at Main Street Cinema (*Main Street U.S.A.*).

frontierland

The Five Bear Rugs. From left: Tennessee, Fred, Zeke, Ted, Zeb and Zeb's young son, Oscar.

Country Bear Jamboree

City slickers may not cotton to it, and it hasn't aged well, but this Audio Animatronic hoedown is still loved by many. Set in an 1880s lumber-camp union hall, it features 18 goofy, life-sized bears singing 14 songs.

Plump, tutu-clad Trixie performs the 1966 Wanda Jackson hit, "Tears Will Be the Chaser for my Wine." Lowered from the ceiling, temptress Teddi Barra sings "Heart, We Did All That We Could," a 1967 Jean Shepard hit. "Ya'll come up and see me sometime!" she coos, channeling Mae West. Replies the emcee: "As soon as I can find a ladder!" The best bear is sad-eyed, tone-deaf Big Al. He butchers the 1960 Tex Ritter dirge, "Blood on the Saddle."

Other songs include Ritter's 1950 "My Woman Ain't Pretty (But She Don't Swear None)" and Homer & Jethro's 1964 "Mama Don't Whip Little Buford (I Think You Should Shoot Him Instead)." Talking trophy heads Buff (a buffalo), Max (a deer) and Melvin (a moose) bicker and banter.

16 min. Capacity: 380. Avg. wait: 8 min. Guests may remain in wheelchairs, ECVs. Assistive listening; reflective captioning. Debuted: 1971.

FUN FACTS ❱❱ Henry's introductory phrase "'cause we've got a lot to give" refers to the 1970s slogan of the show's original sponsor: "You've got a lot to live, and Pepsi's got a lot to give." ❱❱ Tex Ritter provides the voice of Big Al.

Woody's Cowboy Camp is a 20-minute interactive street show based on the "Toy Story" films. Woody, Jessie, Bullseye (and Sam the Singin' Cowboy) do the Hokey Pokey, sing along to "Hey Howdy Hey" and "You've Got a Friend in Me" and giddy-up their way through a cowboy obstacle course, maneuvering around parents donning hats shaped like cacti, mine shafts and mountains. *At various Frontierland locations throughout the day.*

Frontierland Shootin' Arcade

Filled with more than 50 silly sight and sound gags, this old-fashioned arcade is surprisingly fun. The infrared rifles are easy to hold, the targets easy to hit, and every hit causes something to happen — a prisoner escapes from his jail, an ore car comes out of its mine, a grave-digging skeleton pops out of its hole. You get 25 shots for a dollar. There's a bill changer on the side. Guns in the center have the best view of the most targets.

Capacity: 16. Avg. wait: None early morning, 5 min. peak afternoon. Guests may remain in wheelchairs, ECVs. Debuted: 1971.

▶ Each Shootin' Arcade gun is loaded with a secret free round to start the day.

Splash Mountain

✓ This half-mile flume ride in, out, around and down a man-made mountain is the most satisfactual, but least understood, ride in the park. Lined with 68 Audio Animatronic creatures in cartoon-like musical scenes, it takes you through bayous, swamps, a cave and a flooded mine shaft. It includes five short drops and one five-story plummet.

Based on scenes from Disney's 1946 film "Song of the South," Splash Mountain has a storyline that's fun and fascinating to follow. It's based on a series of American folk tales* popular with slaves in the antebellum South. Its obvious lesson: there's no place like home. Its subversive message: if they're crafty enough, the weak can do "pretty good, sure as you're born" against the strong.

You're in the story from the start. Climbing through some barns in rural Georgia, you come upon a secret passageway that leads to Critter Cave, the home of wise old storyteller Brer Frog. "Mark my words," he says to two grandkids, in a shadow diorama along the left side of the queue line. "Brer Rabbit gonna put his foot in Brer Fox's mouth one of these days."

Once in your log (hollowed out by sharptoothed beavers, so the story goes), you travel past the crafty rabbit's briar patch playground (around the ride's outdoor drop) and then head up Chick-A-Pin Hill,

Splash Mountain's final fall is a 52-foot drop into Brer Rabbit's briar patch. Splashdown is in a stream.

home to the tenacious but gullible Brer Fox and strong but stupid Brer Bear.

Floating into a magnolia bayou (i.e., once you go inside), you come upon Brer Rabbit packing up to leave. "I've had enough of this old briar patch," he sings. "I'm lookin' for a little more adventure."

Overhearing the rabbit, Brer Fox and Brer Bear scheme to catch the hare and cook him for dinner. Trouble is, whenever they catch Brer Rabbit he always slips away.

Brer Fox first traps him with a rope, but the bunny bamboozles the bear into switching places.* Then, saying he's headed to a tempting "laughin' place," the rabbit leads the fox and bear far down the bayou and eventually into a hollow, fallen tree. But it's not only filled with bees, it leads straight into a dark flooded mine. "I don't see no laughing place," the bear says. "Just bees!"

* "How Mr. Rabbit Was Too Sharp For Mr. Fox," "Mr. Rabbit and Mr. Bear" and "Brother Rabbit's Laughing-Place," as published in "The Complete Tales of Uncle Remus," an 1895 compilation of 185 African-American folk tales by Joel Chandler Harris, a columnist for the Atlanta Journal Constitution. Though the tales themselves have been widely embraced (Walt Disney loved "their rich and tolerant humor; their homely philosophy and cheerfulness"), Harris' book has not. In its defense, the white Harris described his created narrator, a freed slave named Uncle Remus, as "an old Negro... who has nothing but pleasant memories of the discipline of slavery." Disney's film basically ignored that premise but was still associated with it. The 1987 "The Tales of Uncle Remus" by Julius Lester offers most of the stories — which rival the best European folk tales for charm and humor — in a more unadulterated state.

* In the film, the tied-up Rabbit tells Bear he's a scarecrow, making $1 a minute: "You'd make a mighty fine scarecrow, Brer Bear. How'd you like to have this job?"

▶ **For the driest drop, duck down before the splash, stay down until after the slosh.**

frontierland

"I didn't say it was your laughin' place," the rabbit laughs, rolling on the ground. "I said it was my laughin' place!"

In the mine shaft, Brer Fox slams a beehive over the rabbit and ties him up at his cooking pot. "Well Brer Rabbit, it looks like I'm gonna have to cook ya!"*

But the bunny has one more trick. "You can cook me," he yells, "but whatever you do, please don't fling me in that briar patch!" So that's exactly what Brer Bear does. You experience Brer Rabbit's drop for yourself. He, and you, escape for good.

A singing showboat of friends welcomes him back home, but what's this? Brer Bear and Brer Fox are in the patch, too. Stuck in the thorns, the dim-witted bear is singing "Zip-A-Dee-Doo-Dah" along with the rabbit's friends. "This is all your fault Brer Bear!" Brer Fox says, trying to pull the bear free while fighting off an alligator. "You flung us here. So stop that singing!"

12 min. Capacity: 440. Avg. wait: 10 min. early morning, 75 min. peak afternoon. Fastpass available. Must be ambulatory. Height restriction: 40 in. Fear factor: One small drop is completely dark. The big drop can scare adults. Chicken exit. Best ages: 8 and up. Debuted: 1992 (1989 Disneyland).

FUN FINDS ❶ "Fleas, flat feet and furballs" are all cured by the "Critter Elixir" that's trumpeted on a wagon past the second lift hill. ❷ Around the corner, Brer Bear snores in his house. ❸ "Time to be turning around… if only you could," say vultures above you before the drop. "If you've finally found your laughing place, how come you aren't laughing?"

➡ **The front seat gets the wettest.**

* Alternates with "hang ya!" "roast ya!" and "skin ya!"

FUN FACTS ❭❭ The logs reach 40 mph on the final drop, making the fall the fastest Magic Kingdom moment. ❭❭ The ride uses 956,000 gallons of water, which is recycled every four minutes. ❭❭ In 1993, Great Britain's Princes William and Harry, then ages 11 and 8, visited the park with their mother, Princess Diana. Splash Mountain was William's favorite ride, so the group rode it three times. ❭❭ "Brer" is slang for "Brother." ❭❭ Because of the movie's racial overtones, Disney does not market "Song of the South" on DVDs.

Barrels of fun. A bouncy bridge on Tom Sawyer Island.

Tom Sawyer Island

Accessible only by a natural-gas-powered raft, this hilly, wooded island sits within the Rivers of America waterway of the Liberty Square Riverboat. Lined with paved, shady trails, it's filled with small adventures. Injun Joe's Cave is a cranny-filled cavern with a hidden scary face. Old Scratch's Mystery Mine is a creepy, twisting shaft with wailing winds and glowing crystals. Other spots include a climb-through grist mill (its creaks and groans subtly perform "Down By The Old Mill Stream"; the bird in the cogs is from the 1937 cartoon, "The Old Mill"), a barrel bridge and windmill. Atop a hill is a brook, duck pond, playground with a tiny rope swing and two picnic tables. Along the shore is Aunt Polly's Place, a shady snack bar.

A suspension bridge leads to calvary outpost Fort Langhorn. It has a snoring sentry, robotic horses and a "powder room" that's really the women's restroom. Kids love to find the "secret" escape tunnel at the back wall. Stairs lead to watchtowers with electronic rifles. *Allow 45 min. Capacity: 400. Avg. wait: 10 min. Must be ambulatory. Fear factor: The cave has side niches; preschoolers can get lost. Debuted: 1973.*

▶ **On Tom Sawyer Island, the water in the mine appears to run uphill.**

Big Thunder Mountain Railroad

✓ All curves almost all of the time, this coaster is exciting but never scary. Three series of hairpin turns through caves, mine shafts, hot springs and a flooded town, the 36 mph ride slings you around but there are no big falls and you never go upside down. Sit in the back to go faster over the hills.

It's best at night. The dark track seems faster, its rattling louder, its sulfur pools more colorful, and every dip, drop and turn comes as a surprise. Scattered around the set are hundreds of pieces of real mining gear, barbed wire, cactus and nearly 20 fairly realistic animals, including big-horned sheep, bobcats and javelinas.

The story is one of gods and greed. During the height of the Gold Rush*, men in the town of Tumbleweed were looking for gold on a nearby mountain, which was also an Indian burial ground. Though the mountain "thundered" whenever anyone prospected on it, these miners took ore trains deep down into its caverns and even dynamited new shafts. They removed the gold with glee and celebrated their finds with poker games and parlor girls.

Acts of God struck back. Mysterious spirits took control of the trains and spun them out of control, a flash flood inundated the town and an earthquake hit.

Everything was lost.

In reality, the mountain is a cement and wire-mesh skin over a concrete-and-steel frame. Inside are the ride's computers, electronics and pumps.

3 min. 30 sec. Capacity: 150. Avg. wait: 10 min. early morning, 60 min. peak afternoon. Fastpass available. Must be ambulatory.

* During the mid-1800s, a discovery of gold in a remote mountain area would often bring in a feverish migration of prospectors, who would search stream beds and canyon walls hoping to instantly find their fortune. Later a commercial company often arrived to mine for gold ore, chunks of rock with deposits of the precious metal.

Height restriction: 40 in. Chicken exit. Debuted: 1980 (Disneyland 1979).

FUN FINDS ❶ Lights flicker and dim around the attraction. ❷ As you walk up to the ride a box on your right reads "Lytum & Hyde Explosives Co." ❸ As you head down to the boarding area, a box above you holds whiskey. ❹ On the ride, a bathtubbing prospector on your right has washed down into Tumbleweed from the hills. ❺ On your left, rainmaker Prof. Cumulus Isobar bails himself out. ❻ Inside the Gold Dust Saloon, a whiskey-fueled poker match has been flooded out. ❼ Once the sun sets, drunks and dance-hall dames party upstairs. ❽ Around a bend, a "Flood-ometer" on your left reads "Flooded Out." ❾ Morris Code is the manager of a telegraph office along the left exitway. ❿ The right exit has a canary in a cage (he's not moving!) and ⓫ above a "Blasting in Progress" sign, a plunger. It's pushed in.

Above: The coaster is almost always in a turn

FUN FACTS ⟩⟩ The trains are faster late in the day, after the track grease has melted. ⟩⟩ The train names are I.B. Hearty, I.M. Brave, I.M. Fearless, U.B. Bold, U.R. Courageous and U.R. Daring. ⟩⟩ The "Howdy partners!" announcer is Dallas McKennon, who voiced TV's Gumby and Archie Andrews; Rice Krispies characters Snap, Crackle and Pop; and Ben Franklin at Epcot's American Adventure.

Rounded and out of proportion, Minnie's house (and Mickey's, right) looks as if it was drawn by hand

Minnie's Country House

Though it looks a little like Barbie's Dream House (Minnie Mouse's signature red and white polka dots are nowhere to be found) this walk-through bungalow is a hands-on Disney treat that's filled with detail. The fun starts in Minnie's living room, where the chair and loveseat make good photo props. Children can climb on her potter's wheel in the craft room and check her answering machine in the hall. The best spot is the kitchen, where kids can bake a cake, heat up a teapot, wave some popcorn, open the fridge and try to grab a cookie.

It's all pretend, of course, but still fun.

Silliness is tucked in everywhere. Attila the Mouse is the subject of a book on the coffee table, "Famous Mice in History." Written by Minnie, it's about a misunderstood invader who "merely came to taste the local cheeses." Another entry tells of Leonardo da Moussi, the inventor of the microwave cheese pizza.

The answering machine has a series of playable messages from Goofy, each time calling only to say he forgot why he was calling. In Minnie's kitchen, the spice rack holds Thyme, Good Thyme, Bad Thyme and Out of Thyme.

The best gags are on the sun porch, where pun-prone plants include buttercups (teacups, each with a pat of butter) and palms (with hands for fronds). Each is explained in "Clarabelle's Big Book of Pun Plants," which sits on the room's wicker table.

No detail, it seems, was left out. The porch lamps are flower petals. Wall photos include a portrait of Minnie's great-grandparents, Milo and Mabeline. In the craft room, she's painting Wiseacre Farm, the scene that's visible out her window. Earlier she completed her own version of Norman Rockwell's "Triple Self Portrait."

Capacity: 125. No wait; a slow line takes 15 min. Guests may remain in wheelchairs, ECVs. Debuted: 1996.

➡ **Need to get off your feet?** The loveseat and chairs in Minnie's living room and sunroom are the only indoor spots to sit in Toontown.

FUN FACTS ⟫ The house has no bedroom. ⟫ It sits on the spot of Mickey's Hollywood Theater, a Meet Mickey building from 1988 to 1996.

▶ Out back, Minnie's garden gazebo makes a pretty photo spot.

With its wooded yard, picket fence, and workshop garage, Mickey's house is an archetypical American home

Mickey's Country House

Two attractions in one, this walk-through House of Mouse is also the waiting line for the best place to meet Mickey.

First you tour the house. Mickey's just left, leaving on the television in the living room where he, Donald and Goofy have been watching football. In the bedroom hang many copies of his red-and-black tuxedo, while the den has seen Mickey beat his pals in ping pong. The kitchen is being "remodeled" by Donald and Goofy. Out back you walk through Mickey's appropriately shaped collection of cactus, pumpkins and tomatoes.

Then, if you like, you meet the mouse. He's always right next door, holding court

Mickey-shaped tomatoes in the back garden

in his Judge's Tent. The air-conditioned building entertains you with cartoons while you wait, and magically moves its line much faster than any other character location. (How's it done? Notice all the doors in the final hallway.)

Capacity: 125. Avg. wait: a slow-moving line can take 15 min. in the house; 30 more to see Mickey. Guests may stay in wheelchairs, ECVs. Debuted: 1988.

FUN FINDS ❶ A photo just inside the front door shows Donald, Goofy and Mickey building the house. ❷ The bedroom has photos of Mickey as a baby, posing with Santa and as a Boy Scout. ❸ The bedroom also reveals a secret: Mickey wears glasses! ❹ Mail in the hall includes letters from Buzz Lightyear (return address: "Infinity and Beyond") and Ariel (from "Under the Sea"). ❺ The kitchen's plans are from the "Chinny Chin Chin Construction Co.; General Contractor Practical Pig," a reference to Disney's 1933 Silly Symphonies cartoon "The Three Little Pigs." ❻ The blueprints include a garbage disposal that is simply a pig under the sink. ❼ Scales on the plans read "16 parts = 8.9 parcels," "7 pinches = 2 dollops" and "1 smidgen = 4 oodges."

▶ Want to meet Mickey? Stop by before 11 a.m. to avoid a long wait.

Goofy's plane crashes through a barn. **Below:** Laura Turner of Fort Myers, Fla., rides with her family.

The Barnstormer

With a short steep drop and a tiny tight spiral, this kid-friendly roller coaster is the perfect vehicle to introduce your kids to thrill rides. It's plenty zippy, but its tummy-tickling thrills are condensed into just 19 seconds of high-speed action.

The theme is fun, too. Taking off in a cartoon version of a 1920s crop-duster (Goofy's "Multiflex Octoplane") you immediately veer off course, turning, twisting and eventually crashing through a barn. It's the ideal spot to teach your tike, in the words of '80s funksters Cameo, "wave your hands in the air like you don't care."

1 min. Capacity: 32. Avg. wait: 5 min. until 10:30 a.m., 30 min. after. Must be ambulatory. Height restriction: 35 in. Fear factor: Intense for toddlers. Best ages: 4 and up. Debuted: 1996.

FUN FINDS ❶ Goofy's pants fly above the silo. **❷** Real crops in the gardens often include beets, cabbage, corn, kohlrabi, squash and tomatoes. **❸** Cartoon crops include "bell" peppers, popcorn, and squash that's been squashed by Goofy's feet. **❹** The giant jelly-jar lamps are "real" jelly jars. **❺** The chickens in the barn squawk after each plane passes. **❻** Behind them is a small "chicken exit." **❼** According to the plans on Goofy's drafting table (also in the boarding area), the crop-duster is powered by Dale running on a hamster wheel. **❽** Just outside the barn, a storage closet door labeled "Electrical Main" has been altered to read "Electrical Main Street Parade," a reference to the park's old Main Street Electrical Parade. **❾** A Goofy scarecrow is next, in the garden on your left.

FUN FACTS » The chickens once roosted inside Epcot's World of Motion (1982–1996), on the site of today's Test Track. **»** The first attraction here was Grandma Duck's Farm (1988-1995) a petting zoo with live pigs as well as Minnie Moo, a cow with Mickey-shaped spots. The pigs are now at the Fort Wilderness Campground. Ms. Moo moos no more.

▶ For a healthy treat grab some juice or fresh fruit at the Toontown Farmer's Market.

Donald's Boat

Here's where your toddlers and preschoolers can get soaked, and on a hot day they'll want to.

A leaky yacht-like tugboat, Donald Duck's yellow, blue and red S.S. Miss Daisy features a walk-in control room where pint-sized seafarers can clang a loud bell (by pulling on the right-hand rope) or secretly squirt water on others who have just gone out the back door (the left rope).

The big fun, however, is outside. The ship sits in a spongy duck pond filled with lily pads that spout jumping streams and spray without warning. Bring a swimsuit, or at least a change of clothes so your child can drench himself with abandon. The Pete's Garage restroom — to the left of Minnie's house — makes a good changing spot. Some parents just strip their kids down to their diapers and let 'em romp.

Unfortunately, the water is often turned off.

Next door, Toon Park is a small covered play spot with small slides and tunnels as well as a handful of benches.

Even if you're just walking past you can still admire the boat. The two-story ship looks like it came straight out of a cartoon. Its color scheme mimics Donald's sailor uniform and bill. The roof of the bridge resembles his signature blue cap.

Visiting from Naperville, Ill., 18-month-old Jessa Bergeron plays in one of the shooting fountains

Capacity: 60. No wait. Guests may remain in wheelchairs, ECVs. Best ages: 18 months to 8 years. Debuted: 1996.

How to meet the characters

A variety of characters await you inside the Toontown Hall of Fame tents. One line leads to classic stars such as Chip 'n' Dale, Goofy and Minnie Mouse; another has princesses such as Aurora (Sleeping Beauty), Belle, Cinderella and Snow White; a third goes to Winnie the Pooh and friends that may include Eeyore, Piglet or Tigger. As the fair's presiding judge, Mickey Mouse is in the Judge's Tent — accessible through Mickey's Country House — surrounded by prize-winning fruits and vegetables. Waits for each room can be up to 30 minutes, but the lines are air conditioned and your child will get all the one-on-one time she wants with each star. The princesses are happy to chat. There are no lines at 10 a.m., when this section of Magic Kingdom first opens. The adjacent County Bounty shop sells autograph books.

© DISNEY

Stitch isn't happy in Planet Turo's Prisoner Teleport Center

Stitch's Great Escape!

Featuring elaborate robotics and sound effects, this theater-in-the-round show is geared to those familiar with the 2002 movie "Lilo & Stitch." Its story takes place before the film: When Planet Turo's Prisoner Teleport Center receives an especially naughty detainee (Experiment 626), he breaks free from his guards (that's you) and seems to skitter around in the dark.

The show begins as a sergeant tells you that most prisoners come in two types, and that you, as a new security guard, will be guarding the Level Ones, the "common criminals of the cosmos." Then an alarm sounds. Arriving any second is a rare Level Three! Agent Pleakley orders you into a high-security chamber.

As two DNA-tracking cannons zero in on the little guy, the quick-witted monster breaks free and shorts out the power. As you sit in the dark, it sounds as if Stitch is roaming around the audience. In the show's highlight, you smell, and feel, Stitch burp.

The story is weak (since it takes place before Experiment 626 comes to Hawaii, how is he known as Stitch?) and not that entertaining, but the show's Audio Animatronic technology is impressive. The preshow sergeant shifts his weight from foot to foot and counts down on his fingers. Stitch's ears have multiple, simultaneous movements just like those of a dog; his eyes, arms, fingers and spine move fluidly.

18 min. Capacity: 240. Avg. wait: 10 min. early morning, 30 min. peak afternoon. Fastpass available. ECV users must transfer to a wheelchair. Handheld captions, assistive listening. Height restriction: 40 in. Fear factor: The harnesses and dark periods scare some kids. Best ages: 8 and up. Debuted: 2004.

IN "LILO & STITCH," a mad scientist on the planet Turo uses the genes of ferocious creatures to create Experiment 626, a tiny monster. Programmed to destroy everything it touches, the six-limbed alien can see in the dark and think faster than a supercomputer. When the Grand Councilwoman asks it to "show us there is something inside you that is good," 626 responds with the defiant yell "Meega, nala kweesta!" As it licks its holding glass, the monster is exiled to an asteroid, then guarded by robotic cannons that track genetic signatures. The ingenious creature, however, coughs on the floor. When the guns stalk the spit, 626 breaks loose, knocks out the power grid and escapes to Earth. Landing in Hawaii, the creature is adopted (and named "Stitch"), by Lilo, a lonely 7-year-old misfit. Other characters include Pleakley, a panicky government science advisor; and Gantu, a military captain whose face resembles a largemouth bass.

▶ Sit in back for the best view of Stitch. His platform sits high off the floor.

Monsters Inc. Laugh Floor

This live, improvisational comedy show is unlike any you've ever seen. Though it all takes place on three large video screens, its cartoon characters chat with, tease and read jokes from audience members just like real people. Based on the 2001 film "Monsters, Inc.," the show features eyeball-on-legs Mike Wazowski as its host. Trying to generate electricity by gathering laughter in bulk, Wazowski has created a laugh factory, a place where humans come to watch monsters "make funny with the ha-ha." As you wait for the show to start, you can text-message jokes to the comedians to use during their performance.

The performers choose a variety of adults and children to chat with. To increase your odds of getting picked, wear a colorful shirt or a big hat. The best shows are those with a full house.

15–20 min. Capacity: 400. Bench seats. Avg. wait: 30 min. early morning, 60 min. peak afternoon. Guests may stay in wheelchairs, ECVs. Reflective captioning, assistive listening. Best ages: 6 and up. Debuted: 2007.

FUN FINDS ❶ In the first queue room, an overhead banner that reads "Wow" reflects in a full-width upper wall mirror, making that holding area appear twice as large as it really is. ❷ That effect is ruined by a later addition to the room, a huge sign from the apparently humor-free Disney legal department. It informs you that by text messaging a joke you are giving the company the right "to publish or use the joke in whole or in part in any manner, to distribute the joke in any medium and through any media formats, technologies and channels now known or hereafter devised." ❸ In the second queue room, a candy machine immediately to your left offers such treats as Same Old Raccoon Bar and Polyvinyl Chloride, which small print on its wrapper notes is artificially flavored.

Astro Orbiter

The most thrilling of Disney's four hub-and-spoke rides, Astro Orbiter is fast, high and a little scary. Sitting low in a one-person-wide rocket, you soar up into a tight banked circle 55 feet above the ground. Top speed is 20 mph, plenty fast when you're at a 45-degree angle.

You pass within a few feet of a huge kinetic model of rings, planets and moons (one with its own moon) and look down on everything from the Tiki Room to Toontown. You can even spot the Tower of Terror, five miles away at Disney's Hollywood Studios.

The line is typically awful, but first thing in the morning there's usually no one here. In fact, just after the park opens you can often ride twice, maybe three times in a row without getting off. After dark the rockets' green nose cones and red engine fires light up and the huge central antenna flashes in blue, red and pink neon. The rockets run during drizzles, but are grounded by lightning and downpours.

Unchanged from the attractions's original 1971 Star Jets incarnation, the ride's green, steel-mesh elevator is meant to resemble a Cape Canaveral rocket gantry.

2 min. Capacity: 32. Avg. wait: 10 min. early morning, 60 min. peak afternoon. Must be ambulatory. Fear factor: The height and steep angle scare even some adults. Debuted: 1971 (Disneyland, 1955).

Retro rockets. Astro Orbiter's Art Deco vehicles soar within a ring of twirling planets and moons.

Buzz Lightyear's Space Ranger Spin

✓ This addictive, goofy ride turns the concept of a shooting gallery inside out: the targets stand still while you travel on a track. Piloting an open-cockpit "space cruiser," you use a laser gun to fire at more than a hundred targets. You spin your vehicle to help your aim, while a dashboard display tracks your score. The point? To help Buzz Lightyear, the deluded toy space ranger from the "Toy Story" films, save the galaxy from the Evil Emperor Zurg.

It's more fun when you know the story. As you enter Star Command Headquarters, Buzz thinks you're a new recruit in his Galactic Alliance. And you're just in time: Zurg's robotic henchmen are stealing all the "crystallic fusion power cells" (batteries, in Buzz-speak) from the world's toys to power his new secret weapon. Buzz orders you out to destroy the robots, and his claw-worshipping little-green-alien buddies to go recapture the batteries.

Flying into space, you and a partner battle two huge robots then land on Zurg's volcanic home, Planet Z. You fight his monsters (including the bendy snake from the "Toy Story" bedroom), then sneak onto Zurg's ship and face the evil emperor head-on. His weapon won't fire; his aides have knocked the batteries loose. When Zurg sneaks out an escape hatch you follow him, shifting into hyperdrive. Suddenly Zurg and his scooter reappear, this time as a video image. "Prepare for total destruction!" he roars, darting in front of you. You fire, and (whether you pull the trigger or not) the blast spins him into the next room and right to the squeakies. They capture Zurg and leave him hanging — from a claw.

The whole thing takes place in a world of toys. Buzz gets his information from a Viewmaster; Zurg's lead henchman is a Rock 'Em Sock 'Em Robot. With batteries on its back, your space cruiser is a remote-controlled toy. Its remote hides to your right at the end of the ride, just as you enter the exit area.

5 min. Capacity: 201. Avg. wait: 10 min. early morning, 60 min. peak afternoon. Fastpass available. ECV users must transfer to a wheelchair. Handheld captioning. Debuted: 1998.

"Stop that! I'm invincible!" Zurg bellows as the squeakies take apart his secret-weapon scooter

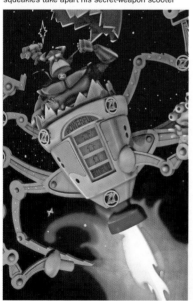

HOW TO SCORE BIG There are five secrets to getting a high score on Buzz Lightyear: ❶ Call dibs on the joystick, so you can keep your vehicle aimed at the right targets. ❷ Let your partner board first, so you sit on the right, the side with two-thirds of the targets. ❸ As soon as your gun is activated, pull the trigger and hold it in for the entire ride. The gun will fire about once per second, and the flashing of its laser beam will help you track your aim. ❹ If the ride stops, keep your blaster fixed on a target. You'll rack up points in a hurry. ❺ Aim only at targets with big payoffs: As you enter the **first room,** aim for the left arm of the left robot (each hit is 100,000 points). As you pass the robot, turn your vehicle to the left and hit the other side of that same arm (25,000). As you leave the first room, turn your vehicle backwards and aim at the overhead claw of the other robot (100,000). As you enter **Planet Z,** aim at the top and bottom targets of the large volcano (25,000). **As soon as you see Zurg,** hit the bottom target of his space scooter (100,000) by firing early and late; your gun can't aim low enough to hit it straight on. **As you go into hyperspace,** aim about six feet to either side of the top of the exit tunnel to hit a circle sitting in the middle of a rectangular plate (25,000). The maximum points possible is 999,999.

Carousel of Progress

Historic Disney robots bring good things to life

Part of the General Electric pavilion at the 1964 World's Fair, this Audio Animatronic show traces how electricity has improved family life. Personally developed by Walt Disney, its theaters rotate around a central stage, like horses on a carousel.

The first scene takes place before electricity, on Valentine's Day, 1904. "Things couldn't be any better," a father proclaims, as he shows off his cast-iron stove which "keeps five gallons of water hot all day on just three buckets of coal" and icebox that holds so much ice that "milk doesn't sour as quick as it used to."

Scene two takes you to the Fourth of July, 1927. "Mr. Edison sure added life to our home," the 'droid daddy says, sitting in a firetrap of cords as he points out his electric oven, refrigerator and vacuum cleaner. "It just can't get any better!"

Next it's Halloween, 1949. "Everything is better than ever now," he says, amazed his new fridge "holds more food than ice cubes." Finally it's the future, a world of laser discs and other wonders from, well, the tomorrow of 1994, the last year this scene was updated.

The vintage script is not exactly PC. Son Jimmy installs fuses and carves the jack-o-lantern while daughter Patty does little but get ready for dates. But listen closely and it is funny. When Jimmy looks through his dad's stereoscope the boy exclaims, "Ooh la la! So that's Little Egypt doing the hoochie-koochie?" When Patty tells her 1940s friend Babs that she's going to a party with "that dreamboat, Wilfred," Babs replies "Wilfred?! What a slug!"

21 min. Capacity: 1,440. Guests may remain in wheelchairs, ECVs. Assistive listening; handheld and activated video captioning available. No flash photography.

I, Robot. Built in 1964, the Carousel of Progress host was Disney's first Audio Animatronic human.

Debuted: 1964 at New York World's Fair, installed at Disneyland in 1967, moved to Disney World in 1975; revised 1994.

FUN FACTS)) The father is voiced by Jean Shepherd, the narrator of 1983's "The Christmas Story.")) His face was modeled from that of actor Preston Hanson, who starred as Marilyn Monroe's manager in the 1975 film "Goodbye, Norma Jean.")) The grandpa is voiced by 1950s singing cowboy Rex Allen.)) Grandma is voiced by Janet Waldo, teenager Judy in the 1960s cartoon series "The Jetsons" and Josie in the 1970s "Josie and the Pussycats.")) Cousin Orville is Mel Blanc, the longtime voice of Warner Bros. cartoon characters.)) Songwriters Richard and Robert Sherman had Walt Disney in mind when they wrote their "Great Big Beautiful Tomorrow" lyrics: "Man [Walt] has a dream and that's the start. He follows his dream in mind and heart...")) The 1904 grandma also rocks in front of the ballroom fireplace at the Haunted Mansion.)) The building has an outer doughnut of six theaters which rotate on railroad-style wheels and tracks.)) The theaters weigh 375 tons.)) They move at 2 feet per second.

▶ **Sit in the center of a back row. Many sound details come from the rear speakers.**

the waist of most people, just thigh-high for taller folks.

The ride is pure joy. You never know where you are going, and rarely know where you are. Projected onto the underside of a smooth dome, twinkling stars and shooting comets have no beginning and no end. Pinpoint projectors and hidden mirror balls put some stars right in your path. In fact, you have no reference points at all. You can't even see the sides of your rocket. It's all sensation, no thought required.

Much of the attraction is a subtle tribute to the seminal 1968 film, "2001: A Space Odyssey." The entranceway's eerie music recalls that of the film's early scenes of a moon transport shuttle, while the hall's angled plastic clapboard walls duplicate those of the transport's interior.

The movie's Discovery One spacecraft shows up three times. In the ride's boarding area, the spool-like corners the rockets pass look just like the axle area of Discovery One's rotating living quarters. The blue strobe tunnel recalls its hexagonal corridor that leads to its EVA pods. On the lift hill, the docked ship has the craft's unique head-spine-and-hip shape. The docked ship also appears earlier in the attraction, outside an entranceway window.

2 min. 30 sec. Capacity: 180. Avg. wait: 10 min. early morning, 60 min. peak afternoon. Fastpass available. Must be ambulatory. The Fastpass queue is wheelchair accessible. Height restriction: 44 in. Fear factor: Many dark drops and turns, but you don't go upside down. Chicken exit. Best ages: 8 and up. Debuted: 1975.

A FUTURISTIC SPACE FLIGHT The story begins as you walk into the building, a futuristic spaceport and repair center that's orbiting high above the earth. Passing the departure board, you walk down a long corridor to the launching platform, an open-air loading zone with its own control tower.

Once you climb into your rocket, a sign to your side flashes "All Systems Go." This

Space Mountain

A roller coaster in the dark

✓ "I want to go again! I want to go again! I want to go again!" said the 8-year-old boy to his parents. "That! Was! Cool!" said the 18-year-old college dude, here on Spring Break. "I rode it daddy! I rode it!" said a fully gowned Cinderella, age 6.

Where are these people? At the exit dock of Space Mountain, climbing out of their rockets after a trip on Walt Disney World's historic roller coaster in the dark.

Now *this* is the happiest place on earth. And no wonder.

The world's first indoor roller coaster when it debuted in 1975, this rocket-in-a-planetarium is still a delight. A series of surprises, its dips and whips leave you in seventh heaven.

Half the fun is the vehicle itself. One of the narrowest coaster cars ever built, your rocket is only slightly wider than you are. The sides are ridiculously low. They're at

▶ **Ask for the front row. You'll fly through the air with a breeze on your knees.**

activates the rocket transporter, which takes you through the energizing portal, a flashing blue tunnel of ever-louder "whoops" that power up your machine and ignite your engine.

Climbing the launch tower (the ride's chain lift), you pass under robotic arms that secure a large ship that has come in for service. As two mechanics work on its ion engines, two control-room operators monitor their progress.

Then you blast off — on a journey through, according to an early Disney press release, "the void of the universe." Zooming through space, "you become engulfed in a spectacular spiral nebula with flashing comets and a whirling galaxy." (Apparently you lose your bearings, as halfway through you fly right back through the launch bay.) Finally you return to the spaceport, creating your own sonic boom in a red de-energizing tunnel before you dock in the entry bay.

FUN FINDS ❶ Just inside the building, destinations on the departure board include Star Sirius, Real Sirius, World Ceres and Beta Beleevit. ❷ As you walk along the corridor, the music changes from a light melody to an ethereal, "2001"-style mix of harmonics, chimes and pings.

FUN FACTS ❯❯ The left track is a little darker, has a longer first drop and covers a slightly greater distance: 3,196 feet compared to the right track's 3,186. The final drop of both tracks is 35 feet. ❯❯ The meteorites projected on the ceiling are *not* pictures of chocolate-chip cookies. They just look that way. ❯❯ The energizing portal has a practical function: its flashing blue strobes shrink your pupils, which makes your space flight seem darker than it really is. ❯❯ Why do the docked ship's engine nozzles look like the plastic caps of spray-paint cans? Because they are! Used by an artist on a pre-production model, they were mistakenly reproduced as-is on the full-scale prop. ❯❯ Your rocket's top speed is only 28 mph. ❯❯ The "sonic boom" in the red re-entry tunnel is the reversed sound of a jet engine starting up. ❯❯ There are 30 rockets, numbered 1 through 31. There is no rocket 13. ❯❯ The building is 183 feet tall with a 300-foot diameter. It covers about two acres. Each of its 72 exterior concrete "ribs" weighs 74 tons, is 117 feet long and narrows from 13 feet wide at its base to 4 feet wide at its top. ❯❯ The building gets its sweeping-pillar look from Israel's Kennedy Memorial. Its shape comes from Japan's Mt. Fuji.

'Where's Mr. Smee?'

With its first passengers NASA astronauts Scott Carpenter, Gordon Cooper and Jim Irwin, Space Mountain opened with an elaborate ceremony on January 15, 1975. Disney officials declared the world's first indoor roller coaster "the nation's most breathtaking thrill ride." But not everyone got the message. As regular guests climbed in their rockets, many expected something along the lines of Peter Pan's Flight, since at the time Disney didn't do roller coasters.

A few seconds later, up came their lunches and out flew their hats, purses, eyeglasses and, on more than one occasion, false teeth. Disney's response included posing two of the ride rockets in a dive up on the attraction's entrance tower, and putting a video in the queue in which Cooper told guests it was A-OK with him if they would rather just head for the exit ramp (or as cast members called it, the "chicken exit") but if not, to "be sure to hang onto anything that's not fastened down: eyeglasses, hearing aids, hats, and even wigs." (Meanwhile, Disney discreetly ironed out some of the ride's most violent jerks and jolts.)

Though it opened during a recession, Space Mountain was an instant smash. By Easter every Central Florida hotel and motel was full, and passenger traffic at the Orlando airport was up 14 percent. When summer came, families with teenagers, many of whom would have never considered a Disney vacation before, began crowding Magic Kingdom turnstiles early each morning, running straight to Space Mountain as soon as the park opened. Afternoon waiting times at the ride would be two, even three hours. By the end of 1975 Magic Kingdom attendance, down 17 percent the year before, was up 20 percent, giving the park its busiest year yet.

Three decades later the only real difference in the attraction is the postshow. Originally it was the elaborate RCA Home of Future Living, as dioramas along the exit ramp showed a dad in a patio chair engaged in a teleconference while kids inside watched videodiscs. In 1985 the area became the RYCA-1 Dream of a New World, where robots built a pod city on a "hostile planet." The goofy Federal Express FX-1 Teleport took over the planet from 1993 to 1998, as "teleportation units" digitized and transported alien fossils back to earth. Remnants of the FedEx scenes remain today. The robotic boy and dog have been around since the beginning. Originally known as Billy, the then-human boy used to film guests for their television appearances on the Speedramp.

The FedEx years also had a preshow. Monitors in the boarding area aired the futuristically wacky "SMTV" network. Commercials featured Crazy Larry selling used spaceships, while a space newscast featured ditzy weather girl Wendy Beryllium: "Our extended forecast: giant comet. Wow, scary!"

Tomorrowland Indy Speedway

Yikes! Your child is at the wheel, pedal to the metal

This winding, wooded "race" track puts your little boy or girl at the controls of a 5-year-old's dream machine — a freewheeling racer with a rough ride and a rumbly, smelly engine. Top speed is, thankfully, just 7.5 mph. You stay in your lane courtesy of a rail underneath your car (expect to hit it every few seconds). The one-lap trip takes you under and over a bridge.

5 min. Capacity: 292. Avg. wait: 5 min. early morning, 60 min. peak afternoon. Must be ambulatory. Height restriction: 52 in. to take a car out alone. Debuted: 1971 (Disneyland 1955). Revised 1996.

➡ **If your child can't reach the gas pedal, have her steer while you work the pedal.**

➡ **Take your spin early in the morning or late at night to avoid a long wait.**

FUN FINDS ❶ Speakers around the track feature famed Indy announcer Tom Carnegie calling your "race." ❷ A brick from the 1909 pavement of the real Indy Speedway is embedded in the "starting line" between lanes 2 and 3, close to the elevated exit walkway.

Above: Jeff Turner of Fort Myers, Fla., cheers on his son, Andrew, 6, as they head for the finish line

Left: Terry's Teen Troupe of Avon, Connecticut, is among the hundreds of bands, choirs, orchestras, dance troupes, and other amateur groups that have appeared at Tomorrowland's Galaxy Palace Theater. They entertain as part of Disney Magic Music Days, an ongoing performance series.

Guest Carol Ravenhorst (in orange) rides with daughters Andrea and Pam and grandson Van. Below, the track goes over Indy Speedway.

Tomorrowland Transit Authority

An elevated tour of Tomorrowland

There are no big thrills, no special effects, not even a story, but this breezy ride does offer a nice way to get off your feet. Traveling alongside, around and sometimes through the four Tomorrowland buildings, you get a great view of Cinderella Castle, go over the Indy Speedway and glide through Space Mountain. A TTA trip is a great way to get out of the rain, or wait out a Fastpass time.

At dusk you get a great view of the Magic Kingdom's most colorful sight: Astro Orbiter in front of a sunset. At night the track glows red. An unsettling time to ride is when Space Mountain shuts down for repairs and you see that ride's usually inky interior fully lit. Like seeing your grandma naked, it's interesting, but you learn things you didn't need to know.

A far cry from its original purpose (see right), the ride is presented as a mass-transit system for a silly future world. Dioramas include a wacky hair salon and a suburban rocket port. A page tells Mr. Tom Morrow his "party from Saturn has arrived; please give them a ring." You also pass by a piece of real retro future: the center section of Walt Disney's working 1960s diorama for his proposed EPCOT community.

10 min. Capacity: 900. Must be ambulatory. Handheld captioning available. Debuted 1975 as WEDway PeopleMover, revised 1996.

Train in Vain

Today's Tomorrowland Transit Authority began life as a sketch drawn by Walt Disney in the mid-1960s. Planning for his Experimental Prototype Community of Tomorrow (EPCOT), he thought a system of small, narrow, electric trains would be an ideal form of mass transportation. It would give people an efficient way to run errands or go to work, as it could snake alongside or circle over convenience stores, offices and monorail stations without creating pollution or traffic problems.

Though Walt Disney died as the idea was getting off the ground, his team developed it fully. Loading is fast, as each train slows but never stops. Clean, efficient and easy to maintain, the power system has no engines and no moving parts except for its wheels. The trains move via an electrical system in the track. Every six feet or so a coil embedded in a shoebox-size rectangle pulses with electricity, turning on to pull the next car to it (its magnetism attracts a steel plate in the car's floor) then turns off to let that vehicle pass over it. These bursts continue around the track (there are 533 numbered electromagnets in its 4,574 feet) moving the trains in a silent, smooth glide of linear induction. The concept won a design achievement award from the National Endowment for the Arts and the U.S. Dept. of Transportation. The Disney company believed in the system so much that it formed a separate division, Community Transportation Services, to market it to other municipalities.

But without Walt, the dream died. EPCOT the city was abandoned, and CTS only sold the idea once: to the Houston International Airport in 1981. A modern version of the power system runs the Rock 'n' Roller Coaster at Disney's Hollywood Studios.

Tigger greets happy fans on Main Street U.S.A.

Disney Dreams Come True Parade

Filled with Disney characters all ready to wave, this procession is your kids' chance to wear out their arms.

Right up front is Mickey Mouse, surrounded by statues of himself that show how he evolved from a gloveless black-and-white imp in 1928's "Plane Crazy" to a colorful cherub in 1983's "Mickey's Christmas Carol." Other floats are filled with stars from the animated films "Aladdin" (1992), "Alice in Wonderland" (1951), "Fantasia" (1940), "Mary Poppins" (1964), "Peter Pan" (1953), "Pinocchio" (1940), "Snow White and the Seven Dwarfs" (1937), "Song of the South" (1946) and the classic Winnie the Pooh featurettes (1966–1974).

Separate floats are devoted to princesses and villains. Also on hand: Minnie Mouse, Donald Duck, Goofy, Pluto and the ever present Chip 'n' Dale.

The procession is an update of the Share a Dream Come True parade (2001–2006), a rolling tribute to Walt Disney. The first character, in fact, is Walt himself, circa 1928. Surrounded by ink-and-paint girls on bicycles, a performer portrays the young animator drawing Mickey Mouse.

Route: Starts in Frontierland; travels Liberty Sq. and down Main St. The 3 o'clock parade gets to Liberty Sq. at 3:07, the castle at 3:15, Town Sq. at 3:25. 15 min. Arrive 30 min. early for a good seat. Special areas for those in wheelchairs, ECVs. Debuted: 2001, revised 2006.

➡ **The best viewing spot: On the curb on the shady western side of Main Street.**

Main Street Family Fun Day Parade

You and your kids can march down Main Street with a Disney character in this fun patriotic procession. Drum major Pluto leads three small floats, five other Disney characters and up to 50 park guests. Guests wave flags with Horace Horsecollar, push strollers with Clarabelle Cow, do a hula-hoop drill with Chip 'n' Dale and shake pom poms with Daisy Duck. Each routine is choreographed, and taught to participants before the parade steps off.

To be included, show up at the popcorn stand in front of Cinderella Castle about 15 minutes early and track down a cast member wearing a red, white and blue costume. Ask early enough and you can even choose the character you walk with. PhotoPass photographers are on hand to take pictures. Counting prep time and a flag-waving finale at Town Square, the whole experience takes about 25 minutes. *Three times daily.*

Mom: "Who's going to be in the parade?" Son, 4: "Piglet!" Mom: "Oh?" Son: "Both Piglets! Piglet and his brother, Piglet Pan!"

park puzzler

How much do you really know about the Magic Kingdom?

1) The girl at right is dressed as which princess?
a. Ariel.
b. Aurora.
c. Cinderella.

2) The flying Tinker Bell at the beginning of Wishes is portrayed by...
a. An Audio Animatronic robot.
b. A beam of light.
c. A cardboard cutout.
d. A real person.

3) Which former attraction star is buried in the Haunted Mansion's pet cemetery?
a. The ExtraTERRORestrial Alien Encounter alien.
b. Minnie Moo from Grandma Duck's Petting Farm.
c. Mr. Toad from Mr. Toad's Wild Ride.

4) At the Pirates of the Caribbean, the auctioneer tells the redhead to...
a. "Bury your treasure!"
b. "Cover your cargo!"
c. "Lower your sails!"
d. "Strike your colors!"

5) In the Enchanted Tiki Room, after Iago hears "In the Tiki Tiki Tiki Tiki Tiki Room" he threatens to...
a. Spill his beans.
b. Toss his crackers.
c. Cut his cheese.

6) The interior decor of Space Mountain re-creates the look of what classic film?
a. 1968's "2001: A Space Odyssey."
b. 1968's "Barbarella."
c. 1971's "The Andromeda Strain."

7) The exterior of Cinderella Castle is made of what material?
a. Concrete.
b. Fiberglass.
c. Stone.

Answers, page 331

Cinderella's twinkling pumpkin transforms into an all-white carriage during the SpectroMagic finale

SpectroMagic

A light parade based on vintage Disney animation

✓ Like a Christmas tree in a dark living room, just the sight of this nighttime light parade makes you feel good. It's a cavalcade of colorful lights, many of which animate into synchronized patterns. Everything is lit — the floats and the characters — but since it all comes from within it's all against a pitch-black backdrop.

But it's more than just lights. Set to a symphonic score and filled with twirling butterfly girls, spinning fish and dancing ostriches, SpectroMagic is like a hallucinatory dream: you can't understand it, but it sure is interesting.

The theme? Disney's cartoons and musicals from the 1930s, '40s and '50s, accented with a couple of modern milestones. The parade features more than 80 characters, 90 percent of them from works released before 1960. Smoke and disco balls add to the fun, as does the mischief of the performers. The "Fantasia" ostriches peck, kick or slap each other. The Three Little Pigs taunt the Big Bad Wolf. Peter Pan has been known to kick Mr. Smee.

A good place to sit is in front of Tony's Town Square Restaurant on Main Street. You'll get a good view of the front and side of every float, as the parade comes right at you and then turns. You'll also be next to the park exit. Running late? Front-row seats are often available in front of the Town Square firehouse until just before showtime. Sit there and you'll be directly across from the barber shop, where celebrities often watch.

A bad spot to sit: In Frontierland, facing the Rivers of America. A spotlight by the riverboat shines right in your face.

FLOATS The procession is lead through the park by the SpectroMen, an exuberant group of green-, orange- and purple-haired trumpeters and whirlyball riders who are literally light-headed.

After Mickey Mouse casts his spell over a lightning ball, Genie conducts a three-float symphony. Goofy, playing the timpani, rides with the Golden Harp from "Mickey and the Beanstalk" (from the 1947 film

▶ Let your kids play in the dark street before the parade. Where else can they?

"Fun and Fancy Free"). Also on board: the bass violins from the 1935 Silly Symphony "Music Land" and a Liberace-like, bench-gliding Chip 'n' Dale playing a grand piano.

A peacock leads in Sleeping Beauty's three-float flower garden. The 1959 film's good fairies Fauna (in green), Flora (blue) and Merriweather (red) turn a multicolor day to a blue and green night. Human butterflies and dragonflies dance alongside.

A 12-foot fish escorts three more to lead in "The Little Mermaid" float. From the 1989 film comes a spinning Ursula, swimming Ariel and singing Sebastian, followed by a sea-horse-drawn King Triton. Also floating by: two flashing, twirling fish. (Watch for the bubbles!)

Next it's back in time to 1940's "Fantasia." Ben Ali Gator, Hyacinth Hippo and the dancing ostriches entertain Bacchus with their "Dance of the Hours" routine.

Then Chernobog, the monstrous bat-winged demon from the film's "A Night on Bald Mountain" segment, is escorted by five winged horses that fly above some dry-ice clouds.

The finale tops it all. Poised before six floats, the Three Little Pigs, stars of a 1932 "Silly Symphony" cartoon, flick paint brushes to change the convoy — including Cinderella's coach and castle, a rotating carousel, Captain Hook's ship and every character's costume — from a silvery white to the full color spectrum.

The lights cause other changes, too, which mimic moments in classic Disney films. Cinderella's coach converts from a pumpkin to a carriage, while in the finale procession the Cheshire Cat entirely disappears except for his mouth and eyes.

Route: Starts on Main Street U.S.A. between the Town Square firehouse and car barn. Continues to the castle hub, through Liberty Square and Frontierland. 20 min. Arrive 30 min. early for a decent seat, an hour early for the best spots. Special viewing areas for guests in wheelchairs and ECVs. Fear factor: The Chernabog float has spooky music and a 30-foot-tall animated monster. Debuted: 1991, revised 2001.

FUN FINDS ❶ The horns of the SpectroMen light up when they're played. ❷ Mickey's 24-tier cape extends up over his float. ❸ His electricity ball sizzles when he touches it and adds rays to his cape. ❹ Other lights on the cape sync to the music. ❺ The bass violins pluck themselves. ❻ Notes project on the ground around them. ❼ A sun changes to a moon on the first garden float. ❽ The insect girls have painted faces. ❾ A waterfall cascades down the back of the last garden float. ❿ Each pair of eyes in the fish school moves differently. ⓫ Ursula stops to chat with some guests ("Hello handsome!"). ⓬ Ariel does the breast stroke. ⓭ The spinning fish wink. ⓮ The ostriches wear heavy eyeliner and tuxedo jackets. ⓯ The pink-lined Bald Mountain turns into the red-lit Chernabog. ⓰ Two buzzards guard the demon. ⓱ Lightning strikes under his horses and on Bald Mountain. ⓲ A crown spins above Cinderella. ⓳ Tinker Bell appears in the castle windows and flies outside of them. ⓴ Two mechanical "Alice in Wonderland" playing cards paint their roses red. ㉑ Mary Poppins' umbrella lights up with her jacket. ㉒ Dumbo is one of the carrousel animals. ㉓ The Three Caballeros (from the 1945 film of that name) appear on the carrousel's top rear panel. ㉔ Capt. Hook's hook lights up. ㉕ His cannons fire in time with the music. ㉖ Flying on Capt. Hook's mast, a Jolly Roger has glowing red eyes. ㉗ Riding with Capt. Hook, the Evil Queen has her magic mirror. ㉘ Tinker Bell appears again, inside the Evil Queen's castle. ㉙ Lights circle the ground around Minnie and Donald. ㉚ Facing backward, a Jiminy Cricket puppet appears at the end of the parade, waving "So long! See ya later!"

FUN FACTS 》 The floats are covered in scrim, a transparent black gauze. 》 The drivers' faces hide behind mesh screens. 》 The parade uses 2,000 car batteries. Walking performers wear battery packs. 》 There are 600,000 miniature lights; 100 miles of fiber-optic cable. Some floats and costumes use fiber-optic thread. 》 The floats carry 204 speakers with 72,000 watts of power. 》 Soundtrack composer John Debney also created the scores for the motion pictures "Elf," "Bruce Almighty," "The Scorpion King," "Spy Kids (1 & 2)" and "The Passion of the Christ." 》 The Sebastian and Jiminy Cricket puppets were added to the parade in 2001, when it returned to the Magic Kingdom after a two-year hiatus.

▶ At Town Square? Get snacks at the line-free locker shop *outside* the train station.

Nearly 700 explosions burst in the air during the Wishes fireworks show

Wishes

Disney's signature fireworks show synchronizes its explosions with dialogue and music

✔ Every! Other! Fire! Works! Show! Emphasizes! Every! Explosion!

Not this one. Disney's signature fireworks show is artistic, even subtle.

Though it explodes 683 different pieces of pyro in just 12 minutes, Wishes paints delicate strokes as well as bold. Sometimes the sky sparkles, sometimes it flashes. Some explosions form stars, hearts, even a face. Some bursts dribble away, others disappear. Comets shoot off by themselves and by the dozen.

But that's just the half of it.

Synchronizing its visuals to a symphonic score, Wishes packs an emotional punch. Narrated by Jiminy Cricket with help from the Blue Fairy, it teaches a heart-tugging lesson about believing in yourself.

The show starts without fanfare, as a quiet chord grows louder and the castle begins to glow and sparkle. Then you hear the Blue Fairy: "When stars are born they possess a gift or two… They have the power to make a wish come true."

Right on cue, a lone star arcs across the sky. *"Starlight, star bright, first star I see tonight,"* a chorus of little girls sings. *"I wish I may I wish I might, have the wish I wish tonight…"* Blue stars — not star bursts but actual five-pointed stars — explode above Cinderella Castle.

"I'll bet a lot of you folks don't believe that, about a wish coming true, do ya?" Jiminy asks. "Well I didn't either. But lemme tell you: the most fantastic, magical things can happen, and it all starts with a wish!"

▶ Watch the show from in front of the castle. Main Street doesn't fill until showtime.

And with that, the spectacle begins.

First Tinker Bell (a real person) steps off the top turret of Cinderella Castle and glides over the crowd to Tomorrowland. Major explosions fill the air as the voices of Cinderella, Ariel, Pinocchio and other Disney stars recall their wishes, then medleys of fireworks (each in its own color palette) express courage and love.

"Fate is kind," a choir sings. *"She brings to those who love... the sweet fulfillment of... their sweet longing."*

A fan of comets wipes the sky clean, then shooting fountains dance to the opening notes of "The Sorcerer's Apprentice." Later, a villains segment features chaotic, crackling bursts, some as bright as strobe lights.

"Wishes can come true," the cricket says. "And the best part is, you'll never run out. They're shining deep down inside of you."

WHERE TO WATCH IT With fireworks that launch directly behind Cinderella Castle as well as symmetrically alongside, Wishes is best seen from in front of the castle, anywhere on Main Street.

The perfect spot is on the crest of the Main Street bridge, between the tip board and the hub. You'll be close enough to see all the castle effects, but far enough away to see all the pyrotechnics. There's always room to stand in this area, as cast members don't let guests out onto the street at this spot until just minutes before showtime.

Avoid Town Square (the lights stay on) and especially the train station balcony (there's no audio).

Want to dash out of the park as soon as the show ends? Stand in front of the Emporium, the closest dark spot to the exit.

But why fight the crowd? Instead, why not embrace the magical mood you'll be in to get an ice cream and relax. Your kids

will be happy; why not talk with them? Ask about their dreams and wishes. Tell them about yours.

12 min. Special viewing areas for wheelchair and ECV guests if arranged 30 min. early. Debuted: 2003.

FUN FINDS **1** Blue stars appear above Cinderella Castle during the opening verse, just after the lines "When you wish upon a star..." "makes no difference who you are..." and "anything your heart desires will come to you..." **2** Tinker Bell starts her flight from the castle just after Jiminy Cricket says "...and it all starts with a wish!" **3** As each Disney character says their wish, the accompanying fireworks are the color of his or her famous wardrobe (i.e., Cinderella's are blue, Ariel's green). **4** After Aladdin tells Genie "I wish for your freedom!" a shout of "Wishes!" brings out another blue star. **5** Red hearts appear above the castle at the end of the song "Beauty and the Beast." **6** More blue stars explode as Jiminy sings "...when you wish upon a star, your dreams... come true!" **7** "Whoa!" Genie says as his fireworks appear. "Ten thousand years can give ya such a crick in the neck!" **8** During the "Sorcerer's Apprentice" sequence, the castle turns into the blue Sorcerer's Hat, complete with its white stars and moons. **9** A red explosion introduces the villains. **10** Images of the Evil Queen's mirror appear on the castle as she commands "Slaves in the magic mirror, come from the farthest space..." **11** A frowning face appears in the sky, and the castle mirrors become faces, when the queen commands "Let me see thy face!" **12** Meanwhile the castle glows in dark greens, oranges and purples and is flashed with lightning. **13** It turns blue again as the Blue Fairy returns.

IN 1940'S "PINOCCHIO," the Blue Fairy (a symbol of kind, patient wisdom) appoints Jiminy Cricket to serve as the boy's official conscience.

"STARLIGHT, STAR BRIGHT," a 19th-century American nursery rhyme, is based on the notion that if you see the first star of the night sky before any others have appeared, any wish you make will come true. (In reality, an evening's first visible "star" is often the planet Venus.)

FUN FACTS ❱❱ The fireworks launch from 11 locations. ❱❱ Tinker Bell is sometimes a man. The role's physical requirements are only that the performer weigh no more than 105 pounds and be no taller than 5 feet 3 inches. ❱❱ Wishes replaced Fantasy in the Sky, the park's fireworks show from 1976 to 1993. Though only five minutes longer, Wishes uses almost three times the fireworks.

▶ Keep an eye on the castle. It sparkles, flashes and changes colors.

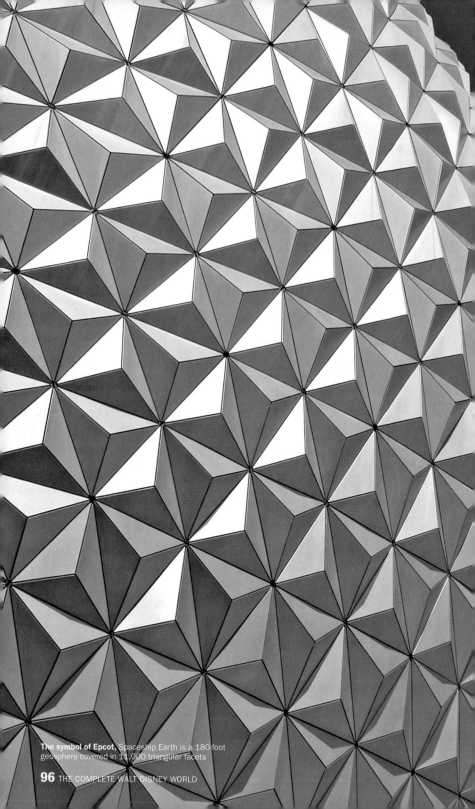

The symbol of Epcot, Spaceship Earth is a 180-foot geosphere covered in 11,000 triangular facets

Epcot

Where can you talk with a sea turtle, crash through test barriers, soar over California, take a rocket ride to Mars, be chosen King of England, buy some exclusive French perfume and feast at a German Oktoberfest? At Epcot, a unique theme park that puts a Disney spin on the science expositions, national pavilions and large, iconic structures of a classic world's fair — all of it set in a relaxing, if huge, musical garden.

TWO PARKS IN ONE The world's fair theme kicks off in Future World, a science-and-technology zone themed to subjects such as agriculture, automotive safety and geography.

Sound dull? It isn't. Each topic is the theme of a ride — a greenhouse boat cruise (Living with the Land), a spin around a General Motors proving ground (Test Track), a hang-gliding flight over California (Soarin'). Other highlights: the interactive "Turtle Talk with Crush" and the realistic Mission Space. In the middle is Innoventions Plaza, a hub with two exhibit halls. Changes for 2008 include a revamped Spaceship Earth attraction (and the restoration of the "ball" itself to its original 1982 appearance, without the Mickey Mouse wand), a better character-meeting setup and a new ice-cream stand.

You'll travel around the world (and stop only in friendly countries) when you take the 1.3-mile trek around Epcot's World Showcase. Lining a 40-acre lagoon, 11 national pavilions are filled with native entertainment, food and merchandise. Most offer an attraction or small museum. Best of all, each is staffed by young natives of its country. Chosen for their outgoing personalities, these participants in Disney's Cultural Representative Program are always willing to chat. For 2008 there's a new film in the Canada pavilion and new restaurants in Japan and Italy.

HISTORY Epcot opened Oct. 1, 1982. For its first four years it was called EPCOT Center. Four pavilions were added during the park's first decade — Morocco (1984), The Living Seas (1986, now The Seas with Nemo & Friends), Norway (1988) and Wonders of Life (1989, now closed). Its biggest change came in 2000, when its futuristic Horizons pavilion was demolished to make way for Mission Space.

THE LAYOUT OF FUTURE WORLD mimics the left-right division of the human brain. As you enter the park, pavilions on your left are themed to analytical, linear or engineering issues (i.e., energy, space travel, automobile) and sit within a landscape of straight-lined walkways. Those on the right cover more natural topics (seas, land, imagination) and rest in a hilly, meandering, watery landscape.

© DISNEY

Eleven international pavilions line a 1.3-mile promenade that circles the World Showcase Lagoon

The word Epcot comes from the acronym for Walt Disney's Experimental Prototype Community of Tomorrow, a working model city of the future he envisioned would be centered on this site. After his death, the company took two of Walt's ideas — a science center that would show ways to improve existing communities, and an international expo that would showcase the culture, history and goals of other nations — and reworked them into a theme park.

A TWO-DAY TOUR With nearly two dozen pavilions spread out over 260 acres, Epcot takes two days to fully enjoy. As shown on the next page, an easy plan is to spend one day in Future World, another at World Showcase. The two areas keep separate hours. Future World closes at 7 p.m. except for major attractions; World Showcase doesn't open until 11 a.m. The theme park typically closes at 9 p.m.

Epcot has two entrances. The main gate is at the front of the park, next to the parking lot and monorail station. A second entry, called the International Gateway, lies between the World Showcase pavilions of the United Kingdom and France. It provides access to guests staying in the Epcot Resort Area hotels — Disney's BoardWalk, Disney's Yacht Club and Beach Club; and the Walt Disney World Swan and Dolphin.

LIBRARY OF CONGRESS

Spaceship Earth (left) was inspired by the Perisphere (above) of the 1939 World's Fair

▶ Rain cancels most of Epcot's live entertainment but only one attraction: Test Track.

Rock 'n' roll bagpiper Jamie Holton and guitarist Mark Weldon lead the Canada pavilion's Off Kilter

FUN FINDS ❶ The central Innoventions fountain offers a five-minute show choreographed to music every 30 minutes. ❷ An upside-down waterfall propels water into a pool in front of the Imagination pavilion. ❸ A single splash of water appears to hop from pad to pad at the Leap Frog Fountain, directly in front of the Honey, I Shrunk the Audience attraction. ❹ Meanwhile, jelly-like blobs of water hang in mid-air after they break off from the streams of the nearby Jellyfish Fountain. ❺ Three Future World drinking fountains imitate submarine sounds, sing opera and offer wisecracks such as "Hey, save some for the fish!" when water hits their drains. One sits in front of MouseGear along the east side of the Innoventions fountain. ❻ A second is near the play fountain between Future World and the World Showcase. ❼ A third fountain sits close to the restrooms behind Innoventions West. ❽ Voices inside a trash can talk to you inside the Electric Umbrella. Swing open the lid of the receptacle marked "Waste Please" (next to the topping bar to the left of the order counter) and you may hear a surfer dude complain "Like, your trash just knocked off my shades!" or a Frenchman exclaim "Zis ees

BY THE NUMBERS ≫ **260** Number of acres in Epcot. **162** Number of acres in the Epcot parking lot.

A DAILY PLAN

Can you get here at least one day by 8:30 a.m.? If so, here's a great schedule. The keys: Getting Soarin' Fastpasses early and making meal reservations far in advance.

DAY 1: FUTURE WORLD

8:30 ARRIVE AT THE PARK

9:00 TEST TRACK

9:30 GET FASTPASSES for Soarin'

9:45 THE SEAS WITH NEMO & FRIENDS See Turtle Talk with Crush, then the 10:45 a.m. marine biology presentation.

12:00 THE LAND Buy tickets to the 2 p.m. Behind the Seeds tour, ride Soarin', then have a 1 p.m. lunch at Garden Grill.

3:00 MISSION SPACE

4:30 INNOVENTIONS

6:00 SPACESHIP EARTH

7:00 DINNER Coral Reef (Seas pavilion)

DAY 2: WORLD SHOWCASE

10:30 ARRIVE AT THE PARK

11:30 U.K. World Showcase Players

12:00 FRANCE Impressions de France

12:30 LUNCH Tokyo Dining. See Miyuki.

2:30 THE AMERICAN ADVENTURE

3:15 GERMANY See the train village.

3:45 OUTPOST OrisiRisi

4:15 CHINA Dragon Legend Acrobats

5:30 NORWAY Maelstrom

6:30 DINNER San Angel Inn (Mexico)

8:30 ILLUMINATIONS

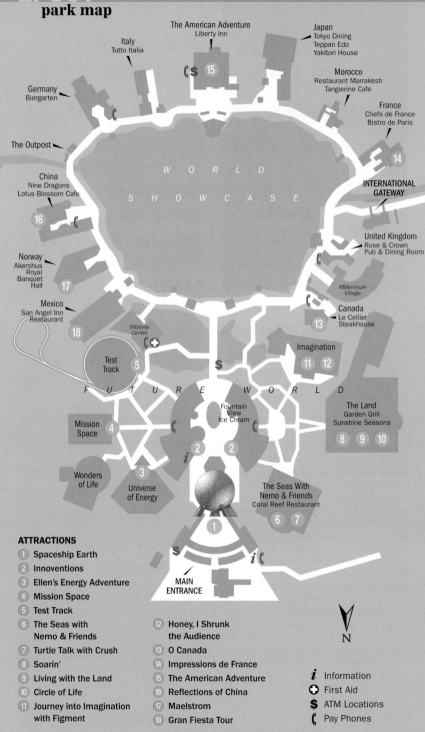

EPCOT
park map

The American Adventure
Liberty Inn

Italy
Tutto Italia

Japan
Tokyo Dining
Teppan Edo
Yakitori House

Germany
Biergarten

Morocco
Restaurant Marrakesh
Tangierine Cafe

France
Chefs de France
Bistro de Paris

The Outpost

China
Nine Dragons
Lotus Blossom Cafe

WORLD
SHOWCASE

INTERNATIONAL
GATEWAY

United Kingdom
Rose & Crown
Pub & Dining Room

Norway
Akershus
Royal
Banquet
Hall

Millennium
Village

Canada
Le Cellier
Steakhouse

Mexico
San Angel Inn
Restaurant

Odyssey
Center

Imagination

Test
Track

FUTURE WORLD

Mission
Space

Fountain
View
Ice Cream

The Land
Garden Grill
Sunshine Seasons

Wonders
of Life

Universe
of Energy

The Seas With
Nemo & Friends
Coral Reef Restaurant

MAIN
ENTRANCE

N

ATTRACTIONS
1. Spaceship Earth
2. Innoventions
3. Ellen's Energy Adventure
4. Mission Space
5. Test Track
6. The Seas with
   Nemo & Friends
7. Turtle Talk with Crush
8. Soarin'
9. Living with the Land
10. Circle of Life
11. Journey into Imagination
    with Figment
12. Honey, I Shrunk
    the Audience
13. O Canada
14. Impressions de France
15. The American Adventure
16. Reflections of China
17. Maelstrom
18. Gran Fiesta Tour

i Information
First Aid
$ ATM Locations
Pay Phones

Kids make souvenir masks at Epcot's Kidcot Funstops, located in pavilions throughout the park

PARK RESOURCES

BABY CARE The Baby Care Center *(inside Future World's Odyssey Center)* has changing rooms, nursing areas and a microwave; and sells diapers and other baby-care products.

CAMERA NEEDS Gateway Gifts *(under Spaceship Earth)* sells cameras and accessories and burns photo CDs.

GUEST RELATIONS The Guest Relations center *(to the left of Spaceship Earth, and at the far right of the park entrance)* has cast members ready to help with any problem. It has maps and Times Guides for all the theme parks, exchanges foreign currency and stores items found in the park that day.

LOCKERS Lockers can be rented at Gateway Gifts *(under Spaceship Earth)* for $5 per day plus a $2 deposit. The lockers are to the right of Spaceship Earth.

LOST CHILDREN Report lost children to Guest Relations or any cast member. Kids who lose parents should tell a cast member.

PACKAGE PICKUP Anything you buy can be sent to Package Pick-Up *(park entrance or International Gateway)* for you to get as you leave. Purchases can also be delivered to your Disney hotel or shipped.

PARKING For day guests parking is $11 a day. Those staying at a Disney resort (and annual passholders) get free parking. A tram takes you to the park entrance.

PETS The Pet Care Kennel *(Entrance Plaza, 407-560-6229)* has clean cages in air-conditioned rooms.

STROLLERS AND WHEELCHAIRS Stands at both entrances rent single strollers and wheelchairs *($10 per day)*, double-passenger strollers *($18)* and Electric Convenience Vehicles *($35)*.

TIP BOARD Tip boards in Future World display waiting times for top attractions

TRANSPORTATION Boats and walkways lead to Disney's Hollywood Studios and the BoardWalk, Yacht and Beach Club and Swan and Dolphin resorts. A monorail connects through the Transportation and Ticket Center to the Contemporary, Grand Floridian and Polynesian resorts and Magic Kingdom. Buses run from every other Disney resort, Animal Kingdom, Blizzard Beach and Disney's Hollywood Studios. There is no direct service from Downtown Disney or Typhoon Lagoon.

my lucky day! French fries!" ❾ Fiber-optic lights are embedded in the sidewalks in front of the Innoventions buildings. Pinpoints of shimmering, flickering stars hide in dozens of small squares. ❿ Larger, colorful changing patterns appear in three 6-foot squares in front of Innoventions West. The lights are on all day, but only noticeable at night. ⓫ Thirty-eight discoveries and inventions are honored in the rarely noticed Epcot Inventor's Circle, five concentric rings embedded into the walkway that leads from Innoventions Plaza to The Land pavilion. Inner-ring discoveries lead to outer-ring ones (i.e., the inner Alphabet leads to the outer World Wide Web). ⓬ The Tower of Terror at Disney's Hollywood Studios appears to be a part of the Moroccan skyline when seen from the promenade area to the right of the Mexico pavilion. The structures share a Spanish influence.

FUN FACTS ›› Epcot has 3.5 acres of flowers and plants, 70 acres of lawn, 12,500 specimen trees and 100,000 shrubs. ›› There are nearly 300 optical, motion and sound effects at Epcot, more than five times the number in the Magic Kingdom. ›› The construction of Epcot was the largest private construction job in U.S. history. The $1 billion project involved 7,500 people (3,000 designers and 4,500 construction workers), and the movement of 54 million cubic feet of dirt.

You enter Spaceship Earth from underneath the ball

Spaceship Earth

✓ For years ridiculed by some as one of Disney's more boring experiences, Future World's original showcase attraction is once again one of its most entertaining. Yes, the ride is still a slow-moving, Smithsonian-quality time-trip through the history of communications, but a 2008 refurbishment has made it much more fun.

New scenes depict a 1960s computer room where two programmers maintain a gigantic reel-to-reel mainframe and a 1977 California garage where an Audio Animatronic hybrid of Apple founders Steve Jobs and Steve Wozniak creates the PC.* There's also a "tech tunnel" in which you become part of a digital data stream.

But that's not all. The ride's 19 other dioramas, which depict man from the days of cave dwellers through the 1960s, benefit from updated decorations, lighting and effects, and include new costumes, hair and movements for their 56 robotic characters. A new narration by Dame Judi Dench emphasizes the roots of technology, and a new musical score features a 62-piece orchestra and 24-voice choir.

* Though the figure combines the clothing style and build of Wozniak with Job's period hair and sideburns, Disney says it officially depicts no one in particular.

As the ride nears its finish, a new touch-screen in your ride vehicle lights up with a series of questions, asking how you'd like to live or work in the future. Then you're treated to a cartoon view of yourself a few decades from now, complete with your face superimposed onto an animated character.

When you get off the ride you head into Project Tomorrow: Inventing the World of Tomorrow, a new post-show area that features four interactive video exhibits, all of which subtly showcase the attraction's new sponsor, Siemens. You learn about automotive accident-avoidance systems on a driving simulator, urban energy management by playing a group shuffleboard game, remote surgery technologies on a digital human body and home medical diagnostic systems through a series of memory, hand-eye coordination and reflex exercises.

A giant globe in the center of the room pinpoints the hometowns of all of that day's Spaceship Earth passengers, while huge video screens include — yikes! — your face, as it appeared in your futuristic video. You can e-mail the image free of charge.

On one of our recent visits, the exit platform was filled with smiling faces. A preschooler refused to get off, demanding to go again. Jumping out of his ride vehicle, a school-age boy shouted "That was awe-

▶ Hop on after 5 p.m. when the line is short. After dark there's often no line at all.

some, dad! Let's go again!" Entering the post-show, a group of teenaged girls giggled as one glanced up at the ceiling and yelled "There I am!"

If only school was this much fun.

Ride: 14 min. Allow 45–60 addl. min. for Project Tomorrow. Capacity: 308. Avg. wait: 45 min. peak morning; 20 min. mid-afternoon. Must be ambulatory. The ride stops intermittently to load mobility impaired guests. Vehicles offer a choice of narration languages: English, French, German, Japanese, Portuguese and Spanish. Fear factor: Low. Debuted: 1982, revised 1994, 2008.

FUN FINDS ❶ The radio station's call letters "WDI" are a reference to Walt Disney Imagineering. ❷ A desk on the right of the 1960s computer room includes a placard with the word "Think," the slogan of IBM founder Thomas J. Watson Sr. It later spawned the Apple slogan, "Think Different." ❸ Nearby lies a manual for the System 360 Job Control Language, used on 1964 IBM mainframes. ❹ On the right is an IBM Selectric typewriter, an icon of nearly every 1970s office. ❺ The snapshot on the garage wall in front of the Jobs/Wozniak character resembles a classic Microsoft photo.

FUN FACTS ❯❯ Serious research went into the show. Science-fiction author Ray Bradbury helped design the attraction, along with consultants from the Smithsonian Institution, the University of Southern California and the University of Chicago. The caveman is speaking a Cro-Magnon language. The cave drawings are based on images found in the Salon-Niaux cave in Ariège, France. The Egyptian hieroglyphics reproduce actual Middle Eastern drawings. The pharaoh's words come from a real letter. ❯❯ The refocused script has changed the meaning of a few scenes. The former Greek thespians are now "teaching an intriguing new subject called mathematics." The burning of Rome is now a fire at "the great Library of Alexandria in Egypt." And though they were once simply "debating ideas," Disney's medieval religious scholars are now "watching over copies of some of these [Egyptian] books to save our dreams of the future." ❯❯ Touchscreen "Work" futures predict "a great big, beautiful tomorrow" — the title of the theme song to the Magic Kingdom's Carousel of Progress. ❯❯ After the futuristic questions, Disney originally planned a pop quiz. "While we're creating your future," Dench was to say, "let's see how much you remember about the past." The segment was cut for technical reasons. ❯❯ Spaceship Earth is Disney World's only park icon with a ride inside.

Building the ball

A 180-foot-high geodesic sphere, Spaceship Earth took 26 months to build, from August 1980 to September 1982. It was created without scaffolding or temporary supports.

First, a foundation team pounded over 100 steel pilings into the ground, to depths of 150 feet. Three pairs of angled legs were placed on top, themselves topped with a six-sided platform about 45 feet off the ground. Secured on that platform, adjustable cranes built a circular frame around themselves, using hundreds of metal-strut triangles. After an outside crane hoisted the preconstructed, 50-foot-wide dome, workers built the bottom, a separate piece that is not load-bearing. Next, rubber-coated panels were secured onto the triangles, creating a giant waterproof black ball. A separate, decorative outer sphere was then added, set off two feet from the core by 4-inch aluminum pipes. The outer sphere is made up of 11,324 triangles of Alucobond*, a rustproof material made of polyethylene plastic bonded to two layers of anodized aluminum.

Spaceship Earth does not drip water: a 1-inch gap between each panel allows the triangles to expand and contract in the Florida heat and lets rainwater flow into two interior gutters that drain through the building's support legs into canals that run alongside the park.

The building weighs 16 million pounds. That's 158 million golf balls.

Disney got the idea for the structure from the entrance icons of the New York World's Fairs of 1939 and 1964, both held in Flushing Meadows, New York. The 1939 event featured the Perisphere, a 180-foot-tall sphere which held a slow-moving, educational ride (a six-minute film portrayed Democracity, a "perfectly integrated garden city" from the year 2068). The focal point of the 1964 fair was the Unisphere, a 140-foot open-grid Earth that symbolized global interdependence. It's still standing. Spaceship Earth can also trace its parentage to the 1940s geodesic domes designed by visionary engineer R. Buckminster Fuller. Billed as homes of tomorrow, his futuristic half-circles were composed of self-bracing triangles. They had no internal supports, got stronger as they got bigger and could be built in one day. The "Bucky balls" caught on as weather stations and airport radar shelters, but never got beyond a following as private homes (one reason: they leaked water). Fuller also coined the name "Spaceship Earth." His 1963 treatise, "An Operating Manual for Spaceship Earth," argued that all the world's peoples must work together as a crew to guide our planet's future.

*A brand name of Alcan Composites, the word is a contraction of "aluminum composite bond." First used in 1978, the material today covers more than 50,000 buildings, including many Honda dealerships.

Innoventions

Most of the exhibits are being changed or updated this year in these two large buildings, which house high-tech, interactive presentations from outside sponsors.

INNOVENTIONS EAST Waste Management's new **Don't Waste It** game gives you your own mini "garbage truck" cart filled with your own virtual trash, which you take to a sorting station, incinerator and landfill as you turn waste into electricity. Kids love to push the truck, which has working headlights and beeps when it backs up. The redone **House of Innoventions** is a guided tour of cutting-edge new household products such as a lift oven with a base that descends for loading, a dining table made of corrugated cardboard and a miniature robot that talks. The Federal Alliance for Safe Homes' **Storm Struck** combines a theatrical show with displays on such subjects as how two differently built Punta Gorda, Fla., homes fared during 2004's Hurricane Charley. Back for a return engagement, Cornell University's **It's a Nano World** is a child-focused look at the world too small to see. It debuted at Epcot in 2004.

A holdover exhibit is Underwriters Laboratories' six-station **Test the Limits Lab,** where you can swing a hammer at a TV, smash a 55-gallon drum onto a helmet and cause other havoc. **Environmentality Corner** is a small display that lets you make paper.

INNOVENTIONS WEST The Velcro Companies' new Slapstick Theater houses **What's Your Problem,** a wacky game show in which live hosts Liza Loopy and Hank Hook select audience members to help solve Seemingly Insurmountable Problems. A reconfigured **IBM Thinkplace** debuts in late 2008 (it had been featuring voice recognition software); also coming soon is **When Pigs Fly,** a T. Rowe Price look at financial planning.

Highlighting the West hall's returning exhibits is Liberty Mutual's **Where's the Fire,** where groups use handheld "safety lights" to find hazards on interactive walls that represent rooms of a home. A companion tour, **Play It Safe,** teaches fire safety to kids, while a real fire truck makes a nice photo prop. **Segway Central** offers test drives on the Segway Human Transporter, a single-axle gyroscopic electric scooter *(1 p.m.–7 p.m., riders must be at least 16 years old. Those under 18 require legal consent).* Also still here: a free-of-charge **PlayStation arcade.**

Each building also has a nice Kidcot area. So what's going away? Say goodbye to The American Farm Bureau's Great American Farm, Kuka's Rockin' Robots and The Society of the Plastic Industries's Fantastic Plastic Works. Also gone: Mr. Tom Morrow. *Presentations avg. 20 min. Allow 2–3 hrs. if you stop at each exhibit. Crowded when the weather is cold or rainy. Guests may stay in wheelchairs, ECVs. Assistive listening. Debuted 1994; revised often.*

Epcot Character Spot

This large air-conditioned room offers a sweat-free way to meet Mickey Mouse, Minnie Mouse, Pluto, Goofy and Chip 'n' Dale. The characters pose in professionally lit stage sets, so every shot is picture-perfect. The characters sign autographs, too. The only downside: there's just one line, and the wait can be at least an hour. To get in

and out quickly, stop by first thing in the morning or after 3 p.m.

Even if you're not interested in meeting the characters, it's worth a stop at the corridor windows to watch the characters interact with guests. Goofy is hilarious.

9 a.m.–5:30 p.m., often later during Extra Magic Hours. Strollers, food, drinks OK.

Free soft drink samples

Located along the right side of the Innoventions Plaza fountain, **Club Cool** offers free samples of eight of the Coca-Cola Company's soft drinks from around the world. Self-service machines dispense beverages from China, Costa Rica, Germany, Israel, Italy, Japan, Mexico and Mozambique. China's watermelon-flavored Smart and Mexico's fruity Lift are pretty good; Italy's bitter Beverly is awful. The store sells frozen sodas and Coca-Cola merchandise. Loud pop music fills the air. *9 a.m. – 7 p.m.*

Ellen's Energy Adventure

This 45-minute multimedia presentation about the history and future of energy combines three theatrical films with a tram ride past Audio Animatronic dinosaurs.

Appearing on a series of large video screens, Ellen DeGeneres displays the same loopy wit she used as Dory in 2003's "Finding Nemo." You meet her in her apartment when Bill Nye* stops by to ask for some aluminum foil, a clothes pin and a candle (she replies "Another hot date, huh?"). Once Nye leaves, she falls asleep while watching her snooty old college roommate Judy Peterson (Jamie Lee Curtis) compete on the game show "Jeopardy!"

Dreaming she's a contestant on the show, Ellen discovers that all the categories deal with one thing she knows nothing about: energy. So she "freezes" her dream and asks Nye for help. He takes Ellen, and you, back in time for a crash course in Energy 101.

Moving into a large theater, you watch as three huge screens dramatically display the Big Bang and the creation of the Earth: billions of years compressed into one stunning minute. As the seating area breaks apart, you travel to the Mesozoic Era — a swamp filled with Audio Animatronic dinosaurs. Ellen is afraid ("Why don't we just skip to the air-conditioning and Jacuzzi period?"), but Nye wants her to get a close-up look at all the flora and fauna that will later turn into fossil fuels. Arriving in yet a third theater, you're brought back to the present through a series of radio broadcasts, then watch as Ellen learns about man's energy use. Finally you return to the first theater, where Ellen unfreezes her dream and becomes the "Jeopardy" champion.

* A one-time mechanical engineer, Nye hosted "Bill Nye the Science Guy," a 1992-1998 PBS preteen program which Disney later sold as a video series.

Jumping for joy in a Future World fountain

Produced back when the average price of a gallon of gasoline was $1.30, the show seems unaware of the problems of fossil fuels. There's no mention of the Middle East, no talk of global warming or even fuel efficiency. The attraction was created in cooperation with Exxon-Mobil, its sponsor until 2004.

Universe of Energy pavilion. 45 min. (new shows begin every 17 min.). Capacity: 582. Avg. wait: 10 min. ECV guests must transfer. Assistive listening; handheld captioning available. Fear factor: Intense for preschoolers; the Big Bang is loud. Debuted: 1996.

FUN FINDS ❶ After Trebek says to Ellen, "Your first correct response!" her lips don't move when she yells "Freeze!" ❷ Nye's lips stay zipped when, in front of a solar mirror, he says "all right."

➡ Sit in the theater's back far right. You'll be with the dinos more and go under a few.

Epcot's best ice cream

The new **Fountainview Ice Cream Shop** (*$3–$5*) is the best place to get an ice cream cone in all of Walt Disney World. It's convenient, rarely crowded, serves hand-dipped Edy's ice cream, and you get to eat inside in air-conditioned comfort. Choose from a dozen flavors including the caramel-rich Dulce de Leche, as well as treats such as floats, sundaes, waffle cones and a made-to-order ice cream sandwich. There are soft drinks and coffee, too. *108 seats, including 68 outside. Noon–8:30 p.m.*

Mission: Space

✓ So intense it includes motion-sickness bags, this flight simulator provides realistic sensations of space travel. Developed with NASA, it's Disney's most advanced attraction ever.

Why do people get sick? Because you spin. You can't tell it when you're in your vehicle, but the ride is a centrifuge, a circular machine with a series of rapidly rotating containers on its spokes. As it spins, it applies centrifugal force to its contents (that's you) that mimic the G-forces of a rocket launch and then the weightlessness of space. The spinning creates forces up to 2 Gs, or twice that of the Earth's gravity. That may not sound like much — it's actually less than many roller coasters — but this force is sustained; you feel it continually throughout the ride. It's one of the ways NASA trained astronauts for decades. "Mission Space is my favorite ride at Disney," says Lance Bass, the former member of the pop group N'Sync who trained to be a Russian cosmonaut. "The experience here is 100 percent on target."

BYE BYE BYE! The story begins as soon as you enter the building. You're in the year 2036 at the International Space Training Center, where astronaut hopefuls come to see if they have the right stuff. You're there to train for an upcoming mission to Mars. (Robots, you soon learn, have already been established on the Red Planet. You are training to be one of the first humans.)

The first room is the Space Simulation Lab. Alongside you is a 35-foot model of a Gravity Wheel, a slowly rotating prop from the 2000 film "Mission to Mars" that's complete with exercise rooms, offices, work areas and sleeping cubicles. Nearby is a Lunar Roving Vehicle display unit, a real one essentially identical to those used on the moon, on loan from the National Air and Space Museum.

After the voice of Mission Control ("CSI" actor Gary Sinise, also known for his roles in 1995's "Apollo 13" and 2000's "Mission to Mars") introduces you to your vehicle, you climb in your trainer and buckle in.

Once a cast member seals the door, an elaborate control panel pivots into place. As you angle up into launch position, you look out into a beautiful blue (video) sky, complete with birds passing overhead. Then the engines power up and the countdown begins.

"3... 2... 1... Zero!" The earth begins to rumble, white clouds of exhaust start to billow and then, in a moment that seems absolutely real, you launch straight up. As the

▶ Disney also offers a mild version of the ride, in which the centrifuge does not spin.

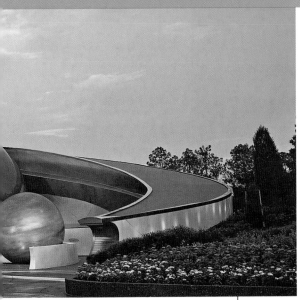

The steely facade has no straight lines. Spheres symbolize Earth, Jupiter, Mars and the moon.

ing headache. To avoid getting sick, continually stare straight at your monitor and do not close your eyes. Don't eat or drink alcohol before you go. Afterward, get lots of fresh air, take it easy and have some saltine crackers or a soda.

6 min. Capacity: 160. Avg. wait: 10 min. early morning, 30 min. peak afternoon. Fastpass available. ECV and wheelchair guests must transfer. Activated video captioning. Height restriction: 44 in. Fear factor: Intense, can cause disorientation, headaches, nausea. Take the warnings seriously: don't ride if you have any serious health issues or a head cold. Chicken exit. Best ages: 8 and up. Debuted: 2003.

G-forces push your body back into the seat, it truly feels like you're on your way to Mars.

Soon Mission Control breaks in with instructions. "Initiate first stage separation, now!" Sinise tells the mission commander. The others get similar orders.

You head past the space station, are slingshot around the moon, feel weightless for a moment, then go into hypersleep. But your three-month nap seems to take only a few seconds, as alarms wake you up. Not only are you in a meteor storm, but your autopilot has broken and Mars is coming up fast.

Your team performs with flying colors. Attempting to follow the instructions of Mission Control, the four of you barely miss some canyon walls, crash through some barriers and nearly go over a cliff, before landing safely.

In reality, two hidden computers on the centrifuge control everything in your capsule — regardless of what you do.

Many adults have no problem with the ride, and children often fare better than their parents. Still, the side effects have landed some riders in the hospital. A few have died, though in each of those cases the rider had existing health problems and ignored the warning signs. The most common troubles are dizziness and a lingering

MISSIONS FOR ALL With entrances from both the exit area and the gift shop, the Advanced Training Lab post-show area is a series of calm, interactive experiences designed for every age group, even toddlers. **Mission Space Race** is a group video game where two teams (each with up to 25 guests) race spaceships from Mars back to Earth. **Space Base** is a preschooler climbing area with a crawl-through rocket, some zany mirrors and a lookout tower. The **Expedition: Mars** video game lets you test your joystick skills as you navigate through dust devils, polar ice and quicksand to rescue fellow astronauts. Everyone will get a kick out of **Postcards from Space,** a video booth which puts your animated face into an alien abduction, saucer invasion or other goofy space scenes and e-mails the results anywhere you choose.

FUN FACTS ❯❯ The logo for Horizons, the attraction previously at this site, appears on the hub of the Gravity Wheel. ❯❯ The Mission Space music was composed by Trevor Rabin, who, as a member of the rock band Yes in 1983, wrote the song "Owner of a Lonely Heart." ❯❯ Besides training astronauts, centrifuges are used to separate fluids of different densities, such as cream from milk.

▶ To avoid getting sick, stare straight at your monitor and do not close your eyes.

© DISNEY

depending on how you and your vehicle hold up," Bill adds, "we'll even throw in a few surprise tests in there."

"Surprise tests?" Sherry asks. "Yeah. Pick one."

With a grin, Sherry chooses the Barrier Test, which slams its car into a wall. Before you can protest, you board your vehicle and off you go.

Heading to the (indoor) testing grounds, you rumble over some blocks, skid through some cones and twist up a hill.

Then things go wrong. Did Sherry forget to turn off those Environmental Test robots? Oh no! You get sprayed with acid! Miss that sign that said to turn on your headlights? Oh no! Here comes a truck! And remember that surprise test? Oh no! You're heading right into the...

At the last second, a hidden door in the building's outer wall slides open and outside you fly for the Handling Run, an elevated series of banked corners that culminate in a burst around the building at 65 mph.

In the post show, a house of mirrors recreates GM's truck plant in Shreveport, La. (can you spot the real walls?), a Fuel for Thought display promotes its alternative-fuel technologies (watch the corn crop on the wall wave as you pass), then a showroom holds current vehicles, unlocked to inspect without any sales pressure.

5 min. Capacity: 192. Avg. wait: 20 min. early morning, 90 min. peak afternoon. Fastpass available usually until 1 p.m. Must be ambulatory. Assistive listening; activated video captioning. Preshow: 4-min. video. Height restriction: 40 in. Fear factor: Intense for those scared by high speeds or sharp turns. Chicken exit. Debuted: 1999.

FUN FINDS ❶ The left anticorrosion robot is labeled "CRUS-T." ❷ The right one is marked "RUS-T."

Test Track

✓ Think of it as Snow White's Scary Adventures with a $60 million budget. Resembling an automobile proving ground, Test Track is an elaborate version of a classic dark ride. Riding in a small vehicle, you speed around corners, through obstacles and over hills. With 34 sharp turns but no corkscrews, falls or loops, the mile-long course is perfect for those who like excitement but hate roller coasters.

A catchy mechanical soundtrack fills the waiting area. Its 22 testing demonstrations make even a 30-minute wait pass quickly. Next, a Briefing Room introduces you to track engineers Bill and Sherry, who appear on a video link (the monitor displays the current time and date, making it seem live). As he determines your test schedule, she programs it into a computer and you watch a short clip of what to expect. "And

▶ The adjacent gift shop offers a unique souvenir: a remote-control Test Track car.

park puzzler

How much do you really know about Epcot?

1) The acronym "EPCOT" stands for...
a. Experimental Polyester Costumes of Torture.
b. Experimental Prototype Community of Tomorrow.
c. Every Person Comes Out Tired.

2) According to the Maelstrom narrator, where is the spirit of Norway?
a. In its kjøttkaker.
b. In its people.
c. In its skolebrød.

3) What goes wrong on your Mission Space flight?
a. Zurg steals your batteries.
b. You hit a meteor storm.
c. You're forced to learn the history of communication.

4) The top speed of your Test Track vehicle is about...
a. 55 mph.
b. 65 mph.
c. 75 mph.

5) The man at right is...
a. Failing to greet guests in "the Disney Way."
b. A drummer in the Epcot street-band Jammitors.
c. Picking up park trash.

6) In the American Adventure attraction, Mark Twain says no dynamic people have ever survived...
a. "Without justice and equality guaranteed forever."
b. "Drought, disease, avalanches and floods."
c. "Success, plenty, comfort and ever-increasing leisure."

7) On Spaceship Earth, one scene depicts...
a. William Bullock's steam-powered printing press.
b. Alexander Graham Bell's early telegraph.
c. Johann Gutenberg's first television.

Answers, page 331

A bottlenose dolphin swims past an aquarium guest

The Seas with Nemo & Friends

✓ There's a lot to like in this revamped pavilion, which is themed to the 2003 Disney/Pixar film "Finding Nemo." Quality attractions combine with live marine-life aquariums, exhibits and demonstrations.

First, there's a ride. Once you enter the attraction, a long, winding walkway takes you under the sea and eventually to a "clam-mobile," a self-propelled vehicle similar to a Haunted Mansion "doom buggy." It takes you past a series of animated dioramas and synchronized, see-through video screens that re-create scenes from the movie. In the finale, the animated fish appear to swim with the real ones in the aquarium.

You exit on the first floor of the two-story pavilion, which includes some interesting sea life exhibits, a stunning theatrical show, and, at various times of the day, fascinating demonstrations.

DOWNSTAIRS "That was cool!" said the 60-year-old man to his wife, as the couple exited **Turtle Talk with Crush.** And he's right. The pavilion's headline attraction, this theatrical show amazes even the most worldly adult. Appearing on a high-resolution video screen that appears to be a window into the sea, the animated sea turtle star of "Finding Nemo" interacts with guests in real-time, spontaneous conversations. He addresses guests individually ("Elizabeth, your polka-dot shell is totally cool!"), asks specific questions ("Is that your female parental unit in the fourth row? She's a total babe!"), and reacts to their responses. His facial expressions are priceless. As the chat continues, the reptile works in some turtle trivia and welcomes a visit by Dory, who can speak whale perhaps a little too well. Crush directs most of his comments to kids who sit down front, but sometimes seeks out guests along the theater's center aisle. The show's queue area holds jellyfish, stingrays, and fish from the Great Barrier Reef. *12 min. Capacity: 130. Avg. wait: 10 min. early morning, 20 min. peak afternoon. Guests may remain in wheelchairs, ECVs. Reflective captioning, assistive listening. Debuted: 2004, moved to a new theater in 2007.*

Also downstairs, a **Nemo and Friends** room displays live versions of many of the movie's stars. Walk-around tubes hold clownfish (Nemo), regal blue tangs (Dory) and Moorish idols (Gill), as well as sea horses, eels, camouflaged frogfish and venomous lionfish and scorpionfish. In a re-creation of the film's sunken submarine, **Bruce's Shark World** has kid-friendly interactive displays and photo props.

▶ To have Crush talk with your child, have her sit down front and wear a funny hat.

UPSTAIRS On the second floor, a huge **salt-water aquarium** simulates a Caribbean coral reef. It's filled with blacknose, brown and sand tiger sharks; some angelfish, cobia, snapper and tarpon; schools of lookdown; a Goliath grouper; sea turtles; and a few rays. An observation tunnel extends into it. There are three daily **fish feedings,** at 10 a.m., 1 p.m. and 3:30 p.m. A diver unloads his pouch in front of you while a narrator adds educational trivia. A side area holds a bachelor herd of **dolphins** — Rainer (born in 1986), Calvin and Kyber (1997) and Malabar (2001). Stop by at 10:45 a.m., 2:15 p.m. or 4:15 p.m. to see a **dolphin training session,** which can include identity-matching, rhythm-identification or echolocation lessons. Huge bars keep the dolphins in their area; otherwise they'd hassle the fish.

A **manatee aquarium** holds two Florida sea cows. You can watch them from above the surface or through an underwater window on the first floor. Five-minute talks are given at 15 and 45 minutes after each hour.

Finally, a **mariculture room** displays how commercial farming can prevent overfishing of clownfish, queen conchs, bamboo sharks and giant clams. There's also an exhibit on coral reef propagation.

The pavilion's **Kidcot table** is upstairs, too, next to the main aquarium.

FUN FINDS ❶ The Audio Animatronic gulls on the rocks outside the pavilion squawk "Mine! Mine! Mine!" ❷ "Hey wait! Take me with you!" says sea star Peach as your clam mobile leaves the aquarium, as the animated fish continue to sing "Big Blue World." "It's a nice song but they just never stop! Never, never, ever, ever, ever!" ❸ Rub Bruce's sandpapery skin in Bruce's Shark World and he'll say "Ooooooo! That's good!"

FUN FACTS ❯❯ The creatures are fed 400 pounds of food a day. Since the parrotfish naturally eat coral, Disney plants synthetic coral (dental plaster) into the artificial reef. ❯❯ Why don't the sharks eat the other fish? Because Disney feeds them tilapia every day, which it raises in the adjacent Land pavilion. ❯❯ The aquarium has 3,500 inhabitants, representing 65 species. ❯❯ The observation area has 61 acrylic windows that are 4 to 8 inches thick. Each of the central panels are 8-by-24 feet and weighs 9,000 pounds. ❯❯ Like all manatees in U.S. waters, these are controlled by the Fish & Wildlife Service. Both are candidates for release.

The big blue world

Here's a brief primer on the fish and other sea creatures found in the Seas with Nemo & Friends aquarium and displays:

A saltwater mollusk related to a squid, the soft **cuttlefish** has an internal shell (the "cuttlebone"), eight short arms and two long tentacles. The tentacles can be pulled into pockets behind the eyes.

One of the world's smartest animals, the **bottlenose dolphin** has the largest brain, in proportion to its body size, of any mammal besides man. It takes in air through a blowhole on top of its head, which is, in essence, a nose with only one nostril. The mammal "holds its nose" underwater by shutting a valve near the blowhole's opening.

Related to sea bass, **grouper** have large heads and broad, down-slanted mouths. The black grouper can lighten or darken its color to match its environment. The goliath grouper can be up to 5 feet long and reach 700 pounds.

A **jellyfish** is like a floating stomach. Coated with a clear, thick flesh, it uses the same orifice for both food intake and waste expulsion. The animal has no heart, blood or bones, and nerves but no brain.

Perhaps drinking a few too many bottles of rum, sailors thought they saw a beautiful, naked woman when they spotted a **manatee,** a mammal with the shape of a cow and the skin of an elephant, its closest relative. Its rear legs have evolved into a beaver-like tail; its front legs have become flippers. Mermaids were thought to be real until the late 1800s.

Known as the Flower of the Sea, the carnivorous **sea anemone** looks like a plant. It feeds by stinging passing small fish with its tentacles then pushing the prey up into its mouth. After hatching from an egg inside its mother's body, a newborn will swim out of its mom's mouth, attach itself to a rock or piece of coral, and stay there forever.

Is there anything stranger than a **sea horse?** This small pipefish has the head of a horse, the tail of a monkey and the pouch of a kangaroo. Its body has prickly, spiny plates instead of scales. To top it off, the male gives birth! Simply put, she has the eggs, but he has the uterus.

Related to a shark, the nonaggressive **stingray** appears to fly through the water. It moves by flapping its wing-like side fins. The fish feeds by sucking up small fish and other sea life into its mouth, which is on the underside of its body.

The huge silver **tarpon** can breathe air. It can get oxygen by rising to the surface, rolling on its side, filling its swim bladder with air, then absorbing it through its flesh.

Green sea turtles can live approximately 150 years. Their ancestors evolved on land.

Don't flush your pet **clownfish** down the toilet. Despite Gill's belief in "Finding Nemo" that "all drains lead to the ocean," they don't. No fish can survive a trip through a sewage plant.

Soarin' flies you high, virtually, over the many sights of California

Soarin'

✓ This one may take you by surprise: it really does give you the feeling of flight. Far more than just a 5-minute film, the attraction uses an innovative theater to immerse you in its experience. Exhilarating but not scary, the ride is a smooth, fun fantasy everyone will love.

After you board a multi-seat "hang glider," Soarin' lifts you up to 40 feet into an 80-foot projection dome. From all sides your vision is filled with the beauty of California. You get the impractical delight of gliding over the Golden Gate Bridge and El Capitan, floating over an aircraft carrier in San Diego Harbor, skimming along the foamy waves of Malibu and zipping through the night lights of downtown Los Angeles. You also get a bird's-eye view of Redwood National Park and the Anza-Borrego Desert State Park, near Mexico. Your glider tilts as you sweep, your legs dangling free underneath.

The seating device is equipped with many effects that make your flight seem real. Hidden fans put wind in your hair, odorizers let you smell pines and oranges, surround-sound speakers re-create a crashing surf and thunderous waterfall.

The ride's entranceway, waiting area and theater resemble an airport. Cast members dress as airline employees, with shoulder boards and brass buttons. The gift stand looks like a ticket counter; the ride's walk-way is a concourse; its boarding areas gates. The theater has runway lights; the gliders navigation lights.

If you wait in the Standby line, you can kill time by playing a series of group video games. Alongside the queue are five 11-by-20-foot screens that let you to tackle challenges such as flying a bird through a narrow canyon and aiming virtual paint balls at a digital canvas. The games get tougher the further you move down the walkway.

The Land pavilion. 5 min. Capacity: 174. Avg. wait: 20 min. early morning; 180 min. peak afternoon. Fastpass available until about 1 p.m. ECV and wheelchair users must transfer. Handheld captioning. Height restriction: 40 in. Fear factor: Those with a fear of heights could be bothered by both the actual (40 feet) and virtual (800 feet) distances off the ground. Debuted: 2005 (Disneyland 2001).

FUN FACTS ⟩⟩ Soarin' cast members may call your flight "number 5-5-0-5," a reference to the ride's opening date of May 5, 2005. ⟩⟩ The boarding video features Patrick Warburton, who played Puddy on "Seinfeld" and was the voice of Kronk in Disney's 2000 film, "The Emperor's New Groove." ⟩⟩ The river is Redwood Creek. ⟩⟩ The vineyards are in Napa Valley. ⟩⟩ The mountains are the Sierras, near Lake Tahoe. ⟩⟩ The orange groves are outside of Camarillo. The golf course is the PGA West golf complex in La Quinta. ⟩⟩ The jets are the U.S. Air Force Thunderbirds. ⟩⟩ The carrier is the USS Stennis. ⟩⟩ The film is projected at 48 frames per second, twice the speed of a normal movie. ⟩⟩ The hang glider you see over Yosemite is computer generated. So is that errant golf ball. ⟩⟩ Why California? Because this is the same film used at Disneyland's Soarin' Over California attraction. Notice the little boy in the preshow wears a Disneyland, not Disney World, T-shirt.

▶ The best Soarin' seats are top-row center. Ask the gate attendant for Row 1, Gate B.

Living with the Land

This indoor boat ride takes a subject usually thought of as dull as dirt — agricultural science — and presents it as an entertaining attraction. A trip through four working greenhouses, the tour is filled with weird plants most Americans never see, as well as some unusual growing techniques. Your slow-moving boat meanders within a few feet of the plants; you can often smell the leaves and fruit.

The crops include four types of banana palms, including the Indonesian "monkey finger" which bears a slender fruit. Papayas (some the size of bowling balls) cover their trees, while 2-foot jackfruit hang from theirs. Vanilla orchids climb trellises. Other sights include 3-foot-long winter melons and pummelos, the world's largest citrus fruit. Some plants are here only for their looks, such as the "nine pound" (ponderosa) lemons in the Temperate Greenhouse that resemble lumpy grapefruit and the nearby 500-pound Atlantic giant pumpkins. The Creative Greenhouse always has at least one three-sphered (i.e., Mickey-shaped) cucumber, pumpkin or watermelon, each grown in a specially shaped plastic mold.

Many plants hang from strings or trellises, roots in the air. Some are on overhead conveyor belts, touring their greenhouse like suits in a dry cleaner.

An aquaculture hut includes elevated, clear-sided tanks of catfish, sturgeon, shrimp, eels, even young alligators.

The ride begins with a trip through three artificial biomes — a rainforest, a desert and a farm. Though elaborate (the dank forest has a real waterfall that sprays your boat) these areas have little to do with the rest of the ride. The dioramas originally played a key role. Until 1993 they illustrated "harsh natural environments" where food can't be grown — look closely and you can see the prairie farmland still catch fire and stir up a cloud of locusts. The original point of the greenhouses? To show innovations for improving harvests in these "unproductive realms."

The Land. 14 min. Capacity: 20 people per boat. Avg. wait: None early morning; 60 min. peak afternoon. Fastpass available. ECV users must transfer to a wheelchair. Handheld captioning. Debuted: 1982 (as Listen to the Land); revised 1993.

FUN FACTS ⟩⟩ Nearly all of the greenhouse produce is served in Epcot restaurants. Most of the vegetables go to The Land's Garden Grill and Sunshine Seasons. The winter melons are used in a soup at China's Nine Dragons. Even some of the flowers make it to meals: the marigolds garnish salads and desserts at Chefs de France. The greenhouses grow 20,000 pounds of produce a year, about 1 percent of the restaurants' needs. Some feed animals at Disney's Animal Kingdom. ⟩⟩ The Aquacell supplies the restaurants with 6,500 pounds of seafood a year. ⟩⟩ The alligators are sold to nearby farms which harvest their meat. ⟩⟩ The greenhouses include the world's most productive tomato plant, a "tree" that produced 20,288 cherry tomatoes (815 pounds) in 2005. Planted in 2004, it was grown from seeds of a similar plant in Beijing, China. ⟩⟩ The greenhouses were developed with help from the Environmental Research Laboratory at the University of Arizona. ⟩⟩ The crops are not grown organically. Disney uses light chemicals and fertilizer. ⟩⟩ The boat moves at 1.3 mph. ⟩⟩ The dioramas have 40 Audio Animatronic animals, including baboons, prairie dogs and a family of buffalo.

Living with the Land's quonset hut uses red light to keep its animals calm and reduce algae growth

Circle of Life: An Environmental Fable

This 13-minute movie uses the stars of 1994's "The Lion King" to teach environmental protection. When Timon and Pumbaa start to clear their savannah to build a tourist resort, Simba tells the story of a creature (man) who at first lived in harmony with nature, but now often forgets that everything is connected in the great circle of life. Live-action sequences show smokestacks, clogged highways, trash dumps and an oil-soaked cormorant, but also wind turbines, electric cars and recycling efforts.

The Land. 13 min. Capacity: 482. Avg. wait: 7 min. early morning; 15 min. peak afternoon. Guests may remain in wheelchairs, ECVs. Handheld and reflective captioning, assistive listening. Debuted: 1995.

Junior Chef

It's hard to tell who has the most fun at this cookie-making lesson: the children on stage or the parents watching them. Twenty kids join two personable cast members in a mock kitchen set for a hands-on experience that teaches them how to make Nestle Toll House chocolate-chip cookies.

But what's supposed to be an easy, four-step process never goes according to plan.

Though all they need to do is mix the wet ingredients, stir in the dry ingredients and spoon the results onto a tray, many of the Junior Chefs dump, shall we say, incredibly generous amounts of salt, sugar and baking soda into their bowls, and seem more interested in eating the raw dough than the finished result. Thanks to a "magic oven," however, each of their recipes always turns out perfect.

Each participant gets two free cookies and a complimentary chef's hat to wear and take home.

Location: The Land pavilion, lower level to the left of the Sunshine Seasons food court. 30-40 min. Typically held daily, every hour on the half hour from 12:30 to 4:30 p.m. Arrive 15 min. early to make sure your child gets a spot. Ages 4–12.

Behind the Seeds

✓ A complement to the Living with the Land boat ride, the extra-cost Behind the Seeds 1-hour walking tour is a fascinating botany lesson. Leaving the main building through a backstage door, your guide takes you into a pest-management room and biotechnology lab before giving you a close-up tour of the greenhouses and fish farm.

Your first stop is the Integrated Pest Management lab, where you see one way Disney controls pests: by using tiny parasitic wasps that hatch within the crop-killing bugs and then eat them (yucko!) from the inside out.

Next is the biotech lab, where scientists from the U.S. Dept. of Agriculture are breeding pear trees. A second program tests reproducing plants without seeds, an idea developed here with NASA to create dwarf wheat that could be grown in space.

Then you head to the greenhouses, where your tour includes some fun, hands-on activities.

Behind the Seeds is conducted a few times each day. The charge is $12 for adults; $9 for children. For reservations stop by the registration desk (the Soarin' "ticket counter") or call (407) WDW-TOUR.

Tour guide Rachel Naegele holds a fluted pumpkin

Journey into Imagination... with Figment

A tour through the Imagination Institute, this tongue-in-cheek indoor ride starts as Dr. Nigel Channing (Eric Idle, shown in the finale as the man in the moon, left) shows how human senses control the imagination. He's interrupted by Figment, a dragon who believes an imagination works best "when it's set free." Eventually you go to Figment's house, an upside-down world. There is one great effect: in a cage past the Sight Lab, a huge butterfly appears to disappear as you go by. Post-show activities include a chance to conduct music by waving your arms.

Imagination pavilion. 6 min. Avg. wait: 5 min. early morning, 20 min. peak after-noon. Guests may remain in wheelchairs, ECVs. Handheld captioning. Fear factor: A dark room has the loud clamor of an on-coming train; a blast of air smells like a skunk; the last room has a sudden flash. Debuted: 1983, revised 1998, 2002.

FUN FINDS The office doors of ❶ 1997's "Flubber" inventor Dr. Phillip Brainard and ❷ 1969's "The Computer Wore Tennis Shoes" principal Dean Higgins line the entrance hall. ❸ There's a page for 1965's "The Monkey's Uncle" chimp-teacher Merlin Jones ("Your monkey is on the loose"). ❹ A door looks into the distorted Dimension Hall. The opposite window (an unmarked pane just to the left of the "Magic Photo Studio") exposes the trick. ❺ On the ride itself, red tennis shoes sit outside the computer room, another reference to that 1969 film.

Honey, I Shrunk the Audience

"Everybody either hates the mice or hates the snake." That's what a cast member says about this theatrical attraction, which features Disney's scariest 3-D effects. The story seems innocent. You're in an auditorium to see Prof. Wayne Szalinski (Rick Moranis, reprising his role from 1989's "Honey, I Shrunk the Kids") accept the Inventor of the Year Award. But when he gets lost in the wings, everything goes wrong. First, the theater fills with scurrying rats (special effects under your seat), then a holographic house cat gets too much power and lunges at your face — first as a lynx, then a lion. The professor returns only to accidentally shrink the theater to the size of a bread box. Then a huge snake slithers in and bares its fangs. Finally, a curious canine looks in, sniffs, and sneezes.

Imagination pavilion. 15 min. Capacity: 570. Avg. wait: 7 min. early morning, 15 min. peak afternoon. Fastpass available. Guests may remain in wheelchairs, ECVs. Assistive listening; reflective captioning. Preshow: 5 min. Kodak slide show. Fear factor: Some children will be terrified. Debuted: 1994.

A giant dog greets the audience during the Honey I Shrunk the Audience finale. *Photo illustration.*

© DISNEY

▶ The "Honey" screen has the best focus if you sit in the center rear of the theater.

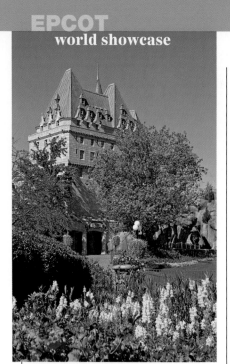

Disney's Hotel du Canada facade recalls Ottawa's 1912 Chateau Laurier as well as the country's 19th-century railroad hotels

Canada

A hillside garden, a tumbling waterfall, an immense French Gothic hotel… it's all part of the landscape at Disney's salute to our northern neighbor.

ATTRACTION Projected on nine screens that wrap around you in a stand-up theater, **O Canada** is a new 14-minute travelogue that introduces you to the people and places of Canada. An update of the film that

---

DEVELOPED IN THE 1950s by Disney video engineer (and original Mickey Mouse animator) Ub Iwerks, the movie's circular projection technique uses nine projectors to display synchronized video onto nine screens arranged above the heads of its audience. Dubbed CircleVision 360, it places its projectors into the gaps between its screens so that everything lines up perfectly. Filming is done by a nine-lens camera that is often hung from a helicopter. (Why nine? Because the concept only works with an odd number.) Originally a major category of Disney attraction, CircleVision 360 theaters now exist only at Epcot. Another one is housed in the China pavilion.

played here from 1982 to 2007, it dumps its predecessor's earnest devotion to the country's rugged outdoors for a joke-filled journey that gives equal time to Canada's cities. As explained by host and Ontario native Martin Short, the movie wants to correct the misconception that the country is simply a Great White North where, as intoned by opening narrator Don Pardo, "it snows 24 hours a day, every day of the year!" and its land is "dotted with igloos, homes for the vast majority of Canadians!"

The new film combines scenes of snowy mountains and towering redwoods with stops in Montreal, Quebec City, Toronto, Victoria and Vancouver. The old New Brunswick video is still present, but you no longer hear from that area's heavily accented locals. As for music, the lumberjack ballads have been replaced by orchestral tracks, and the film's theme song ("Canada, You're a Lifetime Journey") is now sung by 2006 "Canadian Idol" winner Eva Avila.

Unfortunately, the update has also eliminated the idea that you are a part of the action. Whereas the old movie made it appear that you yourself were riding a dogsled or racing a toboggan, the new one makes Short the participant. Now you watch him ham it up as a curler, hockey player and rodeo cowboy.

Little of the new footage forms a seamless wraparound video, the most special feature of these "CircleVision 360" presentations. Instead, the new segments usually simply encircle you with a few versions of the same image, a technique that eliminates the fun of gazing around the theater.

Still, the new movie's visuals are bright and crisp, the sound is fantastic, and Short's antics, while not hilarious, are at least amusing. Besides, there is one nice holdover: the Mounties that originally circled around you to start the show now kick off its conclusion.

14 min. Capacity: 600. Avg. wait: 10 min. Guests may remain in wheelchairs, ECVs. Assistive listening, reflective captioning. Debuted: 1982. Revised 2007.

ENTERTAINMENT Quirky and fun to watch, the kilt-wearing Celtic rock band **Off Kilter** combines electric guitars, a bagpipe and a sense of humor into a 20-minute show. At

▶ The best place to stand for "O Canada" is the middle center of the theater.

The **United Kingdom pavilion's Tudor Street** re-creates many historic facades of Olde England. The cornerside Sportsman's Shoppe mimics the white-stone Abbotsford on its left, the red-brick Henry VIII's 16th-century Hampton Court on its right.

many performances at least a few guests get up and twirl with Deadhead-like joy. The act performs on its own promenade stage.

FOOD AND DRINK Cool, comfy and dark, the stone-walled **Le Cellier Steakhouse** resembles a chateau wine cellar. Its delicious, non-threatening food makes it the toughest Epcot reservation.

SHOPPING Left of the totems, **Northwest Mercantile** stocks Roots apparel and other merchandise from Quebec and real maple syrup, candy and cream cookies from Ontario. The adjacent **Trading Post** has British Columbian dream catchers and cute moose plushies. Out front, the **Canada wood cart** offers personalized leather and pewter goods and plushies of characters from Disney's 2003 film "Brother Bear."

FOR CHILDREN "Brother Bear" characters Kenai and Koda appear on the promenade. Canada's Kidcot tables are under a covered patio at the exit to "O Canada."

ARCHITECTURE At the entrance courtyard to the pavilion, a log cabin, trading post and 30-foot totem poles represent Canada's frontier culture. Carved by a Tsimshian Indian in 1998, the left totem depicts the magical Raven releasing the sun, moon and stars from a carved cedar chest. Up the steps, a stone building reflects the British styles of Canada's east coast. On the right, the French Gothic Hotel du Canada recalls Ottawa's Chateau Laurier, a 19th-century

railroad hotel. In back it's the mountains, complete with a 30-foot waterfall and a mine entrance adorned with shoring and Klondike equipment.

United Kingdom

Even though it doesn't have an attraction, the United Kingdom pavilion has so much to see and do you can spend hours here. The area includes two gardens, lots of entertainment, a restaurant and pub, seven stores and some shady nooks and crannies.

ENTERTAINMENT The **World Showcase Players** butcher classic literature with improvisational street skits. Even the most cynical soul will smile when the audience volunteer playing King Arthur is forced to yell "Ba-boogie-boogie-boogie baby!" (yes, from the Silvers' 1976 disco hit, "Boogie Fever"). Held in the rear park, each 20-minute set from **The British Invasion** consists of spot-on Beatles hits. Evenings in the **Rose & Crown Pub** feature magician Jason Wethington, pianist Leon Gregory or bon vivant storyteller, pianist and Epcot institution Pam Brody.

FOOD AND DRINK The **Rose & Crown Dining Room** has indoor and covered outdoor

▶ U.K. cast members often chalk out a promenade hop-scotch game at 11 a.m.

"Free beer!" A World Showcase Player gathers a crowd for a street performance.

seating, with some tables facing the World Showcase lagoon. The **Rose & Crown Pub** offers beers (typically Bass, Boddingtons, Guinness, Ireland's Harp, even Australia's Strongbow Cider), mixed drinks, appetizers and sandwiches. Try the London broil. *(20 seats)*. The **Yorkshire County Fish Shop** counter-service window serves snack-size helpings of Harry Ramsden-brand fish and chips, as well as Bass ale *(30 seats)*.

SHOPPING **Apparel** includes Beatles T-shirts and Tartan scarves and sweaters. Tartan purses come from Lochcarron of Scotland. In **sporting goods** you'll find rugby and soccer balls. **China** options can include fine bone choices from Dunoon, Royal Albert and Royal Patrician and parian pieces from Belleek. **Bath and body** brands include Bronnley, Burberry, Dunhill and Taylor of London. The pavilion sells **teas** from Jacksons of Piccadilly and Twinings, **toys** such as ELC Pony Club horses, Jellycat plushies and elaborate chess sets. Don't miss the **candy** — creamy Aero Bubbly, Cadbury dairy milk caramel, McVitie's milk-chocolate caramel digestives and knobbly oaten Hob Nobs. Have WASPy blood? The **Crown and Crest** will

look up your family name and create your family's insignia on paper. To the right of the pavilion, the **U.K. wood cart** sells real pub coasters and a great plushie: a tam o'shantered Pluto playing a bagpipe.

FOR CHILDREN Winnie the Pooh, Tigger, Mary Poppins and Alice (from "Alice in Wonderland") appear at The Toy Soldier. On pretty days Alice and Mary come out into Britannia Square. The pavilion's Kidcot table is inside The Toy Soldier.

ARCHITECTURE Building facades re-create many historic sites of Olde England. Out front, the red-brick turrets and medieval crenulation of the Sportsman's Shoppe mimic Henry VIII's 16th-century Hampton Court. The white-stone side of the building is Abbotsford, the 19th-century Scottish estate where Sir Walter Scott wrote many of his novels. Across the street is the 16th-century thatched-roofed cottage of Anne Hathaway, the wife of William Shakespeare. Also on this street: a half-timbered 15th-century Tudor (leaning with age), a plaster 17th-century pre-Georgian, an 18th-century stone Palladian, even an angled-brick home. Meanwhile, the lakeside Rose & Crown Pub combines a medieval rural cottage, a Tudor tavern and an 1890s Victorian bar.

France

Artistic parks, refined roof lines, and a miniature Eiffel Tower let you know you've arrived in Paris, circa 1900. The France pavilion has the best World Showcase movie and some of its best food and shopping.

ATTRACTION Set to an ethereal classical score, the breathtaking movie **Impressions de France** fills your field of vision with the fairy-tale grandeur of the beautiful French landscape. Accompanied by a digital soundtrack, the 200-degree screen packs over 40 scenes into 18 minutes. Starting off over the cliffs of Normandy, your trip include stops at four chateaus, a church, marketplace, a vineyard, the gardens of Versailles, a rural bicycle tour and even a race of antique Bugattis through the streets of Cannes. And that's just the first five minutes. Still to come are hot-air balloons, fishing boats, a train, Notre Dame

▶ The hidden garden behind U.K.'s Tudor Street has a few private, shady tables.

and a trip above the clouds in the French Alps. With great visuals and terrific sound, it's the best film in the World Showcase. In fact, its only sour note is its first spoken line. "My Frahnce awakens with the early dawn," the narrator intones. Well, duh! Based on Napoleon III's elegant royal theater in Fontainebleau, the intimate Palais de Cinema

Surrounded by trees and flowers, Chefs de France recalls a Parisian brasserie of the late 1800s

has padded, if petite, seats. *18 min. Capacity: 325. Avg. wait: 9 min. Guests may remain in wheelchairs, ECVs. Assistive listening, reflective captioning. Debuted: 1982.*

ENTERTAINMENT Appearing in front of Chefs de France, the **Serveur Amusant** juggles vegetables, then gets a "volunteer" to climb a tower of tables and chairs.

FOOD AND DRINK The airy, bustling **Chefs de France** uses rich creams and soft cheeses in many of its provincial dishes. Upstairs, the gourmet **Bistro de Paris** is a quiet second-floor dining room. Sidewalk pastry shop **Boulangerie Pàtisserie** offers over two dozen temptations, including indulgent pastry treats, croissant sandwiches, quiche and cheese plates. There are also coffees, wines and beers (*24 seats outside and in the adjacent Galerie des Halles gift shop*). Walk-up promenade stand **Les Vins des Chefs de France** sells champagne, wine and cheese. Nearby, **Crepes des Chefs de France** offers ice-cream crepes, waffle cones, coffees and beers.

SHOPPING Offering limited-edition and exclusive fragrances, the pavilion's **La Signature** is one of only four Guerlain boutiques in the United States. Its creations include Les Parisiennes, a vintage Guerlain assortment sold in the company's classic sculpted bee bottles; L'Art et la Matiére, a line of new fragrances that focus on raw ingredients; and Quand Vient La Pluie, which comes in bottles decorated with Swarovski crystal. The shop also includes a small Guerlain cosmetics counter. At the nearby **Plume et Palette** brands can include Azzaro, Chanel, Annick Goutai, Givenchy and Thierry Mugler; also here is vegetable-based E. Barrett shea butter soap and gorgeous (and expensive) Limoges porcelain boxes. Elsewhere, **L' Esprit de la Provence** has wooden rolling pins, spoons and other housewares; decorative items; France Lu butter biscuits and fruit-filled Pims; and books about the Provence region of Southern France. **Les Vins de France** features wine by the bottle or glass. In the rear, **Galerie des Halles** stocks touristy fare, Madeline dolls and Babar the Elephant plushies, merchandise themed to the 2007 Disney film "Ratatouille" as well as authentic Beatex berets.

FOR CHILDREN Belle ("Beauty") and the Beast appear each afternoon in a room adjacent to the Plume et Palette shop (its decor includes a book open to an illustration of the couple standing in this very spot, and a bookshelf with, among other titles, the French version of "Cinderella"). Occasionally the pair pose outside along the promenade. Princess Aurora ("Sleeping Beauty") often appears. The pavilion's Kidcot table is in the Galerie des Halles shop.

ARCHITECTURE You approach France head-on, walking over a replica of the historic Pont des Arts footbridge that crosses the Seine, as you gaze upon the Paris of La Belle Epoque ("the beautiful time," from 1870 to 1910). The three-story stone facades have copper and slate mansard roofs, many with chimney pots. Inside the center shop (the Plume et Palette) a curvy wrought-iron railing helps create an Art Nouveau decor. To the right, a canal-side wooded park recalls

▶ Need to get off your feet? The Galerie des Halles shop has air-conditioned tables.

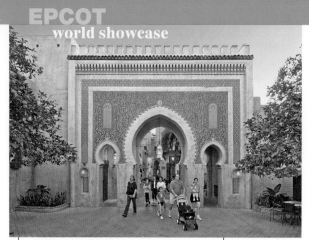

A replica of the Bab Boujouloud Gate of Fez leads to Morocco's main shopping and dining areas

Georges Seurat's 1884–1886 painting "A Sunday Afternoon on the Island of La Grande Jatte." A narrow road ("La Petite Rue") takes you into a rural village. At its end, the Galerie des Halles ("Souvenirs de France") is based on the Les Halles fruit and vegetable market, an 1850 iron-and-glass-ceilinged Paris structure that was demolished in 1971. Towering behind it all is the Eiffel Tower, complete with its period-correct new tawny finish. Disney built the one-tenth-scale replica using Gustave Eiffel's original blueprints.

Morocco

The most exotic pavilion in the World Showcase, Morocco features architecture, food, merchandise and music that is little-known in the West. The complex was created by the Kingdom of Morocco, and is managed independently of the Disney company.

ENTERTAINMENT Sting's 1999 hit "Desert Rose" is among the tunes performed by **Mo'Rockin,** a six-piece band that's fronted by a contemporary belly dancer. The musicians blend authentic Moroccan instruments, such as the darbouka drum, with a violin and keyboards to create a hypnotic sound. The group performs a few 20-minute shows five days a week in a promenade bandstand.

EXHIBIT Used in possession rituals, a guitar-like gimbri is among the antique musical instruments and other artifacts in the three small rooms of the **Gallery of Arts and History,** an overlooked treasure to the left of the front courtyard.

FOOD AND DRINK A traditional belly dancer often entertains at **Restaurant Marrakesh,** which serves roast lamb, kebabs and couscous. The **Tangierine Cafe** offers counter-service chicken and lamb sandwiches and platters served with hummus and couscous. A pastry counter offers baklava, mint tea, liqueur coffees, frozen daiquiris and beer *(101 seats).*

SHOPPING Inside the Medina, **Casablanca Carpets** has rugs from Casablanca, Rabat and Tangier, lamps that filter their light through henna-dyed camel skin; and some handmade furniture from Fez. On the right, **The Brass Bazaar** offers detailed handmade brass plates and platters from Fez and Marrakesh, ceramics, rosewater bottles and aromatic small bowls, boxes and pencil holders made from Thuya, a burled-root wood grown only in Morocco. **The Marketplace in the Medina** is an open-air alley with scarves, bargain-priced seagrass baskets and two strange drums: ceramic tam-tams covered in stretched camel skin and open-top darboukas with bottoms of flounder skin. Tucked alongside is **Tangier Traders,** an apparel shop with caftans, gandouras and other robes and wraps, as well as handmade leather slippers. Out front, the small **Souk-Al-Magreb** ("The Flea Market of Northern Africa") is an enclosed shop with a little bit of everything. Next door, a henna artist will decorate your hands, feet or neck with a choice of designs that last about 10 days.

FOR CHILDREN Aladdin, Princess Jasmine and sometimes Genie pose for photos and sign autographs in a room behind the Marketplace in the Medina. Morocco's Kidcot table is in the Marketplace in the Medina.

ARCHITECTURE Meant to evoke a desert city, the pavilion's buildings are made of brick, tan plaster and reddish sandstone. Like most Moroccan cities, it's divided into two sections, the Ville Nouvelle (new city)

▶ Restaurant Marrakesh often has tables available when other restaurants don't.

and the medina (old city). The new city fronts the promenade. Anchored by two sandstone towers topped with fortress-like crenulation, a fountain courtyard and two buildings recall Casablanca and Marrakesh. Both have interesting interiors. The inside of the Royal Gallery is heavily tiled and molded, with an intricate raised ceiling

A Moroccan cast member waits out a thunderstorm

that's a work of art unto itself. Towering over the courtyard is a large prayer tower, a replica of what is perhaps the most famous building in North Africa, the Koutoubia Minaret in Marrakesh.

The medina of Fez (the religious and cultural center of Morocco) lies in back, behind the pointed arches and swirling blue patterns of that city's 8th-century Bab Boujouloud Gate. On the left is the Fez House, a replica of the central courtyard of a traditional Moroccan home, complete with the sounds of the family. On the right is the open-air marketplace, its bamboo roof loosely lashed to thick beams. Restaurant Marrakesh is a Southern Moroccan fortress, its massive carved wooden doors leading to an interior of arched columns and beamed ceilings. Past the restaurant stands a traditional village fountain, this one a reproduction of the Nejjarine Fountain in Fez. Rising above the old city is another prayer tower, a replica of the Chellah Minaret, a 14th-century necropolis found in Morocco's capital city of Rabat.

Landscaping represents Morocco's agriculture. The grounds include date, olive and sour orange trees, as well as mint and ornamental cabbage plants. Along the shoreline is a working replica of an ancient waterwheel, an ingenious contraption that shuttles water from the lagoon to a grid of nearby desert gardens. The wheel lifts water in compartments inside it, then releases it into a series of wooden troughs.

Moroccan artists supervised Disney's installation of the woodcarvings and created the detailed tiles from nine tons of ceramic pieces. Deliberate imperfections in the work reflect the Muslim belief that only Allah creates perfection.

Japan

Run by the Mitsukoshi company (Japan's oldest department-store business, founded in 1673), this two-story pavilion combines elements of ancient and modern Japan.

Japanese candy artist Miyuki gives away her imaginative, yummy creations to lucky children

▶ An Epcot Friendship boat shuttles between World Showcase Plaza and Morocco.

A Matsuriza Taiko drummer pounds out a beat at the base of Japan's towering pagoda

ENTERTAINMENT Performing on the pavilion's pagoda, the **Matsuriza Taiko Drummers** pound out a traditional, propulsive beat on hand-made instruments. The performers' hypnotic rhythms can be heard throughout the World Showcase, but their intense faces can only be seen here. Arrive early for **Miyuki.** At each performance, the candy artist makes free candy animals for lucky children standing right in front of her. Grabbing a taffy-like ribbon of rice dough, the Tokyo native (and one of our favorite Disney artisans) quickly snips out a child's choice of colorful animals, each with surprising detail. You'll want to save the result as a keepsake; your child will want to eat it. Her stand sits at the front entrance of the Mitsukoshi store.

EXHIBIT What do robots, astronauts, Godzilla and Mickey Mouse have in common? They were all tin toys, a 1950s Japanese creation. With video narration by Pixar guru John Lasseter, **Tin Toy Stories** (at the left rear of the pavilion, in the Bijutsu-kan Gallery) showcases dozens of these colorful period icons.

FOOD AND DRINK New for 2008, Japan's table-service restaurants consist of **Tokyo Dining,** which features a traditional Japanese menu, sushi and remarkably polite service, and **Teppan Edo,** where tableside chefs entertain guests in brand-new dining rooms. The counter-service **Yakitori House** has beef, chicken and shrimp bowls, and good miso soup *(58 seats, including 36 outside).* The **Kaki-Gori** promenade stand sells fruit-syrup snow cones. Choose from honeydew melon, strawberry, tangerine or a rainbow mix of all three.

SHOPPING The pavilion's 10,000-square-foot **Mitsukoshi** department store is divided into four sections. Inspired by the Nishiki Food Market in Kyoto, the Festivity area stocks chopsticks, cooking equipment, ornate porcelain dishes, dozens of teas and sweets (the best: jelly-bean-like Botan Rice Candy, with each piece in a melt-in-your-mouth wrapper). A sake tasting bar offers five microbrews. Apparel (including kimonos, embroidered jackets and tenugui head coverings) and home items (bonsai trees, draperies, lanterns, rice paper, small tables and tatami mats) fill the Zen-themed Silence spot. The store's Harmony zone bridges Japanese and Western cultures with handbags, glass-bead jewelry, sandals, shirts and silver. The largest area, Interest, has a popular Pick-A-Pearl (from an oyster) bar, kitschy Lucky Cats, transforming Rhythm and Seiko clocks and lots of quirky kids stuff. Outside, the walk-in **Mitsukoshi kiosk** sells candy and impulse items. *Founded in 1673, the Mitsukoshi company runs the entire Japan pavilion.*

FOR CHILDREN Japan's Kidcot table is located at the rear of the pavilion, outside of the back entrance of the Mitsukoshi store.

ARCHITECTURE Graceful architecture and landscaping harmonize in this symbolic pavilion. Elements to the left represent culture and religion, including an 83-foot pagoda that recalls the 8th-century Horyuji Temple in Nara. Its five stories represent the five elements from which Buddhists believe all things are created — earth, water, fire, wind and sky. A hill garden's evergreens symbolize eternal life, its rocks the long life of the earth and its koi-filled water the brief life of animals and man. Within the garden, the rustic Yakitori House is modeled on Kyoto's 16th-century Katsura Impe-

▶ During IllumiNations, Tokyo Dining pipes in the soundtrack and dims its interior lights.

rial Villa. Housing the store and restaurants, the building on the right represents commerce. Its architecture recalls the ceremonial Shishinden Hall at the 8th-century Gosho Imperial Palace at Kyoto.

The rear of the complex symbolizes Japan's political history. Once you pass through the 17th-century wood and stone Nijo castle with its sculptures of mounted samurai warriors, you cross a moat to the curved stone walls, white plaster buildings and blue tile roof of the Shirasagijo (White Heron) castle, a 14th-century feudal fortress which overlooks the city of Himeji.

The American Adventure

The focus here is purely on the attraction: a great Audio Animatronic theatrical show.

✔ **ATTRACTION** The only World Showcase attraction that is critical of its country, **The American Adventure** combines film footage with robotic versions of historical figures to review the triumphs, flaws and challenges of the United States. Ben Franklin and Mark Twain lead you from the time of the Pilgrims through World War II.

The robots move convincingly. Franklin appears to walk, Frederick Douglass sits on a rocking raft. Some movements are subtle. In Valley Forge, George Washington shifts his weight in his saddle, and his horse twitches and pulls like a real animal. Each character has its own speaker; its voice projects from it. The film, a combination of real and re-created images, pans across paintings and photographs in a style later made famous by documentarian Ken Burns.

The presentation addresses both proud and ugly episodes of the American story. Chatting with Franklin after the Revolutionary War, Twain says "You Founding Fathers gave us a pretty good start... [but then] a whole bunch of folks found out that 'We the People' didn't yet mean all the people." Civil War images include a close-up of a dead soldier.

A photomontage finale covers events and cultural leaders of the past 50 years. Images added in 2007 include Muhammad Ali at the

The tricorn hats, white wigs and regimental coats of the Spirit of America Fife & Drum Corps recall the formal dress of the Revolutionary War era

1996 Atlanta Olympics torch and former presidents Bush and Clinton working together on humanitarian relief.

30 min. Capacity: 1,024. Guests may remain in wheelchairs, ECVs. Assistive listening, reflective captioning. Debuted: 1982; revised 1993.

ENTERTAINMENT Marching into the promenade a few times most afternoons, the five-person **Spirit of America Fife & Drum Corps** performs "Battle Hymn of the Re-

FUN FACTS ❯❯ The American Adventure show uses three Franklins and three Twains. ❯❯ Twelve statues on the sides of the auditorium represent the Spirits of America. ❯❯ The show uses 35 Audio Animatronic characters on a multi-plane stage. ❯❯ Hidden from view, the staging system is a mechanical marvel. Just beneath your sight line is a mass of wiring and hydraulic-fluid cables which give movement to the figures. Underneath that is a 175-ton scene changer, a steel frame that's 65 feet long, 35 feet wide and 14 feet high. Operated by computer, it wheels in each of the 13 three-dimensional sets horizontally, then raises them into view on telescoping hydraulic supports. Other devices bring in side elements. Behind all that is a 155-foot rear-projection screen that shows the 70-millimeter film.

▶ Stand under an edge of the rotunda. A whisper will carry to the other side.

Italian juggler Sergio puts children in his show

public" and other inspiring tunes. Performing in the rotunda, the a cappella **Voices of Liberty** do more than patriotic numbers; their harmonies on "Amazing Grace," "Ol' Man River" and "This Land Is Your Land" bring to life aspects of U.S. history that are too often ignored. The **American Gardens Theatre** frequently hosts live concerts.

EXHIBIT A small collection of artifacts from the lives of famous Americans, **National Treasures** has some interesting items. Authentic pieces include one of Abraham Lincoln's stovepipe hats (complete with frayed edges), a couple of Thomas Edison's early motion-picture and sound inventions, a microscope used by George Washington Carver, chairs from the homes of Benjamin Franklin and George Washington and a pool cue from the den of Mark Twain. The exhibit is in the American Heritage Gallery, just off the lobby. Items change periodically.

FOOD AND DRINK The counter-service **Liberty Inn** serves cheeseburgers, hot dogs, chicken strips and a kosher meal *(710 seats)*. **Snack kiosks** sell turkey legs, funnel cakes and fried ice cream.

SHOPPING Heritage Manor Gifts sells patriotic clothing and some fun educational items that can help your kids learn history.

FOR CHILDREN The pavilion's Kidcot table is next to Heritage Manor Gifts.

ARCHITECTURE The English Georgian-style architecture recalls the look of many colonial buildings during the Revolutionary War. Its 110,000 hand-formed bricks were laid with an old-fashioned one-then-a-half technique. The structure uses reversed forced perspective to appear just three stories, though it actually rises more than 70 feet to accommodate the large theater. The illusion only works from a distance; up close the second-story windows look huge.

Italy

Gold-leafed ringlets decorate an angel atop the Campanile. Gondolas are tethered to barbershop-striped poles. Where are you? Venice. Or, at least, Disney's Venice, which fronts the World Showcase Italy pavilion.

ENTERTAINMENT Comedic juggler **Sergio** appears weekdays in the courtyard. His 20-minute shows include audience volunteers. The **World Showcase Players** (see United Kingdom) also appear.

FOOD AND DRINK New for 2008, **Tutto Italia** offers a variety of expensive beef, chicken, pasta and pork items. Out front, **snack stands** serve coffee, desserts and gelato.

SHOPPING La Bottega offers made-on-site papier-mâché and fabric Carnivale masks, wines and wine sampling, Bialetti coffee makers and Perugina Baci kisses filled with crushed hazelnuts. **Il Bel Cristallo** has leather clutches and handbags, silk scarves and ties, Murano glass and alabaster accessories, stylish watches and charm bracelets, a variety of Italian perfumes and Giuseppe Armani figurines.

FOR CHILDREN Italy's Kidcot table is behind La Bottega.

ARCHITECTURE The icons of Venice welcome you to the Italy pavilion. Along the lagoon are the city's bridges, gondolas and striped pilings; the front of the pavilion recreates the Piazza San Marco. The two free-standing columns mimic the square's two 12th-century monuments, one topped by the city's guardian, the winged lion of St. Mark the Evangelist, the other crowned by St. Theodore, the city's former patron saint

▶ Don't want to be picked for a street skit? Hold a camera up to your face.

A **Disney horticulturist** plants "trees" in Germany's miniature train village

(shown killing the dragon that threatened the city of Euchaita, an act that gave him the courage to declare himself a Christian). The 10th-century Campanile (bell tower) dominates the skyline, though this version is just 100 feet tall, less than a third the height of the original. At the left is the square's 14th-century Doge's (leader's) Palace. Its elaborate facade replicates nearly every detail of the original. The first two stories rest on realistic marble columns that front leaded-glass windows. The third floor is tiled and topped by marble sculptures, statues, reliefs and filigree. Adjoining the palace, a stairway and portico reflect Verona. The first building on the right is a Tuscany homestead. Sculptures include a version of Neptune and his dolphins that recalls Bernini's 1642 fountain in Florence.

Germany

An animated glockenspiel comes to life every hour at this picture-perfect pavilion, with a look that seems straight out of "Snow White and the Seven Dwarfs."

FOOD AND DRINK The **Biergarten** celebrates Oktoberfest every day with an indoor buffet. An oompah band entertains. Outside, the **Sommerfest** counter has bratwurst and beer *(52 seats on a covered patio)*. **Snack stands** sell pretzels, beers and wine.

SHOPPING Imports include Black Forest cuckoo clocks, made-to-order dolls, hand-painted eggs, Steiff teddy bears, Christmas pickle orna-

The Outpost

✔ This enclave between Germany and China has some terrific African entertainment and folk art. You drum along with **OrisiRisi,** an engaging pair of storytellers who teach timeless truths of life as they relate Nigerian folktales, myths and legends. Don (right) and Tutu Harrell are masters of their craft. And no wonder: he's a music researcher and folklorist; she's a Nigerian native who heard many of these tales as a child. Children love the drumming experience, of course, but you'll be surprised how much you'll like it, too. Show times are available at Guest Relations; arrive 15 minutes early to get a seat. Unified families with intertwined arms are the signature sculptures of African wood and soapstone artist Andrew Mutiso at the open-air **Village Traders.** Other pieces include animals, busts, canes and masks. The **Refreshment Cool Post** offers soft-serve ice cream, frozen yogurt and soft drinks.

Typically 9 to 12 years old, students from the PRC's Puyang Acrobatics Center perform daily

ments, Steinback nutcrackers and limited-edition beer steins. Also available: German schnapps and wine by the glass and bottle. FOR CHILDREN Snow White and Dopey appear to the left of the pavilion. Germany's Kidcot table sits inside the teddy-bear shop. ARCHITECTURE The facade of the Das Kaufhaus shop was inspired by the Kaufhaus, a 16th-century merchants' hall in the Black Forest town of Freiburg. Three statues on its second story recall the rule of the Hapsburg emperors. The huge backdrop combines the looks of two 12th-century castles, the Eltz on the Mosel river and the Stahleck Castle on the Rhine. The plaza centerpiece is a sculpture of St. George (the patron saint of soldiers) with the dragon that legend says he slayed during a trip to the Middle East. Inside, the Biergarten imagines medieval Rothernberg.

China

This serene pavilion combines a thoughtful exhibit, poetic film and calm restaurant and department store. The landscape looks naturally placed. It includes a weeping mul-

berry, a runner bamboo and tallow tree, with a waxy fruit long used to make candles.

✓ ATTRACTION A CircleVision 360 film, **Reflections of China** takes you to ancient areas such as Inner Mongolia and Tibet and modern spots like Hong Kong, Macao and Shanghai. The host portrays 8th-century Chinese poet Li Bai. You stand up to watch. *20 min. Capacity: 200. Avg. wait: 10 min. Guests may stay in wheelchairs, ECVs. Assistive listening; reflective captioning. Debuted: 1982, updated 2003.*

ENTERTAINMENT The **Dragon Legend Acrobats** are a terrific troupe of children. Inside the Temple of Heaven, Chinese harpist **Si Xian** performs before most screenings of Reflections of China.

EXHIBIT You'll see how archeologists uncovered thousands of full-size terra cotta soldiers and horses from a lost tomb in **Tomb Warriors: Guardian Spirits of Ancient China,** in the House of the Whispering Willows gallery. Adjacent cases hold authentic tomb sculptures.

FOOD AND DRINK Choose from the table-service **Nine Dragons Restaurant** or the counter-service **Lotus Blossom Cafe,** which serves egg rolls, grilled chicken, stir-fried entrees and specialty drinks *(100 seats).*

SHOPPING The large **Yong Feng Shangdian** department store is filled with apparel, food, furniture, housewares and jewelry.

FOR CHILDREN Mulan often appears in front of the Lotus Blossom Cafe. A Kidcot table sits at the rear of Yong Feng Shangdian.

ARCHITECTURE China is anchored by a colorful welcoming gate with banners that translate to "May good fortune follow you on your path through life" and "May virtue be your neighbor." The triple-arched gateway and three-tiered, blue-roofed (and half-sized) Hall of Prayer for Good Harvests are based on the main gate and building of Beijing's Temple of Heaven, a summer retreat for Chinese emperors built in 1420. The area also includes facades of an elegant home, a school house, a city gate and shop fronts reflecting European influences. The gallery has a formal saddle-ridge roof line.

The inner rotunda alludes to the cycles of nature. Twelve outer columns represent the months of the year and the years in a cycle of the Chinese calendar. Four central

▶ Giant bullfrogs live in China's reflecting pool. Their heads poke out of the water.

Spelmanns Gledje performs at the Norway pavilion

columns denote the four seasons, a central beam represents earth, a round topping beam is heaven. The center floor stone is cut into nine circling pieces, reflecting the Chinese belief that nine is a lucky number.

A Suzhou-style garden and reflecting ponds symbolize the order and discipline of nature. Keeping with Chinese custom, most of the garden appears old and in a natural state. At the lagoon, large pockmarked boulders demonstrate the Chinese tradition of designing surprising views in landscapes by creating holes in waterside rock formations.

Norway

Welcome to Norway, where men are menn and women are kvinner and meatballs are kjottkakers and all in all there are just way too many consonants. Pronunciation differences aside, the beautiful country is the basis of one of Epcot's best pavilions.

✓ **ATTRACTION** The **Maelstrom** indoor boat ride has a quirky appeal. After you set sail in a dragon-headed longboat, an ancient god urges you to seek the spirit of Norway. Your journey starts off peacefully, as your search takes you past a quaint fishing village, but then things turn into a confused chaos (a "maelstrom") as trolls commandeer your ship. A three-headed ogre sends you backward past some polar bears and nearly off a cliff. Then another troll pops up to send you forward down a waterfall and into a stormy North Sea. You make landfall at a modern fishing village.

Next you head to a small theater to watch "The Spirit of Norway," a 5-minute film that portrays the daydreams of a young boy. As he examines an old Viking ship, he imagines seafarers, oil riggers, ski jumpers, scientists, businessmen and a Constitution Day parade. The point? "The spirit of Norway… is in its people!"

A guide to World Showcase candy

The authors' teenage daughter has sampled the candy and other sweets at every World Showcase pavilion. (It was a tough job, but someone had to do it.) Here are her recommendations: **Canada:** Thick-wafer Coffee Crisp bars and Smarties, an M&M-like candy with a thicker coating and better chocolate. Canada also has delicious maple-syrup candies. **United Kingdom:** Creamy Aero Bubbly and yummy Cadbury dairy milk caramel, as well as two McVitie's tea choices: milk-chocolate caramel digestives and knobbly oaten Hob Nobs. **France:** Lu butter biscuits and fruit-filled Pims. **Japan:** Jelly-bean-like Botan Rice Candy, each piece wrapped in a melt-in-your-mouth wrapper. **Italy:** Perugina Baci kisses filled with crushed hazelnuts. **Germany:** Milka Alpine-milk-chocolate bars. **China:** Ginger candy and peanut-brittle-like nutcakes. **Norway:** Creamy Melkesjokolade chocolate bars and the toffee-like D'aim. **Mexico:** Obleas wafers, a caramelized sweet made with burnt goat milk.

15 min. (5 min. ride, 5 min. wait, 5 min. film). Capacity: 192. Avg. wait: 5 min. early afternoon, 30 min. peak afternoon. Fastpass available. Wheelchair, ECV users must transfer. Assistive listening; handheld and reflective captioning. Fear factor: The ride is often completely dark and has scary faces. In the film, two opening loud flashes will jolt those of any age. Debuted: 1988.

ENTERTAINMENT Mix an accordion and a couple of fiddles with an acoustic guitar and bass and you've got... hand-clapping country music, in this case the Norwegian sounds of **Spelmanns Gledje.** Performing outside, the five-piece group plays short sets of dance and gypsy tunes. Its hoedown sound will show you where American country music got its start.

EXHIBIT A lifesize Rögnvald the Raider stares at you with axe in hand in **The Vikings: Conquerors of the Seas,** a five-display exhibit inside the Stave Church Gallery. The display also includes Erik the Red and King Olaf, as well as authentic swords, arrows and axe blades.

FOOD AND DRINK The **Akershus Royal Banquet Hall** is all princess all the time. Its character meals feature an American breakfast, a Norwegian lunch and dinner. The **Kringla Bakeri Og Kafe** serves open-faced sandwiches (including smoked salmon) and tasty pastries such as coconut-dusted, custard-filled School Bread *(51 seats).*

SHOPPING Finds include stylish Helly Hansen apparel and footwear; Dale of Norway blankets, ski sweaters and caps; Geir Ness perfume (sometimes Ness himself is present); Löfbergs Lila Swedish coffee; troll figurines; and silly plastic Viking helmets, all with horns, some with braids.

FOR CHILDREN Norway's Kidcot table sits inside its shopping area.

ARCHITECTURE Standing at the pavilion entrance is a replica of the 13th-century Gol Church of Hallingdal, one of Norway's stavkirkes ("stave churches") which played a key role in the country's movement from the Viking Age to Christianity. Next door, the bakery has a sod roof, a traditional way to insulate homes in Norway's mountains. The gift shop facades recall coastal cottages. Finally, the pavilion's castle-like restaurant and rear facade re-creates Akershus, a 14th-century fortress that stands in the harbor of the city of Oslo.

Mexico

A great place to get out of the sun, the Mexico pavilion is, for the most part, totally enclosed. Housed in what appears to be a small pyramid, its indoor market and boat ride are cool and dark.

ATTRACTION An update of the pavilion's old El Rio Del Tiempo ride, the **Gran Fiesta Tour** is still a dark, indoor boat tour through the cultural history of Mexico, but now its synchronized video screens feature a storyline based on Disney's 1944 film, "The Three Caballeros." When ladies man Donald Duck, suave parrot José Carioca and hyper cowboy rooster Panchito plan to reunite for a concert in Mexico City, Donald disappears to take in the sights of the country, and his feathered friends try to find him.

The trip includes some strange moments. When Donald finds a pyramid, he climbs its steps, which turns it into an escalator. In Acapulco, his bathing suit falls off. At night, Donald heads to a bar to smooch señoritas.

It's all meant in good fun, of course, but some guests are not amused. "If Gran Fiesta is supposed to be a showcase of Mexico, it is a disrespectful one," a Latin American friend told us. "It seems to me just like a big party, with birds running around looking for a duck."

Look past the videos, however, and you'll notice you actually are seeing the proud cultural history of the country. You start off in the 1st century A.D., sailing through a rainforest before passing a Mayan pyramid and then drifting into a temple. Next it's a Small World-style Day of the Dead, Mexico's annual fall festival when ancestors traditionally come back to visit. Finally you're in modern Mexico, floating along Acapulco's cliffs and grottos before arriving at Mexico City's Reforma Boulevard.

8 min. Capacity: 250. No wait. ECV users must transfer. Handheld captioning. Debuted: 1982, revised 2007.

ENTERTAINMENT **Mariachi Cobre** is an 11-piece group led by trumpets, violins and confident vocals and backed by harmonizing guitars. It's Epcot's best live band. Formed in Tucson in 1971, the group has often played with Linda Ronstadt.

EXHIBITS Wild styles dominate the painted wood carvings of **Animalés Fantâsticos:**

Spirits in Wood, a collection of modern Mexican folk-art animals, humans and mythical creatures just inside the pavilion entrance. The copal-wood creatures are carved with machetes and pocketknives then painted with brushes, cactus spines and syringes. A series of push-button displays introduces you to the art, food, music and regions of modern Mexico inside **Casa Mexicana,** a room off the indoor courtyard.

FOOD AND DRINK The **San Angel Inn** restaurant offers real Mexico City cuisine in a tranquil setting overlooking the Gran Fiesta Tour. A new indoor bar will debut next door in mid-2008. Outside, the counter-service **Cantina de San Angel** serves burritos, tacos, quesadillas, nachos, guacamole, frozen margaritas, beer, and a good Conga fruit drink *(150 seats).* The **Margarita Kiosk** serves frozen margaritas.

SHOPPING The indoor bazaar has everything you expect and plenty you don't. Sure, there are lots of ponchos and super-sized sombreros, but wander around and you'll find many surprises. Food and housewares include jalapeño jelly, salsa and seasonings, tequila, table glasses, goblets and pitchers. There are vivid ceramics and other home accent pieces. Kids will love the hand-painted piggy banks (and teens, the handbags) by Yucatan artist Carlos Millet. Other stands and stores stock peasant blouses and skirts, wool blankets, leather sandals and woven huaraches, hand-tooled leather purses and belts with silver accents and pure-silver and turquoise jewelry.

FOR CHILDREN The Three Caballeros often appear along the shaded walkway to the right of the pavilion. Mexico's Kidcot table is in the Casa Mexicana exhibit room.

ARCHITECTURE The pavilion's pyramid facade is modeled after the Aztec temple of Quetzalcoatl (honoring the feathered-serpent god of life) in the ancient city of Teotihuacan. The god itself is depicted by heads along the priests' steps. Inside, the entry portico to the Plaza de Los Amigos (the "outdoor" market) is that of a Mexican mayor's mansion. The market area was inspired by the 16th-century silver mining town of Taxco. Back outside, the Cantina de San Angel has the look of Mexico City's original 17th-century San Angel Inn.

Disney sells alcohol throughout the World Showcase, including frozen margaritas at the Mexico pavilion

'COME HERE, MY LITTLE ENCHILADA' The most bizarre movie the Walt Disney company has ever produced, 1945's "The Three Caballeros" combines truly psychedelic animation with a storyline that makes Donald Duck a libidinous wolf. Its point? The charms of Latin America. Yes, they don't make 'em like they used to. Still, the film does have a plot, much of which is mirrored in the Gran Fiesta attraction. When Donald has a birthday, his presents include pop-up books about Brazil and Mexico. Cigar-chomping playboy parrot José Carioca (a Disney version of a Brazilian folk character) pops out of the Brazil book, while the one about Mexico brings forth Panchito, a six-gun-shooting cowboy rooster. He tosses sombreros to his new feathered friends, proclaims the trio "three gay caballeros" and takes them on a flying-serape tour of his country. On Acapulco Beach, Donald goes ga-ga for dozens of live-action bathing beauties ("Come to Papa! Come here, my little enchilada!") and keeps losing his swimming suit. At night the duck can't stay away from the clubs, where he dances with still more real-life señoritas. The film's bizarre animation includes illogical color changes and an overdose of morphing gags, though some scenes are beautiful Mary Blair gems that would later inspire the films "Cinderella" and "Alice in Wonderland," as well as the classic Disney attraction It's a Small World. The movie was produced as part of the U.S. government's Good Neighbor Policy, an effort to promote pro-American feelings in Latin America during the Roosevelt administration.

▶ Ask for the first row of a Gran Fiesta Tour boat. You'll have lots of legroom.

IllumiNations' lasers and fireworks light up the sky over the World Showcase Lagoon

IllumiNations: Reflections of Earth

The lights go dark, then a fireball explodes over the stage as thousands stare in awe. As the music begins, fireworks erupt and lasers shoot out from backstage.

Baby boomers may think they're at a Pink Floyd concert, but it's actually the beginning of IllumiNations: Reflections of Earth, Disney's dazzling spectacle of "Wow, man!" effects that concludes every Epcot day. Synchronized to a symphonic world-music score, the extravaganza uses the entire World Showcase lagoon as its stage. Much more than a fireworks show, it includes strobe lights on, and laser beams from, the pavilions. A rotating Earth moves across the water, shows moving images on its continents and unfolds to reveal a torch.

Though there's no narration, the show tells the history of the world in three acts: Chaos, Order and Celebration. It begins with the dawn of time — the Big Bang and the creation of Earth — symbolized by a lone shooting star that explodes into a fiery ballet of chaos.

Act Two starts as the planet is brought under control and gains order. As the spinning globe appears, scenes on it depict primal seas and forests; the development of famous cultural landmarks including the Sphinx, the Easter Island statues and Mount Rushmore; and key historical figures such as Muhammad Ali, the Dalai Lama, Albert Einstein, Martin Luther King Jr., Jonas Salk, Mother Teresa and, if you look closely, Walt Disney.

The coolest image: video of a running horse that transforms into a cave painting.

The third act begins as the globe unfurls into a lotus flower and a 40-foot torch rises from its heart. Celebrating both human diversity and the unified spirit of humankind, this segment features a colorful fireworks finale that heralds a new age of mankind, originally the new Millenium.

IllumiNations ends with a loud crackle, sending you off to embrace the future. As you walk away, the exit music that plays is called "We Go On."

▶ Pick out a viewing spot at least 30 minutes early to get a good view.

The show is directed to the front of the park, directly at Spaceship Earth. The best seats are at the World Showcase Plaza, where you'll see everything symmetrically, as the designers intended it. The photo on the opposite page was taken there.

An added plus: the plaza is the closest viewing spot to Epcot's main exit, so you'll be ahead of the masses when the show ends.

Many locations around the lagoon have a fine view of all the effects, but watching IllumiNations from another location is like sitting at the side, or rear, of a concert stage. It may be interesting, but you really don't get the same show.

If you can't make it to the plaza, better spots include the promenade along the Canadian waterfront; the waterside tables at the U.K.'s Rose and Crown, though they are notoriously tough to snare (you can't reserve one); and the bridge between the U.K. and France, which gives you a more elevated view.

Other good spots include Japan, especially on the balcony above the Mitsukoshi department store; the bridge between China and Germany; and the Cantina de San Angel cafe at Mexico, where you can munch nachos while you watch.

The music can be heard everywhere, as speakers surround the lagoon.

On, above and around the World Showcase Lagoon. 15 min. Guests may remain in wheelchairs, ECVs. Preshow: 30 min. of in-

Torches ring the World Showcase Lagoon

Loading the guns. A cast member packs mortar tubes with fireworks for an IllumiNations show.

strumental music from Japan, South America, Scandinavia and Spain. Fear factor: The loud, bright explosions and fire can be intense for toddlers, some preschoolers. Debuted: 1988; revised 1997, 1999.

FUN FACTS 》 The 2,800 fireworks launch from 34 locations that house 750 mortar tubes. Some ring the shore, just a few feet from unsuspecting guests. 》 The four fountain barges pump 5,000 gallons of water per minute. 》 The 150,000-pound "inferno barge" has 37 propane nozzles. 》 The 28-foot steel globe rotates on a 350-ton barge that houses six computers, 258 strobe lights and an infrared guidance system. Wrapped in more than 180,000 light-emitting diodes, the globe is the world's first spherical video display. 》 The performance uses 67 computers in 40 locations. 》 The pavilions are outlined in more than 26,000 feet of lights — nearly 5 miles worth. 》 For religious reasons, the Morocco pavilion does not participate in the show. 》 The music supervisor was Hans Zimmer, the composer for the 1994 film, "The Lion King." 》 The songs "The Promise" and "We Go On" are performed by country singer Kellie Coffey. 》 There are 19 torches around the lagoon, symbolizing the first 19 centuries of modern history. The 20th torch, in the globe, represents the Millennium. 》 Disney occasionally tests IllumiNations after midnight. If you stay up late at one of the Epcot resorts (the BoardWalk, Swan and Dolphin or Yacht and Beach Club) you may see, or hear, an unscheduled explosion or two.

A performer strikes a pose during High School Musical 2: School's Out, a new street show at Disney's Hollywood Studios

Disney's Hollywood Studios

Celebrating the diverse world of show business, this intimate park — formerly known as Disney-MGM Studios — is one the whole family can enjoy. From preschoolers who love Playhouse Disney television shows to seniors who long for the days of Humphrey Bogart and James Cagney, anyone can have a good time.

Boys are especially well served. There are two stunt shows, two big thrill rides, a mo-tion simulator, a roving rock 'n' roll band and even appearances by the Power Rangers. Other attractions include stage shows that re-create highlights from Disney films.

EASY DOES IT With the smallest public area of any Disney World theme park, Disney's Hollywood Studios is easy to tour. Though the park encompasses more than 150 acres,

Jumping through the flames at the Lights Motors Action Extreme Stunt Show

Authentic down to its warning bell, a two-color traffic light sits alongside Hollywood Boulevard

much of that is backstage. The main thoroughfare, Hollywood Boulevard, is just 500 feet long, and from there nearly every attraction is, at most, just a few minutes away. What's more, you sit down a lot. There are no stand-up theaters and only one walk-through attraction. You may find a long line every now and then, but taken as a whole this is the one Disney park that won't wear you out.

The park is divided into two areas.

The front is Old Hollywood. This 1940s world features palm-lined streets with period-specific shops, signs and stoplights as well as re-imagined landmarks. The

entranceway, Hollywood Boulevard, includes an authentic Brown Derby restaurant and authentic-looking Chinese Theater, which houses the Great Movie Ride. On your right is Sunset Boulevard, a trolley-line theater district that leads to the glamorous Hollywood Tower Hotel. This area is home to the popular Beauty and the Beast and Fantasmic stage shows, the Rock 'n' Roller Coaster starring Aerosmith and the Twilight Zone Tower of Terror.

To your left is Echo Lake, with its Indiana Jones Epic Stunt Spectacular show.

The rear is movie-studio land, with areas that resemble a production center and backlot. Its entrance arch resembles Hollywood's Paramount Studio gate, while side streets are marked by (always open) security gates. Many buildings look like soundstages. The best attractions include the Playhouse Disney and Voyage of the Little Mermaid shows, the Star Tours simulator and the spectacular MuppetVision 3-D.

The park is dotted with curving, shady side streets

Posing for pix in front of the Sorcerer's Hat

© DISNEY

▶ Rain? No problem. Nearly every attraction is inside or under a covered pavilion.

Gee, our old LaSalle ran great. On Sunset Boulevard.

and hidden garden spots. In fact, its friendly feel is a lot like that of the first park Walt Disney himself drew up more than 50 years ago: California's Disneyland.

HISTORY Known as Disney-MGM Studios until 2008, the park opened as a production facility in 1988 and to the public on May 1, 1989. "Welcome to the Hollywood that never was and always will be," then-CEO Michael Eisner said at the dedication. A Hollywood-style gala, the park's Grand Opening featured legends Lauren Bacall, George Burns, Audrey Hepburn and Bob Hope.

Alas, the park is no longer a production center. The company once used the soundstages and backlot streets for movie and television work. Britney Spears, Christina Aguilera and Justin Timberlake worked here on a daily basis as cast members of The Disney Channel's "New Mickey Mouse Club," which was filmed at the park from 1989 to 1994. (Among those who auditioned for the show but didn't make it: Jessica Simpson and Matt Damon.)

The animation building was the East Coast home of Disney Feature Animation. It created the Roger Rabbit shorts "Tummy Trouble" and "Roller Coaster Rabbit;" painted cels for "The Little Mermaid;" produced segments of "Beauty and the Beast," "Aladdin" and "The Lion King;" and cre-

ated the films "Mulan," "Lilo & Stitch," "Brother Bear" and "Home on the Range" in their entireties. At its peak the animation studio had a staff of 350.

Max axe. A 40-foot guitar decks out the Rock 'n' Roller Coaster entrance. Its 320-foot neck becomes a coaster track that rolls out above the walkway.

▶ Coming in 2008 is a new Toy Story ride, parade and Playhouse Disney stage show.

THE COMPLETE WALT DISNEY WORLD **135**

overview

Hollywood Redux

A tribute to Hollywood in its heyday, the park's architecture re-creates the look of Los Angeles during the mid-20th century.

The turquoise **entrance structures** and their white-ringed pylons reflect 1935's Pan Pacific Auditorium, a sports and music hall.

Hollywood Boulevard is a dreamlike 500-foot version of its namesake. Each of its 15 facades is modeled on an actual structure. Kicking things off is the Crossroads of the World gift kiosk, a replica of a Streamline Moderne stand at the 1937 Crossroads of the World shopping center. Sid Cahuenga's is a tribute to the Craftsman bungalows that became Hollywood tourist shops during the 1930s and 1940s. The Disney & Co. store brings back the black-marble-and-gilt Security Pacific Bank building, itself a copy of downtown L.A.'s Richfield Oil Building whose black and gold trim represented the "Black Gold" of the oil industry, and a Hollywood veterinary clinic. Keystone Clothiers includes the scaled-down facades of Hollywood's Max Factor Building and Jullian Medical Building. The right side of the street is equally inspired. The photo center is a clone of The Darkroom, a 1938 Hollywood photo shop known for its front window trim that looked like a giant camera. Celebrity 5 & 10 evokes an Art Deco building that once housed a J.J. Newberry five and dime. Next door, Adrian and Edith's Head to Toe and the adjacent L.A. Cinema Storage recall a two-block Spanish Colonial Revival area. Finally, the Hollywood Brown Derby is modeled from the 1929 second location of the famous restaurant, a legendary dining spot for hundreds of movie stars. Inside the buildings is a ceiling lover's paradise. Cover Story's film-roll theme recalls the style of Frank Lloyd Wright. The tiny Head to Toe foyer towers almost 30 feet. At the end of the road is

Hollywood's Carthay Circle Theatre; Disney's tribute

a full-scale model of Grauman's Chinese Theatre. The front is designed from the same blueprints as the 1927 building and has essentially all the original's soaring trim pieces and intricate detailing. The only real difference: this one has its ticket booth off to the side.

Echo Lake recalls downtown L.A.'s Echo Lake Park, where 1920's silent-movie czar Mack Sennett shot many of his Keystone Comedies. Two snack stands re-create that era's programmatic architecture, when buildings were designed to look like giant objects. Appearing to be a tramp steamer is Min & Bill's Dockside Diner. What appears to be an apatosaurus is Dinosaur Gertie's Ice Cream of Extinction. This tribute to 1914 cartoon star Gertie the Dinosaur includes her footprints in the sidewalk. Nearby, the Hollywood & Vine restaurant evokes a cafeteria that once stood on North Vine, near the actual Hollywood Blvd.

Sunset Boulevard begins with a replica of the 1940 Mulholland Fountain in Griffith Park. On your left, the Colony Sunset gift shop is New York City's Colony Theatre as it appeared in 1928, when it premiered the cartoon "Steamboat Willie," the debut of Mickey Mouse. The Sunset Ranch Market recalls the 1934 Los Angeles Farmers Market, where Walt Disney often ate. On your right, the Legends of Hollywood store features the facade and spiral corkscrew tower of the 1938 Academy Theater. A few doors down, the Once Upon a Time gift shop is a dead ringer for the 1926 Carthay Circle Theatre, which hosted the premiere of Disney's "Snow White and the Seven Dwarfs" in 1937. Next up, the Theater of the Stars is an homage to the 1922 Hollywood Bowl. The entrance to Fantasmic's Hollywood Hills Amphitheater draws its design from the Los Angeles Ford Amphitheater nestled in the Hollywood Hills. The stone entranceway to The Twilight Zone Tower of Terror is a nearly exact replica of the Hollywood Gates, the 1923 entrance to the Hollywoodland real-estate development. The Hollywood Tower Hotel recalls the Spanish Revival look of the 1902 Mission Inn in Riverside, Calif.

In the rear of the park, the "studio" buildings were inspired by the Walt Disney Studios in California. The new Pixar Place structures recall that studio.

Beauties and the Buzz. Guests pose with Buzz Lightyear on the backlot.

FUN FINDS **Hollywood Boulevard:** Second-story offices include those of ❶ tailor Justin Stitches and of ❷ Allen Smythee Productions,* both above the second entrance to Keystone Clothiers. **Echo Lake:** Offices around the right of the pond include ❸ acting-and-voice studio Sights and Sounds ("We've Finished Some of Hollywood's Finest"), run by master thespian Ewell M. Pressum, voice coach Singer B. Flatt and account executive Bill Moore (the door to the left of Keystone Clothiers), ❹ a dentistry office run by doctors C. Howie Pullum, Ruth Canal and Les Payne (to the left of Peevy's Polar Pipeline), ❺ Holly-Vermont Realty, the name of a real business that in 1923 rented its back room to Walt and Roy Disney to use as their first office (to the right of Peevy's) and ❻ grumpy gumshoe Eddie Valiant from 1988's "Who Framed Roger Rabbit" (above the Hollywood & Vine restaurant). Valiant's workplace has two windows; Roger has crashed through one. ❼ A billboard for Roger's employer Maroon Studios sits on the roof above Peevy's. Three crates to the left of Min & Bill's snack stand refer to classic films: ❽ One addressed to "Charles Foster Kane, Xanadu Compound, Gulf Coast, Florida, to the Rosebud Sled Co." refers to 1941's "Citizen Kane." ❾ A crate marked "From Curtiz Wine & Spirits Ltd. to Rick

A DAILY PLAN

Can you get to the park by 8:30 a.m.? If so, here's an easy schedule that includes all the best attractions. The keys: Making meal reservations far in advance and getting to the Tower of Terror before it has a long line.

8:30 ARRIVE AT THE PARK As you wait for the gates to open (usually at 8:45 a.m.), visit the adjacent Guest Relations window to pick up a Times Guide and confirm the 11 a.m. Beauty and the Beast show time. If you haven't already, make meal reservations. When the gate opens, be among the first at the Sunset Boulevard rope barrier.

9:00 GET FASTPASSES for Rock 'n' Roller Coaster Starring Aerosmith

9:05 TOWER OF TERROR

9:30 THE GREAT MOVIE RIDE

10:10 ROCK 'N' ROLLER COASTER

10:30 BEAUTY AND THE BEAST SHOW Be among the first in line for the 11 a.m. show. Sit in the center of one of the first non-handicapped rows.

12:00 LUNCH at the Brown Derby. On your way, send one person to Toy Story Mania for Fastpasses. While you eat, check your Times Guide for the afternoon times of the High School Musical and Indiana Jones shows and fine-tune the following plan:

2:00 HIGH SCHOOL MUSICAL 2 SHOW

2:30 BLOCK PARTY BASH

4:00 INDIANA JONES STUNT SHOW

5:00 TOY STORY MANIA

6:00 DINNER at '50s Prime Time Cafe. Share s'mores for dessert.

7:30 MUPPETVISION 3-D

8:30 FANTASMIC You should get there in time to get good seats for the 10 p.m. show.

Those with young children may want to substitute the Playhouse Disney show for one of the choices above. Assumes park hours of 9 a.m. to 10 p.m.

DISNEY'S HOLLYWOOD STUDIOS
park map

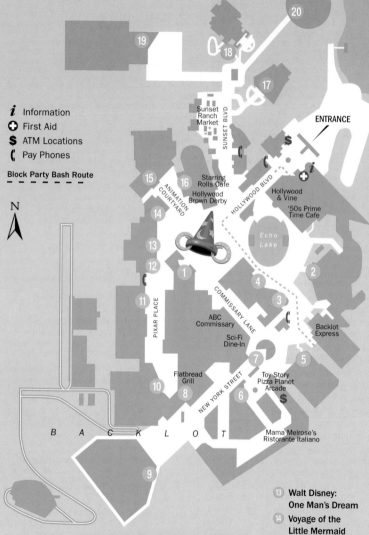

i Information

✚ First Aid

$ ATM Locations

(Pay Phones

Block Party Bash Route

N

Sunset Ranch Market

SUNSET BLVD

ENTRANCE

Starring Rolls Cafe

Hollywood Brown Derby

ANIMATION COURTYARD

HOLLYWOOD BLVD

Hollywood & Vine

'50s Prime Time Cafe

Echo Lake

PIXAR PLACE

ABC Commissary

COMMISSARY LANE

Sci-Fi Dine-In

Backlot Express

Flatbread Grill

NEW YORK STREET

Toy Story Pizza Planet Arcade

B A C K L O T

Mama Melrose's Ristorante Italiano

ATTRACTIONS

1. The Great Movie Ride
2. Indiana Jones Epic Stunt Spectacular
3. Sounds Dangerous
4. ATAS Hall of Fame Showcase
5. Star Tours
6. Jim Henson's MuppetVision 3-D
7. Streets of America
8. "Honey, I Shrunk the Kids" playground
9. Lights, Motors, Action Extreme Stunt Show
10. Backlot Tour
11. Toy Story Mania
12. Journey into Narnia
13. Walt Disney: One Man's Dream
14. Voyage of the Little Mermaid
15. The Magic of Disney Animation
16. Playhouse Disney — Live on Stage
17. Beauty and the Beast — Live on Stage
18. The Twilight Zone Tower of Terror
19. Rock 'n' Roller Coaster Starring Aerosmith
20. Fantasmic

Petite prints. The authors' daughter compares her hands with those of legend Audrey Hepburn.

Blaine, Rick's Cafe Americain, 112642 Rue Renault, Casablanca Morocco," references many aspects of the beloved 1942 movie "Casablanca." ❿ A third crate, marked "From Fleming Fashions Ltd., Atlanta to Scarlett O'Hara, Tara Plantation, 121539 Mitchell Lane, Jonesboro County, Georgia," alludes to the director, premiere city, lead character, main setting, premiere date, novelist and inspiration (Jonesboro, Ga.) for "Gone With the Wind." ⓫ On Sunset Blvd., an office above Villains in Vogue is home to the International Brotherhood of Second Assistant Directors (IBSAD, say it carefully), a union with the motto "We're standing behind you."**

---

* "Allen Smythee" was an official pseudonym-credit used by film, television and music-video directors between 1968 and 1999 when they did not want to be associated with a production. ** During the Great Depression, "Second Assistant Director" was a mercy title given to studio go-fers, who were often told to "Get coffee and stand behind me."

BY THE NUMBERS 》 **122** Height, in feet, of the Sorcerer's Hat. **350** How tall, in feet, Mickey would have to be to wear it. 》 **25,000** Number of outfits created each year by Disney's costuming department, seen on the Backlot Tour. **3.4** Height, in miles, a year's supply of the shop's buttons would reach, if stacked. 》 **300,000** Gallons of water that will fit in the water tower. **0** Gallons of water in the tower, which is just a prop.

hollywood boulevard

Off to see the Wizard, Dorothy and her pals chat in a Great Movie Ride diorama

The Great Movie Ride

✓ The Studio's original showcase attraction creates a dreamlike tribute to the Golden Age of Hollywood. A guided indoor tram travels through 16 classic film scenes, each one brought to life on a soundstage set that is filled with Audio Animatronic characters and special effects.

You pass Gene Kelly "Singin' in the Rain" (1952) and "Public Enemy" James Cagney (1931), get stuck in gangster and Old West shootouts, go under Sigourney Weaver's stalking "Alien" (1979) and head into the Munchkinland of "The Wizard of Oz" (1939) to confront the Wicked Witch of the West. Additional sets portray "Footlight Parade" (1933), "Tarzan and His Mate" (1934), "Fantasia" (1940), "Casablanca" (1942), "Mary Poppins" (1964) and "Raiders of the Lost Ark" (1981). Other robots depict Clint Eastwood and John Wayne. Altogether, the ride depicts nearly every movie genre.

Comedy comes from the tram operator, a self-absorbed projectionist who introduces herself by proclaiming "Let's talk about me!" and "I love movies!" Inspired by Buster Keaton's character in 1923's "Sherlock Jr.," she uses the tram to magically take you into some of her favorite films. Along the way a second performer steps out of a set (a reference to Jeff Daniels in 1985's "The Purple Rose of Cairo") and hijacks your vehicle, but soon meets an untimely demise.

The ride concludes in a theater, with a three-minute montage of film clips.

The best character is the Wicked Witch, a piece of Disney technology that is still the company's most realistic robot. Flexing her backbone, swiveling her hips and pointing her finger, the green-skinned villain has a lifelike face as she confronts your guide: "I'll get you my pretty..."

For the best trip, ask a cast member at the boarding area to let you sit in the first seats in either the first or second row, so you'll be right next to the guide. You may have to wait a few minutes, but the results are worth it. Not only will the guide's spiel make more sense (as you'll always be viewing the same scene), but you'll also get an up-close view of the hijacker, who may direct a few scripted lines your way or talk with you off mic. Once in the "Alien" scene the gangster glanced at the monster, looked over at us and whispered, "I would shoot that but it looks too much like my Aunt Chloe."

The entrance facade and lobby are full-size re-creations of Grauman's Chinese Theatre, a 1927 Hollywood landmark.

Almost two decades after they created it, Disney's Imagineers look back on their

▶ Take your ride before 10 a.m. or at the end of the day, when crowds are light.

Great Movie Ride work with fondness. "It's really dear to my heart," says show producer Eric Jacobson, "not only because of all the effects, but also because of all the work we did. Getting the rights to those movies was not a simple task."

22 min. Capacity: 560. Avg. wait 25 min. late morning, 60 min. peak afternoon (during peak periods, two 70-person vehicles load every 3 minutes). ECV users must transfer. Assistive listening, handheld captioning. Preshow: Highlights from classic movie trailers. Fear factor: Intense for preschoolers. The "Alien" creature moves toward you from the ceiling and then appears suddenly out of the right wall. The Wicked Witch looks real. Best ages: 6 and up. Debuted: 1989.

FUN FINDS ❶ Window displays out front include photos from the real Chinese Theatre's premieres of "Mary Poppins" and "The Jungle Book." ❷ Lobby props include Julie Andrews' "Mary Poppins" carousel horse, which also appears in a queue-line trailer. ❸ The actual theatre is shown in the "Singin' in the Rain" trailer. ❹ The boarding area is lined with actual soundstage equipment. ❺ That area's lights, including those on its Hollywood mural and neon marquee, synchronize to the ride's opening music. ❻ In Gangster Alley, an argument takes place in the flat above Patrick J. Ryan's Bar. One man has a gun. ❼ The Western scene's "Sheriff's Office" sign swings when it gets hit by an illusionary bullet. ❽ Along the left floor of the Nostromo, inside jokes on the first video screen include the ride's "estimated time till next special effects failure" and ❾ a "welcome to all aliens visiting from the Glendale galaxy."* ❿ The third screen lists an astronaut as "still programming the witch." ⓫ Once it captures its victim, the eyes of the Anubis statue glow red. ⓬ Along the left wall of the skeleton room, a snake squirms out of a sarcophagus eye and ⓭ a pharaoh pets a mummified cat. ⓮ A Munchkin pops out of a manhole next to the start of the yellow brick road at the beginning of "Ding Dong the Witch is Dead," just as in the film. ⓯ After the Wicked Witch warns "Just try to stay out of my way, just try," a Munchkin hiding behind her peeks out for a moment.

* Glendale, Calif., is home to Walt Disney Imagineering.

"Maybe nobody will get hoit." Before hijacking the tram, Mugsy the gangster fights off a mob ambush.

FUN FACTS ❯❯ Replicas of statues at the actual Chinese Theatre, two Fu Dogs guard the central entrance doors. Fu Dogs were used in early China to ward off evil spirits. ❯❯ Filling 95,000 square feet, the ride has more than 60 Audio Animatronic characters and nearly 3,000 effects. ❯❯ The Cagney robot wears one of the star's actual tuxedos, donated by his family. ❯❯ Gangster Alley buildings and signs refer to classic movies. Ryan's Bar, J.L. Altmeyer & Sons Novelty Manufacturing, the Red Oaks Social Club and Western Chemical Co. are settings in "The Public Enemy." The signs "Dead End" and "Society for Juvenile Delinquents" refer to the 1937 Bogart film "Dead End." ❯❯ In the Western town, a "Ransom Stoddard" placard alludes to the attorney Jimmy Stewart played in 1962's "The Man Who Shot Liberty Valence." ❯❯ Historical references include the "021-429" license plate on the gangsters' 1931 Chrysler (the Feb. 14, 1929, St. Valentine's Day massacre) and the Western town's Monarch Saloon (the Leadville, Colo., home to outlaw gambler Doc Holliday) and Cochise County Courthouse (the site of Tombstone, Ariz.'s gunfight at the O.K. Corral.) ❯❯ The "No Help Wanted" and "Sheriff's Office" signs are actual props from the MGM backlot. ❯❯ The attraction was built to portray three "Wizard of Oz" scenes. The "Fantasia" room was to be Dorothy's tornado (note the sepia-toned funnel). In the final theater, you were to be told to "pay no attention to that man behind the curtain." Last-minute copyright snags forced the cutback. ❯❯ The oldest of the finale's 247 movie clips comes from a 1925 Charlie Chaplin film, "The Gold Rush."

▶ Want the outlaw? Tell the cast member at the entrance to the boarding area.

hollywood boulevard

High School Musical 2: School's Out

✓ This live street show features six songs from the "High School Musical" movies. More than a dozen young entertainers perform choreographed routines with explosive energy. They invite kids to join them in "Work This Out," "All For One" and "We're All In This Together."

Getting a good viewing spot requires some advance planning. Since the stage rolls down Hollywood Boulevard before it locks down in front of the Sorcerer's Hat, guests are not allowed to stand in front of it until just seconds before showtime, when cast members escort a few dozen guests there. To get these seats, arrive 30 to 40 minutes early and stand along the right side of Hollywood Boulevard, about a hundred feet out from the Sorcerer's Hat, right on the thin brass line that's embedded in the pavement. To get a front-row-center spot, stand directly behind the water meter cover.

20 min. Hollywood Blvd., directly in front of the Sorcerer's Hat. Shows throughout the day. Debuted: 2007.

Dancers bring the Wildcat spirit to life

The Citizens of Hollywood

✓ A witty troupe of improvisational actors, the Citizens of Hollywood are the living, breathing residents of this 1940s Tinseltown. Hollywood wannabes and has-beens, directors and film crews, even some cops and construction workers, up to 20 characters roam Hollywood and Sunset Boulevards at any one time, chatting with guests and holding audience-participation skits (to be picked for one, smile and make eye contact). You'll find them on the streets throughout the day, including during the half-hour before the Block Party Bash. For other times ask the park's Guest Relations office. The performers never break character, a fact that impresses even other actors. "These guys have way more commitment than I do," says actor John Corbett. "I'm supposed to be the 'real' actor, but in my job when they say 'action' I stay in character for about a minute and a half, just until they say 'cut.'"

Citizen of Hollywood Ima Fraudian

park puzzler

How much do you know about Disney's Hollywood Studios?

1) In the Great Movie Ride, what does Clint Eastwood say as you pass him?
a. "Do you feel lucky?"
b. "Go ahead, make my day."
c. He doesn't speak.

2) In Star Tours, your planned destination is...
a. The moon of Endor.
b. The rings of Naboo.
c. The jowls of Jar Jar.

3) The MuppetVision 3-D finale is titled...
a. "A Salute to All Nations."
b. "A Salute to America."
c. "A Salute to All Nations but Mostly America."

4) The Lights, Motors, Action stunt show is introduced as:
a. Bippity Boppity Bang.
b. When You Wish Upon a Car.
c. Voyage of the Little Mermaid.

5) The man at right is...
a. Angry at the price of his turkey leg.
b. A star of the new Studios stage show "Pirates of the Caribbean: Dead Man's Dinner."
c. An actor taking a break from filming a commercial on New York Street.

6) According to its elevator signs, how many floors are in the Hollywood Tower Hotel?
a. 12.
b. 13.
c. 14.

7) What company do you tour at Rock 'n' Roller Coaster?
a. G-Force Records.
b. Fly-By-Night Music.
c. Twist 'n' Shout Studios.

8) In "Beauty and the Beast," Gaston claims he's the size of...
a. A barge.
b. A blimp.
c. A bear.

Answers, page 331

Indiana Jones Epic Stunt Spectacular

✓ Seventeen performers re-create physical stunts from 1981's "Raiders of the Lost Ark" in this outdoor stage show.

First you relive the opening scene, as the actor playing Indiana drops, literally, into a Mayan ruin. Pursuing a golden idol, he dodges spears, hatchet-slamming statues and a giant rolling boulder. Next, Indy and Marion take on a village of Cairo bad guys. Indy fights 'em off with his bullwhip (and, of course, gun), lots of folks fall off buildings and Marion makes a death-defying escape out of a flipping, flaming truck. For the finale, our heroes are at a Nazi airfield in a North African desert. When a Flying Wing taxis in for fuel, Indy and Marion try again to escape. They fight Nazis in, on and around the spinning plane (its iron-fisted mechanic gives Indy quite a battle), fleeing to safety just as leaking fuel sparks a huge explosion.

Indiana Jones punches a sword-wielding assassin

MEAT, WITH CHEESE Basically the same since 1989, this show hasn't lost its appeal. Most of the stunts look real (notice the face punches as Indy battles the mechanic), there's always something to watch and there's plenty of humor. Audience volunteers are made fun of throughout the show, as are some of the cast. The fighting is punctuated by cartoonish sound effects. Listen for the clang-clang of the frying pan when Marion whacks it into two heads.

Between scenes you learn how sets can be quickly dismantled, how heavy-looking props can be feather-light and how to throw a fake punch. To add to the show, Disney pretends it is a real film shoot. Mock cameramen peer through mock cameras; a pretend director barks out pretend directions. When the Assistant Director of the Second Unit explains "We're going to shoot 36 instead of 24 frames per second," his boss declares "I like it!"

The creation of the attraction was overseen personally by George Lucas. The stunts were designed by the late Glenn Randall, one of Hollywood's most famous stuntmen and horse wranglers, and the stunt coordinator for "Raiders."

The first performance of the day usually has the smallest crowd. The last one is often the best looking, as the darker sky makes the pyro more visible. To be in the show, jump and scream wildly when the "casting director" asks for volunteers.

30 min. Capacity: 2,000. Avg. wait: 10 min. early morning, 30 min. peak afternoon. Fastpass available. Guests may remain in wheelchairs, ECVs. Assistive listening; handheld captioning. Preshow: Selection of audience volunteers. Fear factor: None unless kids think the action is real. Best ages: 8 and up. Debuted: 1989, revised 2000.

FUN FINDS ❶ One of the "volunteers" is a professional stuntman. Can you spot him first? ❷ "I have a bad feeling about this." Indy says this signature George Lucas line during the Cairo street scene as he and Marion become surrounded by bad guys. ❸ At the end of the Cairo scene Marion is kidnapped and taken away in a truck, which appears to circle behind a building, reappear, then flip and catch fire. In reality it stops behind the building and a second, empty truck finishes the circle. Attached to the building, the second truck simply rotates over. As for Marion, though she appears to run out of that burning truck, she actually returns through a small gray crate just to the right of the vehicle. ❹ The sidecar motorcycle is a duplicate of the one Harrison Ford commandeered in the 1989

▶ Get here early to sit in the first few rows. You'll feel the heat from the fires.

film "Indiana Jones and the Last Crusade." It even has the same front-fender license: WH38475. ❺ In the last scene the German mechanic is supposedly chopped up by one of the plane's propellers; in truth he falls through an easily visible trapdoor. ❻ Behind the adjacent Outpost gift shop are three vehicles that were used in the filming of the "Last Crusade," in the scenes where Indy and the Nazis are racing to find the Holy Grail. Just off the sidewalk you'll find the Nazi staff car and truck, as well as the "Steel Beast" tank (its side gun barrel still "exploded" from Indy stuffing it with a rock). Each vehicle still displays the symbol of the film's Republic of Hatay. ❼ Just to the left of the Fastpass machines, a British chap has dug a hole and lowered himself down to the bottom of it. Pull on his rope and the irritable archeologist will talk to you ("I say! Stop mucking about up there!").

FUN FACT ⟫ The sound of the airplane is that of a Ford Tri-Motor, the aircraft used in an early scene of 1984's "Indiana Jones and the Temple of Doom."

A CLASSIC ADVENTURE
The plot of 1981's "Raiders of the Lost Ark" begins in 1936. Archaeology professor Dr. Indiana Jones has just returned from the jungles of Peru, where he has failed to recover a sacred idol from the Temple of the Chachapoyan Warriors. Then the Army calls. It tells him that Nazi Germany has plans to find and possess the Ark of the Covenant, the golden casket used by ancient Hebrews to hold the Ten Commandments. Its supernatural powers, legends say, can wipe out entire armies. Uncle Sam wants Indy to find it first. So off he goes, first to reunite with gutsy old girlfriend Marion Ravenwood, then to Cairo, where the Nazis have recruited henchmen to kidnap Marion and steal her medallion, which can reveal the ark's location. Indy fights off a gang of assassins, and Marion knocks one out with a handy frying pan, but soon she is taken away in a truck, which explodes. Indy thinks she's dead, but then finds her at a Nazi excavation camp that's about to load the Ark on a Flying Wing bound for Germany. The couple tracks down the plane and, while it's fueling, takes it over: Marion shoots Nazis from the cockpit while Indy's fight with a mechanic ends when the bad guy is shredded by a propeller. When leaking fuel catches fire, Indy and Marion run to safety just before everything blows up.

Sounds Dangerous

When television's "Undercover Live" incognito investigator Drew Carey shorts out his tiny spy cam, the theater of his test audience — that's you — goes completely dark. You're at the mercy of your imagination when he opens a jar of bees, gets a shave and bumps an elephant.

The show's OK, but the postshow is better. A collection of old but engaging activity stations, **Sound Works** lets you dub your voice to cartoon and movie characters and make your own sound effects with video help from Disney effects legend Jimmy MacDonald. The walls are lined with gadgets MacDonald used to create effects for 20 classic films. To see Sound Works by it-self enter through the Sounds Dangerous exit, the doors to the right of the entrance.

If you're nursing, Sounds Dangerous offers good privacy. For seven minutes the theater is totally dark and, with your headphones off, quiet. But note: After a minute and 45 seconds the screen comes on for 15 seconds, throwing a dim light on the seats. Then it's dark again for five minutes. When you get sprinkled with water you have 15 seconds before the lights come on for good.

12 min. Capacity: 240. Avg. wait: 6 min. Guests may stay in wheelchairs, ECVs. Assistive listening. Preshow: Video trivia about ABC shows. Fear factor: Some sounds portray scary encounters. Debuted: 1999.

'Probably the brother of Julius Caesar'

To the right of Sounds Dangerous, the **ATAS Hall of Fame Showcase** is a small plaza with 15 bronze busts of television stars, all members of the Academy of Television Arts and Sciences Hall of Fame. Included are Lucille Ball, Andy Griffith and Mary Tyler Moore. Plaques on the back wall list all the inductees for each year. Ignored by most visitors, the plaza seems more suited to a museum than a theme park, or perhaps too many of these once-household names are now just ancient history. As one 9-year-old boy said while eyeing a nameplate, "Hmmm... 'Sid Caesar.' Probably the brother of Julius Caesar." Disney stopped adding busts and plaques in 1996.

It's got legs. You enter Star Tours by walking underneath an All Terrain Armored Transport.

port during a time after the 1983 movie "Return of the Jedi." Darth Vader is dead and the Republic and its rebels (the good guys) have a tentative hold on the galaxy. R2-D2 and C-3PO are working for intergalactic airline Star Tours. You're there to board a tourist shuttle to the Ewoks' moon of Endor.

The queue first weaves through a maintenance bay, where C-3PO and R2-D2 are repairing a Star Tours shuttle. Then you step into a "Droidnostics Center," as a robotic mechanic assembles the company's pilots and navigators.

Finally you board your shuttle, known as a StarSpeeder 3000. R2 is its navigator but its pilot is a rookie, RX-24 ("Rex," as he's known). He's sitting in front of you, at the controls.

Rex makes mistakes immediately, sending your ship off its docking ledge and down through a repair bay, barely missing a swinging crane before flying out a side door — then *past* Endor into a field of ice crystals. You tunnel through the biggest crystal and smash your way out.

Star Tours

You journey into space in this elaborate "Star Wars" attraction, which features an early motion simulator.* For a Lucas project it's surprisingly unrestored, but it does have the same mix of wit and action of the early "Star Wars" films.

The story begins as you enter the building. You're in deep space, inside a space-

But an enemy destroyer is nearby, and is pulling you toward it. "Oh no!" Rex yells. "We're caught in a tractor beam!" A rebel fighter pilot breaks in on your video monitor. "Star Tours?!? What are you doing here? This is a combat zone!"

You get free but then get hit, and fall toward a Death Star. Fortunately, R2-D2 repairs your ship just in time, and you escape.

But it's not over. "I've always wanted to do this!" Rex says as he dives toward the Death Star. "We're going in!" You swoop along the surface, zooming under bridges

* Used by airlines and militaries to train pilots, these enclosed, garbage-truck-sized machines create a sensation of flight by synchronizing their tilts, dives and other movements to films that simulate the view out of windshields.

▶ For the calmest ride, sit in the front of the theater. The back row is the bumpiest.

and into a trench, blasting bad guys along the way. Trailing the lead fighter, you watch as he drops two torpedoes down the Star's exhaust port.

You rocket away just as it explodes.

Despite nearly skidding into a fuel tanker on the way in, you return to your Star Tours hangar shaken but sound.

Choose a middle row for a fun ride that won't make you sick, the back seats for lots of rock 'n' roll. The front row is the most calm. Perfect for photos, a climb-on replica of a Speeder Bike (the woods-weaving vehicle of "Return of the Jedi") sits across from the ride entrance.

7 min. Capacity: 240. Avg. wait: 10 min. early morning, 45 min. peak afternoon. Fastpass available. ECV guests must transfer to an available wheelchair. Guest-activated captioning. Height restriction: 40 in. Fear factor: The vehicle's unpredictable sways and dives can cause motion sickness in guests of any age. Chicken exit. Debuted: 1989 (Disneyland 1987).

FUN FINDS ❶ The entrance area is the "stage set" of a village of Ewoks, those teddy-bear creatures that helped save the day in 1983's "Return of the Jedi." Redwood, sequoia and pine "props" are all just tall enough for a film scene (at night you can hear the Ewoks in their tree huts, talking and drumming). The set also includes a captured, 35-foot-tall Imperial Walker, a woodland path (the brown sidewalk) and, just inside, the directors chairs of stars C-3PO and R2-D2. ❷ "Don't insult me, you overgrown scrap pile!" 3PO snaps to R2 in the maintenance bay. ❸ Pages call "Egroeg Sacul" ("George Lucas" backward), Dr. Tom Morrow (the host of 1970s Magic Kingdom attraction Flight to the Moon) and the owner of a vehicle with the ID "THX-1138" (the first Lucas film, 1971). ❹ Little red men chase each other across the bottom of the large video screen. ❺ A watermelon-sized robot circles around the left floor of the Droidnostics Center. ❻ The mechanic asks for your help ("Could you tell me where this goes?") and gets offended by your attention ("Take a picture, it will last longer"). ❼ A wiggling hand and foot hide in a pile of robotic junk on your right. ❽ "Excuse me but you'll have to check the excess baggage," the gate attendant tells you. "Oh, I'm sorry, I didn't realize that was your husband." ❾ As you leave the Center, two robotic hawks above you tend their nests. ❿ Inside your shuttle, a red plastic strip attached to Rex reads "Remove Before Flight." ⓫ "I have a bad feeling about this!" Rex yells as you fly into the crystals, repeating a line used in nearly every Lucas film. ⓬ As you re-enter the maintenance bay Lucas himself appears as a control-room operator. He's standing in an office in front of you. ⓭ Just before the gift shop, a glass case on your right displays some character sketches and a page of the script from 1999's "Star Wars Episode 1: The Phantom Menace."

A SPACE FANTASY that takes place "a long time ago, far, far away," the "Star Wars" films tell a timeless story of good versus evil. Combining a space-opera plot like those of the Buck Rogers serials of the 1930s and '40s with the use of special effects and modeling similar to the 1968 film "2001 – A Space Odyssey," the films created a mix of wit, mythology and simulated reality that has entranced audiences worldwide for decades.

Some classic "Star Wars" vehicles and weapons play key roles in your Star Tours flight. You become caught in an Imperial Star Destroyer's tractor beam, an invisible force field that can capture and redirect rebel ships. Rebel forces fly the X-Wing starfighter. The symbol of the rebel fleet, its double-layered wings separate into an "X" formation during combat. Luke Skywalker flew one in the first "Star Wars" trilogy. The bad guys use the TIE starfighter, named for its twin ion engines. These bare-bolts machines lack hyperdrives and deflector shields. The Empire's most horrific weapons are its Death Stars. Powered by a fusion reactor in its center, each of these moon-sized space stations is staffed with over a million troops. Its main weapon is a superlaser housed in a crater-like cannon well. There have been three Death Stars. The first destroyed Princess Leia's home planet of Alderaan in 1977's "Star Wars," then fell victim to Luke Skywalker when he dropped a pair of proton torpedoes into its exhaust port. The second was never finished; the rebels destroyed it in 1983's "Return of the Jedi." The third appears during your flight. It's destroyed by the X-Wing in front of you.

FUN FACTS ❭❭ Anthony Daniels provided the voice of C-3PO in the maintenance bay as well as the alien voice. ❭❭ In the Droidnostics Center, two of the droids behind G2-9T were background extras in the first "Star Wars" film.

▶ The Tatooine Traders gift shop often carries Darth Tater, a special Mr. Potato Head.

backlot

Jim Henson's MuppetVision 3-D

✓ Built around a funny 3-D film, this inspired attraction mixes vaudeville humor with silly effects. As you sit in the red-velvet theater from the 1970s television series "The Muppet Show," you watch a typical Muppet misadventure that's accented with bubble showers, cannon fire, even Statler and Waldorf.

The Muppets have renovated the auditorium to debut a new film technology. Nicki Napoleon and his Emperor Penguins tune up in the orchestra pit as the Swedish Chef readies the haphazardly assembled projection equipment. As the film begins, Kermit takes you to the lab of Dr. Bunsen Honeydew, the scientist who has created the devilish Waldo, a "living, breathing 3-D effect."

But everything goes wrong. Assistant Beaker gets caught in the machinery, then nearly sucks up the theater when he tries to fix things with a VacuuMuppet. Miss Piggy storms off the set when she learns her special effects are nothing more than plastic butterflies on sticks.

The finale nearly destroys the theater. When patriotic Sam Eagle tries to condense his three-hour extravaganza ("A Salute to All Nations But Mostly America") into 90 seconds, all the performers end up onstage at once. The result is a chaos of falling, tripping, shooting and, in one case, stripping.

Created in 1990, the theater effects look their age, but the show has so much wit it doesn't matter. Despite Kermit's assurance that "at no time will we be stooping to cheap 3-D tricks," his cast does exactly that. (When Sweetums walks on screen and, for no reason, starts knocking a paddle ball into the audience, he's channeling a famously pointless scene from the 1953 Vincent Price horror film, "House of Wax.") The movie uses its 3-D technology creatively. Its scenes often have enormous depth.

Don't miss the preshow, 12 minutes of backstage banter and general confusion that plays out over synchronized monitors. Even the rarely-used outdoor queue area is worth a look. Wrapping around the rear of the building, the covered walkway is lined with zany drawings and posters.

The attraction was Jim Henson's last major project, and his lavish magical touch is everywhere. That's him voicing Kermit and the Swedish Chef.

25 min. Capacity: 584. Avg wait: 15 min. Guests may remain in wheelchairs and ECVs. Assistive listening; reflective and activated video captioning. Fear factor: A few dark moments. Debuted: 1991.

FUN FINDS ❶ Gonzo and Fozzie are filming a brassy Miss Piggy in the courtyard fountain. Clad in a flowing gown and laced sandals, she's re-creating her Statue of Liberty role in the MuppetVision finale. She stands on a half shell, an homage to the 1879 William Bouguereau painting "The Birth of Venus." ❷ Underneath are three rats in the fountain: Rizzo and two friends snorkeling for coins and fishing for dollars. ❸ An outdoor staircase leads to the projection room, where the Swedish Chef runs a combination editing and catering business (its slogan: "Frøöm Qüick Cüts tø Cöld Cüts"). ❹ A tribute to Harold Lloyd's 1923 black-and-white film "Safety Last!" a grayscale Gonzo hangs from the clock tower. ❺ Around the corner is a reference to classic Warner Bros. cartoons: an ACME anvil. ❻ Atop the brick wall to the right, two of the large round planters are actually ice cream sundaes. ❼ One is half-eaten. ❽ Signs lining the outdoor queue area that winds around the building include movie posters for such films as "Beach Blanket Beaker" and "Kürmet the Amphibian" ("So Mean He's Green") and ❾ placards from Dr. Honeydew's MuppetLabs that help you get from "here" to "there" (an eight-step process), perform experiments such as "How to Stick Out Your Tongue and Touch Your Ear" and understand the surprisingly complex 3-D glasses. These last two include the doctor's doodles. ❿ The outdoor waiting area and adjacent covered bus shelter are trimmed out as a salute to a closet Henson, Frank Oz and others decorated in 1963 when the Muppets were booked on "The Jack Paar Program" at NBC Studios in Radio City. Mistakenly arriving six hours early, they killed time by decorating their dressing room's utility

▶ Save this for the middle of the day. Most of your wait will be watching the preshow.

A revolving brass fountain re-creates one of Miss Piggy's roles in MuppetVision 3-D

closet with some Muppet touch-up paint. Henson and his pals covered the walls with loopy designs and faces, incorporating pipes as noses. ⑪ In the entryway the sign at the Security Office saying "Key Under Mat" isn't lying. ⑫ Inside the office there's a wanted poster for Fozzie (for impersonating a comic) and a Piggy cheesecake calendar. ⑬ The directory case includes listings for Statler and Waldorf's Institute of Heckling and Browbeating and Gonzo's Dept. of Poultry and Mold Cultivation. ⑭ A sign above the 8-foot archway reads "You must be shorter than this to enter." A chip at the top indicates someone didn't see it. ⑮ A hall door leading to the MuppetLabs' Dept. of Artificial Reality reads "This is not a door." ⑯ Hanging from the waiting room ceiling is a net full of Jell-O, a reference to 1950s Mouseketeer Annette Funicello. ⑰ Next to it is a bird cage with a perch — a fish, not a pole. ⑱ Down front a crate labeled "2-D Fruities" is filled with flat cutouts of a banana, cherry and lemon. ⑲ Among the items in a box addressed to the Swedish Chef from Oompah, Sweden's "Sven & Ingmar's Kooking Kollection" is "Der Noodle Frooper." ⑳ A box holding Gonzo's stunt props identifies its contents as "mold, fungus, helmets, helmets covered with fungus and mold, helmets with mold — no fungus" and "fungus and mold — no helmets." ㉑ Frankie's Formal Wear

Muppet man

Jim Henson

Jim Henson created the concept of the Muppets when he was a teenager. As a high-school senior in Washington, D.C., in 1954, the 18-year-old combined the features of a marionette with those of a hand puppet.

Success came fast. While attending the University of Maryland Henson got his own local television show ("Sam and Friends," a 5-minute daily program), appeared on NBC's "Tonight" show and became a hot commodity in the advertising world. Out of college he landed a weekly spot on "Today." In 1962 Jim had his first full-time national gig: performing the piano-playing dog Rowlf on ABC's "The Jimmy Dean Show." In 1966 the Muppets began a series of appearances on the CBS "Ed Sullivan Show."

Then the Children's Television Workshop asked Henson to create characters for its new program, "Sesame Street." Henson did it, but feared it could pigeonhole him as a kiddie act.

He was right. Though his new characters were instant superstars, Henson soon learned that no U.S. network would give him a show of his own. In 1975 NBC gave him a limited role on its new "Saturday Night Live," but when he pitched ABC on a half-hour comedy-variety show starring Kermit and a cast of new, more adult-oriented characters, it turned him down flat.

British producer Lew Grade gave Henson the money to produce 24 episodes to syndicate. Hosted by a who's who of 1970s movie and television stars, "The Muppet Show" soon became an international hit. At its peak it was watched by 235 million weekly viewers. After a few years Henson moved to films, and by 1989 the world was at Jim Henson's doorstep.

Specifically, the world of Disney. That August he and the company announced a partnership: Disney would buy the rights to certain Muppet characters and Henson would make movies and television shows for Disney, working from the backlot of the just-opened Disney-MGM Studios. Henson bought a house just a few miles north of the Florida park, and by the next spring he was immersed in projects. While filming the new attraction MuppetVision 3-D in California, he simultaneously worked in Florida shooting "The Muppets at Walt Disney World," a TV movie that would be the first public celebration of the new Disney-Henson relationship. It aired on Sunday night, May 13, 1990.

Two days later, it all went away. Henson contracted an aggressive form of pneumonia, and was rushed to a hospital. He died within 24 hours. He was 54.

WHO'S WHO IN MUPPETVISION 3-D

The show combines characters from "The Muppet Show" with stars from other Henson productions from the 1980s. Known for his scared-witless stare, squeaky meep **Beaker** is the victim of Professor Honeydew's inventions... Known for his big imagination, **Bean Bunny** debuted in the 1986 television special "The Tale of the Bunny Picnic" and starred in the 1984–1991 kids' show, "Jim Henson's Muppet Babies"... The head of MuppetLabs, good-natured inventor **Dr. Bunsen Honeydew** creates elaborate gadgets most people don't know they need... Named for his puppeteer Frank Oz, sweetly insecure **Fozzie Bear** never gives up in his quest to be funny, often accenting his routines with a shout of "Wacka! Wacka!"... A skittish perfectionist, beaked mutant **Gonzo** loves to perform stunts and collect fungus, and has an affection for chickens... Named for rock icon Janis Joplin, hippie chick **Janis** played rhythm guitar and tambourine in the "Muppet Show" house band The Electric Mayhem. She played a nurse in the recurring skit "Veterinarians' Hospital"... The first Muppet, **Kermit the Frog** was created by an 18-year-old Henson in 1954 using two halves of a ping-pong ball and his mom's old green coat. He was named for Henson's friend Theodore Kermit Scott, who later became a philosophy professor at Purdue University... A Rubenesque starlet that loves to kick butt, **Miss Piggy** is the Muppet's diva, or at least thinks she is. She flies into a rage whenever she thinks she has been insulted. During the first year of "The Muppet Show" she was known as Miss Piggy Lee, a reference to purring pop songstress Peggy Lee... Inspired by Ratso Rizzo, Dustin Hoffman's homeless con man in the 1969 film "Midnight Cowboy," streetwise **Rizzo the Rat** has a grating personality and New Jersey accent... Stiff and censorious, patriotic **Sam Eagle** is the group's self-appointed moral watchdog. He wants every Muppet production to promote conservative values and stay orderly... The nephew of the theater's owner, **Scooter** is the group's inept stage manager and all-purpose go-fer... Sitting in a balcony box in the theater, curmudgeons **Statler and Waldorf** heckled Kermit and the gang throughout "The Muppet Show." Statler wears the three-piece suit; Waldorf has the mustache... Lovable but short-tempered, the **Swedish Chef** speaks in nearly indecipherable mock-Swedish. From 1988 to 1989 he had his own General Foods breakfast cereal, Cröonchy Stars... Genial monster **Sweetums** was created for the 1971 television special "The Frog Prince," in which he was the pet ogre of a wicked witch... The world's first digitized puppet, **Waldo C. Graphic** made his debut on the "Jim Henson Hour." His movements were created by a puppeteer wearing an electronic glove, which transmitted signals to a computer to generate a wire-frame image.

has sent "emergency tuxedos" for the penguins in a crate stamped "Open in the event of an event." ㉒ The birds' food has arrived, too, in a box from Long Island Sound and Seafood Supplies ("Everything from Hearing to Herring"). ㉓ Catwalks above include the SwineTrek spaceship used in "Pigs in Space" skits of "The Muppet Show" as well as the frontiersman and some wooden soldiers used in the 3-D film's finale. ㉔ At the front is a hydraulic tube from the MuppetVision machine. ㉕ Along the walls are large reprints from the Kermitage Collection, a series of photo portraits issued as a calendar in 1984. They include parodies of Henri Rousseau ("The Sleepy Zootsy") and Hans Holbein ("Jester at the Court of Henry VIII," a portrait of Fozzie holding a banana to his ear. Its Latin phrase "Bananum In Avre Habeo" translates to "I'm holding a banana in my ear."). ㉖ A photo hanging from the ceiling of a banjo-holding, Henson-like Muppet shows a character in a "Muppet Show" Muppeteer band. ㉗ In the front of the room, a sarcophagus peers through a pair of 3-D glasses. (In the movie, a bust of Beethoven in the lab wears a pair on its head. In the next scene, just after Kermit says "This way, folks," a brass bald eagle has them on.) ㉘ In the theater, the penguin orchestra cackles at Statler and Waldorf's barbs (especially when Waldorf says the penguins "probably took the job for the halibut") and cough when they get squirted by Fozzie's boutonniere. One gets sucked up by Beaker's VacuuMuppet. ㉙ Statler and Waldorf gape in amazement at the MuppetVision machine, nod as Waldo bounces off people's heads, duck from the VacuuMuppet and hide when the Swedish Chef brings out his cannon. ㉚ A chicken wanders behind Kermit as the frog begins the tour of MuppetLabs. Later, another flies off its perch. ㉛ In the lab, two goldfish eventually swim in the beaker just above the Chinese-food takeout boxes. ㉜ When Kermit returns, the theater go-fer Scooter and wanna-be rock star Janis ride a bicycle behind him. ㉝ Miss Piggy loses her head during her waterskiing moment. Watch closely and you'll see it ease backward off her body as she is pulled into the lake. ㉞ In the finale, some members of the marching band

▶ The Stage 1 Co. Store has Beaker, Dr. Bunsen Honeydew and Swedish Chef plushies.

aren't wearing pants. ㉟ Manning the projection room, the Chef reassures Kermit that "der machinen is goin' der floomy floomy" as the show begins. After the penguins fire their cannon at the projector, he yells "Schtupid crazy birds!" ㊱ As you leave the theater, the eight holes created by his cannon fire disappear. (Changes in lighting expose, then conceal, these real holes.) ㊲ Exit posters outside the building include ads for Fozzie Bear ("your full-service

funny bear"), penguin outfitter Frankie ("Large formalwear for the hard-to-fit. Small formalwear for the hard-to-find.") and a record album by Rowlf ("the critics are howling!"). ㊳ The adjacent Stage 1 Co. Store gift shop includes the Muppet lockers and Happiness Hotel registration area from the 1981 film "The Great Muppet Caper" as well as nearly two dozen silly signs. One over a doorway reads "Absolutely no point beyond this point."

Streets of America

This collection of streets and building facades is dominated by Beaux Arts-style New York Street, a 500-foot thoroughfare based on the Big Apple's West 40th St.

Details include graffiti, soot stains and a sidewalk stairway that appears to lead to a subway terminal. The antique stoplights were used on New York City roadways during the 1930s. Background noise includes honking horns, playing kids, screeching buses, talking crowds and whistling police. The best find is the "Singin' in the Rain" umbrella. Hanging off a lamppost near Lights Motors Action, it will often mist you with rain when you stand under it.

The north end, a three-dimensional background piece, includes flat representations of the Chrysler, Empire State and Flatiron buildings. The crossing street recalls London and San Francisco.

The street was used sporadically in the past as an actual movie and commercial set. Some of the outdoor scenes of the 1990 film "Dick Tracy" were filmed here.

The Naked City. Building facades expose their framing along the Streets of America.

Mulch, Sweat and Shears

Driving into the Streets of America a few times each day as a truckful of landscape workers, Mulch, Sweat and Shears is actually a hilarious live rock band. As its vehicle transforms into a stage and power source, the group cranks out a 25-minute set of classic tunes and medleys, grabbing audience members to play cow bells and air guitars in a show that rocks hard but never takes itself seriously. The group changes some lyrics to make them more family-friendly: lead singer and wannabe comedian Morris Mulch delivers a line from the Eagles' 1977 hit "Life in the Fast Lane" as "They had one thing in common, they were good... at sports!" As for Aerosmith's raunchy 1975 classic "Walk This Way," this version has more than one strategic mumble.

High hatch. An Opel Corsa leaps across the stage.

Lights Motors Action Extreme Stunt Show

"That was AWESOME!"

"That was BEAUTIFUL!"

"That was GOOD-LOOKIN' STUFF!"

The hosts sure are enthusiastic at this outdoor stage show, and it is unique. Cars and motorcycles fly through the air, and barely miss each other as they skid and spin on the ground, as skilled stunt drivers demonstrate how chase scenes are created for modern action-adventure films. The premise is the filming of a European spy thriller, with a working crew on a live set.

There are four scenes. First, six Opel Corsas race around in a choreographed ballet chase. The cars return to dodge, weave and jump over a blockade of produce stands and trucks (one car appears to jump backward). Then three motorcycles arrive, one jumping through what appears to be a plate-glass window as the cars drive on two wheels and, for a moment, two guys end up on Jet Skis. This scene ends as a motorcyclist falls and, thanks to a special jumpsuit, catches fire. For the finale, a car jumps directly at the audience as 40-foot fireballs billow in the air.

After each scene unfolds, the director appears to combine his shots into a completed scene that is played on a large video screen. (Actually, the video is prerecorded.)

There's also a car that breaks in half.

The set resembles a seaside village marketplace in southern France (one shop is the Café Fracas, the "restaurant of the noisy rumpus"). The show debuted at Disneyland Paris, hence the French connection.

If you can, sit low in the stands, just in front of the columns. You'll get an unobstructed, fairly close view that's still within range of the large overhead fans.

40 min. Capacity: 5,000. Avg. wait: 20 min. Arrive 30 min. early for a good seat. Fastpass available. Guests may remain in wheelchairs, ECVs. Assistive listening devices. Fear factor: Low. All the action is away from the seating area. Debuted: 2005.

FUN FACTS ⟩⟩ Custom-built in Europe, each car has a 150-horsepower motorcycle engine with four forward gears and four reverse gears, which lets it reach the same speed in either direction. ⟩⟩ Each car weighs 1,300 pounds, less than half that of a similar production vehicle. ⟩⟩ Drivers wear the same suits as professional racecar drivers. ⟩⟩ The stage is 6.5 acres. ⟩⟩ All the "live" video was filmed before the show opened in 2005.

▶ Sit on the left and when you leave you'll pass some interesting backstage sights.

Backlot Tour

The Studios doesn't have a working backlot anymore. Disney has shut down the park's filmmaking, demolished its soundstages and torn down its Residential Street. What's left of the park's Backlot Tour is just what were its added touches — a water-effects demo, a glimpse into a staged prop room, a peek into costume and set-building shops (now used for theme-park work) and a stop at a make-believe disaster set.

Today's tour begins with the filming of a faux movie ("Harbor Attack"), a demonstration of how water cannons and fire bursts can simulate torpedo and bombing attacks. As volunteers get splashed on a PT boat, the scenes are filmed and edited into a comical video. After a quick walk through the prop room you're off on the tram tour. You see the park's Mickey-eared water tower, rumble past the costume and scenic shops, then head out to Catastrophe Canyon, a Mojave-Desert-themed special-effects area that puts you in an earthquake, fire and flood all within a minute (sit on the left to get sprayed with water). As you head back you pass some actual movie vehicles and Walt Disney's real 1960s jet.

Once off the tram you exit through the American Film Institute (AFI) Showcase. This walk-through exhibit most recently has featured costume pieces of movie villains, including a witch hat worn by Margaret Hamilton in 1939's "The Wizard of Oz." A display case is filled with ten antique film cameras and projectors.

To make the tour more fun, tell a cast member you'd like to be in the Harbor Attack demonstration. The first show of the day usually begs for volunteers, as crowds are light. You can see the AFI exhibit without going on the full tour: its entrance (the ride exit) is behind the Prop Shop gift shop.

30-40 min. Capacity: 1,000. Avg. wait: 5 min. early morning, 20 min. peak afternoon. Guests may remain in wheelchairs, ECVs. Handheld and activated video captioning. Fear factor: The water demo has fire. The Canyon simulates an earthquake, fire and flood. Debuted: 1989, revised 2004.

SCREEN GEMS Real movie props line the Backlot Tour walkways. In the queue is the Black Pearl figurehead from 2003's "Pirates of the Caribbean: Curse of the Black Pearl" and a wooden model of the sunken USS Oklahoma used in 2001's "Pearl Harbor." The prop warehouse is filled with fun stuff, though little of it is identified. Look closely to find cans of eyeballs and glue from 1988's "Who Framed Roger Rabbit," the shrinking machine and a giant shoe from 1992's "Honey, I Blew Up The Kid," the Austin of England taxi from 1984's "The Muppets Take Manhattan," an 18-foot Holy Temple statue from 1989's "Indiana Jones and the Last Crusade," furniture from the 1990s television show "Dinosaurs," even props from Epcot's old World of Motion attraction: a hang glider and balloon basket with its pilot and chicken.

'Honey, I Shrunk the Kids' Playground

This soft-floored outdoor playground lets children pretend they're the size of bugs, lost in a suburban backyard. Grass blades tower above kids while they climb over a spider web and explore ant tunnels. A hose drips on unaware heads, grass stalks sound off when stepped on, a giant dog nose sniffs passersby. Kids love it all but parents can get cranky —the playground is crowded and there's almost no place to sit. Come early when the mobs aren't here yet. The playground is based on the 1989 film "Honey, I Shrunk the Kids," in which an inventor mistakenly shrinks his children who then get lost in their own yard.

Racing 'round the Doh at the "Honey" playground

Capacity: 240. Guests may remain in wheelchairs, ECVs. Debuted: 1990.

▶ Want to be in the Harbor Attack demo? Tell the cast member at the entrance gate.

Toy Story Mania

✓ It's tough to keep track of reality at this ride-through video shooting game. Though you travel through a real maze of corridors, everything that happens is a 3-D illusion. It's all created by the use of nearly every high-tech effect Disney can muster, including a cannon that launches virtual projectiles, a series of huge synchronized video screens and even a few "4-D" wind, water and aromatic effects.

The result is an addictive treat.

As the name suggests, everything takes place in the fantastic world of the "Toy Story" films. In this case, Andy has received yet another new toy: an old-fashioned midway games playset. When Andy leaves the room, Sheriff Woody and the other toys set it up and, as their guest, you get to play it.

The fun begins as you hop into a four-seat carnival-tram ride vehicle, don your 3-D glasses and try your luck in a practice round. Using a spring-action shooter that sits right in front of you, you splatter some targets with virtual cream pies.

Then you compete against your partner, who sits right next to you, at five carnival booths, each hosted by different "Toy Story" characters. Hamm has you launch plastic eggs at various barnyard targets. Bo Peep and Wheezy urge you to shoot darts at a landscape of virtual-balloon sheep, trees and other objects — some "filled" with real water. The Green Army Men challenge you to break plates with baseballs, while Buzz Lightyear hosts a ring-toss game that stars the Little Green Men space aliens.

For the grand finale, you launch virtual suction-cup darts in "Woody's Rootin' Tootin' Shootin' Gallery," then fire your shooter as rapidly as possible at one last super-target in "Woody's Bonus Roundup."

The contests are designed to be fun for all ages, as the ride adjusts its difficulty to each player's skill. As the ride ends you see how your score compares with the top results of the day, the hour and all-time.

Rex is the ride's stage manager, while the carnival barker is Mr. Potato Head, a 5-foot 2-inch Audio Animatronic figure you meet in the queue. He offers tips on how to get a high score, engages you in a two-way conversation and sometimes takes off his ear.

The game play is accompanied by variations of "You've Got A Friend in Me."

Apx. 4 min. Fastpass available. The 3-D effects may cause discomfort in guests wearing glasses or contact lenses. Located on the former Mickey Ave., in the building that most recently hosted Who Wants to Be a Millionaire — Play It. Opens May, 2008.

HOW TO SCORE BIG ❶ **Focus on high-value targets.** Most are at the top and bottom of the screens. The biggest hits are often in the corners. ❷ **Fire continuously.** You'll inadvertently hit extra targets you aren't even aiming at. Your cannon can fire up to six shots per second. ❸ **Stay alert.** Sometimes hitting one target triggers another of a higher value. In other cases, taking out a group of identical targets generates bonus points. ❹ **Resist the glitz.** Some of the fanciest targets have low point values.

WHO'S WHO IN THE "TOY STORY" FILMS. Andy Davis is a 6-year-old boy, the owner of most "Toy Story" toys. He shares his room with **Molly,** his baby sister. **Woody** is a pull-string cowboy sheriff doll, with a plastic head and hands. The toys' leader, he's a family hand-me-down based on a 1950s television show, "Woody's Roundup." **Buzz Lightyear** is a high-tech action figure who originally believed he was a real space ranger. In "Toy Story," the **Little Green Men** are promotional squeeze toys from the Pizza Planet restaurant. Prizes in a Claw arcade game, they worship the device, and believe it often chooses one of them to "go on to a better place." In the TV series "Buzz Lightyear of Star Command" they serve Star Command as scientists and inventors. Also from "Woody's Roundup," **Jessie** is an excitable, athletic cowgirl, a female counterpart to Woody, while **Bullseye** is Woody's horse, one of the few "Toy Story" toys who doesn't talk. Though he played an idiot hillbilly on "Woody's Roundup," portly **Stinky Pete the Prospector** is really an intelligent, though bitter, old man, a collectible doll who has rarely been out of his box. A voice of reason, **Bo Peep** is a porcelain lamp base who sits on Molly's cribside table. The **Green Army Men** are small plastic soldiers who have been cheaply molded into fixed positions. **Hamm** is a know-it-all piggy bank who loves to stick his snout into the other toys' business. **Mr. Potato Head** is a sarcastic, synthetic spud with the personality and voice of comedian Don Rickles. He can remove, yet still control, his arms, eyes and ears. **Rex** is a neurotic plastic Tyrannosaurus who always fails to be scary. **Wheezy** is an asthmatic, squeeze-toy penguin who eventually develops the velvety singing tones of Robert Goulet.

Early bird. A 1960s Audio Animatronic parrot at the exhibit Walt Disney: One Man's Dream.

Walt Disney: One Man's Dream

A salute to the life of Walt Disney, this exhibit combines a memorabilia museum with a good short film. It includes the school desk Disney used as a Missouri second-grader, his studio desk from the 1930s and his (re-created) 1960s office.

Walt Disney's role in theme-park history is well represented. Hand-built by Disney himself in 1949, a wooden diorama displays his early ideas for dark rides such as Peter Pan's Flight, while a "Dancing Man" electronic marionette tested figure-movement techniques that led to Audio Animatronic robots. Display cases hold models of early attractions. A simulated TV studio shows Disney filming a video to interest investors in his ultimate dream: the Experimental Prototype Community of Tomorrow. The back room has two Audio Animatronic creatures you can control yourself: a robotic man and Tiki bird.

A 200-seat theater shows a moving biographical film. Narrated by Walt Disney through vintage audio clips, the 16-minute film explores Disney's never-ending drive and the hardships he overcame.

Allow 35 min. No wait. Theater capacity: 200. Guests may remain in wheelchairs, ECVs. Assistive listening, handheld and reflective captioning available. On the walkway between Pixar Place and the Animation Courtyard. Debuted: 2001.

Journey into Narnia

Tucked into one of the park's old sound stages, this "Chronicles of Narnia" promotional exhibit has you stand on a carpeted floor and watch clips from the film series, before a live performer appears briefly. Along the exit route you pass a small selection of props and costumes (look over the pieces quickly; the lights go out after just three minutes). The exhibit will be updated during 2008 to reflect the release of "The Chronicles of Narnia: Prince Caspian."

10 min. Capacity: 150. Avg. wait: 10 min. early morning, 30 min. peak afternoon. Guests can remain in wheelchairs, ECVs. Preshow: Video monitors offer behind-the-scenes glimpses into the films. On the walkway between Pixar Place and the Animation Courtyard. Debuted: 2005.

animation courtyard

Voyage of the Little Mermaid

Black-light puppets, live actors and imaginative effects tell the story of Ariel in this condensed version of Disney's 1989 animated movie, "The Little Mermaid."

As a water curtain opens across the stage, the show begins with a rousing black-light puppet version of "Under the Sea." Then you meet Ariel (she wants legs, and Prince Eric) who belts out "Part of Your World" like a Broadway star. Ursula the Sea Witch — a parade-float-sized Audio Animatronic octopus — slithers in to trick Ariel out of her voice, singing "Poor Unfortunate Soul." Video clips advance the plot to the finale, where the live actress grows her gams and hugs her honey.

The Howard Ashman lyrics alone make the show worthwhile. *"Out in the sun they slave away,"* the puppet Sebastian the crab sings, *"while we devotin' full time to floatin'."* After Ariel's dad forbids her to go to the surface, the teen sulks *"Betcha on land they understand. Bet they don't reprimand their daughters."* The theater's high-backed cloth seats, dark ambiance and cool breezes make it a great place to relax.

17 min. Capacity: 600. Avg. wait: 10 min. early morning, 45 min. peak afternoon. Fastpass available. Guests may remain in wheelchairs, ECVs. Assistive listening, reflective captioning. No flash photography. Fear factor: Real. Ursula causes some toddlers to cry. Debuted: 1992.

FUN FIND Hanging over the right entrance door to the theater is a Disney-fied replica of P.T. Barnum's infamous 1842 "FeJee Mermaid," which the huckster displayed as a real mermaid caught off the Fiji Islands. In truth it was the shriveled body of a monkey stitched to the dried tail of a fish.

REBEL REBEL The 1989 film "The Little Mermaid" broke new ground for a Disney heroine: Ariel's dream comes true because she rebels against her father and takes action herself. Her problem: She wants legs, and the human Prince Eric. Ursula the Sea Witch offers to make the girl human — if Ariel will give up her voice and agree to get it back only if she kisses Eric within three days. Then Ursula transforms herself into a rival beauty — with Ariel's voice — and nearly marries the prince herself. A singing crab and a friendly fish help Ariel land her man. The movie leaves out some grim moments of Hans Christian Andersen's 1836 fable. In that version, when a grandmother puts flowers in the mermaid's hair for her 15th birthday she also clasps eight oysters on the girl's tail, as "pride must suffer pain." The Sea Witch takes the girl's voice by cutting out her tongue. The mermaid and the prince don't live happily ever after; he dumps her for the girl next door. Heartbroken, the mermaid dissolves into the sea foam and becomes a spirit.

She wants more. Gadgets and gizmos aplenty aren't enough for Ariel.

▶ The best seats are in the middle. The front row sits too low to see onto the stage.

Hollywood Studios shopping guide

APPAREL

CHARACTER COSTUMES In Character *(at Voyage of The Little Mermaid, Animation Courtyard)* has princess costumes and a create-your-own-crown station.

CHILDREN'S WEAR The best collections are at L.A. Cinema Storage *(Hollywood Blvd.)* and Stage 1 Co. Store *(next to MuppetVision 3-D, Backlot)*. The Playhouse Disney stands *(Animation Courtyard)* have a few shirts themed to Disney Channel programs.

FASHION Keystone Clothiers *(Hollywood Blvd.)* is the Studios' main fashion store. Legends of Hollywood *(Sunset Blvd.)* has stylish Tinker Bell apparel.

FOOTWEAR You'll find sandals at Keystone Clothiers *(Hollywood Blvd.)*. Stage 1 Co. Store *(at MuppetVision 3-D, Backlot)* has infant and kids shoes.

SPORTS APPAREL Mouse About Town *(Sunset Blvd.)* is the park's sports shop.

T-SHIRTS AND HEADWEAR Mickey's of Hollywood *(Hollywood Blvd.)* has the most. Stage 1 Co. Store *(at MuppetVision 3-D, Backlot)* has Muppet-character shirts. Sunset Ranch Souvenirs *(Sunset Blvd.)* has lots of hats.

OTHER MERCHANDISE

ART Artists at Sunset Club Couture and Once Upon a Time *(Sunset Blvd.)* will sketch a personalized Disney character as you watch. The Animation Gallery *(Animation Courtyard)* sells glass vases, decorative plates and stemware, ceramics, quality lithographs, posters and prints and commercial sericel art.

BOOKS The tiny Writer's Stop *(adjacent to the Sci-Fi Dine-In Theater, Backlot)* has a small selection of paperbacks, hardcovers, cookbooks, and Disney titles. Movie and television books are at Sid Cahuenga's One-Of-A-Kind *(Hollywood Blvd.)* and the AFI Showcase *(Backlot Tour exit, Backlot)*. Tower Hotel Gifts *(Tower of Terror exit, Sunset Blvd.)* has Twilight Zone titles. Tatooine Traders *(Star Tours exit, Backlot)* has Star Wars books. A few animation books are available at the Animation Gallery *(Animation Courtyard)*.

CANDY Sweet Spells *(Sunset Blvd.)* makes its own chocolate-covered strawberries and caramel apples. Other treats include cotton candy, fudge, lollipops and cookies.

CHRISTMAS Once Upon a Time *(Sunset Blvd.)* is the park's Christmas corner. You'll find "Nightmare Before Christmas" items at the nearby Villains in Vogue *(Sunset Blvd.)*.

HOUSEWARES The Writer's Stop *(next to the Sci-Fi Dine-In Theater, Backlot)* has a few items.

JEWELRY AND WATCHES Artists at Sunset Club Couture *(Sunset Blvd.)* draw personalized sketches of Disney characters and reduce them onto watch dials. The store also sells more conventional watches, fine jewelry, Lenox china figurines, snow globes and statuettes. You'll also find watches at the adjacent Mouse About Town. Across the street, Sunset Ranch Souvenirs and Gifts has costume jewelry. The open-air Indiana Jones stand *(at the Indiana Jones Epic Stunt Spectacular, Echo Lake)* has a nice collection of casual jewelry.

PET PRODUCTS The Studios' largest selection of pet products is at Legends of Hollywood *(Sunset Blvd.)*. It carries beds, bowls, clothes, dishes, leashes, toys and treats. The Writer's Stop *(Backlot)* has a small variety.

PINS Pin central is the open-air shop underneath the Sorcerer's Hat *(Hollywood Blvd.)*. The Hollywood Junction kiosk *(Hollywood Blvd. at Sunset Blvd.)* has a decent selection.

TOYS The biggest toy store is L.A. Cinema Storage *(Hollywood Blvd.)*. Among the lures are Disney princess dolls and a create-your-own Mr. Potato Head station. Across the street, Mickey's of Hollywood is packed with just about every other Walt Disney World plaything. The Stage 1 Co. Store *(Backlot)* has Muppet action figures and plushies. Indiana Jones action figures, guns and snakes await you at the Indiana Jones Adventure Outpost *(Indiana Jones Epic Stunt Spectacular, Echo Lake)* and the nearby Indiana Jones stand *(next to the Backlot Express restaurant)*. May the force, or at least willpower, be with you at Tatooine Traders *(at the Star Tours exit, Backlot)*. It's filled with "Star Wars" temptations, including miniature versions of the attraction's Starspeeder 3000 spacecraft. A few Playhouse Disney toys are sold at the Playhouse Disney stands *(Animation Courtyard)*.

A Hollywood Tower Hotel door hanger from the Tower of Terror gift shop

animation courtyard

Top left: Tigger leads the audience in bouncing at Playhouse Disney — Live on Stage. **Top right:** Leo and June from the "Little Einsteins" lead guests in clapping. **Above:** Handy Manny and Mr. Pat fix a bubble machine. **Left:** Kids love seeing the stars of Playhouse Disney programs.

Playhouse Disney — Live on Stage

The stars of the Playhouse Disney programs "Mickey Mouse Clubhouse," "Handy Manny," "Little Einsteins" and "My Friends Tigger and Pooh" star in this elaborate puppet show, which includes animated graphics, catchy songs and many opportunities for children to participate in the fun. As kids watch four short stories from a carpeted floor, they're encouraged to get up and bounce, dance, cheer, shout, clap in rhythm and catch falling bubbles, leaves and streamers.

As soon as the lights dim children sense this is a show all their own. Production values are the equal of any Disney show. The life-like puppets open their mouths and blink their eyes. The studio sound is crisp, and nearly a hundred spotlights provide professional theatrical lighting.

The plot? Mickey Mouse wants to throw Minnie a surprise party, but none of his pals can figure out how to pull it off.

"Whenever I need some help with ideas," says Casey, the show's perky live host, "I

▶ Sit halfway back, not in the front, so your child can see onto the elevated stage.

get them from stories." Soon the stage transforms into three storybook sets, all of which teach gentle lessons about working together. As the show concludes, Minnie's party is a complete success.

Have your kids sit along an inner aisle to interact with Casey.

22 min. Performed several times daily. Capacity: 600. Avg. wait: 25 min. Guests may remain in wheelchairs and ECVs. Assistive listening, reflective and activated captions. Preshow: Outdoor monitors show Playhouse Disney characters. Best ages: 2–6. Debuted: 2001, latest revision 2008.

FUN FINDS ❶ Adults who stand at the rear of the theater can often see the heads of the puppeteers. ❷ When the live host stands to the side of the stage, he (or she) sometimes "chats" with whatever puppets aren't in the spotlight. ❸ When Casey asks Goofy what he learned from the "Little Einsteins" story, for a moment the dippy dog can't think of anything.

FUN FACTS ›› As in the "Handy Manny" television show, Manny is voiced by Wilmer Valderrama, best known as Fez on "That '70s Show." ›› The voice of Manny's hammer Mr. Pat is Tom Kenny, who is also the voice of SpongeBob Squarepants.

DON'T KNOW YOUR MEESKA FROM YOUR MOOSKA? You're not alone. Though the Disney Channel's daily block of Playhouse Disney preschool programs is well-known among the juice-box set, many older kids and adults have never heard of them. Here's a primer: Mickey and his pals help viewers solve problems on **"Mickey Mouse Clubhouse."** When they need assistance they shout "Oh Tootles!," a call which brings forth a magical flying machine equipped with "mouse-ka-tools." The clubhouse itself appears when the characters call "Meeska, Mooska, Mickey Mouse!" **"Handy Manny"** features the adventures of friendly bilingual handyman Manny Garcia and his talking tools. **"Little Einsteins"** uses classical music to urge preschoolers to gesture, sing or otherwise interact with its four smart children as they travel the world on various missions. Helping them out is Rocket, a transformable air-, space- and watercraft. Big Jet, Rocket's nemesis, sometimes interferes. Based on Disney's "Winnie the Pooh" characters, **"My Friends Tigger & Pooh"** adds a new one, a red-haired girl named Darby. The 6-year-old and her pals love to solve mysteries as "Super Sleuths," though impatient Tigger often needs Darby to remind him to "think, think, think." Each show is computer-animated. "Mickey Mouse Clubhouse" represents the first time Disney has used computer-generated versions of its Fab Five characters as stars of a film or television series. They debuted in CGI form in 2003, at Walt Disney World's Magic Kingdom attraction Mickey's PhilharMagic.

The Magic of Disney Animation

This lightweight attraction consists of a short film, a hands-on drawing lesson, some computer games, an air-conditioned chance to meet characters and some exhibits.

The film presentation, "Drawn to Animation," shows how Disney created Mushu, the dragon sidekick in 1998's "Mulan." A large open area is filled with preschooler-friendly computer games. Nearby, stars from a recent Disney movie meet, greet and pose for pictures.

You learn to draw a Disney character at the Animation Academy, a classroom setting in which you sit at a drafting table, follow step-by-step instructions from a live artist and keep your sketch.

The final area is the Animation Gallery, a few small rooms filled with conceptual models and drawings, including Tinker Bell

as a redhead and Buzz Lightyear with a pompadour. A glass case holds a dozen Oscars. The one for "It's Tough to be a Bird" is the actual award from the 1970 ceremony.

Film: 10 min. Animation Academy: 10 min. Rest self-guided. Capacity: Theater: 150; Animation Academy: 50. Avg. wait: 10 min. early morning, 30 min. peak afternoon. Typically no wait after the characters leave (about 5:30 p.m.). Guests may remain in wheelchairs, ECVs; lap boards available for drawing. Reflective, video captioning. Debuted: 1989, revised 2004.

FUN FIND Take too long to make your choices at the Soundstage screens and Ursula, the "Little Mermaid" Sea Witch, will shout "Hurry and make a choice! I have fish sticks in the oven!"

▶ The first Playhouse Disney show of the day is often the least crowded.

Beauty and the Beast — Live on Stage

✔ This uplifting theatrical show fully re-creates the spirit of Disney's 1991 animated film by focusing entirely on its music. "Belle," "Gaston," "Be Our Guest," "Something There," "The Mob Song," "Beauty and the Beast" — they're all here. Most lead vocals are sung live.

The supporting cast is terrific. When Gaston struts on stage the village girls fight over him with flirty passion; when he chooses Belle they stalk off in a huff. The "Be Our Guest" maids squeal in delight when Lumiere announces dinner. Two tickle Belle with their feather dusters; later two whisper to each other, leave the stage and return with a sundae that becomes a warbling diva.

Colorful costumes and special lighting effects add to the theatrical feel. In the first scene the supporting cast wears six different hues. In the ballroom scene Belle's gold gown is offset by the other girls' vivid pink dresses. The stage arch flashes during "Be Our Guest." Dappled lights color "The Mob Song."

25 min. Capacity: 1,500. Guests may remain in wheelchairs and ECVs. Assistive listening. Fear factor: During "The Mob Song" Gaston stabs the Beast, but you don't see the wound. Debuted: 1991, revised 2001.

FUN FINDS ❶ The show begins with a pun: a ringing bell. ❷ As Gaston incites the mob, one couple remains skeptical. One of them never joins in.

Top: Belle yearns for "adventure in the great wide somewhere." **At right:** From stage hands to stage hams, a group of "stage workers" walks on stage 15 minutes before showtime to become the crowd-pleasing a cappella group Four for a Dollar.

FUN FACT ⟫ "The Mob Song" includes a quote from Shakespeare. "Screw your courage to the sticking place" Gaston says as he rallies the villagers to kill the Beast — the same phrase Lady Macbeth uses to urge her husband to kill Duncan.

▶ For a full experience, get in line 45 minutes before showtime and sit down front.

Celebrity impressions

Many Hollywood celebrities have placed their hands and feet into Studios concrete. The Chinese Theatre courtyard has more than 100 prints. Front and center is the work of Warren Beatty (shown above making his mark in 1990); nearby are the marks of Bob Hope, Jim Henson (who brought Kermit) and Dustin Hoffman and Robin Williams (who brought their kids). Others on hand: George Burns, Tony Curtis and George Lucas. On Sunset Blvd., 30 TV stars have left impressions at the Theater of the Stars in a small plaza next to the rear bleachers. "Star Trek's" Scotty, James Doohon, added "Beam Me Up" while "Jeopardy" host Alex Trebek wrote "Who is Alex Trebek?" Also here: Morey Amsterdam from "The Dick Van Dyke Show," Imogene Coca from "Your Show of Shows," Bob Denver from "Gilligan's Island," June Lockhart from "Lassie," George Wendt from "Cheers," even journeyman Martin Mull.

Most prints are from the early 1990s, made at ceremonies during the park's old "Star of the Day" events. During Charlton Heston's 1995 ceremony, a photographer yelled "Charlton!" just as the Hollywood legend was drawing out the "R" in his first name, causing him to look up. When the then-72-year-old star got back to work, he accidentally skipped the next letter of his name, creating a signature that reads "Charton" Heston.

Not all of Disney's prints are on display. Some, including those of Johnny Depp, are stored backstage. All are real except the impressions of Judy Garland's ruby slippers from "The Wizard of Oz," which are replicas of those in the concrete slab at the California theater.

A Tale As Old As Time

"Beauty and the Beast" got its start in Roman mythology. In **"Cupid and Psyche,"** philosopher Lucius Apuleius told the tale of Psyche, the youngest of three mortal sisters. Incredibly pretty, Psyche earns the envy of Venus, the goddess of beauty. But when Venus orders her son, Cupid, to make the girl fall in love with a castle-dwelling snake, Cupid himself falls in love with her, and secretly turns himself into the snake. Cupid gives Psyche a great life in the castle, including invisible servants who prepare her food, and eventually turns himself back to a man.

The story spreads as societies became mobile, and eventually over 200 Eurasian folk tales have a similar plot: a beautiful girl with two mean sisters finds herself living with a beast, who becomes human once she cares for him. A Chinese version makes a few changes — including a "golden shoe" — and becomes the first "Cinderella."

The love of a good woman turns a pig into a prince in the first published beauty-and-beast fable. Produced soon after printing presses became widespread in 1553, **"The Pig King"** was one of many folk tales transcribed by Italian novelist Giovanni Straparola. This beast marries all three sisters, one at a time. He kills the oldest two because they don't like him "climbing into bed stinking with filthy paws and snout."

The Beast is a snake again in 1650, when the story becomes a popular parlor tale among French aristocrats. In this, the first story named **"Beauty and the Beast,"** a king has three daughters, and one day he leaves to get them each a gift. When he comes upon a deserted castle he plucks a rose for his youngest, named Beauty. "Who said you could take my flower?" a voice asks. "I will kill you for that, unless you bring me one of your girls." Beauty volunteers. She doesn't see anyone when she arrives at the castle, but the next morning wakes up to find a serpent in her lap. "You must marry me," it hisses. Beauty says no, but the snake persists. It orders its servants to starve her, and each day repeats its demand. Finally, she gives in. "I won't marry a serpent," she says, "but I will marry a man." The snake turns itself into a handsome prince.

Oodles of *oo-lá-lá* come into the story once French blueblood **Gabrielle de Villeneuve** gets hold of it in 1740. Writing for the pleasure of her salon friends, she turns her prince into a beast after he refuses a promiscuous fairy. When Beauty arrives, he doesn't ask "Will you marry me?" but "Will you go to bed with me?" He stays a beast until after the wedding night.

The story becomes a child's fable 16 years later. In 1756, French tutor **Jeanne-Marie Leprince de Beaumont** publishes her version, a tale she had written to prepare her young charges (girls ages 5–13) for arranged marriages. She bases her story on the earlier serpent tale, but makes the Beast a humble, gentle mammal. Wanting her girls to believe that love can make any man princely, Beaumont contrasted Beauty's beastly fate with that of the girl's two sisters: The first is matched with a handsome man who thinks only of himself. The second gets a smart man who belittles his bride. "Many women," this Beauty ponders, "are made to marry men far more beastly than mine." Beaumont's own arranged marriage had been annulled when her philandering husband contracted a venereal disease. To encourage girls to read, Beaumont makes Beauty a book lover. Her story becomes the definitive "Beauty" fairy tale.

The love of a beauty rescues the soul of a bloodthirsty beast in the first "Beauty and the Beast" movie, a 1947 French film by avant-garde artist **Jean Cocteau.** The adult melodrama grows tedious in its second act (40 minutes of little more than the Beast bellowing "Belle!") but its surreal images (living busts and candelabras, and a disembodied arm that pours wine) make it an art-house favorite. Its Beauty is no role model. She faints when she first sees the Beast and shudders ecstatically when she sees him again. A remake of the film appears in 1983 as an episode of the Showtime television series "Faerie Tale Theatre." Directed by French auteur Roger Vadim, it stars a blond Susan Sarandon.

Can a man sleep in a sewer and still hook up with a society gal? That's the premise of the 1987–1990 **CBS television series** "Beauty and the Beast." Linda Hamilton plays Catherine Chandler, a wealthy New Yorker who wants more out of life. Ron Perlman is Vincent, her beasty boy beneath the streets.

It's no wonder **Disney's** animated "Beauty and the Beast" was nominated for a Best Picture Oscar. Packed with life, humor and music, it also has a great message: A girl can be herself, speak her mind and still end up with a prince of a hubby. Smart, gutsy and with plans for her life, this Belle is no pushover. The villagers say she's a "most peculiar mademoiselle" but she couldn't care less; while street tarts swoon for the town hunk she pushes him off. And when the Beast yells at her, she yells back.

Disney keeps the meat of Beaumont's tale but cuts the fat, eliminating the sisters and downplaying the dad. And it adds a villain: the handsome Gaston, who grows beastly as the Beast grows human.

On a different note, Disney's production is an homage to Broadway and Hollywood.

The song "Belle" gets its bickering villagers and throwaway jokes from "Tradition," the rousing introductory number to 1964's "Fiddler on the Roof." Its "Bonjour! Bonjour!" refrain comes from the "Good Morning! Good Day!" opener to the 1963 stage play "She Loves Me." "Be Our Guest" is a tableware take on Busby Berkeley's "By a Waterfall" sequence in 1933's "Footlight Parade." The title-song waltz features its couple like "Shall We Dance" portrays Anna and her King in 1951's "The King and I." The enchanted objects have their own ancestors. Mrs. Potts is a jollier Mrs. Bridges, the cook from the 1970s British TV drama, "Upstairs Downstairs." Lumiere blends dashing Maurice Chevalier from 1958's "Gigi" with Pepé Le Pew, Warner Brothers' Looney Tunes scent-imental skunk created in 1945.

A Voice of Life

The lyrics in Disney's "Beauty and the Beast" reveal a poet at the top of his game. "Belle" is a prologue, filled with story details that typically take up a first act. "Gaston" is a pub song *("No one's slick as Gaston, no one's quick as Gaston, no one's neck's as incredibly thick as Gaston's")* while "Be Our Guest" bubbles with swing *("Try the gray stuff, it's delicious! Don't believe me? Ask the dishes!")* The title song is elegant: *"Ever just the same, ever a surprise. Ever as before, ever just as sure as the sun will rise."* Ironically, these lyrics, so full of life, were written by a man on his deathbed. Howard Ashman penned them while dying of AIDS.

Howard Ashman

A New York playwright, Ashman had his first success in 1982. Working with composer Alan Menken, his musical version of "Little Shop of Horrors" (a quirky story of a flower-shop worker and a man-eating plant) became the top-grossing off-Broadway musical ever. Ashman later wrote the screenplay. After penning "Once Upon a Time in New York City" for Disney's 1988 "Oliver and Company," Ashman was hired as the lyricist for "The Little Mermaid." His witty wordplay *("bright young women, sick of swimmin'")* helped make the film Disney's first animated blockbuster since Walt Disney died of lung cancer in 1966. In response, the company made Ashman the executive producer as well as the lyricist of its next major film, "Beauty and the Beast." Just after production began in 1989, however, Ashman learned he had contracted HIV.

Given the times, Ashman kept the news to himself. He had loved Disney musicals since he was a kid (you can hear the influence of songs such as "Cruella de Vil" in his lyrics) and wanted to continue his work. When he acknowledged his illness a year later (two days after winning the Best Song Oscar for "Under the Sea") Disney stuck by him. When Ashman could no longer travel it moved the film's development from California to New York, setting up shop at a hotel near his home.

The dying artist gave it his all. To offset Disney's strong Belle, Ashman built a better Beast: a creature with a clear reason to be cursed (he's selfish) and a deadline to fix it (his 21st birthday). He focused the script on men (the Beast and Gaston) as much as women. To add life to the second act, when Beauty and Beast do little but have dinner, Ashman created a comic Greek chorus of enchanted objects. Even when he could no longer leave his bed Ashman still kept working. He finishd the project over the phone.

Then he died, at age 41 in March 1991, six months before the film was released. His second Oscar (Best Song for "Beauty and the Beast," awarded posthumously) was the first to a known AIDS victim.

Some believe Ashman built the story as an AIDS allegory. In 1992 CBS newsman Dan Rather wrote that you could think of Ashman's Beast as a metaphor for an AIDS victim: "He's just a guy trying as hard as he can to find a little love, a little beauty, while he's still got a little time left." In "The Mob Song" some listeners find a commentary on gay bashing. *"The Beast will make off with your children,"* Gaston warns the villagers, who then chant *"We don't like what we don't understand, in fact it scares us, and this monster is mysterious at least.* Sally forth, tally ho, praise the Lord and here we go: Kill the Beast!"*

Regardless of how you interpret his work, Howard Ashman was undeniably a creative genius, cut down at his most productive time by a preventable disease. Just like Walt.

* This line is omitted from the theme park show.

sunset boulevard

The Twilight Zone Tower of Terror features a high-speed drop into the dark mysterious realm of the Twilight Zone.

WARNING!

For safety, you should be in good health and free from high blood pressure, heart, back or neck problems, motion sickness, or other conditions that could be aggravated by this adventure.

Expectant mothers should not ride.

Supervise children at all times.

Persons who do not meet the minimum height requirement may not ride.

Must transfer

A cautionary notice at the ride entrance

The Twilight Zone Tower of Terror

Loaded with spectacular effects and detail, this attraction is painstakingly designed to freak you out. Checking in to an otherworldly hotel, you climb into a freight elevator as souls of earlier guests beckon you to join them. Then you enter the dark, supernatural Fifth Dimension, where you fall up to 130 feet.

And it's never the same ride twice.

Meant to recall the peculiar look and feel of the classic television series "The Twi-

"I tried it, I hated it, I'm never doing it again. Like Brussels Sprouts."

— *Girl, 5, to her mother after riding The Twilight Zone Tower of Terror*

light Zone," the attraction is even more fun if you know its story.

According to Disney lore, the luxurious, 12-story Hollywood Tower Hotel first opened in 1917. Famous for its service, it soon became a gathering place for the Tinseltown elite.

Fast forward to Oct. 31, 1939. As the hotel hosts a Halloween party in its Top of the Tower lounge, many guests check in for the night. But then a freakish thunderstorm sweeps in across the hills and, at 8:05 p.m., a huge bolt of lightning electrifies the hotel. It hits with such force it eliminates two wings and two elevator shafts of the structure and dematerializes the guests in those areas, including five who had just boarded an elevator — a child actress with her nanny, a glamorous couple of young rising stars and a hotel bellhop. The remaining guests run out in horror, leaving their luggage and other belongings behind.

The hotel stands deserted for more than 50 years, but mysteriously reopens in 1994. Strangely, the staff from that fateful night is still there, unaged, and has no memory of the disaster.

As you walk through the entrance gate, you're a guest of the hotel and are arriving to check in. But immediately you sense something is wrong. The misty entrance garden is lush but overgrown. The fountain has no water. The lobby is covered in dust and cobwebs. A bellhop notices you and pre-

▶ Your fall is over when you see the turning spiral from "The Twilight Zone."

Ready to crumble at the next lightning strike, the Hollywood Tower Hotel looms above Sunset Boulevard

pares to take you to your room. Since the lobby elevators aren't working (behind an "Out of Order" sign, their doors hang crooked in their tracks), he asks you to wait for a moment in the library.

Then things really get creepy.

The library power goes out, but then on comes a television set, a black-and-white model circa 1959. Rod Serling appears, describing "tonight's story on 'The Twilight Zone'," a "somewhat unique" fable about a maintenance service elevator. He shows you those five guests, boarding their elevator car just before the flash. When it hits, these guests seem to disappear.

"We invite you if you dare to step aboard," Serling says, "because in tonight's episode, you are the star."

Suddenly a rear door opens, and you're directed into a back boiler room, an industrial area clearly not meant for guests. Still trying to get to your room, you board a service elevator. But as soon as the doors close you learn it, too, has a mind of its own.

First the lights go out. Then it whisks you to the fourth floor, where its doors open to reveal a typical hotel corridor. Do Not Disturb signs hang on most of the doors, while shoes and wine bottles sit outside them.

But as lightning flashes in the hall window, who should flicker into view but those five guests from 1939. They beckon you to follow them but, wrapped in a net of cackling electricity, disappear.

Then the walls disappear, revealing a clear night sky. The hall window floats, then shatters.

You've entered the Twilight Zone.

The doors close and up you go again, to the 13th floor — a level that supposedly doesn't exist. When the doors open, Serling speaks again: "One stormy night long ago, five people stepped through the door of an elevator and into a nightmare. That door is opening once again, and this time it's opening for you."

FUN FACTS ›› When Serling speaks on the library TV, you're actually watching him introduce the 1961 "Twilight Zone" episode, "It's a Good Life," saying "This, as you may recognize, is a map of the United States." On the ride video the camera cuts away just as he pronounces the word "map," and instead you hear him say "maintenance service elevator." All of Serling's lines are dubbed by impersonator Mark Silverman. (Serling died in 1975. There was no "Twilight Zone" episode about a Hollywood Tower Hotel.) ›› The lobby in the video is not the one at the attraction. Disney filmed the shoot on a California soundstage, using an identical set. ›› The elevators have four loading areas but only two exits. The initial four shafts merge into two paths on the top floor. ›› The cast members' break room is between the drop shafts. When you scream, they hear you. "It's very difficult to relax," one says. ›› The ride's engines are at the top and bottom of the shafts. Each develops 110,000 foot-pounds of torque, uses regeneration for deceleration control and is 35 feet long, 7 feet wide, 12 feet tall and weighs 132,000 pounds. ›› The Tower is 199 feet high, just short enough to *not* have aircraft warning lights. ›› In 1993, as it was being built, it was struck by lightning.

▶ The gift shop offers thick, comfortable "Hollywood Tower Hotel" bathrobes.

Your cabin moves forward, out of its shaft and alongside the glowing, moving silhouettes of those same spooky five. Directly ahead is a star field, but it too moves, forming a line which separates with a bright flash. That becomes the edge of another opening door — into one of those shafts that no longer exists.

You move into the space and the doors slam shut. It's completely dark.

Silent. Tense.

Then you move — violently — up, down — down, up — up, up, down — no telling which way. Occasionally doors in front of you open, revealing the open sky. You may see the figures again, or hear rainfall.

After about a minute, however, the madness stops, and the elevator settles down into the basement.

"The next time you check into a deserted hotel..." Serling says, "make sure you know just what kind of vacancy you're filling. Or you may find yourself a permanent resident... of 'The Twilight Zone.'"

The Twilight Zone Tower of Terror is an outstanding attraction — thrilling, full of surprises and with theming that fills every square inch.

4 min. Capacity: 84. Avg. wait: 20 min. early morning, 60 min. peak afternoon. Fastpass available. ECV guests must transfer to a wheelchair. Activated captioning

available. Height restriction: 40 in. Fear factor: Mighty frighty. The drops are smooth, but Disney's mind games start as soon as you come through the entrance gate, when the friendly theme park completely disappears. By the time the library lights go out you'll be ready to scream — and you're still at least five minutes from, as one child called it, "being electrified." Chicken exit. Best ages: 8 and up. Debuted: 1994; revised 1996, 1999, 2002.

FUN FINDS ❶ To the right of the reception desk, a AAA plaque honors the hotel's "13-diamond" status. An actual award, it was presented by the American Automobile Association when the ride opened in 1994. ❷ Abandoned items at the desk include a fedora, topcoat, folded newspaper, open registration book, alligator-skin luggage and mail-slot mail and messages. ❸ A bag, cane and white fedora lean against the concierge desk. ❹ A diamond ring, white glove and two glasses rest on a table on the left. Next to it is a champagne bucket. ❺ A mah-jongg game is in progress on a nearby table.* Tea has just been served to the players; a cart holds cups ready for pouring, roses and a newspaper. ❻ Another teacup rests on the end table in front of a fireplace; a goblet and small plate sit on a table to the right. ❼ The message EVIL TOWER U R DOOMED is formed by letters at the bottom

TRANSCENDENTAL TV "There is a fifth dimension beyond that which is known to man... a middle ground between light and shadow, between science and superstition... it is an area which we call The Twilight Zone." Along with a four-note theme song ("do-do-do-do, do-do-do-do..."), those classic words welcomed viewers to "The Twilight Zone," an imaginative CBS television anthology that aired from 1959 to 1964. Placing ordinary people into extraordinary situations, the episodes often had mind-bending twists, with confused characters in unfamiliar, sometimes supernatural surroundings. Host Rod Serling created the show after getting fed up with censorship hassles at his job as a writer of the dramatic series "Playhouse 90." Though "The Twilight Zone" was as popular as today's "American Idol" (each episode was watched by about one in 10 Americans) Serling had to fight hard to keep it on the air. In the pre-cable world of the 1960s, an audience that size was considered pitiful. Though the show made him a giant in the TV industry, Serling stood only 5-foot-5 and weighed just 137 pounds. A chronic smoker, he died from complications of heart surgery in 1975, at age 50.

A HAUNTED HISTORY While planning the attraction Disney considered a variety of themes. At first it was to be housed in the "Haunted Hollywood Hotel," a real resort with rooms guests could stay in. One idea featured actor Mel Brooks as a madman hotel owner who chased guests into an elevator. Another had movie stars filming a horror picture, with a walk-through segment narrated by Vincent Price. The attraction was built with a reprogrammable ride system, which has let Disney update it three times. At first it was just one gut-grabbing plummet of more than 100 feet. A 1996 revision made it three tumbles, adding a half drop and a false fall. Three years later Disney debuted a seven-fall experience that also brought faster acceleration, more weightlessness and a lot more shaking. Finally, on New Year's Eve 2002, the company introduced "Tower of Terror 4," the current mix of random drops enhanced with physical, sound and visual effects. "We can reinvent the experience as often as we want," says Imagineer Theron Skees. "We can add effects, change timing sequences and alter the way the elevator moves."

of the hotel directory (between the lobby's two passenger elevators) that apparently shook off during the lightning strike. **8** The footage of Serling has been altered to re-move a cigarette from his right hand. **9** The little girl sings the nursery rhyme "It's Raining, It's Pouring" on the video and on the fourth floor. **10** Though the service el-evators' tracking dials only go to "12," their arrows go to an unmarked "13." **11** As your doors close, a hint at your destination — a "1" on the left door and a "3" on the right — disguises itself as a "B," the elevator's letter. **12** The clock in the basement office is stuck on 8:05, the time of the lightning strike. **13** The gift shop windows are still decorated for the Halloween of 1939.

---

* It's a real game, in progress. "One of our designers actually learned to play mah-jongg," Imagineer Eric Jacobson says, "so he could make sure the game pieces would be in a proper position."

PROPS AND ALLUSIONS References to "The Twilight Zone" are scattered throughout the hotel. A poster at the **concierge desk** promotes a show by Anthony Freemont, the name of a 6-year-old boy in a 1961 "Twilight Zone" episode ("It's a Good Life") who uses telepathic powers to terrorize his neighbors. In the **library**, the bookcases hold such items as the devil-headed, "Ask Me a Yes or No Question" fortune-telling machine from the 1960 episode "Nick of Time" (a story of a man unable to make decisions for himself) and the tiny silver robot featured in the 1961 episode "The Invaders" (a tale of a farm woman who kills what appear to be small invading aliens). As you board the **elevator,** the small inspection certificate on its wall is signed by "Cadwallader," a jovial character in the 1959 episode "Escape Clause" who secretly is the devil. Dated Oct. 31, 1939, the certificate has the number 10259, a reference to the date the TV program premiered: Oct. 2, 1959. When your elevator finally stops to unload, you sit next to a basement **storage area** that includes a "Special Jackpot $10,000" slot machine from the 1960 episode "The Fever" (a story of a talking slot that drives a tightwad crazy), two ventriloquist dummies used in 1962's "The Dummy"(a dummy switches places with his human owner) as well as 1964's "Caesar and Me" (a ventriloquist uses his cigar-smoking dummy to commit crimes) and a silver spaceship, the home to the library's "Invaders" robot. Finally, the **bulletin-board** notes to the right of the basement office (the "Picture If You Will" souvenir-photo area) seek finders of items such as "Pocket watch, sentimental value, broken crystal" a reference to the 1963 episode "A Kind of Stopwatch" (in which a bank robber stops time forever when he breaks an unusual timepiece).

The Science of Spooky

What makes the Tower so fun? In part it's the science. Hidden behind all the theming is a unique mix of innovative engineering, classic special effects and modern math. Combining three distinct ride systems, the mechanics of the attraction represent a novel achievement of applied science. Its "elevator" goes up, moves forward, then plummets down and soars up a second shaft, all in one seamless experience.

The first system is obvious: an elevator. When you leave the boiler room, you're in a standard, 50-foot elevator shaft, with typical sliding doors and two distinct stops. The second system kicks in at the top of the shaft. As your elevator car (actually an independent vehicle, which rode up the shaft in a cage) moves forward, it's using the technology of a self-guided palette driver, an automated machine used by companies such as Anheuser-Busch, JC Penney and Sony to move inventory around large warehouses. Controlled by an unseen computer, it rolls on wheels and gets its power from an on-board battery.

The third system is Disney's own. Once your cabin enters the drop shaft, it's silently locked into a second cage that is tightly suspended on a looped steel cable. Pulled by high-speed winches and motors, the cage "falls" faster than the pull of gravity (you reach 37 mph in just 1.5 seconds, about a quarter of a second faster than if you were falling freely) and shoots up with similar speed. The result: though you never actually fall and are never truly free of the ride's grasp, you feel completely out of control.

Though often stunningly realistic, most of the elevator effects are created by simple, time-tested methods. At your first stop, a long corridor filled with translucent people, disappearing windows and sudden star fields is really a shallow area filled with transparent screens, which show images from hidden projectors. Though it looks far away and 8 feet tall, the end of the hall is actually just a few feet in front of you, and only 4 feet high. Once your elevator moves forward, mirrors on the floor and ceiling make it seem those planes have disappeared. The characters to your side are simply independently moving plastic cutouts, split down the middle to make them look warped. In front of you, the changing star field comes from synchronized fiber-optic lights built into the doors to the final drop zone.

Each ride is different, as a computer system chooses the particulars of your fall using a random-number generator based on modulo functions (calculations that search for two numbers that, when divided by a third number, have the same remainder). "The moment that the elevator is entering the shaft, the computer decides what is going to happen," explains Disney software engineer Michael Tschanz.

Rock 'n' Roller Coaster Starring Aerosmith

✓ This popular thrill ride has a lot going for it — a launch that blasts you to 57 mph in 2.8 seconds, two loops, a tight corkscrew, rock music and a fun theme.

The grins begin as you enter the building. Step through the lobby (mimicking guitar necks, its foyer columns are complete with fret boards and strings) and you're off on a time-warp back to the 1970s. As you walk through the halls of G-Force Records, you pass displays of real vintage recording and playback gear. Soon you enter Studio C, where you find the band mixing the rhythm tracks to "Walk This Way."

Suddenly the guys have to leave; they're late for a show. But you're in luck: they want to give you backstage passes, so their manager phones for a limousine to take you to the show. "We're going to need a stretch," she says, counting the crowd. "In fact, make it a super stretch."

"The show is all the way across town," she tells you, "but I got you a really fast car."

You're ushered into the grimy back alley, where up pulls your baby-blue, 24-seat 1959 Caddy convertible. In you climb and off you go, rocketing into the Los Angeles night with Aerosmith blasting on the stereo. You zoom through the HOLLYWOOD sign, through a billboard doughnut, through a half-mile of twists, turns and loops.

Plenty thrilling for most folks, the ride gets mixed reviews from coaster freaks. The launch is exhilarating, but everything after that is rather mild. You slow down after the

© DISNEY

Your Rock 'n' Roll limo loops just after launch

first couple of turns, and average just 28 miles per hour. For the biggest thrill ask to sit in the front seat. With nothing in front of you the launch is hard to predict.

The smooth ride has no steep drops and you're not jerked around in your seat. But the turns are tight, the tunes rock and it's all in the dark. In other words, you won't get sick, but your palms will sweat.

1 min. 22 sec. Avg. wait: 30 min. early morning, 60 min. peak afternoon. Fastpass available. ECV users must transfer. Height restriction: 48 in. Fear factor: Anticipating the launch scares even adults. Chicken exit. Debuted: 1999.

ALL-AMERICAN ROCK 'N' ROLL Known for its spare, driving riffs and suggestive lyrics, Aerosmith formed in Boston in 1970. Its raunchy swagger, highlighted by singer Steven Tyler's prancing stage antics, drew comparisons to the Rolling Stones. Tyler and Mick Jagger even looked similar. Early hits included 1975's "Walk This Way," which, like the Stones' earlier "Satisfaction," used a groove so strong the words didn't matter. Aerosmith also created the first power ballad in 1973, adding strings to the piano-based "Dream On." Plagued by drugs in the late 1970s, the band got back on track in 1986: Tyler and lead guitarist Joe Perry appeared on rap group Run D.M.C.'s cover of "Walk This Way" and the video became an MTV staple.

FUN FACTS ›› The manager is played by actress Illeana Douglas, perhaps best known as Angela on the HBO series "Six Feet Under." ›› The car radio's DJ is voiced by longtime Los Angeles rock jock Uncle Joe Benson. ›› The squeal you hear as each limo peels out is fake. It's coming from barely visible speakers under the driveway. ›› Most of the ride takes place inside "Stage 15," the structure behind the G-Force headquarters building.

▶ Long legs? Ask for an odd-numbered row. They have far more legroom.

FUN FINDS ❶ Equipment in the first display case includes a disc cutter, which, in the days of vinyl, etched sounds from a mixing console onto a master disc, thus creating the phrase "cutting a record." Nearby is a 1958 Gibson Les Paul Standard guitar. ❷ The second case holds vintage record players, from a 1904 external-horn Edison Fireside to a 1970s "Disc-O-Kid." ❸ Put your ear to the doors marked "Studio A" or "Studio B" and you'll hear Aerosmith rehearsing. ❹ The concert posters include one for a 1973 concert from Aerosmith's first national tour, as the opening act for the New York Dolls. It's midway down the right wall. ❺ The alley is full of puns. Signs on the rear of the G-Force building indicate work has been done by Sam Andreas and Sons Structural Restoration. ❻ The parking garage is run by Lock 'n' Roll Parking Systems. ❼ The Dumpster is owned by the Rock 'n' Rollaway Disposal Co. ❽ As you near your limo a glass case lists rates for the Wash This Way Auto Detail. ❾ Each of the limos' license plates sports an apt message, such as 2FAST4U and UGOBABE. ❿ Once you arrive at the show, watch the concert video to see Tyler scream "Rock 'n' Roller Coaster!!!"

Fantasmic

The kitchen sink of evening extravaganzas, this nightcap is quite a spectacle. As you sit in an outdoor amphitheater, your eyes are bombarded with dancing fountains, burning waves, water screens, a huge dragon and before you can say "Great balls of fire!" one of those, too. It takes place in a lagoon dominated by an island with a 60-foot mountain.

The plot: Mickey has a nightmare.

Dressed as the Sorcerer's Apprentice, the dreaming mouse conducts fountains in the lagoon like instruments in an orchestra, creating water screens that then play scenes from 1940's "Fantasia." As his powers increase, Mickey shoots fireworks out of his fingers. Then he imagines dancers who form a giant flower, as well as a wildly colorful elephant, giraffe and rhinoceros who lead a jungle full of animals in a surreal version of "I Just Can't Wait to be King."

As images from classic Disney films appear on large water bubbles, Monstro the whale (from 1940's "Pinocchio") chases Jiminy Cricket, and suddenly lunges right at the audience, splashing guests in the front rows. The theater gets pitch black. "Hey!" Mickey yells. "What's going on?"

Bang! The thunder of a cannon transforms the set into the 17th-century Virginia of Disney's 1995 "Pocahontas." As peaceful Native Americans paddle by in torch-lit canoes, prissy Gov. Ratcliffe claims the land for his king. English settlers sing "Mine Mine Mine" as they burn down trees, dig up land and shoot Indians. Soon, Pocahontas arrives to stop the madness.

After Mickey's dream turns romantic (a boat parade of Ariel, Belle and Snow White) his nightmare returns at full tilt.

The Evil Queen arrives and morphs into the old hag. "Now I'll turn that little mouse's dream into a nightmare Fantasmic!" she cackles, summoning up water apparitions of nearly every Disney villain. Jafar pops onto the land and becomes a live-action snake. Maleficent becomes a 40-foot dragon and ignites the waterway with her breath.

But Mickey fights back. "You may think you're so powerful," he tells the dragon, "well, this is MY dream!" Regaining his powers, he lifts the water up to smother the flames and, finding an oh-so-convenient sword in a stone, slays the dragon.

For the finale a showboat arrives filled with characters, piloted by the black-and-white Mickey from the 1928 cartoon "Steamboat Willie." To end the show there's a burst of fireworks and a delightful now-you-see-him, now-you-don't farewell from your host. The show has 50 performers.

25 min. Capacity: 9,900 (6,900 seats, standing room for 3,000). Arrive 90 min. early to get seats in the center of the theater (a large snack bar helps you kill time). Guests may remain in wheelchairs, ECVs. Assistive listening; reflective captioning. Fear factor: The loud noises, bright flashes and villains frighten some children. Debuted: 1998 (Disneyland 1992).

▶ Often a few seats are available in the front center until 30 minutes before showtime.

street party

"Toy Story" characters Woody and Bo Peep dance in the Block Party Bash

Disney's Block Party Bash

Imagine a line of cheerleaders so long it stretches down the entire length of a football field, from one goal post to the other. Dressed as everything from cowgirls to ladybugs, they shake it like a Polaroid picture to a driving beat of classic disco, rock and Motown songs. Joining them is an assortment of acrobats, stilt jumpers, a caravan of electric scooters and 15 Pixar cartoon characters, including Woody and Buzz from 1995's "Toy Story" and 1999's "Toy Story 2," Mike and Sulley from 2001's "Monsters, Inc." and Flik and Atta from 1998's "A Bug's Life."

Next year's Super Bowl half-time show? No, this year's Block Party Bash, Disney's most infectious street spectacle ever.

The 500-foot-long performance area is anchored by three giant parade-style floats, representing the worlds of "Toy Story," "Monsters, Inc." and "A Bug's Life." Other set pieces include trampoline units, huge orange traffic cones and stacks of toy blocks that double as dance stages, prop boxes and sources of special effects.

There's a lot of audience participation. Guests — who stand within an arm's length of most of the 114 performers — compete in a scream contest, play catch with beach balls and join the entertainers in the street for the "Macarena," "Stayin' Alive," "(Shake, Shake, Shake) Shake Your Booty," "Twist and Shout" and "Y.M.C.A."

Other songs include "Shout," "Footloose," "R.O.C.K. in the U.S.A.," even "Jumpin' Jack Flash" and, yes, a snippet of "Hey Ya!"

Each area is hosted by one of the Green Army Men, a face character who barks out orders such as "I want you... to get down, get funky and be all you can be!" Also on hand: Mr. Potato Head, Jessie and Bo Peep from "Toy Story" and "Toy Story 2"; janitors Needleman and Smitty, scarer George Sanderson and little girl Boo from "Monsters, Inc."; and Heimlich the caterpillar, Gypsy the gypsy moth and Slim the walking stick from "A Bug's Life." During the show's finale, telescoping towers rise to reveal Mr. and Mrs. Incredible and Frozone from 2004's "The Incredibles."

The first show takes place on Hollywood Boulevard. Its best viewing spots are in front of the Hot and Fresh popcorn stand (for the "Toy Story" characters), the in-

tersection of Hollywood and Vine Street ("Monsters, Inc.") and in front of the Cover Story shop ("A Bug's Life"). Either side of the street is fine, as there are two lines of performers, one facing each side. Most shady spots are snared 45 minutes early. A second show, held on the Echo Lake street that passes the former ABC Theater and Sounds Dangerous, was still being blocked out at press time.

Daily at 3 p.m. Each performance consists of a 5-min. arrival and setup period (fully staged and scored), a 12-min. show, and 5-min. departure. Special viewing areas for ECV and wheelchair guests. Debuted: 2008 (Disneyland 2005).

FUN FINDS ❶ On the "Toy Story" float, the brand name of Mike the tape recorder reads "Oldskool." ❷ That float's crayon brand is "Pixola." ❸ On that float's side, the eyes of Lenny the pair of binoculars move as they spy on guests. ❹ On the front of the "Monsters, Inc." float, Sulley's control panel reads, from his point-of-view, "071555," a reference to the July 15, 1955, Grand Opening of California's Disneyland Resort. (The Bash was created for Disneyland's 50th anniversary.) ❺ A sign on that float indicates it has had "4 Accident-Free Days." ❻ Its rear license plate expires in May 2005, the month the Block Party Bash debuted at the Disneyland Resort. ❼ On the "A Bug's Life" float, the back panel of the Casey Jr. box of animal crackers indicates it has 15,000 calories, including "Calories from fat: 14,999."

From top: Crowds compete in a scream contest; guests dance in the street; a Toy Story jump-roper.

Clockwise from top left:
The authors' daughter,
an African gorilla, an
Asian bicycle taxi, the
Expedition Everest
Forbidden Mountain,
a flamingo in Africa,
a Harambe Village
jump-roper

disney's
Animal

Kingdom

overview

Top left: A Discovery Island popcorn cart. **Above:** A Harambe School instructor. **Left:** Chip, safari ready.

though it's not as famous as the Magic Kingdom, in many ways Disney's Animal Kingdom is much more magical. Set in 500 acres of botanical wonder, Disney's largest theme park features a real safari through a 110-acre African wilderness, two Broadway-style shows, a thrilling roller coaster, and up-close encounters with what seems like every strange creature on the planet. The park's mission: to make it easy, and fun, to appreciate the beauty, magnificence and importance of the animal world.

TO ZOO, OR NOT TO ZOO The park's zoo-logical operations are respected worldwide, but are fully hidden, tucked behind, or in, man-made hills, rivers, rocks and streams. Scientists are breeding endangered species, and researchers are studying behaviors such as the low-frequency vocalizations of elephants, but you barely hear about it. The park is a member of the acclaimed Association of Zoos and Aquariums, but the AZA logo appears only on a flag out front.

Why? Because Disney wants you to see the real world of animals, not the artificial world of zoos. "Disney is all about storytelling, and here real live animals help tell the story as their families play out real-life experiences," says the park's executive designer Joe Rohde. "We want people to get a little tug on their heartstrings," adds park vice president Dr. Beth Stevens, "and get people to care about animals."

Laid out in a classic hub-and-spoke style, the park welcomes you with an entranceway free from even a single gift shop. Instead, you meander into this cel-ebration of nature through the aptly named Oasis, a re-created tropical jungle filled with fascinating creatures. Your path leads to the centrally located Discovery Island,

▶ Raining? Try the safari. You'll stay dry, and the animals are often more lively.

Need more cow bell? Not this street performer, who taps out a tune in a Discovery Island band.

PARK RESOURCES

BABY CARE A hidden oasis, the Baby Care Center *(behind Creature Comforts, Discovery Island)* has changing rooms, nursing areas, a microwave, even a playroom; and sells diapers, formula, pacifiers and over-the-counter medications.

CAMERA NEEDS Garden Gate Gifts *(Entrance Plaza)* sells cameras and accessories and burns photo CDs.

GUEST RELATIONS The park's Guest Relations center *(Entrance Plaza; walk-up window outside the gate, walk-in office inside)* has cast members ready to help with any problem. It has maps and Times Guides for all Walt Disney World theme parks, exchanges some foreign currency and stores items found in the park that day.

LOCKERS Lockers large enough to store a couple of large bags can be rented inside the entrance *($5 per day plus a $2 deposit).*

LOST CHILDREN Report lost children to Guest Relations or any Disney cast member. Children who lose their parents should tell a Disney cast member.

PACKAGE PICKUP Anything you buy can be sent to Package Pick-Up *(Garden Gate Gifts, Entrance Plaza)* to pick up as you leave. Purchases can also be sent to your Disney hotel or shipped.

PARKING For day guests parking is $11 a day. Those staying at a Disney resort (and annual passholders) get free parking. A tram takes you to the park entrance.

PETS The Pet Care Kennel *(Entrance Plaza, 407-938-2100)* has clean cages in air-conditioned rooms.

STROLLERS AND WHEELCHAIRS Garden Gate Gifts *(Entrance Plaza)* rents single strollers and wheelchairs *($10 per day),* double-passenger strollers *($18)* and Electric Convenience Vehicles *($35).*

TIP BOARD The park tip board *(Discovery Island)* displays current waiting times for popular attractions.

TRANSPORTATION Disney buses run to Animal Kingdom from all Walt Disney World resorts, Epcot, Disney's Hollywood Studios and Blizzard Beach. Magic Kingdom guests take a monorail to the Transportation and Ticket Center, then a bus to Animal Kingdom. There is no direct service from Downtown Disney or Typhoon Lagoon.

the lush home of the Tree of Life and Its Tough To Be a Bug attraction as well as the best-looking food stands, restaurants and shops you'll find anywhere. From there five lands radiate outward.

Working clockwise, the first land is the smallest. Styled after an Adirondack summer camp, **Camp Minnie-Mickey** is home to two theatrical shows (Festival of the Lion King, Pocahontas and Her Forest Friends) and character meet-and-greet pavilions.

The largest section of the park, **Africa** presents zoological attractions within the context of a small town and its surrounding wilderness. It features the Kilimanjaro Safaris wildlife excursion as well as the Pangani Forest Exploration Trail, a walkway through gorilla and other African-animal habitats. The attractions border Harambe, a fictitious village staffed by real African guides and entertainers.

A short train ride away from Africa is **Rafiki's Planet Watch,** a conservation-themed area that's home to a real animal research center and a nice petting zoo.

The other major Animal Kingdom land, **Asia** is home to a variety of attractions. There's a zoological habitat (the Maharajah Jungle Trek), a bird show (Flights of Wonder), a river-rafting ride (Kali River Rapids) and a thrilling roller coaster, Expedition Everest.

DISNEY'S ANIMAL KINGDOM
park map

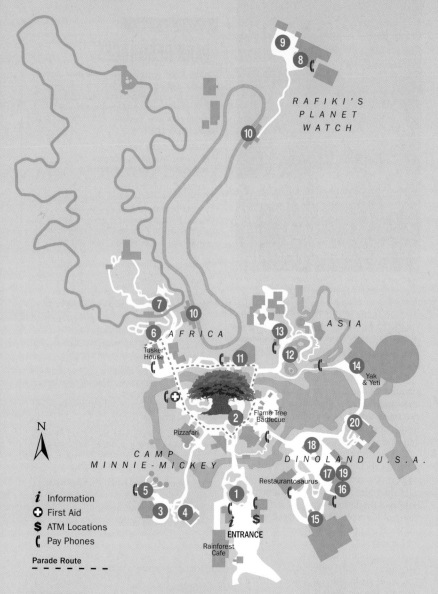

RAFIKI'S
PLANET
WATCH

ASIA

AFRICA

Tusker
House

Yak
& Yeti

Flame Tree
Barbecue

Pizzafari

N

CAMP
MINNIE-MICKEY

DINOLAND U.S.A.

Restaurantosaurus

i Information

✚ First Aid

$ ATM Locations

(Pay Phones

Parade Route
- - - - - - -

ENTRANCE

Rainforest
Cafe

ATTRACTIONS

1 The Oasis

2 It's Tough To Be a Bug

3 Festival of the Lion King

4 Pocahontas and Her
Forest Friends

5 Character Greeting Trails

6 Kilimanjaro Safaris

7 Pangani Forest
Exploration Trail

8 Conservation Station

9 Affection Section

10 Wildlife Express

11 Flights of Wonder

12 Kali River Rapids

13 Maharajah Jungle Trek

14 Expedition Everest

15 Dinosaur

16 Primeval Whirl

17 TriceraTop Spin

18 The Boneyard

19 Fossil Fun Games

20 Finding Nemo
— The Musical

Finally, tongue-in-cheek **DinoLand U.S.A.** has two sections. The Dino Institute presents a lighthearted indoor thrill ride (Dinosaur) and an elaborate Boneyard playground. Next door, DinoRama re-creates a tacky roadside carnival with a spinning roller coaster (Primeval Whirl), hub-and-spoke ride (TriceraTop Spin) and midway amusements (Fossil Fun Games).

HOW MANY DAYS? Some say the park is just a half-day experience, but that's only if you have no interest in wildlife. Actually, it can take up to four days to see everything.

Each of the park's five animal habitats can take up to an hour to fully experience, and each area is far more rewarding early in the morning, before 11 a.m. Likewise, Conservation Station's public animal-care procedures take place only in the morning, and require a separate train trip to get to.

The park has just nine major rides and shows, but they're all worthwhile and,

---

FUN FACTS ❱❱ 150 different animal species have been bred by the park. ❱❱ 2.6 million gallons of water cycles through the park's treated-water system five times a day. It's used in the streams, waterfalls and other water features that come in contact with the live animals. ❱❱ Originally the Camp Minnie-Mickey pathway was to connect Discovery Island with the Beastly Kingdom, a never-built area of the park themed to mythical creatures. ❱❱ The word "Harambe" means "coming together" in Swahili. Tamu Tamu means "sweet sweet," Dawa means "strong medicine," Rafiki means "friend." ❱❱ Kilimanjaro is the most famous mountain in Kenya. ❱❱ Africa's seven thatch huts were built on-site by 13 Zulu craftsmen visiting from Kwazulu-Natal, South Africa, using 15 semi-truck loads of Berg grass harvested by relatives back home. ❱❱ Harambe's coral rock is actually volcanic rock from California. ❱❱ Sanskrit for "place of delight," Anandapur is also the name of an actual East Indian town of 35,000 people. ❱❱ Chakranadi translates to "river that runs in circles." ❱❱ The rusty Asian bicycles were purchased at garage sales. ❱❱ The apatosaurus skeleton that straddles the entrance to DinoLand U.S.A. is a cast of a real 52-foot fossil found in Colorado in 1900. The original is in Chicago's Field Museum. ❱❱ Located between Dinosaur and Dinosaur Treasures, the Cretaceous Trail is the third largest cycad collection in North America. ❱❱ The name of the DinoLand highway (U.S. 498) refers to the month the Animal Kingdom opened: April, 1998. ❱❱ The Restaurantosaurus Airstream once belonged to an Imagineer's grandmother.

A DAILY PLAN

Can you absolutely, positively get to Disney's Animal Kingdom by 8:30 a.m? If so, here's a great plan. The keys: getting Expedition Everest Fastpasses as soon as the park opens, then immediately touring the animal exhibits.

8:30 ARRIVE AT THE PARK As you wait for the gates to open (typically at 8:50), pick up a Times Guide from the Guest Relations window at your left.

9:00 GET FASTPASSES for the Expedition Everest roller coaster adventure

9:10 MAHARAJAH JUNGLE TREK The giant fruit bats will be at their most lively.

9:45 KILIMANJARO SAFARIS

10:30 PANGANI FOREST TRAIL The meerkats and gorillas should be active.

11:30 EXPEDITION EVEREST Ask for the front row for the best views, the back seat for the biggest thrill.

12:30 LUNCH Air-conditioned Pizzafari has good counter-service food and a terrific decor. Close to Everest, the outdoor Flame Tree BBQ offers good food and nice views. While you eat, check your Times Guide to confirm your afternoon's show and parade times. *The new Tusker House buffet and table-service Yak & Yeti will take too much of your time to see the 2 p.m. "Lion King" show.*

1:20 FESTIVAL OF THE LION KING Get in line to see the 2 p.m. Festival of the Lion King show. You'll get a great seat.

3:00 GET FASTPASSES for Kali River Rapids. (Don't want to get wet? Check out a performance by Inka Sikuri across from Flame Tree Barbecue.)

3:30 PARADE It typically starts at 4 p.m.

4:30 KALI RIVER RAPIDS Who cares if you get soaked — you're done! (Don't want to get wet? Check out the character greeting trails at Camp Minnie-Mickey. The waiting lines will be short, or nonexistent.)

Assumes park hours of 9 a.m. to 5 p.m.

A SECOND DAY

Get to the park again by 8:30 a.m. and you'll have another great day.

8:30 ARRIVE AT THE PARK As you wait for the gates to open (typically at 8:50), pick up a Times Guide from the Guest Relations window at your left. Watch for Wes Palm, the talking palm tree.

9:00 THE OASIS Find the anteater, babirusa and wallaby.

9:30 KILIMANJARO SAFARIS You'll see animals and behaviors you didn't before.

10:00 HARAMBE VILLAGE See the entertainers. Check out the school.

11:30 GET FASTPASSES for It's Tough To Be a Bug. The machines are next to the attraction entrance, in front of Disney Outfitters.

11:35 DISCOVERY ISLAND Wander through the paths of Discovery Island. Find the kangaroos, and the lemurs.

12:15 LUNCH at a counter-service restaurant. While you eat, check your Times Guide to confirm afternoon show times.

1:15 IT'S TOUGH TO BE A BUG

2:15 FINDING NEMO — THE MUSICAL Get in line to see the 3 p.m. show. You'll get a great seat.

3:45 FLIGHTS OF WONDER

4:15 CONSERVATION STATION See the indoor exhibits and petting zoo.

5:30 DINNER at Yak & Yeti. *May require advance reservations.*

7:00 DINOLAND U.S.A. Come on a late-night Extra Magic Hours day to see this land after dark. Don't forget Dinosaur, the indoor ride at the back right corner. For a peaceful evening walk, take a stroll around the walkway that leads to Asia, Africa and back to Discovery Island. It's beautiful after dark.

Assumes park hours of 9 a.m. to 9 p.m.

A nutritionist prepares some of the four tons of food that the park feeds to its animals each day, which includes 5,000 worms and 2,500 crickets. Disney also distributes 2,000 pounds of vegetation and browse (clippings of grasses) daily.

counting waiting times, can take up to an hour each. Animal Kingdom's parade is one of Disney's most creative processions.

And the nature of the atmosphere itself — the first-class street performers, the stunning landscaping, the detailed interiors, the museum-like theming — makes you want to slow down and take it all in.

Though its animal attractions close at dusk, the park is sometimes open until 9 or 10 p.m. When it is, it's one of Disney's prettiest night spots. Lit from within the trunk, the upper branches and leaves of the Tree of Life appear to glow. Strings of light bulbs line the paths of Asia, while flashing bulbs add a dose of cheesy charm to the Dino-Rama carnival at DinoLand U.S.A. The dining area of the Flame Tree Barbecue outdoor cafe is especially pretty.

THE PARK TOOK 2.5 YEARS to build. Starting with a 500-acre flat tract of land, Disney re-landscaped the area with 4.4 million cubic yards of dirt (60 dump trucks a day), a hidden water-treatment system and 4 million plants, adding in a million square feet of rockwork, a full theme-park infrastructure, a variety of attractions and 1,500 animals along the way. The park broke ground in August, 1995, and opened on Earth Day, 1998. It employs more than 4,500 people.

Clockwise from above: An African spoonbill honks at the photographer; a college intern displays a spider to a curious guest; the idyllic Oasis sets the stage for your day.

The Oasis

This "A"-shaped collection of tropically landscaped walkways serves as the entrance to the park. Tucked under a canopy of bamboo, eucalyptus and palms, a man-made haven of pools, streams and waterfalls is dotted with flowering jacaranda trees, lianas, orchids and vines. It connects Animal Kingdom's turnstiles and guest services area with Discovery Island, the park's central hub.

In essence its own small zoo, The Oasis is filled with exotic animals. Ever seen a babirusa wild pig? Black swan? Swamp wallaby? You will, with a little luck. Displayed in natural habitats, the creatures are free to roam out of sight. College interns are on hand each morning until about 11 a.m., displaying skulls as well as spiders and other tiny critters in hand-held aquariums.

FUN FINDS ❶ You can see, and touch, the back of the waterfall from within a small cave where the paths converge. ❷ A swaying rope bridge runs alongside the final few feet of the left walkway. It leads into the cave. Water bubbles up from the rocks underneath it. ❸ The Animal Kingdom dedication plaque sits near a lamppost in front of the black swans.

FUN FACT ❯❯ Continually used for bathing, feeding and, yes, pooping by dozens of ducks and wading birds, the water in the ponds, streams and waterfalls is discreetly cleaned and recirculated five times per day. Pipes run under the walkways.

▶ Park animals are most active first thing in the morning and late in the day.

The centerpiece of Animal Kingdom, the Tree of Life is 145 feet tall. It has a 160-foot canopy. **Inset:** Animals "carved" into the Tree of Life trunk include a lounging tiger and, above it, a porcupine

Tree of Life

A symbol of the interconnected nature of plants and animals, this man-made park centerpiece begs you to get closer. A tapestry of 325 animals is sculpted into its gnarled roots, giant trunk and thick branches, and pathways take you through the buttressed root system and right up to the trunk. The park centerpiece, it's meant to resemble an Africa baobab tree.

"We want our visitors to wander up to the tree, to recognize animals and seek out others," says chief sculptor Zsolt Hormay. "Some are more recognizable, some are less so. Finding the balance between the animal forms and the wood textures was a great challenge." Hormay's team of 20 artists included three Native Americans. The tree is "the most impressive artistic and engineering feat we have achieved since Sleeping Beauty castle at Disneyland," says Animal Kingdom Executive Designer Joe Rohde.

FUN FACTS » The concrete trunk is 50 feet wide at its middle, 170 feet at its base. It has 8,000 fiberglass branches and 103,000 leaves. **»** The tree took 18 months to build. An oil-rig-style frame connects to 12 main branches, each of which is encircled in a giant expansion joint which lets it sway in the wind. **»** Disney created the trunk outside the park, then cut it into a dozen segments and flew it to a construction site near its final location. A crane hoisted the pieces up to assemble. **»** Designer Hormay also created the rockwork at Big Thunder Mountain Railroad and the snow and rockwork at Blizzard Beach.

▶ A main branch is the upturned trunk of an elephant. It's to the left of a bald eagle.

It's Tough To Be a Bug

Kids and adults scream with delight at this cartoonish theatrical attraction that combines a 3-D movie with startling theater effects. Hosted by an Audio-Animatronic Flik, the mild-mannered ant of 1998's "A Bug's Life," it has both a cute charm and a wicked sense of humor.

"Take it from an ant. It's tough to be a bug," Flik says. "That's why we've developed some amazing survival techniques." On stage comes a tarantula who shoots poison quills, a soldier termite who sprays acid, and a stink bug who, well, stinks.

Then Hopper crashes the show. What bugs him? People.

"You guys only see us as monsters!" the robot roars at the audience. "Maybe it's time you got a taste of your own medicine!" That cues an attack by a giant fly swatter and a huge can of bug spray, as well as some angry spiders and hornets. "Bug bombs, zappers, sticky little motels," Hopper yells, "nothing can stop us!" Fortunately, a long-tongued chameleon proves him wrong.

The best time to go is the last half-hour of the day. There's no line and you get your choice of seats. For the best focus sit in the middle, toward the back.

8 min. Capacity: 430. Avg. wait: 30 min. morning and afternoon, 4 min. end of day. Fastpass available. Guests may remain in wheelchairs, ECVs. Assistive listening, reflective captioning. Fear factor: Intense for preschoolers. Best ages: 6+. Debuted: 1999.

FUN FINDS ❶ Just outside the holding room, a wall plaque honors Dr. Jane Goodall's chimpanzee commitment. It's next to a carving of David Graybeard, one of her subjects. ❷ Posters in the lobby promote "past" theater shows such as "Beauty and the Bees" and "Little Shop of Hoppers." ❸ A lobby display features the giant dung ball from the earlier "The Dung and I." ❹ The background music is songs from those shows. ❺ The auditorium is the inside of an anthill. ❻ The theater's projection booth is a wasp nest. ❼ The pre-show announcer reports that "the stinkbug will be played by Claire DeRoom." ❽ After the stinkbug performs, Flik tells her "Hey, lay off the churros!" ❾ As the performance ends, fireflies swarm to the exit signs.

One of the most sophisticated robots Disney has ever built, an Audio Animatronic Hopper confronts the audience during It's Tough To Be a Bug

FUN FACTS ❯❯ Voices include Dave Foley (Flik), Cheech Marin (Chili the tarantula) and Kevin Spacey (Hopper). ❯❯ The crying baby that provokes the termite is, of course, prerecorded.

▶ Lean back in your seat to feel all of the show's special effects.

Dressed as animals, dancers perform a choreographed routine

Festival of the Lion King

✓ We dare you to see this show and not walk out with a smile on your face.

An elaborate musical revue of the best songs from the 1994 film, "The Lion King," this dazzling spectacle combines the pageantry of a parade with all the excitement of a tribal festival. Circus acts, stilt walkers, dancers dressed as animals and giant puppets fill your entire field of vision as they celebrate the joy of life.

It's like a revival, without the religion.

It's even funny.

The show opens just like the movie, with the dramatic African chant from "The Circle of Life," but this time instead of watching a cartoon sunrise you see an abstract one, performed by interpretive dancers.

After the introductions of four lead singers dressed in tribal robes, a catchy chorus of "I Just Can't Wait to be King" brings in nearly four dozen additional performers, as well as four parade floats. On one is Simba, a 12-foot animated figure sitting atop Pride Rock. Another float includes Pumbaa. Timon, meanwhile, is the wisecracking master of ceremonies.

After Timon leads the crowd in "Hakuna Matata," he introduces the Tumble Monkeys, a troupe of silly, costumed acrobats who flip, flop and fly across the stage, bounce on a trampoline and perform on still rings, bars and a flying trapeze set.

An ominous "Be Prepared" spotlights a fire-baton twirler on a dark stage between an abstract battle of stilt-walkers. A touching "Can You Feel the Love Tonight" duet features a ballet dancer who, costumed as a bird, soars into the air. Next is a spirited version of "The Circle of Life."

Timon returns to lead an audience sing-along to "The Lion Sleeps Tonight." As sections of the crowd compete against each other, dancers select children from the first few rows to join them in an instrumental parade around the stage.

The performers come together for a rousing finale. A gospel-like reprise of all the earlier songs is synchronized to a choreographed kaleidoscope of dance, lighting and, believe it or not, kites.

Look closely and you'll notice the finale is also a literal circle of life. As the four sing-

▶ Get to the theater 40 minutes early to get one of the best seats.

ers circle on the stage, dancers circle around them and, at times, form circles themselves. Meanwhile, lights, kites and eventually that flying bird twirl overhead.

The dancers' costumes are wildly imaginative. Each combines cuffs, a headpiece, leotard, leggings, makeup, a skirt and yoke to become a colorful abstract animal.

The show is performed in the round, in an enclosed, air-conditioned theater. You sit on a bench.

By the way, there are puppeteers inside the parade floats, and they can see out. If the floats are still present as you leave the theater, stand in front of Simba, Pumbaa, the elephant or giraffe and wave or say hi. They may nod back.

28 min. Capacity: 1,375. Avg. wait: 40 min. to get a great seat. ECV, wheelchair accessible. Assistive listening, handheld captioning. Debuted: 1998.

Timon the meerkat is master of ceremonies

WHERE TO SIT As you enter the theater you'll find four seating areas, two on your left and two on your right. There's not a bad seat anywhere, but a couple of locations offer added benefits.

To see the show the way it's intended, sit in the quadrant at the back right. You'll face Timon during his "Hakuna Matata" number and have the easiest time hearing the float puppets of Pumbaa and Simba, as they'll be right next to you. To be totally immersed in the performance, however, sit on the first front bench on your left. Not only will you be just inches away from the performers, but some will stop to greet you during the show. Note: to snare this front-row bench you'll need to be one of the first few guests in the theater. Even then, Disney sometimes reserves it for VIPs.

WHICH SHOW TO SEE The best shows are those with a full house, as the performers are always more energetic when a huge crowd is cheering them on. The first show of the day, however, is the easiest to get into. Typically held at 9:40 a.m., it's often less

than half full. Usually, you can show up at the last second and still choose your seat.

FUN FINDS ❶ As Timon's float enters and heads into a corner, the Catskills-comic meerkat looks at the animal dancer holding its remote-control device and says "Hey! Whatdya' doin? Slow down! I'm supposed to be center stage!" ❷ The monkeys pick bugs off of audience members and each other. ❸ Their music includes a Tarzan yell, a cow moo, a gargled version of Duke Ellington's 1937 "Caravan" and a snippet of the 1923 ditty "Yes, We Have No Bananas." ❹ Timon is a show all by himself. He cracks up watching the monkeys, trembles during "Be Prepared" and swoons throughout "Can You Feel the Love Tonight?" ❺ The giraffe often mouths the words to the songs. ❻ As you exit, Timon says "Could somebody hose down those Tumble Monkeys? They're starting to smell a little gamey."

LION CUB SIMBA finds his place in nature's circle of life in Disney's 1994 film "The Lion King." After his father is killed by his uncle Scar, Simba thinks he caused it and flees into exile. Befriended by the warmhearted (and oft-pungent) warthog Pumbaa and freewheeling meerkat Timon, Simba adopts the duo's "hakuna matata" (no worries) attitude. When childhood sweetheart Nala comes back in his life, Simba takes his place as king.

FUN FACTS ❯❯ The floats originally appeared in a parade at California's Disneyland. ❯❯ Puppeteers inside them control the movements of the elephant, giraffe, Pumbaa and Simba.

▶ Watch the movie first. It will refresh your memory of the story and its characters.

Pocahontas and Her Forest Friends

Though small in scope, this outdoor theatrical show teaches a nice lesson, and does it in an interesting fashion. A live performer, Pocahontas brings animals onto the stage (some ducks, a porcupine, skunk and a snake) as she learns that man is not only the only animal who can destroy the forest, but also the only one who can save it. Also on hand: Grandmother Willow, an Audio Animatronic tree, and Sprig, a robotic twig.

There's even a bit of philosophy. The rewards of life, the Indian maiden tells you, come not by acquiring the world, but by learning to appreciate it. Or, as she sings, "You can own the earth — and still all you own is earth — until you can paint with all the colors of the wind."

Pocahontas sings "Colors of the Wind"

The first four rows of center seating is reserved exclusively for children under age 10. Kids who sit in the first row will get a close encounter with the snake. For parents, the best seats are in the center or to the left. Sit on the right and you can't see the face of Grandmother Willow.

The show is geared to preschool and early-elementary children. Those older may be bored, or even irritated. "Talking trees?" one middle-school girl complained to her dad. "Give me a break!"

Presented a few times daily, the performance is held in a shady outdoor theater that replicates a forest glen. It's shaded from the sun by a translucent cloth. You sit on a bench.

15 min. Capacity: 350. Avg. wait: 15 min. for a good seat. ECV and wheelchair accessible. Assistive listening available. Debuted: 1998.

TRAINING SESSION You'll see how Disney trains its animals at one special show each day, a "behind-the-scenes" training session. A handler teaches future critter celebrities how to walk or fly to its mark without getting stage fright or, as is often the case, attempting to eat the scenery. Pocahontas doesn't sing, but is on hand to help out.

FUN FIND When Pocahontas sings the accusatory line "You think the only people who are people are the people who look and think like you," the performer makes a point not to make eye contact with the audience.

BASED ON THE TRUE STORY of a teenage Native American girl, Disney's 1995 "Pocahontas" dramatizes the meeting of English settlers in Jamestown with a tribe of Powhatan Indians. With help from her Grandmother Willow — a tree spirit — the young nature lover teaches Captain John Smith to respect the world around him.

Character greeting trails

You'll meet and greet some of Disney's most popular stars at the ends of these short walkways across from the Festival of the Lion King Theater. Waiting for you under the small gazebos should be at least one or two of the Fab Five (Mickey Mouse, Minnie Mouse, Donald Duck, Goofy and Pluto) as well as characters from films such as 1967's "The Jungle Book," 1994's "The Lion King," 2003's "Brother Bear" or the "Winnie the Pooh" series. Late in the day the trails often have no lines at all.

Animal Kingdom shopping guide

APPAREL

CHARACTER COSTUMES Creature Comforts *(Discovery Island)* has the best selection of children's pirate and Minnie Mouse costumes, as well as a create-your-own-crown station. Island Mercantile *(Discovery Island)* stocks pirate costumes.

CHILDREN'S WEAR The children's wear store, Creature Comforts *(Discovery Island)* has collections for kids and infants. Mombasa Marketplace *(Africa)* and Island Mercantile *(Discovery Island)* have some shirts.

FASHION Disney Outfitters *(Discovery Island)* is Animal Kingdom's adult clothing store, a fashion shop with stylish men's and women's apparel. The womenswear selection often has many cute and stylish items. Don't miss the earrings; some are from Kenya.

FOOTWEAR Island Mercantile *(Discovery Island)* has adult and children's shoes. Creature Comforts *(Discovery Island)* has kids' shoes. The Kali Cart *(Asia)* has sandals.

SPORTS APPAREL Disney Outfitters *(Discovery Island)* has character jerseys.

T-SHIRTS AND HEADWEAR Island Mercantile *(Discovery Island)* has the most T-shirts and lots of hats. Attraction-specific items can be found at the Dino Institute gift shop *(DinoLand U.S.A., at Dinosaur)*, the Kali Cart *(Asia, at Kali River Rapids)* and the Serka Zong Bazaar *(Asia, at Expedition Everest)*.

OTHER MERCHANDISE

ART The Art of Disney boutique at Disney Outfitters *(Discovery Island)* stocks Disney posters, fine-quality lithographs and "big figs," two-foot-high figurines of Mickey, Donald and other classic characters. It also has beautiful painted ostrich eggs, Lenox porcelain figurines and oil paintings. Mombasa Marketplace *(Africa)* features authentic items from Kenya and Zimbabwe, such as hand-painted gift boxes, painted gourds and soapstone carvings.

BOOKS Island Mercantile *(Discovery Island)* has a small selection of bestselling paperbacks, hardcovers and Disney titles. General books about animals are at Out of the Wild *(Conservation Station)* and at the Rainforest Cafe gift shop. Creature Comforts *(Discovery Island)* has some general Disney books for children. Mombasa Marketplace *(Africa)* has books about Africa. The Dino Institute gift shop *(DinoLand U.S.A., at Dinosaur)* has dinosaur titles. Serka Zong Bazaar *(Asia, at Expedition Everest)* has Mt. Everest books.

CANDY Beastly Bazaar *(Discovery Island)* has chocolates, cookies, gummies, lollipops, jellybeans, chocolate-covered pretzels, sugar sticks and taffy.

CHRISTMAS ITEMS The Disney Outfitters shop *(Discovery Island)* has a year-round Christmas corner with ornaments, stockings and other holiday items.

HOUSEWARES Animal Kingdom's housewares shop is Beastly Bazaar *(Discovery Island)*. It has some great kitchenware, home accessories and nice picture frames. Island Mercantile *(Discovery Island)* sells frames, photo albums, mugs and snowglobes. Mombasa Marketplace *(Africa)* and the Outpost shop *(Entrance Plaza)* have a few items. Garden Gate Gifts *(The Oasis)* has some picture frames.

JEWELRY AND WATCHES Disney Outfitters *(Discovery Island)* sells fine jewelry and watches. The open-air Mandala Gifts stand *(Asia)* has a nice collection of casual jewelry.

PET PRODUCTS Beastly Bazaar *(Discovery Island)* has Disney-themed pet bowls and dishes, clothes, collars, leashes, toys and treats. Island Mercantile *(Discovery Island)* has a smaller pet-product collection.

PINS The park's best selection is on the cart in front of Island Mercantile *(Discovery Island)*.

TOYS The park has several good toy spots. Island Mercantile *(Discovery Island)* has a large selection of Disney playthings, including animal plushies, character plushies outfitted in safari garb, video games, DVDs and art supplies. Chester and Hester's Dinosaur Treasures *(DinoLand U.S.A.)* has a create-your-own Mr. Potato Head station as well as many dinosaur-themed toys. The Dino Institute gift shop *(DinoLand U.S.A., at Dinosaur)* has toy Time Rovers from the attraction and hand-held snapping dino heads. Mombasa Marketplace *(Africa)* has some great non-Disney animal plushies that include cheetahs, elephants, flamingos, giraffes, hippos, parrots and tigers. Cute-as-a-button Yeti plushies are at Serka Zong Bazaar *(Asia, at Expedition Everest)*. The Rainforest Cafe gift shop *(Entrance Plaza)* sells a wide variety of animal-themed plushies and toys. The most unique toy in the park: the awesome Indonesian dragon kites at the Mandala Gifts stand *(Asia)*.

A Kilimanjaro Safari truck roams through Disney's realistic 110-acre African wildlife habitat

Kilimanjaro Safaris

✓ One of the best zoological attractions in the United States, this jerky, jolty open-air tour takes you through a near-perfect 100-acre re-creation of African jungles and savannas. You'll splash through rivers, cross bridges, climb hills, pass free-roaming elephants, giraffes, rhinoceros and other exotic creatures, including some of the world's rarest species. Though the most dangerous creatures are kept distant by unseen barriers, other animals can come right up to your vehicle. Visit at the right time (such as first thing in the morning, or during a rain) and you may get within inches of a curious wildebeest, or find yourself in a staring contest with a stubborn ostrich.

In fact, you never know what you'll see. Bongos, mandrills, okapi, warthogs... they're all here, feeding, fighting, running, even nursing in what appear to be wide-open forests, rivers, grasslands, hills and streams. It can't be completely real — if it were the animals would be eating each other — but it so clearly seems to be.

'POACHERS MAY BE INVOLVED.' Every Disney ride has a story, and this tale is one of the company's most relevant and, at times, grim. Supposedly an effort by the nearby village of Harambe to replace its timbering economy with eco-tourism, Kilimanjaro Safaris takes you on a "two-week" trip through the "800-square-mile" Harambe Wildlife Preserve. The storyline begins in the queue, as overhead monitors introduce you to the refuge and show you its main problem: its creatures are being killed by poachers. In a jolting — some parents say inappropriate — dose of reality, the video shows slaughtered animals.

On that jolly note, you climb into your truck, a one-time flatbed logging vehicle that's been retrofitted with high bench seats and a canvas top. Once underway, your guide establishes radio contact with the preserve's warden, Wilson Matuah. He flies above you in his spotter plane, watching for poachers and occasionally giving your driver directions to various roaming herds. After about 20 minutes, Matuah radios with

▶ The best trips are early in the day or during a light rain, when the animals are lively.

an urgent plea for help: he's spotted two poaching trucks, one with a baby elephant in back, and he needs your help to stop them. Cutting short your safari, your driver leaves the preserve through a broken gate, chasing the poachers through a flooded gorge and into a clearing where the warden has landed and awaits. Mission accomplished, you rejoin the main road and head to Matuah's office: the ride exit.

A giraffe feeds alongside a Safari truck

Redone in 2007, the radio transmissions are a condensed version of a previous poaching storyline ("They've shot Big Red!") which originally played a much larger role in the experience.

22 min. Capacity: 1,344. Avg. wait: 20 min. early morning, 45 min. peak afternoon. Fastpass available. Wheelchair accessible. Assistive listening; handheld and activated captioning. Debuted: 1998.

FUN FINDS **❶** When the phone rings in the safari office (just inside the standby queue), a machine answers it with the message "Harambe Wildlife Preserve... When it comes to safaris, we go wild!" **❷** The deflated hot-air balloon of the Kinga balloon-safari business (advertised on Harambe posters) is stored in the rafters above the queue. **❸** A grouping of black-faced royal ibis and East African crowned cranes wander a small habitat tucked in between the ride's Fastpass machines and the standby queue. **❹** "Prehistoric" tribal drawings are visible on the gate just past the flamingos and on rocks to your right as you pass the lions. **❺** While chasing the poachers you pass their camp, where a fire is still smoldering and tusks are scattered about.

FUN FACTS ❯❯ Not everything is real. There's a reason your driver says the termite mounds are 'as hard as concrete.' Those ostrich eggs are equally tough to crack. Also, the tusk marks in the red clay pits are man made. ❯❯ An artificial, though realistic, decaying carcass of a zebra originally rested across the road from the lions. Some guests thought was it real and complained. ❯❯ Why does the savannah appear to go on forever? Because the horizon is actually Disney World's 300-acre tree farm, an area not accessible to guests. ❯❯ Disney created the rutted road by coloring concrete to look like soil, then rolling tires through it and tossing in dirt, stones and twigs. ❯❯ The acacias are actually Southern live oaks with close-cropped crew cuts. ❯❯ Animal boundaries include hidden fences, moats and trenches. ❯❯ The safari has the largest collections of Nile hippos and African elephants in North America. ❯❯ The animals respond to sound cues to come in at night. Elephants hear (and feel) beating drums. ❯❯ The entire area used to be a flat cow pasture. Disney brought in 10,000 truck loads of dirt as well as 4 million plants and trees. ❯❯ The trucks run on propane. ❯❯ Kilimanjaro Safaris is the largest Disney attraction worldwide.

Riding in an open-sided truck, a Kilimanjaro Safaris guest videotapes an elephant dusting itself

▶ Taking photos is tough. The bouncy ride makes it hard to keep your camera still.

Stilt-walking performance artist Divine blends into the Animal Kingdom landscape

Meerkats stand guard along the Pangani Forest Exploration Trail

Pangani Forest Exploration Trail

✓ Streams and gentle waterfalls weave through the lush grounds of this self-guided tour of fascinating African animals. It's divided into eight areas.

You'll get a good view of black-and-white colobus monkeys and a yellow-backed duiker at an outdoor hut called the Endangered Animal Rehabilitation Centre. Few Americans have ever seen an okapi, but you will at an observation blind that also has Stanley cranes. Two colonies of naked mole rats crawl from room to room in "study burrows" in a huge wall display inside a replica research station. Other animals include cute spiny mice, a pancake tortoise and a fire skink. You can open some drawers of the research cabinets to find collections of preserved butterflies, feathers, shells, small skulls (including those of bush pigs and dwarf crocodiles), even giant beetles, scorpions and tarantulas.

You never notice that you enter an aviary, a rainforest-like screened-in area with a waterfall and pond. Two dozen species of exotic birds fly above you, rest in the trees and scurry on the ground. Don't miss the gigantic nest of the hammercop stork or the hanging homes of taveta golden weavers. A fish-viewing area features a 4-foot-long lungfish.

A 40-foot glass wall makes for a great underwater hippo viewing area — especially early when the 100,000-gallon tank is clear. Sometimes, if you're quiet, the hippos come right up to the window.

Meerkats stand guard and dig burrows at the savannah overlook, which you view from a thatch hut. Gerenuk roam nearby; meerkat and warthog skulls are on display. Next is a gorilla blind, then a suspension bridge leads to two outdoor gorilla habitats. One side has a family (a silverback, two moms and three kids); the other a bachelor troupe. The gorillas are most active early, when they eat, drink, slap heads and chase each other.

The word "pangani" is Swahili for "place of enchantment."

▶ The fish on display often suck up small pebbles and spit them out. Kids love it.

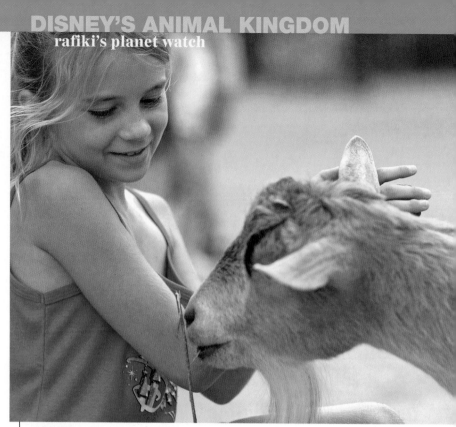

Pleased to meet you. A goat nuzzles the authors' daughter at Affection Section.

Rafiki's Planet Watch

Visiting this animal-care section of the park can be exhausting. To see it means walking to a train station, waiting for a train, taking it to another station and then trekking down a long path. Once you reach the main building, you stay on your feet. To leave, you hike back.

In other words, Rafiki's a beast.

Still, for animal lovers it's terrific. Rafiki's Planet Watch is one of the few places on Disney property where you enter a world that's totally real.

Named after the wise shaman mandrill in the 1994 film "The Lion King," the area features **Conservation Station,** a serious science center with a lot to see. In the mornings, observation windows let you look in on medical procedures on animals up to 500 pounds — expect to see anything from a bandage change on a goat to a root canal on a gorilla. Vets and cast members explain

what's going on. Usually about three animals are brought in each morning.

Other windows peer in on researchers studying elephant vocalizations and tracking a sea turtle off the Florida coast. Adjacent exhibits include a butterfly room, a

---

FUN FACTS ❯❯ Complete with a corrugated-metal water tank, the train's African depot is patterned after British structures built in East Africa during the early 1900s. Next to the formal station is a local plaster-and-thatch addition. ❯❯ Why such a fancy train? Because its track was originally designed to be a safari of its own, before the care facilities grew larger than anticipated. ❯❯ The animals shown in the mural above the Conservation Station entrance represent some of the species helped by Disney's Wildlife Conservation Fund. ❯❯ Luke the goat once ate a guest's $5 bill. ❯❯ The thatched-roof huts that sit along the return-train track are authentic. They were made by hand in Indonesia.

▶ Take the first train of the day and you'll probably see an exam-room procedure.

food preparation area and arachnid, insect and reptile displays.

You can zoom in on the park's primates, elephants, giraffes and other animals with remote-control Animal Cams. You'll hear rain, booming thunder and buzzing insects in the Song of the Rainforest exhibit, a group of cool, dark, family-sized audio booths. Eco Hero kiosks let you "speak" with Dr. Jane Goodall or George Schaller of the Tibet Wildlife Reserve. A Caring for the Wild exhibit includes Dr. Goodall's telescope and notebooks of Dian Fossey. A short film narrated by Rafiki offers a look at endangered creatures.

Cast members often play games with kids (including the ever-popular "Poop-ology") and bring out animals such as lizards, owls, parrots and snakes.

Meet-and-greet characters include Pocahontas, Rafiki and Stanley.

An adjacent petting zoo, **Affection Section** features domestic animals. Roaming free are African pygmy, San Clemente and Nigerian dwarf goats and Gulf Coast native and Tunis sheep. Behind a fence is a Dexter cow, a llama, two rare Guinea hogs and two Sicilian miniature donkeys. The largest goat, a brownish-gray fella named Luke, will steal stuff right out of your pockets.

To get to the area, you take a train from the Harambe Village station in the park's Africa section. Called the **Wildlife Express,** it runs past Disney's "Jurassic Park"-style animal-care facilities.

The long walkway is **Habitat Habit,** a series of signs and displays that offers ways to help foster conservation and attract animals to your backyard. The highlight is a display of cotton-top tamarins. There's also a Kid's Discovery Club spot, a scavenger hunt designed for children ages 3 to 8.

Top: Rafiki meets fans. **Above:** Conservation Station cast members hold animal talks in the lobby.

FUN FINDS ❶ Plastered with posters, the walls of the Harambe station are stenciled "Affixing of Advertisements is Forbidden." ❷ Ankole cattle skulls are strapped on the front of the locomotives. ❸ Impressions of a bird, fish, insect, man, shell, snail, reptile, "Lion King" main character Simba and the Tree of Life in the walkway under the Habitat Habit pavilions come together in a Circle of Life as you reach Conservation Station. ❹ In the restrooms, signs on the back of the stall doors give you The Scoop on Poop. In the men's room, placards above the urinals offer the Whiz Quiz. Did you know elephants pee 20 gallons a day?

▶ Have questions? Cast members cheerfully discuss animal nutrition and health care.

asia

Flights of Wonder

Huge birds fly within inches of the audience during this shaded outdoor show, which demonstrates the natural behaviors of cranes, hawks, vultures and other species. The presentation focuses on endangered and threatened birds but has many fun moments. After the host throws a grape in the air for a hornbill to catch, he asks for a child to come down and try it. "I'll toss the grape," he says, "you fly up and get it." Sit in the front center or near an aisle and a bird may fly right over you. *25 min. Capacity: 1,150. Avg. wait: 15 min. ECV and wheelchair accessible. Assistive listening. Debuted: 1998.*

An owl stars in a Flights of Wonder preshow

Baloo Me Away, Papa-Do-Ron-Rani and So Sad are among the names of Kali River Rapids rafts

Kali River Rapids

✓ Ready to get soaked? You should be if you board this rafting ride, which simulates a trip down a threatened rainforest river. Water slops and sprays into your boat as you bob over rapids and through geysers. Soon there's trouble — illegal loggers are destroying the landscape and filling the river with debris. Then you go over a waterfall and splash down the river. *6 min. Capacity: 240. Avg. wait: 15 min. early morning; 45 min. peak afternoon. Fastpass available. ECV users must transfer. Height restriction: 38 in. Debuted: 1999.*

FUN FINDS ❶ Mr. Panika's Shop (the third queue room) offers "Antiks Made to Order." ❷ Pop star Michael Jackson and the Nike swoosh logo appear on the murals in the last queue room. Jacko rides a raft named the Sherpa Surfer; the Nike icon is painted on a girl's white shirt on the Khatmandoozy. The murals were created in Nepal by a fan of Jackson and the shoe company.

▶ Take your river trip at the end of the day. If you get soaked, it won't matter.

Maharajah Jungle Trek

✓ A re-creation of a decaying hunting lodge turned conservation station, this series of Asian animal exhibits combines exotic wildlife with the architecture of India and Nepal. The trail takes you past a Komodo dragon; into a megabat pavilion; alongside tapir, antelope and tiger habitats; and through a lush garden aviary.

You can skip the bats if you wish, but there's nothing to be afraid of. These are fruit bats, not vampires. They have no interest in people and can't fit through the bars of the viewing area.

Don't miss the tigers. With a large natural habitat, they're often climbing hills, ducking under bushes or scanning the landscape for prey, behaviors you don't see in a regular zoo.

One of Disney's best facades, the buildings and surroundings tell a story of a king and his three sons. As shown in paintings at the second tiger area, one was an architect and built the structures, the second a nature lover who planted the gardens, the third a tiger hunter. The lodge and its forest were later given to locals, who use it today as a wildlife refuge.

FUN FINDS ❶ Just past the footbridge, an environmental history of man is shown in a sequence of stone carvings on a wall to your right. Man emerges out of the water; comes to a paradise rich with wildlife; chops down its tree; experi-

ences floods, death and chaos; and finally gains happiness when he learns to respect nature. ❷ Immediately afterward you enter the tomb of Anantah, the first ruler of the mythical Anandapur kingdom. His ashes are said to be in the large fertility urn in the middle of the room.

An Asian tiger roams the ruins of an ancient royal hunting lodge at the Maharajah Jungle Trek

FUN FACTS » The tiger pool is kept at 70 degrees, and includes fish for the tigers to catch. **»** The bridge over the tiger habitat is actually a wall that separates the carnivores from an area of barred geese. **»** The aviary "weeds" are frayed by hand for a consistent look.

▶ Bats feed first thing in the morning; tigers often play in the water at closing time.

An **80-foot drop** highlights your trip aboard the Expedition Everest tea train

As one 8-year-old girl put it, "That monster was like 100 feet tall!" Actually, he's only 18.

What begins as a peaceful trip through a forest turns into a tense chase through a mountain. It doesn't go upside-down, but your 4,000-foot journey climbs nearly 200 feet in the air, stops twice, switches direction, takes an 80-foot drop and hits a top speed of 50 mph.

"Everest is a ride for the entire family," says executive designer Joe Rohde. "It's just a *fast* ride for the entire family."

If you can, ride it at night. The mountain is lit in eery orange and purple, but the track stays dark. You never know where you're at, or where you're going.

A MONSTER MYTH To deepen your experience Disney has built a full back story — a tale of a mythical creature, weird accidents, wise villagers and clueless entrepreneurs.

Expedition Everest

✓ "I don't know, Charlie. This looks overwhelming to me." Grabbing her husband's arm, the thirtyish blonde stood under waving prayer flags as she looked up at the mountain. She couldn't see what was inside it, but she could hear screams and a distant roar. Every minute or so, out flew a runaway train.

A modern Disney megaride, Expedition Everest combines some sly Disney mind games with coaster-like thrills and the excitement of a close encounter of the hairy kind. Aboard an out-of-control railcar that races forward and backward, you swoop into the mysterious world of the Yeti, the mythical Himalayan creature also known as the Abominable Snowman.

But it's the mental tricks that psych you out. The exotic village looks real. The train is rusty. The mountain looks thousands of feet tall. And you can't see the Yeti until the very last second.

The story, what Disney calls The Legend of the Forbidden Mountain (and has hidden details of throughout the standby queue*) begins in the 1920s, a time when tea plantations flourished in the mountains of the imaginary Asian kingdom of Anandapur. Private rail lines carried the tea to villages, where it was shipped to distant markets. The Royal Anandapur Tea Co. used one such route extensively through the early 1930s, sending "steam-donkey" trains through the mysterious mountains to the village of Serka Zong.

Starting in 1933, however, the railroad was plagued with accidents. Some residents drew a connection between the mishaps and increasing British expeditionary attempts to reach the summit of nearby Mt. Everest, invoking the spirit of the Yeti, the fabled, monstrous creature that guards the sacred area. By 1934, equipment breakdowns and

*If you use a Fastpass you miss much of the back story. You skip the temple, store and museum because, as the story goes, you have already booked your trip and gotten your provisions.

▶ Get your Fastpasses early. A day's entire supply of passes is often gone by noon.

strange track snaps caused the tea company to pull up stakes.

The legend of a guardian beast continued to circulate among locals. It came to a head in 1982, with the tragic disappearance of the Forbidden Mountain Expedition.

Cut to today. Bob, a bohemian American who has wandered into Serka Zong, has decided to set up shop. A hippie who came to Asia many years ago, Bob loves the village's Hare Krishna vibe but doesn't believe in the Yeti.

To earn a living, he has teamed up with a local entrepreneur, Norbu. Together they have restored the old railroad to create Himalayan Escapes Tours and Expeditions, a business marketed as a way to help trekkers get to Everest in a new way. Instead of hiking for two weeks through the foothills and over the smaller ranges, now climbers can get to the foot of Everest in just a few hours, riding safely and quickly on Bob and Norbu's quaint old steam train through the scenic Forbidden Mountain.

The enthusiastic duo have just put on a loud and colorful show for their grand opening. Government officials trumpeted the venture as "a landmark enterprise sparking a new era of prosperity and opportunity for Serka Zong."

Now *you* enter in the story. You've decided to take a trekking trip up to Mt. Everest. Being a weekend warrior, you've heard about Himalayan Escapes and its short-cut train, and have made your way to Serka Zong. As you enter the village, however, locals have fervently posted warnings on the rocks and buildings.

Undeterred, you walk into Bob's office, the converted first floor of his two-story apartment. Crammed with mountaineering gear, this is where you book your trip, get your permit and meet your guide. Unfortunately, Bob has stepped out for a moment — a sign on his chair reads

Fair warning. Advisories from frightened locals try to convince you to cancel your trip.

Sign of a Yeti? Train riders come to the end of the line at the top of the mountain range

"Be right back" — so you move on, deciding to head out on your own.

You work your way through the village and to the train station. It's easy to find your way, thanks to the many handy little signs Bob has taped up.

First you come upon a temple. Carved with images of the Yeti in its columns and eaves, it's been erected by villagers out of respect to the creature.

Next you enter Tashi's General Store and Bar, a chance to get provisions for your trek as well as relax for a moment with a pot of tongba, an alcoholic, tea-like brew that could make you see things that aren't actually there.

Then you pass through the village's Yeti museum, an old tea warehouse that's filled with artifacts so realistic you may forget they're all fake. Included are the mangled climbing equipment, shredded tent and fang-punctured canteens that are the only remains of the ill-fated 1982 expedition, as well as a cast of the creature's footprint. It's run by Professor Pumba Dorjay, a conservation biologist who believes the creature could indeed be real.

Finally you're at the train station, where Norbu and Bob's refurbished Anandapur Rail Service is destined for the foothills of Mount Everest. The hissing transport train has just pulled in and there's an open seat reserved for you. So you board, ready for your calm journey through the mountains.

And that's just what you get. At first.

TRANQUILITY, THEN TERROR Your journey begins as a calm ride. The train rolls over a little hill and around some gentle corners as it passes through bamboo forests and fern groves.

Heading up through an old stone monastery, you do hear some ominous music and maybe a glimpse of a weird totem or mural, but everything is still just hunky dory as you continue into the high, cold (really!) air.

Yeti? Yeah, right.

Then it happens.

Just as you reach the top of the mountain, your train stops. It has to — the rails in front of it have been ripped into a gnarled mass of twisted metal. In a fit of rage, the Yeti has torn apart the track!

As you notice huge footprints in the snow, and a vulture eyeing you from above, your train sits there. Silently.

Suddenly, it loses its grip. You slide backward, careening into a black hole in the mountain's center. But that track leads nowhere, too: you see the skulking shadow of the Yeti smashing it.

Fortunately, your train again breaks loose, sliding forward on still a different track. You drop out of the mountain to safety, only to circle right back in.

Now you meet the Yeti face-to-muzzle. No longer a hypothetical hair man, the massive, mean, monster machine is right in front of you, staring you down. He's ripped up this track too, but just as he takes a swipe at you... you miraculously drop down to another track and hightail it back to the village.

THREE MOUNTAINS IN ONE In reality, the mountain is three free-standing structures. One is the ride, a dynamic system with internal framing that extends all the way down to the foundation. The second is the

▶ Sit in the back for the wildest ride. You'll get whipped harder and fall faster.

building, with its beams and columns. The third is the Yeti, with its own independent supports. Though intertwined like spaghetti, the three structures don't touch. If they did, the mountain's plaster and stucco would flake off. "In some cases we ran building beams down the middle of A-frame columns that support the ride," says project manager Mike Lentz.

Engineering the ride took 15 track designs and more than a year to figure out completely. "I've been here 15 years," says technical supervisor Mark Mesko, "and I've never been through a design collaboration like that."

3 min. Capacity: 170. Avg. wait: 30 min. early morning; 90 min. peak afternoon. Fastpass available, often sold out by noon. Access: ECV and wheelchair users must transfer. Height restriction: 44 in. Fear factor: High. The lift rises high over the ground, you travel backwards in total darkness for 10 sec.; the ride includes one steep, turning drop. Best ages: 8 and up. Debuted: 2006.

FUN FINDS ❶ Plaster on the Fastpass building and gift shop simulates the Himalayan building material of dried yak dung. ❷ A bulletin board note on the wall of Gupta's Gear (left of the main village) reads "Billy — It's a small world after all! Met your brother on the trail... Mikey." ❸ Steam escapes from the train's boiler after it pulls into the boarding area. ❹ It pulls out with a "toot-toot!" ❺ The Yeti's claw marks and footprints appear in the snow to your right at your first stop. ❻ When you stop in the cave, watch the track in front of you. You'll see it flip over.

FUN FACTS ❯❯ The mountain has 1,800 tons of steel, 18.7 million pounds of concrete, 2,000 gallons of stain and paint and 200,000 square feet of rock work. ❯❯ The Yeti has a potential thrust of 260,000 pounds of force — more than a 747 airliner. It's Disney's most advanced Audio Animatronics creature. ❯❯ Much of the queue-line woodwork, including the entire Yeti temple, was handcrafted by Himalayan artists. ❯❯ The Buddha statues, Nepalese Coke bottles, desk phone and pot-bellied stoves are among 8,000 authentic items Disney imported from Asia. ❯❯ The 6-acre area has 900 bamboo plants and 100 types of bushes. ❯❯ The buildings were aged with blowtorches, chainsaws and hammers. ❯❯ "Serka Zong" is Tibetan for "fortress of the chasm."

The Yeti legend

Yetis are not real. Scientists worldwide agree there is no credible evidence of an animal roaming the Himalayas that is not already an identified mammal. Some scholars say people who claim to see a Yeti are probably spotting a golden monkey, a Himalayan primate that shares the mythical creature's face, hairy body, blue skin and ability to live in cold climates.

The Yeti legend, however, is quite real. For hundreds of years, Himalayan natives have told stories about a humanoid monster that fiercely guards the area around Mt. Everest. The reports increased in the early 20th century, when Westerners began to climb the mountains and reported seeing an "Abominable Snowman."

One of the most famous Western reports appeared in 1925. Traveling with a British geological expedition at about 15,000 feet, Greek photographer N.A. Tombazi saw a large creature moving among some lower slopes. He reported its movement was "exactly like a human being, walking upright and stopping occasionally to uproot or pull at some dwarf rhododendron bushes." A thousand feet away from the creature, Tombazi didn't take its picture, but two hours later reached the area and found 15 footprints. He described them as "similar in shape to those of a man, but only six to seven inches long by four inches wide. The marks of five distinct toes and the instep were perfectly clear... undoubtedly those of a biped."

Western interest in the Yeti peaked decades later. Sir Edmund Hillary, who climbed Everest in 1953, led a 1960 trip attempting to prove, or disprove, the Yeti's existence. Sponsored by the World Book Encyclopedia, the expedition was outfitted with infrared film and trip-wire and time-lapse cameras. It found nothing.

But the myth lived on. The villain-turned-good-guy of 1964's stop-motion classic "Rudolph the Red-Nosed Reindeer" is a Yeti named Bumbles. Disney added the creatures to Disneyland's Matterhorn ride in 1978, and the 2001 Disney/Pixar film "Monsters Inc." includes a disgruntled Abominable Snowman voiced by John Ratzenberger. "'Abominable!'" he complains. "Why can't they call me the 'Adorable Snowman,' or the 'Agreeable Snowman,' for crying out loud? I'm a nice guy!" The legend still lives on in Nepal, where the Yeti has a religious meaning to some and is a tourist money maker.

The term "Abominable Snowman" was coined by mistake. While exploring the Himalayas in 1921, British Lt. Col. C.K. Howard-Bury spotted what he thought were gray wolves. When his Sherpa guides told him their prints were those of a "met-teh," or "man-sized wild creature," he misheard them to say "metoh-kangmi," or "snow creature." Reporting this incident, British newspaper editor Henry Newman quoted the words as "metch kangmi," which he said meant "abominable or filthy man of the snow."

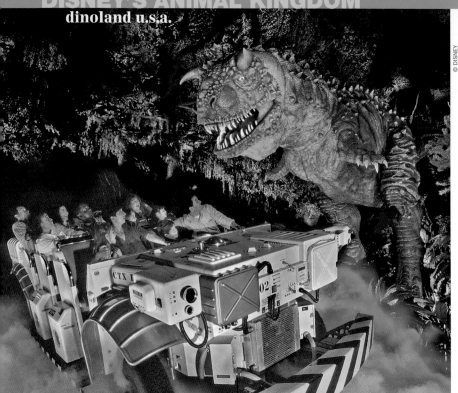

© DISNEY

Too close for comfort. An angry carnotaurus threatens guests riding a Dinosaur Time Rover. **Below,** a McDonald's poster outside the Dino Institute shows a scene from the Dinosaur ride.

Dinosaur

You'll remember the last second of this attraction for days — a ferocious dinosaur gets right in your face and lets loose with an unearthly roar. The rest of this dark indoor ride is almost as tense.

You start off in the rotunda of the Dino Institute Discovery Center, a parody of the Smithsonian's National Museum of Natural History. As you pass earnest murals and displays, a multimedia show explains how an asteroid wiped out the dinosaurs long ago.

In the Orientation Room you meet Director Helen Marsh (Phylicia Rashad, best-known as Claire Huxtable on the 1980s television sitcom "Cosby") via a video hookup. She shows you the Time Rover, a vehicle that will take you back on a peaceful visit to the Age of the Dinosaurs.

But her assistant has a different plan. Once Marsh leaves the room, Dr. Grant Seeker (Wallace Langham, of the television drama "CSI") secretly reprograms her computer to send you back to a time just

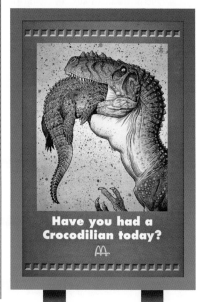

Have you had a Crocodilian today?

THEORIES OF EXTINCTION

ASTEROID IMPACT

CLIMATE CHANGES

EGG-EATING MAM

DISEASE

THE DINO INSTITUTE

A queue-line mural parodies a stuffy museum

before the asteroid strikes, to bring an iguanodon to the present.

Boarding your vehicle, your first stop is a flashing, smoky time tunnel. You emerge 65 million years earlier in a dark prehistoric forest. As you careen forward you see many dinosaurs, including an alioramus swallowing its dinner. Suddenly a huge carnotaurus starts chasing you. Then it gets worse — your power starts to fail. As a massive meteor destroys your trail, it appears that you, too, are about to become extinct.

In a final burst of speed, you find your iguanodon, narrowly miss the last lunge of the carnotaurus and crash back to the present. Security monitors show you did indeed pick up the iguanodon.

3 min. 30 sec. Capacity: 144. Avg. wait: none early morning, 30 min. peak afternoon. Fastpass available. ECV and wheelchair users must transfer. Assisted listening, video captioning. Height restriction: 40 in. Fear factor: Intense. Debuted: 1998 (as Countdown to Extinction).

FUN FINDS ❶ Just outside the building, a dedication plaque is dated April 22, 1978 — exactly 20 years before the attraction opened. ❷ The Smithsonian parody includes a diorama with an obvious plastic rat glued to an obvious plastic tree, beneath which swim plastic fish in a plastic pond. ❸ Dr. Seeker claims flash photography "interferes with the homing signal." ❹ Actually an above-ground warehouse, the "underground research facility" is cooler than the earlier rooms, and has flickering lights. ❺ Monitors in the gift shop show the iguanodon continuing to wander the building. ❻ A cast of an ancient sea turtle hangs over the gift shop.

FUN FACTS ❯❯ An "enhanced motion vehicle," your Time Rover gets its lurching movements from 3,000 PSI of hydraulic pressure. On-board tanks hold 100 gallons of fluid. ❯❯ An iguanodon named Aladar starred in Disney's 2000 film, "Dinosaur."

Dino-Sue

A cast of the largest, most complete Tyrannosaurus rex fossil ever found (Sue, uncovered in South Dakota in 1990) stands in front of the Dinosaur attraction. Named after paleontologist Sue Hendrickson, the 67-million-year-old creature is estimated to have been 45 feet long and 14 feet tall. Much of the real fossil's bonework (now at Chicago's Field Museum) was done in the late 1990s in front of Disney guests, where today's Dino-Rama carnival sits.

The skull of the T-Rex cast

Dumbo XL. Unlike its famous cousin, TriceraTop Spin has short lines... and room for four.

TriceraTop Spin

Toddlers love these friendly dinos, who climb, dive and tilt as they fly around a huge toy top. The colors are vivid — the top alone is orange, blue and red. Extra eye candy includes flying comets and some surprising pop-ups on the top itself. After dark the spokes are outlined with white light bulbs. Add in some manic banjo music and, in the morning or after dark, a nice breeze, and even dad will crack a smile. Each dino seats four, so small families can ride together.

1 min. 30 sec. Capacity: 64. Avg. wait: 15 min. early morning; 30 min. peak afternoon. ECV users must transfer to a wheelchair. Debuted: 2001.

Primeval Whirl

A spoof of the Dinosaur attraction, this spinning roller coaster also takes you back to the age of hitchhiking dinosaurs, but this time in a Time Machine: a 1950s candy-colored car "equipped" with a kitchen timer, clock radio and alarm clock. The scenery combines comic dinosaurs and meteors with cartoon clocks and vortexes. It's a wild trip. The ride whips you into your fellow time travelers as it twists along a switchback track. Once the meteors hit, your car starts to spin. *2 min. 30 sec. Capacity: 52 on each of two tracks. Avg. wait: 5 min. early morning; 20 min. peak afternoon. Fastpass available. ECV and wheelchair users must transfer. Height restriction: 48 in. Fear factor: One steep drop. The spinning can affect those with inner-ear issues. Debuted: 2002.*

FUN FINDS ❶ The time portal in the queue is decorated with egg beaters and hubcaps. ❷ As you come to the exit area Hester says "Please stand up before exiting."

Out for a spin. Primeval Whirl riders.

▶ To avoid getting dizzy on Primeval Whirl, stare at the orange radio in front of you.

The Boneyard

Disney's best playground, this faux dig site combines a towering maze of nets, slides and tunnels for elementary-age kids with a sandy pit for preschoolers. "Fossils" include a triceratops, T-rex and wooly mammoth. You may lose sight of your kids, but there's only one exit.

Dark slides are among the finds at the Boneyard

FUN FINDS ❶ The ambient music (pirate radio station W-DINO) includes the Move's 1970 "Brontosaurus" and the 1977 Blue Oyster Cult classic "Godzilla." ❷ Notes sound when you knock on the "xylobone" behind the Jeep. ❸ Dino tracks in the right corner trigger roars when you step on them. ❹ Debates about dinos appear on signs throughout the area.

A dino double! The authors' daughter is a Fossil Fun Games prize winner.

Fossil Fun Games

It's not that hard to win $15 plushies at three of these carnival games. Use your free hand to cradle the front of your gun at the $2 Fossil Fueler water-squirt game. Don't anticipate the popping heads at the $2 Whac-A-Packycephalosaur. Roll the balls softly at the $2 Mammoth Marathon racing derby.

The easiest way to win: Play these three when there is only one other player. You'll have a 50 percent chance of winning a $10 toy. If you have two kids and no one plays against them, your $4 bet has to pay off.

The extra-bouncy $3 Bronto Score basketball toss and the $3 Comet Crasher ball toss require more luck. Groups of smaller prizes can be traded in for larger ones, and everything can be sent to package pickup.

▶ Wacky Packy (Whac-A-Packycephalosaur) is the easiest Fossil Fun Game for kids.

dinoland u.s.a.

Finding Nemo — The Musical

This 30-minute show is as good as a Broadway musical

✓ "Wow," said the 40-year-old man under his breath, watching the show with his wife. "WOW!!!" said the 3-year-old girl nearby, standing in her seat as she beamed at her older brother.

Singers who somersault as they "swim" high above the stage... giant jellyfish that billow through the theater... a tricycle-pedaling stingray... a chorus line of shimmying sharks... the creativity seems to never end in this Broadway-quality retelling of the 2003 smash-hit movie, "Finding Nemo."

With an appeal every bit as awe-inspiring and broad-based as the film, this beautiful spectacle of color, movement and imagination redefines the meaning of the term "puppet show."

The main characters are costumed live singers who act out their roles as they simultaneously operate larger-than-life animated puppets. Peripheral characters are brought to life by other puppetry styles, including Japanese bunraku (one puppet is operated by multiple puppeteers), shadow and rod. Many of the puppets are huge. Sea turtle Crush is the size of a Volkswagen, and Nigel the pelican stands 22 feet tall.

The dazzling production also includes acrobats, dancers, animated backdrops and terrifically abstract props, like a fish net comprised simply of six bowed ladders in a circle.

Ah, but what about the music? You've never heard it before. Is that a problem?

No. The songs are easily accessible, and presented as fun musical numbers that fit seamlessly into the story, almost as if they were always part of it. Besides, how can you not like a dancing shark?

The production has a big-time pedigree.

The puppetry comes from Michael Curry, who did the Animal Kingdom parade floats as well as the puppets in the Broadway version of Disney's "The Lion King." Its songs were written by Robert Lopez, the Tony Award-winning co-composer of the Broadway musical "Avenue Q," and his wife Kristen Anderson-Lopez, the co-creator of

Broadway's "Along the Way." Anderson-Lopez say the couple took the job of producing the theme-park show "as seriously as we would a Broadway show. 'Nemo' is one of our favorite movies of all time."

The show's director is Peter Brosius, the Tony-winning artistic director of The Children's Theatre Company of Minneapolis. Another sign of quality: all 18 actors are singing live. Unlike Disney World's other stage shows, no one here is lip-synching.

The production takes place in the now-enclosed Theater in the Wild, located along the walkway that runs between DinoLand U.S.A. and Asia.

35 min. Capacity: 1,700. Avg. wait: 30 min. to get a great seat. Fastpass available. ECV, wheelchair accessible. Reflective captioning. Debuted: 2007.

FUN FINDS ❶ As Nemo longs to explore "the big blue world," Marlin warns "Sharks are not our friends, Nemo. Haven't you seen 'Jaws'?" ❷ Later, unsure of his aquarium surroundings, Nemo bangs into the glass. ❸ After the other pet fish welcome Nemo with their "Wannahockaloogie" chant, Peach remarks "I don't know why we can't just say 'Hello.'" ❹ Knocked out after a mine explosion, Dory mumbles "The sea monkey has my money... I'm a natural blue..." ❺ After Crush and the sea turtles perform an elaborate production number, Dory exclaims "Hey look! Turtles!" ❻ She once calls Nemo "TiVo." ❼ As you leave, the movie's "Mine! Mine!" gulls appear to bid you "Bye! Bye!"

IN THE 2003 FILM "Finding Nemo," curious clownfish Nemo defies his overprotective father, Marlin, and swims out to a boat, only to be captured by a diver hunting for aquarium fish. Determined to find his son, Marlin encounters Dory, an absentminded blue tang, as well as sharks, jellyfish and sea turtles. Meanwhile, Nemo, relocated to a fish tank in Sydney, makes new friends who teach him that he's stronger than he thinks, and help him reunite with his dad.

▶ Sit in the middle to see the full spectacle, along the catwalk to be immersed in it.

park puzzler

How much do you really know about Animal Kingdom?

1) During the Festival of the Lion King, Timon doesn't want the Tumble Monkeys to pack up because it's time for...
a. "The Circle of Life."
b. "Hakuna Matata."
c. A "snappy South Seas medley."

2) What song plays in the lobby of the Tree of Life Theater?
a. "Beauty and the Bees."
b. "Herbie and the Fleas."
c. "The Flowers and the Trees."

3) The photo at right is unusual because...
a. It's a girl in a chimpanzee mask.
b. The park doesn't have chimps.
c. The girl is standing in the rain.
d. All of the above.

4) The name of the scientist who sends you back in time at the Dinosaur attraction is...
a. Bunsen Honeydew.
b. Tom Morrow.
c. Grant Seeker.

5) Which animal appears in the logo for Disney's Animal Kingdom but not at the park?
a. A dragon.
b. A mouse.
c. A unicorn.

6) According to your driver, how long is your trip supposed to take on Kilimanjaro Safaris?
a. Two weeks.
b. Two months.
c. Two years.

7) What activity is specifically not allowed on the Wildlife Express Train?
a. Cooking.
b. Camping.
c. Fishing.

8) In Finding Nemo — The Musical, Nemo sings that he wants to explore:
a. A whole new world.
b. The big blue world.
c. Part of your world.

Answers, page 331

A **Party Animal** stilt walker marches down the street

Mickey's Jammin' Jungle Parade

✓ Towering puppets, whimsical stilt-walkers, colorful Jeeps and Land Rovers, dozens of dancers and infectious music combine to celebrate the harmony between man and animals in this lively procession. "I am you. And you are me," the anchor song says. "We're just one great big family." It's all up close and personal, on shady, winding pathways that are often just 12 feet wide.

There are 17 floats and vehicles. The mechanical puppets include an antelope, chameleon, crane, frog, giraffe, monkey, peacock and wildebeest. Handcrafted in a leafy motif from what appears to be natural materials, the abstract animals move like real creatures — the chameleon sticks out its tongue; the frog jumps.

Drummers ride atop four creatures.

Dancing alongside are ten Party Animals (creature-costumed stilt-walkers), ten Party

Patrol safari guides as well as Pluto, Chip 'n' Dale, Timon from Disney's 1994 film, "The Lion King," Terk from 1999's "Tarzan," Baloo and King Louie from 1967's "The Jungle Book," even Brer Bear and Brer Rabbit from the 1946 "Song of the South."

A fun back story ties it all together. Mickey Mouse and Rafiki (the mandrill from "The Lion King") are taking Minnie Mouse, Donald Duck and Goofy camping. Each of the three has his or her own safari truck, but none know how to pack. Donald totes a leaky boat. Minnie brings a bathtub. Goofy's the worst: he's packed everything from his bowling trophy to, literally, his kitchen sink.

The catchy soundtrack features Disney versions of the 1954 New Orleans standard "Iko Iko," South African legend Miriam Makeba's 1960s dance classic "Pata Pata" and "Mas Que Nada," the 1966 signature tune of Brazil's Sergio Mendes.

Selected at random each day, up to 25 park guests ride in the procession.

Travels in a circle around Discovery Island. It starts, and exits, in Africa, at the gate between the Tusker House restaurant and Kilimanjaro Safaris. 15 min. Choose a viewing spot 30 min. early to get a shady, curbside seat. Special viewing locations available for those in wheelchairs and ECVs. Assistive listening. Debuted: 2001.

FUN FINDS ❶ Minnie's bathtub blows bubbles. ❷ It has a rubber ducky: Donald. ❸ Goofy's hood ornament is his bowling trophy. It topples over as his engine overheats. ❹ Strapped onto Goofy's hood is Aladdin's lamp and carpet. ❺ Goofy's vehicle carries a Donald Duck life preserver. ❻ Timon's backpack is full of bugs. ❼ The driver of the hippo rickshaw is the animal's pic-pic bird. ❽ The kangaroo float has a spring for a tail. Its drummer sits in its pouch. ❾ The mane and tail of the zebra-costumed stilt-walker are brooms.

FUN FACT ❯❯ The party animals and safari guides also appear as dancers, stilt-walkers and (hidden) puppeteers at the Festival of the Lion King.

▶ The parade passes through Africa twice — on its way out and back.

Street performers

✓ **The Adventure Begins** is the park's opening ceremony *(Entrance Plaza)*. Rafiki appears at the gate 15 minutes early, then Goofy, Minnie and Pluto meet you at Discovery Island... **The Adventure Continues** *(Asia and DinoLand U.S.A.)* is a character boat that travels past Flame Tree Barbecue and the Dino-Land U.S.A. gate... Roving potted plant **Wes Palm** *(Entrance Plaza)* chats with guests... Covered in a foliage costume, stilt-walking performance artist **DiVine** *(Asia, along the walkway to Africa)* blends into the landscape... Double backflips and mid-air voguing highlight the choreography of the **G-Force** trampoline troupe *(DinoLand U.S.A., at Dinosaur Treasures)*... Children guess the animal when funnyman **Gitar Dan** *(Rafiki's Planet Watch, at Conservation Station)* sings about it... Botswanans, Namibians and South Africans talk about their homelands at the three-bench **Harambe School** *(Africa, behind the fruit market)*. The 1 p.m. lesson is Harambe history... Vibrant costumes and ritualistic dances make Andes panpipe group **Inka Sikuri** *(Discovery Island, across from Flame Tree Barbecue)* fun to watch as well as listen to... The best limbo dancers you'll ever see, the **Karuka Acrobats** *(Africa)* also fly through hoops... So unaffected you'd never guess he's a legendary percussionist who once played with B.B. King, **Mor Thiam** ("Chahm") *(Africa)* is a master of the goblet-shaped Djembe drum and the father of R&B artist Akon... **Pipa the Talking Recycling Can** *(Rafiki's Planet Watch)* chats with guests as he wanders around Conservation Station... Disguised as three dippy painters, **Smear, Splat & Dip** *(DinoLand U.S.A., at Dinosaur Treasures)* is really a balance and juggling troupe... Turn the beat around: you'll love to feel the percussion of the **Tam Tams of Congo** *(Africa, at Dawa Bar)*, a rousing native quintet who call, dance, shout and

Inka Sikuri (top); Tam Tams of Congo (above)

whistle... Strolling steel-drum band the **Tropicals** *(Discovery Island)* sometimes plays Disney tunes... Five drum sets, lots of cow bells and a zendrum create the syncopated rhythms of world-music percussionists **The Village Beatniks** *(Discovery Island, across from Flame Tree Barbecue)*.

▶ Guest Relations has the show times for all Animal Kingdom performers.

animal guide

Western lowland gorilla

ANTEATER

A walking vacuum cleaner, the Latin American **giant anteater** *(The Oasis)* sucks up ants and termites with its toothless snout. It can flick its 2-foot tongue 150 times a minute, eat 30,000 insects a day, yet sleep

Giant anteater

15 hours a day. Growing up to 9 feet long, a giant anteater has the largest claws of any mammal and the longest tongue of any mammal for its size. To protect its claws, an anteater walks on its front knuckles. It uses its tail as a

blanket when it sleeps. Though fed a prescribed diet, Disney's anteater still digs for insects.

ANTELOPE

The beautiful **bongo** *(Kilimanjaro Safaris)* has white stripes on its chestnut coat. This shy, rarely seen creature is known as the Ghost of the Forest. The largest forest antelope, it can weigh up to 600 pounds. The delicate **gerenuk** *(Pangani Forest Exploration Trail)* stands up to feed on the high leaves of trees. Its hip joints swivel to let its backbone line up with its hind legs. The most agile antelope, the **impala** *(Kilimanjaro Safaris)* can leap up to 10 feet in the air and turn in mid-flight. It can run up to 40 mph and take bounds of almost 40 feet. A male attracts females (and scares off other males) by repeatedly sticking his tongue out, a display known as tongue flashing. The **Patterson's eland** *(Kilimanjaro Safaris)* is the world's largest antelope. It can stand 6 feet tall and weigh 1,500 pounds. The aggressive **sable antelope** *(Kilimanjaro Safaris)* drops to its knees to engage foes with its sizable horns. When at rest, a group of the animals will lie in a circle with its heads facing out, protecting young that lie in the middle. The tiny **Thomson's gazelle** *(Kilimanjaro Safaris)* commonly known as the Tommy, stands only 2 or 3 feet tall, but can run at speeds up to 50 mph. Still, it is the favorite prey of the cheetah. The **white-bearded wildebeest** *(Kilimanjaro Safaris)* is also known as the gnu, the sound of its call. The gregarious animal sleeps in rows, gives birth in large groups and migrates annually in a herd of up to 1.5 million — the world's single largest movement of wildlife. Named for its habit of diving into underbrush when frightened, the chunky **yellow-backed duiker** —

"diver" in Afrikaans —
(*Kilimanjaro Safaris*) is the
largest duiker, growing up to 3
feet. Permanently attached,
antelope horns are not shed.

APES
The largest and loudest gibbon,
the 3-foot-tall **siamang** (*Asia, at
the monument towers between
Flights of Wonder and Kali River
Rapids*) inflates a sac at its
throat to produce a hoot that
can reach 113 decibels, nearly
as noisy as a jet aircraft at 100
yards. Early most mornings a
family's adult female will start a
group call that can last 30
minutes. The monogamous
mates sometimes sing duets to
express affection. Family
members often groom each
other and usually don't venture
more than 30 feet apart. The
father shares in raising a baby
and takes over child care after
an infant's first year. A siamang's
arms are longer than its legs, a
feature which lets the ape swing
through tree branches that can
be 30 feet apart.

A crescendo of eerie siren-like
whoops is the territorial call of
the smaller **white-cheeked
gibbon** (*Asia, near the exit to
Kali River Rapids*). It travels up
to a mile each day, farther than
any other forest ape or monkey.
The animal's agility makes it
virtually invulnerable to
predators, but human activities
(rain forest farming, logging and
military activities) have
destroyed most of its habitat. It
lives in southern China, Laos
and North Vietnam. Males and
juveniles are black with white
cheeks. Females and newborns
are blond.

The **western lowland gorilla**
(*Pangani Forest Exploration
Trail*) is the most populous
gorilla subspecies, with about
94,000 animals living in the
wild. The world's largest and
most powerful primate, a gorilla
is also the least aggressive, as
it is generally shy and peaceful.

The iconic chest-
beating is just a
display. The ape
lives in a group of
five to 30 animals,
of which the most
mature male serves
as the benevolent
dictator. Identified
by the silver hair on
his back, this
"silverback" will
even baby-sit an
infant while mom
looks for food.

Like humans,
gorillas have
fingerprints, 32
teeth, can stand
upright, have the
same sexual cycle
(females
menstruate about
every 28 days, births happen
after 9 months, juveniles
mature at around 11 or 12
years), use tools and can learn
sign language. Walt Disney
World has a family of six gorillas
(one silverback, two adult
females, three juveniles) as well
as three bachelors.

BABIRUSA
With a face only a mother could
love, the freakish **babirusa** (*The
Oasis*) looks like a giant pig
with a dental problem. In males,
huge upper tusks extend
through the snout. Like a
macaw, a babirusa eats clay to
cleanse its system. Though its
name means "pig-deer," a
babirusa is more closely related
to a hippo. It lives in Indonesia.

BATS
The largest bat in the world, the
Malayan flying fox (*Maharajah
Jungle Trek*) has a wingspan of
up to 6 feet, so massive it can't
take off from the ground. The
Rodrigues fruit bat (*Maharajah
Jungle Trek*) has a 3-foot span.
Bats are the only flying
mammals. These two species are
vegetarians. *The Disney bats
cling to their hanging food with*

Gerenuk

*their claws and eat it upside
down. They groom and lick each
other to express affection, often
nuzzling snouts. They turn
rightside-up to relieve
themselves. The bats can sense
rain coming. Just before it starts
to sprinkle, the bats fold up, just
as when it's too hot or sunny.*

CAVY
The world's second largest
rodent, the **Patagonian cavy**
(*The Oasis*) can weigh 25
pounds. Related to a guinea
pig, it uses its long legs to run
up to 28 mph and leap up to 6
feet. It lives around the Andes
mountains of South America.

CHEETAH
Using its long tail for balance,
the **cheetah** (*Kilimanjaro
Safaris*) can accelerate from 0
to 70 mph in three seconds.
The fastest land animal, it can
easily outrun any creature, but
only over a short distance.
Adapted for traction, its claws
are only slightly curved and only
partially retract. As the cats
naturally hunt in daylight, safari
guests see them eyeing
intended prey.

Rodrigues fruit bat

CRANES

The **East African crowned crane** (Discovery Island) has the perfect camouflage for the tall grass of its wetland habitat: a

East African crowned crane

brush-like crest of golden feathers. It's the only crane that roosts in trees. Listen for its loud, honking trumpets. Standing 6 feet tall, the **sarus crane** (Maharajah Jungle Trek) is the world's tallest flying bird. Its wingspan is 8 feet. *The courtship ritual of cranes is one of the animal kingdom's strangest behaviors. A pair will bow toward each other and each will hop, jump, strut and flap its wings as it circles the other. The duo also performs a unison call: a lengthy series of coordinated honks and squawks.*

CROCODILES

Much larger than its alligator cousin, the brawny **American crocodile** (DinoLand U.S.A.) can grow up to 15 feet long and weigh 2,000 pounds. It can go up to two years between meals,

using its tail fat for nourishment. Only about 500 are left in the United States, all in southern Florida. Disney's creature often lies with its mouth wide open to keep cool. A croc has no sweat glands. Growing even bigger, the **Nile crocodile** (Kilimanjaro Safaris) can reach 20 feet long. The aggressive animal will run onto land to snatch prey. Life starts off sweet: hatchlings call to their mother from inside their eggs when ready to hatch, then both parents roll the eggs in their mouths to crack the shells. The mom carries her foot-long newborns in her jaws to water, then guards them for up to six months. *Disney's Nile crocs are trained to come in at night. Keepers ring a bell and dangle food in front of an enclosure.*

DEER

Axis deer (Discovery Island) are sure strange. Living in herds of both sexes, the almost-constantly rutting males make loud bugle-like bellows. Meanwhile, the females fight. Like boxing kangaroos, they paw at one another while standing on their hind legs. The world's most endangered deer, the **Elds deer** (Maharajah Jungle Trek) lives only in a 15-square-mile marsh around Loktak Lake in Eastern India. Its unusual antlers curve outward then upward and sport at least six points. The **Reeves muntjac** (The Oasis) is known as the barking deer, due to the sound it can make when alarmed. The male grows large canine teeth that curl from its lips, like tusks.

DUCKS

One of the smallest diving ducks in the world, the **bufflehead** (The Oasis) is less than a foot long. To attract females, a male will puff up its crest, bob its head and show off its diving skills. The duck was originally called the Buffalo

Head, a reference to the male's large noggin. The **white-backed duck** *(Pangani Forest Exploration Trail)* can stay under the water for up to 30 seconds. It's an endangered species. With a high-pitched three-note whistle, the **white-faced whistling duck** *(Discovery Island)* sounds like a squeak toy. When it's afraid, it sounds a single note. The bird lives in Africa, the Caribbean and Latin America. Nearly extinct, the **white-winged wood duck** *(Maharajah Jungle Trek)* once thrived in the rainforests of Southeast Asia. Today most of its habitat is gone.

ELEPHANT

The largest land mammal, the **African elephant** *(Kilimanjaro Safaris)* can weigh 11,000 pounds. It has few natural enemies but has been relentlessly hunted for its tusks, a prize that is actually made of the same ingredient as human teeth: ivory dentine.

An elephant's trunk combines a long nose with an upper lip. It can hold up to 3 gallons of water. Two finger-like projections at the tip can pluck grasses and manipulate small objects. The trunk has 40,000 muscles, more than in a human body.

An African elephant can make a variety of vocal sounds, including low frequency rumbles that are below the human range of hearing, but can be heard by other elephants up to 5 miles away.

An elephant's skin is so sensitive it can feel a fly landing on it.

Females can breed for three to six days every four years. Bulls find mates by listening for female tummy rumbles that can be heard for miles. When mating takes place, the entire herd often takes part in a noisy melee known as the mating pandemonium. Females and calves mill, circle, wave their trunks and trumpet loudly for up to an hour. The gestation period is 21 months.

Three baby elephants have been born at Disney, through both artificial insemination and natural breeding. The first, a male, arrived in 2003. A female was born in 2004; another female in 2005.

When the breeding program began, Disney baby-proofed its elephant habitat by increasing its shade, closing gaps between boulders and installing a shallow backstage pool that allows the calves to safely explore water and learn to swim. "We're the

Reeves muntjac

only zoo in North America that has three African elephant calves on display," reports John Lehnhardt, the park's director of animal operations.

FLAMINGOS

These beautiful birds get their pink color from carotene-rich spirulina, an algae common in brackish lakes in Africa. The paler **greater flamingo** *(Kilimanjaro Safaris)* gets the algae indirectly by eating insects, shrimp and other small creatures that themselves have consumed the algae; the brilliantly colored **lesser flamingo** *(Discovery Island)* eats it directly. Spending much of their day with their heads upside down, flamingos stir up the mud with their webbed feet, then suck and filter the murky water through their bills. *Like most wading birds, a flamingo is most comfortable while standing on one leg, and what appears to be its knee is actually its ankle.*

GIRAFFE

The world's tallest animal, the **reticulated giraffe** *(Kilimanjaro Safaris)* can stand up to 19 feet

Baby Nadirah nuzzles her mom Donna in 2006

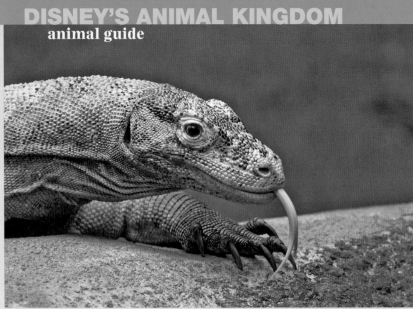

Komodo dragon

tall. Its 6-foot legs support a 6-foot torso that's topped by a 6-foot neck and, finally, a foot-high head. It balances with help from an 8-foot tail (the longest of any land mammal) and rests on feet the size of dinner plates: each one is up to a foot wide. It's an interesting creature

Gray kangaroo

— a giraffe has a stride of 15 feet and can run up to 45 mph; its tongue can be up to 20 inches long; its heart 2 feet wide; its lungs can hold 12 gallons of air; and its neck has only seven vertebrae, the same number as man. Females give birth standing up. Newborns drop head-first to the ground. Babies average 6 feet tall and grow an inch a day. Although generally quiet, giraffes are not mute. Calves bleat; adults can grunt, hiss, moo and snort. Unlike most grazing animals, a giraffe can't lower its head to the ground without splaying its legs.

GOAT

It's the devil! Well, actually it's an **African pygmy goat** (*Rafiki's Planet Watch*), but people have associated it and its relatives with Beelzebub since the animal was domesticated 10,000 years ago. For centuries Satan

was thought to be able to transform himself into a goat at will, and is still often portrayed with the creature's hooves and horns. Some farmers once believed that owning a goat would protect them from the devil, or that when a goat could not be found it was meeting with him. Sailors once thought a goat on board would ensure a calm sea, which helped the 18-inch-tall African pygmy goat become common in North America. Its natural barrel shape makes it appear to always be pregnant.

GUINEA FOWL

The **Kenya crested guinea fowl** (*Discovery Island*) is a black bird covered in tiny white polka dots. It's a rare breed of the creature that Egyptians domesticated in 2400 B.C. Renaissance traders often confused it with a turkey. It's known to take an occasional dust bath.

HIPPOPOTAMUS

A cross between a pig and a whale, the chubby **Nile hippopotamus** (*Kilimanjaro Safaris, also Pangani Forest Exploration Trail*) spends its day in the water. With its ears, eyes and nose on top of its head, the hippo can keep track of its surroundings while hiding its bulk under the surface. It has webbed feet, and can hold its breath for 12 minutes.

The animal feeds after dark, eating land grasses, leaves and bark. With the largest mouth of any land mammal, it can eat up to 150 pounds of food a night.

An aggressive, territorial animal, the hippo kills more humans than any other creature in Africa. Over a short distance the 6,000-pound mammal can outrun a man.

Hippos were once thought to sweat blood. They ooze a pinkish oil that moisturizes and protects their skin from sunburn. Disney's herd is the largest in the country.

IBIS

Easily identified by its large spoon-shaped bill, the **African spoonbill** (The Oasis) fishes for its food by swinging its open bill in the water. The birds have an odd mating ritual. Males will offer a female sticks for her nest. When she accepts one (which isn't often) she has chosen her mate. The behavior can be seen with Disney's birds. The most common bird at

White ibis

Ring-tailed lemur

Animal Kingdom, the **white ibis** is not one of Disney's creatures. Abundant in Florida, thousands of ibis have flown into the park and stayed for its lush habitat and plentiful food. Hundreds roost each evening in the trees along the Discovery River. The bird is easy to identify by its orange downcurved bill that's as long as its legs. It's also known as the mascot of the University of Miami.

KANGAROOS

The only large mammal that hops, a kangaroo can jump 9 feet in the air, leap 40 feet and reach speeds of 30 mph. Tendons in the back legs act like giant springs. At full speed it can outpace a racehorse. At rest, a kangaroo's weight is supported by the tripod of its hind legs and tail.

A newborn resembles a jelly bean. Only an inch long, the hairless, still-developing baby has no back legs. Called a joey, it climbs into its mother's pouch, where it stays put for nine months. A mother produces different milk for different-aged joeys. In some species, a female can control the progress of her pregnancy so that each newborn has an open teat in her pouch. Gestation typically takes 35 days, but can be delayed for nearly a year. The world's largest marsupial, the **red kangaroo** (Discovery Island) can stand 6 and a half feet tall and weigh 200 pounds. It's colored to match the red soil of the Australian desert outback. The red kangaroo can go without drinking as long as green grass is available. The **swamp wallaby**

Cotton-top tamarin

deer, goats, pigs (and other Komodos) and can go six months without a meal. Because adult dragons cannibalize young ones, juveniles often roll in feces as a deterrent. Young dragons also conduct appeasement rituals, pacing around a feeding circle and lurching from side to side in a "circle of death." *To flee an attacker, a Komodo can vomit the contents of its stomach — which can hold 200 pounds of food — to increase its speed.*

LEMURS

The **collared lemur** *(Discovery Island)* sports reddish-blond muttonchops. Living in a group of up to 30 animals, the **ring-tailed lemur** *(Discovery Island)* uses its long tail as a flag — to tell others where it is or warn them of danger. Unlike most mammal groups, a lemur family is led by a female. Males compete for her with a stink fight: Each rubs its tail with a smelly odor from its wrist glands, arches its tail over its back and shakes it at another male while baring its teeth. The competition can last an hour. Found only on the island of Madagascar, the primitive primate is named for its big eyes and haunting howl; the word lemur is Latin for ghost.

(The Oasis) is a small kangaroo, standing no more than 33 inches tall. The **western gray kangaroo** *(Discovery Island)* is the least common large kangaroo in American zoos. *Kangaroos cannot walk backwards. Males box each other to establish dominance. When it's hot, Disney's kangaroos lick their forearms to stay cool.*

KOMODO DRAGON

The world's largest lizard, the **Komodo dragon** *(Maharajah Jungle Trek)* can grow up to 10 feet long and weigh 250 pounds. Using its long, forked tongue as a nose, it picks up scents of animals up to 2 miles away. With a burst of speed that can reach 15 mph, the dragon can kill its prey by simply biting

it... then leisurely following it until it dies. The dragon's saliva contains so much lethal bacteria that death is inevitable. Living in the wild only on a few Indonesian islands, a wild Komodo eats

African lion

Okapi

swim bladders that take oxygen from the air when the animal surfaces. It lives in small pools of water that often evaporate, at which time it uses its long, fleshy fins to plod along in the mud. Its ancestors developed true limbs and evolved into early four-legged land animals.

LION

Known as the king of beasts, the **African lion** *(Kilimanjaro Safaris)* is the largest African carnivore. Its roar can be heard 5 miles away. Living in a pride of about 15 members, females do the hunting, slowly stalking their prey as a team before sprinting forward in a surprise attack. They can run up to 37 mph and leap up to 40 feet. Males defend the pride; their manes protect their necks in a battle. Lions sleep up to 20 hours a day.

LLAMA

Related to a camel, the **llama** *(Rafiki's Planet Watch)* is a domesticated pack animal. Tamed in the 16th century in the Andes mountains of South America, the sure-footed creature can carry up to 100 pounds. In the 2000 Disney film "The Emperor's New Groove," Emperor Kuzco (David Spade) was turned into a llama by his power-hungry advisor, Yzma (Eartha Kitt).

LUNGFISH

The **African lungfish** *(Pangani Forest Exploration Trail)* can breathe air and crawl. It has two

MEERKAT

It takes a village — at least when it comes to meerkats. A type of mongoose, the **slender-tailed meerkat** *(Pangani Forest Exploration Trail)* works with others in organized, multifamily communities of up to 30 individuals. The burrowing animals divide up jobs such as babysitting, food finding and sentry duty, a chore shared by rotating guards throughout a day.

MONKEYS

One of the smallest monkeys, the **cotton-top tamarin** *(Discovery Island)* is about the size of a squirrel, but can still leap 10 feet. It's named for the puffy crest of white fur on top of its head. Living in Colombia, the creatures mate for life and live as a family. Older siblings help care for the infants. Active most of the day, Disney's tamarins usually take a nap about 4:30 p.m. The world's most colorful mammal and largest monkey, the **mandrill** *(Kilimanjaro Safaris)* is the inspiration for the character Rafiki in Disney's 1994 film "The Lion King." The non-aggressive, social creature bares its teeth as a greeting, not a threat. It makes a huge

smile, with the corners of its mouth wide open, exposing its massive canines. The most colorful mandrills are males who have mated with many females. If a mandrill is upset, it may energetically beat the ground.

NAKED MOLE RAT

The giant queen keeps a male harem and rules with brute force, shoving her soldiers and workers around to prod them into action. Everyone's naked, and blind, but all individuals have their own identity — a custom odor achieved by carefully rolling around in the community toilet. Such is the underground world of the **naked mole rat** *(Pangani Forest Exploration Trail)*, the only mammal that organizes itself into ant-like colonies. The animal digs with its four buck teeth but doesn't swallow dirt — the teeth are outside of its mouth in front of hairy lips and side skin folds that close completely. Neither mole nor rat, but plenty naked, the pink, virtually hairless creature is related to a guinea pig.

OKAPI

The only mammal that can lick its own ears and eyelids, the **okapi** *(Kilimanjaro Safaris, also Pangani Forest Exploration Trail)* uses its 14-inch tongue for grooming as well as eating. Its odd appearance combines the body and face of a stubby giraffe with the black-and-white legs and rump of a zebra. Related to a giraffe, its head is topped with the same skin-covered knobs and it walks in the same unique way: simultaneously stepping with the front and hind leg on the same side of its body. It sleeps only five minutes a day. The solitary creature lives only in the dense Ituri Forest of the Democratic Republic of Congo, an area so remote the species wasn't discovered until 1900.

animal guide

White rhinoceros

OSTRICH

The world's largest bird, the ostrich (Kilimanjaro Safaris) has 2-inch-wide eyes, the largest of any land creature. Its eggs, the largest of any living animal, can weigh nearly 2.5 pounds each. An ostrich doesn't fly but can run up to 45 mph — faster than any other two-legged animal. To stay cool the ostrich fans itself with its wings. An ostrich doesn't really stick its head in

Asian tiger

the sand. To hide, it lays its head on the ground.

OTTER

It's hard to leave the Asian small-clawed otter habitat (Discovery Island) when the animals play or feed. The world's smallest otters, they chase each other on the ground at speeds up to 18 mph and swim after each other in the water. They are especially cute when they wash up after a meal: their unique (for otters) non-webbed paws look like hands.

RHINOCEROS

It's been on earth for 60 million years, but today only 10,000 are left — less than 15 percent of the number that roamed Africa as late as 1970. Why? Because poachers continually kill it for its horn — an alleged aphrodisiac in Chinese folk medicine despite the fact that it's really just a big toenail. Growing from the rhino's skin, it's made of

the same material (keratin) as a human nail and grows back when you cut it. The nearly extinct black rhino (Kilimanjaro Safaris) is a solitary herbivore that uses its hooked lip like a finger to select leaves and twigs. It can live 40 years. The larger white rhino (Kilimanjaro Safaris) is a brownish-gray creature that gets its name from its wide upper lip — "white" is a mistranslation of "wijt," the Afrikaans word for "wide." Rhinos wallow in mud to protect their skin, which is sensitive to insects and sunburn. They can charge at 40 miles per hour.

STORKS

The world's largest stork, the 5-foot marabou stork (Pangani Forest Exploration Trail) has a 14-inch bill and an 8.5-foot wingspan. Known as the world's ugliest bird, it has a pickax bill, two unsightly pouches and a naked cranium studded with scab-like spots. The carrion-eating critter communicates by clattering its bill; it has no voice box. The painted stork (Discovery Island) gets a bright pink patch on its back during breeding season. The male saddle-billed stork (Discovery Island, Kilimanjaro Safaris) has a yellow wattle; the female yellow eyes. The best-known stork species, the white stork (Discovery Island) lives in African grasslands. The German legend about the bird bringing babies exists because for centuries it has migrated from Africa to nest on northern German chimneys and roofs in the spring, a time of many human births. Lifelong mates take turns incubating and feeding their young.

TAPIR

The world's largest tapir, the Malayan tapir (Maharajah Jungle Trek) can weigh up to 700 pounds. Looking like a fat black pig with a white saddle, it's actually related to both a horse and a rhino. Its front feet have four toes, but its back feet only have three.

TIGER

One of the world's most beautiful creatures, each Asian (or Bengal) tiger (Maharajah Jungle Trek) has its own stripe pattern, as well as large false eyes and white spots on the backs of its ears. The patterns are on both its fur and skin. Noted for its sheer power, an Asian tiger can drag up to 3,000 pounds, five times its own weight. The 8- to 10-foot animal can leap 30 feet and, thanks to its large webbed paws, swim easily. Its ears turn individually and can rotate 180 degrees. Disney's tigers typically sleep on their backs by the second viewing window, and often play in their fountain area after 4 p.m., especially during hot weather.

TORTOISE

The world's most primitive tortoise, the Asian brown tortoise (DinoLand U.S.A.) has heavy overlapping scales. The largest living tortoise, the 5-foot-long, 500-pound Galapagos tortoise (Discovery Island) lives only in the Galapagos archipelago, 600 miles west of Ecuador. It can live at least 150 years, but it's a slow life. The reptile's top speed is only 0.16 mph.

WARTHOG

No other face looks like that of a male common warthog (Kilimanjaro Safaris). Covered in wart-like growths of skin, it has two sharp 6-inch lower tusks and two curved upper tusks that can grow as long as 2 feet. Perhaps realizing he's no Prince Charming, he relies on his singing skills to attract women — at breeding time a male performs a courtship chant of rhythmic grunts. The creature eats roots and, like other pigs, keeps cool by taking mud baths. The most famous warthog? Pumbaa, from Disney's "The Lion King."

ZEBRA

The unique stripes on every Grant's zebra (Kilimanjaro Safaris) serve as camouflage — the pattern blends right into tall grasses. Even in an open field, a single zebra's stripes break up its silhouette, making it less recognizable to predators, and a herd of complex stripes makes it tough to track any one

Tunis sheep, Rafiki's Planet Watch

animal. Because black absorbs heat more than white, the animal's black areas have an extra layer of protective fat. Zebras themselves are attracted to the pattern. Studies have shown that when stripes are painted on a wall, a zebra will walk over to it. Related more to an ass than a horse, a zebra has the same long ears, short mane, tufted tail and front-leg-only "chestnuts."

Animal guide field and library research by Micaela Neal.

Creatures great and small

Animal Kingdom has 1,500 animals, representing 250 different species. Besides those listed in this guide, fascinating animals in The Oasis include the yellow-bellied slider turtle and rhinoceros iguana and many beautiful birds. Discovery Island has the toothy tambaqui fish. Other animals on Kilimanjaro Safaris include ankole cattle, greater kudu and scimitar-horned oryx. Interesting birds in Africa include the ground hornbill and pink-backed pelican, and, at the Pangani aviary, one of the largest flocks of carmine bee-eaters in North America. The Asian aviary (at Maharajah Jungle Trek) has the most birds of all, including the New Guinea masked plover (shown at right) and the world's largest pigeon. Finally, a huge variety of bugs, butterflies, scorpions, snakes, tarantulas and other small critters live at Rafiki's Planet Watch, including the world's most colorful amphibian, the Latin American poison dart frog. The petting zoo includes the rare Sicilian miniature donkey.

Adventureland, take two

The stories behind the lands of Disney's Animal Kingdom

For decades critics have praised Disney World as an example of how functional urban design can entertain with its form. Only Disney, it seems, can create an area for thousands of pedestrians that is simultaneously its own immersive environment.

Animal Kingdom takes the idea to a new level. Whereas Disney's other parks create visual cues from familiar Western icons such as a European castle, it creates icons out of nonspecific buildings whose designs come from developing countries, with architectural styles and building methods that are virtually unknown in the West.

DISCOVERY ISLAND

The park's central hub of merchandise shops and restaurants, Discovery Island is Disney's own vision. The six buildings and various snack stands are the company's most colorful, and best-looking, ever. The exteriors are bright, happy, patterned and soulful, a combination of styles perhaps best described as a mix of Mexican Wedding Dress and No Worries Caribbean. Each building is covered in whimsical animal wood carvings handcrafted on the Indonesian island of Bali, some 1,500 pieces in all. The interiors are just as attractive, with fanciful animals adorning the ceilings, columns, shelves and walls. The floors are a mix of colorful textured concrete and inlaid stone and broken-tile mosaics.

Each store has its own theme. Migrating and working animals highlight the primary gift shop, Island Mercantile. The main rooms of the Disney Outfitters clothing store are embellished with animals from the four compass directions of North, South, East and West. The right room has animals of the ground; the left has those of the air (a mural has animal constellations). Next door, the Beastly Bazaar housewares shop is decorated with crabs, fish and other water creatures, as well as the animals that catch them. On the pathway to Africa, the Creature Comforts children's store features striped and spotted animals. Street lamps in front are topped with large ladybugs that light up at night.

Bright murals cover the walls of the Pizzafari restaurant. Each of the four rooms portrays a different type of animal — those that carry their homes, camouflage themselves, hang upside down or are nocturnal. Bugs rule the porch in back. Hanging from the walls and ceiling are 570 carved animals from Oaxaca, Mexico.

Predators and prey is the theme of the Flame Tree Barbecue outdoor cafe. Look closely and you'll notice that each structure has its own motif: mongoose eat geckos in the order area, while the seven patio huts have alligators chomping fish, anteaters devouring ants, eagles swallowing snakes, eels sucking down crabs, owls eating rabbits, snakes swallowing mice, or spiders trapping butterflies. At the tables, each chair's backrest features four predatory animals, each of which corresponds to a particular prey on the tabletop.

Decorations on each snack stand subtly relate to its product. Safari Coffee is adorned with hyperactive critters such as kangaroo rats. Safari Popcorn is trimmed with frogs, snakes and fish snacking on clusters of flies, mice and minnows (the popcorn cart has anhingas snacking on lizards and shrimp). Safari Pretzel is decorated with eels, octopus, ostriches and other animals that can contort themselves into strange shapes. Today a sandwich stand, Safari Nacho is covered with antelope, baboons and vultures — animals that stick together like the structure's original snack.

FUN FINDS ❶ Walkway lights are capped with mushroom shades. ❷ Multicolored plastic benches feature two-piece backrests that portray the digestive tracks of alligators, eagles and turtles. ❸ "Ancient" animal-themed statues and large clay pots sit in the foliage in front of the shops and restaurants. ❹ Collages of carved creatures form six windsock poles along the pathway to Camp Minnie-Mickey. **Pizzafari murals:** **UPSIDE-DOWN ROOM:** The front room of the restaurant includes ❺ only one animal that is right side up. A small blue bug stands upright under a purple bird toward the back, painted on the header that frames the room's rearmost seating area. ❻ On the opposite side of that header, an opossum tail without a body appears between the second and third opossums from the right. ❼ Dozens of carved wooden bats hang from the ceiling. **HOME ROOM:** Located on the left side of Pizzafari's main hallway, this room features ❽ hundreds of carved snails and turtles crawling on its ceiling. **NOCTURNAL ROOM:** To the right of the hall, this room features murals with scurrying red mice. On the back wall, ❾ nine white stars join three mice to rush away from a spraying skunk. **CAMOUFLAGE ROOM:** Dozens of animals hide in these murals in this large room at the rear of the building. They include (from left, as you enter the room): ❿ Two bitterns standing in the reeds under the orange fox. ⓫ A frog, resting on the tree trunk under the brown leopard. ⓬ A stickbug, posing on a leaf at the top of a plant to the left of the orange tiger.

AFRICA

The largest section of the park is the mythical East African port town of Harambe, modeled after the real island town of Lamu, Kenya. Appearing worn and weathered by decades of rain and sand storms, the village represents an old gold and ivory trading post that is trying to establish a new economy based on eco-tourism.

Typical of Swahili construction techniques, the buildings appear to have a coral rock substructure that, for the most part, is covered with plaster and topped with either a corrugated-metal or reed-thatch roof.

Foundations of former buildings are still visible in the main streets, while lampposts bear the phrase "Harambe 1961," a reference to the year the village supposedly gained independence from Great Britain. Spread throughout the village are vintage tin signs (mostly real) and Kenyan-English advertising posters (mostly fake). Interiors are dotted with authentic East African canned goods, cots and camping paraphernalia. Harambe's research camp and conservation school (located on the Pangani Forest Exploration Trail) are scattered with letters, notes and journals of field workers and head researcher.

FUN FINDS ❶ A cacophony of murmuring voices, clattering pots and pans and a radio sometimes can be heard from a kitchen behind the back door of Harambe's Dawa Bar. The sounds are meant to be from the residents of the hotel above. Sometimes there's knocking on a door: a landlady trying to collect back rent. ❷ A sly tribute to Animal Kingdom's chief design executive appears in the "open-air market" (the indoor reception area) of the Tusker House restaurant. Looking down on you from the market's second floor, the Jorodi Masks & Beads shop is an homage to famed Disney Imagineer Joe Rohde. The store's "earings" (sic) sign is a reference to Rohde's distinctive lobal adornments. Posters for the shop are plastered throughout Harambe Village.

ASIA

Disney's mythical kingdom of Anandapur is a collage of architectural and landscaping themes that portray another community trying to save its environment. In this Asian story, locals have turned an ancient royal forest and crumbling hunting lodge into a wildlife preserve (the Maharajah Jungle Trek). Other ruins serve as a bird sanctuary (Flights of Wonder). Nearby, a river-rafting business fights with loggers for control of a once-pristine, but still turbulent river (Kali River Rapids).

Detail from a directional sign for Asia's Kali River Rapids ride, originally known as Tiger River Rapids.

The mythical East African port town of Harambe appears weathered by decades of sand storms

Two monument areas, one Thai and one Nepalese, provide homes for hooting gibbons. Supposedly built in 637 A.D., the temples are covered in bamboo scaffolding as cash-starved villagers restore them. Nearby, a crumbling Indian tiger shrine has scarf and garland offerings and bells that celebrate answered prayers. Meanwhile, two entrepreneurs are offering mountain climbers a shortcut to Mount Everest, ignoring warnings from concerned villagers about a Yeti (Expedition Everest).

Like Africa, among Asia's best details are its many rusted signs and aged murals. They're not authentic, but sure look to be. FUN FINDS ❶ The "dried mud" pathways include bicycle tracks and footprints made by barefoot Disney cast members and their children. ❷ Each Anandapur business displays a tax license featuring the kingdom's king and queen. The bigger the license, the more taxes that business pays. ❸ Just right of the tiger shrine, visible seams in an authentic Indian marble pavilion reveal where Disney cut the structure apart to ship it to the United States. ❹ Walls and drain covers shoot water at a small play area between Kali River Rapids and the Maharajah Jungle Trek. ❺ Inside one of the siamang temples is an air-conditioned kitchen. Its door is

protected by an electrified vine that emits a noticeable slow clicking.

DINOLAND U.S.A.

With the most peculiar theming of any Disney land, DinoLand U.S.A. embraces America's fascination with all things dinosaur. Simultaneously, it parodies the stuffiness of scientists and the tackiness of roadside tourist traps and traveling carnivals.

The story begins in 1947, when an amateur fossil-hunter named Chester discovered some dinosaur bones outside his Diggs County gas station. Realizing the importance of the find, the bone-hunter contacted some scientist friends. They banded together to buy the site. In 1949 the scientists transformed its old fishing lodge into the Dino Institute, a non-profit organization dedicated to the Exploration, Excavation and Exultation of dinosaur fossils. For nearly six decades, the site has been inhabited by scientists and graduate students.

During the 1970s the Institute received a large grant from McDonald's (yes, product placement even in a fictitious story), which allowed it to build a formal museum and new research center, and develop a new archeological technique: time travel. The old building's museum became the student cafeteria; its adjacent buildings a dorm and garage. Soon the entire area was opened to the public as DinoLand U.S.A., a "dinosaur discovery park." Tourists poured in.

But when the crowds arrived, so did Chester's newfound interest: money. Teaming up with his wife, Hester, he turned his gas station into a souvenir stand: the gaudy Chester & Hester's Dinosaur Treasures (an "Emporium of Extinction") that sold trinkets of little value, but high profit margin.

As the couple's fortunes grew, the embarrassed Dino Institute pressured Chester and Hester to sell. But the couple refused, and retaliated by turning their parking lot into a cheap carnival ("Dino-Rama," a play on the word "diorama") that openly mocks the scientists. The couple's cousins run the attractions, while two moonlighting Institute interns walk around in a couple of Hester's homemade dinosaur outfits. (An additional story about the three grad students is told by a paper trail of notes and scribbles throughout and around the Boneyard and Restaurantosaurus.)

FUN FINDS Archeological and dinosaur hints abound in the Restaurantosaurus. Among the best: ❶ the shapes formed by greasy hand prints on the walls of the quonset hut; ❷ the cans of Sinclair Litholine Multi-Purpose Grease and Dynoil ("keep your old dinosaur running") on the shelves of that room; ❸ the reproductions of four dino sketches

A DinoLand U.S.A. soft drink cart appears to be marred by graffiti from students at the Dino Institute

for the "The Rite of Spring" sequence in Disney's 1930s film project "Concert Feature" that became the 1940 film "Fantasia;" ❹ the titles in the juke box in the Hip Joint rec room (e.g., "Dust in the Wind"); ❺ the posters in that room for rock bands Dinosaur Jr. and T Rex; and ❻ the ambient music, which includes the 1988 Was Not Was hit "Walk the Dinosaur" as well as obscure tunes such as proto-punk icon Jonathan Richman's "I'm a Little Dinosaur" and "Ugga Bugga," a Bruce Springsteen-like tune by one-time child star Bill Mumy. ❼ The letters A-I-R-S-T-R-E-A-M on the front of the restaurant's travel trailer have been rearranged to spell I ARE SMART. ❽ Four hanging signs above the entrance to the Dinosaur Treasures gift shop read "Rough scaly skin... Making you groan?... Don't despair... Use Fossil Foam" from one direction, "When in Florida... Be sure to... Visit... Epcot" from the other. ❾ Tiny plastic dinosaurs ride trains, snow ski and flee lava flows above the gift shop's main room. ❿ Boxes above Chester's garage floors include "Chester's dig '47," "Chester's pet rocks 1966" and "Train Parts." ⓫ An oil funnel and gas-pump nozzle are among the items that have been turned into dinosaurs on the shop's walls. ⓬ The price of gas is 29.9 cents a gallon on Chester's rusty gas pump alongside the building, as well as on a painted-over sign on the rear roof. ⓭ "I Like Bananas Because They Have No Bones," a 1935 ditty by the Hoosier Hot Shots, is among the bone-themed country songs played on radio station "W-BONE" heard in the adjacent restrooms. ⓮ Two baby dinosaurs hide underneath the adjacent "concretosaurus" folk-art sculpture. One is hatching. ⓯ Though it appears to be a stegosaurus shoulder bone, the Boneyard marquee is actually in the shape of Disney's Animal Kingdom at the time the park opened, before the addition of Asia. An "N" points north. ⓰ "Lost — My Tail" reads one of the notes on the bulletin board across from the Boneyard entrance. It's from the nearby aptosaurus cast, which has a disconnected tailbone. ⓱ DinoLand U.S.A.'s original layout, which included a real fossil prep area and cast display room on the site of today's Dino-Rama, is shown on a map pinned to the board. ⓲ Chester and Hester appear in a photo on one of the shop's walls and on a poster in the main dining hall of Restaurantosaurus.

CAMP MINNIE-MICKEY

A summer camp where Mickey Mouse and his friends have gone on vacation, this T-shaped walkway is lined with birch and cedar trees and hand-hewn benches.

FUN FINDS ❶ As the entranceway crosses the Discovery River, a stone dragon lies along the right bank. What starts in the woods as scattered slabs of stone forms into its head. ❷ Further along that side of the walkway, a figure of Daisy Duck leads Donald's nephews Huey, Dewey and Louie on a hike. ❸ Mickey Mouse and his pals are fishing to the left of a bridge that leads to the Festival of the Lion King Theater and Character Greeting Trails. Donald Duck has caught a boot. Goofy has fallen asleep.

FUN FACT ❯❯ The park has plants from every continent except Antarctica. There are 40 types of palms, 260 grasses and 2,000 kinds of shrubs. DinoLand U.S.A. has many ancient species, including 20 types of magnolia and more than 3,000 palm-like (but cone-bearing) cycads.

Water Parks

giggles, laughs and squeals fill the air. Close your eyes at either of Disney's two water parks and you'll hear more happy people than anywhere else at Disney World. Why? Because it's just so much fun to ride a water slide, float down a lazy river or splash in a pool, especially when you're in such a fully realized fantasy atmosphere.

The United States has more than a thousand water parks, but no others offer the immersive theming of these Disney gems. Instead of plastic culverts and support columns, you see mountain streams and palm trees. Instead of rap and pop songs, you hear reggae tunes and Christmas ditties. And since it's a Disney park, everyone greets you with a smile, and everywhere you look is spic-and-span.

Typhoon Lagoon offers more shade, unique snorkeling and face-first rides, bigger waves and more for preschoolers. Blizzard Beach has more sun; longer, faster slides; and the most for preteens and teens.

The parks share a number of policies. Swimwear can't have rivets, buckles, or exposed metal. You can bring in small sand toys, towels, picnic coolers and food, but not boogie boards, water toys, tubes (all tube rides have complimentary tubes), glass containers or alcohol (beer and mixed drinks are sold in the park).

Strollers and wheelchairs are OK to bring in, but are not available for rent. When the parks close for inclement weather, guests who have been inside less than three hours get complimentary rain checks (conditions apply).

Blizzard Beach

It's a zany combination: a water park that looks like a ski resort. Disguised as ski slopes, water slides extend down the sides of Mt. Gushmore, a 90-foot snow-capped peak. Around it is a beach, wave pool, lazy river and children's areas. The 66-acre park sits east of Animal Kingdom.

A GOOFY IDEA As Disney tells it, in early 1995 Central Florida experienced a freak winter snowstorm. Gazing at the flakes fall outside of their Walt Disney World offices, the company's Imagineers had a brainstorm: "Let's build a ski resort!" Immediately they built a huge mountain, a ski jump, slalom courses, a chairlift, a lodge and more. But just as they finished, the warm weather returned and the snow turned to slush. Reluctantly, the workers began to board things up. But then they spotted a lone alligator, blue from the cold but

full of energy. Strapping on skis, he careened down the jump, flew through the air, landed on the women's restrooms, crashed into the gift shop... and emerged with a smile. Watching this "Ice Gator," as they named him, the Imagineers realized that their failed ski resort would make a great water park. The jump could be a body slide. The slalom, bobsled and sledding

On busy days the water parks often fill to capacity by 11 a.m. They usually re-open at 2 p.m.

A DAILY PLAN

Can you absolutely get to the park by 8:30 a.m.? If so, here's a proven plan. The key: being done with the slides by 11:30 a.m.

8:30 ARRIVE AT THE PARK The gate usually opens early. When it does, get a locker and head to the rope line at the bridge over Cross Country Creek.

9:00 DO THE SLIDES Work your way around the park in a counter-clockwise pattern. Save the kids' areas, the river and the pool until later.

11:30 EAT LUNCH There are a couple of shady picnic tables at Lottawatta Lodge.

12:30 PLAY IN THE POOL Cool off under a waterfall.

1:30 DO THE KIDS' SPOTS Let them work off energy at Tikes Peak (bring a camera!) and the Ski Patrol Training Camp.

3:00 RIDE THE RIVER Want a treat? Climb out for a snow cone from the Snow Balls snack stand at the Ice Gator landing (entry area No. 2).

4:00 RE-RIDE YOUR FAVES The ride lines disappear during the park's final hour.

Assumes park hours of 9 a.m. to 5 p.m.

Topped by beach umbrellas, a chair lift takes you to the top of Mt. Gushmore for easy access to Slush Gusher, Summit Plummet and Teamboat Springs. Skis stretch out beneath your feet. *If there's a crowd, stand in the single-rider line for a much shorter wait.*

runs could be mat and tube rides. The slushy creek? A perfect lazy river. Basking in their genius, they named their creation Blizzard Beach and proudly opened it to the public — on April Fools Day, 1995.

Practical information

FOOD AND DRINK Blizzard Beach has three outdoor counter cafes, five snack shacks, two beach bars and a coffee stand. Meals feature hamburgers, hot dogs, sandwiches, salads and individual pizzas (*$4–$7, at Lottawatta Lodge in the Alpine Village, the Warming Hut on the left side of Melt-Away Bay and Avalunch near the Ski Patrol Training Camp*). Snack stands sell funnel cakes and cotton candy (*MeltAway Bay*), ice cream treats (*$4–$7, Sled Dog Expeditions, Ski Patrol Training Camp*), mini do-nuts (*Alpine Village*), nachos (*Cooling Hut, Alpine Village*), and snow cones (*Snow Balls, near Ski Patrol Training Camp*). Other stands sell coffee, tea and pastries (*Frosty the Joe Man, Melt-Away Bay*) and beer and specialty rum drinks (*Frostbite Freddies at Alpine Village, Polar Pub at Melt-Away Bay*).

SHOPPING The Beach House (*Alpine Village*) has beachwear and swimsuits from Quiksilver, Roxy and Element, Disney beach towels and sundries. Across from the changing rooms, the Shade Shack has sunglasses, sandals, beach towels and disposable cameras, while the North Pearl is a branch of the Hawaii-based Pearl Factory, which sells farm-raised Japanese akoya pearls in their oysters (*6–9 mm, $15*), settings (*$9–$760*) and pearl jewelry.

PARK RESOURCES You enter Blizzard Beach through a re-creation of an alpine village, with buildings that include changing rooms, lockers, food stands and shops.

There's an **ATM** just outside the gate at the ticket and Guest Relations booth (which also serves as Lost and Found).

Inside the turnstiles is the Beach Haus gift shop, which rents **lockers** and **towels** and sells sunscreen. Around the corner, the

▶ Bring hotel soap and shampoo with you for the shower. You'll walk out refreshed.

Clockwise from above: Spraying water at Tikes Peak; tubers take it easy on the Cross Country Creek lazy river; hanging in there on the Thin Ice Training Course

Snowless Joe's stand offers the same services and has complimentary **lifejackets.**

The lockers themselves are in three places. Most are centrally located at Snowless Joe's. Other sit along the right side of the park near the Ski Patrol Training Camp preteen area, and along the left side next to the Downhill Double Dipper tube slide.

A **First Aid** station is to the right of the Beach Haus. Cast members take **lost children** to Snowless Joe's. The park has no package pick-up service or baby care center, but restrooms have **baby changing stations.** Blizzard Beach **parking** is free. The park's **telephone number** is 407-560-3400.

Lazy river

CROSS COUNTRY CREEK Circling the park, this 3,000-foot stream has seven entry points, each with a stack of complimentary tubes. Lined with palms and evergreens, the river flows under bridges, over springs and through a cave with ice-cold dripping water. A round-trip journey takes about 25 minutes. The water is 2.5 feet deep.

Children's area

TIKES PEAK Gentle slides, rideable baby alligators and an ankle-deep squirting "ice" pond highlight this watery playground for preschoolers. There's also a fountain play area, a little waterfall, many small sand boxes and lots of lawn chairs, chaise lounges and picnic tables for parents. Kids may want to wear water shoes: the pavement can get hot. *Height restriction: Must be under 48 in.*

▶ Hit the creek after lunch, when the lines get long at the water slides.

Though her boyfriend chickened out moments earlier, this teen still braved Summit Plummet

A rider gets airborne on Slush Gusher

Preteen area

SKI PATROL TRAINING CAMP This inventive spot features **Fahrenheit Drop,** cabled T-bars that drop kids into an 8-foot pool; and the **Thin Ice Training Course,** slippery walks on floating "icebergs" with overhead rope grids for support. Also here: wide **Snow Falls** slides designed for a parent and child to ride together; **Cool Runners,** two short, bumpy tube slides; and **Frozen Pipe Springs,** a short, steep and covered body slide.

Body slides

SLUSH GUSHER This one fools you. Ninety feet above the beach, you start off slow and stay in control over the first drop. But then… off you go into the wild blue yonder! You definitely get some airtime off the second drop, thanks to some playful Disney designers who followed the second lip with a super-steep drop-off (heavier riders fly higher). The whole trip takes about 10 seconds; top speeds can reach 50 mph. The 250-foot flume has the look of a melting snow-banked gully. *Height restriction: 48 in.*
SUMMIT PLUMMET The tallest, fastest water slide in the country, this 350-foot

▶ To get the most Gusher airtime, lean completely back, your head flat with your body.

chute includes a 66-degree, 120-foot free fall. Looming 30 feet above Mt. Gushmore, the launch platform is a mock ski jump that, if real, would send you flying over the park's parking lot.

Lying down at the top of the ramp, you cross your arms over your chest, cross your feet at the ankles and, in the most unnerving moment of all, push yourself off the edge of this true Tower of Terror. There's a blur of sky and scenery as you fall straight through the lift ramp, then a roar of water as you splash into the run-out lane. The impact can send much of your swimsuit where the sun has never shone. Speeds can reach 60 mph. Unless you wear a T-shirt, the trip can sting your skin.

The fall is so scary even some of its designers don't care for it. "I made the mistake when we were building it of going up the stairs and looking down," says Disney Imagineer Kathy Rogers. "I thought, 'There's no way I'd put my body in there!' I did it once and said, 'Done!'"

There are no exit stairs. If you chicken out you have to squeeze your way back down the narrow entrance stairway, doing what cast members call "the walk of shame."

Don't want to go? There's an observation deck in front of the small chalet, and a shaded viewing area at the end of the ride complete with a real-time display of each

Top: Melt-Away Bay. **Above:** Toboggan Racers.

rider's speed. *Best ages: 10 and up. Height restriction: 48 in.*

Wave pool

MELT-AWAY BAY Nestled against the base of Mt. Gushmore, this one-acre pool appears to be created by melting-snow streams that wash down the mountain into it. Bobbing waves wash through the water for 45 minutes of every hour. Perfect for sunbathing, a sandy beach lines the shore.

Mat slides

TOBOGGAN RACERS Based on an amusement park gunnysack slide, this 8-lane, 250-foot mat slide builds speed as you race down a series of dips — face first. Great for families, it's more fun than scary. To go fast, push off quickly and lift up the front of your mat slightly so it doesn't dig in the water. Regardless of technique, heavier riders usually win.

SNOW STORMERS When you were a kid, did you have a sled? If so, these three rac-

▶ The Bay's shallow water makes it a great spot for a game of Monkey in the Middle.

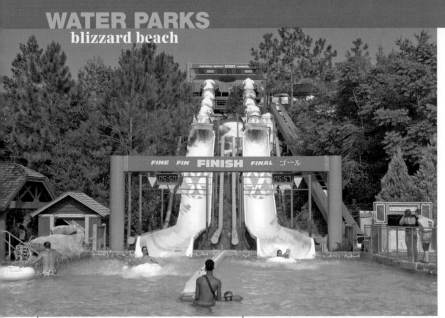

Downhill Double Dipper is Disney's scariest tube ride

ing slides will bring back those memories. Lying face-first on a mat, you weave down a hill of S-curves dug into the ground like high-banked gullies. The 350-foot track is plenty fast, even a little scary — as you careen up the corners the splashing water makes it tough to see. A horizontal line on the wall gives you a point of reference. (Want to win the race? Keep your elbows on the mat and your feet up. To be fair to your lighter-weight kids, give them a second or two head start.) *Best ages: 8 and up.*

Tube slides

DOWNHILL DOUBLE DIPPER Disney's scariest tube ride, this set of two side-by-side racing runs takes you through a tunnel with two drops (steep enough to catch some air) before shooting you through a curtain of water at 25 mph. You race the rider next to you, and your elapsed time is shown at the finish line at the catch pool. The 230-foot ride stands 50 feet high. *Height restriction: 48 in. Best ages: 10 and up.*

RUNOFF RAPIDS You climb up 127 steps to ride these three flumes, but they're worth every huff and puff. Two of them allow two-person tubes, so friends or family members ride together. A third is like a watery Space Mountain, enclosed in darkness except for some starry pinlights. All three 600-foot

Teamboat Springs is a 1,200-foot-long family ride

EACH MORNING Disney opens Blizzard Beach by having the waiting crowd count down a guest who's already perched on Summit Plummet. Want it to be you? Get to the park early, be among the first to the rope line and strike up an energetic, funny conversation with the waiting cast member.

▶ Pull up on your Double Dipper handles just before the pool to fly across the water.

slides make you feel like a bobsledder, sliding you up on their banked curves before shooting you out into a catch pool. *Best ages: 7 and up.*

TEAMBOAT SPRINGS Grumpy papa, moody teenager, creaky grandma… it doesn't matter. Everyone in your family will smile on this, the world's longest family raft ride. Sitting in a raft that's the size of a kiddie pool, you slide down a twisting, splashy, 1,200-foot course. You spin around on the tight curves, which may toss you up high on their banked walls. One thing's for sure: your rear end will get soaked. Thirty holes line each raft's bottom edge. A 200-foot ride-out area takes you under a collapsing roof that's dripping with cool water. *There's often a minimum of four riders per tube. During those times, smaller groups will be grouped together.*

Runoff Rapids allows friends to ride together

FUN FINDS ❶ The park's eclectic soundtrack mixes summertime classics with Christmas songs. Tunes include Jimmy Buffett's 1985 "Jolly Mon" and a Baha Men version of "Hakuna Matata." ❷ Equipment from the Sunshine State Snow Making Co. sits along the queue of Toboggan Racers and on the banks of Cross Country Creek past Reindeer Landing. ❸ Barrels of equipment and "Instant Snow" from the Joe Blow Snow Co. sit along the walkways to Slush Gusher, Summit Plummet and Teamboat Springs. ❹ Snow is melting off a roof of a small building across from the Downhill Double Dipper entrance marked "Safe to Approach Unless Melting." ❺ Just after you enter the park, Ice Gator's ski tracks appear on the roof of the women's dressing room, behind a sign reading "Caution: Low Flying Gator." Directly across that walkway, his silhouette forms a hole in the side of the Beach Haus gift shop. ❻ "Ancient" drawings on the walls of the Cross Country Creek cave include a beach chair with umbrella, Ice Gator, a Yeti, people in tubes, people on skis and a skier with a leg cast. ❼ The Northern Lights shine through the cave's ceiling. ❽ "B-r-r-r-occoli" and "Sleet Corn" are planted in Ice Gator's garden alongside the creek, just past Manatee Landing. ❾ As you float by Ice Gator's house he often sneezes and says "Anybody got a hanky?"

▶ For the fastest Rapids ride go tandem. The more weight, the wilder the trip.

Typhoon Lagoon

With an atmosphere that's one part Hawaii, two parts Gilligan's Island, this tropical park is an unsung Disney masterpiece. Like Magic Kingdom, its perfect theme, passionate design and variety of attractions make it easy to have a great time. The park is divided into four sections: the Harbor Village entrance area, the central surf pool and river, and two attraction areas along the pool's North Shore and South Shore. Across the street from Downtown Disney, the lushly landscaped park covers 61 acres.

A FOOTLOOSE FAIRY TALE Once upon a time there was a bayside Florida village called the Placid Palms Resort, tucked into the valley of a volcanic mountain. Over the years it had been subject to earthquakes and geothermal rumblings, but life remained tranquil. Even when cruise ships arrived, the Placid Palms stayed a quiet, thatch-roofed haven.

Then came Hurricane Connie, in 1955. For one hour furious winds pounded the area. A boat blew through a building. A surfboard sliced through a tree. Crates of fireworks blew in from Mr. Pleasure's nearby island warehouses. A next-door fruit processing plant lost its walls but gained a tractor, which teetered on the roof. A small harbor had been cut off from the sea, trapping an overturned boat, thousands of fish and even a few sharks. Suffering the worst fate: a shrimp boat named Miss Tilly. Blown in from Safen Sound, Fla., it became impaled on the peak of Mt. Mayday.

"No worries!" said the laid-back villagers. Sign paint in hand, they renamed the Placid Palms the Leaning Palms, the center of a new topsy-turvy tropical playground of pools, rapids, rivers and streams. They christened the spot Typhoon Lagoon.

And they lived happily ever after.

Above: Upside-down fun on Castaway Creek

▶ Sunny day? Typhoon Lagoon has plenty of shady palms.

Every half hour Mount Mayday tries to dislodge Miss Tilly with a 50-foot gush of water. A lush trail leads close enough to see the ship's barnacles.

Practical information

FOOD AND DRINK The park has three outdoor counter cafes, five snack shacks, two beach bars and a coffee stand. Meals feature hamburgers, hot dogs, sandwiches, salads and individual pizzas *($4–$7, at Leaning Palms, Harbor Village; Typhoon Tilly's, North Shore; and Lowtide Lou's, South Shore).* Snack stands sell mini donuts *(Harbor Village),* funnel cakes and fried ice cream *(at the Water Works),* ice cream treats *(Snack Shack, North Shore; Happy Landings, Harbor Village; Dippin' Dots cart, South Shore)* and hot dogs and pretzels *(Surf Doggies, surf pool).* Other stands sell coffee, tea and pastries *(Coffee Cappucino, surf pool)* and beer and rum drinks *(Let's Go Slurpin', surf pool).*
SHOPPING Singapore Sal's *(Harbor Village)* has beach and swimwear from Quiksilver, Roxy and Element, Disney beach towels and sundries. The Pearl Factory *(Shark Reef, North Shore)* sells farm-raised Japanese akoya pearls in their oysters *(6–9 mm, $15),* settings *($9–$760)* and pearl jewelry.
PARK RESOURCES Singapore Sal's rents **lockers** and **towels**, sells sunscreen and has an **ATM.** Next to the dressing rooms and showers, a photo pickup stand offers complimentary **lifejacket** use. Most lockers are in Harbor Village; some are at Shark Reef. A **First Aid** station sits behind the Leaning

A MAGICAL DAY

A DAILY PLAN

Can you absolutely get to Typhoon Lagoon by 8:30 a.m.? If so, here's a proven plan. The key: getting the rides done before noon.

8:30 ARRIVE AT THE PARK Once you park your car or get off the bus, it will take nearly 30 minutes to put on sunscreen, get in the park, rent a locker and get in line at the Castaway Creek bridge.

9:00 DO THE SLIDES, TUBES AND REEF Starting with Crush 'n' Gusher, circle the park counterclockwise and do the slides, tubes and Shark Reef. The lines will be short until you're almost done.

11:00 CRUISE CASTAWAY CREEK The lazy river won't be too crowded yet.

12:00 EAT LUNCH Typhoon Tilly's has a first-rate daily rib special. The adjacent Snack Shack has tasty strawberry-banana smoothies and strawberry-watermelon waffle cones.

12:30 PLAY IN THE POOL Check the Surf Report sign for the daily wave schedule.

2:00 RELAX Read a book, or take a nap. Have kids? Sack out at Ketchakiddee Creek.

4:00 RE-RIDE YOUR FAVES The ride lines disappear during the park's final hour.

Assumes park hours of 9 a.m. to 5 p.m.

Palms restaurant. Lost children are taken to High 'N Dry Towels. **Lost and Found** is at the Guest Relations entrance kiosk. The park has no package pickup service or baby care center, but restrooms have **baby changing stations. Parking** is free. The Typhoon Lagoon **telephone number** is 407-560-7223.

FUN FACTS ›› With 10 miles of plumbing, the park circulates 35 million gallons of water daily. **››** The 95-foot Mount Mayday pumps 40,000 gallons of water a minute to its nine water slides. **››** Miss Tilly is actually 17 tons of molded and painted concrete. **››** Lagoona Gator is the park's rarely seen mascot. **››** Early park concepts included a beached cruise ship and a swamped logging camp.

▶ Typhoon Lagoon offers surfing lessons before park hours. Details: 407-939-7873.

Family float. Orlando's Rathbun family relaxes under the lush landscaping on Castaway Creek.

Lazy river

CASTAWAY CREEK This shady, palm-lined stream takes you on a tropical journey around the park. Along the way you'll be sprayed by misters along the shore, drizzled on by the tank and pipes of a broken-down waterworks, and, as you're

Dads join in the water-cannon fun at the Ketchakiddee Creek children's area

forced through a waterfall at a cave entrance, completely soaked. There's a lot to look at. You pass three crashed boats, travel alongside the Ketchakiddee Creek playground and go under a suspension bridge. Once the river splits in two. The 2,100-foot waterway is 15 feet wide and 3 feet deep. It moseys along at 2 feet per second; a round trip takes about 25 minutes. There's never a wait, though the river can get crowded in the afternoon.

Children's area

KETCHAKIDDEE CREEK What was once, according to Disney, a no-man's land of volcanoes and geysers has become an elaborate tyke-sized water park with 18 activity spots. Your toddler will likely break into a huge grin as he or she splashes through the tube slide's three little dips toward the end of this palm-lined, 100-foot course. The surrounding area is filled with ankle-deep pools and creeks and low bubbly fountains. A 12-foot Blow Me Down boiler is topped with hoses that shake, shimmy and squirt. More adventurous kids will hurl themselves down the two slip 'n' slides — cushy 20-foot mats with 20-degree drops. Everyone has a blast at the S.S. Squirt. Using swiveling water cannons, you'll squirt each other with multiple

▶ Hook your ankles over each other's Castaway Creek tubes to create a family flotilla.

Top: Braced for impact, a summertime crowd at the Typhoon Lagoon surf pool awaits a breaking wave. **Above:** Not always heeded, a surf-pool sign warns parents.

STRONG WAVES
OCCUR
AT ANY TIME
PLEASE HOLD
SMALL CHILDRE
BY THE HAND

breakers up to 6 feet. Emerging with a thundering "whoomph!" from two underwater doors, 80,000 gallons of water sweep across the pool every 90 seconds. Each wave is met with hundreds of people who swim into it, swim with it, jump over it or get knocked on their keisters by it. A small sign in front of the pool shows the daily wave schedule.

Twice the size of a football field, the 2.5-acre mushroom-shaped lagoon includes two wading pools with kid-sized slides and two infant-friendly tide pools with bubbling water and climb-on boats. It's bordered by a white sandy beach.

streams of water as you take sides in a battle of oversized sand sculptures. To keep you soaked, a whistle shoots a continuous spray in the air. Many families build sandcastles. When you run out of energy there are many shady chairs and picnic tables. *Height restriction: must be under 48 in. for slides.*

Surf pool

It's not everyone's cup of chowder, but this giant wave pool is a perfect playground to many kids and adults. The surf's up all day, and the waves vary between bobbing swells about 2 feet high and body-surfable

Body slides

HUMUNGA KOWABUNGA Like Splash Mountain without the boat, these zippity speed

---

FUN FACTS >> The pool is 500 feet long and up to 8 feet deep. >> It can hold 1,200 swimmers. >> Its walls are 126 feet apart and rise 7 feet above the static water level. >> The system uses 2.75 million gallons of water. >> The waters are maintained at 75° to 80° F.

▶ **The wave can't be ignored. Even in the shallows its impact can knock you over.**

At left, New Jersey's Amanda Mathus, 14, braces for the splash on the Stern Burner Storm Slide, which goes through a tunnel. **Below,** green means go at Humunga Kowabunga, a 214-foot enclosed tube that drops at a 45-degree angle.

The aquatic world of the Caribbean comes alive in Shark Reef. Family members can watch through underwater portholes of an actual (and upside-down) wrecked ship.

slides drop you and (usually) your swimsuit 51 feet in just a couple of seconds. The three identical dark tubes sit at 60-degree angles and extend 214 feet. Speeds can reach 30 mph. Don't want to go? A waiting bench overlooks the catch pool. *Height restriction: 48 in.*

STORM SLIDES You'll slide up on high banked corners on these swooping body flumes, which take you through rocky gulches on the shady side of Mount Mayday. Each slide is different: Rudder Buster (on the left as you stand at the boarding area) has a small tunnel; Stern Burner (in the middle) has a longer dark tunnel; Jib Jammer (on the right) has no tunnel. Top speed is 20 mph. The slides' average length is 300 feet.

BAY SLIDES Located in the calm left corner of the surf pool ("Blustery Bay"), these two 35-foot slides are for children too old for Ketchakiddee Creek but too young for the Storm Slides or Humunga Kowabunga. One is uncovered, with a few gentle bumps; the other has a 4-foot tunnel. The walkway wanders out of your sight, but it's just 10 steps and it only leads to the slides. Most moms and dads catch their kids at the bottom. *Height restriction: must be under 60 in.*

Saltwater snorkeling

SHARK REEF Darth Vader lives! You hear nothing but your own breathing as you snorkel past "smiling" rainbow parrotfish and other tropical beauties — as well as passive rays and leopard and bonnethead sharks — in the crystal-clear water of this simulated reef. It's the only wild-animal encounter at any Disney park that comes free with park admission. The fish usually swim away from you, but if you're very still one may come close. You're not rushed, and you can stretch out your time by taking a break on the small center island.

A nearby shop provides complimentary use of masks, snorkels and vests. You rinse off in an outdoor shower before entering, and afterward. Changing areas, lockers, showers and a picnic area are nearby. Don't

Top: Masks on, Shark Reef guests get tips from a lifeguard before launching into deeper water. **Above:** Humunga Kowabunga.

want to go? Portholes in an overturned, walk-through sunken tanker let you view your family as they swim by.

For a greater experience, an optional Supplied Air Snorkeling adventure introduces you to the basics of scuba diving.

FUN FACTS 》 Shark Reef holds over 2,000 fish and 362,000 gallons of saltwater. 》 The water temperature is 68° F. 》 The coral, sponges and stationary invertebrates are fiberglass. 》 The fish are fed like those in a home aquarium. Members of Epcot's Seas with Nemo & Friends Animal Care Team toss in food pellets and Romaine lettuce.

▶ Take your time floating at Shark Reef. You're not allowed to reverse your course.

Above: A Toronto 7-year-old splashes into the Keelhaul Falls catch pool as her dad looks on. **Left:** Mayday Falls. **Below:** Gangplank Falls.

Run by the National Association of Underwater Instructors (NAUI), the 30-minute session ($20) includes use of a pony tank, mouthpiece (regulator), flippers and instruction. You can't dive deep, but you get plenty of time in the pool. *Age restriction: 5 and older.*

Tube slides

KEELHAUL FALLS This gentle slide is essentially one big "C" curve. The 400-foot course gets off to a nonthreatening start and slowly builds up speed. It's never scary: the ride ends just after you first slide up on a bank.

MAYDAY FALLS This swervy, rippled flume simulates whitewater rafting. A relatively long, fast course (460 feet at about 15 feet per second, lean back to go faster), it features a triple vortex that can turn you around. There's one small waterfall.

GANGPLANK FALLS The three- to five-passenger rafts on this short family adventure are plenty of fun. You brave water-

▶ Each tube slide lasts less than 30 seconds. Ride them early, when lines are short.

falls, dripping caves and squirting pipes as you twist your way past crates of fireworks on the banks. The course is just 300 feet long, so it's over in about 30 seconds.

CRUSH 'N' GUSHER Wheeeeee! With both lifts and dips, this water-jet-powered tube ride gives you the experience of a roller coaster. Riding in either a two- or three-person tube, you're dropped by a conveyor belt into a flume, then thrust forward with a burst of speed. If you lean back, a lip before each drop may get you airborne (push down with your feet to stay in control). The three slides offer different experiences. Pineapple Plunger has two peaks and three medium-length tunnels. Coconut Crusher has one peak and a long, short, then medium-length tunnel. Banana Blaster is the longest ride by a few seconds, but it doesn't take three-person rafts. It has one peak, with one long tunnel and two medium tunnels. Each ride lasts about 30 seconds. The slides average about 420 feet. A bonus: the waiting line is out of the sun, under a roof.

Hidden behind the dressing rooms, the remote 5-acre area, jokingly named Out of the Way Cay, also includes a small gradual-entry pool and lots of beach chairs and chaise lounges.

The attraction is themed to be the towering remains of a fruit-packing plant. The flumes, as the story goes, were once wash spillways that were used to clean fruit before it was shipped.

Height requirement for slides: 48 in.

FUN FINDS ❶ At the very front of the park, the message spelled out by the nautical flags hanging just to the right of the entrance turnstiles reads "Piranha in pool." ❷ The surf pool wall appears to be a levee ready to burst. Wooden planks spit water between the seams. ❸ Under the clock tower, the decor around Lagoona Gator's shack includes an alligator totem pole. ❹ Inside the window are posters and fly-

© DISNEY

Water jets propel Crush 'n' Gusher riders uphill

ers for The Beach Gators ("So cold blooded, they're hot!") and the film "Bikini Beach Blanket Muscle Party Bingo." A copy of Surfin' Reptile magazine includes the article "How to Get a Golden Tan Without Being Turned into a Suitcase." ❺ At the Happy Landings snack bar, a rack of outboard motors lets you squirt water through their props at Castaway Creek floaters. ❻ The name of the defunct Crush 'n' Gusher fruit company is Tropical Amity (say it slowly). ❼ Ripped open by a long-gone Great White, a "shark-proof" cage sits along the Shark Reef walkway, past the showers. ❽ A sign on a Ketchakiddee Creek slide promotes a boat-washing business: "Keels hauled, decks swabbed. Sorry no sailors washed."

FUN FACTS ❯❯ Each Crush 'n' Gusher water jet puts out 1,350 gallons a minute. ❯❯ The water from one Crush 'n' Gusher slide would fill a standard home swimming pool in about a minute.

▶ Want the most Crush 'n' Gusher airtime? Choose the Pineapple Plunger slide.

Cirque du Soleil
performer Julie
Dionne prepares
to go onstage

Downtown
Disney

The five-story DisneyQuest building is one of the anchors of Downtown Disney West Side

located near the eastern edge of the Disney property, 120-acre Downtown Disney is a mini metropolis of night-clubs, restaurants, shops and the-aters. It's divided into three sections. The largest area, the 66-acre **West Side,** is an entertainment, restaurant and shopping district. It includes a Cirque du Soleil the-ater, DisneyQuest and a House of Blues restaurant and concert hall. Slyly sharing the name of the land where young men turn into jackasses in the 1940 film "Pinocchio," **Pleasure Island** is 72,000 square feet of adult-oriented comedy and dance clubs. Originally known as the Walt Disney World Shopping Village, the **Mar-ketplace** is a 1970s open-air mall. The 25 waterside shops and restaurants wrap around outdoor stands and kiddie rides.

According to Disney lore, the Pleasure Island clubs were once shipping ware-houses of adventurous businessman Merriweather Pleasure. One spot, today's Adventurers Club, was his library. Mr. Pleasure disappeared when the fictional Hurricane Connie destroyed the area (and created the nearby Typhoon Lagoon) and the buildings were converted into night-clubs. Recent renovations have added boat docks that let water taxis shuttle guests be-tween the two ends of the area, the West Side and Marketplace.

RESOURCES Rental **lockers** are located at the Marketplace marina near Cap'n Jack's Restaurant and across from the Motion dance club at Pleasure Island. There are also lockers at the spiral staircase landing of 8TRAX and on the second floor of Man-nequins. **ATMs** are at the House of Blues and Wetzel's Pretzels on the West Side, the Rock 'n' Roll Beach Club at Pleasure Island, near Summer Sands and inside the World of

▶ The parking lot behind Cirque always has plenty of spaces. Others are often full.

© DISNEY

A 3-D pirate adventure at DisneyQuest

Disney store at the Marketplace. **Strollers and wheelchairs** are available at the West Side and Marketplace Guest Relations offices. Downtown Disney has no package pick-up service, first aid station or baby care center, but most restrooms have baby changing stations. Downtown Disney **parking** is free.

AMC Theater

There are 24 auditoriums at this 110,000-square-foot movie complex. Eighteen have stadium seating for unobstructed viewing; two have balconies and screens that reach three stories tall. *5,390 seats.*

DisneyQuest

Virtual reality experiences highlight the attractions at this five-story collection of video and electronic games, which is presented as a one-price indoor theme park. The best games are **Pirates of the Caribbean: Battle for Buccaneer Gold,** which takes a crew of four into an interactive 3-D world for five minutes; **Aladdin's Magic Carpet Ride,** a virtual-reality hunt for the magic lamp; and **Buzz Lightyear's AstroBlaster,** where you battle other guests in cannon-firing bumper cars. Creative types will also love the **Animation Academy,** where 30-minute classes teach you how to draw a Disney character. The 100,000-square-foot building also includes unlimited play on classic arcade games such as Pac-Man. Evening crowds can create 30-minute waits for the most popular games. *Admission: $37 adults, $31 children ages 3–9. Height restrictions: 51 in. for CyberSpace Mountain virtual roller coaster and Buzz Lightyear's AstroBlaster, 48 in. for the Mighty Ducks Pinball Slam life-size pinball game, 35 in. for Pirates of the Caribbean. Open daily from 11:30 a.m. to 11 p.m. Sun.–Thur., midnight Fri. and Sat. Children 9 and under must be accompanied by an adult. Retail shop; two counter-service restaurants. 407-828-4600.*

House of Blues

One of a handful of restaurant and music halls created by Hard Rock Cafe founder Isaac Tigrett and entertainer Dan Aykroyd, this two-story performance venue features lots of original folk art, hardwood floors and quality sound and lighting. A wide range of acts plays here; there are shows almost every night. The adjacent restaurant has free entertainment late. *All ages. General admission. Info and tickets: 407-934-BLUE (2583) or www.hob.com. Restaurant diners get priority admission into the concert hall.*

▶ **DisneyQuest is least crowded on fair-weather weekdays between 4 and 6:30 p.m.**

The Cirque du Soleil theater resembles a Big Top

La Nouba

✓ Created specifically for Walt Disney World, this invigorating Cirque du Soleil spectacle fills you with delight. With costumes, choreography, music and stagecraft that rival the best Broadway extravaganza, it blends the ancient traditions of the European circus with modern acrobatics, dance and street entertainment, captivating you like no American circus can. There are no animals, just humans — acrobats, dancers, clowns, gymnasts and others — putting on a show that's filled with action, color, whimsy and a quirky sense of humor. Designed for a Disney audience, it's performed on a custom-built Elizabethan stage.

The acrobats alone are impressive enough. Up high are tightrope walkers, trapeze artists and, in the show's most beautiful moment, hanging aerialists wrapped in huge red-silk ribbons. Onstage, performers cavort and somersault inside a pair of giant open wheels and jump, spin and twist on two BMX bikes. Four ever-smiling Asian girls dance, flip and climb on each other as they play Diabolo. A finale gymnastic ballet features power-track and trampoline performers. Their surreal diving in and out of windows looks exactly like a film running backwards.

But there's so much more.

Always on stage, sideshow characters participate sometimes as performers, sometimes as spectators. Les Cons ("the nuts"), a quartet of all-white simpletons, automatically dance whenever they hear music. A flightless Green Bird has escaped from her cage. Meanwhile, clowns Balto and Serguei act as children, moving boxes, playing Cowboy and Indian or scaling the moon.

Each scene is presented as a figment of the imagination of a cleaning woman, another stage character who eventually becomes a princess. After all, this is Disney.

There's no master of ceremonies; instead the whole show is scored live by a vibrant band. Hidden in towers alongside the stage, guitar, horn, keyboard and violin players perform in perfect sync with the action. Their zesty mix of classical, jazz, hip hop, klezmer, techno and even bluegrass adds an emotional accent to every performer. Some songs have vocalists — an androgynous male who performs at high alto registers and a spirited female who adds some

FUN FACTS ›› The name "La Nouba" comes from the French phrase "faire la nouba," which means to party. ›› With an average age of 30, the 72-person cast comes from 14 countries. Many are from Russia. ›› There are over 300 costumes and headpieces. Most performers wear three different outfits. ›› The materials include real and synthetic hair, horsehair and feathers. ›› Plaster head molds are made for each performer to ensure that headpieces, masks and wigs fit perfectly.

▶ Get to your seats early. The clowns come out 10 minutes before showtime.

Above: Dressed in pinstripes and a tiny bowler, the Walker roams the stage like Charlie Chaplin. Always optimistic, he feels whatever he sees. **Below:** Based on a Chinese yo-yo game, the Diabolos act features young Asian girls who dance, flip and climb on each other as they toss a wooden spool back and forth. It often steals the show.

Above, Elena Day dresses for her role as the Green Bird, a depressed, awkward creature who has escaped her cage but can't fly. Watching every act from the side of the stage, the audience favorite remains trapped like a marionette with tangled strings. **At left,** the lonely Titan confronts the other characters throughout the show. He marches assertively through the world of La Nouba, like a nightmare waiting to take over a dream. **Below,** the show begins with an invasion by the lock-step Urbanites.

Shoe technican Catherine Delgado stretches new shoes for the Walker. Every day about 250 pairs of shoes are checked and touched up for the show.

society's line. By contrast, the neon circus folk each march to their own beat. Movie buffs will find references to 1997's "The Fifth Element" (the odd music and warbling diva) and 1998's "Dark City" (the looming cityscapes and unexpectedly moving floors). Art lovers will sense Calder and Matisse.

What's it all mean? The show's purpose, its producers say, is to "wake up the innocence in your heart." You'll be surprised how much it succeeds.

$63–$112 adults, $50–$90 for children 3–9. 90 min. show, no intermission. 1,671 seats. Best ages: 4 and up. No photography. Showtimes 6 p.m. and 9 p.m. Tues.–Sat. Tickets can be purchased six months in advance. Info and tickets: 407-939-7600, www.cirquedusoleil.com or at the Cirque box office at Downtown Disney.

WHERE TO SIT Every seat's good, but spending the money to sit down front does pay off — you'll see every costume and makeup detail, every smile and grimace, every tensed muscle. You'll hear the clowns squeak and grunt, and the acrobats shout verbal cues. Catch the eye of a performer and he or she might wink back.

Gospel soul. Both sing exclusively in French. The acoustics are crystal clear.

Though it doesn't tell a tale, La Nouba does have story elements. The opening is a meeting of two worlds, a modern urban society and an early 20th-century circus. Determined, de-personal and de-saturated, the Urbans march in lock step as they toe

FUN FINDS ❶ A rooster crows at the end of the opening parade. ❷ The eyes of the German Wheel performers glow in the dark. ❸ The Flying Trapeze performers are androgynous. The males wear tutus. ❹ The

Le backstage bizarre

As part of the research for this article, the author's husband spent an afternoon with the La Nouba performers as they prepared for a show. His notes:

4:15 I start off in the fitness center. As I chat with a muscleman, three little Asian girls wander in. Dropping their school books and circling around me, they pull out this giant spool thing and FLING IT RIGHT AT MY HEAD! (Well almost! I swear it brushed back my hair.) Then they do it again. And again! They giggle. I leave.

4:30 Hangin' out in the Green Room, I sit down by a nice gray-haired man who, I later learn, is one of the clowns. Watching CNN, we laugh together at the stupid politicians. Then he tells me a long, passionate story. In French. I don't speak French.

5:00 Outside on a patio, a bunch of shirtless guys play backgammon, foosball and ping pong. They look like frat brothers. Except for the eyeliner.

5:15 Makeup and shower time. Wearing only towels, perfect slabs of men half my age file past me in the narrow halls. But I can't feel too inadequate. They're each wearing more makeup than Gwen Stefani.

5:30 Twenty minutes until show time. Back in the gym, a pair of acrobats stretch their legs while a blue-lipsticked bike dude checks his sprockets. In the hall, a trumpeter runs the scales while a white-faced guy greets me with a burst of, I think, opera.

5:45 Yikes! Time to go! I race out to grab my daughter, who's next door at DisneyQuest.

5:50 We race up the steps and into the theater — just two footsteps ahead of the clowns.

▶ Front-row center is Row 1, Section 103. Tickets go on sale six months in advance.

musicians often dance as they perform in the tower. **⑤** During the chair act the cleaning woman hangs her laundry. **⑥** The Diabolo girls return later to watch part of the show from a floating bench.

Pleasure Island Clubs

8TRAX You'll boogie down to '70s rock and disco at this traditional dance club. *Lounge seats 96.*

ADVENTURERS CLUB Convinced they are British world travelers from the 1930s, improvisational actors wander the floor to chat with guests, tell stories and burst into song. Meanwhile, trophy heads speak, masks move their eyes, a beheaded adventurer refuses to shut up. The most unique Pleasure Island nightspot, the club was designed by Joe Rohde, who later created Animal Kingdom. Plan to stay at least 90 minutes.

BET SOUNDSTAGE Run by the Black Entertainment Television company, this hip-hop and R&B club serves appetizers.

COMEDY WAREHOUSE The Who, What & Warehouse Improv. Co. makes fun of everything in sight as they interact with guests. Fine for preteens and older, every show is different. *290 seats.*

MANNEQUINS DANCE PALACE A dance floor rotates as the gyrating Island Explosion dancers add atmosphere at this award-winning club. You enter from a third floor elevator that opens to catwalks, stage rigging and enough mannequins to give the illusion of a theatrical warehouse. *178 seats in the lounge.*

MOTION Backed by a huge video screen, a disc jockey spins the latest dance tunes at this two-story temple of groove. A younger, grinding crowd.

ROCK 'N' ROLL BEACH CLUB Live bands cover songs from the 1950s to the 1990s at this three-story rock 'n' roll mecca, which features a large dance floor.

$9.95 for one club; $20.95 for all clubs. *Adventurers Club and Comedy Warehouse re-*

Top: Rock 'n' Roll Beach Club. **Above:** 8TRAX.

quire the multiclub ticket and admit guests under 18 if they are with an adult. The dance clubs require guests to be 21 or older. Open nightly 7 p.m. to 1 or 2 a.m. Info: 407-WDW-2NITE (939-2648).

▶ The best Pleasure Island family spot: The Adventurers Club.

© DISNEY

Crowds wander the West Side walkway

Downtown Disney shopping guide

WEST SIDE

CANDY CAULDRON This dungeon-style candy shop has lots of jellybeans and an open kitchen that makes candied apples, chocolate-covered strawberries and other treats.

CIRQUE DU SOLEIL STORE Stunning Cirque-branded scarves, purses and fashion apparel (mixing Italian prints and hand beading) make this store more than a souvenir shop. Also here: great masks and circus caps, figurines inspired by the show, even Diabolo games. Located beneath the auditorium, next to the box office.

HOUSE OF BLUES COMPANY STORE Hot sauce, incense, even cornbread mix is tucked into this unique shop. There's some interesting folk art and blues CDs, and lots of funky House of Blues apparel, even for infants.

HOYPOLOI This collection of uncommon art offers often-soulful home-accent pieces made of ceramic, glass, metal, stone and wood.

MAGIC MASTERS You pick a trick from the menu board, then a magician performs it. The family-friendly shop replicates Harry Houdini's private library. Can you find the secret door?

MAGNETRON A tiny shop filled with thousands of fun, unusual, silly refrigerator magnets.

MICKEY'S GROOVE This general assortment of Disney character and other merchandise includes clothing, pins, souvenirs and toys.

PLANET HOLLYWOOD ON LOCATION Attitude and fashion T-shirts and other apparel.

POP GALLERY This bright collection of pop art includes paintings, three-dimensional wall hangings and some wild glass sculptures.

SOSA FAMILY CIGARS This premium cigar shop often has hand-rolling demonstrations.

STARABILIAS This collection of nostalgic memorabilia includes music, movie, political and historical items.

SUNGLASS ICON This sunglasses shop sells Ray-Ban and other brands.

VIRGIN MEGASTORE You'll find a good-sized fashion store (with kooky shirts, caps, purses and figurines) inside this hip 49,000-square-foot shop, as well as a wide-ranging collection of DVDs and CDs and an eclectic selection of books, magazines and video games. The second-story Coco Moka Cafe has sweets, coffees and deli and panini sandwiches that rival those of pricey places nearby. Some of its 50 seats are on an outdoor balcony.

PLEASURE ISLAND

ORLANDO HARLEY-DAVIDSON It's everything Harley but the hogs — apparel for men, women and kids, collectibles, even pet products.

SHOP FOR IRELAND Irish merchandise includes apparel, infantwear and leprechaun hats. Also Guinness apparel; cookbook from chef Kevin Dundon. At Raglan Road.

MARKETPLACE

ARRIBAS BROTHERS This dimly lit, carpeted shop has hand-cut crystal and hand-blown glass items. Glassblowers work before your eyes.

ART OF DISNEY This store stocks Disney-themed oil paintings, lithographs, theme-park attraction posters, Lenox china figurines, plates, vases and other quality art pieces.

BASIN The aroma of this all-natural skin-care store will intoxicate you as you walk in. Massage and shampoo bars, bath bombs, body butters,

The princess room at World of Disney

lotions and salt and sea scrubs. Also a make-your-own candle station.

DISNEY'S DAYS OF CHRISTMAS Filled with ornaments, this year-round Christmas shop also sells collectibles and figurines. An embroidery and engraving area can personalize your find.

DISNEY'S PIN TRADERS This open-air shop has a lot of pins, but many facings of the same one. A good spot to find limited-edition pins, albums, display sheets and carrying cases.

DISNEY TAILS Set in a corner of Pooh Corner, this pet-care and pampering nook has bandanas, clothes, toys, treats and collar-ID tags.

DISNEY'S WONDERFUL WORLD OF MEMORIES Half of this nice shop is a scrapbooking center, half a photo-album and picture-frame boutique. It's also one of Disney's best bookstores.

GHIRARDELLI CHOCOLATE SHOP A great aroma envelops this collection of chocolate candy, fudge sauce, baking cocoa and hot-chocolate mix.

GOOFY'S CANDY CO. Clerks will top an apple, cookie or marshmallow with your choice of crushed candy, nuts and chocolate drizzle. The jellybean and lollipop collection is huge; a coffee counter has lattes and cappucinos.

LEGO IMAGINATION CENTER This crowded store offers dozens of LEGO boxed sets as well as the world's largest Pick-A-Brick wall, where 320 bins let you buy individual pieces. Don't miss the giant display creations, including Brickley the sea serpent outside in Village Lake.

MICKEY'S MART Dozens of small toys and souvenirs, all priced under $10.

MICKEY'S PANTRY This surprisingly complete housewares shop stocks lots of Mickey-styled appliances and kitchen items, as well as non-Disney cooking supplies, tableware, even wine.

ONCE UPON A TOY This 16,000-square-foot toy store has Hasbro classics like Lincoln Logs and Tinkertoys, as well as many fun items based on Disney theme parks. The playful decor includes a huge Game of Life spinner rotating upside down on the ceiling.

POOH CORNER stocks Winnie-the-Pooh apparel, backpacks, pillows, plushies, sleepwear, toys and adorable infant onesies and dresses.

RAINFOREST CAFE STORE Adjacent to the cafe, this shop sells restaurant- and animal-themed apparel, plushies and toys. Kids love the animated creatures along the walls, as well as Tracy the talking tree.

SUMMER SANDS Geared primarily to young women, this swimwear shop features Roxy suits, board shorts and lightweight fashionwear. For the older set — men and women — there's upscale Tommy Bahama apparel.

TEAM MICKEY'S ATHLETIC CLUB Disney character T-shirts, caps, sports jerseys and golf attire. Also Billabong, similar brands. Stocks nice coats and sweatshirts during the winter. Some ESPN items. For 2008, a new Louisville Slugger corner features custom-made bats.

WORLD OF DISNEY This 51,000-square-foot department store stocks the most popular Disney items, though wide hallways consume much of the space and the displays typically have multiple facings of the same item. It *is* organized well. There are separate rooms for girls (here all known as Princesses), Ladies and Juniors, Boys, Men, Infants, Hats and T-shirts, Housewares, Home Accessories, Jewelry and Pins, Candy and Snacks, and Souvenirs. The store's hot spot is the **Bibbidi Bobbidi Boutique,** a styling salon for young girls where Fairy Godmothers apply cosmetics and style hair. Its ten chairs book far in advance. (Info and reservations: 407-WDW-STYLE (939-7895).)

Diversions

Pumping out more than 600 horsepower, Richard Petty stock cars roar around the Walt Disney World Speedway at speeds over 120 mph

Golf

Grouped into three facilities, each of the five Disney golf courses offers a different experience. There's the long course and the short course. The flat course. The water course. And the great-for-kids 9-hole.

Home to deer, egrets, herons, otters, even alligators and an occasional bald eagle, each course is designated as a wildlife sanctuary by the Audubon Cooperative Sanctuary System. All but the Lake Buena Vista course roam far from civilization. From most holes you view no buildings, only nature. The best months to play are September, April and May, when the weather's nice and good tee times are easy to book. *Build some extra time into your round, as the pace may be slower than you expect.*

Magnolia

How's that shoulder turn? It needs to be efficient on this long-game course, a beautiful rolling terrain that sits in a forest of more than 1,500 magnolia trees. The Magnolia features elevated tees and greens and 97 bunkers, the most of any Disney course. And the greens are quick. Host to the final round of Disney's PGA Tour tournament stop since 1971, the course has tested pros from Jack Nicklaus to Tiger Woods. *Yardage: 5,232–7,516. Par: 72. Course rating: 69.4–76.5. Slope rating: 125–140. Designer: Joe Lee. Year open: 1971. Next to Shades of Green, across from the Polynesian Resort.*

The mouse trap. A bunker at Magnolia's No. 6 green

© DISNEY

Palm

Pretty water fountains. Ugly water hazards. This palm-lined beauty has them both. Water hazards line seven holes and cross six. Shorter and tighter than the Magnolia, the Palm is home to most of the play during Disney's PGA Tour event. Rated one of Golf Digest's Top 25 Resort Courses, it has a few long par 4s and a couple of par 5s that can be reached in two using a fairway wood. The large, elevated greens can be maneuvered with good lag putting. Save a sprinkle of pixie dust for hole No. 18. A long par 4, it has been rated as high as fourth toughest on the PGA Tour. *Yardage: 5,311–6,957. Par: 72. Course rating: 69.5–73.9. Slope rating: 126–138. Designer: Joe Lee. Year open: 1971. Next to Shades of Green, across from the Polynesian Resort.*

Oak Trail

This 9-hole walking course is nice for a quick nine, practice, or letting the developing golfer learn the game. With small greens and two good par 5s, the course requires you to be accurate with your short irons. The longest hole, the 517-yard No. 5, features a double dogleg. Water hazards cross three fairways. Most greens and tees are elevated. The score card lists separate pars for children 11 and under and 12 and over. *Yardage: 2,532–2,913. Par: 36. Course rating: 64.6–68.2. Slope rating: 107–123. Designer: Ron Garl. Year open: 1980. Next to Shades of Green, across from the Polynesian Resort.*

Osprey Ridge

This one is flat-out beautiful. Set within uncharacteristically rolling Florida terrain, this course winds through challenging dense vegetation, oak forests and moss hammocks. More than 70 bunkers, mounds and a meandering ridge provide obstacles, banking and elevation changes. Some tees and greens are more than 20 feet above their fairways. The course often has swirling winds. One bit of relief: the waste bunkers along the fairways play differently than regular bunkers. Their sand is fairly hard, so you can play a shot out of one with a more-normal swing. *Yardage: 5,402–7,101. Par: 72. Course rating: 69.5–74.4. Slope rating: 123–131. Designer: Tom Fazio. Year open: 1992. Just east of the Fort Wilderness Resort.*

Lake Buena Vista

The least forgiving Disney course, Lake Buena Vista features narrow, tree-lined fairways and small greens. You tee off at the Saratoga Springs Resort, then weave through Old Key West. Play demands accuracy on the tee shot as well as the approach. Errant shots can fly into windows. Hole No. 7 has an island green; No. 18 is a 438-yard dogleg. Ten holes have water hazards. *Yardage: 5,194–6,819. Par: 72. Course rating: 68.6–73.0. Slope rating: 123–133. Designer: Joe Lee. Year open: 1972. Saratoga Springs.*

Lessons

PGA pros offer year-round programs for all golfers, regardless of age or skill level at all three Disney centers — Shades of Green, Osprey Ridge and Lake Buena Vista. Choose from one-on-one instruction focused on a specific skill, video analysis of your swing or on-course lessons that include course management and strategy, club selection and short-game skills ($50–$150). *Individual lessons, clinics: 407-WDW-GOLF (4653). Group lessons: 407-938-3870.*

Greens fees: $35–$170 for 18-hole courses (required cart rental included); $38 for Oak Trail ($20 for those under 18). Club and shoe rental available. Proper golf attire required. 18-hole courses have putting greens and driving ranges. Transportation provided from Disney-owned resorts. Reservations accepted 90 days in advance for Disney resort guests, 30 days for other players. Cancellations require 48 hours notice. Florida residents can purchase an Annual Golf Membership ($50) that offers savings of up to 60 percent (based upon the time of year) for greens fees after 10 a.m. for the member and up to three guests, and savings of 20 percent on golf instruction. Details at 407-WDW-GOLF (4653) or online at www.disneyworldgolf.com.

Note: Disney's **Eagle Pines** course has been closed. In its place will be a Four Seasons resort development.

All **18-hole greens** have been converted from TifDwarf to ultradwarf TifEagle turf, a shorter type of Bermuda grass that provides a truer, faster roll. Installation on the 9-hole Oak Trail is scheduled for 2009.

Miniature golf

Located next to the Walt Disney World Swan and Dolphin resorts, **Fantasia Gardens** (407-560-4870) is busy at night, when tee-time waits can be an hour. Splashing brooms and dancing-ostrich topiaries entertain you on the Gardens course, while the Fairways course replicates real links, with bunkers, roughs, undulating hills, and holes up to 103 feet long.

Located next to Blizzard Beach, **Winter Summerland** (407-560-7161) is often deserted at night. Its two courses are themed to the activities of a group of elves who, as the story* goes, vacation here. Their tiny trailers dot the landscape. Getting a hole in one is pretty easy; the greens often funnel into the cups.

Rates: $10.75 ($8.50 ages 3–9). Open 10 a.m.–11 p.m. (last tee time 10:30 p.m.). In-person, same-day reservations accepted. Info: 407-WDW-PLAY (939-7529).

FUN FIND ❶ Hoofprints in the Winter Summerland walkway lead from the check-in counter (a sleigh and trailer) to a nearby reindeer barn.

* Late one Christmas Eve as Santa was flying over Florida, he glanced down, saw snow (!), landed and purchased the spot as a vacation retreat for his elves. They built two golf courses: one for their members who enjoyed the snow, another for those who loved the Florida sun.

A snowy style of Magic Kingdom's Cinderella Castle highlights a hole at Winter Summerland

"Mom, that music is freaking me out!" — Girl, 6, referring to the dramatic "Fantasia" background music that plays throughout the Fantasia Gardens grounds.

Surfing lessons

Know how to swim? In decent shape? If so, then you are almost guaranteed to learn how to ride the crest of a wave at the **Craig Carroll Surfing School,** held before park hours (often just after dawn) at Disney's Typhoon Lagoon surf pool. Conducted on dry land, a step-by-step introductory lesson is easy to follow, then instructors plop in the water to demonstrate the technique. Once you're in the pool you get plenty of personal attention. After each attempt Carroll critiques you from the lifeguard stand, then an instructor in the water adds more tips.

Waves average about 5 feet for adults; half that for kids.

Though about 70 percent of students succeed, Carroll says females tend to do the best. "Girls don't think as hard about it, and try to do exactly what you say," he explains. "Boys tend to think it's a macho thing."

A professional surfer since the 1970s, Carroll coached world-champion Kelly Slater and runs the Ron Jon Surf School in nearby Cocoa Beach.

$140. Must be 8 yrs. or older and a strong swimmer. Most students have never surfed. Days and hours vary with season. 2.5-hour lesson has 30 min. on land, 2 hrs. in water. Surf-

Danielle Finke, 20, gets off her knees on her second attempt

boards provided. Spectators welcome. Max. 12 students a day; classes usually sell out quickly. Reservations accepted 90 days early at 407-WDW-SURF (939-7873).

Instructor at his side, a student practices his stand-up technique before getting into the water

Stock car driving

The engine rumbles. You tremble. And then you're doing it: tearing down a real race track at over 100 mph driving a 630-horsepower

RICHARD PETTY DRIVING EXPERIENCE

stock car. And you're the only one in it. Now *this* is no Mickey Mouse ride.

Held at the Walt Disney World Speedway, lessons at the **Richard Petty Driving Experience** start off with a training session that includes some time out on the track. Then, wearing a fire cap, driving suit and helmet, you climb through the window, pop on the steering wheel and strap in.

Before you know it you're on the track. Almost always in a turn, you tail your instructor who's in a car of his own. He watches you in a mirror, and drives as fast as you can handle. I got up to 122 mph (fastest in my class!) and even passed a guy on Lap 7.

Built by Richard Petty's company, your

The author at the wheel

NASCAR-style vehicle features a tube frame, huge V-8 and 4-speed clutch. The doors don't open, and the bodies are covered with logos. Most drivers are men, but women often go faster. "Guys sometimes just want to hear the roar of the engine," my instructor said.

Rides $99. Drives $399–$1249 (8–30 laps). Drives require reservations (call 2 wks. early) and include training. Adj. to the Magic Kingdom parking lot. Must be 16 to ride, 18 to drive. Spectators welcome. Information: 1-800-BE-PETTY or at www.1800bepetty.com.

FUN FACTS ❯❯ Once worn down, the foot-wide tires are sold for $5. ❯❯ Nicknamed the "Mickyard," the one-mile tri-oval was built in 1995 by the Indy Racing League. Many pro races were held here, including five Indy 200s and some Craftsman Truck Series events. A large grandstand held over 51,000 fans. Racing stopped in 2000.

Instructor: "Drive a stick?" Woman, 30: "I can! If you teach me."

Water sports

Working out of two locations, **Sammy Duvall's Water Sports Centre** (407-939-0754) will take you parasailing, water-skiing or tube riding.

Parasailing will give you a birds-eye view of Walt Disney World. Hundreds of feet above the 450-acre Bay Lake behind Disney's Contemporary Resort, you can see everything from Animal Kingdom's Tree of Life to Typhoon Lagoon's Miss Tilly. Attached to an open parachute, you're pulled by a powerboat down below. You never get wet, as you take off and land on the back of the boat. *Single riders $95 for 8–10 min. at 450 ft. or $120 for 10–12 min. at 600 ft. Tandem riders $160 for 8–10 min. at 450 ft. or $185 for 10–12 min. at 600 ft. Min. weight per flight 130 lbs. Max weight 330 lbs.*

You can also water-ski, bounce along on a tube, wakeboard or kneeboard behind a MasterCraft inboard. The instructors are friendly and patient, especially with children. *$155 first hr., $125 per addl. hr. per boat. Up to 5 skiers. Includes equipment, driver, instruction. Extra charge if picked up from Disney's Fort Wilderness, Grand Floridian, Polynesian or Wilderness Lodge.*

The business also rents personal watercraft (see next page). A legendary water skier himself, Duvall has won more than 80 professional championships.

Taking off on a parasailing flight behind the Contemporary Resort

Bike and surrey rentals

Ten resorts rent bicycles and/or multi-seat surreys. You'll find them at the BoardWalk, Caribbean Beach, Coronado Springs, Fort Wilderness, Old Key West, Polynesian (surreys only), Port Orleans, Saratoga Springs, Wilderness Lodge and Yacht and Beach Club (bikes only). *Bicycles $8 an hr., $22 per day. Surreys $18–$22 per 30 min.*

Boat charters

CLASSIC INBOARD You'll cruise in style aboard the Breathless II, a 26-foot mahogany replica of a 1930s Chris-Craft. *Ages 3 and up. 30-min. ride: $85 per group. 90-min. IllumiNations cruise: $250. Yacht Club marina. 407-WDW-PLAY (939-7529).*

PONTOON BOATS You and up to nine friends can float out together into the Seven Seas Lagoon to watch Magic Kingdom's Wishes fireworks show, or head to the World Showcase Lagoon for Epcot's IllumiNations. *$200–$250. 1 hr. Guide, snacks provided. Wishes boats leave from the Contemporary, Grand Floridian and Wilderness Lodge docks; IllumiNations trips leave from the Yacht Club. 407-WDW-PLAY (939-7529).*

YACHT You can charter the Grand 1, a 45-foot Sea Ray, for a cruise on the Seven Seas Lagoon or Bay Lake. Excursions can hold up to 13 people. A captain and deckhand are included. *$400 per hr. Food, butler optional. Leaves from the marina at Disney's Grand Floridian Resort. 407-824-2682.*

Boat rentals

With the world's largest rental-boat fleet and a variety of lakes, lagoons and canals, Disney offers nearly every way imaginable to get on the water. Boats vary by resort; call 407-WDW-PLAY (939-7529) for details. **OUTBOARDS** Choose from two-seat Sea Raycers (*$24 per 30 min., $38 per hr. Ages 12–15 may drive if with a licensed driver. Min. height 60 in. Max. weight 320 lbs. per boat*), 17-foot Boston Whaler Montauks (*$33 per 30 min.*) and 21-foot SunTracker pontoon boats (*$42 per 30 min.*).

SAILBOATS 12-foot Sunfish (*$20 per hr.*), and 13-foot Hobie Cats (*$25 per hr.*).

OTHER CHOICES Some Disney resorts offer canoes (*$6.50 per 30 min.*) or pedal boats (*$6.50 per 30 min.*). The Walt Disney World Swan and Dolphin has swan pedal boats (*$12–$14 per 30 min.*).

PERSONAL WATERCRAFT At the Contemporary Resort, Sammy Duvall's Water Sports Centre rents three-seat Sea-Doo personal watercraft for either non-guided rides on Bay Lake or group excursions that also go into the Seven Seas Lagoon. *Non-guided rides $75 per 30 min., $125 per hr. Morning group rides $125 per hr. Max. 3 riders per vehicle, combined weight under 400 lbs. Operator must be 16 with a valid driver's license; renter must be 18. 407-939-0754.*

Campfire

It's free! Held at a small outdoor amphitheater, **Chip 'n' Dale's Campfire Sing-a-Long** lets you bond with your kids without draining your bank account. You'll roast marshmallows in a fire pit, join in a 30-minute sing-a-long with the chipmunks, then watch a Disney movie on a large (if somewhat dim) screen. There's a different film every night. A snack bar sells s'mores kits, packs of marshmallows and sticks, as well as hot dogs and beer. Note: Sit on the benches instead of the bleachers to interact with the characters. *No charge. Nightly. At the Fort Wilderness Resort & Campground. For schedules call 407-824-2727.*

Carriage and wagon rides

HORSE-DRAWN CARRIAGE RIDES Available at Disney's Fort Wilderness Resort & Campground, Disney's Port Orleans Riverside Resort and Disney's Saratoga Springs Resort, these buggies hold up to four adults or a small family. The Fort Wilderness trips travel through natural areas. Night trips are romantic. (*$35. 25 min. 6–9:30 p.m. Those under 18 must ride with an adult. Reservations accepted 90 days in advance at 407-939-PLAY (7529). Same-day availability information at 407-824-2832.*

WAGON RIDES Fort Wilderness also offers 45-minute wagon rides down its trails. You ride with up to 32 other guests. *$8 adults. $5 children 3–9. Under 3 free. 45 min. 7 p.m. and 9:30 p.m. Fireworks-viewing rides often available. Departs from Pioneer Hall. Children under 11 must ride with an adult. No reservations. Group rides available with 24 hrs. notice at 407-824-2734.*

Diving and snorkeling

EPCOT DIVEQUEST Certified divers can spend 40 minutes inside a 5.7-million-gallon saltwater aquarium at Epcot DiveQuest, a guided tour held at The Seas with Nemo & Friends pavilion at Epcot. You'll swim with more than 65 marine species, including non-aggressive sharks, rays, tropical fish and sea turtles. You suit up in waist-deep water and explore with up to 12 others. The program includes a presentation on marine-life research and conservation and an overview of the pavilion. All gear is provided, as are lockers and showers. *Cost: $140. No theme park admission required. Ages: 10 and up. 3 hrs. Open-water scuba certification required; ages 10–11 must dive with an adult. More info: 407-WDW-TOUR (939-8687).*

EPCOT SEAS AQUA TOUR On this tour you snorkel in the tank for 30 minutes with scuba-assisted snorkel (SAS) equipment. You also tour the aquarium, learn about the marine life you'll see, and are shown how to use the equipment. *Cost: $100. No theme park admission required. Ages: 8 and up. Those under 18 must be with an adult. 2.5 hrs. More info: 407-WDW-TOUR (939-8687). Proceeds from the experiences go to the Disney Wildlife Conservation Fund.*

Dolphin encounter

DOLPHINS IN DEPTH You'll spend 30 minutes in knee-deep water with live bottle-nose dolphins, learn about the anatomy and behavior of these mammals and watch biologists do dolphin research on this 3-hour program. No interaction is guaranteed, but then again you may get to feel a heartbeat. Trainers work with you individually. *Cost: $150. Includes T-shirt, photo of you and a dolphin, refreshments. Wet suits provided. Epcot admission not required. Ages: 13 and up. Those under 18 must be with an adult. No swimming required. 3 hrs. Mon.–Fri. Info: 407-WDW-TOUR (939-8687). Proceeds go to the Disney Wildlife Conservation Fund.*

Fishing

GUIDED EXCURSIONS Catching a largemouth bass is almost guaranteed when you take one of Disney's pontoon-boat fishing excursions. Not only did Disney release 70,000 bass fingerlings into the Walt Disney World waters in the late 1960s, organized fishing tours didn't begin until 1977 (leaving bass to grow and breed undisturbed for years), all fishing is catch-and-release and

The authors' daughter holds one of the many largemouth bass she caught during a morning trip

only a handful of anglers — those who take these tours — are on the water at any time. Guests routinely catch bass weighing from 2 to 8 pounds. Most trips catch five to 10 fish; guests average 2.5 per hour. Trips go out on Bay Lake, the Seven Seas Lagoon, the 25-acre Crescent Lake between Epcot and Disney's Hollywood Studios, the 15-acre Lago Dorado at Disney's Coronado Resort and the 43-acre Village Lake behind Downtown Disney. Bay Lake and the Seven Seas Lagoon are teeming with fish, but the largest (up to 14 pounds) are in Crescent and Village lakes. All programs are run by the Bass Anglers Sportsman Society (BASS). *Cost: $200–$235 for 2 hrs. for up to 5 guests, $405 for 4 hrs., each add'l hr. $100. Includes bait (shiners addl.), guide, equipment, refreshments and digital camera. No license required. Trips leave early morning, mid-morning, early afternoon. More info: 407-WDW-BASS (939-2277). Reservations taken up to two weeks in advance.*

FROM THE SHORE You can fish from the shore with a cane pole or casting rod at Fort Wilderness (407-824-2900) and the Port Orleans Resort Riverside (407-934-6000). *Cost: Poles $3.75 for 30 min., $8.50 all day. Rods $5.25 for 30 min., $9.25 all day. Bait addl. Catch-and-release only. No license required. No reservations.*

other recreation

Horseback riding

Guided 45-minute **horseback rides** along shady pine and palmetto trails inside the Fort Wilderness Resort & Campground are available daily from the Tri-Circle D Livery, beginning at 8:30 a.m. Go early and you'll likely see wild animals, including snakes and deer. *$42. Ages 9 and up. Min. height 48 in. Max. weight 250 lbs. Closed-toe shoes only; no sandals or flip-flops. No trotting. Reservations (required) can be made up to 30 days in advance at 407-WDW-PLAY (939-7529).* Smaller kids can take a short **pony ride** at the resort's petting farm. A parent walks the pony. *$4, cash only. Ages 2–8. Max. weight 80 lbs. Max. height 48 in. 10 a.m.–5 p.m. daily. Info: 407-824-2788.*

Jogging

A wooded 1.5-mile trail threads through the **Fort Wilderness Resort & Campground.** There's a bike path to it from **Wilderness Lodge.** Guests can take a leisurely 1 mile stroll on the **Epcot Resorts** promenade, and continue along the BoardWalk side of the lake to Disney's Hollywood Studios. A 1.4-mile walkway leads around the lake at the **Caribbean Beach Resort.** Two trails weave through the **Port Orleans Resorts** (1-mile and .7-mile) and a mile trek circles Lago Dorado at the **Coronado Springs Resort.** Shorter trails are at the Contemporary, Polynesian and Grand Floridian resorts.

Spas

GRAND FLORIDIAN SPA Signature treatments include an aromatherapy massage and body wrap and citrus-zest facials, sugar scrubs and therapies. Couples can get massages together in a candle-lit room. *407-824-2332. Grand Floridian Resort. Parking at Disney's Wedding Pavilion.*

MANDARA SPA This Asian-inspired retreat includes couples suites, a steam room and two indoor gardens. It features baking-soda micro-therapy, cellulite reductions, Glycolic facials; seaweed wraps, stone therapies and tooth whitening programs. *407-934-4772. Walt Disney World Dolphin.*

SARATOGA SPRINGS SPA Inspired by the spring waters of Saratoga Springs, New York, popular treatments at Disney's newest spa include a maple sugar body polish, Adirondack stone therapy massage, a mineral springs hydrotherapy treatment and a rosemary spring therapeutic bath. The French whirlpool has 72 jets. *407-827-4455. At the Saratoga Springs Resort.*

Specialty tours

All tours: No photography allowed in backstage areas. Photo IDs required at check-in. To book any tour but a VIP outing call 407-WDW-TOUR (407-939-8687).

AROUND THE WORLD AT EPCOT Take a Segway Human Transporter through Epcot. *$85, Epcot admission req. 2 hrs. Daily. Ages 16 and up. Max. weight 250 lbs.*

BACKSTAGE MAGIC This tour takes you behind the scenes at Magic Kingdom, Epcot and Disney's Hollywood Studios. The longest, most elaborate Walt Disney World tour. *$199, lunch included, no theme park admission req. 7 hrs. Mon.–Fri. Ages 16 and up.*

BACKSTAGE SAFARI You tour the vet hospital, elephant barn and other animal facilities of Disney's Animal Kingdom, and may get up-close and personal with a giraffe or rhino. *$65, Animal Kingdom admission req. 3 hrs. Mon., Wed., Thr., Fri. Ages 16 and up.*

BEHIND THE SEEDS An inside look at the four greenhouses and fish farm at The Land pavilion. *$14, $10 ages 3–9., Epcot admission req. 45 min. Daily. All ages.*

DISNEY'S FAMILY MAGIC TOUR A Magic Kingdom primer for first-time visitors with children; a skip (literally) through the park. *$27, Magic Kingdom admission req. 2 hrs. Daily. All ages.*

KEYS TO THE KINGDOM Guides discuss the history and philosophies of the Magic Kingdom, and take you backstage and down into the Utilidor. *$60, includes lunch at Columbia Harbour House. Magic Kingdom admission req. 4 hrs. Daily. Ages 16 and up.*

MICKEY'S MAGICAL MILESTONES TOUR Visits to Magic Kingdom attractions and locations that trace the career of Mickey Mouse. *$25, Magic Kingdom admission req. 2 hrs. Mon., Wed., Fri. Ages 16 and under must be accompanied by an adult.*

THE MAGIC BEHIND OUR STEAM TRAINS An inside look at Magic Kingdom's Walt Disney World Railroad shows how its trains are prepared for operation. Discusses Walt Disney's love of steam trains. *$40, Magic Kingdom admission req. No cameras. 3 hrs. Mon., Tue., Wed., Thr., Sat. Ages 10 and up.*

UNDISCOVERED FUTURE WORLD Learn about Walt Disney's planned Experimental Prototype Community of Tomorrow, visit all Future World pavilions and glimpse backstage areas. *$49, Epcot admission req. 4 hrs. Mon., Wed., Fri. Ages 16 and up.*

WILD BY DESIGN Covers the art, architecture, storytelling and animal care at Disney's Animal Kingdom. *$58, includes light continental breakfast. Animal Kingdom admission req. 3 hrs. Mon., Wed., Thr., Fri. Ages 14 and up. Guests under 16 must be accompanied by an adult.*

WILDERNESS BACK TRAIL ADVENTURE Ride a Segway X2 through the Fort Wilderness Campground. *$85. 2 hrs. Tue., Fri., Sat. at 8:30 and 11:30 a.m. Ages 16 and up. Max. weight 250 lbs. Starts from Mickey's Backyard BBQ pavilion. Same-day walk-up reservations at the Fort Wilderness marina.*

YULETIDE FANTASY Tours the holiday decorations of the Magic Kingdom, Epcot and a few resorts. *$69, Late Nov.–Dec. only. No theme park admission req. 3 hrs. Mon.–Sat. Ages 16 and up.*

WIDE WORLD OF SPORTS GUIDED TOUR An inside look at the complex on selected days when sporting events are scheduled. *(Complimentary. 1 hr. All ages.)*

CUSTOM VIP TOURS Guided tours based on your custom itinerary. *$125 per hr., min. 6 hrs. Daily. All ages. Info: 407-560-4033.*

Tennis

Walt Disney World has 34 lighted courts. **Organized programs** for guests of all ages and abilities are offered on the two courts at the Grand Floridian resort. These include private lessons ($75 per hr.), hitting lessons ("Play the Pro," $75 per hr.) and convention-style tournaments for groups ($25 per person). A pro shop rents rackets and ball machines and re-strings and re-grips guest rackets (407-WDW-PLAY (939-7529), same-day reservations at 407-621-1991; parking at Disney's Wedding Pavilion). All **general court use** is complimentary except at the Grand Floridian ($8 per hr.). Some resorts reserve their courts for

U14 competitor Lauren Matheson breaks past a defender in a U.S. Youth Soccer championship match at Disney's Wide World of Sports complex

their own guests, but the BoardWalk, Contemporary, Fort Wilderness Campground and Yacht Club welcome guests from any Disney-owned resort.

Wide World of Sports

Buzzing with activity, this 220-acre complex resembles a modern-day Olympic Village. On a typical summer day, 15-year-olds from Argentina compete in an international cricket exhibition, while inside a fieldhouse girls basketball teams battle for an Amateur Athletic Union (AAU) National Championship, while next door youth baseball teams slug it out on the fields used by the Atlanta Braves during Spring Training, while nearby softball squads compete on multiple fields for a national fast-pitch title, while on still more fields the Tampa Bay Buccaneers are holding their annual preseason training camp. The Florida Picturesque-style compound includes a 7,500-seat baseball stadium, 5,500-seat old-style indoor fieldhouse, baseball quadraplex, six softball fields, nine multi-sport fields, a 400-meter track and field center and 10 tennis courts. Over 11,000 events are held here each year, an average of more than 30 per day. Participating groups include the AAU, Pop Warner, the United States Specialty Sports Association and U.S. Youth Soccer. Spectators can attend amateur events for a nominal fee. Special-event tickets (such as Braves Spring Training) are available through Ticketmaster outlets or at the Wide World of Sports box office. *For more information call 407-828-FANS (3267).*

Accommodations

Walt Disney World resorts

The Walt Disney company runs 19 resorts on its Florida property, which it divides into five categories. Motel-style **Value Resorts** have food courts, pizza delivery, pools, playgrounds and hourly luggage service. Most rooms sleep four. Large complexes, the **Moderate Resorts** add restaurants, limited room service, pools with slides, bellhops and some on-site recreation. Most rooms sleep four. **Deluxe Resorts** add full room service, club levels, fitness centers, kid's activities, child care and valet parking. Most rooms sleep five. Often available for nightly rentals, **Disney Vacation Club** (DVC) timeshare units have kitchens and sleep up to 12. A category of its own, the **Fort Wilderness Resort & Campground** is a wooded area with campsites, cabins and RV hookups, as well as a lakeside village that includes a restaurant, general store and unique activities.

All resorts have shops, arcades, laundry services and free transportation to Disney theme and water parks and Downtown Disney. For reservations call 407-WDW-MAGIC (939-6244).

Benefits of Disney resorts

Some benefits of a Disney-owned resort are obvious. The themed architecture and decor, landscaping and quality restaurants immerse you in a vacation experience. Disney's reputation as a clean, family environment is well-deserved: grounds crews, maintenance workers and security guards seem to be everywhere. The convenient location makes it easy to take a midday break from theme-park or other adventures.

But that's not all.

Complimentary transportation (boats, buses and monorails) takes you to all theme and water parks, golf courses and Downtown Disney. In some cases, it takes just a few minutes to get from your hotel room to a theme park.

Each day one of the four theme parks opens one hour early, or stays open up to three hours late for Disney resort guests with theme-park tickets. Water parks also participate. These **Extra Magic Hours** offer you uncrowded time in the parks and make it easier to plan out your vacation.

A Disney resort I.D. (your **"Key to the World"**) lets you charge park food, merchandise and other services to your room. Disney's free package pickup and delivery service will take anything you buy from Disney and deliver it to your room.

Resort guests also get preferred tee times at Disney's five golf courses.

Disney's innovative **Magical Express** service offers complimentary shuttle and luggage delivery from the Orlando International Airport (OIA) to your Disney resort. In other words, you don't have to rent a car, you completely bypass baggage claim and your bags are automatically placed in your room. When it's time to return home, you check your luggage at your hotel (domes-

Disney's **BoardWalk Resort** before an evening storm

tic flights only) and then hop on a bus back to the airport. If your flight departs late in the day, you can check out of the hotel, check your luggage at the desk nearby, then go off and still fully enjoy your last day at Disney.

The best part? There's no real catch. You have to book the Magical Express service at least 10 days in advance. Participating airlines for return luggage check-in include American, Continental, Delta, JetBlue, Northwest, Ted and United. The service is extraordinarily popular. On some days more than 10,000 people use it, and that's just on the incoming buses. The Walt Disney World Swan and Dolphin, Shades of Green and the Downtown Disney resorts are not included in the program. *For details call Magical Express Guest Services at 866-599-0951.*

Note: All addresses in the following listings are in the city of Lake Buena Vista, ZIP code 32830. All phone numbers actually go to a central information center.

Guests board a monorail at the Grand Floridian

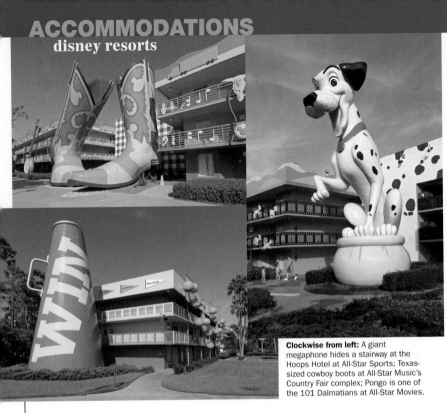

Clockwise from left: A giant megaphone hides a stairway at the Hoops Hotel at All-Star Sports; Texas-sized cowboy boots at All-Star Music's Country Fair complex; Pongo is one of the 101 Dalmatians at All-Star Movies.

All-Star Resorts

Disney's All-Star Movies, All-Star Music and All-Star Sports Resorts offer thousands of rooms at budget rates

Marching bands. Soccer teams. Large families. You'll find them all at these huge complexes, where the low rates bring in everyone who's looking for a deal.

It's quite a crowd. When full, these side-by-side properties can hold 23,556 guests.

Each complex is laid out like a typical American motel, but on a giant scale. A central building holds the registration area, food court and gift shop, and fronts the main swimming pool. Rooms are spread out among detached, three-story rectangular buildings, many with adjacent parking lots. Access is from an outdoor walkway.

All-Star Music includes 298 suites. Designed for budget-minded families with more than two children, they're the least expensive suites on Disney property.

One of only two Disney resort complexes not themed to an exotic land or bygone era*, the All-Star Resorts celebrate Ameri-

* The other: The Contemporary Resort

can culture, specifically movies, music and sports. As for the decorating schemes, they seem to be those of a 6-year-old. Each building has been covered in what appears to be Day-Glo poster paint, then adorned with gigantic props. All-Star Music has 40-foot guitars, huge cowboy boots and a walk-through neon juke box. All-Star Movies is dominated by huge Disney characters, including a 35-foot-tall Buzz Lightyear. All-Star Sports is defined by 38-foot surfboards and gigantic basketballs, football helmets, megaphones and tennis rackets.

DECIDING WHERE TO STAY Besides the fact that All-Star Music has suites, the main difference between the resorts is their food courts. The dining areas at All-Star Music and All-Star Sports are crowded and cranky and serve only standard fast food. The Movies food court, though, is comfortable and well-lit, with a varied, quality menu. Though its breakfast is typical fare, lunch includes fresh deli sandwiches and made-to-order salads, and dinner offers roasted chicken, steak and turkey. (Why the difference? Because All-Star Movies was built last, when Disney understood its needs better.)

Other things to consider: Rooms at All-Star Music and All-Star Sports received new carpet, furniture, mattresses, paint and window dressings in 2007, whereas All-Star Movies was last fixed up in 2006. Also, the Disney buses stop first at All-Star Sports, then Music, then Movies. In other words, guests at Movies have the shortest ride to the theme parks, those at Sports have the fastest trip back.

Each All-Star resort has two themed swimming pools, one at its central hall and a second deeper within its complex. The central pools have adjacent kiddie pools. No pool has a slide, but one at each resort has fountains that shoot water above your head. Each property has a large, sandy playground with climbing areas, monkey bars and a slide.

To be closest to the bus stops, food courts, playgrounds and largest pools, book a room in the Fantasia buildings of All-Star Movies, the Calypso area of All-Star Music, or the Surf's Up section of All-Star Sports.

FUN FINDS All-Star Movies: ❶ Vintage photographs on the back wall of the lobby include many shots of Walt Disney and his team posing with Academy Awards. A 1938 panoramic image shows the entire Biltmore Bowl banquet hall as Shirley Temple and Frank Capra present him with a special eight-Oscar honor for "Snow White and the Seven Dwarfs." ❷ A 1940s movie-theater projector sits in the back room of the food court. You can open its doors. ❸ The stairwells of the 101 Dalmatians buildings are fire hydrants. **All-Star Music: ❹** A lovely spot sits between the two buildings of the Jazz Inn. A ten-foot weathered fountain is surrounded by benches, cobblestones and a wrought-iron fence with climbing roses. **All-Star Sports: ❺** In the courtyard of the basketball buildings, palms are arranged to resemble a basketball team at a tip-off.

FUN FACT 》》 The All-Star Movies Resort kitchen was refurbished in 2007. Its new grilling devices can fully cook a frozen hamburger in 90 seconds.

AT A GLANCE

ALL-STAR RESORTS

RATES Std. room $82–$141 per night, suites $179–$285

LOCATION Southwest corner of Disney property, near Animal Kingdom.

Destination	Distance
Magic Kingdom	5 miles
Epcot	5 miles
Disney's Hollywood Studios	3 miles
Animal Kingdom	1 mile
Blizzard Beach	1 mile
Typhoon Lagoon	4 miles
Downtown Disney	4 miles
Wide World of Sports	3 miles

SIZE 5,740 rooms, 298 suites on 246 acres

ROOMS Std. rooms: 260 sq. ft. and sleep four. Furnished with 2 double beds (1 king bed for handicapped accessible rooms), table, 2 chairs, coffeemaker. **Suites:** 520 sq. ft. and sleep six. Brightly colored bedspreads and carpet. Opt. high-speed Internet srvc. Accessed from outdoor walkways.

FOOD AND DRINK Food courts: Standard American items for breakfast ($3–$6) and lunch and dinner ($6–$9). All-Star Movies has a more varied menu, with salmon and steak salads, deli sandwiches. **Food store:** Each food court has a small food store with fruits, snacks. **Cocktails:** A food court bar serving beer and mixed drinks is open to the main pool area. **Room delivery:** Salads, pizza, desserts (4 p.m. to mid.).

AMENITIES Two swimming pools, kiddie pool. Arcade; gift shop that sells groceries; laundromat; laundry service; playground.

TRANSPORTATION Buses: Disney theme parks, water parks, Downtown Disney.

CHECK IN 3 p.m. **CHECK OUT** 11 a.m.

ADDRESSES
Movies: 1901 W. Buena Vista Dr.
Music: 1801 W. Buena Vista Dr.
Sports: 1701 W. Buena Vista Dr.

PHONE NUMBERS
Movies: 407-939-7000
Music: 407-939-6000
Sports: 407-939-5000

FAX NUMBERS
Movies: 407-939-7111
Music: 407-939-7222
Sports: 407-939-7333

CATEGORY Disney Value Resorts

Clockwise from top: Rooms back up to a wildlife savanna; a giraffe roams behind a lodging building; the huge swimming pool

Animal Kingdom Lodge

Ideal for families, animal lovers and those interested in African culture, this world-class resort is an experience all its own

There's more to see than can ever be seen, more to do than can ever be done at this family-focused resort, which shares its African inspiration with Disney's 1994 film, "The Lion King." Its 19 buildings are interconnected, with all guest service, food and recreation locations right in the center.

WHAT TO SEE The resort's claim to fame is its collection of wildlife. Surrounding three sides of the lodging complex, a 33-acre savanna is home to giraffes, flamingos, zebras, ostriches, gazelles and dozens of other African species. Many rooms have balconies that overlook the animal area; a meandering, elevated walkway extends into the largest section.

African culture is also well represented. The lobby, in fact, is like a museum. Glass cases hold many authentic African pieces, from modern-era Asante gold-dust containers from Ghana and Lobi marriage baskets from Burkina Faso to ancient stone hand axes (circa 8500 BC) from the Sahara Desert. A 16-foot ceremonial mask from the Igbo people of Nigeria stands in the corner.

The resort's greeters, restaurant hosts, savannah guides and activity leaders are young African cultural representatives from Botswana, Namibia and South Africa.

WHAT TO DO Some families spend entire days at the resort, as there are plenty of things to do.

The lodge has Disney's largest resort swimming pool. It features a 67-foot water slide and is open 24 hours. Nearby are two shady and isolated hot tubs and a nice kiddie pool and playground.

Cast members conduct organized children's and family activities every hour of the day, from 9:30 a.m. to 11:30 p.m. Included is everything from cultural lessons about African folklore, music and food to searching for animals after dark with night-vision goggles.

There are three extra-cost programs. A character from "The Lion King" (usually Rafiki) joins a group of children in a **Bush Camp** as they learn about African culture through crafts, games and food sampling (*$70, ages 6–14, Saturdays 1–4 p.m., reservations at 407-WDW-DINE*). The **Wanyama Sunset Safari** takes up to a dozen guests out into the savannas in a specially designed truck to get up-close views of the wildlife. Afterward they have dinner at Jiko, the resort's signature restaurant (*$210, ages 8 and up, reservations at 407-938-4755*). For concierge-level guests, a **Sunrise Safari Breakfast Adventure** offers an extended, early-morning trip through the Kilimanjaro Safaris habitats of the nearby Animal Kingdom theme park (*$55 adults, $28 children, includes breakfast at Tusker House; reservations at 407-938-4755*). The two safaris often sell out 90 days in advance.

FUN FINDS ❶ Between the pool bar and the small spa is a wooden sign that tells the tale of the dung beetle. ❷ A time capsule sits in the Sunset Lounge, to the left of the main lobby. Created by the resort's original cast members, it is scheduled to be opened in 2011. Animal images hide everywhere in the lobby's interior decor. Some examples: ❸ Metal antelopes leap on the outside railing of the fourth floor, visible from the lobby. ❹ Lion and giraffe faces hide in the metal railing around the lobby stairwells that lead to the rear savanna. ❺ At the bottom of those steps, a huge lion face is hiding in plain sight. Two ventilation vents form its eyes, a primitive ladder its nose. The mouth is created by indentations in the rock wall.

Clockwise from top: The resort is surrounded by water on three sides; jogging on the boardwalk itself; the motor lobby; lodging buildings line an inner green

BoardWalk Inn & Villas

The most serene Disney resort is also the most fully realized

Disney's BoardWalk Resort is an entire village, complete with a variety of buildings, a maze of greens and walkways, and an actual lakefront boardwalk lined with restaurants, shops and nightlife. Surrounded by water on three sides, the resort includes an intimate hotel (378 rooms, 20 suites), a 533-unit timeshare property and a 20,000-square-foot conference center.

Meant to resemble a 1940s New Jersey oceanside resort, it seems to be a community that grew and changed over the decades. Mom-and-pop shops have tucked themselves into residental buildings, and "newer" buildings appear to be unrelated to their "older" neighbors. Still, everything blends perfectly together.

Noted architect Robert A.M. Stern restricted his design palette to American building styles common before World War II. He would later repeat that approach as one of the master planners of Disney's

The Keister Coaster water slide at the main pool

nearby residential community, Celebration, which looks remarkably similar.

The BoardWalk has more places to eat than any other Disney resort. Out on the boardwalk are four table-service restaurants, a bakery, sweet shop and, at night, three snack stands. Tucked inside is the Belle Vue Room, a 1930s-style sitting room to the right of the lobby. Furnished with sofas, chairs and small tables, it serves coffee and pastries in the morning and mixed drinks in the evening. Bookshelves are stocked with board games, including, of course, Monopoly. Big Band tunes waft through the air, as do old radio programs like "The Life of Riley."

Designed to look like a 1920s amusement park, the Luna Park swimming pool features the Keister Coaster, a 200-foot water slide with small dips and sweeping turns.

Nightime entertainment includes the Atlantic Dance Hall and Jellyrolls, a dueling-piano bar. Each is restricted to adults and has a $10 cover charge.

FUN FINDS ❶ Photos of all the Miss Americas from 1921 to 2006 hang on the Seashore Sweets walls. ❷ The candy store also displays a Miss America trophy, crown, scepter and robe. ❸ Some of the mutoscopes to the right of the lobby actually work! "The Golfer" features W.C. Fields; "Cat in the Bag" stars Felix the Cat. Drop in a penny and crank.

AT A GLANCE

BOARDWALK INN & VILLAS

RATES Std. room $325–$770 per night, suites $610–$2620, villas $325–$2155

LOCATION Centrally located on Disney property, between the Swan and Epcot.

Destination	Distance
Magic Kingdom	4 miles
Epcot (front entrance, via road)	3 miles
Disney's Hollywood Studios	2 miles
Animal Kingdom	4 miles
Blizzard Beach	2 miles
Typhoon Lagoon	2 miles
Downtown Disney	2 miles
Wide World of Sports	4 miles

SIZE 378 rooms, 20 suites, 533 villas, 45 acres

ROOMS Std. rooms: 385 sq. ft. and sleep five. Furnished with 2 queen beds (1 king bed for handicapped accessible rooms) plus daybed, table, 2 chairs, coffeemaker, small refrigerator, private balcony or patio. **Suites:** Sleep four to eight. **Villas:** Sleep up to 12. Vintage furnishings. Concierge level. Opt. high-speed Internet srvc.

FOOD AND DRINK Table service: Big River Grille & Brewing Works *(lunch, dinner $9–$25)*, ESPN Club *(lunch, dinner $9–$13)*, Flying Fish Cafe *(seafood dinner $28–$40)*, Spoodles *(American breakfast $8–$12, Mediterranean dinner $18–$23)*. **Counter service:** BoardWalk Bakery *(breakfast $1–$6; lunch, dinner $4–$8)*. Seashore Sweets *(ice cream, snacks $2–$4)*. Spoodles pizza window *(lunch, dinner $4 slice, $18+ pie)*. **Cocktails:** Belle Vue Lounge *(4 p.m.–mid.)*. **Pool bar. Room service:** *6 a.m.–mid.*

AMENITIES Three swimming pools with hot tubs. Kiddie pool. Arcade; bicycle and surrey rentals; business center; child-care center; cane-pole fishing; fitness center; gift shop with groceries; laundromat; laundry service; playground; tennis courts; walking trail. 20,000 sq. ft. meeting facility.

TRANSPORTATION Buses: Magic Kingdom, Disney's Animal Kingdom, water parks, Downtown Disney. **Boats and walkways:** Epcot, Disney's Hollywood Studios.

CHECK IN 3 p.m. for Inn, 4 p.m. for Villas

CHECK OUT 11 a.m.

ADDRESS 2101 N. Epcot Resorts Blvd.

PHONE 407-939-5100

FAX 407-939-5150

CATEGORY A Disney Deluxe Resort

Clockwise from top: The Old Port Royale swimming pool resembles a stone fort; small sandy beaches are dotted with hammocks; Centertown at Old Port Royale

Caribbean Beach Resort

Like all of Disney's Moderate Resorts, this centrally located complex is a mixed blessing. It's relaxing, but spread out.

On one hand, this tropical resort is centrally located, has good rates, a fun pool, nice recreation options and a relaxed attitude. On the other hand, it's so spread out that it can take forever to get around, or to even walk to a bus stop, and dining options are poor.

Disney's second largest resort, this sprawling 200-acre property consists of six separate lodging centers that wrap around a 42-acre lake. Lushly landscaped, each of these "villages" has three to six lodging buildings. Three miles of two-lane roads circle the complex, while a 1.4-mile walkway lines the lake. The resort's registration area is located in the Custom House, a separate building along the entranceway.

In the middle of it all is Old Port Royale, a dining, shopping and recreation center. Its indoor area, called Centertown, contains a food court, restaurant, souvenir store and concierge desk.

SWIMMING POOLS Behind Old Port Royale is the main swimming pool, which appears to sit within a stone-walled Caribbean fort. Cannons spray swimmers as they pass. A decent slide has a 90-degree turn. The area also includes a large kiddie pool and a cozy (and very public) whirlpool hot tub. Each village has a small, basic pool.

CHILDREN'S ACTIVITIES The **Islands of the Caribbean Adventure Cruise** *($30, children only, ages 4–10, reservations at 407-WDW-DINE)* is a pontoon-boat trip with tall tales, treasure hunts, even lunch. The two-hour tour casts off a few mornings each week. Centertown holds a 15-minute indoor limbo street dance daily at 12:15 p.m. and 5 p.m. Its food court and gift shop sometimes set up basic activity tables. There are often complimentary basketball, volleyball or other games in the Old Port Royale pool.

The gingerbread charm of the Aruba village

MAKING IT MAGICAL If you stay here, consider renting a car. The resort's large size means many rooms are a long walk away from a bus stop or the Old Port Royale complex, a truth that can be seriously inconvenient during bad weather or late at night. The villages adjacent to Old Port Royale are Martinique and Trinidad North.

Another problem: the dining facilities are too small. Though the resort can hold over 8,000 guests, its food court and restaurant can seat only a few hundred diners at any one time. Breakfast can be especially crowded. At 9 a.m. it can take up to 45 minutes to stand in line for your food, stand in line to pay, stand in line for coffee, and then find an open table. Our advice: Eat breakfast elsewhere — in your room, at the parks, or, if you have a car, another resort.

FUN FINDS ❶ Centertown appears to be an outdoor market. Its two-story walls are building facades with balconies, shuttered windows and thatched roofs. The hall is strung with tin street lamps; its blue ceiling is a sky. ❷ Footbridges over the lake lead to the one-acre Caribbean Cay, a tropical spot with flowers, palms (including banana), benches and hammocks. ❸ Concrete alligators and turtles hide in the beach sand and on the island. ❹ A sign in the Aruba village identifies Caribbean Cay by its former name Parrot Cay, a reference to the birds that once graced its small gazebos.

CARIBBEAN BEACH

RATES $149–$230 per night

LOCATION Centrally located, between Epcot and the Pop Century Resort.

Destination	Distance
Magic Kingdom	5 miles
Epcot (front entrance)	4 miles
Disney's Hollywood Studios	3 miles
Animal Kingdom	5 miles
Blizzard Beach	3 miles
Typhoon Lagoon	1 mile
Downtown Disney	2 miles
Wide World of Sports	3 miles

SIZE 2,112 rooms on 200 acres

ROOMS Std. rooms: 314 sq. ft. and sleep four. Furnished with 2 double beds (1 king bed for handicapped accessible rooms), table, 2 chairs, coffeemaker, small refrigerator. Light oak furniture. Some rooms have bright bedspreads and drapes; others use neutral colors. All are Caribbean themed. Opt. high-speed Internet srvc. Accessed from outdoor walkways.

FOOD AND DRINK Food court: American breakfast items ($5–$7); deli sandwiches, hamburgers, sandwiches, salads and pasta for lunch, dinner ($6–$8). **Table service:** Shutters at Old Port Royale (American dinner with Caribbean influence $17–$21). **Food store:** Small food store with fresh baked goods, fruit. **Pool bar. Room delivery:** salads, pizza, desserts (4 p.m.–11:30 p.m.).

AMENITIES Seven swimming pools, one kiddie pool. Main pool has waterfall and slide. Arcade; beach; bicycle and surrey rentals; pedal-, power- and sailboat rentals; fishing trips; gift shop with groceries; laundromat; laundry service; four playgrounds; volleyball court; walking trail.

TRANSPORTATION Buses: Disney theme parks, water parks, Downtown Disney. A separate shuttle circles within the resort (signs will say "Internal Resort Shuttle.")

CHECK IN 3 p.m.

CHECK OUT 11 a.m.

ADDRESS 900 Cayman Way

PHONE 407-934-3400

FAX 407-934-3288

CATEGORY A Disney Moderate Resort

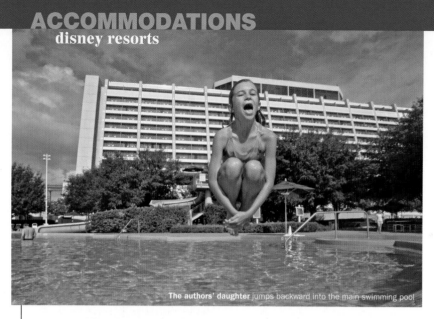

The authors' daughter jumps backward into the main swimming pool

Contemporary Resort

Just a 10-minute walk from Magic Kingdom, this convenient Disney World landmark has just received a modern makeover

An icon of Walt Disney World that's within walking distance of the Magic Kingdom, the Contemporary is easy identified by its central building, a 15-story, open-atrium A-frame that has a monorail track running right through it. A favorite of families and business folk alike, the lakefront resort offers a fun main swimming pool with a spiraling slide, a full range of water sports, a first-class assortment of amenities and an adjacent convention center that's connected via an indoor walkway.

But for 2008, that's not the full story. The resort is finishing up on a near-total renovation, transforming it back to Disney's most modern-themed resort.

Most areas are already done. The atrium boasts a spiffy new open-air gift shop and a new arcade, and will soon have a new snack bar. A new restaurant opens this summer in the main building's lower level. Named The Wave, it will feature dishes created from ingredients such as seared tuna and oven-dried tomatoes.

All rooms and suites were made over in 2007. Standard rooms now have an Asian-inspired decor, with simple white lighting fixtures offset against tan fabrics and dark woods. The bathrooms are especially attractive, with swing-out makeup mirrors and marble baths.

Each room comes with its own computer complete with in-room concierge service and complimentary high-speed Internet access. A cable is provided to hook in your own laptop, and wireless service is an extra-cost option. The computer's flat-screen monitor sits on a small frosted-glass table, with a roll-out side table beside it. Alas, there's no printer, though printing services are available via the lobby concierge.

As always, rooms on the higher floors of the A-frame have great views, though many of their balconies are surprisingly skinny.

Sitting above the atrium on the A-frame's 14th floor, the Tower Suites are heavenly, in particular the one-bedroom units. The size of three standard rooms, each includes a six-seat living area, a six-person dining table, two full baths and three big balconies, one with a large table. The Scandinavian decor features abstract lithographs. Most are used by conventioneers.

A South Wing of additional rooms is still there, but the resort's old North Wing has been demolished. Now under construction in its place, a much taller building is said to be a Disney Vacation Club property.

Monorails travel through the resort's atrium

CRANES, CROONERS AND CROOKS The resort has a fascinating history. Built between 1969 and 1971 by U.S. Steel, the hotel was **an experiment in modular construction.** While its steel skeleton was assembled at the site, the rooms were built at a specially constructed factory about three miles away. As each room moved down an assembly line, workers added in its electrical and plumbing systems, air conditioning units, ceiling, floor, wall coverings, bathroom fixtures and even furniture. An average of 15 rooms were completed a day. Once finished, the nine-ton units were trucked to the resort site, lifted by crane and slid into the steel structure, much like an oversized set of dresser drawers. The result? A real budget-buster. Though each room had been forecast to cost about $17,000, the actual amount was more than five times that much… Reflecting the American Southwest, **the eight-story atrium mural** was created in 1971 by Mary Blair, the Disney artist known for the colorful dolls and abstract background sets of the It's A Small World attraction at Magic Kingdom, as well as the vivid backgrounds seen in the Disney films "Cinderella" and "Alice in Wonderland." Look closely and you'll notice that one of the goats in the mural has five legs. It's facing the monorail tracks at the height of the seventh floor…. **The top floor** of the A-frame was originally a supper club. During the early 1970s, performers in what is today the California Grill restaurant included "I Dream of Jeannie" star Barbara Eden, crooners Lou Rawls and Mel Torme, and even George Clooney's aunt, Rosemary… In perhaps the resort's most infamous moment, President Richard Nixon used one of its ballrooms to speak to the press on November 17, 1973. As part of his address, he declared his innocence in the Watergate cover-up, declaring, **"I am not a crook."**

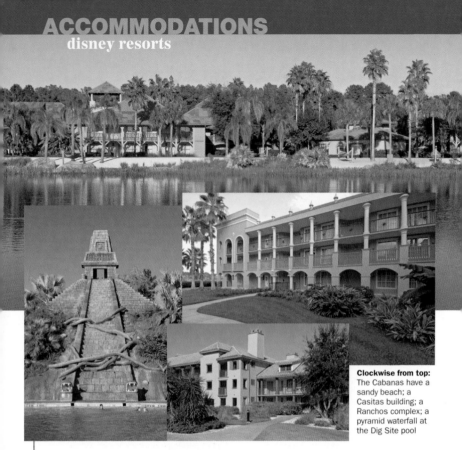

Clockwise from top:
The Cabanas have a sandy beach; a Casitas building; a Ranchos complex; a pyramid waterfall at the Dig Site pool

Coronado Springs Resort

This affordable convention property has many family features

It's not perfect, but with both a terrific recreation center and a large convention facility, this rambling resort can work for either families or business folk. Spread out over 125 acres, it can be a bear to get around. On the other hand, your kids will love it. Architecturally, the property reflects the Spanish Colonial era of Latin America. Building details include arched doorways and windows, tile roofs and mosaic accents.

A CIRCULAR LAYOUT Coronado Springs is anchored by its El Centro complex, which holds the resort's registration, dining and shopping areas as well as its convention center. New for 2008, Rix is a 220-seat upscale lounge with a $15 cover charge. Some evenings have live entertainment. Tables have a $500 minimum charge.

Three distinct lodging areas circle outward from El Centro, wrapping around a 15-acre lagoon and linked together by a paved walkway. Adjacent to the convention center is the Casitas area, with rooms situated in three- and four-story buildings. Halfway around the lagoon, the Ranchos section is more spacious. With sagebrush, cactus and gravel landscaping, these two- and three-story buildings are meant to epitomize arid rural regions of the Southwest. Finally come the Cabanas, on the northern shore of the lagoon. Inspired by seaside resorts along Mexico's Gulf Coast, these two-story buildings are fronted by a beach. The white-sand area is dotted with queen palms, many with swaying hammocks underneath.*

RECREATION CENTER The resort's recreation center is the centrally located Dig

Site, an outdoor complex that offers plenty of things to do. Its large swimming pool features a long, twisting slide that goes under a spitting jaguar as well as an ivy-covered footbridge. An ancient statue blows a continuous stream of water into the pool, while a waterfall flows down the ceremonial stone steps of an adjacent four-story Mayan pyramid.

Surrounding the pool are a huge, soft-surfaced playground (with swings!); a kiddie fountain pool that's just a few inches deep; a pool bar and walk-up food window that serve hamburgers, hot dogs and nachos from 11 a.m. to 6 p.m.; a 22-person outdoor hot tub; a sand volleyball court; and a little-used indoor arcade with an air-hockey table and old-fashioned bowling game.

Organized children's activities include arts and crafts and, weather permitting, swimming pool games such as basketball and water-balloon contests. Billed on its signs as "the lost city of Cibola," the area imagines Francisco Vasquez de Coronado's discovery of a lost Mayan kingdom.

CONVENTION SPACE Disney's least expensive convention resort, the Coronado boasts 220,000 square feet of meeting, ballroom and function space, all on one level. Next to the registration, dining and shopping areas, the convention center includes an 86,000-square-foot exhibit hall, a 60,000-square-foot ballroom and 45 breakout rooms.

As a one-stop meeting and lodging center, however, the resort has an irritating flaw. Spread out like a sun-drenched town, unless you stay in the Casitas it requires you to take a long, outdoor walk to get from your room to your business area. In warm weather, any dressed-for-success look that involves a coat and tie (or, as in my case, pantyhose and heels) is bound to become a frumpy, sweat-soaked mess.

* Which lodging section is right for you? It depends on your needs. The Casitas area is next to the convention center. Stay in rooms 1280–1291 and the convention center is just a few shaded steps outside your door. The Ranchos units neighbor the Dig Site, though Cabanas building 8A (rooms 8100–8257) is actually closer to the rec center's main entrance. The nearest rooms to El Centro are 9500–9657, in Cabanas building 9B. As a family that rarely goes to a convention together, our favorite rooms are Cabanas 8140 to 8147. They're next to the Dig Site entrance, and right in front of a bridge-hopping short cut to El Centro's restaurants and shops.

CORONADO SPRINGS

RATES Std. room $149–$230 per night, suites $340–$1245

LOCATION Next to Disney's Western Way entrance, between Disney's Hollywood Studios and Blizzard Beach.

Destination	Distance
Magic Kingdom	4 miles
Epcot	3 miles
Disney's Hollywood Studios	<1 mile
Animal Kingdom	2 miles
Blizzard Beach	<1 mile
Typhoon Lagoon	3 miles
Downtown Disney	4 miles
Wide World of Sports	4 miles

SIZE 1,877 rooms, 44 suites on 125 acres

ROOMS Std. rooms: 314 sq. ft. and sleep four. Furnished with 2 double beds (1 king bed for handicapped accessible rooms), table, 2 chairs, coffeemaker, small refrigerator. **Suites:** Sleep four to six. Three separate villages: Casitas, Ranchos and Cabanas. Colorful decor features blue, yellow, red. Rooms feature authentic Mexican art. Opt. high-speed Internet srvc.

FOOD AND DRINK Table service: Maya Grill (American breakfast buffet $17; chicken, duck, fish, ribs, steak for dinner $20–$30). **Food court:** Pepper Market (American breakfast $5–$8; hamburgers, chicken, pasta, pizza for lunch, dinner $7–$10). **Food store:** La Tienda (small food store with fresh baked goods, fruit, snacks). **Cocktails:** Laguna Bar (4 p.m.–mid.). **Pool bar** (hamburgers, snacks $6–$8). **Room service:** 7 a.m.–11 p.m.

AMENITIES Four swimming pools with 123-ft. waterslide, kiddie pool, hot tub. Two arcades; bicycle and surrey rentals; kayak, pedal- and powerboat rentals; business center; fitness center; gift shop with groceries; laundromat; laundry service; marina; playground; hair salon; volleyball court; walking trail. 220,000 sq. ft. convention center.

TRANSPORTATION Buses: Disney theme parks, water parks, Downtown Disney.

CHECK IN 3 p.m. **CHECK OUT** 11 a.m.

ADDRESS 1000 Buena Vista Drive

PHONE 407-939-1000

FAX 407-939-1001

CATEGORY A Disney Moderate Resort

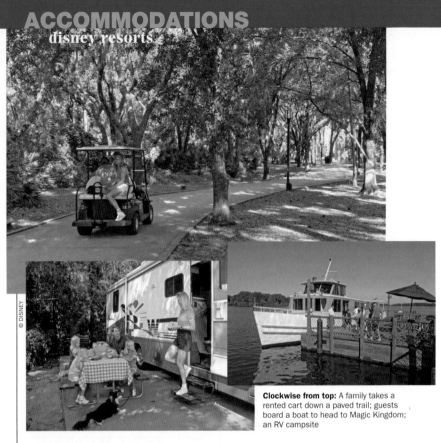

© DISNEY

Clockwise from top: A family takes a rented cart down a paved trail; guests board a boat to head to Magic Kingdom; an RV campsite

Fort Wilderness Campground
Disney's most primitive resort is in many ways the most fun

Packed with organized activities, this wooded campground makes it easy to get in touch with nature. You can ride horses on its trails, fish on its shoreline, rent boats on its lake. At night there are wagon rides and a marshmallow-friendly campfire with its own Disney movie. Best of all, the only decent way to get around is by renting a zippy electric cart. Except to get in and out of your campsite, you're not allowed to drive your car.

Your kids will love it.

Set for the most part in a thick pine forest, Fort Wilderness is a community all its own. The registration building, parking lot and riding stables are at the resort entrance. From there, three main roads branch off into 28 loops, each of which is lined with campsites or cabins. There's a centrally located swimming pool and rec-reation area, and a main "Settlement" at the back, alongside Bay Lake. It includes a general store, restaurant, music hall, marina and Walt Disney World's working stable of Clydesdales and Percherons, which guests are welcome to walk through. There's also a Segway tour.

The nightlife also includes a hokey-but-lovable musical revue and, during every month but January and February, a character barbecue meal.

ACCOMMODATIONS As for a place to stay, you can pitch a tent, hook up an RV or rent a rustic cabin.

The **cabins** are up front, just inside the entrance. Each is air conditioned, and comes with a full kitchen, bathroom, outdoor grill, picnic table and daily house-keeping service.

Roasting marshmallows at the nightly campfire

Located at the extreme eastern and western edges of the resort, tent sites come with water and electric, a combination known as **partial hook-up.** If you don't have a tent, Disney will rent you one for $30 a night. Designed mainly for trailers, campsites with **full hook-up** (water, electric and sewer) are located in the center of the resort, and surround the central recreation area and swimming pool. Meanwhile, **preferred campsites** (water, electric, sewer, cable and Internet) take up the back quarter of the resort. They're usually the choice of large RV owners. All trailer and RV sites are sandy, crushed-shell pads. Each has an adjacent charcoal grill and picnic table.

All sites have close access to air-conditioned comfort stations with private showers, ice dispensers, laundromats, telephones and vending machines.

Fort Wilderness is the only Disney resort that takes pets. They're allowed at select campsites, but not in cabins. The surcharge is $5 per day.

FUN FIND A tree with a push mower embedded in its trunk sits just off of the walkway between the marina and Pioneer Hall, about 100 feet off the lake.

FUN FACTS » The resort has four miles of canals. **»** The Hoop-Dee-Doo Musical Revue serves 800 pounds of ribs each night.

FORT WILDERNESS

RATES Campsites $42–$96 per night, cabins $255–$380

LOCATION Northwest corner of Disney property, southeast of Magic Kingdom.

Destination	Distance
Magic Kingdom	2 miles
Epcot	4 miles
Disney's Hollywood Studios	4 miles
Animal Kingdom	6 miles
Blizzard Beach	4 miles
Typhoon Lagoon	6 miles
Downtown Disney	6 miles
Wide World of Sports	6 miles

SIZE 784 campsites, 409 cabins, 740 acres

ROOMS Campsites: Level, paved pads with electric, water and sewer hookups, charcoal grills, picnic tables. (Partial hookups provide electricity and water only.) **Cabins:** 504 sq. ft. and sleep six. Air-conditioned accommodations that feature vaulted ceilings, fully-equipped kitchens, full bathrooms, TV, VCR, outdoor grills, picnic tables and a private patio deck.

FOOD AND DRINK Table service: "Hoop-Dee-Doo Musical Revue" *(nightly dinner show hoedown at Pioneer Hall $51–$59),* "Mickey's Backyard Barbecue" *(seasonal character dinner show $51–$59),* Trail's End Restaurant *(American breakfast buffet $12, lunch $13, dinner $18. Takeout counter.)* **Cocktails:** Crockett's Tavern.

AMENITIES Two swimming pools. Arcade; basketball, tennis, tetherball, volleyball courts; blacksmith shop; beach; character singalong with campfire and movie; carriage, wagon and trail rides; cane-pole fishing; comfort stations; fishing trips; gift shop with camping supplies, groceries; laundromat; playgrounds; pony rides; riding stables; walking trail; watercraft rentals.

TRANSPORTATION Buses: Theme parks, water parks, Downtown Disney. Separate shuttles run within the resort. **Boats:** Magic Kingdom. **Electric golf carts:** Available for rent for transportation around the property.

CHECK IN 3 p.m. **CHECK OUT** 11 a.m.

ADDRESS 3520 N. Ft. Wilderness Trail

PHONE 407-824-2900

FAX 407-824-3508

CATEGORY Campground

Clockwise from top: The resort sits on the South Seas Lagoon, near Magic Kingdom; SeaRaycer boats for rent; guests stroll in the central courtyard

Grand Floridian Resort & Spa

Walt Disney World's flagship hotel is elegant, yet relaxed

Disney's most opulent resort, the Grand Floridian reflects a theme of old-money elegance. And by old, we mean dead guys, specifically the blue-blooded Yankee tycoons of the late 19th and early 20th centuries. Back during a time when Walt Disney was an overall-clad farm boy in Missouri, many of these suspender-snappin' big-city millionaires would spend their winters in the Sunshine State, taking a train down to one of the many towering resorts that dotted Florida's east and west coasts.

The Grand Floridian brings back both the look and feel of those Victorian vacationlands.* With its red-shingled, gabled roofs; acres of white clapboard siding; miles of moldings, scrolls and turnposts; and thousands of pieces of wicker, leather and floral-fabric furniture, the resort is practically perfectly themed in every way, so much so that Mary Poppins herself drops by each day for breakfast.

The lobby is a five-story atrium. Its ceiling supports two ornate metal chandeliers, and is adorned with three illuminated stained-glass domes. Underneath is a large sitting area dotted with live royal palms, a 20-foot-tall birdcage and an open-cage elevator. Live lobby entertainment alternates between a pianist and the six-piece Grand Floridian Society Orchestra.

The 40-acre grounds include five additional lodging buildings, two pools, a convention center, spa and tennis center, marina and boat dock.

One difference between Disney's Grand Floridian and its inspirational ancestors is its train station. This one welcomes monorails, which pull in and out, on average, every five minutes. The trip to Magic Kingdom takes only two minutes.

* Classic movie buffs (and Disney enthusiasts who realize that the resort was designed in California) will notice that resort also bears a striking resemblance to San Diego's Hotel Del Coronado, the setting of the 1959 film, "Some Like it Hot."

SWIMMING POOLS The resort has two swimming pools — one pretty and peaceful, one lots of fun. In the center of the resort, the quiet **Courtyard Pool** is surrounded by palms and rose bushes. It has an adjacent hot tub and kiddie pool. Best for kids, however, is the resort's **Beach Pool**. Located at the southern end of the property, it features a swerving slide that takes 12 seconds to travel, a 20-foot waterfall that literally pounds you, and a nearby fountain play area that keeps little ones entertained. One side of the Beach Pool is "zero-entry."

CHILDREN'S ACTIVITIES The resort has some indulgent programs for children. Disney's most intimate, expensive and certainly girlie character experience, the **My Disney Girl's Perfectly Princess Tea Party** (*$225 for one adult and one child ages 3–11; addl. adults $75, addl. children $150*) is a 53-person morning affair held in the lobby's Garden View Lounge. It's hosted by Rose Petal, an operatic songstress and storyteller who performs table-to-table. Princess Aurora ("Sleeping Beauty") attends. Besides a tea (with sandwiches) with their parent, children receive an elaborate doll, tiara and other merchandise. Other children's activities include the afternoon **Wonderland Tea Party** (*$43, children only, ages 4–10, at 1900 Park Fare*) hosted by the characters of Disney's 1951 film "Alice in Wonderland," **Grand Adventures in Cooking** (*$49, children only, ages 4–10, at the Mouseketeer Club childcare center*), a lesson in baking cookies, cupcakes and other treats with a take-home apron; and a pontoon-boat **Pirate Adventure** (*$32, children only, ages 4–10*) that searches for treasure on South Seas Lagoon and Bay Lake.

FUN FINDS ❶ The housekeepers twirl their way to work in the Courtyard Parasol Parade, most mornings at 8 a.m. ❷ Among the resort's antiques is an 1890 miniature Ferris wheel. It sits in the main building on a second-floor table, near the entrance to Citricos restaurant. ❸ Out at the motor lobby is an antique car, a white 1929 Cadillac. It can be used as a limousine.

FUN FACTS ❯❯ Why is it called the "Grand" Floridian? Because, as the joke goes, it costs a grand a night.
❯❯ Each lobby chandelier weighs one ton.

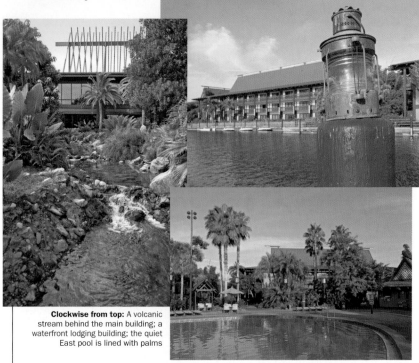

Clockwise from top: A volcanic stream behind the main building; a waterfront lodging building; the quiet East pool is lined with palms

Polynesian Resort

It's not exactly authentic, but no Walt Disney World resort is more family-friendly than this Hawaiian-shirt paradise

The most laid-back Disney Deluxe property, the original Walt Disney World resort is still a great choice for families. It offers large rooms, two nice pools and lots of family-friendly features. What's more, the Magic Kingdom is just a seven-minute monorail ride away. The Polynesian theme is realistic only in a 1970s way, with lush landscaping and exotic trim pieces disguising standard boxy architecture, but a relaxed, Hawaiian-shirt attitude permeates everything.

The front desk, restaurants and shops are located in the two-story Grand Ceremonial House. Topped by 20 clear glass panels, a 40-foot-tall atrium has a volcanic rock waterfall surrounded by tropical plants. A musician performs in the lobby during most evenings, while hula lessons are held there Saturday mornings. Out front, there's usually an evening torch-lighting ceremony that includes a fire-baton twirler.

Torch-lit walkways lead to 11 freestanding two- and three-story lodging buildings, some of which overlook the 172-acre Seven Seas Lagoon.

Refurbished in 2006, the 415-square-foot rooms include hand-carved furnishings and 32-inch flat-screen televisions.

RESTAURANTS The restaurants focus on families. The table-service 'Ohana offers a Lilo and Stitch character breakfast. A converted coffee shop, Kona Cafe has sweet treats such as Tonga Toast (a sort of gigantic, sticky breakfast doughnut) and the Kona Kone (a waffle cone set in chocolate and wrapped in cotton candy). An outdoor dinner show, the Spirit of Aloha teaches kids of any age how to do the hula.

SWIMMING POOLS Located directly behind the Grand Ceremonial House, the Nanea pool is loaded with fun features. Nestled against a simulated volcano, it features a waterfall and, if you listen closely, underwater music. The slide is a dark, two-story slippery tunnel through the volcano, with eerie colored lights and squirting water. Nearby is a kiddie sprinkler area. The far end of the Nanea pool is a "zero-entry" gradual ramp for disabled users. Complimentary wheelchairs can roll right into it. Tucked in to a lodging area, the smaller East pool is less crowded. It has no slide or lifeguard, but hidden behind its lounge chairs are six shady table huts, each with its own ceiling fan. Note: For safety reasons, no lagoon swimming is allowed.

CHILDREN'S ACTIVITIES Free crafts and games are offered in the lobby during most afternoons as well as at the main swimming pool. The Never Land Club, a "Peter Pan"-themed child-care center (kids enter it through Wendy Darling's bedroom window), opens at 4 p.m. each day. Disney's Electrical Water Pageant passes the resort nightly at 9 p.m.

MANAGING THE MONORAIL The fastest way to get to the Magic Kingdom, of course, is by monorail, but in good weather the nicest trip is via the resort's cozy shuttle boat. With open rails and some seats just inches from the water, it's more fun than most park attractions. If you're in a hurry to get to Epcot, meanwhile, the fastest way is to walk — to the adjacent monorail hub known as the Transportation and Ticket Center and take a monorail from there. You'll save about 15 minutes.

FUN FINDS ❶ Behind the Grand Ceremonial House, a volcanic stream appears to flow into the resort's main swimming pool. **❷** Known affectionately as Auntie Kaui, the diminutive Hawaiian woman sitting in the lower lobby stringing leis has been at her job since the resort's opening day in 1971. Before that, she worked at Disneyland. She's really friendly. **❸** A chocolate Lilo and Stitch sculpture graces the Kona Cafe dessert counter. Made in 2003, it stays in pristine shape because it's coated in shellac. **❹** The Cafe's suspended-metal ceiling is meant to be a coffee plant. Its hanging lamps are bean pods.

POLYNESIAN

RATES Std. room $329–$815 per night, suites $575–$2725

LOCATION Northwest corner of Disney property, south of Magic Kingdom.

Destination	Distance
Magic Kingdom	1 mile
Epcot	4 miles
Disney's Hollywood Studios	4 miles
Animal Kingdom	6 miles
Blizzard Beach	5 miles
Typhoon Lagoon	6 miles
Downtown Disney	6 miles
Wide World of Sports	7 miles

SIZE 853 rooms, 5 suites on 39 acres

ROOMS Std. rooms: 415 sq. ft. and sleep five. Furnished with 2 queen beds (1 king bed for handicapped accessible rooms) plus daybed, table, 2 chairs, coffeemaker, small refrigerator, flat-screen TV. Batik-patterned bedspreads and drapes, some hand-carved furnishings. Opt. high-speed Internet srvc. Concierge level. **Suites:** Sleep four to nine.

FOOD AND DRINK Table service: "Spirit of Aloha" dinner show (nightly three-course dinner show with Polynesian entertainers $51–$59), 'Ohana (breakfast character meal $19, Polynesian dinner $26), Kona Cafe (Pan-Pacific-inspired breakfast $8–$14, lunch $10–$14, dinner $16–$26). **Counter service:** Captain Cook's (snack bar, 24 hrs.). **Cocktails:** Tambu Lounge, limited appetizers (1 p.m.–mid.). **Pool bar. Room service:** 6:30 a.m.–mid.

AMENITIES Two swimming pools, adjacent kiddie play area, 2 hot tubs. Arcade; beach; bicycle and surrey rentals; power- and sailboat rentals; child-care center; fishing trips; gift shop with groceries; laundromat; laundry service; playground; fine shops; walking trail.

TRANSPORTATION Buses: Theme parks, water parks, Downtown Disney. **Monorail:** Magic Kingdom, Epcot, Contemporary, Grand Floridian resorts. **Boat:** Magic Kingdom.

CHECK IN 3 p.m.

CHECK OUT 11 a.m.

ADDRESS 600 Seven Seas Drive

PHONE 407-824-2000

FAX 407-824-3174

CATEGORY A Disney Deluxe Resort

Clockwise from top: The Pop Century motor lobby; a squirting-fountain play area; a glowing Rubik's Cube at sunset

Pop Century Resort

Disney's newest Value Resort, this colorful celebration of American pop culture offers a surprising number of benefits

This good-natured resort gets knocked for its small rooms and lack of a real restaurant, but it has a lot to offer. Compared to similarly priced hotels outside Walt Disney World property, it's cornier, but also cleaner, better maintained, more fun, much better landscaped, and, for Disney vacationers, far more convenient.

A celebration of 20th-century pop culture,* the resort is grouped into five themed areas, each representing a decade from the 1950s to the 1990s. Decked out in pop-art color, its lodging buildings are adorned

with huge, decade-appropriate sayings and dozens of gigantic props, such as 41-foot Rubik's Cubes and 65-foot bowling pins. The registration hall features 51 display cases filled with hundreds of cultural artifacts, everything from a 1955 Lionel train accessories catalog to a 1998 Spice Girls videotape.

The lodging areas are meticulously landscaped, but except for their trim pieces the buildings are nothing fancy.

"They're essentially motel buildings," one of its architects tells us, "from a structural standpoint not that much different than those at an old Holiday Inn."

None of the buildings have inside halls, so you enter your room from an outdoor sidewalk or railed walkway.

---

* Only half of the resort is finished, its Classic Years section. On the other side of the 33-acre lake are a few half-completed buildings of the 1900–1940s Legendary Years complex, which has been put on hold.

The guest rooms are identical except for their location. Rooms in the 1960s section are closest to the bus stand, food court and lobby, but come with a $10 surcharge. 1950s rooms are almost as close.

A 650-seat food court offers a varied menu, so no matter how long you stay it doesn't get old. For dinner the four serving stations serve sophisticated flatbreads and salads; hamburgers and hot dogs; pasta and pizza; and Asian noodles and, of all things, 1960s-style TV dinners served in classic molded-compartment tins. Among the desserts are Twinkie tiramisu and tie-dyed cheesecake.

The carpeted dining area has many comfortable booths, and features a soundtrack of songs that includes chestnuts as varied as Van McCoy's "Do the Hustle" to "Fire" by Jimi Hendrix.

None of the three swimming pools have slides, but all are themed. The best is the 1960s Hippy Dippy pool, where four giant metal flowers spray swimmers with water. There's also a 1950s pool shaped like a bowling pin, and a 1990s computer pool (a rectangle) with a spongy keyboard deck. All have adjacent kiddie pools. Other amenities include a nice Memory Lane walking trail. It's lined with signs that identify significant events of each year from 1950 to 1999.

One other benefit: Pop Century has the best Disney bus service of any Disney World resort, with nonstop routes to nearly all theme and water parks. Routes to Disney's Animal Kingdom and Downtown Disney are direct, but each have a stop along the way.

FUN FINDS ❶ A sticker on the giant Big Wheel states that the trike can accommodate a rider that weighs up to 877 pounds. ❷ The 1960s kiddie pool has a flower shower. ❸ Bowling lanes line each side of the bowling-pin pool. ❹ The adjacent laundry building looks like a bowling-shoe bin. ❺ A 1990s service building appears to be a stack of floppy disks. ❻ Cast members join together to do the Hustle every evening at 6 p.m. in front of the resort's check-in counter. ❼ One of the signs along the Memory Lane walking trail has its fact wrong. The St. Louis Gateway Arch opened in 1966, not 1961.

POP CENTURY

RATES $82–$141 per night

LOCATION Centrally located on Disney property, near Disney's Hollywood Studios and Disney's Wide World of Sports.

Destination	Distance
Magic Kingdom	6 miles
Epcot	5 miles
Disney's Hollywood Studios	3 miles
Animal Kingdom	4 miles
Blizzard Beach	4 miles
Typhoon Lagoon	2 miles
Downtown Disney	3 miles
Wide World of Sports	2 miles

SIZE 2,880 rooms on 177 acres

ROOMS Std. rooms: 260 sq. ft. and sleep four. Furnished with 2 double beds (1 king bed for handicapped accessible rooms), table, 2 chairs, coffeemaker. Colorful decor. Opt. high-speed Internet srvc. Accessed from outdoor walkways. Rooms in the 1960s section ($10 surcharge) are closest to the bus stand, food court and lobby. 1950s rooms (no extra charge) are almost as close.

FOOD AND DRINK Food court: American breakfast items ($3–$6); Asian noodles, flatbreads (especially good, with the sophisicated taste of a fine-restaurant entree), hamburgers, hot dogs, pasta, pizza, salads, sandwiches, TV dinners for lunch and dinner ($6–$9). Among the desserts are a Twinkie tiramisu and a tie-dyed cheesecake. 650 seats. **Food store:** The food court includes a small food store with fruits, snacks. **Cocktails:** A corner cocktail lounge in the food court, as well as an outdoor bar at the 1960s pool. **Room delivery:** Pizza (4 p.m. to mid.).

AMENITIES Two swimming pools, adjacent kiddie pools. Arcade; laundromat; laundry service; playground; walking trail.

TRANSPORTATION Buses: Disney theme parks, water parks, Downtown Disney.

CHECK IN 3 p.m.

CHECK OUT 11 a.m.

ADDRESS
1050 Century Drive

PHONE 407-938-4000

FAX 407-938-4040

CATEGORY A Disney Value Resort

Clockwise from top: Port Orleans French Quarter; Port Orleans Riverside; a Riverside restaurant resembles a shipyard

Port Orleans Resorts

One of these two side-by-side Moderate Resorts offers many amenities, the other doesn't even have a restaurant

Though they share a similar name, room layouts and rate structures and are located right next to each other, these two community-style complexes have many key differences. Port Orleans Riverside is a large full-service resort, with an immersive theme, fun swimming pool, many recreational activities and Boatwrights, one of Disney's most underrated basic restaurants. Port Orleans French Quarter, on the other hand, is a much smaller, less inspired lodging area. With theming limited to some shady walkways and wrought-iron railings, it has

a nice pool but little else. In fact, guests who stay at French Quarter are encouraged to use the amenities of Riverside, as long as they don't mind the 10- to 20-minute walk.

PORT ORLEANS RIVERSIDE Filled with towering pines and live oaks, the Riverside grounds re-create classic Old South lifestyles. Buildings are meant to reflect Cajun retreats (16 two-story structures in the resort's heavily wooded Alligator Bayou section) as well as stately Mississippi plantation homes (four two- and

three-story buildings in the more traditionally landscaped Magnolia Bend area).
Nestled alongside a peaceful canal, the central building resembles a riverboat landing. Its food court features an operating
cotton press, with a set of massive working gears powered by a huge water wheel.
The adjacent restaurant is designed as a
boat-building operation.

Parents and children alike will enjoy the
centrally located Ol' Man Island swimming
pool. Surrounded by trees, it's plenty relaxing, but it also has the most waterfalls
of any Disney resort pool, as well as a
swerving slide that dribbles water on those
who go down it.

A nearby Fishin' Hole stand rents cane
poles and sells bait to use off a dock on a
pond stocked with bluegill and sunfish.
Fishing instructions are available. A two-
hour guided fishing trip leaves daily at 6:30
a.m. and 9 a.m., weather permitting *($75–
$80 per person, $160–$185 for a party of five.
Includes use of all rods, reel, and tackle.
Advance reservations required.)*

Other recreation options include a **Bayou
Pirate Adventure,** a kids' pontoon-boat-trip
that searches for hidden treasure as it tells
the tale of John Lafitte *($30, children only,
ages 4–10, reservations at 407-WDW-DINE).*

Until 2001, Port Orleans Riverside was
known as Port Orleans Dixie Landings.

PORT ORLEANS FRENCH QUARTER Located
just south of Port Orleans Riverside, Port
Orleans French Quarter sits alongside the
same man-made canal. A village of seven
three-story lodging buildings surrounds a
central food court and registration area.
French Quarter has a food court but no
table-service restaurant. It's the only
Disney Moderate Resort without one.

Port Orleans French Quarter has few
amenities, but its Doubloon Lagoon swimming pool is fun for families. Its slide goes
down the tongue of Scales, a giant parade
serpent that, if you look closely, is swimming through the cement walkways. Frol-
icking around the pool are a comical band
of fiberglass Mardi Gras alligators. One
plays a water-gushing clarinet, another
squirts a saxophone for tots in the kiddie
pool, while a third gator's umbrella has become a shower. Others pose in front of a
huge water-drizzling clam.

PORT ORLEANS RESORTS

RATES Std. room $145–$225 per night

LOCATION Northeastern Walt Disney World

Destination	Distance
Magic Kingdom	4 miles
Epcot	2 miles
Disney's Hollywood Studios	4 miles
Animal Kingdom	6 miles
Blizzard Beach	4 miles
Typhoon Lagoon	2 miles
Downtown Disney	2 miles
Wide World of Sports	4 miles

SIZE 3,056 rooms on 325 acres

ROOMS Std. rooms: 314 sq. ft., sleep four
(some in Riverside's Alligator Bayou have
trundle beds, sleep five). 2 double beds (1
king bed for handicapped accessible rooms),
table, 2 chairs, coffeemaker, small
refrigerator. Riverside furnishings are hickory
(Bayou) or cherry (Mansion); French
Quarter's are cherry. Accessed from outdoor
walkways. Opt. high-speed Internet srvc.

FOOD AND DRINK Table service:
Boatwright's Dining Hall *(Riverside, Southern
breakfast $9–$12; dinner $17–$30).* **Food
courts:** Riverside *(breakfast $4–$9, lunch
$6–$10, dinner $6–$13),* French Quarter
*(breakfast $2–$8, lunch $3–$8, dinner $6–
$9).* Each resort has a **cocktail lounge, pool
bar** with snacks, and **in-room pizza delivery.**

AMENITIES Riverside: Pool, kiddie pool. Five
quiet pools. Arcade; bike and surrey rentals;
pedal- and powerboat rentals; carriage rides;
cane-pole fishing; fishing trips; laundromat;
laundry service; marina; playground. **French
Quarter:** Pool, hot tub, arcade, laundromat;
laundry service; playground.

TRANSPORTATION Buses: Disney theme
parks, water parks, Downtown Disney.
Boats: Downtown Disney, Old Key West
Resort, Saratoga Springs Resort.

CHECK IN 3 p.m. **CHECK OUT** 11 a.m.

ADDRESSES
French Quarter: 2201 Orleans Dr.
Riverside: 1251 Riverside Dr.

PHONE NUMBERS
French Quarter: 407-934-5000
Riverside: 407-934-6000

FAX NUMBERS
French Quarter: 407-934-5353
Riverside: 407-934-5777

CATEGORY Disney Moderate Resorts

The meandering main swimming pool

Wilderness Lodge and Villas

This 'Faithful homage to Western lodges seems like it's far, far away from a theme park. Actually it's right around the corner.

Isolated yet convenient, a child favorite yet oddly romantic, luxurious yet pomposity free, this Deluxe Disney resort really lets you escape the workaday world. Recreating the geysers, tall timber and Lincoln-Log-like retreats of the American West, the property sits hidden in its own forest of cypress, pine and oak trees on the 450-acre Bay Lake. The four-building complex consists of a central lodge and three guest wings, one of which is a Disney Vacation Club timeshare property.

Reminiscent in particular of the Old Faithful Inn at Yellowstone National Park, Wilderness Lodge features a giant gable roof, hundreds of lodgepole pine logs,* tons of flat granite flagstones and Mission-style furnishings.

The lobby is spectacular. Introduced through two sets of huge log doors, the towering atrium is dominated by four 60-foot bundled log columns which appear to support a wood truss. On the sides are two 55-foot-tall totems, 5 feet wide at their

A buffalo topiary

bases.** Surrounding it all are five floors of wooden balconies.***

At one corner is a three-sided, 82-foot stone fireplace. Viewed from bottom to top, its stone layers illustrate the geological history of the Grand Canyon, complete with fossilized remains of prehistoric animal and plant life. Nearby is a convincing version of a bubbling hot spring. Water from it streams under a picturesque window wall to become an outdoor geothermal area, spills over a 15-foot waterfall and appears to flow into the swimming pool. Behind the pool, a simulated geothermal geyser erupts hourly. Four huge chandeliers hang from pulleys suspended from the ceiling. Resembling teepees, they're circled by torch-cut metal silhouettes of Indians hunting buffalo. Each weighs 500 pounds. The multicolored wood and stone floor includes strips of birds-eye maple, Brazilian cherry, burled walnut and white oak. Underneath is an 18-inch-thick concrete slab.

Teepee-style chandeliers in the lobby

FAMILY FEATURES Portrayed as part of a mountain stream, the large Silver Springs swimming pool features a curving slide that sprays you with mist as you ride down. Nearby are two hot tubs. The Villas has a smaller pool with four bubbling "springs" and an adjacent 15-person whirlpool. The Cub's Den child-care center offers free family craft activities daily from 2:30 to 4 p.m.

FUN FINDS ❶ Hoof prints are embedded into most of the sidewalks. Buffalo prints lead to the front lawn's buffalo topiaries. ❷ The fourth-floor balcony has a few rarely used sitting areas, as well as a front and back porch. The fifth floor has a small back balcony. ❸ Sold at Wilderness Lodge Mercantile, 12-inch souvenir totems are exact replicas of the 12-foot pole that stands in front of the store. They feature Mickey Mouse, Donald Duck, Goofy and the rarely seen Humphrey the Bear.

* The logs were harvested in Oregon, exclusively from dead or diseased trees.

** Though inspired by Native American tales of an eagle and raven, the totems were designed by Disney Imagineers and have no real meaning. They were hand-carved by Washington State artist Duane Pasco. Their odd caramel coloring is the result of a coat of Thompson's Water Seal.

*** None of the wood is load bearing. In the middle of each column is a disguised concrete pole that leads up to equally incognito steel beams.

WILDERNESS LODGE & VILLAS

RATES Std. room $215–$550 per night, suites $485–$1290, villas $305–$1075

LOCATION Northwest corner of Disney property, southeast of Magic Kingdom.

Destination	Distance
Magic Kingdom	1 mile
Epcot	3 miles
Disney's Hollywood Studios	4 miles
Animal Kingdom	6 miles
Blizzard Beach	5 miles
Typhoon Lagoon	5 miles
Downtown Disney	5 miles
Wide World of Sports	7 miles

SIZE 701 rooms, 27 suites, 136 villas, 65 acres

ROOMS Std. rooms: 344 sq. ft. and sleep four. Furnished with 2 queen beds (1 king bed for handicapped accessible rooms) plus daybed, table, 2 chairs, coffeemaker, small refrigerator, flat-screen television. Most rooms have a balcony. Rustic, colorful decor with Native American and animal themes. Concierge level. Opt. high-speed Internet srvc. **Suites:** Sleep four. **Villas:** Sleep four to eight.

FOOD AND DRINK Table service: Artist Point *(Pacific Northwest dinner $20–$51),* Whispering Canyon Cafe *(American meals with all-you-can-eat skillet. Breakfast $8–$14, lunch $10–$15, barbecue dinner $14–$25).* **Counter service:** Roaring Fork Snacks *(snack bar, 24 hrs.).* **Cocktails:** Territory Lounge *(4:30–11:30 p.m.).* **Pool bar. Room service:** 7–11 a.m., 4 p.m.–mid.

AMENITIES Two swimming pools, kiddie pool, 3 hot tubs. Arcade; beach; bicycle and surrey rentals; pedal- and powerboat rentals; child-care center; fishing trips; fitness center; gift shop with groceries; laundromat; laundry service; playground; walking trail. 750 sq. ft. meeting room.

TRANSPORTATION Buses: Theme parks, water parks, Downtown Disney. **Boat:** Magic Kingdom.

CHECK IN 3 p.m. for Inn, 4 p.m. for Villas

CHECK OUT 11 a.m.

ADDRESS 901 Timberland Drive

PHONE NUMBERS
Lodge: 407-824-3200
Villas: 407-938-4300

FAX 407-824-3232

CATEGORY A Disney Deluxe Resort

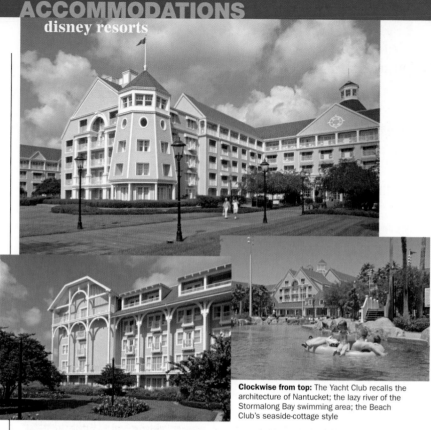

Clockwise from top: The Yacht Club recalls the architecture of Nantucket; the lazy river of the Stormalong Bay swimming area; the Beach Club's seaside-cottage style

Yacht and Beach Club Resort

With an incredible swimming area and a location right next to Epcot, this dual-personality resort is one of Disney's best

This two-in-one resort is a fine choice for families wanting to stay at a Deluxe Disney property. It has a great location, a character-meal restaurant, a soda shop that offers what might be the world's largest ice cream sundae, and a swimming complex that's so complete you can spend hours there.

As for decor, the two resorts are considerably different. Trimmed out decanters of whisky, heirloom statues, gold-fringed drapes and red-white-and-blue carpet that seems straight out of the Hall of Presidents, the Yacht Club reminds us of a wealthy retiree's Florida vacation home. It's meant, however, to evoke the 1870s summer homes of Martha's Vineyard and Nantucket.

The Beach Club, on the other hand, is straight out of the pages of Coastal Living magazine. Comfortable and relaxed, it fea-tures pale-blue-and-white "stick-style" architecture that's meant to resemble 19th-century seaside cottages. Connected to the Beach Club are the Beach Club Villas, a similarly themed collection of suites and studio units that, though part of the Disney Vacation Club timeshare program, can often be rented daily.

The best swimming area of any Walt Disney World resort, Stormalong Bay is, in essence, a miniature water park. Situated between the two resorts, it includes a meandering central pool, lazy river, shallow inlet with a real sandbar, a shady hot tub and an assortment of bubbling fountains, waterfalls and bridges. A spiral staircase on board a life-sized shipwreck leads up to a 300-foot slide. Starting off in a dark tunnel (the inside of the ship's fallen mast)

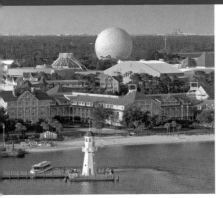

Though landscaping disguises it, the Beach Club sits up against Epcot, within easy walking distance

it plummets into daylight at a rocky outcropping. Riders get showered by two waterfalls before splashing into the central pool. A kiddie pool ("Guppie Bay") with overhead sprinklers has an adjacent sandy play spot, while back on the pirate ship is a second kiddie pool with a tiny slide. Designed so it appears to flow into Crescent Lake, the 2 1/2-acre complex is themed to be a sandy-bottomed Nantucket lagoon. Constantly re-filtering 750,000 gallons of water, it's the largest sand-bottomed chlorinated swimming area in the world.

The marina hosts the **Albatross Treasure Cruise,** which takes children on a pirate-themed pontoon boat that searches for treasure as it stops at the Swan and Dolphin and BoardWalk resorts as well as the Canada and Mexico pavilions in Epcot. Lunch is included. The two-hour excursion sets sail a few mornings each week (*$30 per potty-trained child ages 4–10*).

For couples or families, the marina offer rides in the **Breathless II,** a 26-foot Hacker Craft inboard that's a replica of a 1920s mahogany Chris-Craft.

Other highlights include two specialty restaurants. The Cape May Cafe offers a character breakfast with Goofy, Minnie Mouse and Chip 'n' Dale, while Beaches and Cream is an old-fashioned soda shop.

The two resorts' only flaw: There are hardly any good choices for breakfast. The Yacht Club's buffet is uninspired, and the character buffet will grow old after a visit or two. A hidden treat is the made-to-order yogurt parfaits at the Beach Club's Marketplace gift shop. We eat ours outside, at one of the four wooden tables that sit under a covered veranda just outside the doors.

YACHT AND BEACH CLUB

RATES Std. room $325–$730 per night, suites $575–$2520, villas $325–$1140

LOCATION Centrally located on Disney property, east of Epcot.

Destination	Distance
Magic Kingdom	5 miles
Epcot (front entrance, via road)	4 miles
Disney's Hollywood Studios	2 miles
Animal Kingdom	5 miles
Blizzard Beach	3 miles
Typhoon Lagoon	3 miles
Downtown Disney	3 miles
Wide World of Sports	5 miles

SIZE 1197 rooms, 112 suites, 208 villas

ROOMS Std. rooms: 381 sq. ft. and sleep five. Furnished with 2 queen beds (1 king bed for handicapped accessible rooms), table, 2 chairs, coffeemaker, small refrigerator. Some rooms have daybeds. Concierge level. Opt. high-speed Internet srvc. **Suites, villas:** Sleep four to eight.

FOOD AND DRINK Table service: Beaches and Cream Soda Shop ($4–$22), Cape May Cafe ($19–$26), Yacht Club Galley ($8–$23), Yachtsman Steakhouse ($21–$42). **Counter service:** Beach Club Marketplace ($5–$7). **Cocktails:** Various. **Pool bar. Room service:** 24 hrs.

AMENITIES 3-acre swimming area, 2 kiddie pools. 4 quiet pools. Arcade; beach; boat rentals; business center; child-care center; fishing trips; laundromat; laundry service; marina; massage service; hair salon; fine shops; tennis courts. 73,000 sq. ft. convention center.

TRANSPORTATION Buses: Magic Kingdom, Disney's Animal Kingdom, water parks, Downtown Disney. **Boats, walkway:** Epcot, Disney's Hollywood Studios.

CHECK IN 3 p.m. **CHECK OUT** 11 a.m.

ADDRESSES
Beach Club: 1800 Epcot Resorts Blvd.
Yacht Club: 1700 Epcot Resorts Blvd.

PHONE NUMBERS
Beach Club Inn: 407-934-8000
Beach Club Villas: 407-934-2175
Yacht Club: 407-934-7000

FAX NUMBERS
Beach Club: 407-934-3850
Yacht Club: 407-934-3450

CATEGORY A Disney Deluxe Resort

disney vacation club

The Conch Flats Marina at the Old Key West Resort

OLD KEY WEST

RATES $285–$1645 per night

LOCATION Between Downtown Disney and the Port Orleans French Quarter Resort, in the eastern part of Disney property.

Destination	Distance
Magic Kingdom	4 miles
Epcot	2 miles
Disney's Hollywood Studios	3 miles
Animal Kingdom	5 miles
Blizzard Beach	4 miles
Typhoon Lagoon	2 miles
Downtown Disney	2 miles
Wide World of Sports	3 miles

SIZE 531 villas on 74 acres

ROOMS Studios: 376 sq. ft., sleep four. **1-bedroom villas:** 942 sq. ft., sleep four. **2-bedroom villas:** 1,333 sq. ft., sleep eight. **2-story, 3-bedroom villas:** 2,202 sq. ft., sleep 12. All units furnished with table and chairs, coffeemaker, high ceilings, kitchen facilities, wet bar. Key West decor. Accessed from outdoor walkways. Optional high-speed Internet service.

FOOD AND DRINK Table service: Olivia's Cafe *(American breakfast $9–$10 and lunch $10–$17. Caribbean-inspired dinner $14–$22.)* **Cocktails:** The Gurgling Suitcase *(11:30 a.m.–mid.).* **Pool bar:** Beer, specialty drinks, sandwiches, snacks. **Room service:** Pizza *(4 p.m.–mid.)*

AMENITIES Four swimming pools, each with an adjacent hot tub. Kiddie pool. Two arcades; basketball, shuffleboard, tennis and volleyball courts; bicycle and surrey rentals; pedal-, power- and sailboat rentals; child-care services; DVD rentals; fishing trips; fitness center; gift shop with groceries; laundromat; laundry service; marina; massage services; four playgrounds; walking trail.

TRANSPORTATION Buses: To all Disney theme parks, water parks and Downtown Disney. Internal shuttle bus. **Boats:** Pontoon boats serve Downtown Disney, Port Orleans French Quarter, Port Orleans Riverside, Saratoga Springs resorts.

CHECK IN 4 p.m. **CHECK OUT** 11 a.m.

ADDRESS 1510 N. Cove Road

PHONE 407-827-7700

FAX 407-827-7710

CATEGORY A Disney Vacation Club Resort

Old Key West Resort

Heavily landscaped with palms and other native plants and sitting in a pine forest, this large resort really makes you realize you've come to Florida. Everywhere you look are swaying fronds and falling needles.

A Disney Vacation Club timeshare property, Old Key West often offers nightly rentals to the general public. The two- and three-story lodging buildings are grouped into small, village-like clusters. Replicating the historical look of many South Florida housing areas, they feature clapboard siding, gingerbread accents and tin roofs. Within them are a wide range of accommodations, from studios to three-bedroom units. Many back up to the Lake Buena Vista golf course.

The resort is anchored by the central Conch Flats Community Hall, which holds its registration area, restaurant, gift shop and fitness center. A marina offers complimentary pontoon-boat shuttles to Downtown Disney and the Port Orleans and Saratoga Springs resorts.

Each village has its own quiet pool. The main pool, at Community Hall, has a water slide themed to look like a giant sandcastle.

Some units sit on the Lake Buena Vista golf course

Saratoga Springs lodging buildings

Saratoga Springs Resort & Spa

A world apart from the hustle and bustle of most of Disney's family-oriented resorts, this spacious condominium project is focused on adults. Designed to resemble an upscale country retreat, its amenities are highlighted by a full-service spa, the 18-hole Lake Buena Vista golf course, and a clubhouse-style restaurant with a pool table and bar.

Kids aren't forgotten, of course. The main swimming pool has a short, dark slide and an interactive fountain. It often shows Disney movies at night. The nearby Community Hall features children's activities throughout each day. They include bingo, many arts and crafts projects, even making ice cream.

Saratoga Springs is the largest Disney World property in the Disney Vacation Club timeshare program, but nightly rentals are often available. Accommodations range from studio apartments to a 2,100-square-foot Grand Villa. The resort sits on the grounds of the former Disney Institute.

The low-rise lodging buildings are clustered into five areas (The Springs, The Paddock, Congress Park, The Carousel and The Grandstand), which surround the central registration and recreation center. Three of the areas (The Grandstand, The Paddock and Congress Park) have their own small swimming pools and whirlpool hot tubs. Though actually quite spread out, the resort's small, and relatively uncrowded, gathering spots give it a cozy feel.

A pontoon-boat shuttle provides transportation to Downtown Disney as well as the Port Orleans and Old Key West resorts.

AT A GLANCE

SARATOGA SPRINGS

RATES $279–$1595 per night

LOCATION Eastern part of Disney property, north of Downtown Disney.

Destination	Distance
Magic Kingdom	5 miles
Epcot	3 miles
Disney's Hollywood Studios	4 miles
Animal Kingdom	6 miles
Blizzard Beach	4 miles
Typhoon Lagoon	2 miles
Downtown Disney	2 miles
Wide World of Sports	4 miles

SIZE 828 villas on 65 acres

ROOMS Studios: 365 sq. ft., sleep four. **1-bedroom villas:** 714 sq. ft., sleep four. **2-bedroom villas:** 1,075 sq. ft., sleep eight. **3-bedroom villas:** 2,113 sq. ft., sleep 12. All units furnished with table and chairs, coffeemaker, kitchen facilities. Accessed from outdoor walkways. Optional high-speed Internet service.

FOOD AND DRINK Table service: The Turf Club Bar and Grill (American lunch $10–$20, dinner $12–$23). **Counter service:** The Artist's Palette (American breakfast $4–$7, lunch and dinner $6–$8). **Food store:** Grab 'n' Go with fruits, snacks at the Artist's Palette. **Cocktails:** Turf Club Bar & Grill, with billiard table (Noon–9 p.m.). **Pool bar.**

AMENITIES Four swimming pools, each with an adjacent hot tub. Kiddie play area. Arcade; basketball, shuffleboard, tennis and volleyball courts; bike and surrey rentals; carriage rides; DVD rentals; fitness center; gift shop with groceries; Lake Buena Vista 18-hole golf course; laundromat; laundry service; 2 playgrounds; full-service spa; walking trail. Optional grocery delivery service.

TRANSPORTATION Buses: To all Disney theme parks, water parks and Downtown Disney. Internal shuttle bus. **Boats:** Pontoon boats serve Downtown Disney, Port Orleans French Quarter, Port Orleans Riverside, Old Key West resorts.

CHECK IN 4 p.m. **CHECK OUT** 11 a.m.

ADDRESS 1960 Broadway

PHONE 407-827-1100

FAX 407-827-1151

CATEGORY A Disney Vacation Club Resort

The Swan (left) and Dolphin (above)

Walt Disney World Swan & Dolphin Resort

Not Disney properties, these two Starwood convention hotels are focused on the needs of trade shows and business people

You check in, and the desk clerk is wearing a cap that says "NDB/NMPF/UDIA Annual Meeting." You head to the pool, but it's closed for a "private event." Your teenage daughter heads downstairs for a milkshake, but to get to the snack bar she has to squeeze through a gauntlet of liquored-up conventioneers.

Welcome to the Walt Disney World Swan and Dolphin, where these days about the only thing Disney is the name. Operated by Starwood Hotels, the resorts cater almost exclusively to convention attendees, often at the expense of Disney vacationers. In 2006, the Dolphin removed Santa Claus and his elves from its lobby two weeks before Christmas, to make room for more alcohol stations for an in-house convention.

THE RESORTS TURN OFF their fountain and statue lights at 9 p.m., so guests can get a clear view of Epcot's IllumiNations display.

Over the past few years most of the hotels' moderately priced restaurants have been replaced with more upscale eateries. The last one to go was Palio, a cozy Italian spot that featured a strolling accordionist playing Disney tunes. It closed in 2007 to make way for the high-brow Il Mulino.

As for decor, the two resorts lost much of their interior character last year as well, as a remodeling project trashed the famous whimsical circus and animal theme for a more high-class corporate look. Lobbies now boast woven metal and rosewood paneling, while other areas feature reproductions of classic masterpieces.

Still, families can have fun. When it's not overrun with corporate events, the central recreation area can be a blast for children. The meandering Grotto swimming pool features a huge waterfall that makes it easy to get drenched, and has a decent slide. A volleyball net extends over one of the pool's

The view from the Dolphin's top floor

narrow areas. During the summer, the Grotto shows a Disney movie every Saturday night, and hands out tubes for kids to float on as they watch it.

Nearby is a sandy white beach with two volleyball nets, a basketball court, kiddie pool, boat-like playground piece with covered slides and a small dock that rents swan-shaped pedal boats (*$12–$14 per 30 min.*). Still with its original circus theme, the beach area also includes a statue of a seal that sprays water out of its nose. Across the street are tennis courts and Disney's Fantasia Gardens miniature golf complex.

Meanwhile, Camp Dolphin is an on-site childcare facility open evenings from 5 p.m. to midnight. Staffed by kid-friendly cast members (Thelma is a gem!), it offers arts and crafts, games, Disney movies and dinner at Picabu. (*$10 per hour, for potty-trained kids between 4 and 12. Two hours complimentary for parents who dine at Il Mulino, Shula's Steakhouse, Todd English's bluezoo or purchase a spa service at Mandara Spa. Reservations 407- 934-4241.*)

THE SWAN AND DOLPHIN share a post-modern "entertainment" architectural style, but each has its own appearance. The tallest structure at Walt Disney World, the Dolphin's 27-story triangular tower has two 12-story arching wings topped with 56-foot statues of "mahi-mahi" dolphin fish. A 9-story clamshell fountain cascades down the rear. The Swan, a 12-story arching rectangle with two 7-story wings, is crowned with 47-foot swan statues. The wings of the Dolphin are topped with 20-foot tulip fountains; the wings of the Swan with 20-foot clam shell spouts. The buildings are joined by a palm-lined promenade that splits a lagoon. Seen together, the Swan and Dolphin buildings tell a story. The Dolphin is a tropical mountain. Surrounded by huge banana palms, it has a waterfall flowing from within it. As the water reaches the ground, it splashes onto a huge sand dune: the Swan. The complex was designed by Michael Graves, known for his distinctive line of housewares sold at Target stores.

SWAN AND DOLPHIN

RATES Std. room $279–$555 per night, suites $785–$3500

LOCATION Centrally located, just north of Disney's Hollywood Studios.

Destination	Distance
Magic Kingdom	4 miles
Epcot (front entrance, via road)	3 miles
Disney's Hollywood Studios	2 miles
Animal Kingdom	4 miles
Blizzard Beach	2 miles
Typhoon Lagoon	2 miles
Downtown Disney	3 miles
Wide World of Sports	4 miles

SIZE 2,265 rooms, 191 suites on 87 acres

ROOMS Std. rooms: 360 sq. ft., sleep five. Furnished with 2 double beds (Swan 2 queens) (1 king for handicapped accessible rooms), table, 2 chairs, coffeemaker. "Heavenly" beds. Opt. high-speed Internet srvc. **Suites:** Sleep five to ten.

FOOD AND DRINK Table service: The Fountain *(lunch, dinner $7–$14)*, Fresh *(breakfast buffet $18, lunch $13–$19)*, Garden Grove *(breakfast and character dinner buffets (price varies), lunch $8–$15)*, weekend character breakfast buffet *($17)*, Il Mulino *(Italian dinner $20–$43)*, Kimonos *(sushi bar $5–$24)*, Shula's Steak House *(steak dinner $23–$75)*, Bluezoo *(seafood dinner $20–$52)*. **Counter service:** Picabu *(cafeteria); 24 hrs.; breakfast $3–$12; lunch, dinner $6–$18.* **Cocktails:** Various. **Pool bars:** Two. **Room service:** 24 hrs.

AMENITIES Five swimming pools, 5 hot tubs, kiddie pool. 2 arcades; basketball; volleyball courts; beach; pedal-boat rentals; child-care center; fitness centers; laundromat; laundry service; playground; hair salon; full-service spa; 4 tennis courts. Business center, 254,000 sq. ft. convention center.

TRANSPORTATION Buses: Magic Kingdom, Disney's Animal Kingdom, water parks, Downtown Disney. **Boats:** Epcot, Disney's Hollywood Studios.

CHECK IN 3 p.m. **CHECK OUT** 11 a.m.

ADDRESSES
Dolphin: 1500 Epcot Resorts Blvd.
Swan: 1300 Epcot Resorts Blvd.

PHONE NUMBERS
Dolphin: 407-934-4000 **Swan:** 407-934-4499

FAX NUMBERS
Dolphin: 407-934-4884 **Swan:** 407-934-4710

SHADES OF GREEN

RATES Std. room $89–$129 per night, suites $250–$275

LOCATION Northwest corner of Disney property, southwest of Magic Kingdom.

Destination	Distance
Magic Kingdom	<1 mile
Epcot	4 miles
Disney's Hollywood Studios	4 miles
Animal Kingdom	7 miles
Blizzard Beach	5 miles
Typhoon Lagoon	6 miles
Downtown Disney	7 miles
Wide World of Sports	7 miles

SIZE 575 rooms, 11 suites on 29 acres

ROOMS Std. rooms: 455 sq. ft. and sleep five. Furnished with 2 queen beds (1 king bed for handicapped accessible rooms) plus daybed, table, 4 chairs, coffeemaker, small refrigerator. Light oak woods. All rooms have a balcony or patio. Opt. high-speed Internet srvc. **Suites:** Sleep six to eight.

FOOD AND DRINK Table service: Garden Gallery Restaurant *(buffet breakfast $8–$14, buffet dinner $10–$16; themed buffets vary each day)*, Evergreens Sports Bar & Grill *(burgers, pizza, salads, sandwiches for lunch, dinner $8–$14)*, Mangino's *(Northern Italian dinner $13–$25)*. **Counter service:** Express Cafe *(grab-and-go American breakfast and lunch items)*. **Ice cream parlour:** America, The Ice Cream Parlour. **Cocktails:** Eagle's Lounge. **Pool bar. Room service:** Available for breakfast and dinner.

AMENITIES Two swimming pools, hot tub and kiddie pool. 2 arcades; child-care center; fitness center; AAFES general store with groceries; gift shop; laundromat; laundry service; Kodak photo-taking service; playground; remote-control boats; 2 tennis courts. Golf courses next door. 1,000 sq. ft. meeting space.

TRANSPORTATION Buses: Disney theme parks, water parks, Downtown Disney.

CHECK IN 3 p.m. **CHECK OUT** 11 a.m.

ADDRESS 1950 W. Magnolia Palm Drive

PHONE 407-824-3600

FAX 407-824-3460

CATEGORY The only Armed Forces Recreation Center (AFRC) in the continental United States

Shades of Green

Exclusively for use by active and retired members of the U.S. military and their families, this relaxed resort is the only Armed Forces Recreation Center in the continental United States. Guests are required to show a valid military ID to access the property. Comparable in scope to a Disney Deluxe Resort, Shades of Green features large rooms, full-service restaurants and a great location. Not far from Magic Kingdom, it sits directly across from Disney's Polynesian Resort and within Disney's main golf complex. Surrounding the resort are Disney's Palm, Magnolia and Oak Trail courses.

Originally, Shades of Green was the Disney Golf Resort, a country club with no guest rooms. In 1993 Disney expanded the property and renamed it the Disney Inn. Disney sold the complex to the government in 1996. It was expanded again in 2004.

Room rates offer the best bargains in all of Disney World. They're adjusted on a sliding scale, with prices increasing with rank and pay grade. Even the highest rates are comparable with those at Disney's Value Resorts. Eligible guests and their dependent spouses can each "sponsor" up to three rooms at a time, so large groups of friends and family can stay together.

Shades of Green offers discounted Walt Disney World park tickets to eligible members of the military, including those who don't stay at the property. Located to the right of the main lobby, the Disney ticket office is open daily from 8 a.m. to 9 p.m. A special $55 golf rate is available for tee times after 10 a.m. that are booked no earlier than 24 hours in advance.

The name of the resort refers to that fact that, regardless of branch of service, all U.S. military standard uniforms have some shade of green.

FUN FIND Near the back gazebo, a "Remember the Fun" walkway is lined with bricks engraved with the names and messages from previous guests. One brick is engraved with, of all things, the logo for Universal Studios. Needless to say, it's the only Universal logo at Walt Disney World.

Downtown Disney Resorts

Located at the east end of the Disney property, these hotels are run by outside companies but offer many Disney amenities, including free theme-park shuttles and discounts at Disney golf courses. Developed in the early 1970s as Disney's Hotel Plaza, the area was extensively renovated after the 2004 hurricane season. Its Holiday Inn tower did not reopen.

BEST WESTERN LAKE BUENA VISTA (*$100–$170*) Three restaurants, children's play area, fitness center, 325 rooms. 18-story tower. 2000 Hotel Plaza Blvd. 407-828-2424.

BUENA VISTA PALACE (*$100–$410*) Eight restaurants inc. Australian-themed Outback, Disney character breakfast. Salon, fitness center; tennis, volleyball courts. Large spa (407-827-3200). Top-floor lounge. Largest, tallest Downtown Disney resort. 1,012 rooms. 27-story tower. On 27 acres. 1900 Buena Vista Dr. 407-827-2727.

DOUBLETREE GUEST SUITES (*$135–$400*) Restaurant, fitness center, playground, tennis court. Children's check-in and theater. Sweet Dreams bedding program. Lobby aviary. The only all-suite hotel on Disney property. 229 suites. 7 stories. 2305 Hotel Plaza Blvd. 407-934-1000.

HILTON (*$100–$230*) Six restaurants include Benihana, Disney character breakfast Sun. Hair salon, cyber cafe, health club, golf pro shop. The only Downtown Disney hotel with Disney's Extra Magic Hours benefit. 814 rooms. 1751 Hotel Plaza Blvd. 407-827-4000.

ROYAL PLAZA (*$150–$250*) Restaurants, fitness center, tennis courts. Large rooms, separate sitting areas. Some kitchenettes, wet bars, whirlpool tubs. 394 rooms. 17 stories. 1905 Hotel Plaza Blvd. 407-828-2828.

REGAL SUN (*$100–$210*) Restaurant, English pub, Sat. murder-mystery dinner show, Disney character breakfast Tue., Thur., Sat. Sherlock Holmes museum. Health club. Basketball, shuffleboard, tennis, volleyball courts. 619 rooms, 7 suites. 19-story tower, two wings. On 13 acres. Extensively renovated in 2007. Formerly the Grosvenor. 1850 Hotel Plaza Blvd. 407-828-4444.

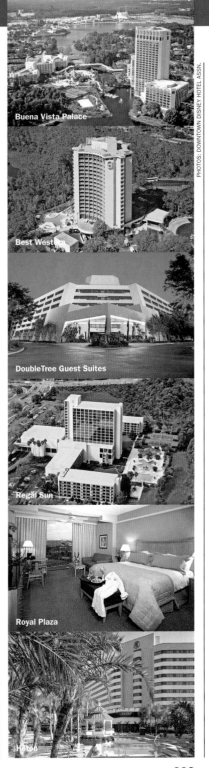

Buena Vista Palace

Best Western

DoubleTree Guest Suites

Regal Sun

Royal Plaza

Hilton

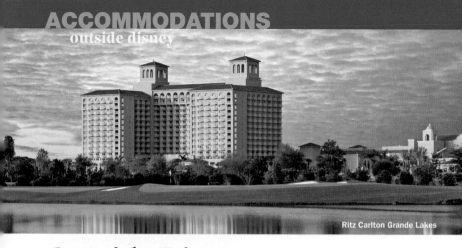

Ritz Carlton Grande Lakes

Outside Disney

BUENA VISTA SUITES $$ *Little Lake Bryan area:* Restaurant. Free breakfast buffet. Fee for pets. 8203 World Center Dr., 32821. 800-537-7737. Free mall and WDW shuttle. 2 mi. from WDW.

CARIBE ROYALE $$–$$$ *Little Lake Bryan area:* Restaurants, pool with slide, waterfall. 8101 World Center Dr., 32821. 800-823-8300. Free shuttle. 2 mi. from WDW.

CELEBRATION HOTEL $$–$$$ *Celebration:* Restaurant. 700 Bloom St., 34747. 888-499-3800. Free shuttle. 4 mi. from WDW.

COUNTRY INN & SUITES $–$$ Kitchens. Free continental breakfast. *U.S. 192 area:* 5001 Calypso Cay Way, 34746. 407-997-1400. Fee for pets. Free shuttle. 5 mi. from WDW. *Int'l. Dr. area:* 7701 Universal Blvd., 32819. 407-313-4200. Free shuttle. 8 mi. from WDW. *Lake Buena Vista:* 12191 S. Apopka-Vineland Rd., 32830. 407-239-1115. Free shuttle. 1 mi. from WDW.

COURTYARD BY MARRIOTT $–$$ Breakfast restaurant. *Lake Buena Vista:* 8501 Palm Pkwy., 32836. 407-239-6900. Free shuttle to outlet mall and WDW. 1 mi. from WDW. *Little Lake Bryan area:* 8623 Vineland Ave. (Marriott Village), 32821. 877-682-8552. Shuttle. 1 mi. from WDW.

CROWNE PLAZA $–$$ *Int'l. Dr. area:* Restaurant. 12000 Int'l. Dr., 32821. 407-239-1222. 4 mi. from WDW.

EMBASSY SUITES $–$$$ Two-room suites with work table, two TVs, wet bar, refrigerator, microwave, coffeemaker. Restaurant(s). Free cooked-to-order breakfast. Evening Managers Reception. Business srvcs. *Airport:* 5835 T.G. Lee Blvd., 32822. 407-888-9339. Free airport shuttle. 15 mi. from WDW. *Downtown Orlando:* 191 East Pine St., 32801. 407-841-1000. 14 mi. from WDW. *Int'l. Dr. area:* 8978 Int'l. Dr., 32819. 407-352-1400. Free shuttle. 5 mi. from WDW. Also: 8250 Jamaican Ct., 32819. 407-345-8250. 6 mi. from WDW. *Lake Buena Vista:* 8100 Lake Ave., 32836. 407-239-1144. Free shuttle. 3 mi. from WDW.

FLORIDAYS ORLANDO $$–$$$ *SeaWorld area:* Restaurant, kitchens, balconies. Two-person jetted tubs. 12550 Floridays Resort Dr., 32821. 866-797-0022. Free shuttle. 3 mi. from WDW.

GAYLORD PALMS $$$ *Adjacent to WDW:* Restaurants, convention space, spa, hair salon. 5-acre tropical atrium with alligators, koi, other live animals. 6000 W. Osceola Pkwy., 34746. 877-677-9352. Free shuttle. 1 mi. from WDW.

GRAND BEACH SUNTERRA $$$–$$$$ *Little Lake Bryan area:* Kitchens, lakefront, water sports. Condo rentals. 8317 Lake Bryan Beach Blvd., 32821. 866-396-0883. 2 mi. from WDW.

HAWTHORN SUITES $–$$ *Lake Buena Vista:* Kitchens. Free breakfast. 8303 Palm Pkwy., 32836. 407-597-5000. Free shuttle. 1 mi. from WDW.

HILTON GARDEN INN $–$$ Refrigerator, microwave, coffeemaker. Garden Sleep System, HDTV. Restaurant. *Airport:* 7300 Augusta National Dr., 32822. 407-240-3725. 15 mi. from WDW. *SeaWorld area:* 6850 Westwood Blvd., 32821. 407-354-1500. 4 mi. from WDW. *Universal Studios area:* 5877 American Way, 32819. 407-363-9332. 9 mi. from WDW.

HOMEWOOD SUITES $–$$$ Studio, one- and two-bedroom suites. Kitchens with full-size refrigerator, microwave, coffeemaker, dishwasher. Free hot breakfast, light meal and beverages Mon.–Thurs. evenings. Business srvcs. *Int'l. Dr. area:* 8745 Int'l. Dr., 32819. 407-248-2232. 5 mi. from WDW. *Universal Studios area:* 5893 American Way, 32819. 407-226-0669. 9 mi. from WDW.

HYATT REGENCY $$$$ *Airport:* Restaurants, beauty salon, spa, convention services. Atop airport. 9300 Airport Blvd., 32827. 800-233-1234. Free shuttle. 16 mi. from WDW. *Lake Buena Vista:* Hyatt Regency Grand Cypress. Restaurants, convention space, lake, 4 golf courses, spa, equestrian center, nature trails, canoeing, air boats. One Grand Cypress Blvd., 32836. 800-233-1234. Free shuttle. 1 mi. from WDW.

MARRIOTT $$–$$$$ *Airport:* Orlando Airport Marriott. Restaurants, indoor/outdoor pool, sauna. 7499 Augusta National Dr., 32822. 407-851-9000. Free shuttle to airport. 16 mi. from WDW. *Downtown Orlando:* Adjoins Amway Arena. 400 W. Livingston St., 32801. 407-843-6664. 16 mi. from WDW. *Lake Buena Vista:* Marriott Cypress: Pools, sauna, kitchens, washer/dryers, marina, water sports. 2 bed./2 ba. villas. 11251 Harbour Villa Rd., 32821. 800-845-5279. 4 mi. from WDW. *SeaWorld area:* Marriott Grande Vista: Lakefront, kitchens, sauna. 5925 Avenida Vista, 32821. 407-238-7676. 5 mi. from WDW. Also: JW Marriott Grande Lakes. Restaurant, pool, spa, sauna, golf course. 4040 Central Florida Pkwy., 32837. 800-576-5750. Free shuttle. 7 mi. from WDW. *World Center Dr. area:* Orlando World Center Marriott. Restaurants, pools (waterfalls, slides), spa, sauna, golf course and instruction, meeting rooms. 8701 World Center Dr., 32821. 800-228-9290. Free shuttle. 2 mi. from WDW. Also: Marriott Royal Palm. Next to Orlando World Center Marriott; free access to its amenities. Lakefront, kitchens, washer/dryers. 8404 Vacation Way, 32821. 407-238-6200. 2 mi. from WDW.

NICKELODEON FAMILY SUITES $$ *World Center Dr. area:* Restaurants, salon. Wacky decor, fun pools, activities, character breakfast. Run by Holiday Inn. 14500 Continental Gateway, 32821. 877-387-5437. Free shuttle. 1 mi. from WDW.

OMNI CHAMPIONSGATE $$$–$$$$ *West of WDW:* Restaurants, heated pool with lazy river, water slides. Two golf courses, golf academy, spa, steam room. 1500 Masters Blvd., 33896. 407-390-6664. 7 mi. from WDW.

PEABODY ORLANDO $$$$ *Convention Center:* Restaurants, beauty salon, spa, convention space. Mallard march at the hotel fountain daily at 11 a.m. and 5 p.m. 9801 Int'l. Dr., 32819. 800-732-2639. 6 mi. from WDW.

RADISSON $–$$ Restaurant. *U.S. 192 area:* 3011 Maingate Ln., 34747. 407-396-1400. Free shuttle. 1 mi. from WDW. Also: 2900 Parkway Blvd., 34747. 800-634-4774. Free shuttle. 2 mi. from WDW.

RENAISSANCE ORLANDO $$–$$$ *Airport:* Restaurant, meeting space. 5445 Forbes Pl., 32812. 407-240-1000. 1 mi. from airport. 16 mi. from WDW. *SeaWorld area:* Restaurants, convention space, spa. Across the street from SeaWorld. 6677 Sea Harbor Dr., 32821. 800-327-6677. Free shuttle. 4 mi. from WDW.

RESIDENCE INN BY MARRIOTT $$–$$$ Kitchens. Free breakfast. Fee for pets. *Int'l. Dr. area:* 8800 Universal Blvd., 32819. 407-226-0288. Free shuttle. 7 mi. from WDW. *Lake Buena Vista:* 11450 Marbella Palm Ct., 32836. 407-465-0075. Free shuttle. 1 mi. from WDW. *SeaWorld area:* 11000 Westwood Blvd., 32821. 800-889-9728. Free shuttle. 4 mi. from WDW.

Hyatt Regency Grand Cypress

RITZ-CARLTON GRANDE LAKES $$$$ S *SeaWorld area:* Restaurants, heated pools with lazy river, beauty salon, convention space, Greg Norman-designed golf course, concierge floors. Life-size chess board. 4012 Central Florida Pkwy., 32837. 800-576-5760. 7 mi. from WDW.

ROSEN CENTRE $$$ *Convention Center:* Restaurants, spa, salon, convention space, concierge floors. 9840 Int'l. Dr., 32819. 800-204-7234. Free shuttle to Fla. Mall. 6 mi. from WDW.

ROSEN PLAZA $$ *Convention Center:* Restaurants, meeting space. 9700 Int'l. Dr., 32819. 800-627-8258. 6 mi. from WDW.

ROSEN SHINGLE CREEK $$$ *Convention Center:* Restaurants, indoor/outdoor pools, spa, salon, convention space, golf course. 9939 Universal Blvd., 32819. 866-996-9939. 7 mi. from WDW.

SHERATON $$–$$$ *Lake Buena Vista:* Sheraton Safari. Restaurants, meeting space. African theme. 12205 S. Apopka-Vineland Rd., 32836. 407-239-0444. Free shuttle. 1 mi. from WDW. *SeaWorld area:* Sheraton Vistana Villages. Restaurants, all suites with kitchens. 8800 Vistana Centre Dr., 32821. 407-239-3100. Free shuttle. 1 mi. from WDW.

SPRINGHILL SUITES $–$$ *Convention Center:* Sauna. Free continental breakfast. 8623 Universal Blvd., 32819. 407-938-9001. 7 mi. from WDW.

STAYBRIDGE SUITES $$–$$$$ Kitchens. Free continental breakfast. *Int'l. Dr. area:* 8480 Int'l. Dr., 32819. 800-238-8000. 7 mi. from WDW. *Lake Buena Vista:* 8751 Suiteside Dr., 32836. 800-866-4549. Free shuttle. 1 mi. from WDW.

VILLAS OF GRAND CYPRESS $$$$ *Lake Buena Vista:* Restaurants, heated pools, 4 golf courses and academy, spa, equestrian center, lake, trails, convention space. 1 N. Jacaranda St., 32836. 800-835-7377. Free shuttle. 4 mi. from WDW.

WESTIN GRAND BOHEMIAN $$$–$$$$ *Downtown Orlando:* Restaurants. 325 S. Orange Ave., 32801. 866-663-0024. 14 mi. from WDW.

WORLDQUEST $$$–$$$$ *World Center Dr. area:* Restaurant. 8849 Worldquest Blvd., 32821. 866-663-0024. 2 mi. from WDW.

WYNDHAM ORLANDO $$–$$$ *Int'l. Dr. area:* Restaurants, sauna. Family suites have bunk beds, play areas. Fee for pets. 8001 Int'l. Dr., 32819. 407-351-2420. 8 mi. from WDW.

➡ Standard room, high season ¢ <$80. $<$110. $$<$160. $$$<$220. $$$$>$220.

World restaurants

...places to eat at Walt ...orld, and most are pretty good. So, where should you eat? In this chapter, we hope to give you the information you need to answer that question. The following pages have reviews of each of Disney's table-service and counter-service restaurants, as well as listings of all theme-park snack stands. Water park options are described in the Water Park chapter. First, here's a quick review of Disney restaurant policies, and the biggest food news for 2008:

Reservations

At Disney, having an advance restaurant reservation is often a must. The best places are often booked to capacity far in advance, especially for the most popular dining times. During peak periods, many Disney restaurants don't accept walk-up diners, regardless of how long you're willing to wait.

Reservations can be made up to 180 days in advance (190 for Disney resort guests) at 407-WDW-DINE (407-939-3463) as well as most restaurant check-in counters and resort concierge desks. Advance reservations are required for dinner shows and Grand Gathering Experiences. Some locations require a credit-card guarantee, while others charge a cancellation fee. Reservations for parties of 13 or more always need a credit card. Most restaurants will hold your reservation 15 minutes beyond its stated time.

The **toughest reservation** is Cinderella's Royal Table, the restaurant located inside Cinderella Castle. It often books in full on the first day of availability. Because of that demand, its meals are charged at the time you book them. Other hot spots include California Grill and Chef Mickey's (at the Contemporary Resort), Le Cellier (Canada pavilion, Epcot) and Victoria and Albert's (Grand Floridian Resort). The **toughest reservation time** is 7 to 8 p.m. To eat anywhere during this hour make a reservation at least a few days early, especially for a party of six or more.

*Artist Point (Wilderness Lodge Resort), California Grill (Contemporary), Citricos and Narcoosee's (Grand Floridian), Flying Fish Cafe (BoardWalk), Jiko (Animal Kingdom Lodge) and Yachtsman Steakhouse (Yacht Club).

All Disney restaurants are nonsmoking and add an automatic 18-percent gratuity to the bill of parties of 8 or more.

Note: At Disney World, making a reservation does not mean the restaurant actually holds a table for you. Instead, it books you into its system, and gives your party the next available table for its size after you arrive at the check-in desk. The policy used to be called Priority Seating, though that term is no longer officially in use.

Kids meals

At theme parks, Disney's Kids Picks meals include many tasty and nutritious entrees. Each comes with unsweetened applesauce, baby carrots or fresh fruit (your choice of two), and a beverage of low-fat milk, fruit juice or water. No more than 35 percent of a Kids Picks meal's calories come from fat, and of those calories, no more than 10 percent come from saturated fat and sugar. Fries and soft drinks can be substituted on request. Kids meals are also available at most resort restaurants.

Dress codes

Some Disney restaurants have a dress code. All Disney Signature Restaurants except the Hollywood Brown Derby* have a business casual dress code. For men, that means dress slacks, jeans, trousers or dress shorts; and a shirt with a collar or T-shirt underneath. Women are required to wear dress shorts, jeans or a skirt with a blouse or sweater, or a dress. Not permitted: Cut-off shorts, men's caps or hats, swimsuits, swimsuit cover-ups, tank tops or torn clothing. Victoria & Albert's (Grand Floridian) requires jackets for men and dresses or dressy pants suits for women.

Special diets

No-sugar, low-fat, low-sodium, vegetarian or vegan diets can be met at table-service restaurants by telling a reservation clerk, host or server (dinner shows need 24 hours notice). With three days notice, these restaurants can accommodate needs such as allergies to gluten or wheat, shellfish, soy, lactose or milk, peanuts, tree nuts, fish or eggs. At buffet restaurants, guests who have had gastric-bypass surgery pay the kids price for an adult meal. Many counter-service restaurants offer low-fat or vegetarian options. Effective Jan. 2008, no Disney restaurant serves food with added trans fats or partially hydrogenated oils.

Kosher meals

Glatt kosher meals are available at most full-service restaurants with 24 hours notice at 407-WDW-DINE (939-3463). The food is prepared in Miami and flown to Disney. Kosher quick-service meals are always available at Cosmic Ray's Starlight Cafe (Magic Kingdom), Liberty Inn (Epcot), ABC Commissary (Disney's Hollywood Studios), Pizzafari (Animal Kingdom), and the food courts at the All-Star, Caribbean Beach, Pop Century and Port Orleans Riverside resorts.

Disney Dining Experience

If you are a Walt Disney World annual passholder (or a Florida resident) but don't want to take part in the Disney Dining Plan (see next page) the Disney Dining Experience card (*$65–$85 annually*) can be a good deal. It saves its holder and up to nine guests 20 percent off food and beverages during non-holiday periods at most Disney table-service restaurants and a handful of other spots, including the food courts at Value Resorts. As of 2008, an automatic 18 percent gratuity is added to all DDE transactions. *For information call 407-566-5858, weekdays 9 a.m. to 5 p.m.*

Secrets to dining success

There are two other things you should keep in mind when dining at Disney.

First, given that you're on what's probably an active vacation, the best food for your needs is often not at the highest-priced restaurants. The fancy sauces, raw fish and indulgent sweets offered at many of Disney's signature restaurants just don't mix that well with day after day of rollicking rides and humid Florida sunshine. Often, you want a restaurant that simply helps you relax, re-nourish and recover. Good choices include Tony's Town Square and the Plaza Restaurant at Magic Kingdom, Le Cellier at the Canada pavilion at Epcot, the '50s Prime Time Cafe and Mama Melrose's Italian Ristorante at Disney's Hollywood Studios and the counter-service Pizzafari at Disney's Animal Kingdom.

Sometimes, some of the best food at Walt Disney World is at unexpected places. Aspiring chefs often work their way up the Disney system by starting at the company's more basic restaurants and impressing upper management with their skills, ideas and enthusiasm. When this happens, a new chef can quickly turn a humdrum eatery a hidden treasure. For 2008, two restaurants that fit this bill are Boatwright's at the Port Orleans Riverside Resort and the Turf Club Bar & Grill at the Saratoga Springs Resort. A third just might be Shutters, at Disney's Caribbean Beach Resort. Its new chef debuted a new menu at the first of the year.

What's new for 2008

In **Epcot**, L'Originale Alfredo di Roma Ristorante in the Italy pavilion closed in 2007, and California-based Patina Restaurant Group will open a new restaurant in the same spot in fall 2008. Patina is operating a temporary Italian eatery, Tutto Italia, in the meantime. Japan's Tempura Kiku and Matsu No Ma Lounge have been replaced with a new spot, Tokyo Dining, with an emphasis on sushi and innovative presentation. The Mitsukoshi Teppanyaki Dining Room has been re-created as Teppan Edo. China's Nine Dragons will be renovated in early 2008. In Mexico, a 50- to 60-seat tequila bar replaces a retail shop in the pavilion's indoor courtyard in the summer of 2008. The pavilion's waterfront Cantina de San Angel is expanding and will offer a new menu by summer.

Inspired by the western Himalayan foothills in India and Nepal, the new Yak & Yeti Restaurant at **Disney's Animal Kingdom** Asia section serves an Asian-fusion cuisine. It offers table-service and outdoor counter-service dining. There's also an outdoor bar and beer garden. In the park's Africa section, Tusker House has been converted into a buffet restaurant that includes a character breakfast. The restaurant features both indoor and outdoor seating.

In November, T-Rex opens at **Downtown Disney.** With an interactive prehistoric environment built around water, fire and ice; a 170-foot dinosaur cast; and $40,000 of fossils in the restrooms alone, it promises to be quite an experience.

The Disney Dining Plan

What it is

The Disney Dining Plan is a pre-paid meal program for those staying at Disney-owned resorts and Disney Vacation Club members. It's an easy way to manage your meal expenses (and possibly save money) at over 100 Walt Disney World restaurants, including those with character meals. There are four different packages available.

The basic **Disney Dining Plan** (also known as "Magic Your Way Plus Dining," about $40 per day per adult, $11 per child) includes one Table Service meal, one Quick (i.e, counter) Service meal and one snack per person, per night of your Disney stay.

The **Disney Deluxe Dining Plan** (about $70 per day per adult, $20 per child) lets you eat all three daily meals at table-service restaurants and comes with two snacks and a refillable drink mug for use at your resort. **Premium** and **Platinum** plans add recreation options (see the Planning Your Trip chapter for details). To purchase a dining plan, go to disneyworld.com or call 407-W-DISNEY (934-7639) from 7 a.m. to 10 p.m. Eastern time.

How it works

You can use your meals and snacks in any combination throughout your stay. For example, you can eat all Table Service meals one day, all Quick Service meals the next, and nothing but snacks the day after that. If one person in your party uses up his or her plan, others can continue to use theirs.

Disney defines a breakfast meal as one single-serving of juice, one entree and one beverage; or a combo meal and a beverage or juice. Lunch and dinner are defined as one entree, one dessert and one beverage; or a combo meal, dessert and beverage.

Participating restaurants include just about every restaurant at Disney World*, and snack locations such as outdoor food carts and shops selling ice cream and popcorn. All food costs are included but, in a

* Restaurants that do *not* participate in the Dining Plan include Downtown Disney's Bongos Cuban Cafe, House of Blues, the Wolfgang Puck Dining Room, Fulton's Crab House and the Portobello Yacht Club (though the last two do accept Disney's Premium and Platinum plans); and, at Epcot, Bistro de Paris in the France pavilion.

big change for 2008, not tips. You can't use the plan for alcoholic beverages and some bottled drinks, in-room mini-bars, souvenir or refillable drink mugs (except in Deluxe plans) or snacks and beverages from recreation rental counters.

The dining plans have four other major conditions: ❶ **They are sold per party, not per person.** If one person in your party buys a Dining Plan, everyone else must, too. The only exception: children under the age of 3. They can eat free from an adult's plate at no extra charge. ❷ **Children ages 3–9 must order from a kid's menu** when one is available. Likewise, those over 10 can't do so. ❸ **Some dining options charge two table-service allotments** for one meal. These include Disney Signature restaurants, dinner shows, Grand Gathering experiences, Cinderella's Royal Table at Magic Kingdom and all room-service meals at Disney Deluxe Resorts. ❹ Like Cinderella's magical accoutrements, **unused meals and snacks expire** at midnight on your check-out date.

To use the plan, you simply present your Key to World Card to your cashier or server, and specify the number of meals or snacks you want to redeem. Your food usage will be tracked electronically. Each time you use your plan, your receipt will show your remaining balance of that particular meal type. Complete summaries of your balances are available from your hotel concierge throughout your Disney stay.

How to take advantage of it

If you manage your plan wisely, you'll have tremendous food and memorable meals. Handle it poorly, however, and your magical vacation can include a frustrating waste of a lot of time and money. Here are four keys to getting the most for your money:

1 DON'T OVERESTIMATE YOUR HUNGER
When determining which plan to purchase, keep in mind that, for most folks, it's tough to eat enough food to justify having three table-service meals a day. And though the Signature restaurants are nice, it's hard to dine at more than one a day, as each takes two or three hours to fully experience.

2
USE YOUR CREDITS WISELY

Appreciate the fact that, except for those at Signature restaurants, nearly all table-service meals are considered equal. Believe it or not, dining with Cinderella or Lilo and Stitch at an all-you-can-eat feast takes no more table-service credits than getting a hamburger at Magic Kingdom's Plaza or a fish sandwich at Cap'n Jack's at Downtown Disney. And beware of room service: getting a meal delivered to your room at Animal Kingdom Lodge costs two meal credits, the same as a gourmet meal at Jiko.

3
KNOW WHERE THE DEALS ARE

Though the Dining Plan charges you exactly the same amount — one credit — for most Table Service meals (and, likewise, Quick Service meals), some one-credit restaurants offer far better food, more memorable experiences, or both.

Among Table Service restaurants, great deals for breakfast include **Boma,** a terrific buffet at Animal Kingdom Lodge; **Donald's Safari Breakfast,** a character buffet at Tusker House, in Animal Kingdom; the **'Ohana Best Friends Breakfast** featuring Lilo and Stitch, an all-you-can-eat character breakfast at the Polynesian Resort; **Playhouse Disney's Play 'n' Dine,** a character buffet at Hollywood and Vine, Disney's Hollywood Studios; **Princess Storybook Dining,** an all-you-can-eat princess meal at the Akershus Royal Banquet Hall at the Norway pavilion in Epcot; and the **Supercalifragilistic Breakfast,** a character buffet at 1900 Park Fare, at the Grand Floridian Resort.

For lunch, you'll get a great value at **Coral Reef,** a near-gourmet seafood restaurant at The Seas with Nemo & Friends pavilion in Epcot; **Le Cellier,** a steakhouse in the Canada pavilion in Epcot; **Liberty Tree Tavern** in Magic Kingdom; the almost-Signature **Turf Club Bar & Grill** at Saratoga Springs Resort; and the **Whispering Canyon Cafe,** an entertaining barbecue meal at Wilderness Lodge.

For dinner, consider the lunch restaurants above as well as **Boma,** Disney's best buffet meal, at Animal Kingdom Lodge; **Cinderella's Happily Ever After Dinner,** Disney's best character meal, at 1900 Park Fare in the Grand Floridian Resort; and **'Ohana,** an all-you-can-eat meat feast at the Polynesian Resort.

The best Quick Service deals are at **The Artist's Palette,** Disney's best resort food court, at the Saratoga Springs Resort; **Columbia Harbour House,** the most comfortable counter-service Magic Kingdom restaurant; **Flame Tree Barbecue,** a first-rate shady outdoor cafe at Animal Kingdom; **Pizzafari,** Animal Kingdom's most comfortable counter-service restaurant; **Starring Rolls Cafe,** the only Disney counter cafe that serves gourmet food, at Disney's Hollywood Studios; and **Sunshine Seasons,** a terrific, healthy food court inside The Land pavilion at Epcot.

4
MAKE YOUR RESERVATIONS EARLY

Once you purchase your plan, make your restaurant reservations as soon as possible. That way, you will be able to dine at the places that best suit your needs and give you the most value for your table-service credits. An added bonus: you'll always have a place to eat.

Cinderella's Royal Table inside Cinderella Castle

MAGIC KINGDOM

COUNTER SERVICE CAFES

Casey's Corner Hot dogs. Main Street U.S.A. *123 seats, including 43 inside.*
Columbia Harbour House ✔ Veggie chili, sandwiches. Nice upstairs. Liberty Sq. *593 seats.*
Cosmic Ray's Starlight Cafe Chicken, burgers, kosher choices, nice condiment bar. Robotic lounge singer. Amusement-park crowd. Tomorrowland. *1,162 seats.*
Main Street Bakery ✔ Yogurt parfaits, quiche, bagels. *Main Street U.S.A. 29 seats.*
Pecos Bill Cafe Burgers, wraps. Good cider-lime-juice slaw. Rooms at the far right stay quiet. Frontierland. *1,107 seats.*
Pinocchio Village Haus Pizza, chicken, sandwiches. Crowded by noon. Many screaming kids. Fantasyland. *400 seats.*

OUTDOOR COUNTER CAFES

Aunt Polly's Dockside Inn Desserts. Tom Sawyer Island, Frontierland. *44 seats.*
Auntie Gravity's Galactic Goodies Soft-serve ice cream, smoothies. Tomorrowland. *12 seats.*
El Pirata y el Perico Restaurante Tacos, taco salads. Adventureland. *Shares seats with Pecos Bill.*
Enchanted Grove Swirls, slushes, coffee, orange juice. Fantasyland. *28 seats.*
Liberty Sq. Market Corn on the cob, baked potatoes, fresh fruit. Liberty Sq. *22 seats.*
The Lunching Pad Turkey legs, pretzels, frozen drinks. Tomorrowland. *83 seats.*
Mrs. Potts' Cupboard Soft-serve ice cream. Fantasyland. *53 seats.*
Scuttle's Landing Bagels, muffins, pretzels. Fantasyland. *80 seats.*
Sleepy Hollow Funnel cakes, caramel corn, soft-serve ice cream. Liberty Sq. *51 seats.*
Sunshine Tree Terrace ✔ Frozen OJ swirled with vanilla soft-serve ice cream. Adventureland. *46 seats.*
Tomorrowland Terrace Noodle Station ✔ Chicken with steamed rice, noodle bowls, teas. Dinner only. Tomorrowland. *500 seats.*
Village Fry Shoppe Hot dogs, fries. Shares seats with Mrs. Potts. Fantasyland.

SNACK STANDS

Aloha Isle ✔ Pineapple/vanilla soft-serve. Juice, pineapple spears. Adventureland.
Frontierland Fries Adventureland.
Westwood Ho Refreshments Muffins, hot dogs. Adventureland.
Plaza Ice Cream Parlor ✔ Hand-dipped cones, floats, sundaes. Main Street U.S.A.
Toontown Farmer's Market Fruit, yogurt, frozen lemonade. Mickey's Toontown Fair.

Theme parks

MAGIC KINGDOM

CINDERELLA'S ROYAL TABLE See the section "Character Meals," later in this chapter.
CRYSTAL PALACE See Character Meals.
LIBERTY TREE TAVERN ✔ AMERICAN Hear ye! Hear ye! Let it be known that this Colonial inn's Butter Griddled Pound Cake is the best dessert in the Magic Kingdom. Large enough to share, it's covered in a warm, pecan-caramel sauce and topped with vanilla bean ice cream. As for the rest of the menu *($9–$17, lunch)*, both the Maryland crab cake and signature pot roast fall apart in your mouth. Also good: the turkey panino and turkey plate. Dinner is Goofy's Liberate Your Appetite character meal (see Character Meals). *Liberty Square. 250 seats.*
THE PLAZA ✔ SANDWICHES The favorite dining spot *($10–$12, lunch and dinner)* of many park veterans, this comfortable Victorian room has good burgers and sandwiches, gigantic ice cream sundaes and a calm, carpeted atmosphere. Good sandwich bets include the Reuben and the chilled vegetable, which has big slabs of mozzarella. *Main Street U.S.A. 94 seats.*
TONY'S TOWN SQUARE ✔ ITALIAN Great for lunch *($8–$17)*, overpriced for dinner *($19–$26)*, this cool and comfortable spot has lots of booths and a central fountain. Lunch is ideal: rarely crowded with a solid, varied menu. The panini are crusty and tasty; our daughter inhales the mild baked ziti. Dinner's more ambitious dishes are just like momma used to make... if her best dish was pizza. Thematically, the eatery is the Tony's of the 1955 movie "Lady and the Tramp." The window in the back right corner looks into the movie's alley. *Main Street U.S.A. 286 seats.*

EPCOT

AKERSHUS ROYAL BANQUET HALL See Character Meals.
CORAL REEF ✔ SEAFOOD You eat fish while you watch fish at this hidden treasure, which looks into The Seas with Nemo & Friends aquarium. As you dine, you watch angelfish, rays, sea turtles and sharks swim by. Both lunch *($12–$26)* and dinner *($17–$32)* are outstanding. The signature appetizer is creamy lobster soup. Like spicy food? Get the blackened catfish. Served on a bed of pepper-jack cheese grits that simmer for at least five hours before they're served, it's my husband's favorite fish dish in all of Disney. Other choices typically include salmon and at least one marine fish, though never anything you see swimming past. Catfish and tilapia often come from The Land pavilion's greenhouses. You eat on brushed-metal tables trimmed in light woods. Dim lighting makes it easy to see into the

aquarium. If you're here right at 11 a.m. you should be able to walk right in. Otherwise book lunch two weeks early, dinner 60 to 90 days in advance. When you arrive, ask for a window-front table or a booth that faces the tank. *The Seas with Nemo & Friends pavilion. 275 seats.*

GARDEN GRILL See Character Meals.

BIERGARTEN GERMAN BUFFET It's always Oktoberfest at this indoor buffet restaurant *($20, lunch; $24, dinner),* which has the look of an outdoor garden. A band plays polkas. The hearty buffet has sausages, red cabbage, sauerkraut, spaetzle, schnitzel and more, all just what you'd expect. *Germany. 400 seats.*

BISTRO DE PARIS ✔ FRENCH This intimate, second-floor dining room overlooks the World Showcase promenade. Gourmet seafood (fish, lobster, scallops) and meats (duck, beef, lamb, venison, veal) highlight a menu *($28–$100, dinner)* that changes often. Great appetizers. Ask for a window table. *France. 120 seats.*

CHEFS DE FRANCE ✔ FRENCH Rich creams and soft cheeses dominate provincial dishes at this bustling bistro. The menu *($11–$20, lunch; $17–$30, dinner)* includes beef, chicken, salmon and seafood dishes; sandwiches at lunch. Don't overlook the Gruyere-topped French onion soup or the rich creme brulee. *France. 266 seats.*

LE CELLIER ✔ STEAKHOUSE This low-ceilinged, stone-walled favorite *($10–$25, lunch; $18–$29, dinner)* resembles a chateau wine cellar. The Alberta-beef steaks are aged 28 days; the best is the filet mignon (dinner only). Made with Moosehead beer, the cheddar-cheese soup makes a great dip for the complimentary soft breadsticks. Other options include salmon, seafood, chicken, entree salads and sandwiches. Young, friendly staff. The toughest World Showcase reservation. *Canada. 156 seats.*

NINE DRAGONS ✔ CHINESE The wonton soup is good at this Epcot staple *($11–$20, lunch; $13–$27, dinner).* Its strong, clear broth is topped with floating scallions. Two nice dinner choices are the Sichuan seafood casserole in a spicy red rice sauce and the Beijing duck. For dessert the thick ginger ice cream tastes like a whipped gingerbread cookie in a wash of thick cream. Children may prefer the Dim Sum over the kid's menu. As you enter the lobby look up; a golden dragon is staring at you. *China. 300 seats.*

RESTAURANT MARRAKESH MOROCCAN A belly dancer often entertains at this traditional Moroccan restaurant, which serves roast lamb, kebabs and couscous *($15–$25, lunch; $20–$40, dinner).* The most popular soup is harira, a smooth blend of lamb, lentil and tomatoes. If you know Moroccan food you'll be disappointed. Green tea, liqueur coffees. *Morocco. 255 seats.*

ROSE & CROWN DINING ROOM ENGLISH Hope you like mashed potatoes! This friendly spot includes them with most of its entrees *($12–*

EPCOT

COUNTER SERVICE CAFES

Electric Umbrella American fast food. Good vegetarian chili. Innoventions East. *426 seats.*

FountainView Ice Cream Shop ✔ Hand-dipped Edy's made-to-order ice-cream sandwiches. Innoventions West. *108 seats inc. 68 outside.*

Liberty Inn Burgers, chicken strips. Kosher meal. American Adventure. *710 seats.*

Sunshine Seasons ✔ Quality sandwiches, noodle plates and bowls, meats, soups, salads, bakery items. The Land. *707 seats.*

Tangierine Cafe ✔ Chicken, lamb platters; sandwiches. Pastries, tea, liqueur coffees, frozen daiquiris, beer. Morocco. *101 seats.*

Yakitori House Bowls, miso soup. Garden setting. Japan. *94 seats inc. 36 outside.*

Lotus Blossom Cafe Egg rolls, chicken, stir-fry, specialty drinks. China. *100 seats.*

OUTDOOR COUNTER CAFES

Yorkshire County Fish Shop Fish and chips, Bass ale. U.K. *31 seats.*

Boulangerie Patisserie ✔ Pastries, croissant sandwiches, quiche, cheese plates. France. *24 seats.*

Sommerfest ✔ Bratwurst, frankfurters. Germany. *52 seats under a covered patio.*

Lotus Blossom Cafe Chinese standards. China. *107 seats.*

Kringla Bakeri Og Kafe ✔ Open-faced sandwiches, pastries. Norway. *51 seats.*

Cantina de San Angel Mexican standards. Mexico. *150 seats.*

SNACK STANDS

Joffrey's Coffee Coffees, baked goods, smoothies, tea. Between Innoventions East and Univ. of Energy; between Canada and U.K.; and at American Adventure.

Cool Wash Sodas, chips. Test Track.

Pizza Cart Individual pizzas. Test Track.

Refreshment Port McDonald's. Near Canada.

Crepes des Chefs de France Crepes, waffle cones, beers, coffees. France.

Les Vins des Chefs de France Champagne, wine, cheese. France.

Kaki Gori ✔ Shaved ice, beer. Japan.

Funnel Cake Kiosk ✔ American Adventure.

Donkey Cart ✔ Gelato, ices. Italy.

Bierline and **Das Kaufhaus Cart** Pretzels, beers, wine. Germany.

Refreshment Cool Post Soft-serve ice cream, coffee, beer. Outpost.

Margarita kiosk Frozen margaritas. Mexico.

BAR

Rose & Crown Pub ✔ Beer, mixed drinks, appetizers, sandwiches (try the London broil). Evening entertainment. U.K. *20 seats.*

$16, lunch; $16–$25, dinner), such as bangers and mash, cottage pie and Guinness beef stew. Nothing's bad, nothing's great. *U.K. 242 seats, including 40 on the covered outside porch.*

SAN ANGEL INN ✔ MEXICAN So dark you can barely read the menu, this quality spot offers flavorful food in a cool, peaceful setting. Chips come with a chunky salsa that delivers an unexpected kick. The ceviche's zesty topping of chilies, cilantro and onions will wake up your mouth so much you may forget about the lime-marinated mahi-mahi buried underneath. A milder choice: tortilla soup, a tasty tomato-based broth filled with veggies and stringy melted cheese. Lunch *($13–$19)* and dinner *($20–$28)* entrees include everything from avocado-topped tilapia to traditional combination plates. Steaks taste like they're from a backyard grill. On-the-rocks margaritas are excellent. Sitting on padded chairs and benches around a candle-lit table, you dine in what appears to be a moonlit courtyard. Off in the distance is a rumbling volcano that, depending on your ingestion of those margaritas, may appear to be the most realistic effect Disney has ever created. A mariachi band performs just outside the dining area. The restaurant is run by the Debler family, the proprietors of the original Mexico City San Angel Inn as well as the Maya Grill at Disney's Coronado Resort. *Mexico. 156 seats.*

TEPPAN EDO ✔ TEPPANYAKI (HIBACHI) An entertaining tableside chef may juggle knives or make a "smoking Mickey train" out of onion stacks at this completely refurbished collection of dining rooms, which now have a stunning red and black color scheme. Using a grill set into your table, the chef's hands fly fast as they slice, dice and stir-fry your choice of beef, seafood or chicken *($16–$30).* You share your table with other guests. *Japan. 192 seats.*

TOKYO DINING ✔ JAPANESE A combination of good food, great atmosphere and absolutely mind-blowing service, this new Epcot treasure is exactly what a World Showcase restaurant is supposed to be — a non-threatening way for you to fully experience the cuisine, and atmosphere, of a foreign culture. A mix of traditional Japanese entrees, the menu *($15–$28)* includes a tender beef teriyaki and nice shrimp tempura. A separate sushi and sashimi menu ($4–$24) has 49 selections, highlighted by a "volcano" California roll that's sliced, stacked and coated with a creamy (and explosively hot) orange chili sauce. For dessert, the green tea pudding melts in your mouth. The sophisticated, peaceful decor has wonderful diffused lighting. Dark cherry tables sit on a tile floor. But what tops everything are the bows. The hostesses and servers bow to you as you enter the restaurant, as you sit down and every time one of them approaches your table. When you leave, the entire staff bows to you

progressively, like a line of falling dominoes. A great place to dine for IllumiNations, the second-story restaurant overlooks the World Showcase Lagoon. Five tables sit right up against the glass. *Lunch, dinner. 116 seats.*

TUTTO ITALIA ITALY The fettucine Alfredo is long gone. This upscale eatery replaced L'Originale Alfredo di Roma in 2007, serving in the same dining room but with a menu that desperately strives for more of your money. The heavily promoted Family Table *($40 per person lunch, $60 per person dinner)* provides your entire party with family-sized versions of one appetizer, two entrees and a dessert. Want something smaller? Regular menus *(lunch: $15–$28, side dishes $8 extra; dinner $24–$36, side dishes $10 extra)* offer a variety of pasta, chicken, pork and beef dishes, but none stand out. The servings are small; the presentations uninspired. Plans call for the place to close again in mid–2008, with a brand-new eatery debuting later in the year. *Italy. 300 seats.*

HOLLYWOOD STUDIOS

50'S PRIME TIME CAFE ✔ COMFORT FOOD This surreal dining spot *($12–$16, lunch; $13–$20, dinner)* puts you in a 1950s kitchen, complete with formica tables, a black-and-white counter TV, "mom" as your waitress and suprisingly good versions of meatloaf, pot roast and, for dessert, s'mores. For the best time, ask for a TV table and an extra-schticky server. One other thing: no elbows on the table and you must eat your vegetables. *Echo Lake. 225 seats.*

HOLLYWOOD & VINE DINNER BUFFET Meant to recall an old cafeteria, this buffet restaurant delivers all too well: it's crowded, noisy and a little greasy. The food *($24)* isn't that bad (the creamed-corn spoon bread and cranberry butter are actually delicious) but for the money you can do better. Breakfast and lunch are Play 'N Dine character experiences (see Character Meals). *Echo Lake. 468 seats.*

HOLLYWOOD BROWN DERBY ✔ AMERICAN A sincere re-creation of the 1929 Tinsel Town landmark, this upscale dining spot features a spacious mahogany and teak interior with a sunken main room and a surrounding indoor terrace. Servers wear white tuxedo jackets and black bow ties. Walls are covered with celebrity caricatures. Lunch *($14–$24)* and dinner *($18–$32)* entrees include chicken, pasta, pork chops, salmon and steak. Marinated in dark ale, the New York strip (lunch only) is so tender you can cut it with a fork. Three items are historic Derby originals. The dinner rolls are the same German Spitzweck hard rolls that an angry Lucille Ball tossed at "Wizard of Oz" tin man Jack Haley in a famous Derby food fight. The finely chopped, tossed-at-your-table Cobb Salad was invented in 1926 when Derby owner Robert Cobb raided his restaurant's kitchen seeking a midnight snack for his friend Sid Grauman. The Chinese Theater owner loved the results so much he returned for another "Cobb's salad" the next day. The grapefruit cake, with juice in its batter as well as in its cream-cheese icing, was first made for gossip columnist Louella Parsons during the 1930s Grapefruit Diet craze. Another throwback: tableside phone service. Arrange it with the check-in desk and your child (of any age) may get a call from Goofy. Gawrsh! *A Disney Signature Restaurant. Hollywood Blvd. 224 seats.*

MAMA MELROSE'S RISTORANTE ✔ ITALIAN There's no theme-park atmosphere in this dimly lit restaurant *($12–$20, lunch; $12–$22, dinner),* which features a yummy caprino-cheese appetizer, good wood-fired individual pizzas and a tasty shrimp and vegetable pasta. The booths are comfortable; the wooden tables too small. On the walls are hundreds of autographed photo cards from the park's old Star of the Day program, which true to their era show many female celebrities with huge permed and teased hair. The 'do on Mary Ann Mobley makes her look like Marge Simpson; each side of Sally Struthers hair is as wide as her face. *Backlot. 250 seats.*

SCI-FI DINE IN AMERICAN You're in the 1950s at this re-created drive-in movie theater, sitting under the stars in a classic convertible as roller-skating carhops bring you your food *($11–$19, lunch; $11–$21, dinner).* Up front the giant silver screen shows a never-ending assortment of science-fiction shlock. The car-seat seating makes it tough for families to talk, but it's still a fun experience. For food, give in to temptation and get an Oreo milkshake. Trivia buffs will love finding Disney World's only topless woman: she's on a poster for the 1959 film "The Giant Gila Monster" on the left-hand side of the theater. Note: Not all tables are cars; be sure to ask for one. *Backlot. 252 seats.*

ANIMAL KINGDOM

RAINFOREST CAFE AMERICAN You dine in an elaborate re-creation of a tropical rainforest at this chain restaurant, located just outside the Animal Kingdom turnstiles. The walls and ceiling are a three-dimensional jungle of plants, trees and waterfalls, dotted with robotic elephants, gorillas and other creatures that come to life every 20 minutes, when the whole place gets struck by a thunderstorm. The rear dining areas feature saltwater aquariums; one has a huge statue of Atlas. The restaurant sits under a two-story waterfall; the entrance walkway has impressions of both child and animal footprints. As for food, the 55-item lunch and dinner *($10–$40)* includes beef, chicken, hamburgers, pasta, pizza, pork, sandwiches, salads, seafood and wraps. There are four

HOLLYWOOD STUDIOS

COUNTER SERVICE CAFES
Flatbread Grill ✔ Grilled chicken, sandwiches, salads. Breezy, mostly-shaded dining area. Backlot. *498 seats.*
Starring Rolls Cafe ✔ Deli sandwiches, bagels (some with smoked salmon), pastries, coffees. Uses the Brown Derby kitchens. Closes about 3:30 or 4 p.m. Hollywood Blvd. at Sunset Blvd. *40 seats.*
Sunset Ranch Market Six-stand outdoor food court. **Anaheim Produce:** Fresh fruit and vegetables, pretzels, frozen lemonade. **Catalina Eddie's:** Individual pizzas, salads. **Fairfax Fries:** McDonald's fries. **Hollywood Scoops:** Hand-dipped Edy's ice cream. **Rosie's All-American Cafe:** Burgers, chicken strips, salads. **Toluca Turkey Co.:** Turkey legs, hot dogs. Sunset Blvd. *400 seats.*

OUTDOOR COUNTER CAFES
ABC Commissary ✔ Comfortable carpeted cafe with cushioned booths, chairs. Good Cuban sandwich (pressed roast beef, pork, cheese and a pickle); decent burgers, fried fish, tabbouleh wrap. Incredibly slow service at peak periods. Skip the Cuban then; it takes 9 min. to cook. Backlot. *562 seats.*
Backlot Express Burgers, sandwiches, hot dogs. Themed as crafts shop, filled with real down-and-dirty clutter (inc. Toon Patrol truck, Bennie the Cab stunt cart from 1988's "Who Framed Roger Rabbit.") Backlot. *600 seats.*
Min and Bill's Dockside Diner Soft ice cream treats, beer, pretzels and other snacks. Echo Lake. *140 seats.*
Toy Story Pizza Planet This noisy arcade looks nothing like the one in 1995's "Toy Story." Individual pizzas. Backlot. *584 seats.*

SNACK STANDS
Dinosaur Gertie's Soft ice cream, waffle cones. Echo Lake.
Dip Site Philly cheese steaks (sometimes), beer, soft drinks. Seasonal. Echo Lake.
Herbie's Drive-In Steamed buns (lousy), frozen drinks. Backlot.
KRNR the Rock Station Frozen lemonade, smoothies and soft ice cream. Sunset Blvd.
Peevy's Polar Pipeline Slushie-style frozen treats. Truly refreshing. Echo Lake.
The Writer's Stop ✔ Bagels, cookies, pastries. Two-table room in back is perfect getaway spot. Comfy chair, sofa. Backlot.

BARS
High Octane Refreshments An alcoholic oasis with beer, wine, margaritas. Backlot.
Tune-In Lounge ✔ Cocktails, full menu from adj. 50's Prime Time Cafe. Echo Lake.

ANIMAL KINGDOM

COUNTER SERVICE CAFES

Pizzafari ✔ Individual pizzas, sandwiches, salads. Beautiful murals, floor mosaics, ceilings. Discovery Isl. *680 seats.*

Restaurantosaurus Burgers, chicken nuggets, hot dogs. Lavishly wacko dino theme. Right-corner Hip Joint room stays peaceful, cool. DinoLand U.S.A. *750 seats.*

OUTDOOR COUNTER CAFES

Flame Tree BBQ ✔ Ribs, pork, chicken with baked beans, corn on the cob. Smoked chicken salad. Shady gardens, riverside pavilions. Discovery Island. *500 seats.*

Yak & Yeti Local Food Cafes Asian. Good egg rolls, mango pie. Asia. *350 seats.*

SNACK STANDS

Anandapur Ice Cream Truck Soft serve. Asia

Dino-Bite Churros, pastries, hand-dipped ice cream, yogurt. DinoLand U.S.A. *50 seats.*

Dino Diner Hot dogs, popcorn, slushies. DinoLand U.S.A. *30 seats.*

Drinkwalla Frozen drinks, whole fruit. Asia.

Harambe Fruit Market ✔ Whole fruit, soft pretzels. Africa. *8 seats.*

Harambe Popcorn Popcorn, churros. Africa.

Hot dog stand Camp Minnie-Mickey.

Hot dog stand Asia.

Ice cream stand Soft-serve treats. Camp Minnie-Mickey.

Joffrey's Coffee Coffees, tea, pastries, fruit, smoothies. Entrance Plaza.

Kusafiri Coffee Shop and Bakery ✔ Coffees, tea, pastries, fruit. Africa.

Mr. Kamal's Ham, turkey sandwiches, chicken strips. Asia.

PetriFries Fries, cookies. DinoLand U.S.A.

Royal Anandapur Tea Co. ✔ Specialty teas, pastries. Asia. *12 seats.*

Safari Coffee Shade-grown, specialty coffee; pastries; fruit; yogurt. Discovery Isl.

Safari Popcorn Popcorn, lemonade, punch.

Safari Pretzel Soft pretzels. Discovery Isl.

Safari Sandwich Discovery Isl.

Safari Turkey Turkey legs, chicken wings. Discovery Isl.

Slush Frz. lemonade, pretzels. Asia *16 seats.*

Tamu Tamu Soft-serve ice cream. Africa.

BARS

Dawa Bar ✔ African beer, liquor, specialty drinks. Africa. *256 seats.*

Tuki's Tiki Bar Specialty drinks, draft beer, smoothies. In the rear outdoor garden of Rainforest Cafe. Entrance Plaza. *30 seats.*

Yak & Yeti Quality Beverages Specialty drinks, Asian beers. Asia. *Shares seats with Local Food Cafes.*

combination plates. The best meal is breakfast *($9–$14)*, when there's usually no wait and the prices are fine. The Pie of the Viper is a huge (12-inch) egg and four-cheese breakfast pizza that two adults can easily share. Tucked under a huge mushroom, a bar offers the full food menus but often has no wait. *Reservations: 407-827-8500. 1,057 seats, including 72 at the bar.*

YAK & YETI ✔ PAN ASIAN The only table-service restaurant inside the Animal Kingdom gates, this two-story Asian affair is run by Landry's Restaurants, the same company that operates Rainforest Cafe. The menu *($16–$23)* has many terrific choices. Among the best are a thick, flaky salmon filet served over white rice with stir-fry vegetables and mahi mahi doused in a hot garlic sauce made with generous amounts of, believe it or not, peanut butter. The strangest dish is Pho, a Vietnamese shrimp noodle bowl. You flavor it yourself, by adding in Thai basil, cilantro, bean sprouts and, if you're daring, a spoonful or two of "fish sauce" made from pressed anchovy filets. The restaurant takes special pride in its pork egg rolls. Each about the size of a huge tamale, they're not hot, but so full of flavor they don't need the included chili-plum dipping sauce. "We worked harder on the egg rolls than anything else," explains Landry's Senior VP and Chief Operating Officer Keith Beitler. "The secret is in the wrapper."

Two desserts stand out. A sorbet sampler is so tangy you can devour it only in small bites. The mango pie is a thick yellow slab with the consistency of cheesecake. Specialty drinks are highlighted by the Yak Attack, a mango daiquiri. Beers include Harbin, a rice beer from China; Singha, a premium lager from Thailand; and Tiger, a light Singapore beer with a strong bite.

Dining areas are lined with hundreds of artifacts from such places as Bali, Burma and Katmandu, including an old hotel registration desk and stairway and some giant 700-pound jeweled puppets. "Collecting all this stuff was fun," says Yak & Yeti creator Steven Schussler, "but the neat thing is to be able to put it all in a place where people appreciate it." *Lunch, dinner. Direct phone: 407-824-YETI. 250 seats.*

TUSKER HOUSE ✔ BUFFET Formerly Animal Kingdom's best counter-service restaurant, Tusker House now offers a great buffet. Similar in concept to Boma at Disney's Animal Kingdom Lodge, the menu combines traditional American favorites with African-themed specialties. A tomato and cucumber salad and spiced top sirloin are great for lunch *($20 adults, $11 children)*; dinner *($27 adults, $13 children)* adds good smoked salmon and and roasted berbere-rubbed prime rib. Both buffets have many vegetarian choices, including a flavorful spiced tofu. Mornings feature Donald's Safari Breakfast (see Character Meals). *1,216 seats.*

Resort restaurants

ANIMAL KINGDOM LODGE

BOMA ✔ AMERICAN/AFRICAN "I heard the prime rib is zebra." "I don't want to eat antelope butt." "It's probably all too spicy." There are plenty of misconceptions about this beautiful buffet restaurant, which serves traditional American comfort foods along with non-exotic African items that share a similar rural heritage. Though some foods are generously spiced with coriander and cumin, most aren't the least bit hot.

Breakfast *($17 adults, $10 children 3–9)* is highlighted by a creamy sausage and biscuit skillet, pap (like grits, but made with smooth white cornmeal; try it with brown sugar) and a house juice produced from guavas, oranges and passion fruit. Conventional American foods include made-to-order omelets and a cinnamon-raisin French toast that is always puffy and warm. Even the ubiquitous bacon and scrambled eggs are the best on Disney property.

Dinner *($26 adults, $11 children 3–9)* offers 60 food choices, again both African and American. Appetizers include delicious mulligatawny and butternut-squash soups, and lavosh bread with three types of hummus, while the salads range from basic field greens to watermelon rind. Entrees include prime rib, baked salmon and beef and lamb bobotie. A kid's station offers American standards such as chicken nuggets, but many children also love the couscous, falafel (mashed chickpeas) and fufu (mashed white and sweet potatoes). The dinner menu changes three times a week.

Though its foods and huge show kitchen are both state-of-the-art, Boma's real secret to success is the design of its buffet line. The hot-food portion is divided into five serving stations, each with its own burners, grills or stoves just a few feet away and its own cooks constantly attending it. The dishes are prepared in small portions so everything stays fresh.

Another key ingredient: relaxed and happy waiters and waitresses. "The entire crew works within just a few feet of our guests, so they have to like people," explains chef Bob Getchell. Turnover is very low. Getchell says 80 percent of his staff has been at the restaurant since opening day in 2001.

Boma's decor outshines anything in its class. Hanging light fixtures are a mix of rustic hand-cut tin and colorful hand-blown glass. Many of the thick wood tables have fabric inlays. A variety of dining chairs features distressed, leather, or hand-carved seatbacks. The concrete floor is colored to look like dirt. Stone walkways wind through it.

Several seating areas sit under thatched huts. The buffet itself is an artistic interpretation of an outdoor market, with each serving station in its own hut or "makeshift" stand. *400 seats. Note: Boma is the authors' favorite Disney restaurant. We eat here often.*

JIKO — THE COOKING PLACE ✔ AFRICAN FUSION Creative comfort food? You'll be surprised at the finds at this sophisticated jewel, which rivals California Grill as Disney's best family-friendly fine-dining experience. The menu *($24–$37)* is always changing and always exceptional, though signature items include flavorful short ribs braised with a Kenyan-coffee barbecue sauce and berbere-braised lamb shank. A great appetizer is the refreshing, mildly sweet cucumber, tomato and red onion salad. The best bet for dessert: pistachio creme brulee. The South African wine selection is the largest in the United States. The dining room is a piece of art in itself. Representing a sunset, the back wall slowly changes color every 20 minutes. Another wall is a translucent piece of orange, green and yellow curved glass. Hanging from the ceiling are stylized kanu birds, flying over diners to bring them good luck. *A Disney Signature Restaurant. Dinner. 300 seats.*

BOARDWALK INN

BIG RIVER GRILLE & BREWING WORKS ✔ AMERICAN Disney World's only microbrewery, Big River offers six handcrafted beers, from light lagers to malty ales. The lunch *($9–$21)* and dinner *($10–$30)* menus include a zingy beer cheese soup and dry-rubbed pork ribs that are marinated in ale. The metal-trimmed restaurant is a good mid-range choice for guests staying at the next-door Swan and Dolphin convention hotels. *190 seats, including 50 outside.*

ESPN CLUB ✔ SPORTS BAR Two restaurants in one, the ESPN club combines a traditional sports bar with a second room that hosts live radio talk shows and encourages comments from the crowd. Television monitors are everywhere, including the restrooms. There are 123 screens altogether. The menu *($9–$13)* includes a good Rueben sandwich, homemade potato chips and full-size chicken wings. There's no one here during most weekday afternoons, but both rooms get packed on the weekend. It's nearly impossible to find a spot to sit during a major college or NFL football game, when fans of competing teams mix together in a face-to-face ruckus. "Only a few times have we had fights," the manager says. (Can't get in? An alternative is the bar at Big River Grille. It has two large-screen TVs, and there's often at least a chair or two empty.) *Lunch, dinner. 450 seats.*

FLYING FISH CAFE SEAFOOD Cramped, crowded and loud, the atmosphere at this boisterous nightspot can interfere with the enjoyment of its food *($28–$38)*. Ask to sit in the back, however, and the quality shines through.

A good appetizer is Chardonnay-steamed Penn Cove mussels, prepared in a heavy cream reduction. Formed into a cake the size of a hockey puck, the yellowfin tuna tartare rivals the creations at Narcoossee's. Our favorite entree is the signature potato-wrapped snapper, a big chunk of comfort food topped with a thick wine sauce. Some of the fish comes from the greenhouses at the nearby Land pavilion in Epcot. *A Disney Signature Restaurant. Dinner. 193 seats.*

SPOODLES ✔ MEDITERRANEAN Wood floors, planked tables and an open kitchen lend this pleasant place a casual, inviting atmosphere, though it gets noisy when crowded. Open for breakfast and dinner, Spoodles offers entrees inspired by the coastal areas of France, Italy, Morocco and Turkey. For breakfast ($8–$12) try the new-for-2008 eggs-and-roasted-vegetable flatbread cooked in a wood-burning oven, or The Italian, which lays two poached eggs on top of toasted focaccia bread and surrounds them with a spicy casserole. New entrees on the dinner menu ($18–$23) include white-bean moussaka and a panzanella (bread salad) done with tomatoes and buffalo mozzarella. Tried-and-true dinner choices include pan-roasted snapper, sausage-and-mushroom rigatoni (the restaurant's signature dish) and steak kabobs, Spoodles' most popular item. The restaurant sells pizza (whole and by the slice) from the takeout window. *205 seats.*

CARIBBEAN BEACH

SHUTTERS ✔ CARIBBEAN Carved out of a corner of the Old Port Royale food court, this grouping of three small dining rooms offers an alternative experience to the nearby hamburger-and-hot-dog world. And finally, it's a better one. Long known for its bland, American food, Shutters debuted a new Caribbean-based menu ($15–$25) at the beginning of 2008. Entrees include a well-seasoned char-crusted strip steak topped with a mango pico; creamy creole pasta with spiced chorizo and goat cheese; plantain-crusted snapper; pineapple chicken served on a black bean paste; and side dishes such as grilled asparagus drizzled with a hot harissa sauce and sweet fried plantains. Black beans are offered as a side dish with rice or as a soup with cornbread. A grilled-and-chilled pineapple shrimp cocktail highlights the appetizer list. Desserts include new raspberry-topped guava enpanadas and a tangy (and appropriately yellow) homemade key lime tart. Though still cursed with Disney's most generic decor — the restaurant's walls are dotted with stamped metal pieces that look like they came from a Pier One sidewalk sale — Shutters is comfortable, with big fat chairs and big wood tables. *Dinner only. 132 seats.*

CONTEMPORARY RESORT

CALIFORNIA GRILL ✔ NEW AMERICAN Superb fare is matched by a terrific view at this Disney landmark, perched proudly atop the signature A-frame tower of the Contemporary Resort. The menu ($23–$36) changes often, but two long-time favorites are the grilled pork tenderloin with goat-cheese polenta and zinfandel glaze, and an oak-fired beef filet that's so tender you don't even get a steak knife. A ravioli appetizer perfectly blends goat cheese and sun-dried tomatoes, but of special note is the sushi. It's prepared by Yoshie Cabral, known as one of the top three sushi chefs in the United States. Famous for her imaginative sauces and use of fruit, the Okinawa native will make a perfect not-on-the-menu novice plate (shrimp tempura with mango and cucumber) upon request. We especially like her Snake in the Grass: eel with shrimp tempura, avocado and cucumber.

There's a magical view. Sit along the west windows, and before the sun sets you'll look into the open cone that is the top of nearby Space Mountain and see the steam of the Liberty Square Riverboat rising off in the distance. After sundown watch for the changing colors of Cinderella Castle, the flashing neon of Astro Orbiter and eventually the Electrical Water Pageant out in the Seven Seas Lagoon. Look the other direction and you can see Wilderness Lodge (so close!), Spaceship Earth, even the Marriott World Center. The view is better than you'd expect, because the land is so flat.

If you're here for the fireworks, you can watch the show from inside the restaurant or from outside, on one of two long rooftop walkways. The best way to see it? Head out to the northwest terrace 10 minutes before the show begins. You'll beat the crowd and be able to cherry-pick your viewing spot. Don't wait too long. At 5 minutes before showtime an announcement encouraging guests to head outside brings a huge crowd. Contrary to popular belief, you can watch Wishes from California Grill without a reservation — the lounge often takes walk-ins, and anyone who has dined here earlier in the evening can return. The northeast terrace is almost never filled to capacity. The dining room, and both walkways, air the show's synchronized soundtrack. Book reservations two to three months in advance for prime dining times; six months for parties of six or more. *Dinner. A Disney Signature Restaurant. 156 seats.*

CONCOURSE STEAKHOUSE ✔ AMERICAN Nestled next to the atrium's monorail tracks, this comfortable dining spot serves you breakfast ($7–$15), lunch ($10–$23) or dinner ($16–$27) while you wave at hundreds of smiling, Mickey-eared faces gliding past you on their way to Magic Kingdom. The decor is a sophisticated take on 1970s Brady Bunch interior design, with black and purple carpet and green-rimmed black tables. For breakfast, eggs Benedict are topped with a zesty tarragon reduction that includes a dash of cayenne pepper. Also with a kick: the new-for-2008 fried mahi mahi lunch sandwich. If you like garlic, a good dinner choice is the beef tenderloin bread salad. *Note: The Steakhouse is scheduled to close in May. In its place will be a new counter-service restaurant. A new table restaurant will then open downstairs in the resort's old arcade area. Nowhere near those gesturing guests on the monorail, it will be called, ironically, The Wave. 220 seats.*

CORONADO SPRINGS

MAYA GRILL AMERICAN WITH LATIN FLAVORS The most honest of Disney's convention-hotel restaurants, the Maya Grill offers straightforward, familiar food in a comfortable atmosphere. The most unusual items, in fact, come before the entrees. Instead of chips and salsa you start off your meal with a far superior light cornbread with a clear garlic-and-onion dipping sauce, and appetizers include a "chicken roll" that's far more interesting than its name. About the size of a small baked potato, its filling of black beans, chopped peppers, rice and warm pepper-jack cheese blends well with its drizzle of mango barbecue sauce and bed of crunchy salad. The main courses, however *($20–$30)*, are a standard expense-account mix of steaks, seafood, chicken and duck, all with just a touch of Latin flavor and all pretty good. In fact, this is the best spot to get a basic steak-and-potato meal in all of Walt Disney World. The rib-eye tastes just like you would hope to grill it at home, but marinated (in that same sauce that's served with the bread) just enough that you don't need steak sauce. The wine list includes selections from Argentina, Chile and Spain. The restaurant also serves an American breakfast buffet *($17 adults, $10 children)*. Run by the same family as Epcot's San Angel Inn, the restaurant has the same low-key service and calm character. Tables have metal tops with wood trim. Chairs are wide and nicely upholstered, like those from an Ethan Allen catalog. The Aztec- and Mayan-themed dining room features torch-style lighting and a three-story open ceiling. *220 seats.*

PEPPER MARKET FOOD COURT Though completely indoors, this food court re-creates the look of an outdoor Mexican market. It places its various food counters under tents, and its tables under awnings and umbrellas. Light bulbs are strung overhead. As for food, breakfast *($3–$9)* is, for the most part, the typical American menu of eggs, meats and oatmeal, though the best choice is waffles, which are prepared to order and topped with fruit. Lunch and dinner *($6–$20)* offer chicken and hamburgers, fajitas and quesadillas, pasta and pizza, salads and sandwiches, even stir-fry plates (the best bet is usually the pasta special). A waiter gets your drinks, which results in an automatic 10 percent tip. *420 seats.*

FORT WILDERNESS

TRAIL'S END ✔ AMERICAN The food is exactly what you want it to be: simple, hearty and plenty good. Operating as an all-you-can-eat buffet, the restaurant serves three All-American meals a day. Breakfast *($12 adults, $8 children ages 3–9)* includes a smooth corned beef hash, a deliciously rich biscuits and gravy and addictive little sticky buns. Lunch *($13 adults, $9 children)* and dinner *($18 adults, $10 children)* feature the same fried chicken served at the Hoop-Dee-Doo Revue next door, prepared, by customer demand, exactly the same way since 1971. You eat off of metal plates and drink from jelly jars. The dining room, meanwhile, is straight out of the roadside Old West of the 1960s. Trophy heads decorate the walls, lights hang from the rims of wagon wheels and rustic pine logs support an open ceiling of white acoustical tile. Full bar at lunch and dinner. Takeout service (4:30 p.m. to 10 p.m.) offers fried chicken dinners and pizzas. *192 seats. 6 counter seats at bar.*

GRAND FLORIDIAN

CITRICOS ✔ MEDITERRANEAN One of Walt Disney World's unheralded gems, this white-tablecloth restaurant *($22–$39)* can be noisy, but it doesn't matter — its sophisticated entrees steal your attention. Top picks for 2008 are the braised veal shank served with surprisingly harmonic carrot mashed potatoes, an oak-grilled filet that rivals those of the Yachtsman Steakhouse and our favorite, grilled swordfish served with a side bowl of clams Provençal, a tomato-based seafood stew so appealing it would steal the show at any coastal oyster bar. Other entrees typically include imaginative takes on chicken, pork and other fishes. For appetizers, try the Gâteau of Crab, a small three-cheese souffle bathed in a subtle citrus cream. Desserts feature a delightfully light little bowl of berries drenched in champagne and Grand Marnier. Share it or you'll get tipsy. Located on the second story of the resort, the restaurant is lit with a soft yellow glow; its window-lined walls overlook the main swimming pool and marina. At night a corner of the room offers a nice view of Magic Kingdom's fireworks. *A Disney Signature Restaurant. Dinner only. 190 seats.*

GRAND FLORIDIAN CAFE ✔ AMERICAN The portions aren't always overwhelming at this large Olde Florida sunroom, but the food is good and the surroundings calm. The breakfast menu *($10–$18)* includes lobster Benedict and a good biscuit skillet, though the best item isn't listed: pancakes with bananas and pecans. Ask your server and the kitchen will whip it up for you. Lunch *($10–$21)* is a decent value. The biggest bargain is the open-faced turkey-and-ham Grand Sandwich ($12), though its Boursin cheese sauce is awfully rich. Better is the ahi (yellowfin) tuna Niçoise salad. Dinner *($12–$28)* ranges from cheeseburgers to surf and turf, but the resort's other restaurants offer more for your money. The airy atmosphere features tall ceilings, lots of white wood, floral wallpaper and, new for 2008, cushy pink floral carpet. You dine on a marble table and sit in padded chairs. Arched windows line the outside wall. (Beware a window seat. In the early morning the harsh sunlight shines right in your face.) *326 seats.*

NARCOOSSEE'S ✔ SEAFOOD When it comes to seafood, my husband and I are tough to impress. Living along all three coasts of Florida over the past 30 years, we've come to think of seafood as something that's still flopping as it's tossed off a boat into a pickup truck, then quickly cleaned, grilled and served up with a few cold beers. That said, Narcoossee's impresses us. This cozy little place knows how to make fish fancy. The best items are the appetizers. Usually smoked salmon and ahi tuna, the tartare starters are always plenty tasty but never have an aftertaste. Same for the mussels. Sauteed in garlic and tomatoes, they're the best we've ever had. As for entrees *($20–$55),* each is prepared as a signature dish, with a carefully tuned mix of flavors and a beautiful presentation. The particular sets change often, depending on the season, the availability of ingredients, and the whims of the chefs. "We could change the menu every day between the three of us," says sous chef Richard Starke. "We've got so many ideas." There's usually a salmon dish and a scallop, and always crab-crusted halibut, a light entree that's balanced by a creamy lemon sauce. Almond-crusted cheesecake tops the dessert menu. As light and flaky as a cream horn, it melts in your mouth. "I get more people asking me for the cheesecake recipe than any other dish on the menu," Starke adds. The circular building sits over the Seven Seas Lagoon. Wood floors and ceilings look nice, but keep the noise level high. Tables are topped in blue cloth; chairs are padded and extra wide. Window-lined walls provide a panoramic view that includes the Contemporary Resort and Magic Kingdom. It's quite a show. Blue-lit shuttle boats pass every few minutes; the colorful Electrical Water Pageant floats by twice. For Magic Kingdom's fireworks spectacular the restaurant turns out its lights and pipes in the show's soundtrack.

The explosions reflect in the water. Your particular seating location makes little difference, as a narrow wraparound porch provides a perfect viewing spot. *Dinner. A Disney Signature Restaurant. 150 seats.*

VICTORIA AND ALBERT'S ✔ GOURMET Everyone fawns about the romantic, personalized experience at this tiny gourmet restaurant, and for good reason. It's designed to be the best meal you've ever had. When you arrive you're greeted by name — reservations are required — by Victoria and Albert themselves, the restaurant's servers, who lead you into one of two small, elegant dining areas. The six-course prix-fixe dinner *($125, $185 with wine pairings)* includes a chilled and hot appetizer, a soup or fish, entree, cheese board or sorbet, and dessert. A harpist plays while you dine, and the chef is always more than willing to come to your table. A day or two beforehand, the restaurant calls you to learn your food preferences, and then creates its menu so it includes your tastes. Female diners get long-stemmed roses. Only well-behaved children are welcome; noisy kids are asked to leave. True foodies will want to reserve the Chef's Table *($175, $245 with wine pairings).* Less formal that the dining room, it's located in an alcove in the back of the kitchen, and can seat up to 10. The experience starts with a champagne toast and a discussion with the chef about your likes and dislikes. He then creates a custom meal for you that can consist of up to 13 courses. As it's being prepared, you tour the kitchen and chat with the cooks. *Dinner. Formal dress code. No kid's menu. Private restroom. Usually two seatings nightly. A AAA Five Diamond Restaurant. 80 seats.*

OLD KEY WEST

OLIVIA'S CAFE ✔ AMERICAN This restaurant reminds us of the cafes on our hometown of Sanibel Island, off Florida's southwest coast. It looks like it's from Key West, but the cuisine seems straight from Minnesota. Like many Florida restaurants, Olivia's has learned that when it comes to meals, folks usually want to stick to the stuff they know. Breakfast *($9–$12)* features huge fluffy pancakes, a best bet for lunch *($10–$17)* is the steak salad, while steak and prime rib highlight the dinner menu *($15–$23).* Feeling adventurous? The menus also include grits, grouper and key lime pie. Some of the walls are covered with snapshots of Old Key West Disney Vacation Club families. *156 seats, including 22 outside.*

POLYNESIAN

KONA CAFE ✔ PAN-PACIFIC AMERICAN Originally a coffee shop, this high-ceilinged, carpeted room is open to the lobby atrium. Dotted with wood tables and a few half-booths, it's been upgraded over the years to a full-service restaurant. It serves a Pan-Pacific-flavored breakfast *($8–$14)*, lunch *($10–$14)* and dinner *($16–$26)* and offers 100-percent Kona coffee as well as a full bar. The best meal is breakfast. With nuts in the batter and a topping made of crushed pineapple, brown sugar and butter, the Macadamia-Pineapple Pancakes are so flavorful you don't need syrup. (Though it has its fans, we say skip the Cafe's Tonga Toast. Two slices of battered, deep-fried, sugar-coated sourdough bread that have been stuffed with a banana, it tastes like little more than a huge doughnut.) Prepared in a small show kitchen, desserts include a pecan-pie-like Chocolate-Macadamia Nut Tart, a Kilauea Torte "brownie volcano" that's filled with warm liquid chocolate and the Kona Kone, a vanilla-and-chocolate ice cream waffle cone that's surrounded by a base of cotton candy and topped with a chocolate Mickey stick. *163 seats.*

'OHANA ✔ POLYNESIAN AMERICAN Carnivores, come hungry. Long skewers of Polynesian-flavored meats and seafood are grilled over an open fire pit and then continually brought to your table at this all-you-can-eat dinner *($26 adults, $12 children)*. They're served with Hawaiian-style appetizers, homemade bread, salads and vegetables. Overlooking the resort's pool and marina areas, some tables offer a distant view of the Magic Kingdom's Cinderella Castle. The restaurant is equally known for its fun character breakfast (see Character Meals). *Dinner. 300 seats.*

PORT ORLEANS RIVERSIDE

BOATWRIGHT'S ✔ SOUTHERN This casual eatery features a Southern-style menu with choices Yankees rarely see. Breakfast *($9–$12)* has soothing sweet potato pancakes, served with a honey-pecan butter so tasty you don't need syrup. Dinner *($17–$30)* features crawfish cakes and a terrific blackened snapper served on grilled grits. Sides include "Southern Greens," the Disney name for collards. The pecan pie is homemade. The wood-table, tile-floor eatery has the look of a 19th-century boat shop, and appears to be in the process of building a 46-foot cotton lugger. Shipbuilding tools line the walls, and some tables sit underneath the boat's wooden frame. *206 seats.*

SARATOGA SPRINGS

THE ARTIST'S PALETTE ✔ AMERICAN (FOOD COURT) Disney's best resort food court, this comfortable eatery offers items unusual except at table-service restaurants. Breakfast *($6–$9)* includes flatbreads topped with bacon, eggs and cheese; lunch and dinner *($7–$8)* includes barbecued-pork flatbreads and sandwiches such as turkey and brie. Many items are made to order; to save time pay for your food while it's being prepared. The dining area has many padded booths, and has drawing easels for children. *112 seats.*

TURF CLUB BAR & GRILL ✔ AMERICAN Gourmet food at good prices makes this cozy, country-club retreat worth seeking out. Tucked into a corner of the Saratoga Springs Resort, the Turf Club is a short drive from the Old Key West and Port Orleans resorts, a pontoon-boat-shuttle away from Downtown Disney. At dinner *($12–$23)*, we like the crusted tuna, two big chunks of sushi-grade yellowfin doused in a red-wine syrup. Don't overlook the unique Caesar salad: it's a full head of romaine, sliced in half and grilled. Remember hot fudge cake? The Club's homemade lava cake dessert is the same thing. Served straight out of the oven, it smells just like a fresh brownie. Stick your spoon in it and hot fudge comes pouring onto your plate. Lunch *($10-$18)* attracts golfers (the restaurant is directly above the pro shop of the Lake Buena Vista course), who find a smaller tuna entree as well as a good cheeseburger. The waiting area has a walk-up bar, a flat-screen television and a billiards table. An outdoor balcony overlooks the golf course as well as a lake. Before moving here, the chef spent time at the California Grill and Yachtsman Steakhouse. Lunch served until 5 p.m. *146 seats, including 52 outside.*

SWAN AND DOLPHIN

THE FOUNTAIN SODA SHOP This classy soda fountain offers a limited menu ($7–$15) of sandwiches, salads and ice cream treats. Everything tastes OK, but the prices are geared more to expense accounts than family budgets. A hot dog with potato chips is $7, a Cuban sandwich is $14. *58 seats.*

FRESH MEDITERRANEAN Try the gray stuff; it's delicious! This buffet restaurant's fresh juice bar mixes up a gray-colored Wheatgrass juice for breakfast that, believe it or not, really does taste great. Unfortunately, that's about the only thing that's interesting about this place, which in the name of Marketing Concept makes you walk up to a buffet line, order, then stand and wait for someone to prepare your food. That way, it's Fresh! Maybe it's just me, but if I'm going to wait for food I'd like to sit down. The food itself is OK if uninspired — a breakfast buffet *($17)* with pancakes, eggs and meats; a lunch buffet *($19)* with rotisserie ham and chicken; a la carte items *($14–$16)* such as salads and sandwiches. The front of the restaurant is noisy; the back verandah is peaceful. *264 seats.*

GARDEN GROVE CAFE AMERICAN "Eighty percent of our cost is in raw materials." "This way you showcase yourself in a market-share system!" "If you look at the history of resin, the market is always volatile." The ambience is dull as dirt at this convention restaurant, where suits, ties and nametags adorn nearly every patron and the conversations echo around the room. Worse, the food is lousy. The breakfast and dinner buffets *($17–$32 adults, $11–$13 children)* generate more customer complaints than any other Swan (or Dolphin) meal. At lunch *($11–$22),* hot sandwiches often come out cold. Order a salad and you're likely to get a bowl of lettuce that tastes like it's been chilling about a month. It's all quite a shame, as the circular dining room has a stunning design. You sit under a huge rotunda, surrounded by lime-green walls dotted with murals of apple trees. Many tables are tucked under a large central tree. *150 seats. Note: On Saturday mornings Goofy and Pluto appear for a character breakfast ($19 adults, $13 children). On Sundays Chip 'n' Dale join them. Dinners always have characters: Rafiki and Timon Mondays and Fridays; Goofy and Pluto other nights.*

IL MULINO ✔ ITALIAN Looking for an upscale Italian dinner? This is your spot. The original Il Mulino is the best Italian restaurant in New York City, and this branch stays right with it. A wide variety of Abruzzi entrees *($16–$45)* are highlighted by creamy risottos and terrific seafood. Especially good are seared snapper and egg-battered shrimp. Unlike the Big Apple legend, this Il Mulino has a relaxing atmosphere and attentive service. *224 seats.*

KIMONOS JAPANESE More of a bar than a restaurant, this friendly, dark little spot combines Karaoke sing-a-longs with some good Japanese food *($4–$24).* It features hot and cold sake, plum wines, Japanese beers and over 50 sushi and sashimi creations. There's also red-bean and green-tea ice cream. Other foods are available for children who don't like sushi. Colorful kimonos hang from the ceiling. *Dinner. Swan. 105 seats.*

PICABU ✔ CAFETERIA Literally hiding behind the Fresh Mediterranean Market, this funky little cafeteria has a lot to offer. The food *($3–$11 breakfast, $6–$18 lunch and dinner)* is honest, the service attentive, and the atmosphere surprisingly clean, comfortable and strangely artistic. The dining area's center columns are trimmed with figures of dancing men who have huge holes where their hearts should be, while the back walls portray a trail of tail feathers left by a small bird who flew down from the ceiling. As you ponder what it all means, eclectic tunes from artists such as David Bowie and Lou Reed fill the air. *140 seats.*

SHULA'S STEAKHOUSE Big steaks for big bucks, for big hats with no cattle. At least that's our take on this testosterone-fueled spot, which seems dedicated to men who are willing to hand over the cash for anything that will make them feel masculine. As you arrive, you're greeted by a young babe in a short black dress, who, if you want her to, will sell you an autographed Don Shula football for $400. The dames disappear once you're seated, as a male server brings out a selection tray of huge raw steaks. Also on the platter (which sits in a corner of the restaurant when it's not in use) is a large, live lobster, slowly dying as the night wears on. As for the food (entrees $23–$75, side dishes $7–$8), it's good but not at the level of the nearby Yachtsman Steakhouse. The dark, clubby decor commemorates Shula's 1972 undefeated season as coach of the Miami Dolphins. *No children's menu. Dinner. Dolphin. 215 seats.*

TODD ENGLISH'S BLUEZOO SEAFOOD This high-style nightspot is all about the show. Designed to look as if it's underwater, the beautiful dining room has glass "bubbles" hanging overhead, animated ambient blue lights and throbbing techno music. Buried under it all is a decent, if overpriced, "coastal cuisine" menu. Appetizers are creative, and often rival those of Narcoossee's. Entrees *($27–$60)* fare less well, except for the decadent, delicious $60 Cantonese lobster. Desserts are the same chocolate and fruit creations you find at any upscale restaurant. The featured specialty drink is the Zooberry martini — fresh blueberries are steeped for three days, then infused into vodka with splashes of fresh lemon juice and rock candy syrup. Television addicts may recognize the restaurant as the setting for a recent infomercial starring the handsome Mr. English himself. *Dinner. Dolphin. 400 seats.*

WILDERNESS LODGE

ARTIST POINT ✔ PACIFIC NORTHWEST The fact that there's no "E" in the name (it's not "Pointe") tells you everything you need to know. This is the real thing, a relaxed, pretension-free dining room with creative offerings that never get too trendy. The entrees *($20–$42)* are seriously Northwestern, but so well-prepared that anyone will find something to love. The signature roasted salmon dish is actually a unique combination of flavors. Coated with a clove, coconut and ginger glaze, the huge chunk of fish is served on a chopped bed of pears, smoked pork and rutabaga. Meanwhile, the grilled buffalo is a sweet treat. An onion-jam topping adds extra zing to the tender steak, while its side of hazelnut-topped sweet potatoes makes a soothing complement. Appetizers include a nice mushroom soup, though the skimpy venison sweet rolls must come from very thin deer. For dessert, a delicious apple tart is topped with buttermilk ice cream and candied pecans. The wine list has bottles from Washington State and Oregon;

a dessert-wine menu also offers herbal teas. With a quiet, adult atmosphere, the L-shaped dining room mixes landscape murals with blond and cherry woods. Chairs are comfortably upholstered. *A Disney Signature Restaurant. Dinner only. 225 seats.*

WHISPERING CANYON CAFE ✔ BARBECUE Open for breakfast *($8–$14)*, lunch *($10–$17)* and dinner *($16–$22)*, this rowdy family favorite features traditional American barbecue and other hearty foods including an all-you-can-eat skillet. Be prepared for the servers: a rambunctious bunch whose hijinks become a free floor show. They specialize in sharing anything that happens at your table with all the other diners. When my husband once scarfed one of our daughter's french fries, our cowgirl server yelled "Everyone! Repeat after me: 'Hey dad! Eat your own stinkin' food!'" *281 seats.*

YACHT AND BEACH CLUB

BEACHES & CREAM ✔ SODA SHOP Clog those arteries! Gigantic sundaes *($8)* are the draw at this old-fashioned soda shop, where the treats are so tempting absolutely no one is thinking about their health. The guilty pleasures include the Milky Way (three scoops of vanilla over a Bundt cake, topped with hot fudge and butterscotch), the Fudge Mud Slide (three scoops over a brownie, topped with hot fudge and Oreo cookies) and our teenage daughter's longtime favorite, the No Way Jose (scoops of vanilla and chocolate sitting in a thick bed of peanut butter and topped with hot fudge). All sundaes are topped with whipped cream, nuts and a cherry. The shop's claim-to-fame is the ridiculous Kitchen Sink sundae *($22)*, made with eight scoops of ice cream, seven toppings, a Bundt cake, an angel-food cake, a brownie, a Milky Way candy bar, and nearly every other sweet in the place, as well as an entire can of whipped cream. It's served, literally, in a kitchen sink. Other treats include banana splits, root-beer floats and cherry Cokes.

Want something really different? Try a Frozen Sunshine, a seltzer soda made with vanilla ice cream and orange sherbet. It's like a carbonated Dreamsicle. There are burgers and sandwiches, too *($7–$11)*, though most of the ice-cream treats are meals in themselves.

The tin ceiling has a tray center with elaborate moldings. Lights above the booths are ice cream cones. An authentic bubble-light Wurlitzer jukebox sits up front. With only three booths and six small tables, the tiny place is usually packed. *Next to the Stormalong Bay swimming area. Takeout counter. 48 seats.*

CAPE MAY CAFE ✔ AMERICAN Though it's billed as a clambake, this comfortable all-you-can-eat buffet *($27 adults, $13 children)* offers a variety of good food. The advertised clams, mussels, corn-on-the-cob and potatoes are here, of course, but they take up just 4 feet of the 52-foot buffet line. The rest of it is filled with a little of everything — salad, chicken, pasta, ribs, soups, grilled vegetables — and except for some heat-lamp pizza and, sadly, run-of-the-mill desserts it's all pretty good, if a little overpriced. The real standout is the carved-to-order top sirloin. Seasoned with just the right touch of garlic, it's perfectly tender and delicious when topped with creamy horseradish sauce. The buffet's general quality comes, in part, because none of its food sits very long. Cooks attend to the line constantly and don't overstock it. The happiest diners seem to be those who have just flown in; the restaurant's large booths, big tables, extra-wide chairs, subdued lighting and soothing background music (occasionally with sounds of sea gulls) make it the perfect place to recover from a day of air travel. Kids will like the carpet, a colorful collage of beach umbrellas. The restaurant's morning meal is Goofy's Beach Club Character Breakfast (see Character Meals). *234 seats.*

YACHT CLUB GALLEY AMERICAN This generic cafe is sort of like a Perkins Pancake House. The food is decent but not memorable, the atmosphere comfortable but not interesting. Breakfast *($8–$16)* features a crab cake Benedict on tomatoes, and a heat-lamp buffet with a creamy bread pudding. Lunch *($10–$14)* is salads and sandwiches, while dinner *($13–$23)* has steaks, fish and seafood. *280 seats.*

YACHTSMAN STEAK HOUSE ✔ STEAKHOUSE The best Disney steakhouse, this understated alternative to the nearby Shula's has better food, fairer prices *($26–$44)*, more personable servers and a far more family-friendly atmosphere. The steaks are the same top-quality cuts found in any fine steakhouse, but here they're more than just plated pieces of meat. The New York strip is brushed in a peppercorn brandy sauce that's both smooth and zesty. The prime rib comes with a savory bread pudding. All meals include onion rolls and sourdough bread, made extra flavorful through the skills of the restaurant's master pastry chef, one of only two on Disney property (the other's at the Grand Floridian). Though it's not mentioned on the menu, the restaurant will hand-cut custom sizes of any steak but the porterhouse. Special occasions can be celebrated with "surprise" homemade cakes of nearly any size; parties of 10 or more can dine off a set menu (call in advance at 407-934-3818). Half of the restaurant is on a wood floor, the other half is carpeted. Tables are covered in white tablecloths. From November through January, about a third of the crowd is conventioneers. *A Disney Signature Restaurant. Dinner only. 286 seats.*

reviews

Character meals

THEME PARKS

A BUFFET WITH CHARACTER WINNIE THE POOH, TIGGER, EEYORE, PIGLET One of Disney's most popular character meals, this Crystal Palace affair is, ironically, the least fun. When you arrive, you wait for your table by standing in the sun. Once you get in, the dining room is so noisy it's tough to talk, and so crowded it can be a challenge to squeeze your way to the buffet line. Worst of all, you hardly see the characters. Besides stopping for autographs and snapshots, Pooh, Tigger, Eeyore and Piglet typically only spend a few seconds with each guest. "Tigger's got to go!" a cast member told a mom as she took too long to pose her daughter. "He's on a certain timeframe!" As for the food, the huge buffet offers a variety of choices, but nothing that isn't better prepared elsewhere. The best times to stop by are 8 a.m. (an hour before the park opens, when afterward you'll still have a full day in front of you), 10:30 a.m. (the last breakfast seating, when the crowd lessens and the characters can relax) or 3 p.m. (when again there's a moment of calm). *At Magic Kingdom's Crystal Palace. Breakfast: $19 adults, $11 children 3–9. Lunch: $21 adults, $12 children. Dinner: $29 adults, $15 children. 400 seats.*

CHIP 'N' DALE'S HARVEST FEAST ✔ MICKEY MOUSE, PLUTO, CHIP 'N' DALE A breath of farm-fresh air from the typical character buffet, this country-style lunch or dinner is served family style, which means it's all-you-can-eat but brought to your table. As you dine, farmer Mickey, Pluto and Chip 'n' Dale mosey up to say hi and, if you invite them, sit down for a spell to "chat." Thanks to the restaurant's small size you see the characters often, at least three times each if you stay for an hour. But that's only half the fun. Originally designed as an experience in itself, the circular restaurant is built like a merry-go-round. The kitchen is the hub, while the seating area around it rotates, circling completely every two hours. The outside rim is an open balcony, and overlooks the rain forest, desert and prairie dioramas of the Living with the Land attraction. The menu features catfish, flank steak, turkey with cranberry relish and a hot skillet of caramel-coated apple crisp.

Ask to sit on the outside of the ring. Not only will you dine in a nicely padded booth and face the dioramas, but your booth's high-backed seats completely block your view to anything else. The benefit? Every character visit will come as a sudden, delightful surprise. The restaurant's only flaw: there's no place to wait for your table. Diners-to-be are forced to stand, or sit, along the pavilion's carpeted indoor walkway, often right in the way of others headed to the attractions downstairs. *At Epcot's The Land pavilion at the Garden Grill restaurant. Beer, wine. Lunch: $21 adults, $12 children 3–9. 11 a.m.– 3 p.m. Dinner: $29 adults, $14 children 3–9. 4:30 p.m.–8 p.m. 150 seats.*

CINDERELLA'S ROYAL TABLE PRINCESSES, FAIRY GODMOTHER, GUS, JACQUES You only meet Cinderella briefly, if at all, and you're rushed through your meal. Unless you absolutely must eat in Cinderella Castle, this pre-plated meal can be disappointing. Various princesses and the Fairy Godmother stop by your table at breakfast and lunch, and the Fairy Godmother and mice Gus and Jacques are on hand for dinner, but bland food and a hurried atmosphere take away the magical feeling. Breakfast *($33 adults, $23 children)* is routine scrambled eggs, bacon and other standard American fare. Lunch *($36 adults, $24 children)* includes a small appetizer plate and pasta, pork, pot pie or salmon. Dinner *($41 adults, $26 children)* features a tasty corn and crab soup with decent entrees of lamb and prime rib. Meal prices include a plastic wand or sword for kids as well as a souvenir photo with Cinderella, who appears only in a downstairs foyer. Guests are subtly urged to get in and out within 60 minutes. When we ate lunch here recently, a cast member literally pushed us into the Cinderella photo line, then grabbed my arm to quickly get us upstairs to make our seating time. The food started arriving almost before we could sit down. The castle is always fully booked far in advance; to get in make reservations *(407-WDW-DINE, 407-939-3463)* exactly 190 days early if you'll be staying at a Disney resort (180 days if not). Reservations must be guaranteed with a credit card; no-shows are charged the full amount of the meal. The Gothic dining hall overlooks Fantasyland. *In Magic Kingdom's Cinderella Castle. 184 seats.*

DONALD AND FRIENDS ✔ DONALD DUCK, DAISY DUCK, MICKEY MOUSE, MINNIE MOUSE African-themed foods spice up the menu at this new breakfast buffet *($19 adults, $11 children)*. A potato-leek frittata, coconut-sweet potato casserole, beef bobotie quiche and mealie pap are the best of the many interesting choices. Made with quality spiced sausage, the all-American biscuits and gravy is outstanding. Don't pass up the mango chutney. Characters spend plenty of time with each guest, and every hour or so invite everyone to grab a noisemaker and join them as they sing and dance around the room. Ask to sit in the main dining room. The smaller side room is too cramped and too loud. After you check in, a cast member will direct you to stand in a line to pose for an optional photo package. You can skip it if you like. *At Animal Kingdom's Tusker House. 1,216 seats.*

GOOFY'S LIBERATE YOUR APPETITE ✔ GOOFY, MICKEY MOUSE, MINNIE MOUSE, PLUTO

With five characters but only 56 tables, this Colonial-style family feast *($28 adults, $13 children)* offers you plenty of time with its Disney stars. Clumsy as ever, Goofy takes his time at every table, though he gets bashful around groups of women. Minnie will give you a kiss, Pluto will lick your head, and Chip 'n' Dale can be downright silly. The food is served family style, which means it's all-you-can-eat but brought to your table. You'll get plates piled high with roasted turkey, carved beef and smoked pork loin, and bowls of mashed potatoes, vegetables, stuffing and macaroni and cheese. Dessert is cobbler topped with vanilla ice cream. It's all good. *At Magic Kingdom's Liberty Tree Tavern. 250 seats.*

Sleeping Beauty meets an admirer at the Princess Storybook Dining experience at Epcot

© DISNEY

PLAY 'N DINE ✔ LEO, JUNE, JOJO, GOLIATH As much of a show as it is a meal, this breakfast and lunch buffet offers so much interaction with its characters kids sometimes forget to eat. Not only do Leo and June (from "Little Einsteins") and JoJo and Goliath (from "JoJo's Circus") come to your table, they also invite you to get up and join them as they sing, dance and cha-cha-cha around the room. The short celebrations take place three times an hour. Little kids really get into it, as do many moms and, surprisingly, teenage girls (as one explained, "Goliath is just so cute!"). The songs come from a variety of Playhouse Disney programs, including "Mickey Mouse Clubhouse" and "Bear in the Big Blue House." Breakfast is rarely crowded. Eat here at 8 a.m. and you'll be finished by 9, right when the park itself opens. Stop by at 11 a.m. and you'll have the characters almost all to yourself. Lunch usually requires reservations about a week in advance. As for food, many breakfast items work fine as a brunch (new for 2008 is a build-own-your-burrito station), while lunch includes a decent baked chicken (topped in a blackberry and wine sauce), seafood Alfredo and creamed-corn spoon bread. Additional kid's items range from chicken nuggets to roasted chicken. Prices are higher than other character meals, as the performers include union actors. *At Disney's Hollywood Studios, in the Hollywood & Vine restaurant. Breakfast: $23 adults, $13 children 3–9. 8 a.m.–11:20 a.m. Lunch: $25 adults, $14 children. 11:40 a.m.–2:25 p.m. Note: The restaurant also serves a dinner buffet, but it does not include characters. 468 seats.*

PRINCESS STORYBOOK DINING PRINCESSES Walt Disney World's most unusual character experience, this bustling meal has four Disney princesses come to your table while you dine, for the most part, on Norwegian food. The particular royalty varies, but almost always includes Jasmine (from 1991's "Aladdin") and, since she's Scandinavian, a fully gammed (and ultra perky) Ariel (from 1989's "The Little Mermaid"). Also usually on hand: Sleeping Beauty and, yes, Cinderella. Occasionally Snow White, Pocahontas or even Mary Poppins substitutes. Breakfast is traditional American, served family style at your table. Lunch and dinner are three-course, all-you-can-eat feasts. Some of the appetizers are acquired tastes (the sliced peppered mackerel is sort of a fish jerky), but the hearty lamb stew and kjottkake will be familiar to anyone raised on American beef stew or meatloaf. Also good: the braised pork and sautéed chicken. Kids can choose from hot dogs, pasta, pizza and grilled chicken. Disney calls it Majesty Cake, but the standout dessert is actually Norwegian napolie cake: a thin slice of raspberry jam-layered sponge cake topped with an inch and a half of iced vanilla cream. Almost as good: traditional Norwegian rice cream. The castle-like room is noisy but no one seems to notice. You'll leave with your stomach full and your family happy. Reservations should be made at least a week in advance, though the last lunch and dinner seatings of each day often have tables available. Optional photo package. *At Epcot's Norway pavilion in the Akershus Royal Banquet Hall. Breakfast: $23 adults, $14 children 3–9. 8:20 a.m.–10:30 a.m. Lunch: $25 adults, $14 children. 11:10 a.m.–2:55 p.m. Dinner: $29 adults, $15 children. 4:10 p.m.–8:25 p.m. 255 seats.*

RESORTS

CHEF MICKEY'S MICKEY AND MINNIE MOUSE, DONALD DUCK, GOOFY, PLUTO These character meals are tough tickets, but their show falls flat. Chef Mickey's features an all-star cast, but none of its characters talk, they rarely interact together and, during peak periods, they don't have much time for you. Often there's only one character in each dining room, dividing their time among up to 100 diners. Though each one will absolutely stop at your table (a supervisor makes sure they do), often none will have any extra time to spare. (To avoid this problem, dine here at an unpopular time, such as 11 a.m.) Taken at face value, Chef Mickey's is an entertaining experience, and for most guests it's the most convenient way to dine with the Mouse, but overall it simply doesn't compare to the character meals at, say, the Grand Floridian. On the plus side, the costumes are cute (Mickey is dressed as a chef, the others are cooks), the huge buffets are constantly kept fresh, and their choices include such goodies as peanut-butter-and-jelly pizzas and made-to-order pancakes for breakfast, prime rib and salmon for dinner. Reserve your table at least a month early. Expect to be asked to pose for an optional souvenir photo package *($32)* when you check in. You can politely refuse. *At the Contemporary Resort. Breakfast: $23 adults, $13 children 3–9. 7 a.m.–11:30 a.m. Dinner: $30 adults, $16 children 3–9. 5 p.m.–9:30 p.m. 405 seats.*

CINDERELLA'S GALA FEAST ✔ CINDERELLA AND FRIENDS The best Disney character meal, this face-character extravaganza *($29 adults, $14 children)* has something for everyone. Little princesses (and, though they are loathe to admit it, many young men) will love meeting Cinderella face to face. Females of any age will blush when Prince Charming arrives to gently ask for their hands. And everyone will love Anastasia and Drizella, Cinderella's evil stepsisters, who wander the room with Lady Tremaine scheming to steal the prince for themselves. The experience is like that of a wacky interactive dinner theater. The crowd includes newlyweds, young couples and many grandparents. And the food! Also in a league of its own, the gigantic buffet includes outstanding strawberry soup, prime rib, rigatoni, snapper, bread pudding… the list goes on forever. *At the Grand Floridian Resort's 1900 Park Fare restaurant. 270 seats.*

GOOFY'S BEACH CLUB BREAKFAST ✔ GOOFY, MINNIE MOUSE, CHIP 'N' DALE The only Disney-operated character meal not in a theme park or on the Magic Kingdom monorail loop, this Beach Club breakfast buffet is calm and relaxed. And, thanks to the design of its host restaurant, it offers great interaction with its characters. Screaming kids are few and far between, as children are an even mix of preschoolers, elementary kids and middle-schoolers, and make up just 40 percent of the patrons. Characters, meanwhile, are more accessible, or at least seem to be. Narrow walkways through the dining rooms continually put them right up next to your table, so besides your official one-visit-per-character, you'll also get plenty of handshakes, waves and slaps on the back.

The characters are a nice mix. Chip 'n' Dale are silly. Minnie is sweet, offering gentle hugs and audible kisses. Goofy, meanwhile, loves to chat. Though he doesn't actually speak, Disney's friendly dog-man may sit down with you if you have an empty chair, ready to mime out an answer to just about any question. The characters dress in swimsuits. Goofy and Chip 'n' Dale wear lifevests and long flowered trunks (the chipmunks' shorts have cutouts for their tails), while Minnie, fitting the resort's Victorian theme, covers up in a vintage three-piece. As for food, the five buffet lines are well attended, so everything generally stays fresh. Offerings include the typical hot entrees (bacon, eggs, sausage), a yogurt bar and plenty of baked goods and fresh fruit. The blitzes, omelets and breakfast pizza change daily.

Everything takes place in a comfortable atmosphere. The cafe is fully carpeted, and includes full and half booths. The background music is a mix of Disney and beach tunes. Listen closely and you'll hear "Disney Mambo No. 5," even Annette Funicello's 1965 duet with the Beach Boys, "The Monkey's Uncle."

If you're not staying at the Yacht or Beach Club the meal is out of your way but easy to get to, especially if you've got a car. The Beach Club is centrally located on Disney property, and if you use its valet parking service ($10) you'll go from your car to the cafe in just 30 seconds, as the restaurant sits just to the left of the resort's small lobby. Most tourists don't know that, however, which makes this the easiest Disney-operated character meal to book at the last second. Small parties can often get in without a reservation. *At the Beach Club Resort's Cape May Cafe. $19 adults, $11 children 3–9. 7:30 a.m.–11 a.m. 234 seats.*

MICKEY AND FRIENDS BREAKFAST ✔ LILO, STITCH, MICKEY MOUSE, PLUTO One of Disney's most popular character meals, this breakfast is a worthwhile, and memorable, time. The reason: kids here *love* Lilo and Stitch. "Hi Lilo!" young girls call to the character across the dining room, ready to beam when she trots over to hug. Stitch, meanwhile, is an absolute superstar, at least with everyone young enough to know who he is. Adored by his fans for his mischievous personality, the alien creature will sometimes "pick bugs" off of unsuspecting dads, get down on all fours to chase kids on the carpet, or sneak up to ruin photos of other children posing with Lilo. Mickey and Pluto are just as accessible, but here they're definitely second fiddle. Characters are always on the floor. Each one appears for 45 minutes at a time, and their schedules overlap. Every hour they come together to lead a maraca-shaking parade of kids around the room. The set menu is served "family style," which means it's all-you-can-eat but brought to your table. Servers will bring you a basket of coconut-pineapple "monkey bread" (fresh baked at 2 a.m. that morning); a platter of scrambled eggs, sausage, bacon, potatoes and a biscuit; another of fruit; and, if you like, some small Mickey-faced waffles. It's all pretty good, but the waffles don't stay warm. Note: After you check in, a cast member will direct you to stand in a line to pose for an optional photo package ($32). You can skip it if you like, which will eliminate the hassle of dealing with a photo salesperson later coming to your table. *At the Polynesian Resort's 'Ohana restaurant. Prime meal times fill 180 days early. $19 adults, $11 children 3–9. 7:30 a.m.–11 a.m. 300 seats.*

SUPERCALIFRAGILISTIC BREAKFAST ✔
MARY POPPINS, WINNIE THE POOH, TIGGER, ALICE, THE MAD HATTER I write each of these reviews on site, using a laptop to jot down a few paragraphs while I eat. It's an idea that works great, except at this meal *($19 adults, $11 children 3–9).*

"She's writing a review!" screamed the Mad Hatter at the top of his lungs, after noticing me working in the corner. "A review?" called Alice, skipping up to my table. "That's not very proper!"

Properly chastised, I have one bite of my omelet, and manage to type *"With face and…"* before Tigger bounces over and starts pounding on my keyboard.

"fgr0-34hsdskjo87…"

When the tiger bounds away, I hit Undo and start over.

"With face and…"

"Make sure you spell my name right!" the Hatter shouts from across the room. "Two T's!"

"…fur characters…"

Then there's a tap on my shoulder. It's Mary Poppins "I hear you're working? That is not something we do on vacation!"

It goes on for an hour. Once, Mary comes back and examines my work. "You sure are messy!" she says, staring at my screen full of cut-and-pasted phrases. "Tidy up!"

"Two T's!" yells the Hatter, off in a side room.

Eventually, the characters take a break ("We went to have tea!" Alice later insists), and I'm able to finally write that, with face and fur characters from three different films, this character breakfast has something for everyone. Infants squeeze Pooh's nose and offer Tigger cereal. Mary Poppins engages in practically perfect conversations with grandparents. Alice, meanwhile, romps around the room, cheerfully greeting guests even if they don't know who she is. ("They call me Alison," she confides.)

Best of all, all of the characters are perfectly in character, with personalities, even voices that match those in the Disney films. The reincarnation of Ed Wynn, the Mad Hatter has the late actor's comical lisp down to a T.

The 40-item buffet is terrific. It includes extravagances such as lobster Benedict, an $18 entree at the Cafe next door. Omelets are made to order at two stations, so there's rarely a wait.

Though reservations can be hard to come by, there are dozens of no-shows each morning, so tables are often available. *At the Grand Floridian's 1910 Park Fare restaurant. 270 seats.*

Dinner shows

DISNEY'S SPIRIT OF ALOHA DINNER SHOW
POLYNESIAN MUSIC AND DANCING A dancing, drumming and musical tour of Hawaii, New Zealand, Samoa, Tahiti and Togo, this venerable dinner show *($51–$59 adults, $26–$30 children)* features gorgeous (and skimpy!) costumes, lots of authentic booty shaking, an outstanding fire dancer and an odd first half that consists of corny jokes and sitcom-style skits. Kids learn the hula. The meal is an all-you-can-eat feast of pork ribs, chicken and rice. If you go, splurge for the more expensive, front-of-the-house seats. Folks who sit in back have a hard time hearing. Also, note that it takes about 10 minutes to walk to the theater from the Polynesian Resort lobby. *At the Polynesian Resort's Luau Cove. 420 seats.*

HOOP-DEE-DOO MUSICAL REVUE ✔ COUNTRY WESTERN SALOON SHOW The food's nothing special, yet everyone swears by it. The songs and skits, if you analyze them like a cold-hearted guidebook reviewer, are never that funny, yet the whole room keeps laughing. Why? Because the good-natured spirit of this thing *($51–$59 adults, $26–$30 children)* is just so contagious! Kids in particular love the corny humor of the rootin', tootin' troupe of six Wild West performers, as well as their frequent forays into the audience. The food is all-you-can-eat fried chicken, ribs, mashed potatoes and, if you want, unlimited draft beer. The handsome heartthrob, the dumb blonde, "Call me butter! I'm on a roll!" — nothing's changed in decades. And, really, why should it? *At the Fort Wilderness Resort's Pioneer Hall. 360 seats.*

MICKEY'S BACKYARD BBQ COUNTRY MUSIC This corny celebration of country music *($45 adults, $27 children)* is an acquired taste, but if you've taken a cotton to line dancing and your kids are dying to meet Mickey Mouse you may love it. Held in an outdoor pavilion, the experience includes a live band, line-dance instruction and appearances by Mickey and Minnie, Goofy and Chip 'n' Dale. It's hosted by two live performers, Tumbleweed and Sarsaparilla Sal. The all-you-can-eat buffet includes pork ribs, baked chicken and corn on the cob. You share a long picnic table with other guests. Sound like fun? Get there early for a good seat. *Thur.–Sat. except during Jan., Feb. At the Fort Wilderness Resort. 300 seats.*

Downtown Disney

MARKETPLACE

CAP'N JACK'S SEAFOOD/AMERICAN Though its worn wood decor is decades past due for a makeover, this unpretentious 1970s throwback has some surprisingly good food. Lunch *($9–$17)* features a mozzarella crab cake melt topped with zesty horseradish sauce. It's served on a giant slice of focaccia bread. At dinner *($15–$33)*, the pot roast falls apart in your mouth. Both menus include white and red clam chowder. If you ask the kitchen will mix them together into a smooth pink treat. *113 seats, including 15 at the bar. Direct line for reservations: 407-828-3971.*

EARL OF SANDWICH ✔ AMERICAN/ENGLISH There are many tasty hot-sandwich choices at this popular counter-service restaurant *(breakfast $2–$5, lunch and dinner $5–$6)*. Our faves are the Beef 'n' Bleu (roast beef and bleu cheese) and the Ultimate Grilled Cheese (bleu, brie and Swiss, with bacon and tomato). The crusty bread is baked all day; beef is roasted every morning. A good side dish: the chunky cole slaw with touches of garlic and sour cream. The best deal: the $1.25 cup of steaming hot, creamy-orange tomato soup. Owned by the ancestors of the fourth Earl of Sandwich. *190 seats, including 65 outside. 407-938-1762.*

FULTON'S CRAB HOUSE SEAFOOD There's usually no wait at lunch *($10–$18)* at this white-tablecloth restaurant, when the best crab bet is an appetizer, a filling bowl of crab-and-lobster bisque *($8)*. For dinner *($21–$55)*, there are crab cakes, claws and legs. Don't want crab? Try the generous fried seafood combo. You'd never guess this 20,000-square-foot building isn't a real paddle-wheeler. Inside, its narrow halls, creaky floors and wooden ceilings suggest a long life on the water. Actually, it was built by Disney and is not floating. Ask to sit on the lake side of the Constellation Room, a semicircular, window-lined area on the second deck. Its ceiling glows blue at night. *Direct line for reservations: 407-934-BOAT (2628). 660 seats, including 24 outside.*

GHIRARDELLI SODA FOUNTAIN ICE CREAM You can eat at a booth, table or bar at this busy ice-cream parlor, which features cones, waffle cones, banana splits, chocolate drinks, floats, milkshakes and specialty sundaes *($3–$25)*. The hot fudge sauce is made daily. A small chocolate shop is adjacent. *88 seats, including 22 outside. Direct line for info: 407-934-8855.*

MCDONALD'S FAST FOOD The chain's standard menu *($1–$4)*. The quietest tables are in back. *254 seats, including 114 outside.*

PORTOBELLO YACHT CLUB ITALIAN This nondescript white-tablecloth place belongs in a shopping mall. Except for some display-case model ships there's no real theme, just stucco walls and industrial-grade carpet. Lunch *($10–$16)* is a decent value with soup-and-sandwich combos, but dinner *($22–$40)* is overpriced. The signature gorgonzola-topped filet ($40) is about $10 more than the same item at Orlando's gouge-happy convention restaurants. A kid's menu *($5–11)* includes grilled fish. *Full bar. 390 seats, including 64 outside. Direct line for reservations: 407-934-8888.*

RAINFOREST CAFE AMERICAN A robotic rain forest comes to life every few minutes as you choose from beef, chicken, pork and seafood dishes, pasta, pizza, salads, sandwiches or hamburgers *($10–$40)*. See our review of the sister restaurant at Disney's Animal Kingdom theme park. *575 seats. No same-day reservations. 407-827-8500.*

WOLFGANG PUCK EXPRESS CALIFORNIA FUSION This indoor counter serves individual pizzas, omelettes, waffles and a Crispy Cornflake French Toast for breakfast *($4–$6)*; pizzas, quesadillas, sandwiches and signature butternut squash soup for lunch and dinner *($5–$10)*. *133 seats, including 109 outside. 407-828-0107.*

PLEASURE ISLAND

RAGLAN ROAD IRISH PUB & RESTAURANT ✔ IRISH Run by Irish proprietors and an Irish chef, this pretension-free restaurant and bar is the real thing. The decor is filled with antiques, including two 130-year-old bars that feature large dividers with leaded glass. The bar has a full selection of ales, stouts, lagers and whiskies. The food *(lunch $9–$15, dinner $13–$28)* is a step beyond tradition — pub classics that have gone to cooking class. The tender meats are topped with subtle glazes; the smooth mashed potatoes with crispy braised cabbage. Desserts include a rich bread pudding served with creamers of warm butterscotch and creme anglaise. The best dish is the creamy, subtle Rustic Chicken soup. It will warm your soul. The tab here can approach $40 per person with a couple of ales, but with the live band and table step-dancer (after 8 p.m. every night but Sunday) it's still a great value. Ask to sit at the center table (an old parson's pulpit) for an unforgettably up-close performance. The restaurant is named after a street on the south side of Dublin immortalized in a 1960s folk song. The adjacent **Cooke's of Dublin** offers counter-service fish and chips, with fried candy bars for dessert. *600 seats, including 300 outside. Merchandise shop; two outdoor bars. Pleasure Island admission not required. Children welcome. Direct line for reservations: 407-938-0300.*

WEST SIDE

BONGOS CUBAN CAFE CUBAN Housed in a whimsical building that's dominated by a three-story adobe pineapple, this festive eatery has fair food but great nightlife. There's dancing and live entertainment Fri. and Sat. starting at 10 p.m. Entrees *($16–$33)* range from Ropa Vieja (shredded beef in a tomato sauce) to surf and turf. Lunch also offers sandwiches *($8–$9)*. Side dishes include yuca (a boiled root vegetable, similar in taste to a potato) and plantains (sweet pan-fried bananas). The interior features bamboo bars and mosaic murals that recall the B.C. (Before Castro) Cuba of the 1940s and 1950s. Ask to sit in the pineapple, where every booth is a different color, or on the second-story patio. The restaurant was created by pop-star Gloria Estefan and her husband Emilio. *560 seats, including 60 outside and 87 at the bar. Direct line for information: 407-828-0999.*

HOUSE OF BLUES ✔ SOUTHERN With good food and a cool, dark, comfortable atmosphere, the family-friendly restaurant is an ideal spot to refresh from too much Mickey. Based on tried-and-true recipes of the rural South, the menu ($10–$27) offers dozens of entrees. Awesome pork ribs are plenty tender and coated with Jim Beam barbecue sauce. Don't overlook the rosemary cornbread, a soothing side dish that melts in your mouth. Locals return just for the white-chocolate banana bread pudding. Southern folk art covers the walls, ceilings, railings, window frames, lamps, even the stalls in the bathrooms. There's free acoustic live entertainment on the Front Porch bar from 6 p.m. to 11 p.m., and a complimentary plugged-in show in the restaurant Thursdays–Saturdays from 10:30 p.m. to 2 a.m. Kids will love the art, the big booths, the bucket of crayons in the lobby, and the fact that at night, any noise they make will be drowned out by the live music. *578 seats, including 158 at outside tables and 36 at the outdoor bar. No reservations. Info: 407-934-BLUE (2583) The adjacent Music Hall (250 seats) offers a buffet brunch with live gospel music each Sunday at 10:30 a.m. and 1 p.m. ($33 adults, $16 children 3–9; reservations 407-934-BLUE).*

PLANET HOLLYWOOD AMERICAN Shaped like a planet, this three-story cafe is filled with celebrity and movie memorabilia, including one of the blue gingham dresses Judy Garland wore in 1939's "The Wizard of Oz." The menu *($12–$23)* has a little of everything, but is uninspired. The atmosphere is loud; the service irritating. *Lunch, dinner. 800 seats. Direct line for information: 407-827-7827.*

WETZEL'S PRETZELS ✔ SNACKS This indoor counter stand serves yummy hot hand-rolled soft pretzels with a variety of coatings. There's also fresh-squeezed lemonade, as well as Haagen-Dazs ice cream, milkshakes, sundaes, sorbets and waffle cones. *36 outdoor seats.*

WOLFGANG PUCK CAFE ✔ CALIFORNIA FUSION This large, noisy cafe *(lunch $10–$18,*

GREAT IRISH PUBS FLORIDA

Shepherd's pie at Raglan Road

dinner $12–$28) features signature Puck entrees such as veal weinerschnitzel and butternut squash soup. Steak and chicken choices are served with deliciously creamy garlic mashed potatoes. The sushi bar is noteworthy. The boldly colored restaurant was designed by Puck's ex-wife, Barbara Lazaroff. *586 seats, including 30 at the sushi bar. Direct line for reservations: 407-938-WOLF (9653). Takeout window adjacent.*

WOLFGANG PUCK DINING ROOM ✔ CALIFORNIA FUSION No one can blend flavors like Wolfgang Puck, and this white-tablecloth gem does him proud. Duck, goat cheese and chutney? Seared tuna with spinach and poached eggs? Though those and most other dishes are, in fact, created by local chefs, Pucks' signature California Fusion style is well represented. Mr. Puck himself stops in once or twice a year. A worthwhile appetizer is Duck Napoleon, a towering delight of layered wonton skin, braised duck, goat cheese and apple chutney. Entrees *($25–$41)* include chicken, fish, steak and veal dishes; new for 2008 are beef short ribs with polenta and lobster ravioli with marscapone cheese and truffles. Prix fixe three-course and four-course meals *($50, $60)* are also available. Desserts include banana beignets. Kid's choices *($10–$17)* range from chicken tenders to a 4-ounce filet. Located on the second floor of the Wolfgang Puck building at Downtown Disney, the room overlooks the Downtown Disney waterfront and the Saratoga Springs resort. Dotted with celebrity caricatures, its orange walls are dominated by a gigantic ornamental hookah. *120 seats. Direct line for reservations: 407-938-WOLF (9653).*

THE COMPLETE WALT DISNEY WORLD **317**

Stormtroopers parade during a Star Wars Weekend

Special events

WINTER

MARATHON WEEKEND A pair of running events — a 26.2-mile full marathon and a 13.1-mile half marathon — highlight this weekend. Typically more than 30,000 athletes compete; participants travel through the theme parks. There's also a 5K run for families and children as well as a health and fitness expo at the Wide World of Sports Complex. *Early January. Entry fees: $75 (26.2), $45 (13.1), $25–30 (5K). Disabled runners welcome. Advance registration is required; the entry deadline is typically early Nov. but the events can reach capacity much earlier. Note: A Minnie Marathon Weekend women's endurance event (15K, 5K and kids' races) follows in May. Details at 407-939-7810 or disneysports.com.*

SPRING TRAINING The Atlanta Braves hold their Spring Training at Disney's Wide World of Sports. Workouts start in February; more than a dozen Grapefruit League exhibition games follow in March. *February–March. Training sessions $11, games $14–$22. Tickets on sale in Jan. Info and tickets: 407-939-1500, 407-839-3900 (Ticketmaster) or at disneysports.com.*

SPRING

ESPN: THE WEEKEND Legendary athletes join popular ESPN broadcasters during this no-extra-charge fan-fest at Disney's Hollywood Studios. The events include Q&A sessions, celebrity motorcades, interactive sports activities and live telecasts. *Early March.*

ST. PATRICK'S DAY Two locations mark the Irish holiday with special events: The Raglan Road restaurant at Downtown Disney's Pleasure Island, and the U.K. pavilion at Epcot's World Showcase. *March.*

INTERNATIONAL FLOWER AND GARDEN FESTIVAL This two-month Epcot garden party decorates the park with about 70 character topiaries, 80 floating water gardens, 300,000 bedding plants and 30 million blooms. Disney's most elaborate one-park promotion, the festival includes dozens of daily hands-on seminars, planting demonstrations and celebrity guest speakers. Kids love the walk-through butterfly garden, which often includes a live exhibit showing how a caterpillar forms a chrysalis and emerges as a butterfly. Themed weekends celebrate art, bugs and Mother's Day. Nightly concerts feature acts from the 1960s and 1970s, such as Monkees singer Davy Jones. Vendor booths line some walkways. *April–May. No extra charge. Info: 407-W-DISNEY (934-7639).*

EASTER The Magic Kingdom Easter Day parade includes the Easter Bunny and the colorful Azalea Trail Maids from Mobile, Ala. *March or April.*

STAR WARS WEEKENDS This fan-fest includes autograph booths featuring Star Wars characters and others involved in the creation of the classic motion pictures. Other highlights: roving characters, special motorcades, question-and-answer sessions, trivia games and children's activities. Merchandise includes an incredibly popular Darth Mickey plushie and a Darth Tater version of Mr. Potato Head. Many guests dress up. Get there when the park opens to get the

318 THE COMPLETE WALT DISNEY WORLD

full effect. *May–June. No extra charge. Info: 407-W-DISNEY (934-7639).*

GAY DAYS Tens of thousands of gay adults come to Walt Disney World (especially Magic Kingdom) during the first weekend in June, most wearing red shirts in a sign of solidarity. Straight parents can be uncomfortable, but those who aren't get to show kids that even some old folks and yes, parents, can be gay. A few guests are flamboyant. There is, naturally, less demand for strollers as well as shorter lines at Fantasyland attractions. Disney does not sponsor the event but doesn't interfere with it. *First weekend in June. Info: 407-896-8431 or at gaydays.com.*

SUMMER

INDEPENDENCE DAY Usually the most crowded day of the year, Independence Day features a Magic Kingdom fireworks show that surrounds guests watching from Main Street U.S.A. *July 4th.*

PIRATE & PRINCESS PARTY These nighttime events include a unique parade and one of Disney's most spectacular fireworks shows. There are interactive events for children and treasure hunts for a bibbity-bobbity-booty of beads and candy. Most major attractions are open, too, with short lines. Many guests dress up. Though the parties run from 7 p.m. to midnight, party-goers can come into the park as early as 4 p.m., which makes the price a bargain. Popular with young singles as well as families. *August–September. $37 adults; $30 children 3-9. Apx. a dozen evenings. Info and tickets: 407-W-DISNEY (934-7639).*

LITTLE ONES TRAVEL TIME Magic Kingdom's Fantasyland opens an hour early (at 8 a.m. instead of 9) a few days each week for Disney resort guests during late September and early October, with characters on hand to play games and sometimes go on rides with kids. A series of Playhouse Disney concerts at Disney's Hollywood Studios are free with park admission. Over the last few years parents have often been arriving at the Studios as early as 4 a.m. to get in line for tickets to the Doodlebops, effectively "selling out" those shows by 6 a.m. *Info at 407-W-DISNEY (934-7639). September–October.*

NIGHT OF JOY Live concerts by at least a dozen Contemporary Christian artists accent this Magic Kingdom event. Most attractions are open. *Early September. Adv. tickets $40, $68 for two nights. Day of event $5 more. Often sells out. Info and tickets: 407-W-DISNEY (934-7639).*

FALL

MICKEY'S NOT-SO-SCARY HALLOWEEN PARTY There's nothing but fun at this charming Magic Kingdom event, which includes a terrific parade (which starts with a galloping headless horseman) and a spectacular fireworks show. There are lots of free-candy stations; most attractions are uncrowded. Many families wear homemade costumes. *September–October. $43 adults; $36 children 3–9. Many dates offer $6 advance savings. Friday events near Halloween, and the holiday itself, often sell out. Info and tickets: 407-W-DISNEY (934-7639).*

INTERNATIONAL FOOD AND WINE FESTIVAL Booths around Epcot's World Showcase feature food and wine samples from Spain, India, Italy, Turkey, Ireland, Poland and other countries during this six-week festival. The 2007 event even had a booth from Oklahoma. Other events include cooking demonstrations, gourmet dinners and wine seminars. Nightly concerts feature classic pop acts such as Little Richard and Three Dog Night. The demonstrations, seminars and entertainment are included in the regular Epcot ticket price. *October–November. Info: 407-WDW-FEST (939-3378).*

CHILDREN'S MIRACLE NETWORK CLASSIC You'll be just a few feet away from the top names in golf with a pass to this PGA Tour tournament. Tiger Woods usually plays. $10 practice-round days, $30 championship-round days, $50 for all rounds. *Late October–Early November. Held at the Magnolia and Palm courses at the Shades of Green resort. Food packages avail. Info and tickets: 407-835-2525 (the Greater Orlando Chamber of Commerce).*

FESTIVAL OF THE MASTERS One of the top art festivals in the country, this Downtown Disney event features 200 artists, each of whom has won a primary award at a juried art show within the past three years. Works include paintings, photographs, sculptures and jewelry. Even more interesting are the pieces at the adjacent House of Blues folk-art festival, which features self-taught creators, many of whom are fascinating. Cirque du Soleil artists perform in front of their theater each afternoon. Chalk artists cover 6,000 square feet at the Marketplace. Held annually since 1975. *November. No charge. Info: 407-824-4321.*

ABC SUPER SOAP WEEKEND Dozens of hot hunks and daytime divas from the ABC programs "All My Children," "General Hospital" and "One Life to Live" are on hand to sign autographs and participate in question-and-answer sessions during this enthusiastic two-day fan-fest at Disney's Hollywood Studios. Other festivities include motorcades and a nighttime Street Jam where stars rock out on a Hollywood Boulevard stage. You know if you're in this cult; if not it's still tons of guilty-pleasure fun. Either way, get here when the park opens; the crowds are thick. *November. No extra charge. Info: 407-397-6808.*

Santa's elves coax their gingerbread men down the street during the Magic Kingdom parade

Christmas

Even the most determined Scrooge will warm up to Disney World in the weeks between Thanksgiving and Christmas. The mood is most contagious at Magic Kingdom, which salutes the community spirit of the American secular holiday with four special shows, a new parade and an amazing fireworks display. Epcot is filled with cultural performances, while Disney's Hollywood Studios embraces the bright lights and big-city charm of an urban holiday. Disney's Animal Kingdom joins in, too. *To avoid long lines, plan to see the regular attractions early, saving your time after lunch for Christmas fun.*

MAGIC KINGDOM

CELEBRATE THE SEASON Remember when your neighbors got together for holiday sing-a-longs? When carolers came to your door? When your town held its big Santa Claus parade? No? Well Disney does, and brings it back with this campy outdoor stage show, a musical revue that parents enjoy as much as their kids do. The show kicks off with "Let's Have a Joyous Celebration," as a dozen gliding ice skaters remember "the shopping and the traffic and the holiday sights!" Leading the others in the "Santa Claus Parade," Pluto uses his bone as a baton, whistling in a kitschy klatch of dancing reindeer, hoofing horses and elves who appear to have had just a little too much eggnog. After high-kicking Santa Goofy arrives to "Must Be Santa," a quartet of bake-shop coquettes sweet-talk him with "Mr. Santa." But when Mickey gives Minnie her gift (a performance of "The Nutcracker Suite"), Donald Duck gets steamed. Angry that there

was no present for him, he knocks the jester aside and attempts the dance himself. Chip 'n' Dale do the same to an Asian dancer, then Country Bears Wendell, Shaker and Liver Lips mimic the leaps of a Russian Cossack duo. Everyone is back onstage for the finale, a medley of classics (watch the reindeer act out "Rudolph the Red-Nosed Reindeer": at first they don't let poor Rudolph Pluto join in their reindeer games). The nighttime shows are best, as spotlights add a theatrical flair. *20 min. Cinderella Castle forecourt stage.*

MICKEY'S 'TWAS THE NIGHT BEFORE CHRISTMAS This outdoor stage show is a tongue-in-cheek take on the classic poem.* "While visions of sugar plums danced in their heads" brings out the Sugar Plum Fairy, a serious ballerina who performs to "The Nutcracker Suite" until a pair of tutu-trimmed hippos (from the "Dance of the Sugar Plum Fairy" segment of the 1940 film, "Fantasia") steal the show. "When what to his wondering eyes should appear but a miniature sleigh and some tiny reindeer" delivers an antler-wearing Pluto and a guitar-playing Rudolph, who performs "Run, Run, Rudolph." "When down the chimney Saint Nicholas came with a bound" cues Santa Goofy to roll out of the fireplace. A great moment takes place out of the spotlight. Aghast as Minnie recites her Christmas wish list during "Santa Baby," Mickey nearly faints when she sings "Think of all the fellas that I haven't kissed." The music comes from a live orchestra. *20 min. At Tomorrowland's Galaxy Palace Theater.*

CINDERELLA'S HOLIDAY WISH To mirthful holiday music, Mickey, Minnie and the gang appear at dusk on the Cinderella Castle stage, admiring the festive lights illuminating Main Street, U.S.A. But what to do about the darkened, unadorned castle? As they bandy about ideas, the Fairy Godmother appears. It is Cinderella who should decide, she insists. Enter the princess herself, with her Prince Charming. All agree with Cinderella that her castle should sparkle the way her beloved glass slippers do — like shimmering ice and snow. With a wave of Fairy Godmother's wand — and guests joining in to make the wish come true — Cinderella Castle magically morphs into a glorious wintry confection, with 200,000 tiny white lights twinkling in the sky. *Nightly at 5:45 p.m.*

BELLE'S ENCHANTED CHRISTMAS The friendly Disney heroine uses audience volunteers to share the story of her first Christmas in the Beast's castle, the tale told in the 1997 video "Beauty and the Beast: The Enchanted Christmas." Six kids go on stage; a dad plays the Beast. Get there 30 minutes early to get a good seat, 15 minutes early for any seat at all. Sit by the stage steps and your child may be in the show. *16 min. Fairytale Garden, to the right of Cinderella Castle.*

COUNTRY BEARS CHRISTMAS SPECIAL These hillbilly bears are certainly an acquired taste, but they do spout some funny lyrics in this Audio Animatronic concert. During "Tracks in the Snow," host Henry warbles "When the snow begins a'fallin' and your blood begins to freeze, it's time to stomp and holler and slap your hairy knees." The Five Bear Rugs sing "This Christmas, dear ol' Santa won't show up I bet. If he comes down our chimney, he might just get et." On the theater's wall, talking trophy head Melvin the moose sports outdoor Christmas lights in his antlers; his deer buddy Max has a red light bulb on his nose. *18 min. Frontierland.*

MICKEY'S ONCE UPON A CHRISTMASTIME PARADE Choreographed to a medley of songs, this elaborate Santa Claus parade was updated

Epcot's Lights of Winter syncs its lights to holiday music

for 2007. Themes include a Friends and Family Christmastime Party, a sleigh ride through a Winter Wonderland, a romantic Fairy Tale Christmas, a display of holiday sweets and Santa and Mrs. Claus. It still has marching toy soldiers and dancing reindeer. *15 min.*

HOLIDAY WISHES Explosions form Christmas images in the sky during this six-act pyrotechnic show that's synchronized to "Rudolph the Red-Nosed Reindeer" and other songs. During "O Christmas Tree" the castle turns green, a star explodes at its top and boxed presents float around it. Smiley-face fireworks introduce the "Nutcracker Suite;" later sparklers twirl on the castle. The castle lighting is filled with detail. "March of the Wooden Soldiers," brings projected images that portray cranking toy gears and marching toy soldiers. The best viewing spot is on Main Street, between the Casey's Corner hot dog stand and the Walt and Mickey statue. *12 min.*

HOW TO AVOID THE HOLIDAY RUSH The week between Christmas and New Year's is Magic Kingdom's most crowded of the year, and not, frankly, the best time to visit. Not only does the park often close (reach its 80,000-person capacity) around lunchtime, the throng is largely made up of people who appear to have IQs somewhere south of Goofy's. They clog the rides, crowd the restaurants and wander the park aimlessly. We've even seen guests drunk. The other theme parks can be almost as bad, and service at the resorts suffers as well. If you must visit Magic Kingdom during this week, arrive at the park by 7:30 a.m. Use the morning for attractions, see the noon parade, then leave for a long lunch, time in a pool, or nap. Return after dark for the castle show, Holiday Wishes and, after the crowd is gone, more attractions. The week *before* Christmas is much better. All the holiday events are happening but the monster crowd isn't here yet. An easy way to enjoy the Magic Kingdom fun is **Mickey's Very Merry Christmas Party.** Held every few nights from Thanksgiving through a few days before Christmas, these events have crowds of only 10,000 to 25,000 but give you all the park's holiday events, plus cookies and hot chocolate. All major rides are open, too. For the best time get to the park before 6:30 p.m. and see the second parade, which is far less crowded. The least crowded party is the Sunday after Thanksgiving; those on December Fridays and Saturdays sell out early. *7 p.m.–mid. Advance tickets: $41 adults, $34 kids 3–9.*

EPCOT

HOLIDAYS AROUND THE WORLD STORYTELLERS Sharing legends and traditions from all over the globe, these actors perform for small crowds outside of each World Showcase pavilion. In **Canada,** comic lumberjack Nowell describes Boxing Day, the Inuit's impish Nalyuks and the legend of "people who come to homes dressed in strange outfits. We call them… relatives!" At the **United Kingdom,** Father Christmas tells how holiday cards and decorating with holly and mistletoe began in his countries. In **France,** Père Noël comically explains how children leave shoes on their doorsteps for him to put presents in. In **Morocco,** a drummer describes the Festival of Ashura, which gives presents to kids who behave well. In **Japan** a vendor explains Daruma dolls, pupil-free good-luck charms that children paint eyes on as they make wishes. At the **American Adventure** one storyteller explains Hanukkah, another describes the principles of Kwanzaa. In **Italy,** good witch La Befana, who slides down chimneys to leave treats for kids, explains why she travels on the day the Three Kings came to Bethlehem. **Germany's** St. Nicholas fills you in about the first Christmas tree and Nutcracker as well as the Christmas pickle, a hidden tree ornament that rewards its finder with an extra present. At the **China** pavilion, the Monkey King spins a tale of how he defeated a monster and found a magic stick. In **Norway,** Epcot's strangest storytelling skit has farm girl Sigrid sure that Christmas Gnome Julenissen doesn't really exist, though you can see him easily. At **Mexico,** the Three Kings explain the customs of Posada. Each storyteller performs every hour or so from noon until dusk. Some appear after dark. *20 min.*

CANDLELIGHT PROCESSIONAL This inspirational pageant recounts the birth of Jesus Christ with a 50-piece orchestra and more than 400 singers (a different group for each show!). Narrated by a different celebrity every few nights, it often includes "O Come All Ye Faithful," "O Holy Night" and "The Hallelujah Chorus." The show takes place three times a night at the 1,950-seat America Gardens amphitheater. Though free with park admission, it's so popular that on peak days the only way to see it is to buy a Candlelight Processional Dinner Package (407-939-3463), which includes dinner at an Epcot table restaurant and is priced so the show is still, in essence, free if you order a pricey entree. Otherwise you wait in a standby line for hours and are not guaranteed a seat. *60 min.*

LIGHTS OF WINTER After sunset, the walkway that links Future World and World Showcase becomes the Lights of Winter, a lit archway synchronized to holiday music as well as the nearby Innoventions fountain. Don't miss the oboe accents in its rendition of "The Dance of the Sugar Plum Fairy."

DISNEY'S HOLLYWOOD STUDIOS

CITIZENS OF HOLLYWOOD Portraying fictitious old movie stars, hangers-on and has-beens, these improvisational actors perform holiday street skits. In its "Hollywood Glee Club," the characters sing "O Christmas Tree" using only those three words, and "Jingle Bells" to the music of "Joy to the World." Show times are available at the Guest Relations office. *Hollywood and Sunset Blvds. 20 min.*

THE HOLLYWOOD HOLLY-DAY PARADE A tribute to the song "Winter Wonderland," this procession is a reworked Disney Stars and Motor Cars Parade. Led by Santa Goofy and Rudolph Pluto, dozens of characters skip and shimmy past Echo Lake and down Hollywood Blvd. while others ride in a classic-car motorcade. Everyone's bearing gifts and decked out in holiday gear. One of Miss Piggy's presents is tagged "To Moi, From Moi." *15 min.*

OSBORNE FAMILY SPECTACLE OF DANCING LIGHTS Christmas lights cover two dozen facades throughout the Streets of America. Hundreds of strands flash in time to

On tape with Regis and Kelly

Though ABC implies the Walt Disney World Christmas parade is live when it airs on TV on Christmas Day, the event is actually taped during the first weekend in December. Hosted by Regis Philbin and Kelly Ripa, the production fills Main Street and the Cinderella Castle stage with cameras, crews and celebrities. The work moves at a snail's pace. Hang out for awhile and you'll see stars painstakingly perform take after take of the same sequence. Want to be on camera? Come early, be happy and wear bright, festive clothes without advertising slogans. *Special access may be available at www.lightshiptv.com.*

the music as they hang from rooftops in huge nets, while a spinning carousel, giant rotating globe and other animated displays tower above. Dozens of rope-light angels fly over the square at the end of New York Street; others pray to a nativity creche. The five million lights use 12 miles of extension cords and 800,000 watts of power.* Disney sprays "snow" (soap bubbles) from overhead spouts.

DISNEY'S ANIMAL KINGDOM

MICKEY'S JINGLE JUNGLE PARADE A reworking of Mickey's Jammin' Jungle Parade, the 12-minute procession adds a holiday touch to its characters, animal floats and safari trucks. Her Jeep topped with a tub of marshmallows, Minnie is baking treats (you can smell the chocolate) and has set out some for Santa. Donald is making it snow, while Santa Goofy has hung his vehicle with stockings, each for a different character (including himself), and put Donald on both his naughty and nice list. The parade's animal floats are all redone (the giant parrot has become a partridge in a pear tree) and its soundtrack has new lyrics. Its shout of animal movements ("and stomp and jump and leap and soar!") has been tagged with "and thumpity-thump-thump!"

* The Spectacle began at the Arkansas home of business tycoon Jennings Osborne in the 1980s, when he strung 1,000 red lights as a gift to his daughter, Breezy. In just a few years he had his huge home covered with millions of lights and giant animated displays, a visual overload some neighbors didn't appreciate. Osborne moved the display to Disney in 1995. Look for the family's giant Christmas stockings, which usually hang above a fireplace.

The Osborne Family Spectacle of Dancing Lights at Disney's Hollywood Studios

CAMPFIRE CAROLERS These a capella singers aren't above a few jokes. When one says she wants an "opotamus" for Christmas, the others correct her. "You must mean a hippopotamus!" "No, he doesn't have to be very cool." *Camp Minnie-Mickey. 20 min.*

New Year's Eve

The **Magic Kingdom** typically stays open until 1 a.m. on the last night of the year, with a special fireworks show at midnight. **Epcot** events can include a big band orchestra, dancing and DJs spinning world music. A late IllumiNations show adds a New Year's countdown and a coda of "Auld Lang Syne." **Disney's Hollywood Studios** often hosts a street party, with a band and disc jockey, free hats and horns and midnight fireworks. All the theme-park events are included with regular admission. That's not the case at the biggest bash, held at **Downtown Disney's** Pleasure Island. Priced about $90 per person, it's restricted to those 21 or older.

HOLIDAY HITS Walt Disney World's holiday celebration is filled with the vintage pop songs that were once the universal soundtrack of the American Christmas experience. **"The Christmas Waltz"** was a Top 40 hit for The Carpenters in 1978. Written in 1954 for Frank Sinatra, its music is simply a finger-exercising routine... **"Deck the Halls"** combines a 17th-century Welsh tune with lyrics from an anonymous 19th-century American... Cowboy star Gene Autry got the idea for 1947's **"Here Comes Santa Claus"** as he rode his horse in the 1946 Hollywood Christmas parade. Though Autry was billed as the procession's major draw, he noticed children were more interested in the guy behind him, yelling "Here comes Santa Claus! Here comes Santa Claus!"... 1963's **"It's the Most Wonderful Time of the Year"** was penned by George Wyle, who later wrote the theme to the 1960s TV show "Gilligan's Island"... First published in 1840 as "One Horse Open Sleigh," **"Jingle Bells"** is a tribute to sleigh races that took place down snow-filled Salem Street in Medford, Mass. 1955's **"Mr. Santa"** is a novelty version of the 1954 Chordettes hit, "Mr. Sandman"... **"Must Be Santa"** debuted on the "Sing Along with Mitch [Miller]" TV show in 1961... Tchaikovsky's **"The Nutcracker Suite"** is a medley of tunes the Russian composer created from his own Nutcracker ballet. First performed in 1892, it includes the tale of a family whose Christmas presents include two life-sized dolls, which each take a turn to dance... **"O Christmas Tree"** is an English version of the 16th-century German carol, "Oh Tannenbaum" ("Oh fir tree")... Based on a 1939 newspaper ad for the Montgomery Ward department store, Gene Autry's 1949 hit **"Rudolph the Red-Nosed Reindeer"** is the best-selling single in the history of Columbia Records... In 1958 **"Run, Run, Rudolph"** peaked at No. 69 for rock and roll pioneer Chuck Berry... **"There's No Place Like Home for the Holidays"** was a No. 8 hit for TV singer Perry Como in 1954... **"Santa Baby"** was a No. 4 hit in 1953 for Eartha Kitt... **"We Wish You A Merry Christmas"** is a 16th-century English Christmas carol... Published in 1934, **"Winter Wonderland"** became a million-seller hit for both Perry Como and the Andrews Sisters in 1946.

A mischievous painter has converted hearts on a pair of boxer shorts on the mural in the Snow White's Scary Adventures loading area to the three-circle shape; the silhouette also appears on the cottage chimney, directly under two flowers.

Hidden Mickeys

The image of Mickey Mouse is hidden everywhere in Walt Disney World. Throughout the resort's history, architects, painters and landscapers have subtly placed the three-circle, head-and-ears silhouette of the company's mascot (and occasionally a profile or full-figure shape) into theme-park attractions, building architecture and interiors and even the general landscape. *Note: the Hidden Mickeys in the following list are all three-circle silhouettes unless noted.*

MAGIC KINGDOM

ENTRANCE AREA ❶ As wedding-bell clappers on souvenir bricks in the walkway. **ADVENTURELAND** LANDSCAPE ❷ On the entrance bridge, as white flowers on the first shield on both sides of the walkway. JUNGLE CRUISE ❸ "You're a Bendel bonnet, a Shakespeare's sonnet, you're Mickey Mouse!" go the lyrics of Cole Porter's 1935 hit "You're the Top," which plays occasionally on the radio in the queue. ❹ On the crashed airplane,

between and below the windows. ❺ As yellow spots on the back of a giant spider on your right in the Cambodian temple, just past the snakes. ❻ In the temple's framing directly above each of the statues on your left, nearly impossible to see because of the darkness. Some are Hidden Minnies, as they have bows (three smaller circles) on their heads. THE ENCHANTED TIKI ROOM UNDER NEW MANAGEMENT ❼ On the entrance doors, as 2-inch berries on a stem underneath a bird's tail, four feet off the ground. ❽ On the bottom of Iago's perch, where a small carved face is wearing Mickey ears. THE MAGIC CARPETS OF ALADDIN ❾ As a 3-inch impression in the woodgrain hub floor (facing the Sunshine Tree Terrace, most visible after a rain). ❿ Set in the pavement behind the camel facing the ride, as a design painted on two yellow stones of a four-piece bracelet. **FRONTIERLAND** SHOOTIN' ARCADE ⓫ The back-wall target triggers a ghost rider in the sky wearing Mickey ears and gloves. SPLASH

MOUNTAIN ⑫ As stacked barrels on your right along the second lift. ⑬ As a three-orbed fishing bobber on your left (left of a picnic basket, inside the mountain just past Brer Frog toe-fishing on top of Brer Gator). ⑭ As a hanging rope in the flooded cavern (on your right, behind a lantern, past a turtle on a geyser). ⑮ After the big drop, reclining as a full figure in the sky to the right of the riverboat, as the upper outline of a cloud. Mickey's head is to the right. BIG THUNDER MOUNTAIN ⑯ As three rusty gears on your right after you go under the dinosaur rib cage.

LIBERTY SQUARE HALL OF PRESIDENTS ⑰ At the tip of George Washington's sword in a painting in the lobby, just to the right of the theater entrance. HAUNTED MANSION ⑱ The foyer and two stretching rooms form the shape. ⑲ As the left-most place setting on the near side of the ballroom banquet table. ⑳ As a black silhouette in the final scene of the graveyard, at the end of the uplifted arm of the Grim Reaper (visible on your extreme far right just after your doom buggy turns away from the tea party). ㉑ On the right side of the souvenir cart, on the index finger of a painted hand (beneath the word "Parlour"). COLUMBIA HARBOUR HOUSE ㉒ As circular wall maps in the room across from the order counter. LIBERTY TREE TAVERN ㉓ As painted grapes at the top of a spice rack in the lobby, right of the fireplace.

FANTASYLAND MICKEY'S PHILHARMAGIC ㉔ As seven 1-inch-wide white paint splotches in the lobby mural. From the right, they appear between the third and fourth bass violin, between the second and third clarinet, above the second trumpet, below the second trumpet, to the left of the fourth trumpet, and twice to the left of the sixth clarinet (one's a stretch). ㉕ In the tubing of the French horn in the theater's right stage column. ㉖ As shadows on the table in the film's "Beauty and the Beast" scene, visible as Lumiere sings the word "it's" in the lyric, "Try the gray stuff, it's delicious!" (Lumiere's hands cast Mickey's ears; his base Mickey's face). ㉗ As a hole in a cloud made as Aladdin's carpet flies through. ㉘ As three domes atop a tower on your left when the carpets dive toward Agrabah. ㉙ In the gift shop, as music stands along the top of the walls. PETER PAN'S FLIGHT ㉚ As scars on the fourth painted trunk on your left as you face the turnstile, 4 feet off the ground. IT'S A SMALL WORLD ㉛ As 6-inch purple flower petals in the Africa room, on a vine between the giraffes on your left. PINOCCHIO VILLAGE HAUS ㉜ As a dark blue sparkle of fairy dust in the Blue Fairy room, above the "a" in "dreams." ㉝ As a cutout on the back of *one* of the restaurant's wooden chairs. SNOW WHITE'S SCARY

A hanging skillet and two pots form a Hidden Mickey in the kitchen of Minnie's Country House at Magic Kingdom

ADVENTURES ㉞ In the loading area mural, on a pair of shorts on the dwarf's clothesline and ㉟ among the stones on the cottage chimney. ㊱ In the ride's first dark scene, on top of the Queen's magic mirror. ㊲ On the lower right of the entrance to the dwarfs' mine, a full-figure dwarf-nosed Mickey wears dwarf clothes and has a shovel. THE MANY ADVENTURES OF WINNIE THE POOH ㊳ On the radish marker in Rabbit's garden. POOH'S PLAYFUL SPOT ㊴ On the front-door transom of the house.

MICKEY'S TOONTOWN FAIR THE BARNSTORMER ㊵ In the queue, on a helicopter seat-back above Goofy's drafting table. MINNIE'S COUNTRY HOUSE ㊶ As a hanging kitchen skillet and pots. MICKEY'S COUNTRY HOUSE In the garage, as ㊷ hubcaps, ㊸ paint stains on an apron and ㊹ a tiny Mickey-eared bale of hay.

TOMORROWLAND LANDSCAPE ㊺ As a softball-sized impression in the concrete between the entrances of the Tomorrowland Transit Authority and Astro Orbiter. BUZZ LIGHTYEAR'S SPACE RANGER SPIN ㊻ In the queue room, a Mickey profile appears on a poster as a green land mass on the planet Pollost Prime. The planet also appears to the left of the Viewmaster in the queue, on the right as you battle the video Zurg and in the final battle scene (the photo room) on the left. ㊼ A Mickey profile appears on your left as you enter Zurg's spaceship, behind the battery-delivering robot and under the words "Initiate Battery Unload." ㊽ As an image on a painted video monitor on a mural, across from the souvenir-photo monitors. ㊾ In a painted window to the left of the full-size pink character Booster, as a cluster of three stars at the top center of a star field. ㊿ As a second star cluster at the bottom right of that field. CAROUSEL OF PROGRESS ⑤ In the 1940s scene, Mickey's sorceror's hat sits on a stool to the right of the exercise machine. In the finale, ㊿ a nutcracker Mickey sits on the mantel, ㉥ a Mickey plushie rests under the Christmas tree, ㉦ a white Mickey salt shaker sits to the right of a knifeholder on the bar, ㉧ an abstract painting of Mickey as the Sorceror's Apprentice hangs on the wall to the right of the dining table and ㉨ the three circles appear on the television as engines of a spaceship during the first moments of a video game. TOMORROWLAND TRANSIT AUTHORITY ㉩ On a customer's belt buckle in the beauty salon, on your right just after you enter the Buzz Lightyear/Laugh Floor building. MICKEY'S STAR TRADERS In a wall mural as ㉪ loops of a highway, ㉫ train headlights, ㉬ glass domes of the building, ㉭ satellite dishes, ㉮ clear domes covering a city and ㉯ Mickey Ears on top of two windows.

EPCOT

FUTURE WORLD SPACESHIP EARTH ❶ As blots on the top right of a piece of parchment, made by the sleeping monk. ❷ As bottle rings on the table of the first Renaissance painter. INNOVENTIONS WEST ❸ As a blue mole on the cheek of a boy in an IBM ThinkPlace mural. Wearing a fez, he appears on the wall of the left Thinking of You video-postcard station. ❹ A girl in the ThinkPlace video wall is wearing a Mickey hat. MISSION SPACE ❺ As overlapping craters on the moon in the courtyard, above and to the left of the Luna 8 impact site. ❻ As tiny round tiles in the courtyard patio, 40 feet from the Fastpass entrance. The ears are blue; the head black. ❼ In the queue a notepad on the left desk reads "Mickey and Goofy are scheduled to launch at exactly 3 p.m." ❽ As craters on Mars on the far left and ❾ right monitors above the desks. ❿ As part of the grid on a circuit board to the upper left and right of the joystick consoles for the post-show video game, Expedition Mars. ⓫ As black craters in the mural behind the cash registers in the gift shop, under Minnie's foot. ⓬ A profile of Mickey appears in the reddish dust in the photos of space on the gift shop ceiling. He's in the center of the room, directly above a Space Mickey statue. ⓭ As three electrical boxes on the gift shop walls (one is a Mickey profile). TEST TRACK ⓮ As washers on the edge of the left side of a desk near queue area 7b. ⓯ Mickey has signed off on inspection stickers on a test car in the queue. Appearing on a vehicle in area 5b, the signature on the Fastpass and Single Rider side of the car reads "M. Mouse;" on the Standby side "Micky" (yes,

misspelled). ⓰ As stains on a fender on the left side of the Corrosion Chamber. ⓱ As similar stains on a car door on the right side of the chamber. ⓲ As crash-test stickers on a car to your left in the Barrier Test area. They're on an open gas-tank filler door. ⓳ As a coil of hoses on the left floor, just before the Barrier Test wall. MOUSEGEAR ⓴ As wall gauges behind the main cash registers. SOARIN' ㉑ As a blue balloon at the beginning of the Palm Springs scene, held by a man behind a golf cart at the far lower left. ㉒ As a small silhouette on the golf ball that flies toward you (flinch and you'll miss it). ㉓ In the second burst of Disneyland fireworks, in the center of the screen. LIVING WITH THE LAND ㉔ Bubbles in the mural on the waiting area's back wall (under the word "nature," a Mickey profile). ㉕ In the mural behind the loading area, one green and two blue circles form an angled Mickey (about 7 feet from the right wall, a half-foot off the floor). ㉖ As trays of red-leaf lettuce surrounded by trays of green. ㉗ In the final greenhouse, as green test-tube caps behind the lab windows. SUNSHINE SEASONS FOOD COURT ㉘ As snowflake crystals on the food trays. JOURNEY INTO IMAGINATION WITH FIGMENT ㉙ A Mickey-eared headphone sits in the Sight Lab, on top of the left wheeled table. ㉚ As two small circular carpets and a flowered toilet seat in Figment's bathroom. ㉛ Between the "I" and "M" in the ImageWorks logo. ㉜ In place of a letter in the eyechart in the Kodak demonstration area at the entrance to ImageWorks. **WORLD SHOWCASE** CANADA ㉝ On both sides of the left totem pole underneath the top-most set of hands. ㉞ As wine-rack bottles behind the Le Cellier check-in counter. U.K. ㉟ As a tennis racket, soccer ball and rugby ball on a hanging sign for the Sportsman's Shoppe. FRANCE ㊱ The courtyard's metal grates incorporate the three circles into their design. ㊲ As a bush in the fleur-de-lis hedge garden. ㊳ In a second-floor window behind the "Impressions de France" wedding reception. MOROCCO ㊴ As brass plates on the left green door of the Souk-Al-Magreb shop. ㊵ As a window in the dome of a minaret on the photo backdrop in Aladdin's indoor meet-and-greet area. Mickey's in the upper right-hand segment, next to a small ladder. JAPAN ㊶ In the courtyard's metal tree grates. ㊷ As the center of a koi-pond drain cover, near a bamboo fence. GERMANY ㊸ In the center of the crown of the left-most Hapsburg emperor statue on the second story of Das Kaufhaus. ㊹ Mickey's often in the train village, standing in a window of the hilltop castle. NORWAY Mickey appears three times in the mural behind the Maelstrom loading area: ㊺ As Mickey ears on a Viking in the middle of a ship toward the left, **46** as shadows on a cruise-line worker's blouse (her right pocket is Mickey's head, her clipboard ring is his nose) and **47** at the far right on the watch of a bearded construction worker wearing a hardhat. **48** As black circles on King Olaf II's tunic embroidery in the Stave Church.

HOLLYWOOD STUDIOS

HOLLYWOOD BOULEVARD COVER STORY
1 The shape of Mickey's ears repeats in the black molding beneath the second-floor windows. GREAT MOVIE RIDE **2** As a silhouetted profile in the second-story windows of the Western Chemical Co. building, on your left side as you enter Gangster Alley. **3** Mickey's tail and one of his shoes are visible on a poster underneath the one for "The Public Enemy" on the alley's left wall. **4** As a profile on a piece of broken stone below the Ark of the Covenant in the Well of Souls. Facing left, the light-gray Mickey hides in plain sight on a dark-gray rock. **5** A full-figure Mickey pharoah appears on the Well's left wall, just past the second statue of Anubis. An Egyptian Donald Duck is serving him some cheese.
ECHO LAKE TUNE-IN LOUNGE **6** As washers used to secure the top of coffee tables. PRIME TIME CAFE **7** As dining-table red napkin and utensil holders.
BACKLOT STAR TOURS **8** An Ewok child holds a Mickey doll in the pre-boarding video. TOY STORY PIZZA PLANET **9** In a mural above the cash registers, as star clusters left of the spaceship, near the pizza-slice constellation. **10** As craters in the moon in a wall mural above the arcade (a three-quarter Mickey profile). JIM HENSON'S MUPPETVISION 3-D **11** On Gonzo's inflatable ring float in the courtyard fountain. **12** In a small sketch of a DNA model in the "5 Reasons" poster along the back outdoor queue area. **13** As a test pattern in the early moments of the preshow video. **14** In the film's final scene, park guests behind the fire truck hold Mickey balloons. STAGE 1 COMPANY STORE **15** Outside, as purple paint drips on a recessed light under a bronze lion head. **16** As green drips on a shelf of a wood bureau along a side wall. **17** Mickey's red shorts hang above the hotel desk. MAMA MELROSE'S RISTORANTE ITALIANO **18** As a spot on the right shoulder of a dalmation in a lobby statue. **19** As a leaf on a vine to the right of the check-in podium, at the bottom right of a lattice fence. THE WRITER'S STOP **20** As yellow stickers on ceiling stage lights. LIGHTS MOTORS ACTION EXTREME STUNT SHOW **21** A vintage full-figure Mickey appears in the window of the Antiquites Brocante ("Secondhand Antiques") shop. **22** As a gear and two circular belts in the top right corner of the motorcycle shop window. BACKLOT TOUR

23 As a blue-sky cutout in the white clouds of the "Harbor Attack" backdrop. **24** In the prop room on the door of the yellow "Marvin's Room" refrigerator and as cannon balls hanging from the ceiling. **25** At Catastrophe Canyon, as gauges on your right on top of the third barrel from the exit. **26** A full-figure Mickey hides in a mural to your right just as you enter the AFI exhibit. He stands on top of a gravestone about halfway up the right third of the scene.

SUNSET BOULEVARD LANDSCAPE
27 Impressions along the curbs read "Mortimer & Co. Contractors 1928," a reference to Walt's original name for his mouse when he created him in 1928. ROSIE'S ALL-AMERICAN CAFE **28** As three gauges on a welding torch behind the order counter. ROCK 'N' ROLLER COASTER STARRING AEROSMITH **29** Twice on the building's sign: Steven Tyler's shirt has Mickey silhouettes and the boy is wearing mouse ears. **30** As three pieces in a beige section of the foyer's floor mosaic, just before you leave the room. **31** As a distorted carpet pattern in the first display room of G-Force Records. **32** As cables on the floor of the recording studio. **33** On the registration sticker on each of the limo's rear license plates. **34** As the "O" in the phrase "Box #15" on a trunk along the ride exit walkway. THE TWILIGHT ZONE TOWER OF TERROR **35** As a pair of folded wire-rim glasses on the lobby's concierge desk (the temples form Mickey's face, the eye rims make his ears). **36** 1932's "What! No Mickey Mouse?" is the song featured on some sheet music in the left library, on the bookcase directly in front of the entrance door. **37** The little girl in the TV video is holding a 1930s Mickey doll. **38** As large, round ash doors beneath the fire box on a brick furnace in the boiler room (on your right just after you've entered the boiler area). **39** As water stains just left of a fuse box on the boiler room's left wall, just past where the queue divides. **40** On the 13th floor, in the center of the stars as they come together to form a single beam of light. FANTASMIC **41** As bubbles in the water screens. Pinocchio's bubble forms Mickey's head; two others form his ears.

ANIMAL KINGDOM

DISCOVERY ISLAND TREE OF LIFE **1** As moss on the trunk, to the left of a buffalo, near a tiger, facing the park entrance. **2** Upside down, above a hippo's eye on the side of the trunk that faces the walkway from Asia to Africa. IT'S TOUGH TO BE A BUG **3** As spots on a root in the lobby, left of the theater's handicapped entrance. PIZZAFARI **4** As an orange firefly in the nocturnal room, to the left of a large tiger, behind a frog.

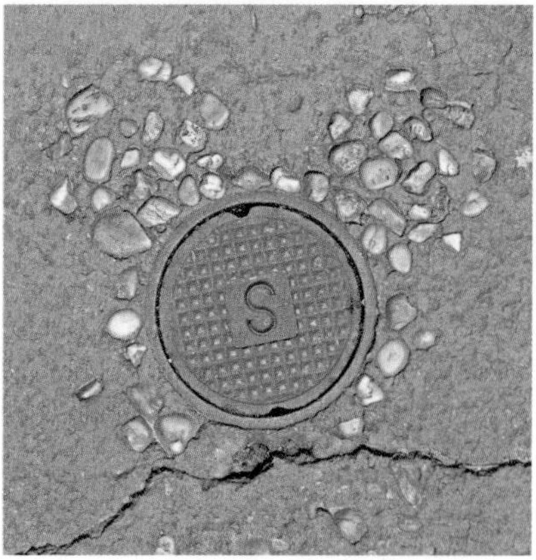

A walkway drain cover and two pebble groupings form a Hidden Mickey near Animal Kingdom's Tamu Tamu Refreshments

CAMP MINNIE-MICKEY LANDSCAPE ⑤ A profile appears as the hole of a birdhouse that hangs in the courtyard. POCAHONTAS AND HER FOREST FRIENDS ⑥ As a shadow in the grass between two trees and as another shadow (a profile) above a fallen tree on the left of a stage backdrop, and as rocks on a dirt path on the backdrop's right. ICE CREAM STAND ⑦ In the carved woodwork, as sideways accents.
AFRICA HARAMBE VILLAGE ⑧ As a large shape of gray pavement on the walkway in front of Harambe School, behind the Fruit Market. A bench may be sitting on it. ⑨ As a drain cover with the letter "D" on it and two round pebble groupings, just left of the main entrance to Mombasa Marketplace, across from Tusker House. ⑩ As another drain cover (this time with the letter "S") and two round pebble groupings in front of Tamu Tamu Refreshments, facing Discovery Island. KILIMANJARO SAFARIS ⑪ As the flamingo island. PANGANI FOREST EXPLORATION TRAIL ⑫ In the research station, as a small shape on a backpack to the left of the naked mole rat exhibit.
RAFIKI'S PLANET WATCH PLANET WATCH TRAIN STATION ⑬ As blue circles in the rafter's cross beams. LANDSCAPE ⑭ As overlapping circles in the grates of Affection Section trees and in the Conservation Station lobby. CONSERVATION STATION On the left wall of the entrance mural, left to right: As a pupil of a squirrel, ⑮ wrinkles on a hippo's chin (a profile), ⑯ a scale behind the eye of a crocodile, ⑰ a shadow on a walrus's neck to the right of his tusks, ⑱ an owl's pupils, ⑲ a spot on a yellow fish (obscured by an octopus), ⑳ black spots on a butterfly's left wing (above a bat). On the right wall, right to left: ㉑ As a pink spot on a spider's abdomen (above a white owl chick), ㉒ in the pupil of an opossum, ㉓ as black spots on the yellow wings of a butterfly (above a praying mantis arm). Middle wall, right to left: ㉔ As an ostrich's pupil, ㉕ scales on the back of a green snake, ㉖ a sucker on the bottom of a starfish (a profile), ㉗ on the top of a butterfly body (a smiling, detailed face), ㉘ as spots on the wings of a butterfly (under a monkey) and ㉙ a silver frog's left pupil (a profile). Many Mickeys hide in the "Song of the Rainforest" area. Left to right: ㉚ As the petals of a yellow flower, ㉛ a white spot on a fly above a flower, ㉜ a shadow on a tree in front of the rainforest doors (a profile), ㉝ a white spot on a tree to the left of "The Accidental Florist" sign, ㉞ a spot on the tree bark, across from a fly, about 4 feet off the ground, ㉟ an impression in tree bark in the "Song of the Rainforest" sign to the lower right of Grandmother Willow's face (a profile), ㊱ a nearby painted hole in a leaf, ㊲ spots on a wooden cockroach inside a tree in the front of the rainforest area, ㊳ three dark green spots on the side of a chameleon above the "Giant Cockroach" sign at the right of the rainforest area, ㊴ and three round petri dishes in the far left window of the reptile display room. AFFECTION SECTION ㊵ As a pattern on a sheared sheep. ㊶ As orange spots on a stage wall, right of a lizard door.
ASIA MAHARAJAH JUNGLE TREK ㊷ At the second tiger viewing area, as swirls of water under a tiger in the first mural to your right. ㊸ As a golden earring and ㊹ three small bushes in the first mural to your left. ㊺ As rocks in a mountain range above a flying dove in the second mural to your left. ㊻ As swirls in a cloud formation in the second painting to your right. ㊼ Past the tigers, as a leaf in a mural to your left, about 9 feet off the ground. ㊽ In the top right of a mural left of the Elds Deer habitat, an orange flower and two leaves create a detailed Mickey face and waving arm. ㊾ As beads on a necklace in the middle stone carving, just before the aviary entrance. EXPEDITION EVEREST ㊿ In the queue, as a tiny Mickey hat worn by a Yeti doll in Tashi's Trek and Tongba Shop, on the top shelf of a cupboard to the right. (51) As black water bottle caps in a display of patches in the same shop. ㊿ As a dent and two holes in a tea kettle that's part of the wreckage of a camp in the Yeti museum. (51) On the left wall after the museum, a Mickey with eyes, a nose, and a Sorcerer's hat appears as wood stains in a photograph that shows a woman with a walkie-talkie.
DINOLAND U.S.A. LANDSCAPE (52) As cracks in the asphalt in the parking area next to the Cementosaurus, to the left of Dinosaur Treasures. (53) On a Steamboat Willie cast

member pin on the right of the fourth hump on the back of the Cementosaurus. **54** As three small, black scales on the back of the red and green hadrosaurus at the start of the Cretaceous Trail. BONEYARD **55** As a water stain under the drinking fountain near the entrance. **56** As a quarter and two pennies on a table behind a fenced-in area, on the second level by the slides in the back. **57** As a fan and two hardhats in a fenced-off area at the back of the wooly mammoth excavation. PRIMEVAL WHIRL **58** As three meteor craters throughout the Primeval Whirl attraction. DINOSAUR **59** Along the queue, as lily pads in the second diorama on your right. **60** As green spots on that diorama's largest tree trunk, to the left of its lower right branch. **61** Just before the gift shop, as clouds above a carnotaurus tail (below the meteor) on a poster advertising souvenir ride photos (with the phrase "We took your photo 65 million years ago!"). **62** As three scales on the neck of a carnotaurus on a mural behind the souvenir photo counter. FINDING NEMO THE MUSICAL **63** As three blue bubbles, two lit and one drawn, at the bottom left of the stage wall.

WATER PARKS

BLIZZARD BEACH BEACH HAUS **1** As three rocks in a painted scene, on a wall light fixture near the changing rooms. CROSS COUNTRY CREEK **2** As four stones on a bridge over the creek at the back of the park. The top stone is Mickey's Sorcerer's hat. CHAIRLIFT **3** As rocks on a ledge of Mount Gushmore, under the chairlift track.

TYPHOON LAGOON CRUSH 'N' GUSHER **4** On the second floor of the tower, as paint circles on the floor in front of the elevator. STORM SLIDES **5** As an extension on a step halfway up the walkway, across from a lantern, just before an anchor on the right. CASTAWAY CREEK **6** On the bridge past Shark Landing, on a railing strut. KETCHAKIDDIE CREEK **7** As a hole in the wall of the cave, a foot off the ground, left of a drain.

DOWNTOWN DISNEY

MARKETPLACE LANDSCAPE **1** As a 20x20-foot arrangement of fountain squirters in the pavement at the Marketplace entrance to the right of Earl of Sandwich. **2** The squirters themselves are small Mickeys. ONCE UPON A TOY **3** As robotic claws that hold toys, suspended from a hanging track. **4** As blue support bars under stands that hold plushies. WORLD OF DISNEY **5** In a mural in the Women and Juniors room, as a red and white design on a blue flag to the left of the Queen of Hearts and as a golden design on Tweedledee's red sumo cloth. **6** In a mural in the facing room, as a design above the doors to the Chinese Theater behind the floating Three Little Pigs.

WEST SIDE DISNEYQUEST **7** As repeating ancient symbols in the carpet in the Adventureport and the 5th-floor cafe. CIRQUE DU SOLEIL **8** Outside the box office, as black floor tiles inside the doors of both restrooms.

DIVERSIONS

GOLF COURSES MAGNOLIA **1** As a sand trap near the green of hole No. 6. (called "the Mouse trap"). OSPREY RIDGE **2** A practice green (a Mickey profile).
MINIATURE GOLF FANTASIA GARDENS **3** As the 12th green of the Gardens Course. WINTER SUMMERLAND **4** On the 16th hole of the Winter Course, as a gingerbread cookie that pokes out of a mantelpiece stocking (a full-body Mickey). **5** On the mantelpiece on the Summer Course 16th hole, in a sleigh with Minnie and Pluto.
WDW SPEEDWAY LANDSCAPE **6** As the infield pond (visible on Google Earth).

ACCOMMODATIONS

ALL-STAR MUSIC **1** Around the Jazz Inn, as a screw top on top of a cymbal. **2** As beige designs on the front and back of the boots of the County Fair buildings.
ALL-STAR SPORTS **3** Between the buildings, as a large round platform and two gray pavement ovals. **4** As a repeating pattern of a baseball and two white circles in the carpet in the gift shop.
ANIMAL KINGDOM LODGE **5** Outside the front entrance, as a design in the mouth of the second tall figure left of the motor lobby, above the lower roof. **6** As a yellow spot on the middle of the back of the right spotted creature just inside the entrance. **7** As a design on the right middle chandelier in the lobby, facing the check-in counter. **8** As a leaf about two-thirds of the way up the left outdoor vine staircase at the rear of the building, visible from the Sunset Savanna Overlook (a profile). **9** To the left of that overlook's pelican viewing area, as spots on the tallest giraffe in the stone carving. **10** As dents in rock on that overlook's planted walkway, about 4 feet off the ground. **11** Behind the pool slide as three dents in a brown rock wall, 3 feet off the ground. **12** As a small green shape to the right of a wall above the Mara snack bar. **13** Inside the snack bar, as a hole in a painted leaf on a wall in front and above the wine selection, and in another leaf on the upper left wall, the third leaf from the left tree. **14** As three circles in the ceiling of Jiko, formed by the tops of a column and two wood-burning ovens alongside the show kitchen.
BOARDWALK **15** In the resort's main entrance foyer, as a brown spot on the neck of a white carrousel horse. **16** As a second brown spot on its rump. **17** As a cloud on the sign for

other areas

Seashore Sweets to the top right of the left woman. **18** As repeating red berries in the carpet in front of many elevators.
CORONADO SPRINGS 19 Jutting out from a bolt, a detailed Mickey face is on the top left of the left door of the main entrance. **20** As impressions in the sidewalk near the lamppost closest to the resort's boat and bike rental.
GRAND FLORIDIAN 21 As repeating tan designs on the border of the carpet on the lobby staircase. **22** As a repeating white pattern on the tan wallpaper. **23** As a hot-air balloon, on the painted ceiling of the convention center rotunda.
OLD KEY WEST 24 As three seashell imprints in the walkway that leads from Building 36 to parking spaces.
PORT ORLEANS RIVERSIDE 25 As a design on an Indian's sandal in the food court.
SARATOGA SPRINGS 26 As a white design at the bottom of the spa signs outside of the spa.
SHADES OF GREEN 27 As the Millpond Pool.
WILDERNESS LODGE 28 As three stones above and to the right of the lobby fireplace. **29** Behind the main building, as lumps of earth about a third of the way up a stream that flows from the geyser by the pool. **30** As nuts in a small bulletin board at the entrance to Roaring Fork Snacks. **31** As leaves in the wallpaper in the guest room hallways. **32** As dents in the wood on a beam to the right of the exit to the Boat and Bike Rental. **33** As dents in the wood on the second closest post to room 4035 and **34** on the post closest to room 5066.
YACHT AND BEACH CLUB 35 On the wallpaper in the guest room halls, as repeating white designs on a tan background. In the entrance hall to the Solarium, as wheels of trunk-mounted tires of **36** the far left yellow car and **37** the far right blue car in the first painting to the left (Mickey faces). **38** In that same painting, as the hood ornament on the right red car and right blue car. **39** As a cloud in the second painting to the left (a detailed face). **40** As a red balloon held by a girl at the right of the third painting on the left wall. **41** As a yellow balloon held by the girl next to her.

CHRISTMAS DECORATIONS
MAGIC KINGDOM MICKEY'S 'TWAS THE NIGHT BEFORE CHRISTMAS SHOW **1** As a snowman standing on the left side of the opening backdrop. **2** As the top of a hatrack on the right of the stage. HOLIDAY WISHES **3** As crystals along the edge of each snowflake projected on the castle.
DISNEY'S HOLLYWOOD STUDIOS THE OSBORNE FAMILY SPECTACLE OF DANCING LIGHTS **4** Twenty-two Hidden Mickeys can shift locations from year to year. One is formed by a hat and "ears" of a lifesize toy solder, another is

created by the face and ears of a snowman. The best one is in the smoke of a large toy train. (Kermit the Frog and other Muppets characters hide in the giant Christmas bulbs decorating the apartments to the left of Al's Toy Barn.)
ANIMAL KINGDOM ENTRANCE AREA **5** As ornaments on the park's main Christmas tree.

OTHER HIDDEN CHARACTERS
MAGIC KINGDOM Stitch hides in the exit of Buzz Lightyear's Space Ranger Spin, **1** riding in a tiny red spaceship behind the photo counter (left of "8 x 10") and **2** across the hall in a star field in the Captain Nebula mural. **3** Donald Duck's abstract face and hat are on an upholstered chair's backrest in the Haunted Mansion, left of the endless hallway.
EPCOT 4 An abstract Donald Duck and Pluto hide in the Mission Space gift shop ceiling. Donald's head and neck are to the Hidden Mickey's right. Close to the exit, **5** Pluto's face points toward the cash registers.
DISNEY'S HOLLYWOOD STUDIOS 6 Minnie Mouse hides in the center of the Great Movie Ride boarding-area mural. Facing left, her profile is just above and to the right of a tile roof, tucked under some palm fronds. **7** On the left wall on the ride's Well of Souls, a center carving two blocks up from the floor shows a pharaoh holding "Star Wars" character R2-D2 while C-3PO repairs him with a screwdriver. (The carving appears on the same wall in the "Raiders of the Lost Ark" movie). **8** On an outside wall of the Star Tours gift shop (along the walkway that leads to MuppetVision 3-D), an abstract Goofy face is formed by a center box of a fake light fixture, with his ears as its light covers. **9** Gonzo appears as a chalk drawing wearing 3-D glasses on the right wall of the MuppetVision 3-D building. **10** The name "Walt Disney" hides in the Tower of Terror lobby. Often covered in dust, the cover of a Photoplay magazine on the concierge desk promotes "Four Pages of Hilarious Star Caricatures by Walt Disney."
DISNEY'S ANIMAL KINGDOM 11 Baloo's head and neck appear as peeling, cream-colored paint on a wall in the Harambe Village fort, behind Tamu Tamu Refreshments, next to the area where Baloo appears.
BLIZZARD BEACH 12 A hidden Ice Gator alligator appears in the hill at the rear of Melt-Away Bay. A high rock is its snout, the rock below is his front left foot.
WINTER SUMMERLAND 13 Goofy and Donald Duck nutcrackers are on the left side of the mantelpiece on the 16th hole of the miniature golf course.

Hidden Mickey field research by Micaela Neal. ("This took forever!")

books

Anderson, Philip Longfellow. "The Gospel in Disney: Christian Values in the Early Animated Classics." Augsburg Books, 2004.

"The Annotated Classic Fairy Tales" edited by Marie Tatar. W.W. Norton & Company Ltd., 2002.

Appelbaum, Stanley. "The New York World's Fair 1939/1940." Dover Publications, 1977.

Barrie, J. M. "Peter Pan." Charles Scribner's Sons, 1911, 1985.

Borgenicht, David. "The Classic Tales of Brer Rabbit." Running Press, 1995.

Brode, Douglas. "From Walt to Woodstock: How Disney Created the Counterculture." University of Texas Press, 2004.

Canemaker, John. "The Art and Flair of Mary Blair: An Appreciation." Disney Editions, 2003.

Connellan, Tom. "Inside the Magic Kingdom." Bard Press, 1997.

Corey, Melinda and Ochoa, George. "The American Film Institute Desk Reference." Stonesong Press, 2002.

Dunlop, Beth. "Building a Dream: The Art of Disney Architecture." Harry N. Abrams, 1996.

"E.Encyclopedia Animal." DK, 2005.

Eisner, Michael and Schwartz, Tony. "Work in Progress." Random House, 1998.

Finch, Christopher. "The Art of Walt Disney." Harry N. Abrams, 2004.

Finch, Christopher. "Jim Henson: The Works: The Art, the Magic, the Imagination." Random House, 1993.

Finch, Christopher. "Walt Disney's America." Abbeville Press, 1978.

Fjellman, Stephen M. "Vinyl Leaves: Walt Disney World and America." Westview Press, 1992.

Flower, Joe. "Prince of the Magic Kingdom: Michael Eisner and the Re-making of Disney." Wiley, 1991.

Greene, Katherine and Richard. "The Man Behind the Magic: The Story of Walt Disney." Viking, 1991, 1998.

Griswold, Jerry. "The Meanings of 'Beauty and the Beast,' a Handbook." Broadview Press, 2004.

Hahn, Don. "Disney's Animation Magic." Disney Press, 1996.

Harris, Joel Chandler. "The Complete Tales of Uncle Remus." Houghton Mifflin Company, 1955.

Heide, Robert and Gilman, John. "Mickey Mouse: The Evolution, the Legend, the Phenomenon!" Disney Editions, 2001.

Hench, John. "Designing Disney: Imagineering and the Art of the Show." Disney Editions, 2003.

"The Imagineering Field Guide to Epcot at Walt Disney World." Disney Editions, 2005.

"The Imagineering Field Guide to the Magic Kingdom at Walt Disney World." Disney Editions, 2005.

Kinney, Jack. "Walt Disney and Assorted Other Characters." Harmony, 1988.

Koenig, David. "Realityland: True-Life Adventures at Walt Disney World." Bonaventure Press, 2007.

Kurtti, Jeff. "Since the World Began: Walt Disney World's First 25 Years." Hyperion, 1996.

Lamb, Bob. "Field Guide to Disney's Animal Kingdom Theme Park." Roundtable Press, 2000.

Lambert, Pierre. "Mickey Mouse." Hyperion, 1998.

Malmberg, Melody. "The Making of Disney's Animal Kingdom Theme Park." Hyperion 1998.

Maltin, Leonard. "The Disney Films." Disney Editions, 1995, 2000.

Maltin, Leonard. "Of Mice and Magic: A History of American Animated Cartoons." Penguin Books, 1987.

Mannheim, Steve. "Walt Disney and the Quest for Community." Ashgate Publishing, 2002.

Marling, Karal Ann. "Designing Disney's Theme Parks: The Architecture of Reassurance." Hyperion, 1997.

Milne, A.A. "Winnie-the-Pooh." Puffin Books, 1926, 1992.

Mosley, Leonard. "Disney's World." Scarborough House, 1990.

Neary, Kevin and Smith, Dave. "The Ultimate Disney Trivia Book Vols. 1–3." Hyperion, 1992, 1994, 1997.

"Official Guide: New York World's Fair 1964/1965." Time Inc., 1964.

Philip, Neil. "The Complete Fairy Tales of Charles Perrault." Albion Press Ltd., 1993.

Philip, Neil. "The Illustrated Book of Myths: Tales and Legends of the World." DK, 1995.

Price, Harrison "Buzz." "Walt's Revolution! By the Numbers." Ripley Entertainment, 2004.

Rafferty, Kevin. "Walt Disney Imagineering." Disney Editions, 1996.

Samuelson, Dale. "The American Amusement Park." MBI, 2001.

Schickel, Richard. "The Disney Version: The Life, Times, Art and Commerce of Walt Disney." Simon & Schuster, 1968, 1985, 1997.

Schroeder, Russell K. "Disney: The Ultimate Visual Guide." Dorling Kindersley Ltd., 2002.

Schroeder, Russell. "Walt Disney: His Life in Pictures." Disney Press, 1996.

Smith, Dave. "Disney A to Z: The Official Encyclopedia." Hyperion, 1998, 2006.

Smith, Dave. "The Quotable Walt Disney." Disney Editions, 2001.

Smith, Dave and Clark, Steven. "Disney: The First 100 Years." Hyperion, 1999.

Surrell, Jason. "The Haunted Mansion: From the Magic Kingdom to the Movies." Disney Editions, 2003.

Surrell, Jason. "Pirates of the Caribbean: From the Magic Kingdom to the Movies." Disney Editions, 2005.

Taylor, John. "Storming the Magic Kingdom." Knopf, 1987.

Thomas, Bob. "Building a Company: Roy O. Disney and the Creation of an Entertainment Empire." Hyperion, 1998.

Thomas, Bob. "Walt Disney: An American Original." Hyperion, 1994.

Thomas, Frank and Johnston, Ollie. "The Illusion of Life: Disney Animation." Disney Editions, 1995.

Tieman, Robert. "The Disney Treasures." Disney Editions, 2003.

Twain, Mark. "The Adventures of Tom Sawyer." Fine Creative Media, 2003.

"25 Years of Walt Disney World." Disney's Kingdom Editions, 1996.

"Walt Disney Imagineering: A Behind the Dreams Look at Making the Magic Real." Hyperion, 1996.

"Walt Disney Resort: A Magical Year-By-Year Journey." Hyperion, 1998.

Watts, Steven. "The Magic Kingdom: Walt Disney and the American Way of Life." Houghton Mifflin, 1997.

Zicree, Mark Scott. "The Twilight Zone Companion." Silman-James Press, 1982, 1989.

Zipes, Jack. "The Complete Fairy Tales of the Brothers Grimm." Bantam, 1992.

video

Cocteau, Jean. "Beauty and the Beast." Criterion, 2003.

"Frank and Ollie." Walt Disney Pictures, 2003.

"Modern Marvels: Walt Disney World." A&E Home Video, 2006.

"Walt Disney Treasures" series. Walt Disney Video, 2002–2007.

"Walt: The Man Behind the Myth." Walt Disney Home Entertainment, 2004.

New York Times archive

Orlando Sentinel archive

PARK PUZZLER ANSWERS Magic Kingdom 1b, 2d, 3c, 4d, 5b, 6a, 7b Epcot 1b, 2b, 3b, 4b, 5b, 6c, 7a Disney's Hollywood Studios 1c, 2a, 3c, 4c, 5c, 6a, 7a, 8a Animal Kingdom 1c, 2a, 3d, 4c, 5a, 6a, 7a, 8b

Phone directory

GENERAL INFO
Birthday parties:
407-939-2329
Boat charters and rentals:
407-939-7529
Carriage rides:
407-939-7529
Disney Institute:
407-566-2620
Disney operator:
407-824-2222
Disney reservations:
407-934-7639
Disney's Wide World of Sports:
407-828-3267
Sammy Duvall's Water Sports:
407-939-0754
Fantasia Gardens miniature golf:
407-560-4870
Fishing excursions:
407-939-2277
Florist:
407-827-3505
Foreign Language Assistance:
407-824-2222
Golf reservations:
407-939-4653
Horseback riding:
407-824-2900
Merchandise Guest Services:
407-363-6200
Pony rides:
407-824-2788
Post office:
Lake Buena Vista:
407-238-0223
Recreation reservations:
407-939-7529
Restaurant reservations:
407-939-3463
Resort reservations:
407-934-7639
Richard Petty Driving Experience:
1-800-237-3889
Scooter, stroller and wheelchair rentals:
EZ Street Rentals:
866-394-1115
SunTrust Bank:
407-828-6103
Surfing Lessons:
407-939-7873
Tennis:
407-939-7529

Tours:
407-939-8687
Travel packages:
407-934-7639
VIP Tours:
407-560-4033
Weather line:
407-824-4104
Winter Summerland miniature golf:
407-560-3000
LOST AND FOUND
Blizzard Beach:
407-560-5408

Disney's Hollywood Studios:
407-560-3720
Disney's Animal Kingdom:
407-938-2785
Downtown Disney:
407-828-3150
Epcot:
407-560-6646
Magic Kingdom:
407-824-4521
Typhoon Lagoon:
407-560-6296
After 24 hours:
407-824-4245
MEDICAL CARE
Florida Hospital Emergency Dept. (Celebration):
407-303-4034
Centra Care:
Walk-In Clinic:
407-239-6463
In-Room Care:
407-238-2000
Turner Pharmacy:
407-828-8125

RESORTS
All-Star Movies:
407-939-7000
All-Star Music:
407-939-6000
All-Star Sports:
407-939-5000
Animal Kingdom Lodge:
407-938-3000
Beach Club:
407-934-8000
BoardWalk:
407-939-5100

Caribbean Beach:
407-934-3400
Contemporary:
407-824-1000
Coronado Springs:
407-939-1000
Fort Wilderness:
407-824-2900
Grand Floridian:
407-824-3000
Old Key West:
407-827-7700
Polynesian:
407-824-2000
Pop Century:
407-938-4000
Port Orleans French Quarter:
407-934-5000
Port Orleans Riverside:
407-934-6000
Saratoga Springs:
407-827-1100
Wilderness Lodge:
407-824-3200
Yacht Club:
407-934-7000

Shades of Green:
407-824-3600
WDW Dolphin:
407-934-4000
WDW Swan:
407-934-3000
DOWNTOWN DISNEY RESORTS
Best Western:
407-828-2424
Buena Vista Palace:
407-827-2727
DoubleTree Suites:
407-934-1000

Tweedledum takes a call at Magic Kingdom

Hilton:
407-827-4000
Holiday Inn:
407-828-8888
Royal Plaza:
407-828-2828
Regal Sun:
407-828-4444
TRANSPORTATION
Car Care Center:
407-824-0976
After-hours service:
407-824-4777
Alamo Rent A Car:
407-824-3470
Hess Express:
Magic Kingdom:
407-938-0143
Epcot Resort Area:
407-938-0151
Downtown Disney:
407-938-0160
Magical Express:
866-599-0951
Mears (cabs, etc.):
407-423-5566